If this first instalment is any indication, Douglas Kelly's three-volume Systematic Theology is sure to set a new standard. Harvesting decades of steady scholarship and equally steady engagement in all facets of the church's life and ministry, Kelly displays the richness of the Christian faith, particularly in its Reformed expression. Christians of all traditions will benefit greatly from the catholic breadth, appropriate but not bewildering depth, and exegetical insight of this remarkable work.

Michael Horton
J. Gresham Machen Professor of Systematic Theology and Apologetics
Westminster Seminary in California, Escondido, California

Douglas F. Kelly is one of the English-speaking world's leading Reformed theologians. A brilliant Patristics scholar and a gifted linguist, with a grace-wrought passion for the Triune God, a love for truth, and a commitment to godliness, Dr. Kelly is a hearty advocate for supernaturalism in its fullest Christian sense (and you will not read far before you see his polemic against rationalism in every form). I know of no one who is better at making the unseen world of spirituality reality vivid and tangible. Here we begin to enjoy the fruits of his labors of more than three decades as a doctor of the church and servant of the Word in the teaching of systematic theology. What a feast it is. Few Protestant theologians in our day know the terrain of the doctrine of the Trinity, and the Person of Christ, as well as Professor Kelly. Consequently, he is at his best when opening up to us the unrealized importance and glory of these foundational truths about our Savior God. For those who yearn for an orthodox Reformed catholicity, Kelly shows the way forward.

Ligon Duncan
Chancellor and CEO of the Reformed Theological Seminary System,
John E. Richards Professor of Systematic and
Historical Theology at Reformed Theological Seminary

This is the fruit of decades of research, thought and teaching. Kelly's procedure is entirely sound; Scripture is his basis, the primary authority, but he engages throughout the past teaching of the church.. In this he follows in the footsteps of Calvin and the Westminster and the Westminster Assembly. His breadth of coverage is wide.

Evangelicals Now

SYSTEMATIC THEOLOGY

VOLUME ONE

Grounded in Holy Scripture and understood in the light of the Church

DOUGLAS F. KELLY

THE GOD WHO IS: THE HOLY TRINITY

MENTOR

ISBN 978-1-84550-386-4 – Book
ISBN 978-1-78191-387-1 – ePub
ISBN 978-1-78191-388-8 – Mobi

10 9 8 7 6 5 4 3 2 1

Published in 2008 and reprinted in 2014 and 2021
in the
Mentor Imprint
by
Christian Focus Publications Ltd.,
Geanies House, Fearn, Ross-shire,
IV20 1TW, Scotland, Great Britain

www.christianfocus.com

Cover design by Daniel van Straaten
Printed by Bell & Bain, Glasgow

MIX
Paper from
responsible sources
FSC® C007785

Contents

Hoc volumen filio quarto meo
Patrick Blue McMillan Campbell Kelly
diligatione aestimationeque dedicatum est

Haec est autem vita aeterna,
ut cognoscant te solum Deum verum,
et quem misisti, Iesum Christum.

Ioannes XVII:iii

Author's Preface

I was born and brought up in the Presbyterian Church in the United States (the old 'Southern Presbyterian Church'). At the age of twenty-four, I was ordained into the ministry of this church, and have always believed its basic teachings as I learned them at the feet of my believing family and local church. Particularly, I grew up trusting in Christ as my personal Lord and Savior, God as my heavenly Father, and the Holy Spirit as my sanctifier. From family and church, I learned, and still believe in the Holy Scriptures as the written Word of God, 'the only infallible rule for faith and practice.' I cannot claim to have lived up to all I believe, but such has been my sincere and lifelong desire.

While every Christian denomination has its own limitations, the Reformed churches do have the considerable advantage of seeing themselves as true branches of a much larger, ancient and worldwide body: the body of Christ; the bride of Christ, as part of the Holy Catholic Church (and not the whole of it). The Church of Scotland, which is the mother church of American Presbyterians, saw itself, not as a new denomination, but simply as the Catholic Church *Reformed* in Scotland.

A Manual of Church Doctrine according to the Church of Scotland explains how the Reforming Catholics in sixteenth-century Scotland (and much of Europe) understood themselves:

> While retaining in common the Divine Ordinances and the Catholic Creeds, they [the sixteenth century European Reformers] adopted, each for itself as it was reformed, 'Confessions' or statements of doctrine, for the guidance of teaching and for testimony: and they regulated their internal policy on different models. They have not thereby changed their identity or broken their continuity. They are the same national churches now reformed, and members of the one visible and Catholic Church which our Standards [i.e. the Westminster Standards of the 1640s] define.
>
> The Reformers believed that it was the Roman Church that had departed from the Apostolic faith. It was by the Church itself that the Reformation had been effected. The Reformers sought not to destroy the Church as a united and visible body, but to strengthen it and cleanse it by restoring its Apostolic and primitive form. In the eyes of the Reformers there was no real disruption at the Reformation – baptism and ordination were held as valid and the Reformed presbyter emerged from the Roman priesthood;

> the Catholic Church Reformed was no national sect, but The Universal Kirk [according to the *Scots Confession* of 1560, art. xvi] …
>
> The word 'Catholic' has also a canonical and juristic sense which is decided by the Edict of Gratian, Valentinian, and Theodosius (A.D. 380): that those are to be called Catholics who believe in 'the one Godhead and equal majesty and holy tri-unity of the Father, the Son and the Holy Ghost'. The Scottish Reformers in 1558 had this definition in view when they required that 'the Church be reformed in accordance with the precepts of the New Testament, the writings of the Ancient Fathers, and the Godly and approved laws of the Emperor Justinian' (in whose code the Theodosian Edict had been incorporated) … As a branch of the Reformed Church the Church of Scotland has consistently followed the example of Calvin who sought to restore the face of the Apostolic and Catholic Church by reforming it in accordance with its apostolic foundation and in agreement with the Catholic doctrine of the Ecumenical Councils of the undivided Church …[1]

Therefore, I have written this first volume of *Systematic Theology*, thinking of my heritage as both Reformed and Catholic; gladly appropriating crucial insights, as best I could understand them, of the whole people of God over the last two thousand years – Eastern Orthodox, Western Catholic, and Reformation Protestant – as they sought to explicate and live out the foundational truths of the inspired Word of God.

I like what Dr. (often called 'Rabbi') John Duncan (Free Church of Scotland minister, former missionary to the Jews, and erudite professor of Old Testament in nineteenth-century New College in Edinburgh) once said: 'I'm first a Christian, next a Catholic, then a Calvinist, fourth a Paedobaptist and fifth a Presbyterian. I cannot reverse this order.'[2]

For all of these reasons, I entitle this work: *Systematic Theology: Grounded in Holy Scripture and Understood in Light of the Church*. Christ promised that the Holy Spirit would be with the Church to the end of time, so as to guide her into all truth (John 16:13-15). The Apostle Paul makes it clear that all parts of the universal Church need one another in order to see the fullness of this truth (Eph. 1). It takes the whole Church to understand the whole truth. God reveals His life and truth within the covenant community (of Israel and of the Church). Dissociated individuals, cut off from the covenant community of faith and the covenant Word in the Scriptures, are in no position accurately to grasp and articulate God's saving truth. They need the Church in order to see and experience the Word of God in God's own light (cf. Ps. 36:9), and this volume seeks to call them into this believing fellowship of grace. This believing fellowship of grace has been divinely called out from all ages, cultures, tribes and tongues. That is why I have not hesitated to draw from its rich resources from a wide array of denominational traditions, who have often vehemently disagreed among themselves on important issues, but nonetheless, have ultimately agreed on

---

[1] H. J. Wotherspoon and J. M. Kirkpatrick, *A Manual of Church Doctrine according to the Church of Scotland* (Second Edition), Revised and enlarged by T. F. Torrance and Ronald Selby Wright (London: Oxford University Press, 1960), 9, 10.

[2] William Knight, *Colloquia Peripatetica: Conversations with John Duncan* (Edinburgh: Oliphant, 1907), p. 8.

far more than divided them, since it is a God-ordained characteristic that 'the sheep hear Christ's voice and follow Him' (John 10:27). It is my humble prayer that the bread of heaven and the living waters may be multiplied to many of God's people (and to some outside the fold who may thereby find their true spiritual home), as they read this volume.

Thanks and Acknowledgements

It remains my happy task to thank many who have helped me in so many different ways while this first volume has been in preparation. I started on it during a sabbatical leave from Reformed Theological Seminary in Charlotte, North Carolina, to the University of Edinburgh (1998–99), and largely finished it during a second sabbatical leave (from and to the same places) in 2005–06. Of necessity, I have done plenty of other things during these years, so that I had to lay aside this book for long stretches of time, but it has remained my major project. Since it has stretched over seven or eight years, I fear that I shall forget some who have been of significant assistance. If I did not keep a personal daily diary, this task of acknowledgments would indeed be hopeless. And even with the diary, I am likely to neglect important servants of God, who have done much for me. If so, I apologize to them ahead of time. But no doubt they did it primarily for Christ, 'who is not unfaithful to forget their labour of love.'

First, I am grateful to Reformed Theological Seminary (RTS) for these two academic leaves of absence, and to my alma mater, New College (University of Edinburgh), which allowed me to be a visiting scholar during these periods of study. I thank Professor (and Dean) David Fergusson for his help. Also I thank the Free Church of Scotland College in Edinburgh, who (under Principal Donald Macleod) kindly provided me with an office during these sabbaticals. Holyrood Abbey Church of Scotland in Edinburgh helped me with housing during the first sabbatical, and the Banner of Truth Trust in Edinburgh provided housing during the second period (with the assistance of former director, Iain Murray, and the current director, Jonathan Watson). Rutherford House of Edinburgh was of great help, as was Dr. Frank Gibson of Edinburgh. Elder Jim Shipway, Elder and Mrs. Tom Maxwell, and Elder and Mrs. Ken Colville rendered us much help during our time in Edinburgh.

The first trip was made possible by generous assistance of several of the Lord's people: the Rev. William Fulton of Austin, Texas; Elder Tommy Peaster of Yazoo City, Mississippi; Mrs. Betty Edwards of Jackson, Mississippi; the session of Second Presbyterian Church in Yazoo City, Mississippi; Dr. Michael Brown of Dillon, South Carolina; Elders Jim Atkins and Coble Adams of Dillon, South Carolina; the session of Reedy Creek Presbyterian Church of Minturn, South Carolina; and the session of Sovereign Grace Presbyterian Church of Charlotte, North Carolina; and also the late Mr. Jerre Pearson of Auburn, Alabama and Mrs. Jane Moore of Charlotte, North Carolina.

My long-time secretary, Mrs. Tari Williamson, the RTS-Charlotte librarian, the Rev. Ken McMullen, and a number of able student assistants have strengthened my hands. Among them are Scott Lingle, Matthew Miller,

Chris Finnigan, Paul Mulner, Mark Miller and Blake Schwartz. I am grateful to the former President of RTS, Dr. Luder Whitlock, and to his successor, Dr. Ric Cannada, Chancellor of RTS, for all of their help. Mr. Alex Mark, minister to the youth of First Presbyterian Church of Dillon, South Carolina (with generous contributions from Mr. and Mrs. Jack McInnis, Mr. and Mrs. Earl Rich Alford, Mr. and Mrs. Neill Alford, Mr. John Manton Alford, and Dr. and Mrs. Michael Brown, all of Dillon) provided for me a laptop computer on which I have composed most of this volume. Thanks go to Mr. F. E. Hobeika of Dillon, South Carolina who makes it possible for us to be away for long periods by looking after our house.

Monsieur Jean-Marc Berthoud, a lay scholar (in the Reformed tradition) of Lausanne, has been of inestimable service as he has constantly interacted with me on the preparation of this volume. He has offered insightful critique and suggestions throughout all its chapters, and has provided books, articles and papers, which always seemed to come at just the right time. For whatever the book may be worth, much of its value will go back to his highly knowledgeable and perceptive theological mind. He has made my pathway much less lonely. And I am grateful for discussions on aspects of feminist theology with the Rev. David Jones, of Reformed University Fellowship at Stanford University in California.

Also I wish to thank cordially two distinguished scholars from other major Christian traditions (Eastern Orthodox and Roman Catholic) for generously taking the time to look over the manuscript: Protopresbyter George Dion Dragas (a former New College, Edinburgh, classmate of mine), now Professor of Theology of Holy Cross Greek Orthodox School of Theology in Massachusetts, and Father Joseph Koterski, S.J., Associate Professor and Chair of the Philosophy Department of Fordham University in New York.

Above all others, I thank my noble wife, Caroline, for all she is and does, and I thank the hundreds of Christians who have reminded me of how much they have prayed for this long project. The head of Christian Focus Publications in Scotland, Elder William Mackenzie, and my chief editor, the Rev. Malcolm Maclean of the Free Church of Scotland on the Isle of Scalpay, have made it possible for this work finally to appear. I am particularly grateful to my youngest son, Patrick, who has spent a great deal of time, care, and love, proofreading this work and suggesting changes to improve it.

My prayer for all of these good people, and for all who will ever read this volume, is that of the Psalmist:

> Lord, bless and pity us,
> Shine on us with thy face:
> That th' earth thy way, and nations all
> May know thy saving grace.
> Let people praise thee, Lord;
> Let people all thee praise.
> O let the nations be glad,
> In songs their voices raise.
>
> (Ps. 67:1-4; Scottish metrical version).

Chapter One

Knowledge of God: God Reveals Himself

God reveals Himself in the light of who He is by means of His Word and Spirit personally within the context of the covenant community. Thus, the pressure of the revelation of His truth gives rise to faith within this chosen community of grace throughout the Old and New Testaments. Faith is marked by believing assent and occurs within the atmosphere of prayer. God's revelation of Himself is validated the same way it was revealed: in the gracious community context created by His Word and Spirit. To enter this context of life and truth, one must look out of every unbelieving framework to Him who is 'the way, the truth and the life.'

I. God Makes Himself Known

The living God has made Himself known. That is the basic meaning of 'Theology', composed of two Greek words *Theos* (God) and *Logos* (word, or meaning or rationality). It is the essence of scientific procedure to seek to know a given reality in accordance with its nature. We must put questions to this reality in a way that is appropriate to what it is, so that it can reveal itself to us. The sort of questions we pose must be determined by the nature of the object (in the case of God, our 'object' is the supreme 'Subject' in control of all reality).

To know God, we must start our inquiry at the very place where He has chosen to make Himself known. The Living God has made Himself known in His Word in the Scriptures of the Old and New Testaments, and supremely in the person and work of His Son, the Lord Jesus Christ, God made flesh, 'the one Mediator between God and men, the man Christ Jesus' (1 Tim. 2:5). The Old Testament is the background and preparation for Christ, and the New Testament is His full manifestation (see Luke 24:25-27 and John 5:39). As Novatian of Rome said in the mid-third century: 'This Jesus Christ, I say again, the Son of this God, was promised, as we read in the Old Testament, and we find Him set before us in the New Testament, fulfilling the shadows and types of all mysterious foreshadowings, by the presence of the embodied truth' (*De Trinitate* IX.46). Or in the famous words of Saint Augustine, 'Novum testamentum in vetere latet, vetus testamentum in novo patet' (*Quaest. 73 in Exod.*).[1]

Those who wish to know this true and living God are in a most happy position, for He reveals Himself both in His written Word and, above all, in His Son as a speaking God. The very first chapter of the Bible begins with God speaking the cosmos into existence, and then in the heart of the New Testament, we are told that God the Father's last word has been spoken to us 'in his Son ... by whom also he made the worlds' (Heb. 1:2). And as we shall see, the very 'worlds he made' also speak of Him in their own appointed way (see Ps. 19:1-6 and Rom. 1:18–2:16).

Holy Scripture does not begin with arguments for the possibility of God's existence. It starts with reality, not possibility: 'In the beginning God created the heaven and the earth' (Gen. 1:1). Probably 'beginning' (בראשית) refers to the beginning of the space/time cosmos; to the origin of what the Nicene Creed calls 'all things visible and invisible'; that is, to the beginning of everything that is not God.[2] Thus the Old Testament begins with the majestic reality of God who creates all things 'out of nothing'.

Strange as it may seem to human logic, the New Testament takes us (to use human time words) 'much further back' than that! For John 1:1, with obvious reference to Genesis 1:1, tells us that 'In the beginning was the Word (Λόγος), and the Word was with God and the Word was God.' That is to say, Word (Λόγος) existed with God the Father before there was ever a world. This Word is identified in John 1:14 and 18 as God's 'only begotten Son.' The Son being fully God is as eternal as His Father.

Hence, from all eternity there has been 'Word' in God; there has existed a community of speaking, sharing and communication within God. That is why it should not be thought strange that this speaking, communicating God, who at a chosen point created humanity in His own image in order to know Him (Gen. 1:26, 27; Eph. 4:24; Col. 3:10), should speak to us so as to reveal Himself to us and reveal who we are and the meaning of the world around us. As John Calvin says, to know Him is to know ourselves; to know ourselves is to be confronted with Him (*Institutes of the Christian Religion* I.1.1).

II. How Ultimate Truth Can Be Known

In our world today, which is suspicious of truth claims, especially those with a transcendent reference, the question is certain to arise: how do we know that these assertions concerning God, Christ, Scripture and valid knowledge are true? After all, many contrary assertions to explain reality (or perhaps to deny that it can even be known) are available in the marketplace of ideas. What claim then do these biblical teachings have on us?

---

[1]'The New Testament is in the Old concealed, the Old Testament in the New revealed.'

[2]In the original Hebrew text of Genesis 1:1, the term – הַשָּׁמַיִם וְאֵת הָאָרֶץ –'the heavens and the earth') – functions as a 'merism'. That is to say, this term is all inclusive of every sort of reality apart from God, the Creator Himself.

From beginning to end, it must clearly be recognized that the only way humans can properly test truth claims to ultimate reality must be in light of who that ultimate reality is and how He acts and speaks. The supreme reality makes Himself known as the personal God, and hence the supreme truth He reveals at its very heart partakes of His personal reality and is, for that reason, what the Greek Church Fathers called αὐτουσία (that is, 'self-existence' or 'self-evidence'). That is to say, the supreme truth of the personal God does not depend on anything outside itself to validate itself, for why should that which is ultimate be dependent on that which is subordinate for its power to convince?

Professor Thomas F. Torrance has seen this with clarity, and two references should help us grasp this point:

> There is no way to demonstrate this Truth outside of the Truth; the only way for the ultimate Truth to prove Himself is to be the truth, and the only way for us to prove the ultimate Truth is to let Him be what He is before us, in His αὐτουσία and αὐτεξουσία. That is the majesty and prerogative of the Truth of God as it is in Jesus, Truth who is ultimate in identity with the Being and Act of God, Truth who is and cannot be established by us, Truth who will not be mastered and yet will not remain closed to us, Truth who unveils Himself for us and who is known only through Word and Grace on God's part and faith and thankfulness on our part. It is He who says, 'I am the way, the truth and the life; no man cometh to the Father but by me' (John 14:6) (*Theological Science*, 144).

> With us human beings authority is not something that functions by itself but depends on something else that gives it its impelling force and something else again through which it is implemented; but this is not the case with God in whom will and action and the power of his divine Being perfectly coincide. This was the point recognized by the Alexandrian theologians when they spoke of God's Authority as Αὐτοεξουσία in the same way in which they spoke of his Truth as Αὐτοαλεθειὰ Ἀληθεία and Ἐξουσία are one in the ἐγώ ἐιμι, of his very Being as God, so that Αὐτοαλεθεία and Αὐτοεξουσία represent cognate ways in which we have to do with the ultimate Reality and Majesty of God himself (*Theological Dialogue Between Orthodox and Reformed Churches*, 108).

An understanding of this αὐτουσία of God's supreme truth in Person and Word lies behind John Calvin's teaching that the final proof of the truth of the Holy Scriptures is that, since they are given by God, they are αὐτοπίστος (or 'self-evidencing').[3] They shine in their own light, when the One who inspired them illumines the mind of the recipient. No auxiliary, creaturely light is needed to convince the reader of their ultimate authority.[4]

God who is truth and lives in truth reveals Himself truly to His image-bearers so that they may respond to Him in truth. God, the Creator,

---

[3]John Calvin, *Institutes*, I.vii.2 and .5.

[4]See Calvin, ibid., I.vii.5 and III.ii.33: 'And this bare and external proof of the Word of God should have been amply sufficient to engender faith, did not our blindness and perversity prevent it. But our mind has such an inclination to vanity that it can never cleave fast to the truth of God; and it has such a dullness that it is always blind to the light of God's truth. Accordingly, without the illumination of the Holy Spirit, the Word can do nothing. From this, also, it is clear that faith is much higher than human understanding. And it will not be enough for the mind to be illumined by the Spirit of God unless the heart is also strengthened and supported by his power.'

comes first, and His created image-bearers come second. As the medieval Scholastics said in a different context, *'operari sequitur esse'* ('operation follows being'). This means that the order of knowing follows the order of being and determines it. As we do not prescribe to God how He shall be, so we do not prescribe how we shall know. The fact that God is God means that only He can reveal Himself to His creatures, for forcefully to draw information out of God would take a power greater than God.[5]

As Tertullian said to the heretic, Marcion, in the early third century: 'In what manner then has he been revealed? If [you suggest] by human surmisings, I answer that a god cannot be known except on his own showing, and I appeal not only to the method employed by the Creator, but also to the conditions imposed as well by divine greatness as by human insignificance. Otherwise the man might appear greater than the god, for he would, without the god previously consenting to be known, have as it were by his own power dragged him out into the publicity of being known – though human insignificance has, by the trial and error of all the ages, found it easier to invent gods for itself than to attend upon the true God, of whom they are already aware by nature' (*Adversus Marcionem*, I.xviii, translated and edited by Ernest Evans, Oxford, 1972).

In our own day, Karl Barth has stated it well in a number of places:

> Divine determination and revelation, and not man's approval, are the criterion of what is appropriate to God and salutary for us. It is not for our human approval to precede the divine approval, but to follow it up. The God-created fact of revelation is the manifestation of this divine approval. And therefore it is the judge of our convictions and not *vice versa* (*Church Dogmatics* I.2, p. 5).
>
> ... God is known through God and through God alone. God speaks to man in His Word. Thereby He gives Himself to him to be known; therein He is known by him. In this way, as the One who speaks to him, God stands before man, and it comes to pass that man stands before Him, and that man for his part – as happens in the Church of Jesus Christ – can speak and hear about Him (*Church Dogmatics* II.1, p. 44).

III. Truth Is Known within a Covenant Community

Scripture teaches throughout that God, who is truth, makes Himself known to mankind by means of both Word and personal communion within a covenant context. God speaks His Word to His image-bearers, not in a vacuum, but

[5]Origen states this point forcefully against the Neo-Platonic adversary of Christianity, Celsus, as follows: 'Celsus supposes that we may arrive at a knowledge of God either by combining or separating certain things after the methods which mathematicians call synthesis or analysis, or again by analogy, which is employed by them also, and that in this way we may as it were gain admission to the chief good. But when the Word of God says, "No man knoweth the Father, but the Son, and he to whom the Son will reveal Him," He declares that no one can know God but by the help of divine grace coming from above with a certain divine inspiration. Indeed it is reasonable to suppose that the knowledge of God is beyond the reach of human nature, and hence the many errors into which men have fallen in their views of God. It is then through the goodness and love of God to mankind, and by a marvellous exercise of divine grace to those whom He saw in His foreknowledge ...' (*Contra Celsum*, VII.44).

within a personal relationship. And this personal relationship in which God's speaking occurs is always in the bounds of a covenant community. God is in charge of the speaking, of the persons who are addressed, and of their covenant relationship to Him and to one another within the wider creation.

The Sovereign God chooses to speak to those whom He has made for relationship with Him in what must be termed a gracious community context, or Covenant of Grace. Even prior to and apart from the fall of mankind into sin, God's condescension to know and be known in a personal and intimate way by His infinitely inferior subject, man, constituted sovereign grace and infinite loving kindness. The first three chapters of Genesis indicate that man was made in such a way that when he functions properly, he may know truth.

IV. Within that Community Truth Gives Rise to Faith

God's being and speaking in truth and grace to mankind are intended to evoke an appropriate response from His image-bearers, and that is faith, which is found only within a community of faith (or context of inter-relationship that depends on grace). The Church Fathers frequently noted three points about this movement: first, faith is caused by truth; second, faith is the only appropriate response to truth; and third, faith arises within a community context.

Faith is caused by truth

Truth causes faith; that is to say, objective reality always has priority over subjective response. The early Church Father, Irenaeus of Lyon, stated in the late second century: 'And faith is produced by the truth; for faith rests on things that truly are...' (*Demonstration of Apostolic Preaching*, 3). God created all things out of nothing; created mankind for fellowship with Himself, and graciously spoke to them, as the Gospel of Luke clearly implies, as a Father (Luke 3:38). After their disobedience and expulsion from His immediate presence (Gen. 3:22-24), God made promises of grace to them (Gen. 3:15) and over the long centuries continued to speak to them by the prophets, and 'hath in these last days spoken unto us by His Son by whom also he made the worlds' (Heb. 1:2). Throughout the entire process of making Himself known, what God says is always the ground on which He is to be known. Hilary of Poitiers wrote around A.D. 350: 'For He whom we can know only through his own utterances is a fitting witness concerning himself' (*De Trinitate*, I.xviii).[6] Or as Clement of Alexandria had written earlier: 'The voice of the Lord is the only demonstration of Himself' (*Stromateis* VII.xvi).

Faith is the appropriate response to truth

Second, the appropriate response to truth is faith. God's reality imposes itself upon those whom He has made to know Him, as Paul brings out

[6]This statement of Hilary is quoted by John Calvin in *Institutes*, I.vii.4.

in Romans 1 and 2. Clement of Alexandria describes how truth begets a response: 'Knowledge is excited by outwardly existing objects' (*Strom.*, VI.viii).

T. F. Torrance writes:

> The question must be raised as to how we get inside this new world of meaning... The answer given, for example by Clement of Alexandria, was that here we have to reckon with realities which, like the first principles in geometry or the simple facts of perception, are known on the strength not of anything else but of themselves, that is, through a basic act of assent or faith in recognition of and in response to those realities. The right way to break through into the new realm of meaning or truth, therefore, is the way of faith, for unless we believe, we will not understand [Isa. 7:9]. Now faith involves a conceptual assent to the unseen reality, for the proof of an unknown reality is its own evidence and the evident assent it calls forth from us. That is to say, if we are really to understand, we must willingly allow our minds to fall under the compulsive self-evidence of the reality, otherwise we merely lapse back uncritically into our own false preconceptions (*Reality and Evangelical Theology*, 102).

Far from being antithetical to reason, 'Faith is the orientation of the reason toward God's self-revelation, the rational response of man to the word of God ... a fully rational acknowledgement of a real Word given to us by God from beyond us.'[7] Put another way, faith is an utterly scientific (that is, appropriate) response to the reality of the God who speaks in His Word. Much of the research of T. F. Torrance has shown that humble belief before the Word of God is, in its own field, in line with the way scientific reasoning functions in other (creaturely) realms of knowledge:

> In the first place, the reorientation that has been taking place in the foundation of scientific knowledge, which we have traced from Clerk Maxwell through Einstein to Polanyi, demands that we must recognize belief or intuitive apprehension once more as the source of knowledge from which our acts of discovery take their rise, for it is in belief that we are in direct contact with reality, and through belief that our minds remain open to the invisible realm of intelligibility independent of ourselves... Regarded in this way, faith and rationality are intrinsically bound together. It must be granted ... that by their nature beliefs of this kind are not themselves directly or logically demonstrable, for they have what Einstein called 'extra-logical' status, but they are nonetheless rational. They are concerned not with the relations of ideas or indeed with relations of matters of fact, but with the relations of ideas to being which cannot be put into logical or rationalistic form. They are logically prior to any demonstration for they have to do with the bearing of reason on the nature and structure of things, which all explicit forms of reasoning are intended to serve and without which they are blind and impotent. In this event it is unreasonable to throw faith and reason into a Lockean 'contradistinction', for faith is the very mode of rationality which the reason takes in its faithful adaptation to what it seeks to understand and explain (*Christian Theology & Scientific Culture*, 69).

---

[7]T. F. Torrance, *Theological Science*, (London: Oxford University Press, 1969) 33.

Faith is neither non-cognitive nor mere emotion

Thus, faith is not a non-cognitive or merely emotional approach to God, nor is it a psychological projecting of human desires and needs into a supposed 'infinite' realm. On the contrary, faith is an intelligible and obedient response, like that of the child, Samuel, to the voice of that reality which is infinitely great, yet tenderly near: 'Speak, Lord, for thy servant heareth' (1 Sam. 3:10). Faith in a sense restores our access to the cognitive first principles on which reason properly functions. Faith puts us into direct contact with ultimate reality, which cannot be seen by mortal eye, for 'faith is the substance of things hoped for, the evidence of things not seen' (Heb. 11:1). It takes us through the visible up to that which is invisible and absolute (which is the very foundation of that which is visible): 'Through faith we understand that the worlds were framed by the word of God, so that things which are seen were not made of things which do appear' (Heb. 11:3).

Even where, because of the hostility to God's existence caused by human sin, faith is not exercised, still those who do not believe are inexcusable, because of the powerful, inescapable evidence they wilfully and irrationally reject. As Paul states in Romans 1:19, 20: 'Because that which may be known of God is manifest in them; for God hath shewed it unto them. For the invisible things of him from the creation of the world are clearly seen, being understood by the things that are made, even his eternal power and Godhead; so that they are without excuse...'

Unbelief as foolishness

In terms of ultimate reality, instead of unbelief being wise (and thus, somehow 'scientific') and faith being foolish (and 'unscientific'), it is the exact opposite, as St. Hilary says: 'Thus all unbelief is foolishness, for it takes such wisdom as its own finite perception can attain, and measuring infinity by that petty scale, concludes that what it cannot understand must be impossible. Unbelief is the result of incapacity engaged in argument. Men are sure that an event never happened, because they have made up their minds that it could not happen' (*De Trinitate*, III.24).

The New Testament gives us a model of one whose foolish unbelief seemed to him to be wise (in that it was in accordance with the physical limitations of what he previously understood). This is 'doubting Thomas', who rejected the testimony of other believers who had witnessed Christ's resurrection body, with the words: 'Except I shall see in his hands the print of the nails, and put my finger into the print of the nails, and thrust my hand into his side, I will not believe' (John 20:25). Eight days later, the risen Christ meets Thomas and invites him: 'Reach hither thy finger, and behold my hands; and reach hither thy hand, and thrust it into my side: and be not faithless, but believing' (v. 27). Thomas passed from the folly of unbelief to the wisdom of faith, for unmistakable reality made him cry out: 'My Lord and my God' (v. 28). As the Fathers would have said it, truth caused faith, and faith was the only appropriate, fully rational response to what was really there.

It is no different with the whole range of the true knowledge of God. God confronts us with the reality He wishes us to know, and faith is the only fully rational response, especially when it is childlike and humbly receptive, for that is the only way we can enter into the kingdom of God (Matt. 18:3).

Circular reasoning and faith

If it be objected that it is 'circular reasoning' to be asked to exercise faith in a God who cannot be known outside His own witness to Himself, we must note that all forms of true knowledge must work with initial assumptions or beliefs:

> ... what we are concerned with ... here is the proper circular procedure inherent in any coherent system of thought operating with ultimate axioms or beliefs which cannot be justified or derived from any other ground than that which they themselves constitute. Thus in coherent conceptual systems with which we are familiar today in various fields of scientific knowledge, we are committed to certain ultimate axioms or beliefs for which we can offer no independent demonstration, but without which the scientific system concerned, together with the knowledge it yields, would not be possible at all.[8]

The proper mode of response to reality (or 'faith') of course varies in ways appropriate to the object it seeks to know. The necessary differences between a receptive response to the nature of creaturely realities (in the physical sciences, for instance) as contrasted with that called for by the nature of uncreated Being (in theology) has been explored by Professor Torrance, but will not be discussed here in any detail.[9] Obviously the way one seeks to uncover the patterns in a crystalline formation or the purity of water in a well is different from the way one seeks to make sense of the psychology of a human being, which is yet different from the way one must seek to know the eternal God. But there are similarities. In all cases of rational procedure (or 'scientific thinking' or true 'faith') one distinguishes between one's mind and the objective reality one seeks to know, thus assuming the reality of the external world; one seeks to understand a reality out of itself in accordance with what it really is, and hence one adapts one's mode of enquiry in accordance with the object to be known.

V. The Faith Occurring within this Community is Rooted in the Son's Knowledge of the Father in the Bonds of the Holy Spirit

Moreover, as far as the mode of rational response (or faith) elicited by the reality of God is concerned, we have seen that it always arises within a community of personal relationship (or 'covenant'). While faith is exercised by individuals (or it would not exist), yet it is never strictly individual. For

---

[8]T. F. Torrance, *The Christian Doctrine of God, One Being Three Persons*, (Edinburgh: T & & Clark, 1996) 28.

[9]T. F. Torrance, chapter 6, 'Theological Science among the Special Sciences,' in *Theological Science*, 281-352.

it arises in the speaking and hearing process (Romans 10:17: 'faith cometh by hearing'), which requires a community of more than one person for this dialogue to take place. Indeed, faith is exercised by persons, and the very concept of person (which arose in Western culture only under the impact of the doctrine of the Holy Trinity) means that there has to be relationship with others for a person to exist.[10] Knowledge of God can only arise within community because God Himself is, in a certain sense, 'community' within Himself. That is, the one God has always existed as three co-equal, sharing, speaking, loving Persons in one 'substance' or reality, in which each divine Person (intrinsically distinct in terms of being unbegotten, engendered and proceeding) indwells or coheres in the others. The divine Persons constitute the relations, and the relations are also constitutive of the Persons.

Thus, the ultimate theological knowledge is the inner-Trinitarian knowledge that God has of Himself, referred to by Jesus in Matthew 11:27: '... no man knoweth the Son, but the Father; neither knoweth any man the Father, save the Son, and he to whomsoever the Son will reveal him.' God, in whom is the Word (John 1:1), created mankind through the agency of His Word, whose 'life was the light of men' (John 1:4), and was 'the true light, which lighteth every man that cometh into the world' (v. 9). Even before the formation of Eve, the first man Adam was already in a community of knowing with God through the light of the Word and the speaking of the Father in a realm which had been ordered (Gen. 1:2), and in the words of Basil the Great, 'perfected' by the Spirit.[11] After the formation of Eve, God makes of the two 'one flesh' (Gen. 2:24), dealing with them, and later with their descendants in community or covenant terms. What Adam does affects all of his and Eve's descendants (that is, the entire human race) to the end of time (see Gen. 3:15-24; Rom. 5:12-21; I Cor. 15:21, 22, 45-47).

First promise of the gospel

Even in the midst of God's curse upon the serpent, He announces to Adam and Eve a promise of grace, often called 'the first promise of the gospel': 'And I will put enmity between thee and the woman, and between thy seed and her seed; it shall bruise thy head, and thou shalt bruise his feet' (Gen. 3:15; see also Rom. 16:20).[12] All the rest of the Scriptures show God dealing with

[10]As we shall see later in this volume in more detail, the definition of person as inherently involving relationship with other persons was given classical formulation by Richard of St. Victor in the twelfth century in his *De Trinitate*: 'persona est ... intellectualis naturae incommunicabilis existentia' ('a person is the incommunicable existence of intellectual nature'), IV.16, 22, 24.

[11]Basil, *De Spiritu Sancto*, 16.37, 38.

[12]In the words of Geerhardus Vos: 'As to the word "seed" there is no reason to depart from the collective sense .... The seed of the serpent *must* be collective, and this determines the sense of the seed of the woman. The promise is, that somehow out of the human race a fatal blow will come which shall crush the head of the serpent. Still, indirectly the possibility is hinted at that in striking this fatal blow the seed of the woman will be concentrated in one person, for it should be noticed that it is not the seed of the serpent, but the serpent itself whose head will be bruised. In the former half of the curse the two seeds are contrasted; here the woman's seed and the serpent. This suggests that as at the climax of the struggle the serpent's seed will be represented by the serpent, in the same manner the woman's seed may find representation in a single person; we are not warranted, however, in seeking an exclusively personal reference to the Messiah here, as though He alone were meant by

and speaking to the fallen descendants of Adam and Eve in terms of His redemptive purposes that they should be restored by grace to His family favor and communion. While we must deal with election elsewhere, let us notice here that God chooses representative figures from among the descendants of the first pair to be the bearers of His divine purposes to the others: Seth, Noah, Shem, Abraham, Isaac, Jacob, Joseph and Judah, David and others, culminating in 'Great David's greater Son' (see Ps. 110), Jesus Christ, God made man, who – as the genealogies of Matthew and Luke make plain – is the 'grand finale', the supreme offspring of all these preparatory forebears.

The line of godly seed

Seth, the third son of Adam, through whom the promise of a godly seed came, and Noah, whose family survived the universal flood, are the direct ancestors of Abraham, to whom and whose seed the Covenant of Grace is promised afresh (see Gen. 12, 15, 17, 21 and Rom. 4; Gal. 3:6-9; Heb. 11). Through Abraham's 'son of promise', Isaac (Gen. 21:12; Rom. 9:7), the one in whom 'his seed shall be called', came Jacob, the 'supplanter', who by wrestling with God had his name changed to Israel or 'prince with God' (Gen. 32 and 35:10). The entire Old Testament is centered in the history of Israel; Jacob and his descendants, who are elected to be the bearers of God's blessings to the entire world, thus fulfilling God's promise to Abraham that 'I will bless thee… and thou shalt be a blessing ... and in thee shall all the families of the earth be blessed' (Gen. 12:2, 3).

Israel as 'the womb of Christ'

Israel has been spoken of as 'the womb of Christ', the community with which He is in solidarity and out of which He is born, for 'salvation is of the Jews', as He Himself says to the Samaritan woman at the well (John 4:22). Christ chooses twelve apostles to reflect the continuity and fulfillment with the twelve tribes of Israel. God's Word was spoken by the prophets in the Old Testament community of Israel; Christ, the Word Incarnate, is born within Israel as the fulfillment of that prophetic Word, and then He chooses and empowers His apostles to be His witnesses and to receive the Holy Spirit that they might write down the authoritative and inspired account of His person and work for the Church, and through it to the whole world unto the end of time (see John, chapters 14 and 16, and especially verses 12-15 of chapter 16: 'I have yet many things to say unto you, but ye cannot bear them now. Howbeit when he, the Spirit of truth, is come, he will guide you into all truth: for he shall not speak of himself; but whatsoever he shall hear, that shall he speak: and he will shew you things to come. He

---

"the woman's seed". Old Testament Revelation approaches the concept of a personal Messiah very gradually. It sufficed for fallen man to know that through His divine power and grace God would bring out of the human race victory over the serpent. In that faith could rest. The object of their faith was much less definite than ours, who know the personal Messiah. But none the less, the essence of this faith, subjectively considered, was the same, viz., trust in God's grace and power to bring deliverance from sin' (*Biblical Theology*, Grand Rapids MI, Wm. B Eerdmans, 1948) 43, 44.

shall glorify me: for he shall receive of mine, and shall shew it unto you. All things that the Father hath are mine: therefore said I, that he shall take of mine, and shall shew it unto you.')

Martin Luther appositely summed up this truth: 'Since the Gospels and Epistles of the apostles have been written to direct us to the writings of the prophets and of Moses in the Old Testament so that we might read and see for ourselves how Christ was wrapped in swaddling clothes and laid in the manger – that is, how he is contained in the writings of the prophets.'[13]

The apostles' dependence on the Old Testament

The Holy Spirit's 'showing the things of Christ' to the apostles so that they could authoritatively interpret them to the Church in the writings of the New Testament for all time to come was the culminating point of the receptive activity of faith within a God-created community. From the very beginning of Israel's history, going back through Abraham, Shem, Noah and Seth to Adam and Eve 'the mother of all living' (Gen. 3:20), God has used the corporate life and responses of His chosen people as a way to make His Word understandable in their interactions with Him, with one another, and with the world around them, both positively and negatively. God uses the promises and threats of the covenants, the Mosaic Law, the sacrifices, ceremonies and offices of the Levitical System, the words and enacted parables of the prophets, slavery and Exodus, obedience and disobedience in the Promised Land, captivity and return to make His Word plain to His people; to work it deeply into their lives (rather like the Hebrew sense of כָּרַתִּי בְּרִית or 'cutting the covenant' into their very fleshly existence as His people).

Their intellectual and moral understanding of the infinitely great and Holy God could only occur in community; a community of life and faith in which He was binding themselves ontologically and covenantally to Himself ever more profoundly through the generations until the final appearance of His own Son in the flesh. Some sense of this movement to fulfilment of covenant knowledge seems reflected in Luke's Gospel in the blessings that Simeon and Anna gave to the Christ child when he was presented at the Temple (Luke 2:21-38), as well as in the 'Magnificat' of the Virgin Mary (Luke 1:46-55) and the Prophecy of Zacharias, father of John the Baptist (Luke 1:67-79).

Hence faith arises within the communion God has established with His people. While it is true that God makes Himself directly known to individuals, yet at the same time, they need one another to know him accurately. An illustration of this necessity of community for discernment of God's Word is found in the experience of the child Samuel. God spoke to him when he was by himself at night in his bed. The first three times that God called him, Samuel could not understand, and thought it was Eli, the priest, to whom he went running. After the third time, Eli

---

[13] Martin Luther, *A Brief Instruction on What to Look for and Expect in the Gospels, Church Postil,* 1522, *LW* 35, 122.

perceived what was happening, and instructed young Samuel to say, 'Speak, Lord, for thy servant heareth' (1 Sam. 3:9). Samuel obeyed Eli, and then was able to understand the voice of the Lord. Hence, it took someone else in the believing community for Samuel to be able to grasp the Word of God.

The Church: 'pillar and ground of the truth'

This is at least part of the meaning of Paul's description of the Church in 1 Timothy 3:15 as 'the pillar and ground of the truth.' Faith arises within the Church in its Old and New Testament phases, and it takes the Church together to know, interpret and be transformed by the blessings of the Triune God, as Paul prays:

> Wherefore I also, after I heard of your faith in the Lord Jesus, and love unto all the saints, Cease not to give thanks for you, making mention of you in my prayers, That the God of our Lord Jesus Christ, the Father of glory, may give unto you the spirit of wisdom and revelation in the knowledge of him: The eyes of your understanding being enlightened; that ye may know what is the hope of his calling, and what the riches of the glory of his inheritance in the saints, And what is the exceeding greatness of his power to us-ward who believe, according to the working of his mighty power, Which he wrought in Christ, when he raised him from the dead, and set him at his own right hand in the heavenly places (Eph. 1:15-20).

John teaches that one cannot love (perhaps the fullest sense of 'to know') God, whom one has not seen, without also loving (and thus knowing together with) the brother whom one has seen (1 John 4:20). A number of the Church Fathers reflect the understanding that faith necessarily occurs within the community established by God to know him together.[14] Novatian speaks of God as 'He whom the church knows and worships as God' (*De Trinitate* VIII.40) and goes on to say a few paragraphs later: 'In order that the whole world should not dry up in its aversion to the streams of his grace, He willed that through His Son apostolic messengers should be sent into all the world to instruct our race, that mankind in its condition might recognize its Creator, and if it would then follow Him, could have one whom it might address in its prayers as Father instead of God' (*ibid.*, VIII.42).

The community of faith needed to interpret the Scriptures

In his great work on interpretation of the Holy Scriptures, Augustine explains that one can properly understand the message of the inspired text only within the community of faith in which we are taught by other humans:

[14] e.g. Augustine, *De Trinitate*, VIII.12. Similarly, in the sixteenth-century Reformation, Calvin – commenting on Isaiah 60: 19 ('the Lord shall be thy everlasting light') – applies it to the Church: 'He there testifies that the light of God will arise in the church alone; and leaves only shadows and blindness outside the church [Isaiah 60: 2: 'shadows will shroud the earth and darkness will cover the peoples']. (*Institutes of the Christian Religion* II.3.1).

Let us not tempt the one in whom we have placed our trust, or we may be deceived by the enemy's cunning and perversity and become unwilling even to go to church to hear and learn the gospel, or to read the biblical text or listen to it being read and preached, preferring to wait until 'we are caught up into the third heaven, whether in the body or out of the body' (in the words of the apostle) [2 Cor. 12:2-4], and there hear 'words that cannot be expressed, which a human being may not utter' or see the Lord Jesus Christ in person and hear the gospel from him rather than from men.

Let us beware of such arrogant and dangerous temptations, and rather reflect that the apostle Paul, no less, though cast to the ground and then enlightened by a divine voice from heaven, was sent to a human being to receive the sacrament of baptism and be joined to the church [Acts 9:3-8]. And Cornelius the centurion, although an angel announced to him that his prayers had been heard and his acts of charity remembered, was nevertheless put under the tuition of Peter... All this could certainly have been done through an angel, but the human condition would be wretched indeed if God appeared unwilling to minister his word to human beings through human agency. It has been said, 'For God's temple is holy, and that temple you are' [1 Cor. 3:17]: how could that be true if God did not make divine utterances from his human temple but broadcast direct from heaven or through angels the learning that he wished to be passed on to mankind? Moreover, there would be no way for love, which ties people together in the bonds of unity, to make souls overflow and as it were intermingle with each other, if human beings learned nothing from other humans' (*De Doctrina Christiana*, Preface, 5-6, translated by R. P. H. Green, Oxford University Press, 1997)

The sixteenth-century Reformer, John Calvin, who in many respects was a follower of Augustine, spoke in much the same way, as he commented on Ephesians 4:10-13:

We see how God, who could in a moment perfect his own, nevertheless desires them to grow up into manhood solely under the education of the church. We see the way set for it: the preaching of the heavenly doctrine has been enjoined upon the pastors. We see that all are brought under the same regulation, that with a gentle and teachable spirit they may allow themselves to be governed by teachers appointed to this function. Isaiah had long before distinguished Christ's Kingdom by this mark: 'My spirit which is upon you, and my words which I have put in your mouth, shall never depart out of your mouth, or out of the mouth of your children, or out of the mouth of your children's children' [Isa. 59:21]. From this it follows that all those who spurn the spiritual food, divinely extended to them through the hand of the church, deserve to perish in famine and hunger. God breathes faith into us only by the instrument of his gospel, as Paul points out that 'faith comes from hearing' [Rom. 10:17]. Likewise the power to save rests with God [Rom. 1:16]; but (as Paul again testifies) He displays and unfolds it in the preaching of the gospel...

But as he did not entrust the ancient folk to angels but raised up teachers from the earth truly to perform the angelic office, so also today it is his will to teach us through human means.[15]

[15]*Institutes of the Christian Religion*, IV.1.5.

Three Reformation prayers for the Holy Spirit to help the Church understand and obey the truth

The truest theology is expressed in the prayers of the Church, in all of its branches. Since I know the Reformed stream of Christianity best, I include here three prayers from the Reformation era that indicate the profound piety in which these (and countless other) teachers of the Church sought God's help in order to understand and communicate His truth.

Pierre Viret (1511–1571)

Pierre Viret, Swiss Reformer, colleague of John Calvin, and preacher at the Cathedral of Lausanne, often began his sermons with the following prayer:

> Recognizing our faults and imperfections, and that we have nothing of ourselves that we did not receive from above, we humble ourselves before the high majesty of our good God and Father, full of all goodness and mercy, praying to Him that He would not enter into judgment with us so as to punish us and correct us in His anger and fury [Psalm 6] in regard to our faults and iniquities, but that instead He would look upon the innocence, righteousness and obedience of His Son, Jesus Christ, whom He gave over to death for us.
>
> For the love with which He pleases His Father, may the Lord have mercy upon us all, and by His celestial light chase away all darkness, error and ignorance from our hearts, filling us with His grace and with His Holy Spirit. Thus, may He lead us into full confidence in all truth, and open to us the true understanding of His holy Word, so that it may not be corrupted by our carnal sense and understanding. Instead, may He give us the grace by which He spoke by His holy prophets and apostles, so that being led by the same Spirit, we may declare to His honour and glory and to the edification of all. And may we not listen only with carnal ears to our own judgment and condemnation like the infidels and hypocrites, but rather may we be enabled to receive it in our hearts as true children of God, by a true and living faith, which will be efficacious and active by love.
>
> In this way may we learn to renounce ourselves, so that we no longer follow any idolatry, superstition or wicked carnal affections, so that we may fully place all our trust in Him, and consecrate ourselves and confirm ourselves completely to His holy will. Hence, may we know the favour of our Lord Jesus Christ, so that we may be found irreproachable and without spot before His face.
>
> Together with all of these blessings, let us ask of this good God and Father all other things which He knows are necessary for us. Thus, as this great Saviour and Redeemer, Jesus Christ, His dear Son, our sovereign Master, has taught us all to pray with one heart: 'Our Father, which art in heaven…'[16]

Theodore Beza (1519–1605)

Theodore Beza, successor of John Calvin in Geneva, poet, theologian, textual critic and statesman wrote the following prayer for God's light in

[16]Pierre Viret, *Instruction Chrétienne, Tome Premier*, édition établie, présentée et annotée par Arthur-Louis Hofer (Lausanne: L'Age d'Homme, 2004), 365, 366.

understanding His Word. First he refers to Hebrews 1:1 and 1 Timothy 3, and then prays:

> Lord God eternal, who knoweth that every man is but flesh, and that flesh is but corruption, so that although thou hast endued him with a reasonable soul which doth distinguish him from other creatures, yet his light is notwithstanding converted into darkness, when thereby he seeketh to penetrate into the glory of thy Kingdom and the mysteries of thy grace; who knoweth that this poor blind creature, born destitute of thy supernatural light, doth in lieu of his God, forge to himself an idol, and instead of truth, talketh lies; for thy word, his own inventions; for goodness, vanity; and for the path to life, the way to death. And albeit thou hast even from the beginning made thy self as it were visible to man, in the table of the universal world, that thou hast many times revealed thy self unto him in a lively voice, by the eternal word in *Eden*, *Horeb*, in the burning bush, and elsewhere, afterward by thy Prophets, insinuating thy self by thy [S]pirit into their hearts and thoughts, to the end by their ministry to instruct thy people; and finally that thou hast also manifested thy self in greater light by thy own word made flesh for our redemption, and speaking unto us by his mouth. Yea which is more, that thou hast so far graced us, that this thy word of life hath been, and still remaineth amongst us, faithfully collected in the sacred registers of the holy Scripture, so to be unto us, the image of thy glory, the Law of thy Kingdom, the ladder to heaven, the gate to Paradise, the trumpet of salvation; to be brief, the treasury of piety, virtue, wisdom, consolation and perfection. Yet the flesh nevertheless ignorant, rash and perverse, hath neither eyes to perceive these spiritual riches, nor ears to hear the wholesome doctrine, but doth rather disdain it, as it were some devised discourse, and unprofitable voice; or howsoever it be, suffering itself to be carried away with it[s] own and feeble imaginations, taketh in this vall[e]y, the thorn for the rose, the leaf for the fruit, and the husk for the kernel. And thus are we all born in this error, in this calamity, in this way to mortal ruin, until that thou (O merciful God) makest us to be born again, of the [S]pirit, and in will to make our thoughts capable of the light of thy word; and through true faith, to apprehend the mysteries of thy kingdom, the covenant of life, the gospel of thy peace, and the assured testimonies of thy mercies. Unto this grace of inestimable value doth my timorous soul direct her vows in searching thee (O great King of heaven) throughout the course of thy faithful testimonies, which minister wisdom to the ignorant (the holy Scriptures). I beseech thee therefore (my God) vouchsafe to direct and guide me in the understanding of this eternal truth, through the operation of thy [S]pirit, (the true teacher of our souls), that being by him instructed, I may accomplish and make my self perfect in these four chief principles of the doctrine of salvation, which are fully taught at large. (The knowledge of thee the true God, and the God of thy people, and the knowledge of faith, of piety, and of righteousness.) Whereby I may obtain the end of my being, and therein even my Sovereign felicity, which is to know thee, to glorify thee for my God, to believe thee, and in thee, Jesus Christ, and in Jesus Christ, to love, and fear and serve thee, according as thou dost command us and in all things to observe equity towards all men. For thus are thy children bound to learn, according to the measure of the gift of thy grace, thy fatherly love in thy well-beloved Son, namely, by conjoining thereto the fear of thy name that is to say, that reverence that causeth us in humility and obedience, to shun evil, to do good, and to embrace righteousness and charity. Walking

> in this sort, O Lord, under thy conduct, in the communion of Saints I shall want nothing to my comfort or perfection, and in good time, a departure, (my life being ended), to receive peace and perfect joy, in the eternal habitation of the blessed souls. So be it.[17]

The Book of Common Prayer (Church of England)

This is a prayer for Pentecost (Whitsunday) from the Anglican Book of Common Prayer:

> O God, who on this day didst teach the hearts of thy faithful people by sending to them the light of thy Holy Spirit; Grant us by the same Spirit to have a right judgment in all things, and evermore to rejoice in his holy comfort; through the merits of Christ Jesus our Savior, who liveth and reigneth with thee, in the unity of the same Spirit, one God, world without end. *Amen.*[18]

VI. This Community of Faith has been Reconciled to the Truth in and through Christ

The Fathers and Reformers also teach that the community in which true knowledge of God is received by faith is a particular type of community; one that has been reconciled to Him by divine grace. In other words, one cannot actually know the truth (in the biblical sense of both intellectual and relational knowledge) without being reconciled to the truth. Origen said that we can only know God by grace (*Contra Celsum* VII.44). Clement of Alexandria wrote that God can only be known in Christ by the Holy Spirit (*Strom.*, V.1), and both of them teach that God's grace, ministered by the Holy Spirit, is experienced within the community of faith. Calvin writes:

> For while Moses speaks of God's dwelling place, at the same time the place where God has put the memory of his name he calls the 'place of God's name' [cf. Exod. 20:24]. He plainly teaches thereby that there can be no use of the place apart from the doctrine of godliness... By his Word, God alone sanctifies temples to himself for lawful use.[19]

The foundation of this community of faith and its crowning goal is that knowledge which the Son has of the Father, and the Father of the Son (cf. Matt. 11:27), which the Son by becoming incarnate brings within the being and thought-forms of our humanity, so that on that basis our human knowing and speaking of God is grounded in God Himself (for, as Matthew says, the Son 'reveals it to us'). Hence Christ established this reconciled community of being and knowing both in his pre-incarnate[20] and then

---

[17] *Master Bezaes Household Prayers For the Consolation and Perfection of a Christian Life* (London: Printed for John Barnes, 1621), 'Seventh Prayer' – 'To crave of God the light of his word', 25-27. The French original of this little volume has been lost.

[18] *The Book of Common Prayer...According to the use of the Episcopal Church* (New York: The Church Hymnal Corporation, 1979), 175.

[19] Calvin, *Institutes* IV.1.5.

[20] John, for example, conveys something of the relationship of the pre-incarnate Lord to Israel, when in reference to the vision of God's glory in the Temple seen by Isaiah (see Isa. 6:1ff.), he writes: 'These things said Isaiah, when he saw his glory, and spake of him' (John 12:41). Similarly, Paul writes concerning the rock from which the complaining Israelites drank in the wilderness (see Exod. 17:6

supremely in his incarnate existence,[21] so that (as John Calvin writes) '... the original adoption of the chosen people depended upon the Mediator's grace... God cannot without the Mediator be propitious toward the human race, under the law Christ was always set before the holy fathers as the end to which they should direct their faith.'[22] Hence, for both Old and New Testament believers, '... salvation flows from the Head to the whole body.'[23]

The Church knows and is reconciled to the Father by the hypostatic union

Christ then establishes a reconciled community of mutual fellowship and knowing between God and man, which is based on that union and communion in which He knows the Father and the Father knows Him in that eternal relationship of love, who is the Holy Spirit, as Augustine phrases it (*De Trinitate* VI.7). But the Holy Spirit is not only an inner-trinitarian relationship of love, He is also a distinct Person. Richard Haugh paraphrases Photius on this point:

> From within the general framework of the Greek triadological 'model' the Father begets his Son whom he loves and this love, the Holy Spirit, simultaneously proceeds, or springs forth, from the Father to embrace the Son. The Son, loving the Father in return, embraces the Father also. Hence, according to this scheme, the Holy Spirit proceeds eternally from the Father to the Son and through the Son to the Father. According to this idea, the Holy Spirit is not the result of the love between the Father and the Son but is rather the very hypostatic love of the Father for the Son and the Son for the Father.[24]

St. Irenaeus describes how Christ brings humanity into his knowing of the Father:

---

and Num. 20:11): 'and that rock was Christ' (1 Cor. 10:4). The verb used in John 1:14 for 'dwelt' ("and the Word became flesh and *dwelt* among us') – ἐσκήνωσεν – means 'to tabernacle'; a clear reference to the Old Testament wilderness tabernacle, as thus foreshadowing and being fulfilled in Christ. And Christ himself speaks of his physical body as being 'the temple' which would be destroyed and raised up in three days (John 2:19), thus showing to the yet uncomprehending Jews that He was the fullness of all that their temple typified. The Puritan theologian, John Owen, seems to be right in suggesting that the meaning of Hebrews 8:2 ('A minister of the sanctuary, and of the true tabernacle which the Lord pitched and not man') is actually the human nature of Christ (John Owen, *Exposition of Hebrews*, Edinburgh: Banner of Truth, 1991,Vol. 6, 21) toward which the Old Testament appointments were directed and from which they drew all their meaning.

[21]In addition to Matthew 11:27 (already quoted), see the high priestly prayer in John 17, and especially – 'And this is life eternal, that they might know thee the only true God, and Jesus Christ, whom thou hast sent ... I have manifested thy name unto the men which thou gavest me out of the world: thine they were, and thou gavest them me; and they have kept thy word. Now they have known that all things whatsoever thou hast given me are of thee. For I have given unto them the words which thou gavest me; and they have received them, and have known surely that I came out from thee, and they have believed that thou didst send me ... And I have declared unto them thy name, and will declare it: that the love wherewith thou hast loved me may be in them, and I in them' (vv. 3, 6-8, 26).

[22]*Institutes of the Christian Religion*, II.vi.2.

[23]Ibid., II.vi.3.

[24] Richard Haugh, *Photius and the Carolingians: The Trinitarian Controversy* (Belmont, MA: Nordland Publ. Co., 1975), 177.

> Now this is His Word, our Lord Jesus Christ, who in the last times was made a man among men, that He might join the end to the beginning, that is man to God. Wherefore the prophets, receiving the prophetic gift from the same Word, announced His advent according to the flesh, by which the blending and communion of God and man took place according to the good pleasure of the Father, the Word of God foretelling from the beginning that God should be seen by men, and hold converse with them upon earth, should confer with them, and should be present with His own creation, saving it, and become capable of being perceived by it, and freeing us from the hands of all that hate us, that is, from every spirit of wickedness; and causing us to serve Him in holiness and righteousness all our days, in order that man, having embraced the Spirit of God, might pass into the glory of the Father (*Adversus Haereses*, IV.20.4).

As we shall see in a later chapter, classical Christian theology refers to Christ, the Word and eternal Son of the Father, taking human nature into 'personal union' with Himself, as 'the hypostatic union' (ὑπόστασις being a Greek word adapted by the early Church to mean 'personal'). Thus the foundation of both our reconciliation with God and our knowing of Him (by means of His revelation to us) ultimately reposes upon the hypostatic union of the two natures (humanity and deity) in the one, unconfused and undivided person of Jesus Christ. The hypostatic union then carried through in the life, death, resurrection and ascension of Christ as representative head of his people (cf. Rom. 5:12-21), reconciles us to the Father, and in so doing reveals the Father to us most fully.

In the words of Origen:

> ... as John writes in his Epistle, 'God is light and in Him there is no darkness at all' [1 John 1:5]. Truly He is that light which illuminates the whole understanding of those who are capable of receiving the truth, as is said in the thirty-sixth Psalm, 'In thy light we shall see light' [Ps. 36:9]. For what other light of God can be named, 'in which any one sees light,' save an influence of God, by which a man, being enlightened, either thoroughly sees the truth of all things, or comes to know God Himself, who is called the truth? Such is the meaning of the expression, 'In thy light we shall see light;' i.e., in Thy word and wisdom, which is Thy Son, in Himself we shall see Thee, the Father' (*De Principiis* I.1.1).

Some twelve hundred years later, John Calvin writes:

> For since 'God dwells in inaccessible light' [1 Tim. 6:16], Christ must become our intermediary. Hence, he calls himself 'the light of the world' [John 8:12], and elsewhere, 'the way, the truth, and the life'; for no one comes to the Father, who is 'the fountain of life' [Ps. 36:9], except through him [John 14:6] because he alone knows the Father, and afterward the believers to whom he wishes to reveal him [Luke 10:22]...
>
> Indeed, it is true that faith looks to one God. But this must also be added, 'To know Jesus Christ whom he has sent' [John 17:3]. For God would have remained hidden afar off if Christ's splendor had not beamed upon us. For this purpose the Father laid up with his only-begotten all that he had to reveal himself in Christ so that Christ, by communicating his Father's benefits, might express the true image of his glory [cf. Heb. 1:3]. It has been said that we must be drawn by the Spirit to be aroused to seek Christ; so,

in turn, we must be warned that the invisible Father is to be sought solely in this image.[25]

Christ is the head of a new humanity that knows and loves God

In terms of Romans 5 and 1 Corinthians 15, Christ, the image of the invisible Father, becomes the head of a new humanity, more than undoing the damage done by 'the first Adam', who brought the old humanity into sin and alienation from God, so that 'they do not like to retain God in their knowledge' (Rom. 1:28), but instead, '*hold down* [κατέχω in Greek, meaning 'to suppress'] the truth in unrighteousness' (Rom. 1:18). St. Athanasius spoke of fallen mankind as having its face turned away from God, and so Christ comes into the race as its Savior in order to turn its face back to the Father in obedient knowledge and filial love (see *De Incarnatione* 15. 2-7). The first Adam, tempted by the serpent, makes a choice based on the attitude 'my will be done', whereas the Last Adam, both in the temptations that came from the same evil one in the wilderness as he began his ministry, and in the Garden of Gethsemane, as he, on the verge of completing it, says 'Thy will be done' (cf. Matt. 26:42).

In reconciling our will to God in and through His own person and work, He at the same time opens our ears to hear Him,[26] our eyes to see Him and consciences to serve Him,[27] and our hearts to know Him.[28] On that basis, the Apostle John says: 'And we know that the Son of God is come, and hath given us an understanding, that we may know him that is true, and we are in him that is true, even in his Son Jesus Christ. This is the true God, and eternal life' (1 John 5:19, 20). As St. Hilary says (commenting on Col. 2:11, 12): 'For we rise again in Him through faith in God, Who raised Him from the dead; wherefore we must believe in God by whose working Christ was raised from the dead, for our faith rises again in and with Christ.'[29] According to Calvin, 'Now, both repentance and forgiveness of

---

[25]*Institutes*, III.2.1.

[26]See Psalm 40:6 ('mine ears hast thou opened') and compare Hebrews 10:5-7, which applies this passage to Christ, quoting the Greek Septuagint ('a body hast thou prepared') rather than the Hebrew Masoretic text ('mine ears hast thou bored').

[27]The Epistle to the Hebrews, commenting on the inability of the High Priest to enter the Holy Place but once a year, and that 'not without blood' (Heb. 9:7) as he represented the chosen, but sinful nation of Israel, contrasts what the universal church now has in its High Priest, Christ: 'The Holy Ghost this signifying that the way into the holiest of all was not yet made manifest, while as the first tabernacle was yet standing ... But Christ being come an high priest of good things to come, by a greater and more perfect tabernacle, not made with hands, that is to say, not of this building; Neither by the blood of goats and calves, but by his own blood he entered in once into the holy place, having obtained eternal redemption for us... How much more shall the blood of Christ, who through the eternal Spirit offered himself without spot to God, purge your conscience from dead works to serve the living God?' (Heb. 9:8,11, 12, 14).

[28]Jeremiah 31 promises that the central characteristic of the New Covenant will be: 'After those days, saith the Lord, I will put my law in their inward parts, and write it in their hearts; and will be their God, and they shall be my people. And they shall teach no more every man his neighbour, and every man his brother, saying, Know the Lord: for they shall all know me, from the least of them unto the greatest of them, saith the Lord: for I will forgive their iniquity, and I will remember their sin no more' (vv. 33,34). Hebrews 8:8-13 quotes these very verses in the context of Christ, the true and great High Priest, who alone puts this New Covenant into force.

[29]*De Trinitate*, IX.9.

sins – that is, newness of life and free reconciliation – are conferred on us by Christ, and both are attained by us through faith.'[30]

Christ, the eternal Word, now incarnate, is the one whose Spirit inspired the prophets of old (1 Peter 1:11 and Rev. 19:10), whose writings testify of Him (John 5:39 and Luke 24:27), in whom 'all things [including the writings of Holy Scripture] cohere' (Col. 1:17). After His resurrection, He empowers the apostles to write of Him with dominical authority the texts recognized by the Church as the canon of the New Testament (see John chapters 14 and 16). Thus the incarnate Word lived out and fulfilled the written word of the Old Testament (inspired by his Spirit to point to Him), and in fulfilling the Old, gave rise to the New, so that He is 'the sum and substance' of both Testaments.

VII. The Holy Spirit Brings Us into the Son's Knowledge of the Father

As T. F. Torrance writes: '... within the hypostatic union of divine and human nature that took place in Jesus Christ, there is included a union between uncreated and created rationality and between uncreated and created word, so that it is in the rational form of creaturely word that Jesus Christ mediates God's Word to all mankind' (*Reality and Evangelical Theology*, 91). It is through the work of the Holy Spirit that the whole world – i.e. both Jew and Gentile – are brought into union with Christ, and thus enabled to share in His knowing of the Father in a way appropriate to their capacities which He assumed in the incarnation.

Our participation in the Son's knowing of the Father

Paul explains in Ephesians chapter 2: '... at that time ye were without Christ, being aliens from the commonwealth of Israel, and strangers from the covenants of promise, having no hope, and without God in the world: But now in Christ Jesus ye who sometimes were far off are made nigh by the blood of Christ. For he is our peace, who hath made both one, and hath broken down the middle wall of partition between us ... for to make in himself of twain one new man, so making peace; And that he might reconcile both unto God in one body by the cross, having slain the enmity thereby... For through him we both have access by one Spirit unto the Father' (vv. 12-14, 15b, 16, 18).

Elsewhere, Paul gives us more detail of how the Spirit brings us, through union with Christ, into the deepest knowing of God:

> 'But as it is written, Eye hath not seen, nor ear heard, neither have entered into the heart of man, the things which God hath prepared for them that love him. But God hath revealed them unto us by his Spirit: for the Spirit searcheth all things, yea, the deep things of God. For what man knoweth the things of a man, save the spirit of man which is in him? even so the things of God knoweth no man, but the Spirit of God. Now we have received,

---

[30]*Institutes*, III.3.1.

> not the spirit of the world, but the spirit which is of God; that we might know the things that are freely given to us of God... For who hath known the mind of the Lord, that he may instruct him? But we have the mind of Christ' (1 Cor. 2:9-12, 16).

Athanasius the Great, in his *Letters Concerning the Holy Spirit* (or *Ad Serapionem*), richly meditates from the Scriptures on how the Spirit makes us participate in the Son's knowledge of the Father:

> As then the Father is light and the Son is his radiance ... we may see in the Son the Spirit also by whom we are enlightened. 'That he may give you' it says, 'the Spirit of wisdom and revelation in the knowledge of him, having the eyes of your heart enlightened' [Eph. 1:17-18]. But when we are enlightened by the Spirit, it is Christ who in him enlightens us. For it says: 'There was the true light which lighteth every man coming into the world' [John 1:9]. Again, as the Father is fountain and the Son is called river, we are said to drink of the Spirit. For it is written: 'We are all made to drink of one Spirit' [1 Cor. 12:13]. But when we are made to drink of the Spirit, we drink of Christ. For 'they drank of a spiritual rock that followed them, and the rock was Christ' [1 Cor. 10:4]. Again, as Christ is true Son, so we, when we receive the Spirit, are made sons. 'For you have not received', it says, 'the spirit of bondage again to fear; but you have received the Spirit of adoption' [Rom. 8:15]. But if by the Spirit we are made sons, it is clear that it is in Christ we are called children of God. For: 'So many as received him, to them gave he the power to become children of God' [John 1:12].[31]

St. Basil the Great, not long after Athanasius, shows how the Holy Spirit binds us into the Son's knowledge of the Father:

> When, then, the apostle 'thanks God through Jesus Christ' [Rom. 1:8], and again says that 'through Him we have received grace and apostleship for obedience to the faith among all nations' [Rom. 1:5], or 'through Him have access unto this grace wherein we stand and rejoice' [Rom. 5:2], he sets forth the boons conferred on us by the Son, at one time making the grace of the good gifts pass through from the Father to us, and at another bringing us to the Father through Himself. For by saying 'through whom we have received grace and apostleship' [Rom. 1:5], he declares the supply of the good gifts to proceed from that source; and again in saying 'through whom we have had access' [Rom. 5:2], he sets forth our acceptance and being made 'of the household of God' [cf. Eph. 2:19] through Christ. Is then the confession of the grace wrought by Him to usward a detraction from His glory? Is it not truer to say that the recital of His benefits is a proper argument for glorifying Him (*De Spiritu Sancto* VIII.17).
>
> It results that in Himself He shows the glory of the Only begotten, and on true worshippers He in Himself bestows the knowledge of God. Thus the way of the knowledge of God lies from One Spirit through the One Son to the One Father, and conversely the natural Goodness and the inherent Holiness and the royal Dignity extend from the Father through the Only-begotten to the Spirit (Ibid., XVIII.47).

---

[31] *The Letters of Saint Athanasius Concerning the Holy Spirit*, translated by C. R. B. Shapland, London: The Epworth Press, 1951, I.19.

The Holy Spirit is the bond of the Trinity and the bond of unity of believers

Epiphanius indicates that the Holy Spirit is not only the bond of the Trinity, but also the bond of unity among believers, uniting them to Christ in His knowledge of the Father. He speaks of Him as 'the seal of grace' and 'the bond of the Trinity' (*Ancoratus* VII). Commenting on 1 Corinthians 3:16, 'For you are the temple of God, and the Spirit of God dwells in you,' Epiphanius notes how the indwelling Holy Spirit reveals the Father within the believers (Ibid. IX), and causes them to know 'the deep things of God' [1 Cor. 2:10] (Ibid. XII). The same Holy Spirit also bonds believers together as we are baptized into the one name of the Father, the Son and the Holy Spirit [Matt. 28:19] (Ibid. VIII). Thus the Holy Spirit is the bond of believers one to another and is the bond of their relationship to God and knowledge of Him.

The necessity of our union with Christ

In a later age, John Calvin much more systematically works through the biblical doctrine of true knowledge of God through the Son in the Spirit. While we postpone a careful discussion of this teaching until a later chapter on union with Christ, here we merely note the basic outline of it, as regards what is essential to our grasping of true theological knowledge. Calvin shows first, the necessity of our union with Christ in order to know God, which is salvation itself:

> First, we must understand that as long as Christ remains outside of us, and we are separated from him, all that he has suffered and done for the salvation of the human race remains useless and of no value for us. Therefore, to share with us what he has received from the Father, he had to become ours and to dwell within us. For this reason, he is called 'our Head' [Eph. 4:15], and 'the first-born among many brethren' [Rom. 8:29]. We also, in turn, are said to be 'engrafted into him' [Rom. 11:17], and to 'put on Christ' [Gal. 3:27]; for, as I have said, all that he possesses is nothing to us until we grow into one body with him. It is true that we obtain this by faith (*Institutes* III.11).
>
> We know, moreover, that he benefits only those whose 'Head' he is [Eph. 4:15]... But he unites himself to us by the Spirit alone. By the grace and power of the same Spirit we are made his members, to keep us under himself and in turn to possess him (Ibid., III.1.3).

What our union with Christ is not and what it is

Calvin notes that this union is a spiritual reality, not a 'gross mixture of Christ and ourselves' (Ibid., III.11.10), and that it surpasses the ability of the human mind to understand (*Commentary on Ephesians*, at ch. 5:32).[32] This relational union of true theological knowledge is (1) bonded by the Holy Spirit and (2) by faith, and (3) is made effective in the preaching of the Word and in the administration of the sacraments.

[32]This outline is taken from the excellent work of Ronald S. Wallace, *Calvin's Doctrine of the Christian Life* (Tyler, TX: Geneva Divinity School, 1982) especially Chapter III, 'The participation of the Church in the sanctification of Christ'(17-27). See also Chapter XIII, 'The Mystery of Sacramental Union' (159-74), of Wallace's *Calvin's Doctrine of The Word and Sacrament* (Tyler, TX: Geneva Divinity School, 1982)

Ronald S. Wallace summarizes Calvin's teaching on (1) the Holy Spirit's bonding believers on earth with Christ in heaven:

> It is therefore the Holy Spirit alone who can effect this union, for it is the Holy Spirit alone who can so join things in Heaven and things on earth that heavenly things can be grasped by human minds and that the life and virtue of what is in Heaven can be shared by those who are yet on earth [*Comm. on Gal. 2:20, Calvini Opera*, 50, 199. And Sermon on *Job* 15:11-16, *Calvini Opera* 33:720]. It is the Holy Spirit alone who can bring into real being that wonderful relation of mystery between Christ's heavenly body and His church on earth which is so clearly depicted in the act of participation in the Lord's Supper and in Baptism [Sermon on *Acts of the Apostles* 2:1-4, *Calvini Opera* 48:634].[33]

Calvin notes that this union is (2) bonded by faith. Again, Wallace draws together the crucial references:

> ... faith actually unites us to Christ and inserts us into His body [*Institutes* 3:2:30, cf. 2:13.2 and *Commentary on 1 John* 4:15, *Calvini Opera* 55:356], creating the bond that enables us to receive, possess and enjoy Christ Himself [*Commentary on 1 John* 4:14, *C. O.*, 55:368] – for the blessings which are His gifts cannot be received and enjoyed by us apart from communion with Himself by faith [*Commentary on Hebrews* 5:9, *C.O.* 55, 64; cf. *Institutes* 3.3.1]...
>
> ... it is equally true that we are united to Christ by the Holy Spirit alone and by faith alone... Faith, rising from the human heart, can penetrate the heavens [*Commentary on 1 Peter* 1:4, *C.O.*, 55:211]... Faith is thus an entirely supernatural gift – a new capacity created within man whereby what is in Heaven is really possessed and enjoyed by him. It effects such a secret and wonderful communion with Christ that even though Jesus Christ remains entire in Heaven, He is nevertheless grasped so firmly and possessed so completely that He may be said actually to dwell in our hearts [*Sermon on Ephesians* 3:14-19, *C. O.*, 51: 491]... Faith unites man to God and makes God to dwell in man [*Commentary on 1 John* 4:15, *C.O.*, 55:356].

(3) Calvin's teaching on how true knowledge of God that can only occur on the basis of union with Christ is made effective in the preaching of the Word and the administration of the sacraments must be postponed.[34] We merely note here that his assumption is the same as that of the Church Fathers; God makes Himself truly known in the Church, where the Holy Spirit blesses the preaching of the Word and the administration of the sacraments. Faith takes its rise in this covenant community which is baptized in the Spirit (1 Cor. 12:13).

God the Father, who makes Himself known through the Son, in the Spirit (as Athanasius and Basil say[35]), calls forth faith from men and women and children to whom He reveals Himself in the covenant community. Let us look briefly at two of the constituent activities that are involved in the response of faith, making further and deeper knowledge of God possible: assent and prayer.

---

[33]Ronald S. Wallace, *Calvin's Doctrine of the Christian Life*, 20.

[34]See Wallace, *Calvin's Doctrine of The Word and Sacrament*, especially Chapters VII – XVIII.

VIII. Faith And Assent

Scripture shows that when God speaks, there is a response. In the account of creation, for instance, 'And God said, Let there be light, and there was light' (Gen. 1:3). The physical elements have no choice but to respond, whereas with persons created in God's image, proper response involves mind, will and affections, traditionally summed up in the concept of 'assent.'

The prototype of faith for both Old and New Testaments is Abraham, who according to the Apostle Paul, is 'the father of all them that believe' (Rom. 4:11), so that 'they which are of faith, the same are the children of Abraham' (Gal. 3:7). When God renews the Covenant of Grace to Abraham, He promised to be his God and the God of his seed: 'And he believed in the Lord; and he counted it to him for righteousness' (Gen. 15:6). That is, he assented to the gracious promise of God. Stated another way, he 'amened' the covenant.[36] This idea of profound assent to God's covenant seems to be reflected all through the worship of both the Old and the New Testament Church in the liturgical usage of this word 'Amen' ('so let it be'; 'may it be established'), as we particularly see in the book of Psalms,[37] in the response of the people to the announcement of the blessings and cursings of the covenant (cf. Deut. 27), in the writings of Paul (cf. 2 Cor. 1:20) and in Revelation (e.g. Rev. 3:14; 22:20).

True assent is pictured in the Tabernacle

After the Exodus from Egypt, at the very center of Israel's life was the Tabernacle (and later, in the Promised Land, the Temple), with 'the Holy of Holies' in its midst. Enshrined in 'the Holy of Holies' (often called 'oracle' or 'word-house' in the books of Kings and Chronicles) was the Ark of the Covenant, bearing within it 'the ten words', or law of God, which revealed the divine character and His will for His people. The entire history of Israel turned on a proper or improper response (an assent or refusal) to the God, whose clear Word was in their midst. The prophets made it plain that a mere liturgical response to God would lead to disaster unless that Word were lived out in the lives of the people (e.g., cf. Isa. 1:10-20).

True assent is presented in the Wisdom literature

In the later history of Israel, the Wisdom literature equated 'the fear of the Lord' with 'the beginning of wisdom' (Prov. 1:7), and saw a listening ear as the only door to this reverential understanding: 'A wise man will hear, and will increase learning; and a man of understanding shall attain unto wise counsels' (Prov. 1:5). Thus, assent is at the basis of all true wisdom.

---

[35]Athanasius writes: 'For it was God himself who, through the Word, in the Spirit [Isa. 63:14] led the people ... For when the Spirit was with the people, God, through the Son in the Spirit, was with them' (*Ad Serapionem*, I.12). Acording to Basil: 'Thus the way of knowledge of God lies from the one Spirit through the one Son to the one Father' (*De Spiritu Sancto*, 18.47).

[36]The Hebrew verb employed for 'Abraham *believed* the Lord' in Genesis 15:6 is a form of *aman* (to assent, to confirm), from which the formula '*Amen*' is taken.

[37]The Book of Psalms, the largest book in the Bible, is divided into five parts. The first four of these five parts all end with 'Amen': Psalms 41:13; 72:19; 89:52; 106:48.

True assent manifested in Christ

In the New Testament, He who was the fullest revelation of God in the flesh, had a heart attuned above all to the Word and will of His Father. Luke indicates this in his frequent references to the prayer life of Jesus (cf. Luke 9:18; 10:21; 11:1; 22:32, 40-46, etc.), as does John in a different way, in his references to the God-centered motivation of Jesus for the Father's will and glory (cf. John 4:34: 'My meat is to do the will of him that sent me, and to finish his work'; and 12:27-28: 'Now is my soul troubled; and what shall I say? Father, save me from this hour: but for this cause came I unto this hour. Father, glorify thy name. Then came there a voice from heaven, saying, I have both glorified it, and will glorify it again'). And Matthew's Gospel approaches this responsorial assent in a still different way: the very events of Christ's life were done 'that the Scripture might be fulfilled' (e.g. 1:22; 2:15, 17-18, 23; cf. 3:3, etc.); that is, all aspects and every event of Christ's life were to fulfil the ancient Word of the Father 'in the fullness of the time' (Gal. 4:4), as though they were a mighty choir of voices crying out, 'Thy will be done.'

Paul teaches that at the centre of the salvation experience, 'faith cometh by hearing, and hearing by the Word of God' (Rom. 10:17). Heart-assent to God's Word is the essence of salvation: 'That if thou shalt confess with thy mouth the Lord Jesus, and shalt believe in thine heart that God hath raised him from the dead, thou shalt be saved' (Rom. 10:9). So then, Abraham, the Tabernacle, the prophets, the Wisdom literature, Christ Himself and then His apostles demonstrate faith to involve at its deepest level whole-hearted assent to the Word, will and glory of God.

Excursus on 'Assent': The Church Thinks Through how the Human Mind Can Know Objective, External Reality in order to Assent to It

A. The Relativistic Culture into which the Church had to Proclaim the Gospel

In taking the gospel to the pagan, relativistic and skeptical culture of their day, the early Church Fathers laid much emphasis on the subjective response of assent to the objective truth brought from another world in the glad tidings of God made man, crucified and risen for mankind, and now present in the Holy Spirit. It was their task to penetrate the intellectual and ethical darkness of skeptical relativism in the Hellenistic world with the absolute truth of Him 'who brought life and immortality to light through the gospel' (2 Tim. 1:10) so that people could be set free by giving their 'Amen' or response to it. But because of the relativistic assumptions underlying the pagan thought-world of the early centuries of the Christian Era, the Church had no small task in hand. Since our so-called 'Post-Modernist' culture is inundated in relativistic confusion not unlike that facing the apostles and their successors, it is worthwhile to look in some detail at the way they conveyed absolute truth to people who denied its very existence. Their approach turned on calling skeptics and relativists to assent to absolute truth.

To ask people to assent to truth means that they can actually come to know the truth to which they are called to respond. But that was the point at issue both in Hellenistic relativism before the Constantinian settlement (declaring the Roman Empire to be Christian in the fourth century) and also in the decayed 'Enlightenment' thinking now at the beginning of the new millennium (with its intellectual rejection of the Christian revelation after the eighteenth-century European Enlightenment, our own culture has in many ways reverted to the philosophical and moral confusion of Classical paganism).

The Christian Church faced (and faces once again) a culture which operates on the assumptions of skepticism (how can one really know anything?), relativism (since we cannot be certain of reality, all truth-claims and values are equally valid, or perhaps equally invalid), and the natural offspring of the two: eclecticism (illustrated in how 'New Age' thought attempts to merge elements of Christianity, Eastern religions and Western scientism). At the heart of this relativistic skepticism of ancient times (as well as in our post-Enlightenment situation) lay the assumption of a deep dualism between knowing and being, that tended to tear apart concepts from experience, thus negating scientific advance in general, and ethical certainty and personal security in particular.[38] The ultimate issue here is whether the human mind and heart can know and assent to truth that is outside itself or not. Ancient and modern skeptics deny this possibility. The Church, in continuity with Old Testament Israel, asserts the opposite: God has spoken truth and is assented to (or 'amened') by His people. This position is generally known as 'realism,' and is the contrary to skepticism. To explain the gospel to a skeptical culture, the teachers of the Church had to interact with the assumptions of that culture in order to liberate it from deadening skepticism in a realist direction, to set them free to add their own 'amen' to the Covenant of Grace. To see how they achieved this, it will be well to look into the background of the cultural relativism with which the Church Fathers had to deal.

B. Ancient Realism And Skepticism

The ancient search for realism in knowledge

From one point of view, much of the history of the development of Greek and Hellenistic philosophy from the time of the Sophists (who were sceptics in an early form in the time of Socrates in the fourth century B.C.) to the beginning of the Christian Era could be considered in terms of the search to achieve realism in knowledge.

Plato: a realist

The great 'dogmatic' system of Plato has at its heart an attempt to establish a realist epistemology (i.e. how knowing is related to being). Against the

---

[38]This epistemological crisis is carefully explored by Thomas F. Torrance in *Theological Science*.

nominalistic (i.e. 'names' or words do not take one to objective reality) Sophists and against the relativism that ensues from the constant 'flux' of Heraclitus (i.e. everything is changing so constantly that one cannot establish unchanging, external truth), Plato established the theory of a transcendent world of ideas (or 'forms') above the flux of this world, by means of which objective truth can be established in knowledge (above the mere 'opinion' of the world of 'becoming' which is characterized by 'flux'). Although his intention was to be realist, it seems that his world of 'reified' ideas became more real than the creation, so that the 'spiritual' notion of reality tended to decrease or even deny the value of the created order.

Aristotle: a realist

Aristotle, also a realist, severely criticized the Platonic doctrine of 'forms' (or 'transcendent ideas'). Instead of seeing Plato's intention of guaranteeing objectivity of science in his doctrine of ideas, Aristotle takes it as an unnecessary 'reification' of concepts – i.e. projecting into spatial and material existence imaginary forms of things – which would thus tend to confuse the pursuit of true knowledge of external reality, rather than add to its clarification and objectivity (see *Metaphysics* A). With Aristotle, universal ideas are known from actual artifacts. Hence he denied the reality of Plato's eternal ideas as such, but held that another sense of universals can be deduced from the concepts of species and genera. Here he was closer to created realities than had been Plato.

Aristotle's four causes

For Aristotle, reality is to be explained in terms of the four famous causes. Reality is hence bound up within, if not exhausted by, material existence within limited space. His approach to knowledge is very different from Plato. A. E. Taylor says:

> Aristotle denies the thought of sensation as suggestive of what it is powerless to reveal. The work of the intellect in construing science consists simply in educing and disentangling from sensuous experience what is implicitly contained in them. The one function of thought is thus to abstract and generalize ... Hence a reduction of thought to the capacity for abstraction and generalization...[39]

In effect, Aristotle gives the impression of reducing knowable reality from the broader, less confined view of Plato in seeing objective, universal realities express themselves through individual phenomena, to a more narrow, spatially confined state, in which one through individual sense experiences draws out the essential reality of specific, singular objects; which is entirely contained in the object itself.

Plato's Universal Terms

The Aristotelian approach to knowledge was definitely realist (holding that thought follows being),[40] but in attacking the Platonic view of universal

[39] A. E. Taylor, *Platonism*, (New York: Longmans, Green & Co., 1927), 48

[40] F. Copleston, *A History of Philosophy*, Vol. I, Part II (New York: Image Books, 1962), 24.

terms, it tended to bring in scepticism (at that point at least, though perhaps properly in terms of Plato's theory of eternal 'forms'), and to restrict the scope of reality in knowledge from the broad realist view of the objective actuality of universal terms to a more materialist, narrower frame of reference.

Skepticism: anti-realist

The great Aristotelian synthesis was itself soon under attack. Aristotle had attacked Platonist realism at the heart of its thesis: namely, the reality of significant universal terms. The Aristotelian explanation of realist knowledge was in turn attacked at its very heart: the reliability of sense experience in the knowledge of facts. Thus realist epistemology and objectivity in science suffered further decline. At the hands of the Skeptics, a widespread relativism began to ensue. A long line of Skeptics from Pyrrho, Timon of Phlius, to Arcesilaus, Carneades, and finally Sextus Empiricus (the source of most of our information on Skepticism) attacked the very possibility of man possessing true knowledge of 'things in themselves' in the external world. Because of the differences in opinion of various observers, unreliability of sense organs, etc. the Sceptics counseled ἐποχή, – suspension of judgement as to the objectivity of knowledge.

C. Stoic Realism

Into this background of the relativizing of the great dogmatic systems of Plato, and then of Aristotle in the face of the sceptical onslaught, a new philosophy with a realist epistemology first came to light in the person of Zeno, its founder (c. 336–264 B.C.). Zeno and his successors, Cleanthes and Chrysippus (heads of the 'early' Stoa) all worked to re-establish and maintain the possibility of objective science through the demonstration of realism in knowledge. This third great 'dogmatic' (as opposed to 'sceptic') system continued on its realist basis through its middle and later phases.

The general Stoic philosophy

No wonder then that many Christian apologists and Fathers turned here for instruction and equipment in evangelizing the Hellenistic culture. A number of studies have documented the pivotal importance of Stoic realist epistemology on early Christian theology; in particular, the works of Spanneut, Verbeke, Pohlenz and Lebreton.[41] Such works point out the influence of the Stoa upon the Church Fathers in teaching the unity of the world, natural law, 'conspiration,' and using vocabulary taken from the idea of the Stoic 'world cycle,' etc. Cyprian of Carthage, for instance, accused the schismatic theologian, Novatian of Rome (c. A.D. 250), of being a (Stoic) philosopher in his rigorism (that refused to grant repentance of Christians who failed to confess Christ during Roman persecution), rather than a Christian. Much the same could be said of Tertullian.

---

[41]See Spanneut, *Le Stoicisme des Pères de l'Eglise* (Paris: Editions due Seuil, 1957), 78-128; G. Verbeke, *L'Evolution de la Doctrine du Pneuma du Stoicisme à St. Augustin, Etude Philosophique* (Paris: D. de Brouwer, 1945); M. Pohlenz, *Die Stoa, Geschichte einer geistigen Bewegung* (Gottingen: Vandenhoek & Ruprecht, 1959 with 50 pages on the Church Fathers); J. Lebreton, *L'Histoire du Dogma de la Trinité*, 2 vols. (Paris: Gabriel Beauchesne, 1927-28).

Stoic concepts and vocabulary are in abundant presence throughout the works of the early Christian writers.

This, however, is not to suggest that Stoicism was the strongest influence on the Church Fathers. Clearly, the various phases of Platonism, and then, later in the Middle Ages, the philosophy of Aristotle (taken through the Arab commentators and Moses Maimonides) were far more influential than the Stoic philosophy. But my concern here is with epistemology, rather than with the larger range of metaphysics and ethics. Therefore, I will not enter into any serious discussion of the general philosophy of the Stoics in its three phases.[42]

The Stoic epistemology and the Church Fathers

Far more important to the early theologians however than the Stoic idea of ethics or nature was the preponderant influence of their epistemology and logic. The Bible itself, as we have seen, has a powerfully realist view of language and being, but the Stoic structure helped the early Church think out and enunciate this fact with its many implications for evangelism, science, and culture.

Details of Stoic concepts of how the mind knows outside reality

Reality comes first, and the mind second

Stoic logic and the epistemology on which it is based served Christian theology well because of their ability to give a credible explanation of how the human mind can know reality outside itself, and assent to it. At the basis of the whole Stoic system is the assumption that the real world imposes itself on the recipient mind of man. Man's mind does not impose its own structure and form on the real world (as is the position in much of post-Kantian thought). According to Sextus, 'A real object is that which excites an apprehensive presentation (καταληπτικὴ φαντασία).'[43] Hence the starting point of knowledge is the fact that outer reality presses in on the mind (through the senses). Outer reality makes itself truly known, 'for the starting points of nature are never perverse' (Diogenes Laertius, VII.89).

The mechanism by which objects in the real world are faithfully grasped by the mind is known, as we have seen, as the 'apprehensive presentation'. 'They (the Stoics) declare that "presentation" is an impression on the "regent part" [of the soul] (ἐν ̔ηγημονικῷ).'[44] 'The apprehensive presentation must be in accord with the object itself. Moreover, it must be imaged and stamped in the subject, in order that all the characteristics of the presented objects may be reproduced with artistic exactitude...'[45]

---

[42] For general background, you are referred to: E. Zeller, *Stoics, Epicureans and Sceptics* (London: Longmans, Green & Co.,1870); E. V. Arnold, *Roman Stoicism* (Cambridge: University Press, 1911); M. Pohlenz, *Stoa und Stoiker, die* (Artemis Verlag); Gründer, *Panaitios, Poseidonios* (Zurich, 1950); T. V. Smith, *Philosophers Speak For Themselves: From Aristotle to Plotinus* (Chicago: University of Chicago Press, 1956); Von Arnim, *Stoicorum Veterum Fragmenta* (Teubner, in Aedibus B.G., 1903); G. Verbeke, *L'Evolution de la Doctrine du Pneuma du Stoicisme à St. Augustin: Etude Philosophique* (Paris: E. de Brouwer, 1945); H. A. Wolfson, *The Philosophy of the Church Fathers* (Cambridge, MA: Harvard University Press, 1976); Emile Brehier, *Histoire de la philosophie: Antiquité et Moyen Age* t. I (Paris: Presses Universitaries de France, 1994).

[43] Sextus Empiricus, *Adv. Log.*, I.426.

[44] Sextus, *Pyr. Hp.*, II.70.

[45] Sextus, *Adv. Log.*, I.249-251.

Zeno likened the operation of the 'cataleptic phantasm' to the imprint of a seal on wax. Chrysippus called it a 'change' (ἀλλοίωσις) that takes place in the soul under the impact of a presented object. The Stoics then held that outer reality is powerful to make itself truly known. According to Sextus, they said: 'Truth kindles its own fire,' and truth 'drags us by the hair.'[46] Truth reveals itself with absolute precision: '... of such a kind as could not be derived from a non-existent object...'[47]

The place of assent in Stoic epistemology

And yet the Stoics taught that the mind does have a part to play in knowledge, by way of the exercise of 'assent' (συγκατάθεσις). At one time the Stoics apparently held that all sensation was true. Later, according to Mme. Virieux-Reymond: 'Zénon introduit l'assent pour sauvegarder le libre arbitre, et qu'ainsi l'homme puisse être tenu résponsable de ses actions...'[48] Man's assent to clear presentations brings sufficient certainty of knowledge. The process of knowledge was illustrated by Zeno by the closing of the hand. Simple sensation was like an extended finger; assent was the first activity of the power of judgment, and was illustrated by the closed hand. Conception was likened to the fist, and scientific knowledge was seen as one fist fully grasped by the other. In other words, these steps represent the steps through which one arrives at true knowledge; by observation, comparison, abstraction and classification.[49]

The Jewish Hellenist philosopher, Philo of Alexandria, in *De Congressu Quaerendae* mentions (following the Stoics) the work of assent:

> The mind is the eye's eye and the hearing's hearing, and the purified sense of each of the senses; it uses them as ushers in its tribunal, but itself passes judgement on the nature of the objects presented; giving its assent to some and refusing it to others...[50]

The individual hence does have a personal decision to make in the events leading up to knowledge. It was the genius of the Stoic epistemology to affirm the individual's choice in the process, without weakening the objectivity and given reality of that process. In fact the Stoic emphasis on assent even strengthened the realism of their epistemology in that it led them to clarify and develop the central point and keystone of their whole realist system: the cataleptic phantasm. This was the one point more than any other, that they used to assert their confidence that man can and does know reality as it is in itself.

'The cataleptic phantasm' (correct recognition of reality)

The cataleptic phantasm proceeds directly from the 'mental assent' that the mind has given to a faithful picture (or 'presentation') of some object in reality.[51] Diogenes Laertius explains it this way:

---

[46]Sextus, *Adv. Log.*, I.257-259.

[47]Ibid., I.252.

[48]'Zeno introduced assent in order to safeguard free will, and thus man might be held responsible for his actions...' (A. Virieux-Reymond, *L'Epistémologie* [Paris: Presses Universitaires de France, 1966], 3).

[49]T. W. Levin, *On the Philosophical Writings of Cicero* (Cambridge, 1871), 74.

[50]Philo, *De Con. Qr.* XXV (Loeb translation, 533).

[51]See Cicero, *Acadm.* I.11.42; II.12.38; *Fin.* V.26.76; Sext., *Math.* VII.253.

> Freedom from precipitancy (in dialectic) is a knowledge when to give or withhold the mind's assent (συγκατάθεσις) to impressions... Earnestness (absence of frivolity) is a habit of referring 'presentations' (φαντασίας) to right reason. Knowledge itself is either unerring apprehension (κατάληψις ἀσφαλῆ), or a habit or state which in reception of presentations cannot be shaken by judgement... The presentation meant is that which comes from a real object ... and is accompanied by yielding and assent on our part... The standard of truth is the apprehending presentation ('ηκαταληπτικὴ φαντασία') – i.e. from a real object.[52]

The Stoa in explaining how the cataleptic phantasm flows from assent, showed it to be the standard of truth and reality. As Zeller writes:

> A true perception is one which represents a real object as it really is. This can be known by the degree of strength with which certain perceptions force themselves on our notice. Perception by itself does not carry assent (συγκατάθεσὶ) until the faculty of judgement is directed to the perception. While assent rests with us, some perceptions are of such a kind as to force assent as corresponding with the actual nature of things. Such perceptions produce in us that strength of conviction which Stoics call a conception (hence a 'conceptual perception' – φαντασί αι καταληπτικαί – or 'irresistible perceptions'). These are the standard of truth. Hence the test of 'irresistibility (κατάληψις) is first applied to outer sensations – which supplied the material for knowledge; and secondly, an equal degree of certainty is attached to terms deduced from originally true data either by universal exercise of thought, or by scientific processes of proof. Since these derivative terms (among them κοιναὶ ἔννοιαι [i.e. common concepts, basic beliefs or 'common sense assumptions of humanity' – ed.]) serve as the basis for deriving others; in one sense sensation and primary conceptions [πρόληψεις – ed.] are both standards of truth. However the real standard lies neither in sensation, nor in primary conceptions, but in the power inherent in certain perceptions of carrying conviction – τὸ καταληπτικόν – a power belonging first to sensations, and next to 'primary conceptions formed from them in a natural way (κοιναὶ or πρόληψει).'[53]

'Absolute clarity' of the cataleptic phantasm

The great strength of the 'cataleptic phantasm' lay in the absolute clarity (ἐναργεία) with which it presented reality to the knowing mind. No philosophy has ever been able to state exactly how the mind knows reality. The closest the Stoics came to doing so is stated by Cicero: 'There was no need to define the essential nature of knowledge, of perception, of "mental grasp" ... because there was no thing clearer than ἐναργεία ... truths so manifest did not need defining.'[54] The mind ultimately had to 'yield' to what is evident.[55]

How notions and class concepts develop in the mind. From the 'mind pictures' ('presentations' which lead to λεκτά, – 'pictures' or 'conceptual expressions')

---

[52]Diog. Laert., II (Loeb Translation, 156).
[53]E. Zeller, *Stoics, Epicureans, and Sceptics* (London, 1870), 89-91.
[54]Cicero, *Acadm.* (Loeb Series), 489.
[55]Cicero, *Lucullus*, 12.

were built up 'notions' that are stored in the mind, making 'experience' (ἐμπειρία), which help to form class concepts. On the other hand, the Stoics taught the presence of some sort of 'innate' preconception (πρόληψις) of class concepts, which served to give the mind 'clues' into the objectivities of reality. These πρόληψις were 'tools' (called by Cicero '*instrumenta*') to grasp real objects.[56] Or stated otherwise, they are instruments through which the real thing reaches the mind. And the only proper response to them is 'assent.' Thus, the mind experiences intuitive apprehensions and then intellectually consents to them. That is how one can know objective truth outside one's own mind, and on that basis assent to it.

The senses point to reality (but do not determine it). The Stoics did not overemphasize the mechanics of sense perception in a way that turned the interest away from (or even excluded) the outer reality that this process was supposed to convey. The senses were a means to an end, not an end in themselves. They pointed beyond themselves to objective reality in such a manner that reality was not understood to be 'enclosed' in them. They were in a certain sense windows opening up to what is there. Thus the emphasis is not laid on the senses, per se, but rather by means of them one moves beyond them to a more precise view of things as they are.

Put in other terms, 'percepts' lead to 'concepts,' and the mind by use of these developed concepts is able to move from a restricted (though correct) view of one particular object, to a broader, higher view of reality in general – including class concepts and an understanding of cause, effect and purpose in the external world. According to Cicero:

> For the mind itself which is the source of the sensations and even is itself sensation, has a natural force which it directs to the things by which it is moved. Accordingly, some sense perceptions it seizes on so as to make use of them at once; others it as it were stores away; these being the source of memory, while all the rest it unites into systems by their mutual resemblances; and from these are formed the concepts of objects which the Greeks term sometimes ἔννοιαι and sometimes πρόληψεις. When thereto there has been added reason and logical proof, and an innumerable multitude of facts, then comes the clear perception of all these things, and also this same reason having been by these stages made complete, finally attains to wisdom.[57]

D. Use of Stoic Epistemology by the Church Fathers

Many Church Fathers made heavy use of these aspects of Stoic epistemology, while rejecting the materialist philosophy that originally underlay it (i.e. all things, including the cosmos and the human mind are ultimately composed of a sort of 'rational fiery substance' or 'λόγος', which makes possible the interconnections in the knowledge-event. On the contrary, the Fathers held that both world and human minds are creatures which are illuminated by the uncreated Λόγον in terms of John 1:4, 5, 9). This confidence that reality

[56] Cicero, *Acadm.*, II.10.

[57] Cicero, *Acadm.* (Loeb Translation, 508).

is knowable and that the senses are open channels to what is there so that knowledge (γνῶσις) and science are possible, constituted an important philosophical and terminological heritage, employed by much Christian theology to explain the obligation imposed on the mind of man calling for assent, as God reveals Himself in His Word.

Clement of Alexandria

Clement of Alexandria, for instance, makes uses of these Stoic concepts to describe how objective theological knowledge takes place:

> For prophecy is full of knowledge (γνῶσις) inasmuch as it was given by the Lord. And is not knowledge (γνῶσις) an attribute of the rational soul, which trains itself for this, that by knowledge it may become entitled to immortality. For both are powers of the soul, both knowledge and impulse. And impulse is found to be a movement after assent. For since learning is older than action ... knowledge turns out the beginning and author of all rational action. So that rightly the particular nature of the rational soul is characterized by this alone; for in reality impulse like knowledge is excited by existing objects. And knowledge is essentially a contemplation of existences on the part of the soul, either of a certain thing, or of certain things (*Stromateis* VI. VII.343).

Church writers closely followed the Stoic understanding that 'assumption' (or preconception – ὑπόληψις) and 'assent' are closely connected to 'faith.' Wolfson mentions one definition of faith by the Stoics: 'It is said of them that they defined faith as a "strong assumption" (ὑπόληψις ἰσχυρά) confirming that which is assumed' (Stobaeus, *Ecologae* II.7), reproducing Aristotle's statement that faith is a vehement assumption... What the Stoics seem to have done here, therefore, is to extend the meaning of that term (i.e. συγκατάθεσις – [assent]) so as to include also the meaning of Aristotle's term faith, and thus to use it as a judgement of the truth of a thing as well as a judgement of the goodness of a thing.'[58]

Stoic 'assent' is close to Patristic 'faith'

With a number of the Fathers, who followed the Stoic epistemology at this point, 'assent' to objective reality was quite close to 'faith' – which was the proper way of knowing the God who presented Himself in compelling revelation. Clement of Alexandria says in *Stromateis* II, that 'assent is faith.' Irenaeus shows the priority and compelling power that outer reality (of God) has over the assent when he says, 'Faith is produced by the truth.'[59] Later, Hippolytus of Rome reflects the Stoic teaching of the mind having to assent to reality when he says in speaking of the Holy Trinity, 'And we cannot otherwise think of one God, but by believing in truth in Father, Son and Holy Spirit.'[60] He says in another section of the same treatise, 'A man therefore, even though he will it not, is compelled to acknowledge God, the Father Almighty, and Christ Jesus, the Son of God ... and the Holy Spirit; and that these therefore are three.'[61] Origen, speaking of untrue, unreal,

---

[58]H. A. Wolfson, *The Philosophy of the Church Fathers* (Cambridge, Mass: Harvard University Press, 1964), 116,117.

[59]Irenaeus, *Demon.* , 3.

[60]Hippolytus, *Contra Noetum*, 14.

[61]Ibid., 8.

and therefore uncompelling doctrines of God, states: 'Christians will not yield their assent to such opinions...'[62]

Novatian of Rome, a theologian who 'Christianized' certain aspects of Stoic epistemology, ethics and physics,[63] in his famous *De Trinitate* begins this earliest work in church history on the Trinity (around A.D. 250), with the simple assent of faith to the reality of God revealed in 'the rule of truth'[64] (a summary and development of the baptismal formula used in all parts of the Church): 'The rule of truth requires that we should believe first of all in God the Father and Lord Almighty...' (I.1).

Some seventy years after Novatian (A.D. 325), the first ecumenical council of the whole Christian Church at Nicea summarized the heart of orthodox Christianity in the words of the Nicene Creed (with certain supplements being added at the Council of Constantinople in A.D. 381). It is of utmost significance to note exactly how this ancient and universally accepted Creed begins. As the Serbian theologian, Justin Popovitch, explains:

> The Orthodox Church founds all its knowledge of God on faith, and for this reason the Symbol [i.e. Nicene-Constantinopolitan Creed] purely and simply begins with the words: *I believe*, and not with the words: *I know*. God is the object of faith and that is why the knowledge of God is the fruit of faith...[65]

Faith then is the divinely appointed mode for humans to know God, and at its heart is the response of assent (in the words of the Creed, the whole Church says, *I believe* ...). Assent, as we have seen in the Church Fathers' Christian adaptation of elements of Stoic epistemology, included both intuitive apprehension of what is there, and also intellectual consent to that supreme Reality that is external to the mind and objectively real. Hence, they employed several Stoic terms to express the more clearly to their own generation profound biblical realities as concerns the perennial question of how knowing is related to being, particularly to that Being whom to know is life eternal.

IX. Faith and Prayer

The Patriarchs

God and the pressure of His truth give rise to faith, as we are shown in Scripture and the Church Fathers, and faith works by means of the assent of the human personality, and the entire body of Christ on earth. Assent on the part of the persons (and covenant community) who know God, and inevitably wish to know Him better, deeper and more devotedly and

---

[62]Origen, *Contra Celsum*, IV. lxxxiii.

[63]See Douglas Floyd Kelly, *Novatian of Rome* (2 Vols.), Ph.D. Dissertation, University of Edinburgh, 1972, *passim*.

[64]'The rule of truth' will be discussed in Chapter two in some detail.

[65]My translation of the French rendition of the Serbian original: Père Justin Popovitch, *Philosophie Orthodoxe de la Vérité: Dogmatique de l'Eglise Orthodoxe* ,Vol. I (Paris: Collection La Lumière du Thabor L'Age d'Homme, 1992), 106.

obediently always functions in the context of prayer. One of the antediluvian Patriarchs, Enoch, knew God so well, and walked so closely to Him, that we are told, 'And Enoch walked with God: and he was not; for God took him.' After the Flood, Noah built an altar and made appropriate sacrifices of clean animals (in a typological way, pointing to 'the Lamb slain from the foundation of the world' – cf. Gen. 8:20 and Rev. 13:8). God heard his prayer and made him covenant promises of grace (cf. Gen. 8:21–9:17).

The prayers of *Abraham*, father of the faithful, were initiated by God sovereignly and unexpectedly, calling him into a gracious covenant relationship with him (cf. Gen. 12–24). Abraham hears from God and speaks to Him in prayer as he comes to know God's person, will and ways more deeply. Thus in the New Testament, James calls him 'the friend of God' (James 2:23, quoting Isa. 41:8), especially in light of his willingness to sacrifice his 'son of promise,' Isaac, in the surrender of utter devotion (the supreme 'assent' of faith) 'to him who is invisible' (cf. Heb. 11:27), whom he was constantly meeting in the place of prayer.

Moses – on the basis of the divine choice – knew God so well as to lead millions of His people out of captivity in Egypt towards the Promised Land, and to give them the revealed Law received on Mount Sinai. After a lifetime of 'assenting' to God's Word from the initial crisis of the burning bush in the wilderness (Exod. 3:14), to the plagues on Egypt (Exod. 5–11), to that of the Red Sea (Exod. 14), and the renewal of the covenant through the giving of the Law (Exod. 19–21), and his intercession for the idolatrous people (Exod. 32–34), Moses was – at one stage – so close to God that his face was literally shining with divine light (cf. Exod. 34:28–35; 2 Cor. 3:4–18). Yet this same Moses prays that he might know God even more directly: 'And he said, I beseech thee, shew me thy glory...' (Exod. 33:18).

The same context of prayer for deeper knowledge of God is the case for *David*: 'As for me, I will behold thy face in righteousness: I shall be satisfied, when I awake, with thy likeness' (Ps. 17:15).

The same must be said of the Prophets, as with *Isaiah*: 'With my soul have I desired thee in the night; yea, with my spirit within me will I seek thee early...' (Isa. 26:9); 'And it shall be said in that day, Lo, this is our God; we have waited for him, and he will save us: this is the LORD; we have waited for him, we will be glad and rejoice in his salvation' (Isa. 25:9). So with *Jeremiah*, who looks forward to the time when God 'will satiate the soul of my priests with fatness, and my people shall be satisfied with my goodness, saith the Lord' (Jer. 31:14), so that '... After those days, saith the LORD, I will put my law in their inward parts, and write it in their hearts; and will be their God, and they shall be my people. And they shall teach no more every man his neighbour, and every man his brother, saying, Know the LORD: for they shall all know me, from the least of them unto the greatest of them, saith the LORD: for I will forgive their iniquity, and I will remember their sin no more' (Jer. 31:33-34; cf. Heb. 8:9-13). And so with *Ezekiel*, who foresaw the waters of the glory of God once again filling the temple (Ezek. 43:1-12) and the land (Ezek. 47:1-12), so that '... the name of the city from that day shall be, The LORD is there' (Ezek. 48:35).

In line with Ezekiel, the last book of the Old Testament promises that '... the Lord, whom ye seek, shall suddenly come to his temple, even the messenger of the covenant, whom ye delight in: behold, he shall come, saith the LORD of hosts' (Mal. 3:1). This Lord of hosts, the messenger of the covenant, whose glory is usually hidden during the days of his incarnation on earth, is the one who supremely reveals the knowledge of God to man, thus representing God to man and man to God (cf. Matt. 11:27) in the Covenant of Grace. He represents His people in faith (cf. Gal. 2:20: 'the faith of the Son of God'), obedience (cf. John 17:4: 'I have finished the work which thou gavest me to do'), and prayer (John 17 and Heb. 4:14–5:10; 6:15-20; 7:14-28; 9:11-28; 10:1-22). Ultimately, eternal life is possible only in the context of that prayer 'without ceasing' (1 Thess. 5:17) and 'not fainting' (Luke 18:1) that is found in that theological knowledge which occurs in union with Christ (John 17:3: 'And this is life eternal, that they might know thee the only true God, and Jesus Christ, whom thou hast sent').

True and ever fuller knowledge of God granted to the assenting response of faith in the context of prayer is equally the case with the *apostles*. After Peter and John were forbidden by the Jewish authorities to preach Christ and to heal in His name, they – and the whole apostolic company in Jerusalem – gave themselves to prayer, on the basis of the Old Testament promises, in the name of the Father's 'holy child Jesus,' and 'were filled with the Holy Ghost, and they spake the word of God with boldness' (Acts 4:23-31). It was the same with the first Christian martyr, Stephen, who in being stoned by the Jews for his public witness to Jesus, turned to prayer: 'But he, being full of the Holy Ghost, looked up steadfastly into heaven, and saw the glory of God, and Jesus standing on the right hand of God, And said, Behold, I see the heavens opened, and the Son of man standing on the right hand of God... And they stoned Stephen, calling upon God, and saying, Lord Jesus, receive my spirit' (Acts 7:55, 56, 59). The Apostle to the Gentiles, Paul, who had been caught up 'to the third heaven ... into paradise, and heard unspeakable words...' (2 Cor. 12:2, 4), is the very one who instructs us to 'pray without ceasing' (1 Thess. 5:17; 1 Tim. 2:28; Eph. 6:18; 1 Thess. 3:10). The last chapter of the final revelation given to the Church through the beloved Apostle, John, concludes with promises and prayers for the one whose glory has been majestically revealed, to come quickly (Rev. 22:16-17; 20), so that the knowledge of faith may be replaced with that fuller knowledge of sight: '... But we know that, when he shall appear, we shall be like him; for we shall see him as he is' (1 John 3:2). All true theological knowledge then, from beginning to end, lives and breathes in an atmosphere of prayer to the One whose fuller vision will at last totally transform us.

Theology to be done in the atmosphere of prayer

Athanasius

Many, if not most, of the greatest of the Church Fathers have pursued their theological work in the context of prayer, as the only appropriate atmosphere for true faith from start to finish. St. Athanasius writes that true faith functions in vital piety, rather than a bare logical demonstration,[66] and this vital piety requires '... constant prayer to God, godly knowing, and supplications offered not in some casual way but with the consent of the whole heart.' In *Epistle* 11, he writes: 'For faith and godliness are allied to each other, and sisters; and he who believes in Him is godly, and he also who is godly, believes the more [cf. John 7:17]... For such meditation and exercise in godliness, being at all times the habit of the saints, is urgent on us at the present time, when the divine word desires us to keep the feast with them if we are in this disposition. For what else is the feast, but the constant worship, and the recognition of godliness, and unceasing prayers from the whole heart with agreement?'[67] In *De Incarnatione*, Athanasius explains why piety and prayer are so essential:

> But for the searching of the Scriptures and true knowledge of them, an honourable life is needed, and a pure soul and that virtue which is according to Christ; so that the intellect guiding its path by it, may be able to attain what it desires, and to comprehend it, in so far as it is accessible to human nature to learn concerning the Word of God. For without a pure mind and a modelling of the life after the saints, a man could not possibly comprehend the words of the saints ... thus he that would comprehend the mind of those that would speak of God must needs begin by washing and cleansing his soul, by his manner of living, and approach the saints by imitating their works; so that associated with them in the conduct of a common life, he may understand also what has been revealed to them by God... (57.1-3)

Athanasius frequently verbalized prayers for God's help in trying to explain the true meaning of the Scriptures concerning the deity of Christ against the heretical Arians in *Contra Arianos*.[68] And he began his *Letters to Serapion Concerning the Holy Spirit* with a comment on the comforting providence of God in preserving his life for the difficult task at hand (I.1).

Hilary of Poitiers

St. Hilary of Poitiers, who though he lived in the West, spent considerable time in exile (at the hands of the Arian civil government) in the East, reflects at the deepest level in his theological work Athanasius' insistence that God can only be known and spoken about by those who live a life of prayer. Hilary's *De Trinitate* (c. A.D. 350), rather like the book of Nehemiah, is interspersed with prayers:

> ... I must pray also for the gift of Thy help and compassion, that the breath of thy Spirit may fill the sails of faith and confession which I have spread,

[66] Athanasius, *Letters to Serapion Concerning the Holy Spirit* (translated by C. R. B. Shapland; London: The Epworth Press, 1951), I.20 (pp.114-115): 'For tradition, as we have said, does not declare the Godhead to us by demonstration in words [1 Cor. 2], but by faith and by a pious and reverent use of reason. For if Paul proclaimed the saving Gospel of the Cross, "not in words of wisdom, but in demonstration of the Spirit and of power" [1 Cor. 2: 4]; and if in Paradise he heard "unspeakable words which it is not lawful for a man to utter" [2 Cor. 12:4]: who can declare the holy Triad itself ...'

[67] Sections 9 and 11.

[68] See I.25 – 'After many prayers then that God would be gracious to us ...'; III.63 – '... be propitious, O Lord ...'

> and a favouring wind be sent to forward me on my journey of instruction. We can trust the promise of Him Who said, *Ask, and it shall be given you, seek, and ye shall find, knock, and it shall be opened unto you* [Luke 11:9]; and we in our want shall pray for the things we need. We shall bring an untiring energy to the study of Thy prophets and apostles, and we shall knock for entrance at every gate of hidden knowledge, but it is Thine to answer the prayer, to grant the Thing we seek, to open the door on which we beat. Our minds are born with dull and clouded vision, our feeble intellect is penned within the barriers of an impassable ignorance concerning things divine; but the study of Thy revelation elevates our soul to the comprehension of sacred truth, and submission to the faith is the path to a certainty beyond the reach of unassisted reason.
>
> And therefore we look to Thy support for the first trembling steps of this undertaking, to Thy aid that it may gain strength and prosper. We look to Thee to give us the fellowship of that Spirit who guided the prophets and apostles, that we may take their words in the sense in which they spoke and assign its right shade of meaning to every utterance.[69]

Far from Hilary merely writing a prayer as a formal preface to his work, throughout the book he is frequently turning to God for help: 'Language is exhausted by the magnitude of the theme... Still, under the necessity that is laid upon us, with a prayer for pardon to Him whose attributes these are, we will venture, enquire and speak; and moreover – it is the only promise that in so grave a matter we dare to make – we will accept whatever conclusion He shall indicate' (II.5). Three substantial sections of Book VI, and six more in Book VII constitute other prayers in the midst of his theological argumentation; indicating that for Hilary, prayer and theology are inseparable companions. The reasons are clear, according to him: no mind can understand the divine,[70] God cannot be known except by devotion,[71] and thus, it is the Lord who will give us understanding.[72]

- *Eastern Orthodox piety*

It is a strong characteristic of Eastern Orthodox piety over the centuries that theology has always been thought through in the atmosphere of prayer and worship. Prayer for God's light to speak worthily of Him is a constituent part of the broader piety of Orthodox worship and life in the Church. That piety is specifically Trinitarian, as Bobrinskoy states: '…Eastern trinitarian piety is always placed in a personalistic context of relations within the Trinity, the Father, the Son, and the Holy Spirit. It is not a Unitarian piety.'[73]

And prayer for God's presence and light is viewed as a part of the larger reality of 'deification'.[74] That is, the believer, as part of the Church, is made 'a partaker of the divine nature' (2 Pet. 1:4) – by grace and adoption, but

[69] I.37,38.

[70] X.53; XII.56.

[71] XI.44.

[72] XI.23.

[73] Boris Bobrinskoy, *The Mystery of the Trinity*, translated by Anthony P. Gythiel (Crestwood, NY: St. Valdimir's Seminary Press, 1999), 257.

[74] I shall address 'deification' in Volume Two of this Systematic Theology.

does *not* become part of the absolute substance of God. That is, by virtue of the Holy Spirit, the believer is vitally united to the humanity of Christ, the head of the Church, hence becoming a member of His body. It is their understanding that the Christian partakes in the uncreated energies of God, but not His substance.[75] While the Holy Spirit alone can regenerate the believer into union with Christ, still the believer is called on to a life of holy discipline, including faith, prayer, the sacraments and general obedience of love to God and mankind. Thus the Church 'participates' in the life of God, so that theology is one aspect of knowing God (John 17:3).

As Stăniloae says:

> … the Holy Spirit makes spiritual the humanity assumed by the Son and deifies it, which is to say, makes it fit to participate in the love which the divine hypostasis of the Son has toward his Father. The revelation of the Trinity has no other purpose than to draw us after grace, to draw us through the Holy Spirit into the filial relationship the Son has with the Father. The trinitarian acts of revelation that save and deify, acts that raise us up into communion with the persons of the Holy Trinity.[76]

Justin Popovitch specifically includes the theologian in this necessary context of Church piety:

> It is also necessary for the dogmatician with all of his heart and all of his spirit to penetrate by prayer into this holy, catholic, apostolic and universal conscience of the Church, so that all of his work may receive – by her and for her – the norms for dogmatic science. Above all, he must not forget this blessed word of the Lord Jesus, that only those who are 'pure in heart shall see God' (Matt. 5:8) and the eternal truths of God.[77]

In the context of monastic theology, John Meyendorff speaks of the place of prayer in our union with Christ:

> Union then becomes possible through prayer. It is Evagrius who first coins the term 'prayer of the mind' which will become standard in Byzantine hesychasm. Prayer is 'the proper activity of the mind' [Pseudo-Nilus (Evagrius), *De Oratione*, 84; PG 79:1185a], 'an impassible state' [Ibid., 52], the 'highest possible intellection' [Ibid., 34A]. In this 'state' of prayer, the mind is totally liberated from every 'multiplicity'; it is 'deaf and dumb' to every perception of the senses [Ibid., 11]. According to Evagrius, as we know now, prayer also means that the mind is an 'essential union' with the deity …[78]

By the time of the high Middle Ages in the Eastern Church, 'the Jesus prayer' had become very important, as a sort of method to be in touch with the Lord. Meyendorff summarizes it:

> Although this method is held by some as a return to the origins of monasticism, it appears only in explicit, written documents of the late-

[75] The distinction the Orthodox make here between the substance of God and the uncreated energies of God will be dealt with in Appendix I to Chapter 3.

[76] Dumitru Stăniloae, *Orthodox Dogmatic Theology: The Experience of God*, translated and edited by Ioan Ionita and Robert Barringer (Brookline, MA: Holy Cross Orthodox Press, 1998), 249.

[77] Justin Popovitch, *Philosophie Orthodox de la Verité: Dogmatique de L'Eglise Orthodoxe, Tome Premier*, 92 [my translation].

[78] John Meyendorff, *Byzantine Theology: Historical Trends & Doctrinal Themes* (London & Oxford: Mowbrays, 1975), 68.

> thirteenth and early-fourteenth centuries ... Undoubtedly, the method was widely known, for Gregory Palamas quotes, among its adepts, such major figures of the Church as Patriarch Athanasius I (1289–93, 1303–1310) and Theoleptus, Metropolitan of Philadelphia (1250–1321/26).[79] The method consisted in obtaining 'attention' (*prosoche*) – the first condition of authentic prayer – by concentrating one's mind 'in the heart,' retaining each breath, and reciting mentally the short prayer: 'Lord Jesus Christ, Son of God, have mercy upon me.'[80]

No doubt, this 'Jesus prayer' was connected to the much earlier *kyrie eleison!* found in the Mass of the ancient, undivided Church.[81] Far broader than 'the Jesus prayer', however, was the insistence on a Spirit-filled life in the context of the disciplines of the Christian Church in order to express theology faithfully. Symeon the New Theologian (949–1022) describes its necessity:

> Therefore a Christian must always think and speak and do only what is good, for as the Lord says, *A house divided against itself shall not stand* (Matt. 12:25). But one must always keep in mind also that it is impossible for thoughts always to be good (and from such thoughts are usually produced words and deeds which are similar to them), unless first Christ the Lord has come to dwell in the mind, for which we should struggle as far as we have strength – that is, so that Christ the Lord should come to dwell in our mind ... And so for those who are called Christians and do such works of the devil [*sc.* 1 John 3:8], what benefit is there from the fact that they are called Christians, when the manifestation of the Son of God has not destroyed in them these works of the devil?
>
> If anyone will say that some of those who are like this explain the Divine Scripture, theologize, preach Orthodox dogmas – let them know that it is not in this that the work of Christ consists. John the Theologian does not say, *to this end was the Son of God manifested* [1 John. 3:8], that certain ones should theologize and orthodoxize (that is, pride themselves on their Orthodoxy – *tr. note*), but *that He might destroy the works of the devil.* Concerning such ones, I shall say that first one must clean the vessel of every filth and then place in it the myrrh, lest the myrrh itself become defiled, and in place of fragrance there should come from it an evil smell. The Son of God, the Word, did not become man in order that men should believe in the Holy Trinity, glorify It, and theologize about It, but in order to destroy the works of the devil. In whomsoever among those who have received the faith of Christ the works of the devil shall be destroyed, to him may be entrusted the mysteries of theology and Orthodox dogmas...for how is it possible that a mind which is darkened by a defiled conscience should think rightly and purely? ...[82]

---

[79] Gregory Palamas, *Triads*, I, 2; ed. J. Meyendorff, *Défense des saints hesychastes*, Spicilegium Sacrum Lovaniense 30 (Louvain, 1959), 99.

[80] Meyendorff, *Byzantine Theology*, 76. See also *The Jesus Prayer by A Monk of the Eastern Church*, by Lev Gillet with a foreword by Kallistos Ware (Crestwood, NY: St. Vladimir's Seminary Press, 2006).

[81] As in *The Apostolic Constitutions*, VIII, 6, 3-9. Although an apocryphal compilation, Book VIII goes back to the early third century *Apostolic Tradition* of Hippolytus of Rome. See Lucien Deiss, *Springtime of the Liturgy* (Collegeville MN: The Liturgical Press, 1979), 215-227.

[82] St. Symeon the New Theologian, *The First Created Man: Seven Homilies*, Selected and translated with an Introduction by Fr. Seraphim Rose (Platina, CA: St. Herman of Alaska Brotherhood, 2001), 62. 63,65.

That devout prayer should inform not only the teaching and writing of theology, but also the daily life and thinking and suffering of the entire laity as well as the ministry, is illustrated beautifully in what happened among the Orthodox Christians of Romania during the long years of Marxist oppression.

The new *Cambridge History of Christianity: Eastern Christianity* discusses the Jesus Prayer as part of the Christian 'subversion' of the Marxist totalitarianism over Eastern Europe before its liberation from 1989 to 1991:

> A significant example of subversion was the practice of the 'prayer of the heart' by political prisoners. This tradition of unceasing prayer, known in the Balkans as hesychasm, or the attainment of inner stillness through prayer (specifically the Jesus Prayer), flourished in Romanian prisons like Aiud, Ocnele, Mari and Gherla, where copies of Dumitru Stăniloae's translation of the Greek *Philokalia* (an anthology of ascetical and mystical texts on hesychast spirituality dating from the third to the fifteenth century) had been smuggled in. Stăniloae is an example of an intellectual who, while appearing to make concessions to the status quo, in fact through his writing undermined the very principles on which the political structure was based.[83]

Augustine

Passing from East to West, a generation after the time of Athanasius and Hilary, we find the same emphasis on the necessity of theology being produced in the atmosphere of piety and prayer in the greatest of the Western Church Fathers, Augustine. The entirety of Book I of his *Confessions* is one long prayer to God, without whose constant aid one cannot speak: ' ... Yet, O my God, my life, my holy Joy, what is this that I have said? What can any man say when he speaks of Thee? But woe to them that keep silence – since even those who say most are dumb' (I.5). It is the same with his great work, *De Trinitate*:

> And it is necessary, therefore, to purge our minds, in order to be able to see ineffably that which is ineffable; whereto not having yet attained, we are to be nourished by faith, and led by such ways as are more suited to our capacity, that we may be rendered apt and able to comprehend it. And hence the apostle says, that 'in Christ indeed are hid all the treasures of wisdom and knowledge' [Col. 2:3]... (I.3).
>
> Wherefore, our Lord God helping, we will undertake to render, as far as we are able, that very account which they so importunately demand: viz., that the Trinity is the one and only and true God ... in such wise ... that they may find by actual trial, both that the highest good is that which is discerned by the most purified minds, and that for this reason it cannot be discerned or understood by themselves, because the eye of the human mind, being weak, is dazzled in that so transcendent light, unless it be invigorated by the nourishment of the righteousness of faith ... and thus, if there be anything in them of either love or fear towards God, they may return and begin from faith in due order: perceiving how healthful a medicine has been provided for the faithful in the holy Church, whereby a heedful piety, healing the

[83] Michael Angold, ed., *The Cambridge History of Christianity: vol. 5 Eastern Christianity* (Cambridge: Cambridge University Press, 2006), 565, 566.

> feebleness of the mind, may render it able to perceive the unchangeable truth, and hinder it from falling headlong, through disorderly rashness, into pestilent and false opinion. (I.4)
>
> Further let me ask of my reader ... there to go on with me ... so that we may enter together upon the path of charity, and advance towards Him of whom it is said, 'Seek His face evermore' [Ps. 105:4]... And I would make this pious and safe agreement, in the presence of our Lord God, with all who read my writings... This I pray for, and this my trust and desire I commit to Him, who is sufficiently able to keep those things which He has given me, and to render those which He has promised'. (I.5)
>
> And to be sure, when they have steadfastly believed the Holy Scriptures as most true witnesses, let them strive, by praying and seeking and living well, that they may understand, i.e. that so far as it can be seen, that may be seen by the mind which is held fast by faith (XV.49).

Similarly, in his classical work on biblical interpretation, *De Doctrina Christiana*, Augustine, after discussing the rules of the Donatist Tychonius for interpreting difficulties in Scripture, states: '... and especially – this is paramount, and absolutely vital – to pray for understanding.' [84] Later he writes:

> Or are we rather to understand two things at once – that through the abundant gifts of the Holy Spirit the human task of teaching even the teachers themselves must not cease, and that 'neither the one who plants nor the one who waters is anything, but it is God who produces the growth?' [1 Cor. 3:7]. That is why even with the ministry of holy men, or indeed the co-operation of the holy angels, nobody properly learns the things that appertain to a life with God, unless, through God, he becomes responsive to God, to whom it is said in the Psalm: 'Teach me to do your will, since you are my God' [Ps. 143:10].[85]

And again, Augustine shows the necessity of prayer and piety for understanding and conveying of true theological knowledge:

> Whether they are going to speak before a congregation or any other body, or to dictate something to be spoken before a congregation or read by others who are able and willing to do so, speakers must pray that God will place a good sermon on their lips. If Queen Esther, when about to plead before the king for the temporal salvation of her people, prayed that God would place a suitable speech on her lips [Esther 4:16], how much more important is it for those who work for people's eternal salvation 'by teaching God's word' [1 Tim. 5:17] to pray to receive such a gift?[86]

Anselm

St. Anselm of Canterbury, who is considered by some to have been the first, and certainly one of the greatest, of the Scholastic thinkers in the West (in the eleventh century), is biblical, Patristic, and particularly Augustinian in his constant practice of formulating theological knowledge on his knees in prayer. This is seen with particular stress in *Proslogion*, where he discusses

[84] Book Three, XXXVII, 56 – translation of R. P. H. Green.

[85] Book Four, XVI, 33.

[86] Book Four, XXX, 63.

the ontological proof for the existence of God. Anselm's discussion was brought back to the fore of contemporary theology by Karl Barth's *Anselm: Fides Quaerens Intellectum: Anselm's Proof of the Existence of God in the Context of his Theological Scheme* in 1930. Barth's thesis that Anselm was thinking through the impossibility of the serious contemplation of God's non-existence 'from faith to faith', rather than attempting a 'neutral' sort of logical demonstration, has been disputed by many.[87] But no one who has actually read Anselm would wish to deny that Barth is at least right about the crucial practice of prayer for Anselm at the heart of his theological enterprise.

He begins by calling those who wish to know God to prayer:

> Speak now, my whole heart, speak now to God: 'I seek Your countenance, O Lord, Your countenance I seek' [Ps. 27:8]. Come then, Lord my God, teach my heart where and how to seek You, where and how to find You. Lord, if You are not present here, where, since You are absent, shall I look for You? On the other hand, if You are everywhere why then, since You are present, do I not see You? But surely You dwell in 'light inaccessible' [1 Tim. 6:16]
>
> ... When will You enlighten our eyes and show 'Your countenance to us [Ps. 79:4]? ... Look upon us, Lord; hear us, enlighten us, show Yourself to us ... Have pity upon our efforts and our strivings towards You, for we can avail nothing without You ...[88]

Then Anselm in the context of prayer and faith repeats the statement as the ground of his theological procedure, taken from Isaiah 7:9 (and used previously by such Church Fathers as Augustine and Clement of Alexandria):

> I do not try, Lord, to attain Your lofty heights, because my understanding is in no way equal to it. But I do desire to understand Your truth a little, that truth that my heart believes and loves. For I do not seek to understand so that I may believe; but I believe so that I may understand. For I believe this also, that 'unless I believe, I shall not understand' [Isa. 7:9].[89]

John Calvin

Half a millennium after Anselm, the biblical and Patristic scholar and magisterial Reformer, John Calvin, stands on the same ground as regards the necessity of piety and prayer constituting the only atmosphere in which true theological knowledge can take place. Calvin writes in a very different style from Anselm (who wrote in a different style from Hilary and Augustine), as would be expected for such different ages. Calvin's theological writing is not interlaced with prayers, as is that of his patristic and scholastic predecessors. Although very pastoral and intended for 'the flock', Calvin's is still a more academic and systematic approach, and thus less dialogical. But as to substance, at this point he is at one with these luminaries of the early and medieval Church.

---

[87]e.g. M. J. Charlesworth, *St. Anselm's Proslogion* (Notre Dame: University of Notre Dame Press, 1979), 'Karl Barth's St. Anselm' (pp. 40–46).

[88]*Proslogion* I (Charlesworth translation, pp. 114, 115).

[89]Ibid., 115.

Piety (which includes prayer) is central to the thought of Calvin (more so, undoubtedly, than even the doctrine of predestination, by which he is popularly remembered). Near the beginning of his major theological work (*Institutes of the Christian Religion*), Calvin defines piety:

> I call 'piety' that reverence joined with love of God which the knowledge of his benefits induces. For until men recognize that they owe everything to God, that they are nourished by his fatherly care, that he is the Author of their every good, that they should seek nothing beyond him – they will never yield him willing service. Nay, unless they establish their complete happiness in him, they will never give themselves truly and sincerely to him.[90]

A few pages later, he notes that although 'the seed of religion has been divinely planted in all men,' because of the universal effects of human sin and 'revolt from God... As a result, no real piety remains in the world...'[91] Rather than worshipping God in God's way, because 'the blindness [of sin] under which they labor is almost always mixed with proud vanity and obstinacy... They do not therefore apprehend God as he offers himself, but imagine him as they have fashioned him in their own presumption.'[92] Calvin, of course, includes here in worship, the knowledge of God and the description of it in theology, which is intended to result in a life of purity, praise and service within the Church. But instead, because of the rebellion of sin and its continuing effect on the children of Adam, 'Accordingly, we see that many, after they have become hardened in insolent and habitual sinning, furiously repel all remembrance of God, although this is freely suggested to them inwardly from the feelings of nature.'[93]

The Holy Scriptures as 'spectacles'

Thus Calvin shows that because of the willful blindness of sin, mankind needs 'spectacles' in order to see God's truth clearly, '... so Scripture, gathering up the otherwise confused knowledge of God in our minds, having dispersed our dullness, clearly shows us the true God. This, therefore, is a special gift, where God, to instruct the church, not merely uses mute teachers, but also opens his own most hallowed lips.'[94] But to make proper use of these 'spectacles' of Scripture, fallen humans must personally undergo an inner change or renovation of personality, attitude and thus 'sight'. For as Christ said to Nicodemus, 'except a man be born again, he cannot see the kingdom of God' (John 3:3). Calvin explains:

> ... Flesh is not capable of such lofty wisdom as to conceive God and what is God's, unless it be illumined by the Spirit of God. As Christ testified, the fact that Peter recognized him was a special revelation of the Father [Matt. 16:17]...
>
> If we were convinced that our nature lacks everything that our Heavenly Father bestows upon his elect through the Spirit of regeneration [cf. Titus 3:5]

---

[90] *Institutes*, I.2.1.
[91] Ibid. I.4.1.
[92] Ibid.
[93] Ibid. I.4.2.
[94] Ibid. I.6.1.

> – a fact that should be beyond controversy – we would have no occasion to doubt...
>
> It therefore remains for us to understand that the way to the Kingdom of God is open only to him whose mind has been made new by the illumination of the Holy Spirit...[95]

'Internal testimony of the Holy Spirit'

But in addition to the spiritual renovation and 'enlightening of the eyes' known as the new birth, members of the redeemed community have to be continually given 'the internal testimony of the Holy Spirit' to hear 'God in person speaking in it,' and whereby 'The same Spirit, therefore, who has spoken through the mouths of the prophets must penetrate into our hearts to persuade us that they faithfully proclaimed what had been divinely commanded.'[96] To know God and his truth, one needs the continuous help of the Holy Spirit. Discussing Paul's prayer in Colossians 1:9-10 ('We ceased not to pray for you and to ask that you may be filled with the knowledge of God in all spiritual wisdom and understanding in order that you may walk worthily before God...'), Calvin adds:

> Nor does Scripture teach that our minds are illumined only on one day and that they may thereafter see of themselves. For what I have just quoted from Paul has reference to continuing progress and increase. David has aptly expressed it in these words: 'With my whole heart I have sought thee; let me not wander from thy commandments!' [Ps. 119:10]. Although he had been reborn and had advanced to some extent in true godliness, he still confesses that he needs continual direction at every moment, lest he decline from the knowledge with which he has been endowed.[97]

'Accordingly,' Calvin sees that 'without the illumination of the Holy Spirit, the Word can do nothing.'[98]

Therefore, since the Holy Spirit is given in prayer, as Christ tells us (Luke 11:13), Calvin – with Athanasius, Hilary, Augustine, Anselm and the whole company of the Church Fathers – holds that prayer for the illumination of the Holy Spirit is the atmosphere of true theological work.

> Clearly, then, to pray rightly is a rare gift ... our intention is that, loathing our inertia and dullness, we should seek such aid of the Spirit. And indeed, Paul when he enjoins us to pray in the Spirit [1 Cor. 14:15], does not stop urging us to watchfulness. He means that the prompting of the Spirit empowers us so to compose prayers as by no means to hinder or hold back our own effort, since in this matter God's will is to test how effectually faith moves our hearts.[99]

The Holy Spirit and preaching

For Calvin, the major purpose of theological knowledge seems to be the goal of informing the preaching of the Word of God. Most of his commentaries

---

[95]Ibid. II.2.19, 20.
[96]Ibid. I.7.4.
[97]Ibid. II.2.25.
[98]Ibid. III.2.33.
[99]Ibid. III.20.5.

on various books of Holy Scripture draw their sources from his sermons or homilies delivered in the Cathedral of St. Pierre in Geneva. He clearly states that '... nothing is accomplished by preaching him [Christ] if the Spirit, as our inner teacher, does not show our minds the way.'[100] It is 'a two-way street': the Spirit enables us to understand the doctrines of the preached Word, and sound doctrine helps us call upon the Spirit in such a way as to increase our confidence in God, who gave that Word. Thus, in his discussion of the doctrine of election, he holds that doctrines are to inform our prayers. In the case of election, he says:

> The practice of this doctrine ought also to flourish in our prayers. For even though faith in election prompts us to call upon God, still, when we frame our prayers, it would be preposterous to thrust this upon God or to bargain upon this condition: 'O Lord, if I have been chosen, hear me.' For it is his will that we be content with his promises, and not inquire elsewhere whether he will be disposed to hear us.[101]

Therefore, for the primary theological work of God's people, reading Scripture and hearing the sermon, prayer for the aid of the Holy Spirit is absolutely essential:

> When we come to hear the sermon or take up the Bible, we must not have the foolish arrogance of thinking that we shall easily understand everything we hear or read. But we must come with reverence, we must wait entirely upon God, knowing that we need to be taught by His Holy Spirit, and that without Him we cannot understand anything that is shown us in His Word.[102]

Prayer at the heart of the Church's Life

From beginning to end, therefore, the purpose of true theological knowledge is a vital relationship to God, characterized by continual prayer. 'We are called into the Church in order that we may call on God; for in vain do they boast who neglect prayer and true calling upon God, and yet hold a place in the Church.'[103] Thus the grasping and conveying of Christian theology (which is always within the Church) is directly and constantly dependent on the Spirit who comes in answer to prayer:

> As the seed covered with earth lies hid for a time, so the Lord will illuminate us by His Spirit, and will cause that reading which, being barren and void of fruit, causes nothing but wearisomeness, to have plain light of understanding. The Lord never keeps the eyes so shut, but that, as soon as they are once entered, the way of salvation appears unto them in the Scripture... Yet He suffers them to stick fast oftentimes, and permits their course to be hindered by some bar which is laid in the way both that He may try the patience of faith in them, and also that He may teach them humility ... that He may make them more fervent in prayer; that He may prick them forward to love the truth more dearly; that he may set forth the excellence of His heavenly wisdom, which is otherwise not so esteemed as it ought.[104]

---

[100]Ibid. II.2.20.
[101]Ibid. III.24.5.
[102]*Commentary on 2 Timothy*, at chapter 3: 16.
[103]*Commentary on Isaiah*, at chapter 56: 7.
[104]*Commentary on Acts*, at chapter 8: 34.

We may summarize what the Church Fathers and one of the leading Reformers teach as to how a human being may come to know God by two passages from Holy Scripture. In the context of gracious promises by God to deliver his sinful people from captivity in Babylon after seventy years, God declares that these promises must be prayed into execution: 'Then shall ye call upon me, and ye shall go and pray unto me, and I will hearken unto you. And ye shall seek me, and find me, when ye shall search for me with all your heart' (Jer. 29:12-13). The prophet Daniel is a bright example of this, especially when he 'prays into execution' the promises of God given through Jeremiah concerning the return home of the Jews after seventy years of captivity in Babylon (cf. Dan. 9 and Jer. 29:10-14).

And then the incarnate Christ, to whom Jeremiah and all of true Israel were ultimately looking forward, promises in controversy with the Jews of His time, many of whom accused Him of deceiving the people: 'If any man will do his will, he shall know of the doctrine, whether it be of God or whether I speak of myself' (John 7:17). The covenant God of Israel and the Church, the Creator, Sustainer and Redeemer of heaven and earth can still be found by sincere seekers, who earnestly pray and search out His written Word, particularly where it is proclaimed in the power of the Spirit in churches where 'the Word is rightly preached and the sacraments purely administered.'

X. God's Truth is Validated the Same Way it is Revealed

This inevitably raises the question of the validation of these high theological (and indeed, intensely personal) claims on humanity. Some references from Thomas F. Torrance should make the way clear:

> Michael Polanyi reminds us in his Gifford lectures that we cannot convince others by formal argument, for so long as we argue within their framework, we can never induce them to abandon it. 'Formal operations relying on one framework of interpretation cannot demonstrate a proposition to persons who rely on another framework' (*Personal Knowledge*, p. 151). That applies to theological communication as much as scientific controversy, and yet this is precisely the erroneous line taken so often by apologetics, whether by the theologian or the preacher. Whenever we take that line we are simply reducing ourselves to be servants of public opinion or popular ideas of science and religion, and in that event we have nothing at all to offer to people which they do not already know or cannot tell to themselves much better than we. Moreover, by taking this line we eliminate from theological knowledge its real meaning, for we deprive it of its proper message. That is why theological statements inevitably appear meaningless and impossibly paradoxical if we claim for them validity within a frame of reference which is the correlate of ordinary observable and empirically verifiable experience.
>
> When we are faced with the problem of communication between two different frames of reference separated by what Polanyi calls a 'logical gap', then the first step in understanding is to explore the nature and depth of the difference. The only proper road to take at that point is to persuade those operating from the other frame to look away at the realities we seek to indicate, and to persuade them to take, in the face of it, the kind

> of 'heuristic' step forward which we always have to make in any genuine scientific discovery, for only then will they discern and know for themselves what we are speaking about. That is to say, in theological language, we have to bear witness to the divine Truth, and try to get from others a genuinely open hearing, but if they take the heuristic step which they must if they are really to know, it will involve on their part a self-critical act in reconstruction of their prior understanding, i.e. what the New Testament calls *metanoia* [repentance].[105]

Elsewhere, Torrance discusses the only proper grounds of verification of ultimate truth:

> ... theological concepts and statements have their justification through the Grace of God alone. They have their proper right and their proper truth, not through some process of verification which we put into effect by linking them to a ground in our prior knowledge, far less to some vaunted 'self-understanding' on our part, as though we could compel God to be the truth of what we think and say of him, but solely through the self-giving of God in Jesus Christ, the Way and the Truth and the Life... To seek verification on any other ground than that which God has freely provided for us is to falsify the gospel at its very basis... Hence justification or verification by the grace of God's truth alone brings us with all our preconceptions and prior knowledge radically into question.[106]

> It is as such [i.e. having its own reality and truth wholly and in every respect within itself] that revelation proceeds from God to man, breaking sovereignly into human life and thought, calling into question what people claim to know, and directing their thinking beyond themselves altogether... In point of fact it actually conflicts sharply with generally accepted beliefs and established ideas in human culture and initiates a seismic reconstruction not only of religious and intellectual belief but of the very foundations of human life and knowledge... The fathers and theologians of the Early Church reflected upon the fact that, since the proof of an unknown reality is its own evidence and the conceptual assent or basic belief it calls forth from people, the right way for people to break through into a completely new realm of meaning or truth is the way of *faith* – hence the principle widely promulgated in the Church: 'unless you believe you will not understand.' This is certainly the case whenever we have to do with *ultimates* which carry their own authority calling for the intelligent commitment of belief, and provide the irreducible ground upon which rational knowledge and theological formulation take place.[107]

In summary, for the validation of theological truth claims, (1) we do not step off the grounds where the living God has given Himself to be known (His Word and Spirit), and hence, (2) we operate outside all frameworks of unbelief so as to call their inhabitants forth in faith and repentance into an utterly new 'paradigm' (God's revealed truth in the power of the Holy Spirit), where they can experience the liberation of a 'new creation', in which 'old things are passed away; behold, all things are become new' (2 Cor. 5:17).

---

[105]Thomas F. Torrance, *Theology In Reconstruction* (London: SCM Press, 1965), 27,28.

[106]Thomas F. Torrance, *Reality and Evangelical Theology*, (Philadelphia, PA: The Westminster Press, 1982),148.

[107]Thomas F. Torrance, *The Christian Doctrine of God, One Being Three Persons*, (Edinburgh: T & T Clark, 1996), 19, 20.

XI. It Is Necessary to Look Outward and Upward from Frameworks of Unbelief to Him who is the Truth

There are many illustrations in Holy Scripture of this transforming shift from a framework of unbelief to that of faith. One of the most famous is that of the distinguished 'ruler of the Jews' (John 3:1) and 'master of Israel' (John 3:10), Nicodemus, who came to Jesus by night to ask the way into the kingdom of God. Though his intellectual framework prevented him from recognizing it at the time, Nicodemus had indeed come to the right place, for the very person to whom he was speaking was actually the true King of the kingdom into which Nicodemus wished to enter. Jesus showed him what a radical shift is required to move from one kingdom to another; from one intellectual/moral/theological framework to another: 'Jesus answered and said unto him, Verily, verily, I say unto thee, Except a man be born again, he cannot *see* the kingdom of God' (John 3:3), and 'Except a man be born of water and of the Spirit, he cannot *enter* into the kingdom of God' (John 3:5).

Nicodemus at first could not grasp the spiritual reality of what Jesus said, and could only allude to the physical absurdity of such instruction to a grown man, who could not 'enter the second time into his mother's womb and be born' (v. 4). Jesus of course replied that this birth is a supernatural event; a miraculous action in the sphere of the Holy Spirit (John 3:5-8). And then in his gracious, accommodating manner, in order to help Nicodemus understand the one way into the kingdom of God, Jesus gives him an Old Testament picture of the spiritual dynamics that are involved in saving faith, as one passes from death (which is housed in the far end of the framework of unbelief) to life (which is housed in Christ, who says 'I am the resurrection and the life' John 11:25).

The upward look and the new birth

To help Nicodemus look out of one framework into the other, Jesus takes this Old Testament scholar to the story in Numbers 21, when the complaining, distrusting Israelites in the wilderness were punished by being bitten by fiery serpents, so that numbers of them were dying. Moses interceded for these sinful people, and God told him quickly to make a brass serpent and put it high on a pole. The people were then instructed to look upwards to that serpent on the pole, and they would be healed. Elsewhere, Scripture pronounces that everyone who hangs on a tree is cursed (Deut. 21:23, quoted in Gal. 3:13). And presumably the lifting up of the serpent speaks of the draining off of the venom of the Satanic tempter with all its consequences into the ultimate Messianic substitute on the tree. The people who looked up in Moses' time were undoubtedly healed through the virtue of Him who would come in the fullness of the time (Gal. 4:4) in order, through his atoning work on the cross, 'by himself to purge our sins' (cf. Heb. 1:3). In taking away human guilt and the punishment it deserves, Christ thus removes the sting of death, which is sin (1 Cor. 15:56) and in its dread place, gives us abundant and eternal life (John 3:16 and 36).

The parallel that Jesus draws between Numbers 21 and his interview with Nicodemus makes the position clear. Only the outward, upward look can save; for the suffering Israelites, it involved a physical look to the image of a snake on a pole. For Nicodemus, and all others to this day, it involves the upward look of faith to Christ as Savior and Lord. Thus, Christ says:

> And as Moses lifted up the serpent in the wilderness, even so must the Son of man be lifted up: That whosoever believeth in him should not perish, but have eternal life. For God so loved the world, that he gave his only begotten Son, that whosoever believeth in him should not perish, but have everlasting life (John 3:14-16).

It is clear that the testimony of Jesus to Himself did cause Nicodemus to look up to the one who would be 'lifted up' (John 3:14); to the one who said, 'And I, if I be lifted up from the earth, will draw all *men* unto me' (John 12:32).[108] Nicodemus' looking upwards out of his old framework of understanding was part of the miracle of the 'new birth' (or 'birth from above'), which is essential to 'seeing' and 'entering' the kingdom of God (John 3:3, 5); the realm of eternal life and joy. It is significant that the Greek word for *new* birth ('ἄνωθεν) is often translated 'from above.'[109] Hence, Nicodemus is told to look up to the Christ who 'came down from heaven' and yet at the same time 'is in heaven' (John 3:13), and so is 'above all' (John 3:31). He looks to the highest place and to Him who is above all, and that precisely is whence the 'birth from above' comes.

Multitudes of others since Nicodemus' day have also received the testimony of Christ's words through the apostolic writings, and have been divinely drawn upwards from the deadness and darkness of unbelief into the new life and light of saving faith in Him.[110] This is the only way to true theological knowledge and to life itself: 'And this is life eternal, that they might know thee the only true God, and Jesus Christ, whom thou hast sent' (John 17:3). This way which God has provided for sinners to know Him will remain open 'until the day break and the shadows flee away' (Song 2:17).

Some lines from a hymn by Thomas Binney capture this upward movement:

---

[108]Nicodemus later spoke out in the Sanhedrin against the judging of Christ without evidence (John 7: 50), and after the crucifixion assisted in the burial of Christ (John 20:39).

[109]The term 'ἄνωθεν [literally, 'from above'], which in the English versions of John 3:3 and 5 is generally translated 'born *again*', is rendered as 'again' in Galatians 4:9, but 'from above' in Mark 15:38; John 3:31; 19:11; James 3:15. In Luke 1:3 and Acts 26:5, it is rendered 'from the beginning.'

[110]This 'looking upwards' to Christ in faith is described as a *divine giving* in John 6: 37 ('All that the Father giveth me shall come to me; and him that cometh to me I will in no wise cast out') and v. 65 ('... no man can come unto me, except it were given unto him of my Father'); a *divine teaching* in John 6:45 ('It is written in the prophets [cf. Jer. 31: 34], And they shall be all taught of God, Every man therefore that hath heard, and hath learned of the Father, cometh unto me'), and a *divine drawing* in John 6: 44 ('No man can come to me, except the Father which hath sent me draw him: and I will raise him up at the last day'). John 6 also describes this life-giving transaction as 'eating Christ's flesh and drinking his blood' (vv. 50-58). Verse 63 shows that Christ is speaking of spiritual, rather than literal, physical realities ('It is the spirit that quickeneth; the flesh profiteth nothing: the words that I speak unto you, they are spirit, and they are life'). It must be kept in mind here that spiritual realities are no less 'real' than physical ones.

There is a way for man to rise to that sublime abode;
An offering and a sacrifice,
A Holy Spirit's energies,
An Advocate with God.

These, these prepare us for the sight of holiness above;
The sons of ignorance and night
May dwell in the eternal Light,
Through the eternal Love![111]

[111]Thomas Binney, 'Eternal Light, Eternal Light' in *Church Hymnary* (Oxford: Oxford University Press, 1928, Second Edition), 38.

Chapter One Appendix One

Some Traditional Theistic Proofs

The first chapter has already noted that we do not consider it necessary to attempt to prove God's existence logically, before we begin the work of theology. We need not repeat the reasons here (dealt with in the early pages of Chapter 1, as well as in much of Chapter 2, which follows). I agree with Paul Evdokimov, that since the character of the 'I am that I am' (Exod. 3:14) is the supreme personal reality, there can be no strictly rational proof of God. He writes:

> The insufficiency of the proofs for the existence of God is explained by the fundamental fact that God alone is the criterion of His truth, God alone is the argument for His being. God can never be subject to logical demonstrations nor enclosed in the causal chain...This means that faith is not invented; it is a *gift* ...[1]

Yet in a textbook on systematic theology that interacts with the various traditions throughout the Christian ages, it would surely be amiss not to discuss at least a few representative examples of some of the best theologians who believed in offering proofs for God's existence. Certainly, some of the most consecrated and brilliant effort of Christian theologians of all the centuries has been expended on this very question. If what they seek to establish logically is not considered necessary by us, at the very least in 'the communion of the saints', we owe them a thoroughly respectful hearing.

For our purposes here, I shall select only three major (Western) theologians,[2] as illustrations of this type of serious and influential theological work: St. Anselm, St. Thomas Aquinas and Duns Scotus. First, we consider St. Anselm of Canterbury.

I. St. Anselm of Canterbury (1033–1109)

St. Anselm was born in 1033 in Piedmont, educated by Benedictine monks at Aosta, and went to the Abbey of Bec in Normandy as abbot in 1078,

[1]Paul Evdokimov, *Les âges de la vie spirituelle* (Paris: Desclee, De Brouwer, 1980), 46.

[2]Since this approach was not taken in the East, we do not find Eastern Orthodox theologians 'proving' God's existence. Hence, we must remain in the West.

succeeding Lanfranc. Then, as a result of the Norman conquest of England in 1066, he was called once again to succeed Lanfranc; this time as Archbishop of Canterbury, in 1093. He died in 1109 in England. He was both a great theologian and brave churchman against the kings of England, who wished to control the church. He wrote a number of theological works: *Monologion*, *Proslogion* (or *Fides Quaerens Intellectum*), and its complementary volume, *Liber Apologeticus*, as well as *De Veritate*, and his great book on the atonement: *Cur deus homo*, along with many others.

His writings exude a spirit which combines deep, fragrant devotion, keen logical insight and intelligence, thorough knowledge of Scripture and the historic Christian tradition of theology. He is certainly in the line of St. Augustine, who taught that 'I believe in order that I may understand.'

Anselm devoted two works to proving the existence of the God of Holy Scripture (in whom, of course, he already believed, in order to understand Him). His first attempt was *Monologion*, which was based, as Copleston points out, on an *a posteriori* argument.[3]

Proof of *Monologion*

That is, he starts with facts that we observe in our experience, and then works from those back to God. He seeks to prove God's existence from the varying degrees of perfection that we observe in creatures (not unlike St. Thomas's 'fourth way'). Etienne Gilson summarizes Anselm's proof here:

> Therefore, since all particular goods are unequally good, they can only be good by their participation in a single and same good...Now nothing of what is good by another is superior to what is good by itself. This sovereign good then surpasses all the rest to the point of having nothing above itself. That is to say, what is sovereignly good is also sovereignly great. There is, therefore, a primary being, superior to everything that exists, and it is him whom we call God...Thus, therefore, one single hypothesis remains acceptable; namely, that everything which exists, exists in virtue of a single cause, and that cause which exists by itself is God.[4]

Anselm writes:

> We have found, then, that there is something supremely good (because all good things are good through some one thing, namely that which is good through itself). But in the same way we arrive at the necessary conclusion that there is something supremely great, since whatsoever is great is great through some one thing, namely that which is great through itself. I do not mean great in terms of size, like some sort of body; but something which, the greater it is, the better or more valuable it is, like wisdom. And since only that which is supremely good can be supremely great, it is necessary that there is something that is best and greatest – i.e. of everything that exists, the supreme.[5]

---

[3]Frederick Copleston, *A History of Philosophy, Volume 2: Medieval Philosophy, Part I, Augustine to Bonaventure* (New York: Image Books, 1962), 180.

[4]Etienne Gilson, *History of Christian Philosophy in the Middle Ages* (New York: Random House, 1955), 131.

[5]Anselm, *Monologion*, 2, in *Anselm of Canterbury: The Major Works*, Edited with an Introduction by Brian Davies and G. R. Evans (Oxford: Oxford University Press, 1998), 13.

Weakness of *Monologion*

As Karl Barth noted, Anselm decided upon later reflection that the heart of his proof in *Monologion*, that God is '*quod est maius omnibus*' ('that which is greater than all') 'might also be conceived of as not-existing'.[6] Barth continues:

> The invalidity for proof which Anselm himself asserted of the *quod est maius omnibus* stood in very close connection with a second consideration, namely that as a Name of God it did not possess that self-sufficiency that belongs to and benefits the nature of its subject. For the *quod est maius omnibus* to become admissible as proof, it required certain presuppositions not contained within itself. That is, in order to be the highest, it must first presuppose the existence and nature of *omnia*, that is of objects which in their existence and nature point beyond themselves to the 'highest' which forms their peak. Without the rest of the pyramid the peak could not be a peak.[7]

It was to overcome this deficiency that Anselm composed a second type of proof for God's existence. This one would be *a priori* rather than *a posteriori*. Hence, his most famous proof is formulated in *Proslogion*, and it turns on the very meaning of the name that Anselm gives to God, in and of itself, without necessary reference to the *omnibus*.

A different kind of proof in *Proslogion*

Although Barth has been criticized for allegedly reading himself back into Anselm,[8] it seems to me that he is right, at least in his account of what Anselm set out to accomplish in *Proslogion* that he had not achieved in his earlier *Monologion*:

> In order to be valid for proof the conception of 'the highest' requires in the second place to be supplemented by such another concept as excludes the very possibility of this mode of thinking. This vital concept is just the *quo maius cogitari nequit* ('than which no greater can be conceived'). In so far as the *maius omnibus* is thought of as identical to the *quo maius cogitari nequit*, the existence and perfection of what it describes can be proved – but not otherwise. Therefore it has none of that self-sufficiency with which it would correspond to its object. This self-sufficiency does, however, belong to the Name of God discovered in the *Proslogion*. The designation of God as the *quo maius cogitari nequit* does not assume the existence of any creature, certainly not of God himself, neither as actually conceived nor as being conceivable. It simply says that if God should or could be conceived – that both these are in fact so is obviously the other assumption, the substance of the Proof – then nothing else may be conceived of as greater than God…*Quo maius cogitari nequit* is designed to exclude just this conceivability of the non-existence or imperfection of God…[9]

That is to say, the very notion of God implies his existence, when one understands Him as *quo maius cogitari nequit*. Anselm makes this clear in

[6]Karl Barth, *Anselm: Fides Quaerens Intellectum (Faith in Search of Understanding)* (Cleveland and New York: Meridian Books, 1962), 86.

[7]Ibid., 87.

[8]M. J. Charlesworth, *St. Anselm's Proslogion; with A Reply on Behalf of the Fool by Gaunilo, and The Author's Reply to Gaulino* (Oxford: Oxford University Press, 1965), 40-46.

[9]Barth, *Anselm*, 88,89.

chapter two of *Proslogion*, where he refers to Psalm 14, which speaks of 'the fool who hath said in his heart, there is no God':

> But surely, when this same Fool hears what I am speaking about, namely, 'something-than-which-nothing-greater-can-be-thought', he understands what he hears, and what he understands is in his mind, even if he does not understand that it actually exists. For it is one thing for an object to exist in the mind, and another thing to understand that an object actually exists...Even the Fool, then, is forced to agree that something-than-which-nothing-greater-can-be-thought exists in the mind, since he understands this when he hears it, and whatever is understood is in the mind. And surely that-than-which-a-greater-cannot-be-thought cannot exist in the mind alone. For if it exists solely in the mind, it can be thought to exist in reality also, which is greater. If then, that-than-which-a-greater-cannot-be-thought exists in the mind alone, this same that-than-which-a-greater-*cannot*-be-thought is that-than-which-a-greater-*can*-be-thought. But this is obviously impossible. Therefore there is absolutely no doubt that something-than-which-a-greater-cannot-be-thought exists both in the mind and in reality.[10]

In other words, this argument has three steps: (1) Our mind understands that God is, by definition, a being than whom nothing greater can be conceived; (2) It is greater to exist both in the mind and in reality, rather than only in the mind; (3) Therefore, God is the greatest being, which means that He exists both in the mind and in reality.

Anselm according to Karl Barth

To the best of my knowledge, I would hold Barth to be essentially correct in arguing that for Anselm, a 'proof' was never constructed off the grounds of Christian faith,[11] nor did he ever allow the 'neutral human mind' to be a final judge of faith.[12] But at the same time, a close reading of Anselm's *Monologion*, *Proslogion* and also *Cur deus homo* will also indicate that Nicholas Wolterstorff correctly perceives what he was trying to accomplish in his proofs '*remoto Christo*':

> Knowing a proposition was in general, for Anselm, a state of mind preferable to taking that proposition on faith. Hence Anselm's goal in constructing the ontological argument, as the remainder of the *Proslogion*, was to bring it about that what already he believed he now would know. In his view an essential component in this process of transmuting belief (faith) into knowledge (understanding) was constructing proofs.[13]

Precisely what Anselm was trying to accomplish has been carefully discussed by D. P. Henry, who is no doubt rather closer to Wolterstorff than to Barth.[14]

---

[10]Anselm, *Proslogion* 2, (Davies & Evans, op. cit.), 87, 88.

[11]Barth, op. cit., 60.

[12]Ibid.

[13]Nicholas Wolterstorff, 'Can Belief in God Be Rational?', a chapter in A. Plantinga and N. Wolterstorff, editors, *Faith and Rationality: Reason and Belief in God* (Notre Dame and London: University of Notre Dame Press, 1983), 141.

[14]D. P. Henry, *Medieval Logic and Metaphysics* (London: Hutchinson & Co. Ltd., 1972), 101-118.

Jonathan Barnes argues, contrary to Barth, that there is 'a decisive passage' in Anselm's *Epistola de Incarnatione Verbi*[15] '...where Anselm states that his intention in the *Monologion* and the *Proslogion* was to prove "by necessary reasons" and "without the authority of Scripture" that certain Christian beliefs were true.'[16] But still, I believe, that does not refute Barth's contention that Anselm never thought he needed to stand off the ground of faith to demonstrate to unbelievers the existence of God. Certainly, he *did* think that he was proving his point to outsiders (that cannot be doubted), but from firmly within the context of Christian faith and prayer to God for help.[17]

Bonansea agrees with this assessment:

> More precisely, the argument is not meant to convince an atheist or an agnostic – no theistic argument will ever do so – but only those who have been enlightened by faith and are favourably disposed towards it. It is true that in his reply to Gaunilo's objections Anselm writes: 'It was a fool against whom the argument of my *Proslogion* was directed.'[18] However, this does not mean that the argument was written *for a* fool but rather *against* a fool, i.e., one whom we would today call an unbeliever.[19]

Alexander Broadie argues similarly, that *Proslogion* is 'not a demonstration of the existence of God, but instead a systematic investigation into God's mode of existence.... If this is a correct interpretation, then the question he addressed was not *whether* God exists but *how* He does.'[20]

E. Gilson, from a committed Thomist viewpoint (not Barthian!), has underlined this from a different perspective when he raises the interesting and neglected question of why there had been no trace of an ontological argument in Greek thought, and why it was Christians who first formulated it. He replies:

> Once the question is asked the answer is obvious. Thinkers like Plato and Aristotle, who do not identify God and being, could never dream of deducing God's existence from his idea; but when a Christian thinker like St. Anselm asks himself whether God exists he asks, in fact, whether Being exists, and to deny God is to affirm that Being does not exist....The inconceivability of the non-existence of God could have no meaning at all save in a Christian outlook where God is identified with being, and where, consequently, it

---

[15]Anselm, *De Incarnatione Verbi* 20.16-21.

[16]Jonathan Barnes, *The Ontological Argument*, (London and Basingstoke: MacMillan, 1972), 6.

[17]It seems to me that Barth is right in his statement (backed by references in Anselm) that the Name (or Definition) Anselm gives to God [i.e. *aliquid quo nihil maius cogitari possit*] presupposes divine revelation: '...it is a genuine description (*signfiicatio*), one Name of God, selected from among the various revealed Names of God...in such a way that to reach a knowledge of God the revelation of this same God from some other source is clearly assumed. All that can possibly be expected from this Name is that in conformity with the programme of Anselm's theology, it should demonstrate that between the Name of God and the revelation of his Existence and Nature from the other source there exists a strong and discernible connection.Only in that way and to that extent will statements about the existence and Nature of God inevitably follow from an understanding of this Name' (in *Anselm: Fides Quaerens Intellectum*, 75,76).

[18]Introduction to *Liber Apologeticus*, PL 158, 247.

[19]B. M. Bonansea, *Man and His Approach to God in John Duns Scotus* (Lanham: University Press of America, 1983), 175.

[20]Alexander Broadie, *The Shadow of Scotus* (Edinburgh: T & T Clark, 1995), 9.

> becomes contradictory to suppose that we think of him and think of him as non-existent.[21]

So, without needing to step off 'Christian ground' himself, Anselm argues that the very concept of this definition of God is so self-evident that one does not need to resort to the Scriptures and Church tradition for subsidiary help in its proof. Rather, he believes that this name or definition alone should bring 'fools' into the realm of truth, which will be explicated by the Scriptures once they are there.

But not everyone agreed that Anselm had accomplished what he had set out to do in his proofs for God's existence. Some felt (and some still feel) that he by no means transmuted faith into knowledge.

Contemporaneous criticism of this proof by Gaunilo

The monk Gaunilo, a contemporary of Anselm,[22] who lived in the Benedictine community of Marmoutier, did not accept this 'proof.' Against it he wrote *Liber pro insipiente* ('A Book on behalf of the Fool'), to which Anselm replied in his *Liber apologeticus*. Gaunilo argues that one cannot conclude the existence of something from an idea that one has of it. He illustrates this absurdity by saying that one could imagine 'the most perfect isles of the blest' in the midst of the ocean. But that alone does not make them have existence.

Anselm responds by admitting that the objection is correct for all ideas *except* for that of God Himself. The isles of the blest are not the greatest being of all, and thus do not include existence among their perfections. The basic concept seems to be that a certain kind of 'logical essence' necessarily implies 'ontological existence.' That is not true of all 'logical essences'; only of one: namely, that which is of infinite and absolute being. This is what Kant called 'the ontological proof.'

Anselm's proof has been criticized by many major thinkers, and accepted (and modified) by many great thinkers. Somehow, it has never gone far away from theology and even philosophy.

Later critics of Anselm's ontological proof

A theologian as great as St. Thomas Aquinas could not accept this proof on the grounds that it seems to presuppose an equivalence between the logical universe and the ontological universe. Thus, he saw it as a *petitio principii* (a 'begging the question'), which already presupposes that which it set out to prove.[23] In spite of this critique of Anselm's logical procedure, St. Thomas did not think that it is necessary for lines of *a posteriori* evidences to be available before one actually believed in God. For he states in chapter six of *Summa Contra Gentiles* that 'to give assent to the truths of faith is not foolishness even though they are above reason.'

---

[21]Etienne Gilson, *The Spirit of Medieval Philosophy*, English translation by A.H.C.Downes (Notre Dame and London: University of Notre Dame Press, 1991), 59.

[22]Gaunilo died in 1083.

[23]St. Thomas Aquinas, *S.T.* I. Q. 2, art. 1.

Kant

Immanuel Kant, not entirely unlike the monk Gaunilo, has this against it: existence is not a quality of essence.[24] Or, 'existence is not a predicate.' That is, the quality of existence is wholly of another genre than such qualities as good, great, large or evil. However, Philippe Thiry interestingly points out that Kant himself in fact employs a sort of 'ontological argument' to establish the existence of 'things in themselves', which no one has ever seen! Thiry states that these are 'necessary to establish the Kantian epistemology. Therefore, Kant concludes that they exist!'[25]Perhaps some kind of 'ontological argument' really is necessary in order to establish any system, whether theistic or otherwise!

Alvin Plantinga discusses Kant's critique of Anselm's proof in Chapter X of *The Nature of Necessity*.[26] Plantinga responds:

> But Kant never specified a sense of 'is a predicate' such that, in that sense, it is clear both that existence is *not* a predicate and that St. Anselm's argument requires it to be one. Nor are the mere claims that no existential propositions are necessary...impressive as refutations of St. Anselm – after all, he claims to have an *argument* for the necessity of at least one existential proposition.[27]

After a careful and thorough logical reworking of Anselm's argument, Plantinga concludes that the fact that the ontological proof of *Proslogion* has been for so long strongly contested is insufficient to make us reject it:

> Were we to believe only what is uncontested or for which there are incontestable arguments from uncontested premises, we should find ourselves with a pretty slim and pretty dull philosophy. Perhaps we should have *Modus Ponens*; certainly not much more. The policy of accepting only the incontestable promises security but little else.[28]

Jonathan Barnes provides a careful and complex chapter on 'Existence and Predication' with reference to Kant's (and others') refutation of the Ontological Proof in terms of 'existence is not a predicate'.[29] He concluded '... the most prominent type of objection to the Ontological Argument is the objection that the argument rests on a false notion of existence.'[30] He divided the main objection into several points:

> ...that existence is not a logical predicate; that existence cannot be a *differentia* since all things exist; that individuals cannot be properly said to exist; and that the notation of quantificational logic contains the correct expression of the logical status of existential propositions.[31]

---

[24] I. Kant, *Critique of Pure Reason*, 'Transcendental Dialectic', Book II, ch. 3, translated by Norman Kemp Smith (London: Macmillan, 1929)

[25]Philippe Thiry, *L'Existence de Dieu: Les arguments de l'agnosticisme, de l'athéisme et du théisme* (Namur, Belgium: Presses universitaires de Namur, 1996), 180 n.

[26]'God and Necessity', ch. x of Alvin Plantinga, *The Nature of Necessity* (Oxford: Clarendon Press, 1982), 196-221.

[27]Ibid., 196,197.

[28]Ibid., 22

[29]Jonathan Barnes, *The Ontological Argument* (London and Basingstoke: MacMillan, 1972), 39-66.

[30]Ibid., 65.

[31]Ibid.

After working through these disputed points, Barnes concludes that 'Each of these views is interesting in itself and valuable in the issues it raises; but none appeared to be both true and fatal to the Ontological Argument.'[32] The interested reader is referred to Barnes for the logical details.

Hume

Kant followed in some measure the contention of the earlier Scottish philosopher, David Hume in section ix of his *Dialogues on Natural Religion*:

> I shall begin with observing, that there is an evident absurdity in pretending to demonstrate a matter of fact: or to prove it by any arguments *a priori*. (i) Nothing is demonstrable, unless the contrary implies a contradiction. (ii) Nothing, that is distinctly conceivable, implies a contradiction. (iii) Whatever we conceive as existent, we can also conceive as non-existent. (iv) There is no Being, *therefore*, whose non-existence implies a contradiction. (v) *Consequently* there is no Being, whose existence is demonstrable. I propose this argument as entirely decisive, and am willing to rest the whole controversy upon it.[33]

Jonathan Barnes dissects Hume's 'disproof' of the ontological proof by means of careful logical procedure, which I need not recapitulate here.[34] He then concludes 'that Hume's argument does not establish his thesis that necessary existence is impossible. Hume's successors have not to my knowledge produced any better argument…'[35]

Proponents of some form of the ontological proof

St. Bonaventura

St. Bonaventura (1221–1274) took from the ontological proof the position that one's intuition of such values as the good, the true and the beautiful clearly implied a sense of God's necessary existence. In these and in other ways, God is always present to us, so that it is impossible for us to think that God is not, without contradiction. As Gilson has summarized Bonaventura on this point:

> To become aware of this fact [that it is impossible to think that God is not] is to see that the very notion of God implies his existence. Since he is being pure and simple, immutable and necessary, it is one and the same thing to say that God is God, or to say that he exists: *si Deus est Deus, Deus est* [quoting Bonaventura's *I Sent.*, 8, 1, 1, 2].[36]

Bonaventura showed that for the ontological proof to work, it was necessary to draw a strong distinction between a necessary being and a defective being. It was a reply to the objection of Gaunilo: 'When I talk of an island than which no better can be imagined, there is a repugnancy between the subject and the predicate; for island means a defective being.'[37]

---

[32]Ibid.

[33]David Hume, *Dialogues on Natural Religion*, ed. Norman Kemp Smith (Oxford: Clarendon Press, 1935), section ix.

[34]Barnes, op. cit., 29-38.

[35]Ibid., 34.

[36]E. Gilson, *History of Christian Philosophy in the Middle Ages*, (New York: Random House, 1955), 353.

[37]Quoted in Barnes, op. cit., 28.

Descartes

We shall discuss presently what John Duns Scotus makes of Anselm's ontological argument. R. Descartes, in some respects the fount of the Enlightenment, formulated two forms of proof of God's existence, both reworking aspects of *Proslogion*.[38] Whereas Anselm defines God as 'that than which no greater can be conceived', Descartes defines Him as 'a sovereignly perfect being.' His argument is as follows: since God is sovereignly perfect, He possesses all perfections. Since existence is a perfection, therefore, God exists.[39]

In his 'Fifth Meditation', Descartes says that 'there is a repugnancy in imagining God (that is, a being supremely perfect) to whom existence is lacking (that is to say, to whom some perfection is lacking)...'[40] He adds:

> ...whenever it pleases me to imagine a first and supreme being, and as it were to bring down an idea of him from my mind's treasury, it is necessary that I should attribute to him all perfections, even though I neither then enumerate them all nor attend to each one; and this necessity is plainly sufficient that afterwards, when I notice that existence is a perfection, I rightly conclude that a first and supreme being really exists...[41]

Gassendi criticized this formulation of the ontological proof by Descartes in terms not unlike those later raised by Kant.[42] But neither Gassendi nor Kant have been able to dispose of the continuing influence of this 'proof.' As Richard Swinburne wrote in 1977: 'There have been some very thorough discussions of the traditional ontological argument, and variants thereof, over the past twenty years; and although almost all philosophers argue that it is not a good argument, it has proved very difficult indeed to show exactly where it goes wrong.'[43]

Leibniz

Leibniz also made use of Anselm's proof, though in his own way.[44] He establishes God's existence, by means of a form of the ontological argument, as the 'Necessary Being', or the 'original simple substance, from which all monads, created and derived, are produced'.[45] In a very different spirit from Anselm, Leibniz argues that the ontological proof is valid if one first establishes that the idea of God is logical, that is to say, non-contradictory, and then one can conclude that God must exist since He is in this way logical or possible. Leibniz says that this proof

> Is not a paralogism, but it is an imperfect demonstration which assumes something which must still be proved in order to make it mathematically

[38] See R. Descartes, *Discours de la Méthode* (1637), Parts III and IV. He returns to these proofs in his *Méditations métaphysiques* (1641), III, IV and V. English translation in *The Works of Descartes,* ed. by E.S. Haldane and G.R.T. Ross (Cambridge: Cambridge University Press, 1911) Vol. 1.

[39] See his 'Third Meditation.'

[40] Descartes, 'Fifth Meditation', in the English translation of his *Works* by E. S. Haldane and G. R. T. Ross (Cambridge; Cambridge University Press, 1911), vol. I, 181.

[41] Ibid., 182.

[42] See Ibid., 186.

[43] Richard Swinburne, *The Coherence of Theism*, (Oxford: Clarendon Press, 1986), 263.

[44] See Leibniz, *Monadology* (1714), xlv. English translation by M. Morris in Leibniz, Philosophical Writings (London: Everyman, 1934).

[45] Ibid.

evident; that is, it is tacitly assumed that this idea of an all-great or all-perfect being is possible, and implies no contradiction.[46]

Leibniz then argues that the idea is possible, and believes that he has improved the proof. Here we see that in both attitude and detail, Leibniz is far removed from St. Anselm.[47]

Two 'process theologians'

I will not attempt to enter into the modification of the ontological proof by the leading 'process theologians' (i.e. who read evolution into the very being of God), Norman Malcolm and Charles Hartshorne, simply because I deem the God they 'prove' to be so far afield of the sovereign God of Scripture and Christian tradition. For instance, they hold that God is as dependent on the world as the world is on Him: scarcely a biblical proposition![48]

Yet the logic by which they argue for this severely reduced 'God' is of interest for its own sake. Hence, it is appropriate to mention their serious and painstaking attempts to establish a proof of God in terms of modal logic: i.e. necessity and possibility. Malcolm's article on 'Anselm's Ontological Arguments'[49] has been deemed fallacious by both Alvin Plantinga[50] and Jonathan Barnes.[51] And Hartshorne's *The Logic of Perfection*[52] has fared no better at the hands of these very able philosopher/logicians.[53] And Thomas V. Morris has judiciously and fairly critiqued these theologians and their modal proofs in chapter 7 of his *Anselmian Explorations: Essay in Philosophical Theology*: 'God and the World: A Look at Process Theology.'[54] And years before, E. L. Mascall accurately portrayed the teaching on an evolutionary deity by A. N. Whitehead, and his 'two grave defects' in logical and theological procedure.[55]

Is a sort of 'ontological proof' hidden in the closet of every all-sufficient system?

As a theologian (and above all, a simple Bible believer), and not a trained logician (much as I respect them), I would hazard to add that what I take from Anselm is this: unless we presuppose God as the one than whom

---

[46]Quoted in Plantinga, *The Ontological Argument*, 55.

[47]The German Idealist philosopher, G. F. W. Hegel, also employed a certain kind of 'ontological proof' of God, but since his God is so vastly different from the God of Holy Scripture, I will not attempt to discuss it here. Gilbert Ryle argued against the validity of Hegel's use of this proof in a long article: 'Systematically Misleading Expressions', *Proceedings of the Aristotelian Society*, xxxii (1931-2), 139-170.

[48]Thomas V. Morris shows how this works with Charles Hartshorne in particular, in Morris, *Anselmian Explorations*, (Notre Dame, IN: University of Notre Dame Press, 1989), 139.

[49]In *Philosophical Review*, lxix (1960), 41-62.

[50]Alvin Plantinga, 'A Valid Ontological Argument?' in *Philosophical Review*, lxx (1961), 93-101.

[51]Barnes, op. cit., 65.

[52]C. Hartshorne, *The Logic of Perfection* (La Salle, IL: Open Court, 1962).

[53]Barnes, op. cit., 18,19; and Plantinga, *The Nature of Necessity*, 212, 213.

[54]Thomas V. Morris, *Anselmian Explorations* (Notre Dame, IN: University of Notre Dame Press, 1989), 124-150.

[55]E. L. Mascall, *He Who Is*, (London: Libia Books, 1966), ch. XI, 'The Cosmology of Whitehead,' 150-160.

no greater can be conceived, then we cannot make sense of anything else in our experience of life. Certainly, Anselm meant much more than this; but at least, he meant no less than this. Indeed, I would add that some kind of 'ontological' presupposition seems necessary for any and every comprehensive system of reasoning, although – especially in non-theistic systems – it is usually hidden (perhaps even from those who employ it). Those, like Kant, for instance, who deny it for the existence of God, seem to bring it in somewhere else to shore up their system (e.g., as Thiry points out, Kant 'ontologically' assumes 'things in themselves' or 'the noumenal', which are not provable, to make sense of the categories of the human mind, which impose structure on 'the phenomenal', thus making the God of Holy Scripture and his creational orders quite unnecessary as 'ontological assumptions'. Even so his reasoning is still in its own fashion 'ontological.'). Something of the same ontological assumption appears to be hidden deep in Darwinism.[56]

This is *not* to suggest that the various systematizers are directly borrowing Anselm's proof, and then willfully misusing it. After all, for Anselm there is only one ontological proof: that which relates to the one necessary Being[57]. Rather, the point is this: systems of thought that reject the Holy Trinity need some other ultimate reference point to make their system work; some *necessary thing*. It would appear that truly ultimate reference points impose themselves; that is, they have to be 'ontologically assumed,' although this will not usually be stated (nor is it necessarily conscious in most cases). Thus, by 'ontological proof', I do not mean a direct one, or even a conscious one, but an indirect, usually hidden one. And its indirectness or its hiddenness does not imply that it is insincere for the systematizer to use it. Maybe it is a 'given' condition of human thought.

As a vague illustration, I wonder if something like this necessity of some kind of unprovable faith (or, if you will, 'ontological assumption') is what one of the characters in Boris Pasternak's *Dr. Zhivago* could have meant in his discussion of 'history' in the context of atheism (which has – probably unwittingly – borrowed certain finally 'ontological assumptions' from historic Christianity)?

> Now what is history? It is the centuries of systematic explorations of the riddle of death, with a view to overcoming death. That's why people discover mathematical infinity and electromagnetic waves, that's why they write symphonies. Now, you can't advance in this direction *without a certain faith*. You can't make such discoveries without spiritual equipment. And the basic elements of this equipment are in the Gospels. What are they: To begin with, love of one's neighbor, which is the supreme form of vital energy. Once it fills the heart of man it has to overflow and spend itself. And

---

[56]See, for instance, Phillip E. Johnson, *Evolution as Dogma: the Establishment of Naturalism* (Dallas, TX: Houghton Publishing Co., 1990).

[57]Richard Swinburne explicates a 'necessary being': 'For the scholastics God differed from other necessary beings [e.g. angels and stars] in being an 'unconditioned necessary being – i.e. unlike them, he did not owe his necessary existence to anything else. The necessity of a proposition is then a matter of the eternal truth of what it states' in *The Coherence of Theism*, 251.

> then the two basic ideals of modern man – without them he is unthinkable – the idea of free personality and the idea of life as sacrifice. There was no history in this sense among the ancients. They had blood and beastliness and cruelty and pockmarked Caligulas who do not suspect how untalented every slaver is. They had the boastful dead eternity of bronze monuments and marble columns. It was not until after the coming of Christ that time and man could breathe freely. It was not until after Him that men began to live toward the future. Man does not die in a ditch like a dog – but at home in history, while the work toward the conquest of death is in full swing; he dies sharing in this work…[58]

Perhaps these words of the great Anglican theologian, Richard Hooker, though written for a different context, will illumine how something like the ontological proof can stand on its own, without long trains of subsidiary justifications being finally or absolutely necessary:

> The main principles of reason are in themselves apparent. For to make nothing evident of itself unto man's understanding were to take away all possibility of knowing anything. And herein that of Theophrastus is true, 'They that seek a reason of all things do utterly overthrow reason.'[59]

Anselm rightly saw that our personalities and therein, our reason, are created to make sense of reality, by a certain type of 'ontological assumption'. He who is the supreme reality has made himself supremely clear to the thinking human, perhaps even by means of such a far-reaching concept as the one 'than whom none greater can be conceived'. It is not easy to formulate exactly how this works psychologically.[60] One cannot, without hopeless distraction, keep basing one reason upon another reason, upon yet another reason. And yet, though we cannot state the precise 'logical mechanics' of it all, we can know reality, and we can know the supreme reality (for He has chosen to make Himself known, and has created us so that we can know Him). The ontological assumption appears to me to be in the category of 'insight' in the one place where it necessarily imposes itself on us (namely, God, who is the ground of all else), but merely to be a gratuitous assumption when we use some aspect of it to replace God as the ground of basic meaning (as for instance, Kant's *noumenal*).

---

[58]Boris Pasternak, *Dr. Zhivago*, translated by Max Hayward and Manya Harari (New York: Modern Library, 1958), 13.

[59]Richard Hooker, *Ecclesiastical Polity*, (Cambridge and New York: Cambridge University Press, 1989), I.8.5.

[60]Thomas V. Morris states this in terms of 'intuitions': 'For if an Anselmian God exists and creates rational beings whose end is to know him, it makes good sense that they should be able to come to know something of his existence and attributes. It makes sense that he create them capable of recognizing important truths about him as well as about themselves. Such a being could, in his creation of us, render us at least capable under the right conditions of having reliable intuitions such as those which yield the Anselmian conception of God and provide for a modal argument to his existence. So once he comes to believe in the existence of such a being, the Anselmian can retrospectively provide some reason for thinking that those intuitions which brought him to belief, or which strengthen his cognitive hold on that belief by way of a modal ontological argument are formed by a reliable belief-producing mechanism' (*Anselmian Explorations*, 190).

II. The Fivefold Proofs of St. Thomas Aquinas (1224–1274)

In our second chapter, the issues of the historical and intellectual contexts in which St. Thomas formulated his classical and perennial 'viae quinque' are discussed, as well as the relationship of the 'preambles' of faith to the content of faith. These need not be stated here. But instead, let us simply look at *how* St. Thomas seeks to prove the existence of God.

We have noted above St. Thomas's rejection of Anselm's ontological proof, as insufficient because it is deemed to have been a 'begging of the question' (i.e., assuming the very thing you go on to prove). On the contrary, Thomas seeks to demonstrate God's existence not *a priori*, or by means of a definition, but *a posteriori*, or by means of actual facts that we observe. That is, he will look at our experience in the physical world, and then by way of that move us up to the world's Creator.

In order to make sense of the 'fivefold ways' to God, it is first necessary to consider a basic distinction made by St. Thomas, that underlies all of the proofs. This distinction is central to the Thomist revolution or reformation of Aristotle's thought: the distinction between essence and existence.

St. Thomas's distinction between essence and existence

Fr. Copleston explains the all-important difference between Aquinas and Aristotle:

> ...it is in emphasizing the existentialist aspect that Aquinas goes beyond Aristotle. For the latter did not raise the problem of the existence of finite things; and this means, of course, that he did not see that there is any problem. And he did not see that there is any problem because he concentrated on what a thing is, on the ways in which something is or can be, and not on the act of existing itself...Thus in general, while it is perfectly true that Aquinas took over the Aristotelian metaphysical analysis of substance and accident...it is also true that his concentration on being considered as existence (as *esse*) set in a new light the world which Aristotle described in his metaphysics.[61]

Ralph McInerny notes that Aquinas derives this crucial distinction from Boethius' work, *De Hebdomadibus* (on which Aquinas wrote a commentary). Boethius says: '*diversum est esse et id quod est*' ('what a thing is and that it is are diverse').[62] This distinction has not been easy to grasp. Some interpreters have held that all Boethius (and St. Thomas) mean is the difference between nature (or essence) and the individual (or supposit), but as McInerny states, this is not the point.[63] Norman Geisler is closer to the meaning, when he suggests that the difference is that between potency and act,[64] although this is still not a full explanation.

Let us follow McInerny here:

---

[61]F. C. Copleston, *Aquinas* (Harmondsworth, Middlesex: Penguin Books, 1961), 79,80.

[62]Ralph McInerny, *St. Thomas Aquinas* (Notre Dame and London: University of Notre Dame Press, 1982), 94.

[63]Ibid., 95.

[64]Norman Geisler, *Thomas Aquinas: An Evangelical Appraisal* (Grand Rapids, MI: Baker Book House, 1991), 100.

When that-which-has-existence is in itself composite, as any natural thing is, since it is a compound of matter and form, then, Thomas argues, it is clear that that-which-has-existence is really different from existence. Here is his argument [See exposition of Boethius' *De Hebdomadibus*, lectio 2, n.32].

> (1) Existence itself (*ipsum esse*) does not partake of or participate in anything.
>
> (2) Existence itself cannot have anything extraneous; it cannot be the subject of an accident.
>
> (3) Therefore existence itself is not composed, is not compound.
>
> (4) Therefore no composed thing is identical with its existence.
>
> ...It is the transition from (3) to (4) that may seem problematic. Why does it follow from the fact that existence *itself* is not composed that no composed thing is identical with *its* existence?
>
> (5) That-which-has-existence, an existent thing, a being, is designated such from its existence.
>
> (6) A being is composed of that-which-has-existence and the existence it has.
>
> (7) That which exists is not existence alone.
>
> (8) Its existence is simple, noncompound.
>
> (9) That-which-has-existence is not its existence, is distinct from, diverse from, it.
>
> ...Whenever existence is the existence of something, there is a distinction between what is and existence – not merely a conceptual distinction, but a distinction *realiter*. Thus a simple or noncomposed essence, form alone, enters into an existent thing as one component of it distinct from existence as another component. As a being, therefore, it is composed, even though its essence is not a composed essence. A truly simple being would be one in which there is no composition of essence and existence, a being in which existence would not be the existence *of* something, inherent, but rather subsistent existence. There can be only one simple being of this kind.
>
> This however would be unique, because if *ipsum esse* has nothing admixed with it and is nothing other than existence itself, it is impossible that it be diversified or multiplied...This one and simple thing is God himself.

What Thomas says in *On Being and Essence* is perhaps easier to understand concerning this distinction between essence and existence:

> Whatever does not enter into the understanding of an essence or quiddity comes to it from without and enters into composition with the essence, since no essence could be understood without the parts that make it up. Every essence or quiddity, however, can be understood without its being understood that it exists in fact; for I can understand what a man or a phoenix is, and yet not know whether they are given in reality. Therefore, it is clear that existence is other than essence or quiddity, unless indeed there should be some thing whose quiddity is its existence; and such a thing could only be unique and first.[65]

[65]Thomas, *On Being and Essence*, ch. 5, n. 3, quoted in McInerny, 96, 97.

McInerny summarizes St. Thomas's distinction:

> It seems clear enough that natural things do not exist by definition, as if existence were what they are or part of what they are, since, if that were so, they could not not be. But natural things are simply things which come into being, then cease to be. If there is something which exists by definition, which cannot not exist, it is unique and first, it is God.
>
> The upshot of the teaching is quite clear. God alone is a being for whom to be is *what* he is; God alone is such that he cannot not be. He is, in short, a necessary being. Whatever other than God exists does so, not because it is of its nature to exist, a definitional necessity, as it were, but because it has received existence.[66]

St. Thomas on how we know God and reality

St. Thomas appears to be saying that the creation of existing things which come into being and then pass away cries out for an explanation in some being that always **is**, who needs nothing outside its own existence to explain it, and therefore can stand behind the reality of all things else. But then the question arises: how can a human (who is described as composed of essence and existence, and thus is not pure existence) be able to know this ultimate existent One? As far as the human act of knowing is concerned, the mind starts with *the empirical*; or, one could say that St. Thomas, like Aristotle, puts physics before metaphysics.

As Copleston explains, 'It is the senses which first set the mind in contact with existent things and which supply it with the materials for the formation of ideas...Sense perception is ultimately presupposed by all our knowledge.'[67] From our experience learned through sense perception, we can determine causality:

> According to Aquinas we first have experience of, for example, actual things coming into being and of causal agents...But once we have the concepts and understand the terms, analysis reveals a necessary connexion or relation...[concerning] efficient causality...Thus once we have had the requisite experience we can know *a priori* that if at any time something begins to exist it does so as the result of an already existent extrinsic thing.[68]

This relationship then of knowing to being, and of uncaused being to caused being is at the basis of the five proofs of St. Thomas. Copleston shows how Thomas moves from physical facts to God, the cause of those facts:

> The main point is that according to Aquinas, the world reveals itself to the reflective mind as dependent on an ultimate reality which he calls 'Good'...The argument...is that unless there is a supreme cause which is itself uncaused, there is no explanation of the existence and activity of any subordinate cause.[69]

It is generally recognized that the methodology of Aquinas that moves from physical reality to ultimate or metaphysical reality lies in our ability

---

[66]McInerny, op. cit., 95,96,97.
[67]Copleston, op. cit., 26.
[68]Ibid., 27,30.
[69]Copleston, *A History of Medieval Theology* (London: Methuen & Co., 1972), 194.

to discern a difference between the two in terms of the essence/existence distinction. Peter A. Redpath asks:

> What is it about the way things around us exist which demands that we conclude there is a God? In other words, what is the central link in Thomas's demonstration for God's existence?
>
> … The answer to our question is that the act-of-existing of sensible things is the central link to his demonstration. In other words, it is precisely the central metaphysical intuition of St. Thomas that the existence of sensible things is other than their essence which lies at the center of his demonstration of God's existence.
>
> The problem however, is how does one recognize this distinction in things? The answer to that is this… One recognizes the distinction between essence and existence wherever one sees things operating in a limited way, sometimes doing something and sometimes not. This indicates that they 'participate in existence rather than possess it by nature.'[70]

The underlying procedure used in the fivefold proofs

Redpath finds an underlying procedure used by St. Thomas in all five of his proofs. Consistently with what was said above, Thomas in five different ways argues that once you 'identify something in the world of sensible experience which, in one way or another, sometimes does something and sometimes does not, you go on to conclude that the feature in question is not caused by the power or nature of this being, and hence recognize that the feature in question must be caused by some external source, which is God.'[71]

This means that in each of the five proofs, Thomas takes as his starting point some feature of sense reality which indicates limitation in existence, and then works back to its ultimate explanation, which is the uncaused being of God. Or, as Barbellion has correctly noted, these five ways are precisely intended to be 'ways of access to God', in the truest sense of an *a posteriori* demonstration.[72] Each of the five ways 'begins with a human experience (realities which are moved, contingency, etc.) and then leads up to a cause.'[73]

These proofs proceed by means of 'the natural light of reason' (which St. Thomas distinguishes from 'the light of divine revelation').[74] This methodology is in the category of St. Paul's teaching in Romans 1:19, 20 ['Because that which may be known of God is manifest in them; for God hath shewed it unto them. For the invisible things of him from the creation of the world are clearly seen, being understood by the things that are made, even his eternal power and Godhead; so that they are without excuse…']. E. Gilson comments on St. Thomas's usage of these verses:

---

[70]Peter A. Redpath, *A Simplified Introduction to the Wisdom of St. Thomas* (Lanham, New York: University Press of America, 1980), 120.

[71]Ibid., 121.

[72]Stephanie-Marie Barbellion, *Les "Preuves" de l'Existence de Dieu* (Paris: Les Editions du Cerf. 1999), 224.

[73]Ibid., 252.

[74]St. Thomas, *ST*, Ia, q. 1, a. 1, ad 2.

> All theologians and Christian philosophers who have spoken about the existence of God have quoted these words, but Thomas took them in all their living force. For him, they mean that we can begin with God's effects and come to know his existence, and that we can only know it by demonstrating it from his effects. We go from the existences we experience to the inferred existence of their cause.[75]

In the *Catechism of the Catholic Church* (1992), this procedure is discussed, with one significant reference to St. Thomas:

> These 'ways' of approaching God from creation have a twofold point of departure: the physical world and the human person.
>
> **32** The *world*: starting from movement, becoming, contingency, and the world's order and beauty, one can come to a knowledge of God as the origin and the end of the universe…
>
> **34** The world, and man, attest that they contain within themselves neither their first principle nor their final end, but rather that they participate in Being itself, which alone is without origin or end. Thus, in different ways, man can come to know that there exists a reality which is the first cause and final end of all things, a reality 'that everybody calls "God"' [St. Thomas, *ST* I, 2,3].[76]

The five proofs (or 'ways' to God)

The first proof: from motion or change

The first proof is based on change or motion. In this sensible world around us we see things in process of change (or motion).[77] Redpath explains:

> Now anything in process of change is being changed by something else. This is so because it is characteristic of things in process of change that they do not yet have the perfection towards which they move, though able to have it; whereas it is characteristic of something causing change to have that perfection already…one is bound to arrive at some first cause of change not itself being changed by anything, and this is what everybody understands by God.[78]

Redpath then lays out this argument in a logical form, which I follow here:

1) Everything which is changed must be changed by another.

2) Some things in the world are changed.

3) For this to be possible these things must be changed by agents working without the aid of an infinite number of other agents.[79]

---

[75]E. Gilson, *Thomism: The Philosophy of Thomas Aquinas*, translated by Laurence K. Shook and Armand Maurer (Toronto, Canada: Pontifical Institute of Medieval Studies, 2002), 52.

[76]*Catechism of the Catholic Church* (San Francisco, CA: Ignatius Press, 1994), 15.

[77]While Redpath opts for 'change' to translate *movere*, others – such as Barbellion – argue that it really means local movement. See Barbellion, op. cit., 270. F. C. Copleston, holds that with Aquinas, as with Aristotle, *movere* means more than 'local motion'; rather, it is something like 'reducing from a state of potentiality to one of act'. See Copleston, *Aquinas*, (Hammondsworth, Middlesex: Penguin Books, 1955), 110,111.

[78]Redpath, op. cit., 122.

[79]This is the issue of the possibility of an 'infinite regress'. St. Thomas deals with it in *ST* I.2.3c. E. L. Mascall lays out in logical fashion both a direct proof and an indirect proof of the impossibility of an infinite regress:

4) But all this is possible only if there be an agent which can change other things without itself changing.

I. DIRECT PROOF
From two propositions

1. *Everything set in motion is so moved by something else.*
   Three proofs of this:
   i. For a thing to be in motion of itself:
      a. It must have the principle of its movement in itself.
      b. It must be moved primarily, i.e. by its whole and not by any part.
      c. It must be divisible and have parts.
      Now, since it is moved primarily, if one part were at rest the whole would be at rest. For if one part were moved while another were at rest, not the whole but a part would be moved primarily. But if the quiescence of the whole depends on the quiescence of a part, the movement of the whole would depend on the movement of the part. Hence the whole is not moved by itself. And this is a contradiction.
   ii. By induction. Things are moved either accidentally or *per se*.
      a. If accidentally, they are not moved by themselves. Or
      b. By nature,and so either
      aa. By something in them (as animals). Or
      bb. By something not in them (as heavy bodies). *Ergo*
   iii. Nothing is at the same time and in the same respect both in act and in potency.

2. *It is impossible to proceed to infinity in the series of movers and things moved.*
Three proofs of this:
   i. All the members would move at the same time as any one of them. But one, being finite, is moved in a finite time. Therefore, so are the infinite number of them. Which is impossible.
   ii. There would be no first mover, and so nothing would be moved.
   iii. All would be instrumental movers. Which is impossible.

From 1 and 2 the existence of an immobile First Mover follows.

II. INDIRECT PROOF
Suppose 'Whatever moves is moved' is true. It is then true either *per accidens* or *per se*.

1. Suppose it is true *per accidens*.
   Then:
   i. 'Whatever moves is moved' is true. But 'Nothing that moves is moved' is possible. Therefore 'There is no motion at all' is possible. But it is impossible that there should ever be no motion at all. Therefore the proposition is not true *per accidens*.
   ii. Alternatively:
   If *moving and being moved* occur together *per accidens*,
   And, as we know, *being moved* sometimes occurs without *moving;*
   Then probably, *moving* sometimes occurs without *being moved*.
   Thus the proposition is not true *per accidens*.

2. Suppose it is true *per se*.
   Then either:
   i. A mover receives a movement of the same kind as it imparts, which is contrary to experience. Or
   ii. It receives a different kind, and either
      a. We get an infinite regress, which is impossible, since the number of different kinds of movement is clearly finite. Or
      b. After a finite number of steps we get to the same kind, and so the case is reduced to case i.
      Thus the proposition is not true *per se*.
      Therefore it is not true at all.

But: we have proved that the First Mover is unmoved by anything outside itself.
However: if it moved itself, then either:

> 5) There must, then, be such a being and this is what everybody understands the name 'God' to signify.[80]

Garrigou-Lagrange notes that all of the sophisticated complexities employed in the five proofs can be 'boiled down' to one basic proof, that is understandable to ordinary, non-philosophical people:

> The principle of this general proof, 'The greater cannot arise from the less,' condenses in effect into one single formula the principles on which our five typical proofs rest: becoming can emerge only from determinate being; caused being only from uncaused being; the contingent only from the necessary; the imperfect, composite and multiple only from the perfect, simple and one; order only from an intelligence. The principles of the first three proofs place in relief especially the dependence of the world upon a *cause*, the principles of the last two insist on the *superiority* and *perfection* of this cause. All of them can be summed up in this formula: 'The greater does not arise from the less; only the higher explains the lower.'[81]

Before moving on to the second proof, let us address the frequent criticism of how St. Thomas concludes his logical proofs by saying, 'And this is what everybody understands by God.' Copleston states this not uncommon

---

i. The whole moves the whole, and it is in potentiality, and in act at the same time and in the same respect, which is impossible. Or
ii. Part of it moves another part, and so again we have an immobile First Mover. *Therefore*: there exists an absolutely immobile First Mover. From E. L. Mascall, *He Who Is*, 41, 42 n.

Or, as Norman Geisler summarizes these logical steps in verbal fashion: '...an infinite series of simultaneous and existentially dependent causes is not possible...An ungrounded infinite regress is tantamount to affirming that the existence in the series arises from nonexistence, since no cause in the series has a real ground for its existence. Or, if one cause in the series grounds the existence of the others, then it must be a First Cause (and hence the series is not infinite). Otherwise it turns out to be a cause that causes its own existence (which is impossible), while it is causing the existence of everything else in the series' (op. cit., 127, 128).

In slightly different terms, R. P. Phillips appositely notes that even if one supposed some eternal series of contingent beings, the supposed eternality of this contingent series, 'does not in any way account for their existence, or relieve us of the necessity of demanding a necessary being as the cause of such eternal existence. Even if the series is eternal, it is eternally insufficient' (R. P. Phillips, *Modern Thomistic Philosophy* [London: Burns, Oates, 1934-35], 2 vols., II, 285.

But Anthony Kenny questions the sufficiency of St. Thomas's logical proof of the impossibility on an infinite regress in Chapter 1 ('The First Way') of *The Five Ways: Thomas Aquinas' Proof of God's Existence* (London: Routledge & Kegan Paul Ltd., 1969 [1980]), 6-33. He concludes this chapter by quoting the sixteenth-century Jesuit commentator, Suarez: 'Taken by itself, this argument is shown in many ways impotent to prove there is anything immaterial in reality, let alone that there is a first and uncreated substance' [*Disputationes metaphysicae* XXIX, 1, 7]. Some of Kenny's objections are addressed (in favor of St. Thomas) by Barbellion (op. cit., particularly from pp. 270-83).

I wonder if finally, the impossibility of an infinite regress is not something that has to be assumed by the human mind in order to make sense of our experience in the world? Some things that are difficult to demonstrate logically have to be assumed to make sense of everything else. That point is made by Jacques Maritain in *Sept Leçons sur l'être et les premiers principes de la raison spéculative* (Paris, Tequi, 1932-33), where he states that the impossibility of an infinite regress (which lies behind the principle of causality) is 'a principle of causality', that is part of the 'first principles of speculative reason' (p. 50). Thus he holds that this intuitive origin of the principle of causality has no need of a real justification which would then have to be based upon yet another analysis.

[80]Redpath, op. cit., 127.

[81]R. Garrigou-Lagrange, *God, his Existence and Nature*, English translation by Bede Rose (St Louis, MO: Herder, 1934), 2 vols., I, 252.

[82]Copleston, *Aquinas*, 125.

protest to the theistic proofs as follows: 'For it might be argued that even if it is granted that there is a first or supreme unmoved mover, a first efficient cause and an absolutely necessary being, it does not immediately follow that this being can with propriety be called "God".'[82] Joseph Owens, for instance, held that this first proof of St. Thomas provided only a mover (or motor), not a person.[83]

I hope these two brief responses may be sufficient. First, Aquinas makes it clear that his theistic proofs are in the class of 'preambles' of the faith, rather than constituting the content of the faith.[84] Secondly, although not a Thomist (perhaps, however, I could be vaguely fitted into the category of what Ralph McInerny has termed a Protestant 'Peeping Thomist'![85]), it seems to me that *if* St. Thomas has indeed proved that a finite world requires an infinite 'unmoved Mover', then He who began everything – in order to have done so – would of necessity be infinite, eternal, and of unbounded power. And that is who the Scriptures tell us God is.

The second (or aetiological) proof: from an ordered series of efficient causes
This second proof is based on the nature of causation, and in particular with *how* causation takes place, or the way agents operate in things. Let us follow Redpath's summation again:

> 1) That in the sensible world we discover an order of efficient causes.
>
> 2) That in every order of efficient causes there is a hierarchy or causal support in which one cause directly depends on another cause in order to exist.
>
> 3) That it is impossible to proceed to infinity in such a hierarchically ordered series of causes.[86]

Redpath illustrates this procedure by mentioning electricity going through a television tube:

> The point is that the series of beings from which it is getting this force which it is transmitting must be finite in nature because no force can be transmitted across an infinite medium...There must be a first efficient cause to make the present operations of efficient causes intelligible, and this is God.[87]

I note that the first point is obvious from our empirical experience. We have already discussed the third point (infinite regress). As to the second point, Thomas states that if one thing were not caused by another thing, then something would be its own efficient cause; thus, prior to itself, which is impossible. That is, if there were no cause to bring forth the act, then

---

[83]Joseph Owens, *Thomas Aquinas on the Existence of God (Collected Papers of Joseph Owens)* (Albany, NY: State University of New York Press, 1980), 167.

[84]St. Thomas, *ST* Ia, q. 2. a. 2, ad 1.

[85]See Alvin Plantinga in Plantinga and Wolterstorff, *Faith and Rationality*, 40.

[86]Redpath, op. cit., 128.

[87]Ibid., 129.

[88]See Barbellion, op. cit., 285.

everything would remain in mere potentiality. There would be no actual world around us to observe or discuss.[88]

Anthony Kenny has written off at least part of this second proof as 'starting from an archaic fiction'.[89] By this he refers to Thomas's attempting to illustrate his second way by an example from astrology. Yet Thomas uses less questionable illustrations, such as a father begetting a son. Barbellion shows that Thomas's understanding of the efficient causality of his second proof can be taken in a much broader sense than mere local motion (which is more appropriate to the first proof):

> The soul is the efficient cause of the being and the life of the body. A father also has an efficient causality upon his son. An artist by the same token has an efficient causality over the work which he carries out.[90]

Copleston seems correct in stating that

> ...in every proof the idea of ontological dependence on a transcendent cause appears in some form or other...which ...involves seeing the dependence of these facts on a transcendent cause. The existence of things which change, for instance, is, in his opinion, not self-explanatory: it can be rendered intelligible only if seen as dependent on a transcendent cause, a cause, that is to say, which does not itself belong to the order of changing things.[91]

Although the second way seems very close to the (easier to understand) first one, there is a difference, pointed out by Barbellion. It is the distinction between movement and change. 'The phenomena of life are not always explained by movement; if generation for example is not a movement, then there would need to be another proof for this kind of change...'[92] Barbellion hence believes that our human life is more fully covered by this second proof than by the first.[93]

The third proof: from possibility and necessity (or the cosmological proof)
This cosmological proof and the first proof (from motion) are certainly the most comprehensible, and perhaps – for that reason – the most popularly known of St. Thomas's fivefold ways. Even so, I think, the third proof is not so clearly understandable as the first one. St. Thomas starts from our normal experience in this world, where we find that some things may be, and may not be; things are born, die and pass out of view. Sometimes this proof is called the argument *e contingentia mundi*.

Ralph McInerny lays out the steps of this argument in clear logical fashion:

> (1) Some of the things that are, since they are generated and corrupt, can either be or not be.

---

[89]Kenny, op. cit., 44.
[90]Barbellion, op. cit., 286.
[91]Copleston, *Aquinas*, 113.
[92]Barbellion, op. cit.
[93]Ibid.

(2) It is impossible that everything that is should be such that it can either be or not be.

(3) Whatever is such that it cannot be at some time is not.

(4) Thus if everything were such that it could either be or not be, at some time there was nothing.

(5) But if once there was nothing, there would be nothing now, since that from which not being comes to be requires a cause which is.

(6) Therefore if once there was nothing, nothing could have come to be, and even now there would be nothing, which is clearly false.

(7) Therefore not everything is possible and there must be something which is necessary.

(8) That which is necessary either has a cause of its necessity from elsewhere, or it does not.

(9) It is impossible that all necessary beings should have a cause of their necessity outside themselves.

(10) Therefore there must be a necessary being whose necessity is not caused by another but which is necessary of itself.

(11) Such a necessary being we call God.[94]

In other words, we see things which come into existence, and these things (which can also go out of existence) must have been caused to exist:

> ...of course the father is a cause of the son's coming to be, as the grandfather is a cause of the father's coming to be, but Thomas wants us to ask why there should be things of that kind at all. What the first stage of the proof seeks to establish is that in order for there to be things of this kind, things that *can* be, there must be things of another kind, things that *must* be.[95]

Underlying this cosmological proof are two premises, pointed out by Etienne Gilson:

> The first is that what is possible is contingent, that is, it can either be or not be, and thus it is opposed to what is necessary. The second is that what is possible does not have its existence from itself or from its essence but from an efficient cause that gives it existence.[96]

And, as we saw, St. Thomas shows that necessary being is by definition not contingent; it cannot not be. The existence of things that come into being and then decay requires the existence of the One who always is. To state it another way: 'Not everything, for Thomas, however, can be merely a possible being. For if all things were only possible beings Thomas thinks there would be nothing in existence at present.'[97]

Perhaps this is a good answer to the perennial philosophical query, famously posed by Leibniz: *why is there something and not nothing?*[98] That

---

[94]R. McInerny, *St. Thomas Aquinas*, 164, 165.
[95]Ibid., 166.
[96]E. Gilson, *Thomism*, 65.
[97]Redpath, op. cit., 132.
[98]See E. Gilson, *The Spirit of Medieval Philosophy*, 77.

may be why there has been so much interest in the cosmological proof over the centuries. Hegel makes a certain use of this proof.[99] He holds that every particular substance is contingent insofar as its truth is necessary in the measure that the truth of this particular is the universal. He places all this into his main category: that of the finite and the infinite. He writes: 'Thus while one considers that the being of a finite [thing] is uniquely its own being, and not the being of another, it is thereby shown this way that there is no possible passage from the finite to the infinite.'[100] But, as Philippe Thiry has seen, in the context of Hegel's assumption of the multiplicity of the finite and its unity, 'If one underlines unilaterally this unity, one would deem that quite properly Hegel is a pantheist.'[101]

And this 'third way' of Aquinas, like the ontological proof of Anselm, has been of some interest to modal logicians. Philippe Thiry has turned the steps of this proof into the symbols of modal logic, to which you are referred.[102]

David Hume attacked the cosmological proof, in particular its basis, that no substance can begin to exist without a cause. He argues:

> It is easy for us to conceive any object to be non-existent this moment, and existent the next, without conjuring to it the distinct idea of a cause or productive principle. The separation, therefore, of the idea of a cause from that of a beginning of existence, is plainly possible for the imagination; and consequently the actual separation of these objects is so far possible, that it implies no contradiction nor absurdity.[103]

As part of his effort to discredit the use of the existence of the cosmos as a proof for its Creator, he actually went so far as to deny causation:

> Before we are reconciled to this doctrine, how often must we repeat to ourselves, *that* the simple view of any two objects or actions, however related, can never give us any idea of power, or of a connexion betwixt them: *that* this idea arises from a repetition of their union: *that* the repetition neither discovers nor causes anything in the objects, but has an influence only on the mind, by that customary transition that it produces: *that* this customary transition is therefore that same with the power and necessity; which are consequently qualities of perceptions, not of objects, and are internally felt by the soul, and not perceived externally in bodies?[104]

This denial of cause and effect seems to be a total dereliction of all good sense! Why would a very clever man like Hume have seriously attempted to establish such a position? What Stanley Jaki said about the Idealists in his Gifford Lectures in the University of Edinburgh (not far from where Hume once lived) seems to be the correct answer: 'The Idealists got rid of rationality to avoid God.'[105] By the same token, it would seem that Hume

---

[99]Barbellion, op. cit., 224

[100]Hegel, op. cit., 152.

[101]Thiry, op. cit., 153.

[102]Ibid., 151, n. 253.

[103]David Hume, *Treatise of Human Nature,* L. A. Selby-Bigge, ed. (Oxford: Oxford University Press, [1902] 1961), I, III, III.

[104]Ibid. I. III. XIV.

[105]Stanley Jaki, *The Road of Science and the Ways to God,* (Port Huron, MI: Real View Books, 2005), 142.

got rid of causality to get rid of God. But in so doing, Hume would also have made modern science impossible, had his assumptions been followed. Thus, Jaki writes on Hume's denial of causality (in relation to 'matters of fact not being subject to demonstration'):

> The result was the abolition of God as well as of science, for the existence of both God and science could be justified only if the world were demonstrably ordered…His starting point was empiricism carried to its extreme, that is, sensationalism in which sensations stood as lonely data with no intrinsic relation to mind and world.[106]

George Romanes (as cited by Stanley Jaki) put his finger on the ridiculous nature of this denial of causality:

> Of all philosophical theories of causality the most repugnant to reason must be those of Hume, Kant and Mill which … attribute the principle of causality to a creation of our own minds, or in other words deny that there is anything objective in the relations of cause and effect, i.e. in the very thing which all physical science is engaged in discovering particular cases of it.[107]

Probably the best answer to such a claim that flies in the face of the experience of every human being every day of their life is a commonsense one: 'you have to assume causality even to articulate a sentence, walk or make a cup of tea! You have to assume causality even to argue against it!' These convoluted arguments to replace cause and effect with our mental habit of association of events that occur near the same time may sound impressive to some people, but the philosopher making such a claim could never have lived by it!

Of course this observation does not constitute a formal philosophical proof of causality. But such a proof has never been needed. Causation is a basic axiom which all who live in the world have to assume in order even to survive, and after basic survival, it has to be assumed in order to make any sense of the realities around us. Nevertheless, since Hume thought he had established his point in a responsible way philosophically, he deserves some kind of thoughtful philosophical answer.

A. E. Taylor[108] believed that the Scottish Common Sense philosopher, Dr. Thomas Reid, had answered Hume's attempt to deny the principle of causation more successfully than others, in spite of some weaknesses, in his *Essays on the Intellectual Powers of Man*, Essay II – 'On our external senses', chapters 7–16, and Essay VI – 'On Judgement', chapter 6. These are briefly summarized in Appendix II to this chapter, as I wish to make the core of them available to Church people who so often hear that Hume has destroyed the cosmological argument by disproving causality.

Another way that Hume sought to discount the cosmological proof, which looks at the whole of physical reality, and sees it as requiring for both the entirety of its existence and all of its particular physical operations, an infinite Creator and Sustainer, was to argue (in nominalistic fashion) that

---

[106]Ibid., 108.

[107]George Romanes, 'A Candid Examination of Religion' in *Thoughts on Religion*, edited by Charles Gore (London: Longmans Green and Co., 1895), p. 119; quoted in Jaki, op. cit., 153, 154.

[108]In A. E. Taylor, *Platonism and its Influence* (New York: Longmans, Green and Co., 1927), 55, and 138, n. 32.

if we can explain physically the dependence of the various parts upon one another, then no explanation of the whole can be called for. Thus Hume writes in his *Dialogues on Natural Religion*:

> In... a chain ... or succession of objects, each part of which is caused by that part which preceded it, and causes that which succeeded it. Where then is the difficulty? But the *whole*, you say, wants a cause. I answer that the uniting of several parts into a whole, like the uniting of several distinct countries into a kingdom, or several distinct members into one body, is performed merely by an arbitrary act of the mind, and has no influence on the nature of things. Did I show you the particular causes of each individual in a collection of twenty particles of matter, I should think it very unreasonable, should you afterwards ask me what was the cause of the whole twenty. This is sufficiently explained in explaining the cause of the parts.[109]

Richard Swinburne replies to Hume's nominalism at this point: 'I conclude that if each state of the universe at each instance of time has a complete explanation which is a scientific explanation, then the existence of the universe at each instance of time and its having certain permanent features have no explanation at all.'[110]

No doubt Hume is teaching that humans through empirical examination of numbers of facts establish what needs to be known, pure and simple. But Aquinas is right: the whole is so much greater than the parts, that the parts need an explanation. Hume, however, by holding that we have everything in the discrete parts, leads us to a sort of closed, mechanistic viewpoint of the world and of life itself. He gives us a kind of blocked paradigm; wilfully shut off from higher reality required to explain it. As Swinburne states it: 'The choice is between the universe as stopping-point and God as stopping-point.'[111]

The cosmological argument says that sound reason cannot stop with the disparate parts, or even with the larger universe, but only with God Himself. In this light, Swinburne summarizes the weightiness of the cosmological proof:

> There is quite a chance that if there is a God he will make something of the finitude and complexity of a universe. It is very unlikely that a universe would exist uncaused, but rather more likely that God would exist uncaused. The existence of the universe is strange and puzzling. It can be made comprehensible if we suppose that it is brought about by God. This supposition postulates a simpler beginning of explanation than does the supposition of an uncaused universe, and that is grounds for believing the former supposition to be true.[112]

While Hume claimed that the particularities of the world are self-explanatory, T. F. Torrance argues that to the contrary, the work of twentieth-century

---

[109]David Hume, edited by Norman Kemp Smith, *Dialogues Concerning Natural Religion*, (Indianapolis and New York: Library of Liberal Arts, Bobbs-Merrill, 1947), 59.

[110]Richard Swinburne, *The Existence of God* (Oxford: Oxford University Press, 1979), 125.

[111]Ibid., 127.

[112]Ibid., 131, 132.

physics on the nature of light in the universe does clearly call for a higher explanation, outside the world, for,

> While all entities and events in the universe are defined relationally in terms of space and time, and space and time are defined in terms of light, light is not defined by reference to any contingent reality beyond itself. In other words, 'light has a unique metaphysical status in the universe.' That was the point discovered by Einstein when he established that the speed of light remains the same irrespective of any motion on the part of the observer.[113]

Elsewhere, Torrance shows that the discoveries of modern physics have not confirmed the self-sufficient nominalism (which Hume employed to undo the cosmological argument):

> … the realization of the utterly contingent nature of the universe and of its inherent intelligibility raises with us the question as to the mystery of its origin, and as to the transcendent ground on which the universe as a contingent and intelligible whole rests. By its very nature as contingent and intelligible, the universe embodies a semantic reference beyond itself, for it requires an explanation for its own intelligible state of affairs that it cannot provide out of itself…
>
> It is within that same created universe that natural science operates and thus within the relation of contingent intelligibility to the Creator who sustains it beyond its contingent capacities and makes it terminate on his own reality and rationality. Therefore, when scientists seeking to understand the universe in its contingent nature and intelligibility find themselves close to those zero points where their science no longer proves adequate but where they must continue to ask rational questions – not least as to the transcendent ground and sufficient reason for the coherent singularity of the universe – we must regard them as sustained and upheld by God within the ontological and semantic reference of the universe to himself as the Creator, which is the ground of that imperious constraint upon them.[114]

It would appear then that much of modern scientific work, instead of confirming Hume's skepticism and nominalism, would instead point in the direction of something like the cosmological argument, formulated long ago by St. Thomas.

The fourth proof (or henological proof): from diverse grades of existing

This proof is based on the gradation observed in things; some are more good, true and noble than others. But these comparative terms require a superlative. When many things possess some property in common, the one most fully possessing it causes it in the others, and 'this is God.' This is one of the most difficult of the five to understand. St. Thomas writes:

> …this consideration of God's works leads to admiration of God's sublime power, and consequently inspires in men's hearts reverence for God. For the power of the worker is necessarily understood to transcend the things made.[115]

---

[113]T. F. Torrance, *Christian Theology & Scientific Culture*, (New York: Oxford University Press, 1981), 78.

[114]T. F. Torrance, *The Ground and Grammar of Theology*, (Charlottesville, VA: University of Virginia Press, 1980), 104, 106.

[115]St. Thomas, *Summa Contra Gentiles*, II, 2, translated by James F. Anderson (Notre Dame and London: University of Notre Dame Press, 1975), 30.

The basic concept in the proof from gradation is that non-necessary, finite things possess some virtue imperfectly; in a limited manner. Thus 'there must be some absolutely perfect being which is the cause of existence and other perfections in things. This we call "God".'[116]

Accordingly, Redpath states the basic steps in this fourth proof:

> (1) That we observe a gradation in things based upon the degree in which things more or less completely, thoroughly, or perfectly possess existence (that is, are good, true, noble, and so on).
>
> (2) Any property shared in varying degrees by all the members of a genus is caused in the other members by the member most perfectly possessing the property.
>
> (3) There must be a being which perfectly possesses the act-of-existing and all other attending perfections.[117]

It is important to see with Barbellion that this 'fourth way' leads to only One First True or One First Good, for 'if they [the "transcendentals" of good, true and noble, etc., as Maritain calls them[118]] were multiple, they would be ordered in terms of one another (that is, by some other power). The act of *the* true is no longer a pure act if it is submitted to some higher order outside itself. This proof thus implicitly deals with the unicity of the first cause, where we were left in suspense in the first proof.'[119]

Although developed in a Christian direction, scholars generally accept that Aquinas is here influenced by Plato's exemplarism and Augustine's idea of participation.[120] To that degree, this fourth proof, and the earlier ones, may be considered as 'Platonic'. But Gilson clarifies what this would specifically mean:

> [The proofs are Platonic]...to the extent that, through Augustine and Dionysius, Thomas borrowed Plato's conception of a participation of things in God by way of resemblance. This invited Thomas to think of the universe as arranged in a hierarchy according to the various possible degrees of finite participation in the causality of the first cause, in the actuality of the unmoved mover, in the goodness of pure goodness, in the nobility of the purely noble, and in the truth of the pure truth. But this is not so in the doctrine of Thomas Aquinas, who...began by changing the Platonic notion of participation into an existential notion of causality.[121]

In terms of biblical thought, we might say that the character of God *is* the standard, origin and power of goodness, beauty, truth, and so forth. 'God is light'; 'God is love'; 'God is good'; 'God is holy.' Love and holiness (and every other moral standard) are what they are because of who God is. These standards (or 'transcendentals') do not come from 'somewhere' above God or outside God. They are the 'attributes' or 'qualities' of God's own being. Without his holiness and truth, there could be no moral standards in the

---

[116]Redpath, op. cit., 138.
[117]Ibid., 137, 138.
[118]J. Maritain, *Approches de Dieu*, (Paris: Alsatia, 1953), 64.
[119]Barbellion, op. cit., 294.
[120]See E. Gilson, *Thomism*, 71-73.
[121]Ibid., 73.

universe. He has built the universe on moral lines. Every exemplification of goodness, beauty, truth and love in some way or other points up to God, the source and standard of them all. By the miracle of the new birth (see John, 3), God through the Holy Spirit brings us into His light, so that we are 'children of light' (1 Thess. 5:5); He brings us into His truth, so that 'we walk in truth' (3 John 3); He brings us into His love, so that 'the love of God is shed abroad in our hearts by the Holy Spirit who is given unto us' (Rom. 5:5). Then, as the Psalmist says, 'the beauty of the Lord our God is seen upon us' (Ps. 90:17). All of these heavenly-born beauties penetrate ever more thoroughly into human personality through the disciplines of the Christian life in the fellowship of the Church, and from there they shine into a dark world (cf. Matt. 5:16).

Two passages in the New Testament might in a rather general sense be consistent with what Augustine and Thomas meant by causal exemplarism: 2 Corinthians 3:18: 'But we all, with open face beholding, as in a glass the glory of the Lord, are changed into the same image from glory to glory, even as by the Spirit of the Lord', and 1 John 3:2: 'Beloved, now are we the sons of God, and it doth not yet appear what we shall be: but we know that, when he shall appear, we shall be like him; for we shall see him as he is.'

I do not hereby suggest that this is how St. Thomas's fourth proof works! But I would suggest that it might help make sense of it in biblical and theological categories, though these remarks in no sense add to the power of its proof (if proof it be).

The fifth proof (or teleological proof): from design

This proof from design has been the most popular, along with the cosmological proof. It has also been strongly attacked. Dr. Geisler summarizes the steps of this argument from design:

1. Every agent – even a natural agent – acts for an end.
2. Now what acts for an end manifests intelligence.
3. But natural agents have no intelligence of their own.
4. Therefore, they are directed to their end by some Intelligence.[122]

This proof, as E. L. Mascall explains it, 'simply asserts that, when we are confronted with any being, however insignificant, the question, "What is its purpose?" is just as valid and necessary as the question, "What began it?" or "Why does it go on?"'[123] In terms of Aristotelian philosophy, the fifth proof deals with 'the final cause' of things.'[124] That is, what is the goal for which the world was created and ordered?

---

[122]N. Geisler, op. cit., 122.

[123]E. L. Mascall, op. cit., 54.

[124]Aristotle held to four causes: final, formal, efficient and material. For example, in building a house, the final cause is the reason for which it was built; so that one could comfortably live in it. The formal cause is the shape it takes in accordance with the blueprint of the architect. The efficient cause is the work done by the builders, such as sawing planks, installing electricity and water pipes, and putting on a roof, etc. The material cause includes the materials: wood, bricks, pipes, shingles, etc. Enlightenment thought has tended to eliminate final causes and formal causes. John Calvin made use of Aristotle's four causes in describing salvation. He sees the efficient cause

Design indicated in the whole system of nature

St. Thomas says on this matter:

> We see that things which lack intelligence, such as natural bodies, act for an end, and this is evident from their acting always, or nearly always, in the same way, so as to obtain the best result. Hence it is plain that not fortuitously, but designedly, do they achieve their end. Now whatever lacks intelligence cannot move towards an end, unless it be directed by some being endowed with knowledge and intelligence; as the arrow is shot to its mark by the archer. Therefore some intelligent being exists by whom all natural things are directed to their end; and this being we call God.[125]

He gives illustrations of this directedness towards an end from nature. 'The leaves in plants are arranged to protect the fruit; the foot is made by nature apt for walking; front teeth are good for biting, back teeth are good for chewing.[126] As examples of instinctive activities of brutes, he mentions the swallow's building of its nest and the spider's weaving of its web.'[127]

Although these observations seem to fit with common sense, yet modern science has been intensely uneasy with the concept of formal and final causation, because during the Middle Ages these concepts of 'design' often functioned to keep researchers from carefully considering natural realities in their own light, since they were pre-determined to formal or final ends in light of eternity. For a long time, 'finalism' tended to entail a sort of 'rationalistic simplification' (under the cover of 'biblical fidelity'),[128] by which researchers could not seriously look at an object in its own light. Hence teleology was functionally discredited in much of post-seventeenth-century science, and one can understand the reason why.

T. F. Torrance explains this seventeenth-century movement against medieval forms of finalism:

> In the Augustinian and mediaeval outlook the whole focus of man's mind was directed *upward and away from* nature to God, and therefore nature had only symbolic significance as it was seen to reflect eternal verities and forms... But with the Reformation the stress was upon the turning of God in all his compassion and love *toward* the world he had made...The Reformation man turned his eyes outward to the great world which God had made...Natural science thus becomes a religious duty, for in its pursuit man is gratefully and obediently fulfilling his divinely appointed functions in relation to nature.[129]
>
> In other words, for mediaeval theology nature was thought of as impregnated with final causes so that...an eternal pattern [could] be read off the face of

---

as the mercy of the Heavenly Father; the material cause as Christ's obtaining righteousness for us; the formal cause as faith, and the final cause as the proof of divine justice and the praise of God's goodness (*Institutes*, III. xiv. 17).

[125]St. Thomas, *S.T.*, I.2.3.

[126]St. Thomas *Summa Contra Gentiles*, 3, taken from Aristotle, *In Physics* II.12.252.

[127]Aristotle, *In Physics* II, 13 259, quoted in Kenny, op. cit., 98.

[128]To borrow terms from Jean-Marc Berthoud, *Les Différentes Formes de Causalité et la Pensée de la Bible*, in the quarterly 'Positions Creationnistes': No. 25, Sept. 1996 (Lausanne: Association Vaudoise de Parents Chretiens), 9.

[129]T. F. Torrance, *Theology in Reconstruction*, (London: SCM Press, 1965), 274.

> nature...But to interpret nature in the light of final causes left little room for the element of real contingency, to the recognition of which all modern science owes its existence...only through observation and interpretation of the creaturely processes themselves, could the more or less static science of the ancient and mediaeval world give way to the great movement of modern science.[130]

Nonetheless, teleology did not completely disappear from the foundations of modern physics. Anthony Kenny shows how it endured, though in a transmuted form, in the thought of Sir Isaac Newton:

> Considered merely as a fund of *ex post* explanations of motions, Newtonian physics is no less teleological than Aristotelian. For Newton defined gravity as a centripetal force; and a centripetal force is 'that by which bodies are drawn or impelled, or in any way tend, towards a point as to a centre.' ... What made this a fundamentally teleological account was that the natural place for each body was supposed to be the place in which it was best for that body to be, the place in which it was most likely to survive as it was.[131]

Again, I think that Kenny is right that evolutionary theory was unable, even if one granted its assumptions, to displace some sort of teleological structure:

> If Darwin is correct in ascribing the origin of species to natural selection, then the production of a teleological structure may be due in the first instance to factors which are purely mechanistic. But both may be right and yet the ultimate explanation of the phenomenon would be finalistic. The only argument refuted by Darwin would be one which said: wherever there is adaptation to environment we must see the immediate activity of an intelligent being. But the argument from design did not claim this; and indeed it was an essential step in the argument that lower animals and natural agents did not have minds. The argument was only that the ultimate explanation of such adaptation must be found in intelligence; and if the argument was correct, then any Darwinian success merely inserts an extra step between the phenomena to be explained and their ultimate explanation.[132]

Objective design indicated in the consciences and desires of humans

But not only is overall design seen in non-intelligent plants and physical systems, it is also seen in the inevitable functioning of humans in terms of a moral system to which they feel somehow accountable; a moral system which is ordered from outside their own wills; one they did not create and cannot finally escape. This moral system definitely shapes or 'teleologically orders' the lives of human in directions that they might not otherwise go. In his volume on the philosophy of realism, Robert C. Koons, Professor of Philosophy, has addressed this strong evidence of teleological design (very close to what was meant by the concept of 'final cause'):

> Moral virtue is the disposition to make decisions that promote eudaimonia [well being]...Moral truths have the power to provide both reasons and

[130]Ibid., 63.
[131]Kenny, op. cit., 109, 110.
[132]Ibid., 118.

> motivation, since the human capacities for reasoning and desiring have the natural disposition to respond to moral truth…Our ultimate aim is not up to us, nor merely the product of accidental contingencies. It is our being objectively ordered to the ultimate end of human eudaemonia that makes us human and thereby constitutes us as capable of desiring and wanting.[133]

There is no doubt that St. Thomas would have considered this teleological ordering of the human conscience an illustration of the correctness of his fifth proof. This objective and insistent moral code is part of the design of the holy Creator for the directing of his image-bearers in the created order where they must live. It is not the only way that He providentially directs their paths, but it is a very important way, and it indicates both design in our lives and thereby points to the Designer.

The 'question-begging' of David Hume

It is frequently assumed that David Hume disproved the argument from design once and for all in the late eighteenth century. He sought to avoid the evidences of design all around us by claiming that any universe would have to have the appearance of being designed.[134] He says that there could be no universe at all unless its various parts were adapted to one another in order to function. But surely, this is a classical instance of 'begging the question.' To pretend that other universes would have to look like this one is something that he could not know, for he only lived in this one. Such a groundless, non-empirical assertion is a very poor attempt to dispose of massive evidence of design that the only universe he knew exhibits on every hand!

This question-begging procedure of Hume is not the attitude that has advanced modern science. Albert Einstein wrote a letter to Maurice Solovine on 30 March 1952 dealing with his amazement at the sheer intelligibility of the physical cosmos. Although not a Thomist or a Christian, the approach of this giant of physics is rather closer to St. Thomas's 'fifth way' than to the short-circuiting of evidence by David Hume:

> You find it curious that I consider the comprehensibility of the world to be like a miracle or an eternal mystery. Well, *a priori*, one ought to expect a chaotic world, which in no sense could be grasped by thought. One could, and even should expect that the world would be submitted to law only in the measure where we could intervene with our organizing intelligence. This would be a sort of order like the alphabetical order of the words of a language. But the sort of order created, for example, by the theory of gravitation of Newton, is of a totally different character. For even if the axioms of the theory are set up by man, the success of such an enterprise supposes an order of a higher degree than the world, objective, which one would not have been at all authorised to expect. That is the miracle which becomes more strongly apparent with the increasing development of our knowledge.[135]

---

[133]Robert C. Koons, *Realism Regained: An Exact Theory of Causation, Teleology, and the Mind* (Oxford: Oxford University Press, 2000), 139.

[134]David Hume, op. cit., 59

[135]A. Einstein, quoted in P. Thiry, op. cit., 157.

The skepticism of Hume about the invalidity of induction from complex realities that act harmoniously together, thereby implying an intelligent designer, exercised powerful sway within philosophy, but modern science had to go in a very different direction in order to accomplish its wonders. In the eighteenth century, Hume's contemporary opponent, Thomas Reid, showed that the study of even ancient medical science concerning the design of the human body pointed in a profoundly different direction from Hume's skepticism over design.[136] And at the end of the twentieth century, Reid's insight (from Galen, the ancient Greek medical doctor) was confirmed by the microbiologist, Michael Behe, an expert on the structure of the human cell. Behe noted that Hume's objections to design in the universe have been long since surpassed by science:

> Although Hume's objection to the inductive argument might have been valid in his day, it has been destroyed by the advance of science. Modern biochemistry routinely designs biochemical systems, which are now known to be the basis of life. Therefore we *do* have experience in observing the intelligent design of components of life. There have probably been tens of thousands of experiments in which new biochemical systems were put together, and in the future there will be many, many more.[137]

Kant's epistemology surpassed by modern science

Kant's objection to the argument from design was even more influential on subsequent thought than that of Hume. He termed it the 'physico-theological proof.'[138] Kant agreed with the teleological proof to this degree: the physical world indicates order and purpose beyond what individual component parts of it could have achieved themselves. However, he denies that this argument actually proves the existence of a God who designed it all, because of the severe limitations of what the human mind can know.

Kant denies that our minds can accurately know what is actually outside or above the world we experience. He imposes a radical dichotomy between the world as it is in itself (or *noumenal*) and the world as it is for us (or *phenomenal*). He claims that when our senses perceive the raw material of the external world, we do not really know what they are in themselves: 'while much can be said *a priori* as regards the form of the appearances, nothing whatsoever can be asserted of the thing in itself, which may underlie these appearances.'[139]

He holds that what we perceive is not 'things in themselves' (the *noumenal*), but rather the world as it comes through our minds (the

---

[136] He writes: 'When the structure of the human body was much less known than it is now, the famous Galen saw such evident marks of wise contrivance in it, that though he had been educated an Epicurean, he renounced that system, and wrote his book of the use of the parts of the human body, on purpose to convince others of what appeared so clear to himself, that it was impossible that such admirable contrivance should be the effect of chance' (Thomas Reid, *Essays on the Intellectual Powers of Man*, Derek R. Brookes, ed. [University Park, Pennsylvania: The Pennsylvania State University Press, 2002], 510).

[137] Michael J. Behe, *Darwin's Black Box: The Biochemical Challenge to Evolution* (New York: The Free Press, 1996), 219.

[138] I. Kant, *Critique of Pure Reason*, E. T. by Norman Kemp Smith (London: Macmillan, (1929, 1964), 'Transcendental Dialectic', 500.

[139] Ibid., 'Transcendental Aesthetic', 87.

phenomenal). Our minds are the shapers, or perhaps creators, of such concepts as design, because the mind conditions all that comes through it through its forms of intuition (such as of space and time)[140] and categories of understanding (such as quantity and quality).[141] He concludes that because our mind so shapes our perception of reality, we cannot finally get beyond the human mind to know, for instance, that there actually is an intelligent designer. That is to say, our 'phenomenal' perceptions of organization around us do not imply that there really is a finality, or a designer of the universe 'in himself', or independent of what we perceive. Such human concepts as God, freedom and immortality are 'regulative ideas', but not objects or independent realities as such. While Kant denies the validity of such concepts for 'natural theology',[142] he says that they do have a place in ethics.[143]

But modern physics had to go in precisely the opposite direction of Kant's assumptions about our inability to know the real world (or 'the thing in itself') in order to make its unparalleled discoveries. T. F. Torrance refers to an essay of Albert Einstein on the work of Sir James Clerk Maxwell on electromagnetic field theory. In this essay, Einstein contrasted the Kantian position with Clerk Maxwell's 'belief in an external world independent of the perceiving subject as the basis of all natural science.'[144]

Clerk Maxwell and Einstein held that one has to assume certain beliefs, such as the reality of the external world (which is not non-existent outside our minds, or hidden in an unknowable 'noumenal'), as well as the inherent comprehensibility of the universe. As Torrance remarks:

> These are beliefs that have to be assumed and put to the test, but they are not open to logical derivation or proof for they are prior to reasoning and have to be employed as premises in any attempted proof. There could be no science without belief in the inner harmony of the world or without the belief that it is possible to grasp reality with our theoretical constructions. Belief of this kind, Einstein claimed, is and always will remain the fundamental motive for all scientific work.[145]

In light of the thought and scientific achievements of Clerk Maxwell and Einstein, Torrance shows that the Kantian dualism between *phenomenal* and *noumenal*, between empirical and theoretical, had to be rejected for science to advance:

> The history of modern science has shown that when we operate with phenomenalist and dualist assumptions of this kind, the observable pattern of things in nature is torn away from a frame of objective structures in reality and loses its underlying coherence, with the result that it suffers serious distortion and disintegration. However, when these assumptions are set aside, a much profounder and more integrated understanding of nature becomes possible in terms of the dynamic-field structures inherent

---

[140]Ibid., 67-91.

[141]Ibid., 111-19.

[142]In Ibid., 528, he calls such proofs of God 'null and void.'

[143]Ibid., 528, 531.

[144]T. F. Torrance, op. cit., 58.

[145]Ibid.

> in the ongoing processes of the universe. Hence, for example, as we see in scientific understanding of the fields of radiation that pervade the universe, explanation in terms of mechanical connection has had to give way to explanation in terms of dynamic onto-relations.[146]

Quite specifically then, Kant's dualistic epistemology which denied *a priori* real knowledge of the actual universe (or 'things in themselves'), including the intelligent design indicated by the teleological proof, had to be rejected for true scientific advance. Torrance states clearly this necessity for science to leave Kant's epistemology:

> In natural science this is the point where we part company with Immanuel Kant, for here we are concerned with penetrating through the level of our empirical and early theoretical understanding of reality into its internal relations, for if nature is not in itself that which we claim to know of it in its relations toward us, then we do not really know nature but are merely operating with convenient symbols or useful arrangements of observational data. This is the decisive point of Einstein's critique of the phenomenalist and Kantian approach to knowledge, when he broke through it and grounded scientific knowledge on the objective intelligibility of the universe: that is, upon an inherent relatedness that characterizes the universe independently of our perceiving and conceiving of it... our knowledge of the universe is not cut short at appearances or what we can deduce from them, but is a grasping of reality in its ontological depth...we operate with the ontological integration of form and being, or of structure and matter, which is, after all, what $E = mc^2$ entails.[147]

Concluding reflections on the proofs of St. Thomas

The fivefold proofs of St. Thomas, then, seek to establish in an *a posteriori* fashion the existence of God from what we experience in the world of change, contingency and intelligibility around us. I am not able to accept the complaint of Kant that all of these proofs are finally ontological (or *a priori*). Indeed, as Thiry has shown (as we saw earlier), Kant himself employs an 'ontological proof' in the matter of assuming without evidence the existence of the *noumenal* realm.[148]

What E. L. Mascall says of the fourth proof, which some have claimed is a disguised 'ontological proof,' could be said of all five:

> For that argument [*sc.* the Ontological] claimed to deduce the existence of God from the mere concept of him, whereas the argument now under review [*sc.* that from degrees of goodness] does not claim to deduce the existence of maximum goodness from the mere concept of goodness. On the contrary, its starting-point was the concrete existence of things which, albeit imperfectly, are good. There is no transition from the order of concepts to that of existence. The only question is whether the argument can in fact prove what it claims to; whether the concrete existence of finite good necessarily implies the concrete existence of an absolute maximum good...[149]

---

[146]T. F. Torrance, *Reality and Evangelical Theology*, 57.
[147]T. F. Torrance, *The Ground and Grammar of Theology*, 162.
[148]I. Kant, *Critique of Pure Reason*, 521.
[149]E. L. Mascall, *He Who Is*, 53.

Certainly, St. Thomas does assume some basic axioms for his proofs to work, such as the existence of the real world outside one's mind, the reality of causation, and the impossibility of an infinite regress. But these are essential to any kind of valid reasoning, and do not constitute proof of an ontological argument as such. As we have just seen, the axioms of St. Thomas are far more consonant with the findings of modern science than the denials of them by Hume and Kant. This alone ought to tip the balances in favor of a sympathetic reading of the proofs of St. Thomas.

I cannot see any essential error in the procedure of St. Thomas in these five proofs, which we have just discussed. I do not think that they are necessary as a foundation for the exposition of true theology (for reasons we have seen in Chapter 1), but that would not imply that they are wrong. At very least, I would have to agree with the Dutch Reformed theologian, Herman Bavinck, about these proofs: 'But though they are weak as proofs, they are strong as testimonies. They do not force the mind of the unbeliever, but they are signs and testimonies which never fail to leave an impression on the soul of any person.'[150]

By 'weak', Bavinck does not mean that they are wrong, or that they have no final value:

> Analyzed, isolated, taken separately and one by one they can be attacked at every point of reasoning; instead of promoting faith they retard it, for faith is spontaneous and unforced. But taken in the sense of testimonies, and proclaimed as the revelation of that God, of whose existence every person is by nature and apart from reasoning or study assured in the very depths of his soul, they are of great value.[151]

Fideism?

Does refusal to place such proofs at the necessary foundations of true theology constitute a sort of 'fideism'? 'Fideism' is defined as 'exclusive or basic reliance upon faith alone, accompanied by a consequent disparagement of reason and utilized especially in the pursuit of philosophical or religious truth.' Alvin Plantinga has devoted a section of his 'Reason and Belief in God' to whether or not Reformed Christians are fideists.[152] Plantinga rightly denies that the Reformed epistemologist is committed 'to thinking that faith and reason conflict.'[153]

He also holds that the existence of God and our responsibility to Him are not only deliverances of faith, but also among the deliverances of reason.[154] He quotes John Calvin to that effect (*Institutes* I. 3. 1). Thus, 'the belief that there is such a person as God is as much among the deliverances of reason as those other beliefs.'[155]

> From this vantage point we can see, therefore, that the Reformed epistemologist is not a fideist at all with respect to belief in God. He does

[150]Herman Bavinck, *The Doctrine of God*, (Edinburgh: The Banner of Truth, 1979), 79.
[151]Ibid.
[152]A. Plantinga in Plantinga and Wolterstorff, *Faith and Rationality*, 87-91.
[153]Ibid., 88.
[154]Ibid., 89.
[155]Ibid., 90.

> not hold that there is any conflict between faith and reason here, and he does not even hold that we cannot attain this fundamental truth by reason; he holds, instead, that it is among the deliverances of reason…
>
> …Nor is he [the Reformed epistemologist] committed to the view that argument is irrelevant to belief in God if such belief is properly basic. Furthermore, belief in God, like other properly basic beliefs, is not groundless or arbitrary; it is grounded in justification-conferring conditions. Finally, the Reformed view that belief in God is properly basic is not felicitously thought of as a version of fideism.[156]

III. The Proof of Duns Scotus (1266–1308)

The 'subtle doctor', a major metaphysician and Franciscan from Scotland, who taught in Oxford, Paris and Cologne (where he died at an early age after a prodigious output of writings), formulated a very complex proof for God's existence. In doing so, he went in a different direction from St. Thomas, and to a limited degree, was influenced by Anselm's ontological proof (to which he gave a different 'coloration').

Scotus's view of God's Being different from that of St. Thomas

We have seen that St. Thomas approaches the capacity of man to grasp God's being in terms of analogy. Thomas writes in *Summa Contra Gentiles*: 'The names of God and creatures are predicated neither univocally nor equivocally but analogously, that is, according to an order or reference to some one thing.'[157]

Bonansea explains the methodology of St. Thomas:

> Starting from the Aristotelian principle that knowledge is possible only through the process of abstraction from the objects of our experience, Aquinas goes on to discuss man's knowledge of God in terms of the triple way laid down by Pseudo-Dionysius, namely, the way of affirmation, the way of negation, and the way of eminence.[158]
>
> This process whereby the human mind arrives at some sort of knowledge of God from the perfections found in creatures is what is termed the method or theory of analogy…[159]

Unlike St. Thomas, who holds that the being of man is *analogical* to the Being of God, Scotus declares that the relationship between the two is *univocal*. Why this radical change from the general Christian tradition? Etienne Gilson says that Scotus thought that according to Thomas's analogy of names, we were left with only a certain likeness, not precisely the same quality. 'This is why [Scotus was] anxious to uphold the doctrine of the univocity of being, as well as of all the terms signifying divine attributes.'[160]

156Ibid., 90,91.

157Thomas, *SCG*, I. 34.

158Bonansea gives references to Dionysius from Thomas' *De pot.*, q. 7, a. 5, ad 2; *In Sent.*, d. 34, q. 1, a. 1, and *de malo*, q. 16, a. 8, ad 3 (in Bonansea, op. cit., 96).

159Bonansea, 97.

160Etienne Gilson, *Jean Duns Scot. Introduction à ses positions fondamentales* (Paris: Vrin, 1952), 107.

Instead of – with Thomas and most theologians of the Christian past – speaking of analogous being, Scotus speaks of the univocity of being between God and humankind, or of 'being as being'. Copleston asks the right question:

> Very well, but what is being as being? It is not a thing. Rather is it the universal concept of being which applies to infinite and finite being, to spiritual and material being, to existent and possible being. Being as being is, in other words, the most abstract of all concepts, considered prior to all determination. It is opposed simply to not-being.[161]

Since Scotus holds that we have no direct intuition of being, '… the only way to find for metaphysics an object endowed with a sufficient unity is to posit a notion of being so abstract and indeterminate that it may apply indifferently, always in the same sense, to everything that is … at the ultimate degree of abstraction …it becomes applicable in one and the same sense to all that is. This is what we mean when we say that being is "univocal"…'[162]

But, in light of Holy Scripture and of nearly the whole Christian theological tradition, univocal predication of the being of both God and man seems at first sight to run contrary to the most basic biblical and theological distinction of all: that between the Creator and the creature. That is, if we start with the concept of man, the creature, sharing the same being with God, his Creator, we may wind up with a God created in man's image; even though He be greater and more perfect. Would He not still be a sort of 'superman'?

It appears, however, that Duns Scotus is using univocity in a more limited and careful sense than that. Bonansea points out that Scotus does not mean the same thing that Thomas means when he speaks of univocity:

> For Scotus, univocity means identity of term, concept, and the specific reality or modality to which the term is applied, but not the identity of the total reality of the beings concerned. Thus he can speak of being as a univocal term applicable to God and creatures, even though God is an infinite being formally distinct from being itself, just as truth, goodness, and the other perfections are. For Aquinas there is no such distinction.[163]

André De Muralt explains that Duns Scotus tries to avoid the theologically unacceptable fusion of being suggested by univocal predication as opposed to the generally acceptable analogical predication that safeguards the Creator/creature distinction by means of 'adding the mode of *intrinsic* to his univocal notion of being in order to attribute it legitimately to God.'[164] This *intrinsic* mode proper to the being of God is infinity.[165]

In a way that will not be intuitively obvious for most of us, Duns Scotus strives to maintain a certain difference between God's and man's 'univocal

[161]Copleston, *A History of Medieval Philosophy*, 217.

[162]E. Gilson, *Christian Philosophy in the Middle Ages*, 455.

[163]Bonansea, op. cit., 104, 105.

[164]André De Muralt, *Néoplatonisme et Aristotélisme dans la Métaphysique Médiévale* (Paris: Vrin, 1995), 55n.

[165]Ibid., 62 n.

being' by distinguishing between two sorts of predication; one appropriate to propositions concerning the being of man, and the other proper to affirmations concerning God's being. The type of predication proper to dealing with propositions concerning creatures is called by Scotus 'formal', while the predication proper to propositions concerning the being of God is called that of 'identity.' De Muralt explains:

> The first predication [*sc.*, 'formal'] is that which permits one to speak 'quidditatively' concerning the univocal predicates of every creaturely subject, as in the proposition: 'man is an animal.' This is the only mode of predication which is found in propositions bearing on creatures, for in the created order there is no predication by identity which is not also a formal predication. [But] the second predication [*sc*, 'identity'] permits one in divine things to speak of in and by means of the divine identity, the divine attributes between themselves and within the divine essence. The divine essence being the subject of attributes that are formally distinct *ex natura rei* because of their univocity, these attributes such as *being, wise, good,* are identical with one another and with the divine essence by means of the mode of infinity which cannot fail to posit them in God, and not only because they could be said to be in God, as some sort of inherent form. The reasons of being, of wisdom, of goodness are thus identical even as they are infinite in God, but not formally.[166]

To say the least, this is a very difficult way to attempt to maintain something of the necessary Creator/creature distinction, which is explained much more simply in St. Thomas's analogical predication! That alone makes one wonder at its value.

So, with univocity of being in mind, Duns Scotus sets out on his proof of the existence of God inferentially. As Copleston very truly states: 'Scotus's line of argument, as given in the Oxford Commentary on the *Sentences* and summarized in *On the First Principle*, is complex, involved and difficult to follow.'[167] As Gilson points out, 'The univocity of being imposes a certain method in the demonstration of the existence of God.'[168]

Scotus does not wish to start 'from the existence of sensible things to infer from it the existence of their cause…'[169] He holds that to take that approach, as did Aristotle, leaves one with only a physical cause. Gilson explains:

> In other words, if it is the function of physics to prove the existence of God, the God whose existence physics can demonstrate does not transcend the physical order; as a keystone is gripped in the arch, this God is gripped in nature, even if it holds together only through him. To attain a primary principle, which causes the world its very being, one cannot build upon *sensible being*, but on *being*.[170]

This brings us to the key of Scotus's demonstration of God's existence; it is his concept of the univocity of being. According to Gilson:

---

[166]A. De Muralt refers to Scotus, I S., d. 4, d. 8 in op. cit., 79, 80.
[167]Copleston, op. cit., 220.
[168]Gilson, op. cit., 455.
[169]Ibid.
[170]Ibid., 456.

> The univocal notion of being as being is therefore the condition of the very possibility of a science transcendent to physics and the indispensable point of departure for metaphysics...Taken in its logical predictability with respect to all that is, being is the emptiest of forms; no matter how it is considered, no *real* knowledge can come from it.[171]

The importance of infinity in Scotus's proof

Bonansea notes that Scotus then takes the richest and most encompassing characteristic of God's being as crucial to his proof: namely, God's infinity, for 'the infinite contains in itself really and by way of identity all simple perfections.'[172] Scotus believes that 'all the other divine [attributes] can be more easily derived from radical infinity ...'[173] As Copleston says, 'Infinity is for Scotus the basic "absolute" property or attribute of God.'[174]

Bonansea then explains how Scotus proceeds from this point of univocity and infinity:

> Given such a notion of the infinite, it is little wonder that, in approaching the problem of God's existence, Scotus should introduce the question by asking, 'Whether among being something exists that is actually infinite' (*Ord.*, I, d. 2, no. 1). Having formulated the question in these terms, he proceeds in scholastic fashion to state a few arguments against the possibility of an actually infinite being, which he then counters with arguments favouring such a possibility. But before taking up the issue...he feels the need to discuss a preliminary question...whether the proposition 'An infinite being exists' or 'God exists' is self-evident (*Ord.*, I, d. 2, no. 10). [175]

Scotus's 'coloration' of Anselm's ontological proof

Then Scotus discusses Anselm's ontological proof, which perhaps surprisingly, he to a degree accepts, though with some refinement, 'coloration' as he calls it. Chapter V of Bonansea's *Man and His Approach to God in John Duns Scotus* refers to 'Duns Scotus and St. Anselm's Ontological Argument.'[176] Briefly, as Copleston points out, '...the Anselmian argument ...must be colored or retouched by addition of the words "without contradiction" (*Opus Oxoniense*, Bk. I, Dist. 2, Q. 2, No. 137).'[177] With Scotus's 'coloration', God is the being which, conceived without contradiction, is so great that a greater being cannot be conceived without contradiction. According to Scotus, 'the mind perceives no repugnance or contradiction in the concept of infinite being; and no greater being than the actual infinite can be conceived. God must therefore be infinite.'[178]

As to how much use Scotus really makes of Anselm's argument (even reformulated), scholars are not agreed. Though no expert, I think that Bonansea's conclusion is probably right:

---

[171] Ibid.
[172] Bonansea, op. cit., 120.
[173] Ibid., 121.
[174] Copleston, op. cit., 221.
[175] Bonansea, op. cit., 121.
[176] Ibid., 173-186.
[177] Copleston, op. cit., 221.
[178] Ibid.

> Yet despite some 'persuasive reasons' in support of the Anselmian argument, Scotus refrains from endorsing it as a demonstrative proof of God's existence. It is only by an argument *a posteriori* that such a proof is possible. This is what he means when, in introducing his answer to the question, 'Whether among beings something exists that is actually infinite,' he says that, although it is not possible to demonstrate *a priori* (*propter quid*), it is necessary and altogether possible to demonstrate it by a demonstration *a posteriori* (*quia*) beginning with creatures (*Ord.* I, d. 2, no. 39).[179]

Gilson shows that Scotus proceeds in two phases: (1) he proves that a Primary exists in the order of being, and then (2) that this Primary is infinite.[180] Closely related to this is the 'dividing line' between infinitude and finitude that must be drawn in the act of being between God and creatures. The role played in Thomism by the existential purity of the divine act of being, is played in Scotism by the divine will. Thus, 'the very essence of Scotism is in the formal distinction between the intellect of God and His will… In Scotism, the will of God intervenes to bridge the ontological gap there is between the necessary existence of Infinite Being and the possible existence of finite beings… Between the necessary and the contingent the only conceivable link is a Will.'[181]

The first part of Scotus's proof

As an illustration of the detailed and complex thought of Scotus, I shall reproduce here *the first part* of his proof of God's existence as laid out by Bonansea, and then comment on Part A of it (from Scotus's *De Primo Principio*), immediately following the outline.

A. *The Relative Properties of God*

1. The Triple Primacy
   a. First Efficient Cause
      i. Its possibility
      ii. Its uncausability
      iii. Its existence
   b. An Ultimate Final Cause
      i. Its possibility
      ii. Its uncausability
      iii. Its existence
   c. Most Perfect Nature
      i. Its possibility
      ii. Its uncausability
      iii. Its existence

---

[179]Bonansea, op. cit., 122.
[180]Gilson, op. cit., 457.
[181]Ibid., 460.

2. Interrelation of the Three Primaries
3. The Triple Primacy of Efficiency, Finality and Eminence Belongs to One Nature

B. *The Absolute Properties of God*

1. The Infinity of the First Being
    a. Preliminary Theses
        i. The First Being is endowed with intellect and will
        ii. Self-knowledge and self-volition of the First Being are the same as its essence
        iii. Knowledge and volition of other things are also the same as the First Being's essence
        iv. Distinct and necessary knowledge of all intelligibles by the First Being
    b. Proofs of the Infinity of the First Being
        i. From its infinite power
        ii. From its infinite knowledge
        iii. From its infinite goodness
        iv. From its infinite perfection
2. The unicity of God

    Proofs from:
        i. The infinite intellect
        ii. The infinite will
        iii. The infinite goodness
        iv. The infinite power
        v. The notion of necessary being
        vi. The nature of necessary being
        vii. The notion of omnipotence[182]

Summary and commentary on the first part of Scotus's proof

Next, let me summarily condense the main proofs offered by Scotus in his *De Primo Principio* (Chapter 3 in the English translation: 'The Triple Primacy of the First Principle').[183] And the ones I go through from this third chapter

---

[182]Bonansea, op. cit., 134, 135.

[183]I draw from the English translation, *John Duns Scotus: A Treatise on God as First Principle*, Translated and edited with commentary by Allan B. Wolter (Chicago, Il: Franciscan Herald Press: , 1983). Unless otherwise stated, all of the quotations or paraphrases that follow come from Wolter's translation.

are only *a part* of the vast series of his proofs of God in terms of his vision of univocal predication! But they will give us some idea of his painstaking methodology and the tightness of his logical argumentation.

The first conclusion

The first conclusion states that *'some natures among beings can produce an effect'* (**3.4**). As proof, Scotus says that (1) some nature is contingent and thus producible by another, while (2) some nature, being changeable or mobile, and lacking perfection, is able to be produced (**3.5**). That is, if something can be effected, something can effect it. This implies that some existent cause could create it or produce some change in it (**3.5**).

'Some nature is producing, because some nature is produced…' (**3.6**).

Bonansea explains that in this first conclusion, a being is producible only in terms of the being itself, of nothing, or of another being. It cannot proceed from nothing; nothing can cause only nothing. The production of the being cannot be by the being itself. It would in that case have to act before existence; an evident contradiction. Thus, since the first two options are inconceivable, one must conclude that a producible being can only be produced by another being.[184]

The second conclusion

The second conclusion states that *'something able to produce an effect is simply first, that is to say, it neither can be produced by an efficient cause nor does it exercise its efficient causality in virtue of anything other than itself'* (**3.7**). Like Aquinas, Scotus denies an infinite regress, because 'whatever has nothing prior is not posterior to anything posterior to itself, for the second conclusion of chapter two does away with a circle in causes' (**3.8**).

His goal is to rule out a possible infinite in a sequence of essentially ordered causes. Here he speaks against Avicenna (**3.9**). Then he discusses what is involved in essentially and accidentally ordered causes, holding that several kinds of causes co-operate simultaneously, with material, formal, efficient and final causes working together to produce a common effect (**3.10,11**).

As Wolter notes in his Commentary on this text, some philosophers (Averroes and Avicenna) in line with the thought of Aristotle, claimed that God acted only through a hierarchical chain of 'intelligences,' related in terms of causality. Each higher intelligence, including God, was responsible for the continuing existence of each intelligence below it, and since the latter 'could exercise no causality of its own unless it were continually conserved by the ongoing causal action of the intelligence above it, the cocausality of the higher was required for any effect the lower intelligence might produce. A series of such efficient causes would not be *accidentally ordered* as an eternal sequence of generative causes might be, but they would be *essentially* ordered in causing their common effect.'[185]

---

[184]Bonansea, op. cit., 135, 136.
[185]Wolter, op. cit., 229.

Scotus explains that efficient causes (in light of the above) differ from accidental causes in three ways: (1) Each lower or 'second' cause depends upon the highest or 'first' in the act of causing. (2) The higher intelligence (as with Aristotle) is not a more powerful version of the lower intelligence, but that of a specifically different nature and order, being more perfect, and (3) All essentially ordered causes required for an effect must employ their causality simultaneously (**3.11**).

Scotus maintains that 'if cause A is not first, but depends upon another cause B, one can argue of B as one did of A that either it is first in the order of efficiency or if dependent upon a still higher cause C, one cannot continue to postulate higher and higher causes *ad infinitum*.'[186]

Three theses concerning infinity

Thus, in light of the differences between accidentally and essentially ordered causes, Scotus posits three theses concerning infinity: (A) an infinity of essentially order causes is impossible; (B) an infinity of accidentally ordered causes is impossible unless a terminus in an essentially ordered series is assumed, and (C) if no essential order exists, then an infinite number of causes is impossible (**3.12**).

Five arguments support premise A

Five arguments support the first premise: that an infinity of essentially ordered causes is impossible (Proof A). According to Wolter's Commentary, we note that Duns is dealing with a theory that claims a series of infinite intelligences, both created and creative. These intelligences constitute a class apart from God ('the first Intelligence'), with each one caused by a prior member in the series. But if nothing were outside, then the infinite sequence could rightly be viewed as self-sustaining (*a se*) and existing as its own cause. Even so, the chain is not made independent by increasing the number of dependents. If an infinite number of simultaneously existing links existed in the causal chain, one would still have to account for an outside cause.[187]

A series of essentially ordered causes, in which each member depends on the prior one for its causation, calls for a cause outside the series itself (as already established). All of the causes are also effects with respect to the preceding causes, and if no outside cause exists that comprises the effect of anything else, then the series either depends upon an effect without a cause or a cause that is its own effect – either way a contradiction.[188]

Concerning the second argument, Duns states that in a series of essentially ordered causes, all the causes must act simultaneously in the production of any effect. If the series is infinite, an actual infinity of causes would then all act at the same time, apart from any first cause, a situation not claimed by any philosopher. Aristotle himself related that there must be a beginning, with no infinity of causes.

---

[186]Ibid., 228-30

[187]Ibid., 230-31.

[188]Bonansea, op. cit., 139.

In his third argument, he appeals again to Aristotle, and points out that if there is no first, there is no essential order. Where there is no beginning (as with an infinite series of causes), nothing is essentially prior to anything else.[189]

The fourth argument states that the higher cause is more perfect in its causality than the lower, in a series of essentially ordered causes. Therefore, an infinitely higher cause must be infinitely more perfect, both in itself and its resultant causality. However, it cannot occur in terms of a cause that acts only in virtue of another, and thus a cause is needed that is outside the series and 'simply first.'[190]

The fifth argument (which concludes this particular series on Proof A) appears to assume that creativity (in terms of efficient causality) is a pure perfection, implying no imperfection or essential limitation. Scotus had reminded us that extrinsic causes imply no imperfection of necessity (as in **2.26,27**), since the effect is produced in the 'patient', not the agent. If 'it is not necessarily imperfect' is made equivalent to 'if it is not necessarily not perfect', then it is possible for it to be perfect. Scotus states that if every cause were dependent upon some prior cause, then efficiency would never lack perfection, which is a proof that denies the initial premise, that extrinsic causes are not necessarily imperfect. Thus he concludes that an independent power to produce something can exist in some nature, being 'simply first.'[191]

Premise B

As for Proof B, if its thesis is combined with that of A, one can conclude that an infinity of essentially ordered causes is possible (**3.14**). Wolter summarizes Scotus' subsequent argument by noting that the 'higher' or 'superior' nature of the cause responsible for periodically changing phenomena (accidentally ordered causes) lies outside the causal chain of univocal causes as an equivocal cause.[192]

In an infinity of accidentally ordered causes (even if such were possible), the causes in question do not act simultaneously but only in succession; the activity of one cause flows from the activity of the others. However, no dependence is exhibited among the causes, for each cause creates its own activity apart from the actual concurrence of the previous one.

An infinite series of such causes is not possible unless it depends upon something which is equally infinite in duration. A succession of new beings or forms of beings is only conceivable in terms of something permanent that is separate from the succession. All the components of such a succession are comprised of the same nature; since none of them can co-exist with the entire succession without altering its temporal character, then something must exist that is prior to the succession itself. The whole series of accidentally ordered causes so depends on an essentially ordered cause as its foundation, that no causality and no series is possible without it.[193]

---

[189]Wolter, op. cit., 231.

[190]Bonansea, op. cit., 140.

[191]Wolter, op. cit., 231.

[192]Ibid., 232-34.

[193]Bonansea, op. cit., 140-41.

Premise C proved by nineteen conclusions

Proof C states that if no essential order existed, then the being referred to in the first conclusion would be identical to the being referred to in the second conclusion. Since it is able to produce an effect, it is uncaused and does not cause in virtue of another cause (**3.15**).

If the first cause were not self-existent, it could never exist at all, unless it came from nothing, since no other being could give it existence. Therefore, since from nothing nothing comes, this being would be possible, but unable to exist – a contradiction. Furthermore, to cause itself is still to be caused, and that is uncharacteristic of a being proven to be uncausable. Thus, Scotus demonstrates that if the first efficient cause can exist of itself, then it will.[194]

For the third conclusion, Scotus states that if what is able to cause effectively is *simply first*, then it is incapable of being caused, since it cannot be produced and is thus able to produce independently (**3.16**).

The fourth conclusion maintains that a being that is *simply first* and able to exert efficient causality actually exists. Only an actually existent nature is capable of exercising this degree of causality (**3.18**).

Scotus proves this as follows: 'Anything to whose nature it is repugnant to receive existence from anything else, exists of itself, if it is able to exist at all. To receive existence from something else is repugnant to the very notion of a being which is first in the order of efficiency' (**3.19**).

Such a cause is prior to all others, with none others prior to it. Because such a cause is first, it exists. The essential idea of such a being implies both its inability to be caused and its self-existence.

According to Wolter, the proof given above for the fourth conclusion affirms that if something exists or can exist in actuality, it is because 'it is already existing in actuality or if it is not now existing, something does not actually exist, or something can exist that will bring it into existence at some future time.' A being incapable of being caused can only actually exist in the present.[195]

As to the second proof for the fourth conclusion, Scotus mentions 'the impropriety of a universe in which the highest possible degree of being is lacking' (**3.19**).

The fifth conclusion affirms that a being unable to be caused is necessarily existent (**3.21**). He proves this by saying that 'Nothing can be nonexistent unless something either positively or privatively incompatible with it can exist, for one of two contradictories is always true' (**3.22**).

Wolter's Commentary on this fifth conclusion notes that it clearly states that the uncausable actually exists. The possibility of a contingent existence is eliminated in favour of a necessary existence.[196]

The sixth conclusion states that *It is characteristic of but one nature to have necessary being of itself* (**3.23**). He then proves this assertion two ways. First,

---

[194]Bonansea, op.cit., 144.
[195]Wolter, op. cit., 238.
[196]Ibid., 238-41.

if two natures of themselves could be necessary being, then necessity of existence would be a common feature, shared by means of an essential or generic unity. But two inconsistencies would arise from this concept. (1) Each necessary being would reflect a common nature (less actual), rather than a distinctive nature (more actual). (2) Neither would necessarily exist by virtue of that common nature, which is presumed to be the primary reason why each is necessary. Indeed, two natures included in a common genus are unequal, with one being more perfect than another. But Scotus adds that nothing is more perfect than a being having necessary existence of itself (**3.24,25**).

In his second proof for the sixth conclusion, Scotus explains that neither one of two natures having necessary being would depend upon the other for existence, and thus, no essential order would exist between them. In fact, one nature would not belong to this universe, because in this universe, all beings are related by an essential order to each other. If two *first natures* are assumed, then two orders would reside within two universes (**3.26**).

Scotus maintains in his seventh conclusion that *Among beings some nature is able to function as final cause* (**3.27**). He proves it by referring to his previous work in this treatise, and hence holds that 'something is able to be ordered to an end, so that it is even more evident here than in the case of the efficient cause, that an essential order is involved' (**3.28**).

The eighth conclusion states that '*Something able to be an end is simply ultimate, that is to say, it can neither be ordained to something else nor exercise its finality in virtue of something else*' (**3.29**). He proves this by five arguments similar to those given for the second conclusion of this third chapter (**3.30**).

The ninth conclusion: *Such an ultimate end cannot be caused in any way* (**3.31**). He proves this from the fact that it cannot be ordained for another end: otherwise it would not be ultimate, and refers also to some earlier conclusions (**3.32**).

The tenth conclusion: *The being which can be an ultimate end actually exists, and that this primacy pertains to some actually existing nature* (**3.33**). His proof here is rather like his fourth conclusion of chapter three (**3.34**). Duns now goes on to discuss four further conclusions about 'the order of eminence' (of which the eleventh will constitute the first):

The eleventh conclusion [i.e. the *first of four* conclusions concerning 'the order of eminence']: *Among beings, there is some nature which excels* (**3.35**). 'This is proved from the fact that something is ordered to an end; therefore, it is excelled' (he refers here to earlier conclusions) (**3.36**).

The twelfth conclusion [i.e. the *second of four* re the order of eminence]: *Some eminent nature is simply first in perfection* (**3.37**). 'This is clear because we have an essential order' (referring to Aristotle). 'And in such an order, an ultimate nature is to be found. This is proved by the five reasons given above for the *second conclusion*' (**3.38**).

The thirteenth conclusion [i.e. the *third of four* re eminence]: *The supreme nature cannot be caused* (**3.39**). Proof is found in the fact that it cannot be ordained to an end, and therefore it cannot be caused by an efficient cause.

(He refers here to previous proofs) (**3.40**).

The fourteenth conclusion [i.e. the *fourth of four* re eminence]: *The supreme nature is something actually existing* (**3.41**). The proof of this is like that of conclusion four of this chapter. Corollary: It is contradictory that any nature should be more perfect or higher than this. (He refers to a previous proof) (**3.42**). Wolter comments that if a supreme nature is both possible and uncausable, it is actual.[197]

The fifteenth conclusion: *In some one and the same actually existing nature, there is the triple primacy in the aforementioned triple order, namely, of efficiency, finality and eminence* (**3.43**). Duns Scotus then writes:

'This fifteenth conclusion comes as the fruit of this chapter…If to exist necessarily of itself is characteristic of but one nature (from the sixth conclusion of this chapter) and if such existence is proper to whatever possesses a primacy in any of the aforementioned three ways…then each of these primacies belongs to that unique nature to which the others belong…' (**3.44**). Scotus further summarizes: 'This is a very fertile conclusion, containing as it does, six others virtually…' (**3.45**).

The sixteenth conclusion: *It is impossible for the same being to depend essentially on two things in such a way that its total dependence terminates with each* (**3.46**). His proof: 'If for a given causal category one cause is the total cause of something, then it is impossible that another cause of the same category should cause the same thing, for then one and the same thing would be twice caused or neither would be the total cause…For if it still depends on the other, the first does not sufficiently terminate its dependency. Similarly then it would depend upon something without the existence of which it would still exist, and in the same order of being. But this runs counter to the very notion of dependence' (**3.47**).

The seventeenth conclusion: *There is but one nature which is first as regards any given type of extrinsic causality* (**3.48**). He proves this by showing the incoherence of such a primacy pertaining to more than one. As to secondary beings, he shows that a supposed twofold dependence of the same type would also exist. Furthermore, if the secondary beings comprise a distinct set, they would constitute a distinct universe, because the members of the two sets are neither ordered to each other nor to the same thing. Duns refers to Aristotle, who 'assumes the principal goodness of the universe to consist in its single end' (**3.49**). To confirm this proof, among other points, he adds: 'The ascending progression in an essential order is from more to less. Consequently, it terminates with one (**3.50**). 'Again, it seems clear enough that the primacy of eminence pertains to one nature, for if two natures cannot be so ordered that one does not excel the other (for in this respect they are like numbers), then it is even more impossible that two different natures should be first to the same degree (**3.52**). The implication is, he says: '…no nature would contain virtually the perfection of every other nature. But without contradicting ourselves, we cannot think that no nature is most perfect (**3.54**).

---

[197]Ibid., 254.

The eighteenth conclusion: *That being which is first able to produce an effect is most actual since it virtually contains all possible actuality. The first end is the best, virtually containing all possible goodness. The first of those beings which can excel is most perfect, containing eminently all possible perfections* (**3.55**).

In Wolter's comments on this eighteenth conclusion, he considers it not to be a conclusion in itself, so much as 'the nature of a proof for the last three virtual conclusions.' Wolter adds: 'What Scotus seems to be doing is showing that each of the three essential orders culminates not only in a first, specific to that order, but in a first which is all perfect. Since the efficient cause is one which gives being or actuality to all that is produced, it must contain in itself the fullness of what it imparts to others. It has to contain virtually the actuality of what it can give…As such it is "whole" as he points out, and that is also what it means to be "perfect" (i.e. to be a complete or finished thing). Similarly, the final cause "motivates" qua good, in the sense that it tends to give or communicate of its goodness to others. As that from which all goodness stems, it must be the ultimate goodness.'[198]

The nineteenth conclusion: *But one existing nature is first in the aforesaid triple way with reference to every other nature, so that any such is, therefore, posterior to it in a threefold way* (**3.57**). Scotus refers to previous proofs of his to establish this point (cf. **3.58, 59**). In the background of his argumentation here seems to lurk Aristotle's theory of a plurality of unmoved movers that function as final causes for the various retrograde movements of the planets, though without having efficient cause.[199]

Also, Scotus as a Christian who believed in creation out of nothing, had to overcome Aristotle's view of 'primary matter as eternal and uncreated… and posterior in perfection to everything else in the universe.[200] As Wolter comments: 'But if necessary existence pertains to only one being or nature and this enjoys a triple primacy of efficiency, finality and eminence, one could argue, as Scotus did, that this other Aristotelian theory could not be correct. Consequently, all posterior beings would have to be caused, since they do not exist of themselves, and hence all would be posterior also in the orders of efficiency and finality as well as eminence. Conversely, whatever is not posterior in this way is a necessary being and hence would enjoy the aforesaid triple primacy' (**3.59**).[201]

A concluding prayer of Duns Scotus

Duns Scotus concludes this difficult chapter with a prayer of praise to the Lord:

> Indeed, O Lord, in wisdom you have made things so ordered that any reasonable intellect may see that every being is ordered. Consequently, it was absurd for the philosophers to deny order of some. From the universal statement 'Every being is ordered,' then, it follows that not every being is posterior and not every being is prior, since in either case an identical thing

[198]Wolter, op. cit., 260.
[199]Ibid., 262.
[200]Ibid., 262,263.
[201]Ibid., 263.

> would be ordered to itself or else a circle in the ordered world would be assumed. Consequently there is some prior being which is not posterior, and is therefore first. And there is some posterior being which is not prior. You are the unique first, and everything besides you comes after you by reason of a threefold order, as I have explained to the best of my ability. (**3.63**)[202]

Concluding reflections on the proof of Duns Scotus

The high genius and sheer acuity of the intellect of Duns Scotus certainly leaves its mark in this amazing third chapter of *De Primo Principio*. It is also marked, I think, by his genuine piety. The complexity and harmony of its construction makes one think of the manner in which the vaulted arches and flying buttresses of a Gothic cathedral somehow elegantly maintain its weight and contribute to its beauty. Along these lines, the monk and man of letters, Thomas Merton, said about it: 'It is getting to be rather generally admitted that, for accuracy and depth and scope, this [Scotus'] is the most perfect and complete and thorough proof for the existence of God that has ever been worked out by any man.'[203]

While I cannot but admire the beauty of its 'architecture', I cannot creditably judge its effectiveness or even its overall accuracy. Not being a professional logician, I, therefore, lack the ability to find any particular errors (assuming that there are any) in the complex proof of Duns Scotus, insofar as I have been able to follow it. So, unless I am shown otherwise, I shall assume that he has proved what he set out to prove: that an infinite God exists. Yet three matters still seem problematical to me.

Three problems with the proof of Scotus

First, his replacing the traditional Christian analogical mode of predication with univocal predication. Duns Scotus argues, as we have seen, that univocal being is a superior way to St. Thomas's assumption of analogical being between infinite and finite being. He holds that univocal predication constitutes a tighter proof of God's existence than analogical; that it gives us a richer view of God, and one harder to overturn. But I am not convinced, although it may be that I lack the intellectual capacity to grasp the subtleties of the 'subtle doctor.' On my view, St. Thomas's doctrine of analogy is closer to what the Bible seems to assume in its usage of the names of God (e.g. 'The Lord is my shepherd'; divine and human shepherds are in some ways alike and in some ways different. This is precisely what is assumed by analogical predication, though of course the Church's doctrine of analogy is much more complex than that).[204] Philosopher Thomas V. Morris has a very sensible discussion in clear English of how a word can accurately convey to us information about

---

[202]I will not deal with his fourth chapter, where he proves God's attributes of simplicity, infinity and intellectuality.

[203]Thomas Merton, *The Seven Storey Mountain* (1948), 94; quoted in Bonansea, op. cit., 107.

[204]See a classical discussion of analogy in E. L. Mascall, *Existence and Analogy* (London: Darton, Longman & Todd Ltd., 1966), Chapter 5 – 'The Doctrine of Analogy' (92-121); and more recently an illuminating section on analogy in part of Chapter 3 of Alan J. Torrance, *Persons in Communion* – 'Theological Language, Vestigiality and the Question of Continuity between the Human and Divine Realms' (Edinburgh: T & T Clark, 1996), 120-212.

both God and man, without our thinking that the being represented by this term is either exactly the same (as required by the univocal theory), or totally different (as required by the equivocal theory).[205]

What analogy does is to make us aware of a necessary 'shift in meaning' when we speak in ordinary language concerning the being of God:

> The application of our ordinary language to speak about God involves a fundamental shift in its meaning. We cannot but use language taken from our common experience in this world when we make theological statements, but even so it is the subject that must be allowed to determine the meaning. It would be inherently wrong to use expressions like 'right' or 'bosom' or even 'father' and 'son' as if they meant when applied to God the same thing they mean when used of creatures. It is thus one of the most important elements of theological activity to discern the basic change in meaning which our ordinary speech undergoes, lest we should speak in merely human terms of God or speak in unwarranted ways of creatures.[206]

To teach that 'being' applies univocally to both God and man (as Duns Scotus appears to teach) seems to veer towards a blurring of the Creator/creature distinction that runs from Genesis 1 to Revelation 22. If so, it opens the door for some very grave errors of thought that lower God and elevate man to a similar level (although Duns sought to guard against this himself, as we saw earlier).

This univocal predication seems to be placing God and man in a similar category of being, where some form of causation is therefore used in a similar fashion of them both. Karl Barth issues a needed warning here:

> If the term *causa* is to be applied legitimately, it must be clearly understood that it is not a master-concept to which both God and the creature are subject, nor is it a common denominator to which they may both be reduced. *Causa* is not a genus, of which the divine and creaturely *causa* can then be described as species. When we speak about the being of God and that of the creature, we are not dealing with two species of the one genus being. When we speak about the divine nature and the human nature of Christ, we are not dealing with two species of the one genus nature.[207]

Alan Torrance comments on Barth's meaning in this passage:

> For Barth, however, not only the content but the very fact of revelation suggests a divine ratification of the *non-parallelism* between the divine and human natures and the attendant *non-parallelism* between the different contexts in which the term 'cause' might be used…
>
> What is plain is that Barth refuses to determine the nature of the free Self-giving of God to be spoken of *independently* of the event of God's actually giving of himself to be spoken in and through the Logos and by the Spirit… The point is that Barth refuses to establish *a priori* as foundational any particular set of parameters in terms of which the nature of God-talk – its meaning, function and capacity to refer – requires to be understood.[208]

---

[205]Thomas V. Morris, *Our Idea of God: An Introduction to Philosophical Theology* (Downers Grove, IL: Intervarsity Press, 1991), 16-26.

[206]T. F. Torrance, *Theology in Reconstruction*, 30, 31.

[207]Karl Barth, *Church Dogmatics* III/3, (Edinburgh: T & T Clark, 1998), 102.

[208]Alan J. Torrance, op. cit., 148, 149.

Eberhard Jüngel, I believe, gives us a safer and sounder way concerning the use of similar terms for both God and man, when he notes that: 'The criterion of the truth of theological statements is, for Barth, given rather in the fact that in all theological statements the freedom of the subject of the revelation remains safeguarded.'[209] He adds: 'God's presence in the parable of the sacramental reality must not be allowed to lead to equating God with our reality, if God is not to be objectified by man.'[210]

On the contrary, Jüngel speaks of language itself being 'commandeered' by revelation...which is '*demanded* of language from outside it' [referring to Barth's *Church Dogmatics* I/1, 339].[211] Further, 'But where revelation commandeers language, *the word of God* takes place. The word of God brings language to its true essence.'[212]

What T. F. Torrance says concerning the usage Athanasius makes of the classical term παράδειγμα can help us grasp the significant concept of Jüngel:

> Athanasius uses it to refer to some aspect of the visible or physical world which is adopted and adapted to point out something that cannot be reduced to words or to point upward to a divine reality that is ultimately ineffable or to reflect the glory of God which we are unable to see. He does not think of παράδειγμα as a simile of man's choosing or devising, but rather as an image taken from human things which divine Revelation has laid hold of and uses in a special way for its particular purpose – that is why we cannot really understand παραδέιγματα apart from the condescending grace of God in divine Οικονομία.[213]

This is a far different approach from supposing that language about the being of God and the being of man has to be used univocally in order to make sense. Thus, I think that Athanasius is far more in accord with the way Holy Scripture uses language than is Duns Scotus.

Secondly, the highly abstract nature of Scotus's proof. It is necessary to be careful here in criticizing abstraction. The mere fact of abstraction, in the sense of drawing a particular doctrine of God from the Scriptures and then stating it in a very different, less concrete, and more theologically abstract form, cannot in and of itself, be fairly urged against Duns Scotus, unless it is urged against every other theologian. All theology and all preaching does this in some way or other. As Geerhardus Vos has pointed out, even those types of theology which seek to be closest to Scripture (such as 'biblical' or 'historical redemptive' theology, as compared to 'systematic' or 'dogmatic' theology) are alike in that '...both equally make the truth deposited in the Bible undergo a transformation... Biblical theology draws a line of development; systematic theology draws a circle.'[214]

---

[209]Eberhard Jüngel, *The Doctrine of the Trinity: God's Being is in Becoming* (Grand Rapids, MI: Wm.B. Eerdmans Publ. Co, 1976), 59.

[210]Ibid., 60.

[211]Ibid., 13.

[212]Ibid., 14.

[213]T. F. Torrance, *Divine Meaning: Studies in Patristic Hermeneutics* (Edinburgh: T & T Clark, 1995), 255.

[214]Geerhardus Vos, *Biblical Theology*, (Grand Rapids, MI: Wm. B Eerdmans Company, 1975), 15.

But the kind of theological/philosophical abstraction employed by Duns Scotus goes far beyond this. What Torrance notes about the even more extreme form of abstraction employed by William of Occam (which cannot be directly charged to Duns Scotus) sounds a proper warning about theological abstractionism: 'But if, as Ockham taught, abstractive knowledge abstracts from actual existence, then abstractive knowledge prevents us from knowing God in accordance with his own personal mode of being.'[215]

By 'abstracting' the peculiar characteristics of the being of God in order to consider Him univocally with mankind, something happens to the God whom he is proving. He seems more like 'the God of the philosophers than the God of Abraham, Isaac and Jacob' (to paraphrase Pascal). What T. F. Torrance says would accord, I believe, with the concerns of Pascal: 'And knowledge of God is gained not through abstraction from knowledge of sensible realities but by direct intuitive experience of God which we are given through his Word and Spirit.'[216]

Yet in favor of Scotus, it has been already noted that he attributes infinity to God, and not to creatures, and that he definitely believes in the Holy Trinity as a relationship of love within God.[217] Also, in his favor, he devotes Chapter IV of his *De Primo Principio* to establishing important attributes or qualities of the Being of God: 'The Simplicity, Infinity and Intellectuality of the First Being.' But the way he achieves his proof by abstracting so much of the biblical witness to God's personal characteristics, to explain 'being as being', gives the appearance at least of becoming so abstract that he lets philosophy run far beyond, and far afield, of the biblical and traditional theological testimony of the Church at the risk of obscuring the personal nature of God. Where does this sort of thing stop? Perhaps that is answered by the Nominalists, who in some respects (though not all), followed Scotus, but in a much more heterodox direction.

It is very interesting to note with A.–A. Upinsky that 'The fourteenth century was marked by the production of abstract words. Orême [a Nominalist, slightly later than Scotus] brought in three hundred Latin words to enrich French.'[218] Among these words was 'abstraction'! Something was taking place in the fourteenth century (the century of the Black Death, the Hundred Years War, the split of the Papacy, the 'little ice age,' etc.) that was 'shaking' Western Christendom 'loose' from its calm Patristic and earlier Scholastic certainties and approaches. It would have been surprising if Duns had not been influenced by this changing atmosphere of abstraction and freer philosophical speculation.

While Duns was a realist on the question of universals, and not a nominalist,[219] still his abstract methodology that is little controlled by a reading of Scripture seems to have opened the door for the Nominalists who soon followed him, who were far more abstract, and much further

[215]T. F. Torrance, *Theology in Reconstruction*, 84, 85.

[216]T. F. Torrance, *Theology in Reconstruction*, 273.

[217]See A. Broadie, op. cit., 36.

[218]A. – A. Upinsky, *La Tête coupée: Le Secret du Pouvoir* (Paris: Le Bec, 1998), 275.

[219]A. Broadie, op. cit., 25,47.

removed from Scripture. If André De Muralt is right, this abstractive and speculative methodology of Scotus would in several respects prepare the way for the Nominalist, William of Occam, whose metaphysical and especially political ideas, when carried to their conclusions much later, would eventually wreak havoc with the social and political structures of Western Christian society.[220] But of course, Scotus never intended nor foresaw such developments. Yet his abstractive speculation seems to have been a factor in the serious theological decline found in nominalism.[221]

Thirdly, the length and complexity of Scotus's proof, as contrasted with those of Anselm and Aquinas, raise questions about the possibility of its usefulness to the Church (even to the high levels of the intellectual leadership of the Church). Certainly, complexity is never enough to demonstrate that something is untrue or unuseful. If that were the case, then the discovery by Watson and Crick of the DNA Code would be written off, as would the 'irreducible complexity of the human cell' (to quote Michael Behe), or the mechanical complexity of the jet engine of an airplane! But as far as the usefulness of a proof for God for human minds (even very bright ones), the work of Duns Scotus (which I cannot help but respect) does seem very tenuous at best.

It is probable that in the nearly seven hundred years after Scotus, some pilgrims have been helped along their way by his proof. If so, then his pains were worthwhile. Presumably this has been the case for many in the Franciscan order, and no doubt for others. That could be part of the reason why the Roman Church in 1993 elevated him to the title of *Beatus*. But as for this *viator*, all I can say is that if I were looking for convincing theistic proofs, I would turn towards either St. Anselm or St. Thomas Aquinas. But as it is, I think that the pressure of the reality of God imposes itself upon all humans in creation, in conscience, and above all, in the revelation of His Word, so that I am not sure that proofs are needed. Still, with Herman Bavinck, I feel that the theistic proofs are 'strong as testimonies,' and I respect them as such.

This, I hope, is not the same as 'fideism', for I always assume that finally the true deliverances of faith[222] are consonant with the valid deliverances of non-autonomous reason,[223] if both are properly understood in light of who God is and how He has revealed Himself and His truth. And that seems to be the assumption of such biblical passages as Psalm 19, John 1 and Romans 1 and 2, to mention only a few significant texts out of hundreds.

Although I would take a much higher view of theistic proofs as valid testimonies than does Fr. Justin Popovitch, major theologian of the Serbian

---

[220]André de Muralt, *L'Unité de la Philosophie Politique de Scot, Occam et Suarez au Libéralisme Contemporain* (Paris: Vrin, 2002), 146-156.

[221]I am aware that the famous Reformation and Late Medieval scholar, Heiko Oberman, in *The Harvest of Medieval Theology: Gabriel Biel and Late Medieval Nominalism* (Durham, NC: The Labyrinth Press, 1983), holds that Nominalism was not a 'decline' in theology (see his 'Introduction': 1-7).Yet from the point of view of biblical orthodoxy, it could scarcely be denied that Nominalism loosed its moorings from Scripture, and tended towards a Pelagian view of the nature, with extremely elevated views of the intellectual powers of man that were not consonant with Christian orthodoxy.

[222]Never contradictory to God speaking in Scripture.

[223]Never setting itself up as an independent authority with the right to overrule or reject God speaking in Scripture.

Orthodox Church, nevertheless I wish to conclude with his words on this matter:

> For the church, as for the revelation itself, the truth concerning the existence of God is not a logical hypothesis which must be demonstrated by way of logical syllogisms; it is a truth revealed by God and therefore, incontestable. Since it is a divine reality, this truth does not flow from a proof, from a demonstration, or from logical functions of reason.[224] The logical proofs hide God as much as they uncover Him. Also man loses himself in the antinomies [involved in such proofs], because he cannot find through them this bridge of faith which helps him pass over towards God above the uncrossable abyss of irreconcilable antinomies. It is because the dogma of the existence of God is a revealed and eternal truth that it draws it main demonstrative force from the holy Revelation…[225]

[224]I believe that Fr. Popovitch means here 'autonomous reason', for he knows that we have to employ reason to receive the witness of Scripture.

[225]Justin Popovitch, *Philosophie Orthodoxe de la Vérité: Tome Premier,* 104.

Chapter One
Appendix Two

Thomas Reid Answers David Hume on Causation

Decades ago, the great Edinburgh philosopher, A. E. Taylor, pointed out the acuity of the responses Dr. Thomas Reid gave to the philosophy of David Hume, particularly as concerns the validity of the universal assumption of cause and effect.[1] Hume denied this assumption in order to escape its testimony to the existence, activity and final judgement of the Creator God. In this appendix, I shall abstract (without much comment) several of the crucial points argued by Reid against Hume's skepticism and in favor of the overwhelming belief in cause and effect. I believe that Reid's writing is so clear in these extracts that it requires almost no explanation, other than to be put in its context.

These extracts are taken from a recent edition of Reid's *Essays on the Intellectual Powers of Man*.[2] First, we refer to Essay II – 'Of the Powers we have by means of our external senses.'

The philosophical assumption of 'ideas' 'in-between' the mind and the object perceived (or in place of the object perceived)

In Chapter 7 of Essay II, Reid pinpoints the great point at issue:

> Plato's subterranean cave, and Mr. Locke's dark closet, may be applied with ease to all the systems of perception that have been invented: For they all suppose that we perceive not external objects immediately, and that the immediate objects of perception are only certain shadows of the external objects. Those shadows or images, which we immediately perceive, were by the ancients called *species, forms, phantasms*. Since the time of Des Cartes, they have commonly been called *ideas*, and by Mr. Hume *impressions*. But all philosophers, from Plato to Mr. Hume, agree in this, That we do not perceive

[1]A. E. Taylor, *Platonism and its Influence* (New York: Longmans, Green & Co., 1927), p.55 and 138, n. 32.

[2]*Thomas Reid: Essays on the Intellectual Powers of Man*, edited by Derek R. Brookes, annotations by Derek R. Brookes & Knud Haakonssen; introduction by Knud Haakonssen (University Park, Pennsylvania: The Pennsylvania State University Press, 2002).

> external objects immediately, and that the immediate object of perception must be some image present to the mind.[3]
>
> It seems, therefore, that their opinion is, That we do not really perceive the external object, but the internal object only; and that when they speak of perceiving external objects, they mean it only in a popular or in a figurative sense…The way in which Philosophers speak of ideas, seems to imply that they are the only objects of perception.[4]
>
> [Descartes held] That the external object itself is not perceived, but only the species or image of it in the mind…it is only a representative image, in the mind, of the external object that we perceive, and not the object itself… [Descartes and his successors hold] that the objects we immediately perceive are ideas only. All their systems are built on this foundation.[5]

In Chapter 9 of Essay II, after a discussion of the epistemology of John Locke, Reid rightly shows the problem of not distinguishing the mind from the things it knows: '…that it should lead ingenious men who adopt it to confound the operations of the mind with their objects, and with one another, even when the common language of the unlearned clearly distinguishes them.'[6]

In Chapter 11, Reid answers as follows:

> In sensation, properly so called, I can distinguish two things, the mind or sentient being, and the sensation. Whether the last is to be called a feeling or an operation, I dispute not; but it has no object distinct from the sensation itself. If in sensation there be a third thing, called an idea, I know not what it is.
>
> In perception, in remembrance, and in conception, or imagination, I distinguish three things, the mind that operates, the operation of the mind, and the object of that operation. That the object perceived is one thing, and the perception of that object another, I am as certain as I can be of anything… There must be an object, real or imaginary, distinct from the operation of the mind about it. Now, if in these operations the idea be a fourth thing different from the three I have mentioned, I know not what it is, nor have been able to learn from all that has been written about ideas. And if the doctrine of Philosophers about ideas confounds any two of these things which I have mentioned as distinct; if, for example, it confounds the object perceived with the perception of that object, and represents them as one and the same thing, such doctrine is altogether repugnant to all that I am able to discover of the operations of my own mind; and it is repugnant to the common sense of mankind, expressed in the structure of all languages.[7]

In Chapter 12, Dr. Reid deals with the teaching of David Hume, particularly from his two *Treatises of Human Nature*. He shows that Hume:

---

[3]Ibid., op. cit., 105.
[4]Ibid., 106.
[5]Ibid., 125, 126.
[6]Ibid., 137.
[7]Ibid., 161.

> … adopts the theory of ideas in its full extent; and, in consequence, shews that there is neither matter nor mind in the universe; nothing but impressions and ideas. What we call a *body*, is only a bundle of sensations; and what we call the *mind*, is only a bundle of thoughts, passions, and emotions, without any subject…[8]
>
> …But in Hume's [system], the idea or the impression, which is only a more lively idea, is mind, perception, and object, all in one…Mr. Hume adopts Locke's account of the origin of our ideas, and from that principle infers, that we have no idea of substance corporeal or spiritual, no idea of power, no other idea of a cause, but that it is something antecedent, and constantly conjoined to that which we call its effect; and, in a word, that we can have no idea of any thing but our sensations, and the operations of mind we are conscious of…and the mind is nothing but that succession of impressions and ideas of which we are intimately conscious.
>
> He thinks, therefore, that our impressions arise from unknown causes, and that the impressions are the causes of their corresponding ideas. By this he means no more but that they always go before the ideas; for this is all that is necessary to constitute the relation of cause and effect…causation, according to him, implies no more than contiguity in time and place.[9]

David Hume holds that we perceive 'ideas', not real things

In Chapter 14, Thomas Reid gets to the heart of the issue between sceptics and 'the common sense' public, by arguing that what we directly perceive are 'real things, not ideas.'[10] But on the contrary, philosophers such as Hume held that

> …we do not see the sun immediately, but an idea; or as Mr. Hume calls it, an impression, in our own minds…But say the philosophers, beside those objects which all men acknowledge [e.g. the mind, its operations, and objects of perception], there is a more immediate object which really exists in the mind at the same time we remember or imagine. This object is an idea or image of the thing remembered or imagined.[11]

Reid gives five arguments against interposing 'ideas'

Reid responds to this philosophical interposition of 'something in between' the perceiving mind and the perceived object with *five* reflections:

(1) It is contrary to universal common sense

> The *first* reflection I would make on this philosophical opinion is, That it is directly contrary to the universal sense of men who have not been instructed in philosophy. When we see the sun or moon, we have no doubt that the very objects which we immediately see, are very far distant from us, and from one another… But how we are astonished when the Philosopher informs

[8]Ibid., 162.
[9]Ibid., 164, 165.
[10]Ibid., 171.
[11]Ibid., 171, 172.

> us, that we are mistaken in all this; that the sun and moon which we see, are not, as we imagine, many miles distant from us, and from each other, but that they are in our own mind; that they had no existence before we saw them, and will have none when we cease to perceive and to think of them; because the objects we perceive are only ideas in our own minds, which can have no existence a moment longer than we think of them…[12]

(2) Its supporters hold it without proof

> A *second* reflection upon this subject is, That the authors who have treated of ideas, have generally taken their existence for granted, as a thing that could not be called in question; and such arguments as they have mentioned incidentally, in order to prove it, seem too weak to support the conclusion.[13]

Reid realizes that 'though we are conscious of perceiving objects, we are altogether ignorant how it is brought about; and know as little how we perceive objects as how we were made.'[14] Yet he then closely argues that this universally held supposition makes more sense of how we perceive and deal with external reality than to conclude that all we can know is 'something in between' our mind and the supposed object of knowledge. Which one, he asks, makes the most sense of reality?

> Shall we say that a false supposition, invented by the rude vulgar, has been so lucky in solving an infinite number of phaenomena of nature? This surely would be a greater prodigy than philosophy ever exhibited: Add to this, that upon the contrary hypothesis, to wit, that the objects of sight are internal, no account can be given of any one of those appearances, nor any physical cause assigned why a visible object should, in one case, have one apparent figure and magnitude rather than another.
>
> Thus I have considered every argument I have found advanced to prove the existence of ideas, or images of external things, in the mind: And if no better arguments can be found, I cannot help but thinking, that the whole of philosophy has never furnished an instance of an opinion so unanimously entertained by Philosophers upon so slight grounds.[15]

(3) Philosophers are unclear as to what ideas mean

> A *third* reflection I would make upon this subject is, That Philosophers, notwithstanding their unanimity as to the existence of ideas, hardly agree in any one thing else concerning them. If ideas be not a mere fiction, they must be, of all objects of human knowledge, the things we have best access to know, and to be acquainted with; yet there is nothing about which men differ so much.[16]

---

[12]Ibid., 172.
[13]Ibid., 174.
[14]Ibid., 178.
[15]Ibid., 183,184.
[16]Ibid., 184.

(4) The assumption of 'in-between ideas' does not clarify the operations of the mind

> A *fourth* reflection is, That ideas do not make any of the operations of the mind to be better understood, although it was probably with that view that they have been invented, and afterwards so generally received.[17]

How then does Reid account for perception? Reid freely admits the difficulty of accounting for perception: 'We are at a loss to know how we perceive distant objects; how we remember things past; how we imagine things that have no existence.' Then, he notes that the theory of ideas or 'something in between' the mind and what it knows, 'seems to account for all these operations'.[18] He then argues that this representative theory of perception actually makes things worse, for it tends to confound the mind with what it knows.

It is best simply to accept that we have been created with the capacity to perceive:

> ... there must therefore be in the percipient a power to feel or to perceive. How this power is produced, and how it operates, is quite beyond the reach of our knowledge. As little can we know whether this power must be limited to things present, and in contact with us [*sc.* as required by Hume's theory]. Nor can any man pretend to prove, that the Being, who gave us the power to perceive things present, may not give us the power to perceive things past, and to conceive things that never existed.[19]

Not to assume the proper functioning of perception of external reality leads to confounding one's mind with reality itself and necessitates an unnatural language:

> ...this theory has led Philosophers to confound those operations of mind, which experience teaches all men to be different, and teaches them to distinguish in common language; and that it has led them to invent a language inconsistent with the principles upon which all language is grounded.[20]

(5) The consequences of this theory are repulsive to common sense

> The *last* reflection I shall make upon this theory, is, That the natural and necessary consequences of it furnish a just prejudice against it to every man who pays a due regard to the common sense of mankind.[21]

Reid lists some of these consequences, particularly as they flow from the systems of Berkeley and Hume:

> That there is no material world: No abstract ideas or notions: That the mind is only a train of related impressions and ideas, without any subject on

[17]Ibid.
[18]Ibid., 185.
[19]Ibid.
[20]Ibid.
[21]Ibid.

> which they may be impressed: That there is neither space nor time, body or mind, but impressions and ideas only: And, to sum up all, That there is no probability, even in demonstration itself, nor any one proposition more probable than its contrary.[22]

Metaphysical first principles as regards causation

In Essay VI, 'Of Judgment', Thomas Reid discusses in Chapter 6, 'First Principles of necessary Truths.' Some of these are very relevant to establishing the case for belief in cause and effect, specifically, to accepting evidence of the existence of the Creator by means of what we perceive in the created order. For our purposes here, we need not examine what he says (correctly, I think) about those first principles in grammar, logic, mathematics, taste and morals.

Instead, we will keep to his observations concerning first principles in metaphysics, as these most directly bear upon David Hume's denial of causation, and thus, of creation of the universe by God. Reid comments in particular upon *three* metaphysical first principles which had been denied by Hume.

(1) We must assume a body and a mind

> The *first* is, That the qualities which we perceive by our senses must have a subject, which we call body, and that the thoughts we are conscious of must have a subject, which we call mind...The difficulty which some Philosophers have found in admitting this, is entirely owing to the theory of ideas...in the style of Mr. Hume, from what impression is the idea of substance derived? It is not a copy of any impression; therefore there is no such idea.[23]

Reid's answer is that the very structure of languages naturally assumes a distinction between the mind and what it perceives, and that without this distinction one cannot deal with the real world:

> The distinction between sensible qualities, and the substance to which they belong, and between thought and the mind that thinks it, is not the invention of Philosophers; it is found in the structure of all languages, and therefore must be common to all men who speak with understanding. And I believe no man, however sceptical he may be in speculation, can talk on the common affairs of life for half an hour, without saying things that imply his belief of the reality of these distinctions.[24]

First Principles require no proof, for they make possible proof for everything else. As Reid shows, the very nature of a *first principle* is that it is a *given*; it is something essential for us to make sense of life and the world. Proof outside it, above it or beyond it, is neither available, nor necessary, for these first principles. That is precisely what makes

---

[22]Ibid., 187.
[23]Ibid., 495,496.
[24]Ibid., 496.

them *first* principles: we necessarily start with them in order to get anywhere else.

> ...there are principles of belief in human nature, of which we can give no other account but that they necessarily result from the constitution of our faculties; and that if it were in our power to throw off their influence upon our practice and conduct, we could neither speak nor act like reasonable men.
>
> We cannot give a reason why we believe even our sensations to be real and not fallacious; why we believe what we are conscious of; why we trust any of our natural faculties. We say, it must be so, it cannot be otherwise. This expresses only a strong belief, which is indeed the voice of Nature, and which therefore in vain we attempt to resist.[25]

(2) Whatever begins to exist must have a cause

The *second* metaphysical principle mentioned by Reid is 'That whatever begins to exist, must have a cause which produced it.'[26] He shows that it is, indeed, a first principle: 'That it is self-evident and needs no proof, but ought to be received as an axiom, which cannot by responsible men be called into question.'[27] Reid enumerates various attempts to prove this axiom of causation, and agrees with Hume that 'they take for granted the thing to be proved...'[28]

Reid, while unable to prove this (or any other *first principle*), does offer reasons for the universal assumption of cause and effect. (1) 'This universal belief of mankind is easily accounted for, if we allow that the necessity of a cause of every event is obvious to the rational powers of a man. But it is impossible to account for it otherwise.'[29]

His second argument for it is, 'That the practice of life is grounded upon it in the most important matters, even in cases where experience leaves us doubtful; and it is impossible to act with common prudence if we set it aside.'[30] Reid then shows from Hume's own writings that he has to assume the necessity of causes in order to make his case.[31]

(3) Intelligent design may be correctly inferred from signs in the creation

The third metaphysical principle discussed by Reid in his debate against Hume's denial of causation and creation is: 'That design, and intelligence in the cause, may be inferred, with certainty, from marks or signs of it in the effect.'[32] This holds true both in moral and

---

[25]Ibid., 497.
[26]Ibid.
[27]Ibid.
[28]Ibid., 498.
[29]Ibid., 501.
[30]Ibid.
[31]Reid shows how Hume does this in his *Treatise of Human Nature*, I.iii.5, in op. cit., 502, 503.

physical judgments.

> Yet it is to be observed, that we judge of men's talents with as little doubt or hesitation as we judge of the immediate objects of sense...From this it appears, that it is no less a part of the human constitution, to judge of men's characters, and of their intellectual powers, from the signs of them in their actions and discourse, than to judge of corporeal objects by our senses: That such judgments are common to the whole human race that are endowed with understanding; and that they are absolutely necessary in the conduct of life.[33]

Reid shows that this is truly a *first principle*, in that it is 'too universal to be the effect of reasoning...of those who are governed by it, not one in ten thousand can give a reason for it.'[34] Moreover, it is not something we learn merely by experience, because it has to be in place for us to make sense of our experience.[35]

Reid goes on to apply the concept of inferred design to the created order. What he says here is the normal syllogism[36] and requires no comment, except for one point, particularly aimed at Hume's attack on the principle. Hume had argued, 'That the universe is a singular effect, and therefore, we can draw no conclusion from it, whether it may have been made by wisdom or not.'[37]

Reid explains that Hume hopes to avoid the power of this argument from design in creation by holding that we would need to have seen several worlds produced, 'some by wisdom and others without it...[in order to conclude] that such a world as this which we inhabit was always the effect of wisdom; but having no such experience, we have no means of forming any conclusions about it.'[38]

Reid exposes the pivot of Hume's argument here:[39]

> Whence it appears that this reasoning of Mr. Hume is built on the supposition, that our inferring design from the strongest marks of it, is entirely owing to our past experience of having always found these two things conjoined. But I hope I have made it evident that this is not the case. And indeed it is evident, that, according to this reasoning, we can have no evidence of mind or design in any of our fellow-men.[40]

---

[32]Reid, op. cit., 503.

[33]Ibid., 503, 504.

[34]Ibid., 504.

[35]Ibid., 507, 508.

[36]i.e. '*First*, That design and intelligence in the cause, may, with certainty, be inferred from marks or signs of it in the effect (the major proposition). The *second*, (the minor proposition) is That there are in fact clearest marks of design and wisdom in the works of Nature; and the conclusion is, that the works of Nature are the effects of a wise and intelligent cause', from ibid., 509, 510.

[37]Ibid., 511.

[38]Ibid.

[39]Hume, *Treatise on Human Nature*, I.iv.5.

[40]Reid, op. cit., 511.

That is, Reid has already demonstrated that the concept of cause and effect is in the category of *first principle*. Because of its nature as a *given* axiom by which we make sense of everything else, it neither admits of, nor needs philosophical proof, and it – precisely as a first principle – is not derived from our experience (whether of one world or a thousand). Hence, Hume's attempt to discount causation and thereby, the witness of the creation to the Creator, by requiring past experience of several worlds coming into existence is utterly beside the point.

Chapter Two

Knowledge of the Triune God through Creation and Conscience

An inescapable sense of religious obligation is felt by all mankind. It arises from the presence of the Triune God pressing upon us in external creation and internal conscience. Old and New Testaments testify to a certain binding knowledge of God within pagan nations. This pressure from God or 'revelation' has traditionally been spoken of as 'natural' or 'general' (from creation and conscience; non-verbal) and 'supernatural' or 'special' (given to the covenant community; verbal). Sin has caused humans to misinterpret what they know of God in nature in self-serving directions. But God has from the beginning established a covenant community, to whom has been given a gracious personal relationship with Him and words by which to understand Him and His will. Attempted explanations of who God is apart from this community relationship and verbal revelation of the Trinity are inadequate. The Triune God in all His Being, works and ways is properly known only in a saving, covenant relationship to Him. From this perspective, the universe, with its intelligibility and reliability, is found to be open upwards, not closed in upon itself. One level of being after another is open to yet a higher level. Ultimately the universe itself is caused by its Creator and Sustainer to function as a way of bringing believing mankind into the beatitude of personal relationship with the Trinity. Those in this favoured position are commissioned to spread the light to the rest of mankind; to call them to faith and repentance.

I. The Reality of Religion

Even in this time of advanced secularism that grips the intellectual centers of much of Western civilisation, it is still generally recognized that some sense of religion is all-pervasive throughout the world, including those areas whose cultural leaders have rejected one religious system after another: biblical Christianity, Enlightenment Deism, the various Western syntheses between liberal Christianity and democracy theory that resulted in the civil religion so popular up to the 1950s, and finally the peculiarly religious aspects of Marxism. Although Karl Marx in the early nineteenth century wished to explain away religion as 'the opium of the people',[1] and expected this 'drug dependency' soon to be renounced in favour of his economic interpretation of reality as the only way to human happiness, traditional religion has outlasted the Soviet Empire, and to a certain degree determines the various divisions and armed conflicts that recently engulfed central and eastern Europe. At the end of the second millennium, whether an ethnic group was Eastern Orthodox, Roman Catholic or Muslim seemed more basic to the borders they choose than any particular theory of economics.

Since the overthrow of the secularist Shah of Iran by the Muslim 'Fundamentalists' in the 1970s, and the geopolitical upsurge of militant Islam, the 'historicist' assumption that 'the pendulum can never swing backwards' (from a secularist to a religious organization of society) is, to say the least, lacking in empirical validation. Those who reject the truth claims of the various religions, and particularly those who predicted the obsolescence of traditional belief systems in the light of modern progress, are far from having proven their case in the court of current events, impressive though their arguments may have appeared in the realm of some philosophical theories.

The continuing universal experience of religion among humankind calls for analysis, whether one approves of the perennial phenomenon or not. The basic idea of religion lies in a sense of God, or spiritual reality, and is marked by a feeling of obligation to Him. John Calvin wrote:

> There is within the human mind, and indeed by natural instinct, an awareness of divinity…To prevent anyone from taking refuge in the pretence of ignorance, God himself has implanted in all men a certain understanding of his divine majesty. Ever renewing its memory, he repeatedly sheds fresh drops…
>
> Men of sound judgment will always be sure that a sense of divinity which can never be effaced is engraved upon men's minds. Indeed, the perversity of the impious, who though they struggle furiously are unable to extricate themselves from the fear of God, is abundant testimony that this conviction, namely, that there is some God, is naturally inborn in all, and is fixed deep within, as it were in the very marrow.[2]

There is a good reason for this. The one true God who has revealed Himself in His written Word, and supremely in Jesus Christ, is none other than the Creator of heaven and earth. God created this world to reflect His glory (e.g., see Ps. 8 and 19), and created mankind as His image-bearers to perceive and articulate that glory in obedience and praise back to its Creator (e.g., see Ps. 65, 66, 67, 135, 146–150). Therefore, both the external created order and the internal, conscious being of humankind speak of the existence, glory and authority of God, the holy, mighty and beneficent Creator. But, as we see from the Scriptures, the *fact* of creation is not to be interpreted apart from the *purposes* of creation. These purposes come to light in the concept of covenant.

---

[1]Karl Marx, *Contributionà la philosophie du droit de Hegel*, in *Oeuvres Philosophiques*, (Paris: Champ Libre, 1981), t.l, p. 84

[2]John Calvin, *Institutes*, I.iii. 1, 3 translated by Ford Lewis Battles (Philadelphia, PA: *The Library of Christian Classics*: The Westminster Press, 1960), vol. 1.

Covenant and creation

Much of classical theology has taught that creation itself is to be seen within the context of a divinely ordered covenant.[3] Pierre Courthial has drawn together covenant and creation as follows:

> Everything [concerning the Covenant of Grace] begins with the first part of Genesis, the indisputable fountainhead of the Bible, and with the first man, Adam. That is where one finds the beginning of the Covenant and of the history of the Covenant...It is only with Noah that the word 'Covenant' (in Hebrew בְּרִית) actually appears for the first time in the Bible. In Genesis 6:17-18, one reads this word from God to Noah: 'I will cause a flood to come upon the earth ... but with thee will I confirm my covenant.'
>
> An all too frequent French translation is found here, 'I will establish my covenant.' However, even though the form (known as *hiphil* in Hebrew) of the Hebrew verb *qum* can signify 'to establish', it can also just as well signify 'to ratify', 'to confirm'. And in chapters 6, 9 and 17 of Genesis, as in Exodus 6, every time covenant appears, one must choose the translation 'to confirm' rather than the translation 'to establish'. Why? Simply because the preceding general context reveals, as we have seen, the Covenant of Grace already existed since the time of Adam (and even before the Fall of Adam!) and that the immediately preceding context also shows us that Noah is already in the Covenant before this one is 'confirmed' for him, for his family and his descendants. In Genesis 6:8-9 (thus before 6:18) it says: 'Noah found grace in the eyes of the Lord...Noah was a righteous and just man in his generation. Noah walked with God.' Now no-one could obtain favour of the Lord, no-one could be righteous and just, no-one could walk with God, unless it were *within* the Covenant of Grace, this Covenant which God calls *my Covenant*.[4]

Some of the seventeenth-century Reformed theologians spoke of this as part of a 'Covenant of Redemption' (among the three persons of the Holy Trinity in relation to the future creation, fall and redemption of the cosmos), and others have thought of it as the 'pre-temporal' aspect of the one great Covenant of Grace. Karl Barth, for instance, speaks of creation as 'the external basis of the covenant', and the covenant as 'the internal basis of creation'.[5] He states: 'Creation sets the stage for the story of the covenant of grace...Creation must not be separated from this context.'[6]

Strictly speaking, Scripture itself never uses the term 'Covenant of Redemption' (nor ever actually applies the word 'covenant' to any arrangement pre-dating the creation of humankind). Yet some kind of pre-

---

[3]The word 'covenant' [בְּרִית] is not found in Genesis chapters 1 to 5. It is first used regarding God's promise to Noah in Genesis 6:18, 'But with thee will I establish my covenant...' W. J. Dumbrell suggests that since the phrase 'establish', rather than 'cut' a covenant (which implies newness) is employed, the idea is to re-establish something already in force, hence implying an original covenant which contemplated the earth, now to be destroyed by a flood. (W. J. Dumbrell, *Creation and Covenant*, Nashville, TN: Thomas Nelson, 1984, 32). Dumbrell also refers to Hosea 2:18, where God makes a covenant between Israel and the earth, thus implying that the earth was already 'covenanted'. Hosea 6:7 speaks of Adam (or mankind) 'breaking the covenant', and Jeremiah 33:19-20, refers to the covenant of day and night which cannot be altered, which covenant would have to go back to 'creation week' of Genesis 1 and 2.

[4]Pierre Courthial, *Le Jour Des Petits Recommencements: Essai sur l'Actualité de la Parole (Evangile-Loi)* (Lausanne: Messages: L'Age D'Homme, 1996), 3, 6.

[5]Karl Barth, *Church Dogmatics*, III. 1, section 41.

[6]Ibid., III. 1, p.44.

temporal 'covenant concept' seems to be implied in its teaching that Christ is 'the lamb slain from before the foundation of the world' (Rev. 13:8) and in the high priestly prayer of Christ: 'Father, I will that they also, whom thou has given me, be with me where I am: that they may behold my glory, which thou has given me: for thou lovedst me before the foundation of the world' (John 17:24). Thus, from all eternity the Father and Son encompass the knowledge of the world that is to be in the bonds of the mutual knowledge characterized by the love and glory that they share with one another and with the Holy Spirit.

God the Father Almighty, Creator of heaven and earth (cf. Gen. 1:1), spoke the cosmos into being through the agency of His eternal Son (cf. John 1:3), to be a 'theater' (in Calvin's words) through which His glory would shine to the sons and daughters of Adam and Eve. Thus, creation was planned in terms of the descendants of the first Adam, and its agent was He whom Paul speaks of in Romans 5:12-21 as the 'last Adam'. Hosea 6:7 speaks of Adam (or, as most translations have it, 'man' in the generic) 'breaking the covenant.' 'In the fulness of the time' (Gal. 4:4) the Father sends His own Son, who will keep the covenant both from God's side and from the side of humankind.

The context in which the Son keeps the covenant is the created order, blighted by sin through the covenant breaking of Adam. Only the Agent of creation is sufficient to be the Redeemer of creation. And it is in this context of a creation needing redemption (and then unilaterally being redeemed) that Scripture discusses the reality of human religion. Thus the covenant (and the divine revelation in which it is established) is prior to 'the sense of the divine' that characterizes humankind's understanding of God within creation.

This universal sense of the divine has two major roots, according to the Holy Scriptures: first, the testimony of God within the external created order, and second, His speaking through mankind's internal conscience. We must survey some central scriptural passages on both of these realities.

A. The Testimony of God within the Created Order

Romans 1:18-23 is a classic text describing the reality and severe limits of fallen mankind's sense of God within the creation:

> 18. For the wrath of God is revealed from heaven against all ungodliness and unrighteousness of men, who hold the truth in unrighteousness;
>
> 19. Because that which may be known of God is manifest in them; for God hath shewed it unto them.
>
> 20. For the invisible things of him from the creation of the world are clearly seen, being understood by the things that are made, even his eternal power and Godhead; so that they are without excuse:
>
> 21. Because that, when they knew God, they glorified him not as God, neither were thankful; but became vain in their imaginations, and their foolish heart was darkened.
>
> 22. Professing themselves to be wise, they became fools.

> 23. And changed the glory of the uncorruptible God into an image made like to corruptible man, and to birds, and fourfooted beasts, and creeping things.

These verses are part of a larger section (Rom. 1:18–3:20), which establishes the universal sinfulness of all mankind, both Gentile and Jew (see 3:29); their lack of righteousness (3:23: 'All have sinned and come short of the glory of God'), and inability to save themselves (3:20: 'Therefore by the deeds of the law there shall no flesh be justified in his sight…'). All of this is to demonstrate the universal need of the gospel of grace (described in Rom. 3:21–5:21), which is a revelation of the righteousness of God, received through faith (see especially 3:21-31).

Details of the passage

Significantly, the term 'revelation' (ἀποκάλυψις – 'is revealed') is used in verse 17 of the righteousness of God, and immediately afterwards, in verse 18 of the wrath of God. Both of these verses follow the declaration in verse 16 that 'the gospel of Christ is the power of God unto salvation.' Cranfield describes the meaning of this parallelism between the two contiguous verses:

> In v. 17 he has stated that δικαιοσύνη θεοῦ in the gospel events themselves, a revelation indicated by the perfect πεφανέρωται in 3.21. In view of the parallelism between vv. 17 and 18, the most natural way of taking v. 18 is to understand Paul to mean that ὀργὴ θεοῦ also is being revealed *in the gospel*, that is, in the on-going proclamation of the gospel, and to recognise that behind, and basic to, this revelation of the wrath of God in the preaching, is the prior revelation of the wrath of God in the gospel events…The two revelations referred to in these two verses are then really two aspects of the same process…In the gospel the divine mercy and the divine judgment are inseparable from each other…[7]

In other words, the good news (the revelation of God's free gift of righteousness) makes sense only in the light of the bad news (the revelation of his wrath against our ungodliness and unrighteousness). The dark backdrop of the bad news about mankind (which makes the light of the gospel of Christ so glorious) is that our ungodliness and unrighteousness[8] cause the wrath of a holy God to be revealed against that which is contrary to his character of perfect holiness. Verses 18 through 23 show the inexcusability of mankind before God for failing to be godly and righteous.

'Holding Down' the Truth

The key concept is found in verse 18b: '…who *hold down* [κατεχόντων] the truth in unrighteousness…'[9] C. Spicq renders the sense of κατέχω (as used

---

[7]C. E. B. Cranfield, *A Critical and Exegetical Commentary on the Epistle to the Romans* (Vol. I), (Edinburgh: T. & T. Clark, 1975), 109, 110.

[8]It is significant that a wrong relationship to God (ἀσέβειαν) leads to immorality or unrighteousness (ἀδικίᾳ).

[9]The verb κατέχω in the New Testament predominantly means 'to hold fast' (Edited by G. Kittel, translated by G.W. Bromiley, *Theological Dictionary of the New Testament*, Grand Rapids, MI: Wm. B. Eerdmans, 1964), Vol. II, 829, but it also bears the figurative meaning of 'to suppress' or 'to hold down' (cf. H. Balz and G. Schneider, eds., *Exegetical Dictionary of the New Testament*, Grand Rapids: Eerdmans, 1991, Vol. 2, 277).

in this verse) as follows: '...human godlessness and unrighteousness "hold the truth" captive in the chains of unrighteousness. By not adhering to the truth from the heart and not submitting their conduct to it, they somehow shackle the divine truth and hold it in check.'[10] That is to say, men *suppress* what they know.[11] Verse 19 then explains *why* people suppress the truth.[12] Like Adam and Eve hiding in the Garden from God against whom they had sinned, all of their descendants are still attempting to hide from the reality of God. In order to do this, they must 'hold down' (or 'suppress') 'that which is known of God' [τὸ γνωστὸν τοῦ θεοῦ]. Cranfield's paraphrase is to the point: 'The phrase as a whole must mean "that which is knowable (to man) of God", i.e. "God, in so far as He is knowable (to man)."'[13]

The gravity of the sin involved in this kind of hiding from God is multiplied by the fact (brought out in v. 19b) that to do so, one is 'suppressing' what God Himself has revealed [ὁ γὰρ Θεὸς αὐτοῖς ἐφανέρωσε] to the one who desperately seeks to evade it. '...God's being manifest in His creation is the result of His own deliberate self-disclosure and not something in any way independent of His will.'[14] Verse 20 specifies the content of what God has clearly manifested to the human race about Himself, and the context in which He has made it known.

Visibility of God's qualities

God has manifested or, 'made visible' [ἐφανέρωσεν] those supreme realities which are invisible [ἀόρατα]; namely, His own personal properties of 'eternal power and divinity' [ἀΐδιος αὐτοῦ δύναμις καὶ θειότης]. Scripture constantly refers to the power of God from Genesis 1, where He speaks the cosmos into existence, to the last chapters of Revelation, where he brings all of space/time history to its glorious consummation of 'a new heaven and a new earth' (Rev. 21:1), planned by Him from before the beginning. '...power is so characteristic of God that ἡ δύναμις can be used as a periphrasis for the divine Name' (Matt. 26:64; Mark 14:62).[15] God has made it clear that his power does not come into being and then go out of existence, but rather is eternal [ἀΐδιος].

Along with his eternal power, God has also manifested clearly his divinity [θειότης]. This word is used only this once in the New Testament, and is related to the term deity [θεότης], which is also used only once in the New Testament (Col. 2:9). While deity refers to God's divine personality,

---

[10]Ceslas Spicq, *Theological Lexicon of the New Testament*, J. Ernest, translator, (Peabody, Mass.: Hendrickson Publ., 1994), Vol. 2, 288.

[11]Cranfield, *op. cit.*, 112, shows that the present participle of the verb κατεχόντων is to be understood as having a conative force, and thus to be translated as 'hold down' or 'suppress'.

[12] γὰρ ('for' or 'because') could be taken either to give the reason for the revelation of the wrath of God, or to explain why it is that humans resist the truth in unrighteousness. Either is possible, but the latter seems to fit more clearly into the sequence of thought introduced in the next words of verse 19 and explicated in verses 21-23.

[13]Cranfield, op. cit., 113, immediately adds: 'Paul's main purpose in putting as the subject of this sentence τὸ γνωστὸν τοῦ θεοῦ rather than ὁ θεός was probably to safeguard the truth of the mysteriousness and hiddenness of God.'

[14]Cranfield, op. cit., 114.

[15]Ibid., 115.

divinity seems to refer to the various divine qualities or perfections of His nature. That is to say, God's transcendent ('invisible') reality from 'above this world', and also His eternal power which brings into being and directly controls this world have both been made 'visible' by Him to humanity.

The context within which both of these transcendent realities have been 'manifested' is the created order within which mankind lives: 'from the creation of the world...being understood by the things that are made.' [ἀπὸ κτίσεως κόσμου τοῖς ποιήμασι νοούμενα καθορᾶταῒ.] 'From the creation of the world' is speaking temporally, and means that this knowledge has been communicated clearly from the very beginning of space/time history.[16] 'Being understood by the things that are made' can be interpreted in various senses, but most probably is to be taken 'as an ordinary participle clause explanatory of καθορᾶται ['are clearly seen'].[17] In other words, physical sight of the created order, indicated in the verbal forms – 'being understood' [νοούμενα] and 'are clearly seen' [καθορᾶται] – is the context in which humankind are unmistakably confronted with the knowledge of God's 'eternal power and divinity'.

The conflict between 'visibility' and 'holding down'

Cyril of Alexandria discusses the way this *ought* to work:

> We say that the knowledge of God has been deposited in the nature of man and that the Creator has inspired in him a natural knowledge of things which are useful and necessary for salvation. It ought to be the case that those for whom such very great things were prepared would be able to go directly to the Truth from the creation of the world, from the order by which it is governed, from its beauty, from the permanence of these things, and that they would be able to see how very great (passing description) are the wisdom and the power of Him who brought all these things into existence.[18]

The consequence of this clear revelation of God within the created order is specified in the causal clause at the end of verse 20: 'so that they are without excuse.' Rather than gratefully recognizing God from what they have clearly seen of him by means of 'the things that are made,' mankind's response is inexcusable. The nature of that inexcusable human response is stated in verses 21-23. These verses give a more detailed account of how the human mind 'holds down the truth in righteousness' (v. 18). Verse 21 begins with an explanatory clause, stating why people are without excuse (as stated at the end of verse 20): 'Because that, when they knew God, they glorified him not as God...' In spite of their objective knowledge of God, they refused to glorify him. Paul uses the verb 'to glorify' [δοξάζω] five times in Romans (8:30; 11:13; 1:21; 15:6 and 9). Here, as well as in 15:6 and 9, it is used with God as the object and man as the subject; man is to give the glory to God by gratefully and obediently acknowledging him as Creator

---

[16] κτίσεως refers to the act of creating (by God), and is used with this temporal sense frequently in the New Testament; cf. Matthew 24:21; 25:34; Mark 10:6; 13:19; Luke 11:50; 2 Peter 3:4; Revelation 13:8; 17:8.

[17] Cranfield, op. cit., 115.

[18] Cyril of Alexandria, *Contra Julianum* III; PG 76, col. 653 D.

and Lord. The supreme example of thus glorifying God is given by Christ to the Father, when He says: 'I have glorified thee on the earth: I have finished the works which thou gavest me to do' (John 17:4). But the sons and daughters of fallen Adam, rather than having 'the Lord always before them' (Ps. 16:8), 'did not like to retain God in their knowledge' (Rom. 1:28), and thus 'became vain in their imaginations, and their foolish heart was darkened' (Rom. 1:21b).

Darkness and Emptiness of Human Religion

The key to the nature of their inexcusable ingratitude ['neither were thankful' – ἢ ηὐχαρίστησαν] is found in the verb 'and *became vain* [ἐματαιώθησαν] in their imaginations.' While this is the only occurrence of this verb [ἐματαιώθησαν] in the New Testament, its root word ματαιόω is used some thirteen times; particularly in connection with idols, which Scripture refers to as vanities [μάταιος], or 'mere useless nothings.'[19] This same verb and related substantive are both used in the LXX version of Jeremiah 2:5, where the Lord asks this question: 'What iniquity have your fathers found in me, that they are gone far from me, and have walked after vanities [ματαίων] and are become vain [ἐματαιώθησαν]?'

Instead of following the revelation of God in nature in the direction of the true religion of glorifying God, humankind perverts its testimony and so descends into the depths of the false religion of idolatry. As Meyer stated: 'For heathenism is not the primeval religion, from which man might gradually have risen to a knowledge of the true God, but is, on the contrary, the result of a falling away from the known original revelation of the true God in His works.'[20] Idolatry results from the appalling choice of 'changing the truth of God into a lie' (Rom. 1:25). It indicates a devastating, perverted condition, first in the human mind, and then, inevitably in human behaviour.

The human mind is full of 'vain (or 'idolatrous') imaginations' (Rom. 1:21). 'Imaginations' [διαλογισμός] is a word used by Paul 'which in the Bible often has a distinctly pejorative connotation (e.g. Mark 7:21; Luke 5:22; 6:8; 9:47, and Ps. 94 [LXX: 93]:11, which is quoted in 1 Cor. 3:20). All their thinking suffers from the fatal flaw, the basic disconnection from reality involved in their failure to recognise and to glorify the true God.'[21] The next clause of verse 21 gives, if possible, an even deeper description of the vanity of human thoughts when confronted by knowledge of God in nature; 'and their foolish heart was darkened.' As Cranfield writes:

> Paul uses καρδία to denote a man's inward, hidden self as a thinking, willing and feeling subject. The fact that καρδία is qualified by ἀσύνετος ('uncomprehending', 'void of understanding') suggests that it is the intellectual element of their inner lives which here is particularly in mind... it is a sober acknowledgement of the fact that the ἀσύνετος as the inner self of

---

[19]Cranfield, op. cit., 117.

[20]H. A. W. Meyer, quoted in John Murray, *The Epistle to the Romans*, Grand Rapids, MI: Wm. B. Eerdmans, 1971), 41.

[21]Cranfield, op. cit., 118.

> man shares fully in the fallenness of the whole man, that the intellect is not a part of human nature somehow exempted from the general corruption, not something which can be appealed to as an impartial arbiter capable of standing outside the influence of the ego and return a perfectly objective judgement.[22]

The utter folly (though boasted in as highest wisdom) of willfully exchanging the glory of the 'uncorruptible God' for the worship of various aspects of the 'corruptible' created order (such as man and beasts) leads down into sexual perversion and even into violent transgressions of basic morality (as is charted in vv. 24-32). This passage, therefore, indicates that God's clear revelation of his eternal power and divinity in nature, far from leading mankind to proper recognition, worship and service of Him, is actually misused and perverted in terrible ways that deny and dishonor the true God.

Luther on the perversion of human religion

In commenting on Romans 1:20 – 'The invisible things of Him from the creation of the world are clearly seen,' Luther writes:

> This statement tells us that from the beginning of the world invisible things of God have always been recognised through the rational perception of the (*divine*) operations (*in the world*). All men therefore, in particular all idolators, had a clear knowledge of God, especially of His Godhead and His omnipotence...There was in their hearts a knowledge of a divine sovereign Being. How else could they have ascribed to a stone, or to the deity represented by a stone, divine attributes, had they not been convinced that such qualities really belong to God! Manifestly they knew that God is mighty, invisible, just, immortal and good. But they erred in ascribing to their idols the divine attributes (*that belong only to the true God*).[23]

This is the origin of human religion, and Paul describes it in the context of the revelation of the wrath of God (Rom. 1:18). Human religion then, though in a sense flowing from God's original revelation of Himself in nature, is marred and blinded so that it refuses to see what has been made clear [Rom. 1:20: τοῖς ποιήμασιν νοούμενα καθορᾶται] because of hearts 'darkened' [καὶ Ἐσκοτίσθη 'η ἀσύνετος αὐτῶν καρδία – v. 21] by sin. Paul connects the individual sin of hard human hearts to the fall of our universal ancestor, Adam, in Romans 5:12-21. And he discusses God's glorious remedy for all human sin as he sets forth the righteousness of God as manifested in the gospel of Christ in Romans 3:21–5:21.

Idolatry of Greek religion calls for repentance

In two other biblical passages,[24] in very different cultural settings, Paul (as reported by Luke) comments on the reality of a sense of God from creation among the pagans and the idolatrous direction in which they have

---

[22]Ibid.

[23]Martin Luther, *Commentary on Romans*, Translated by J. Theodore Mueller (Grand Rapids: Kregel Publications, 1976), 43.

[24]Acts 14 and 17.

taken it.[25] During the missionary tour of Paul and Barnabas to Lystra, Paul healed a cripple, in reaction to which the people (including the priest of Jupiter) wished to pay honour to these missionaries as gods. According to Acts 14:

> 14. Which when the apostles, Barnabas and Paul, heard of, they rent their clothes, and ran in among the people, crying out,
>
> 15. And saying, Sirs, why do ye do these things? We also are men of like passions with you, and preach unto you that ye should turn from these vanities unto the living God, which made heaven, and earth, and the sea, and all things that are therein:
>
> 16. Who in times past suffered all nations to walk in their own ways.
>
> 17. Nevertheless he left not himself without witness, in that he did good, and gave us rain from heaven, and fruitful seasons, filling our hearts with food and gladness.
>
> 18. And with these sayings scarce restrained they the people, that they had not done sacrifice unto them.

Paul's speech (as Howard Marshall writes) '...begins very naturally where the people are and asks them to consider what they are *doing*.'[26] They are engaging in idolatry; attempting to offer worship to human beings that belongs only to God (i.e. 'they called Barnabas Zeus [or Jupiter] and Paul Hermes [or Mercury]' – Acts 14:12). In verse 15, the apostle immediately condemns their idolatry, and calls them to repent or turn from 'these vanities' [τούτων τῶν ματαίων, as they are also called in the LXX version of the Old Testament, e.g. Esther 4:17; Jer. 2:5; 8:19, etc.][27] 'Like the speech at Athens this one begins with a description of the creator in biblical phraseology.'[28] Idolatry indicates a perverted sense of the divine present in all humanity, and Paul calls them from that to the true Creator God, whose self-witness to them in nature leaves them without excuse for not turning. That is, while condemning their current idolatrous practices, the apostle seeks to show that the mighty Creator, to whom they should turn, has already been with them, so that in a sense to turn to Him is to come home.

---

[25]Some scholars have questioned whether the two speeches reported in Acts 14 and 17 actually go back to Paul, since they differ from his communications to audiences with Jewish, biblical backgrounds (as, for instance, chapter one of his epistle to the church in Rome). F. F. Bruce has responded as follows: 'Preachers to such audiences [pagans with no knowledge of the Hebrew Scriptures] would not be expected to insist on the fulfilment of Old Testament prophecy, as they did in addressing synagogue congregations; instead, an appeal to the natural revelation of God the Creator is put in the forefront. Yet this appeal is couched in language largely drawn from the Old Testament' (*The Book of the Acts Revised Edition* (Grand Rapids: Wm. B. Eerdmans, 1989), 276). He writes further: 'If the author of Romans 1–3 had been invited to address an Athenian audience on the knowledge of God, it is difficult to see how the general purport of his words could have been much different from what Luke here reports Paul as saying. The tone of the *Areopagitica* is different from that of Romans 1–3, but Paul knew the wisdom of adapting his tone and general approach to the particular audience or readership being addressed at the time' (Ibid., 334).

[26]I. Howard Marshall, *Acts of the Apostles* (Leicester: Inter-Varsity Press, 1996), 238.

[27]This call to turn from idols to the true and living God is similar to Paul's words to the former pagans of the Christian congregation in Thessalonica (I Thess. 1:9f).

[28]K. Lake and H. J. Cadbury, *The Beginnings of Christianity Part IV: The Acts of the Apostles*, English Translation and Commentary (London: MacMillan and Co., Ltd., 1933), 166.

God's goodness to the pagans

The Creator God has shown His goodness towards the pagans in the kindness of His providence in nature, supplying their physical needs and bringing them gladness through blessing the regularity of agricultural seasons and sustaining the crops with rain (v. 17). These natural blessings have constituted a witness [μαρτύρος] to their ancestors and to them: 'The world of nature should thus have led men to recognise the existence, power and goodness of the Creator.'[29] Cyril of Alexandria suggested that the very decay within the order of nature should have made people look up to the One who does not decay.[30] But instead of recognizing Him, they manufactured idols, and were doing so on the very day they wished to give divine honours to Paul and Barnabas.

A time of overlooking

In verse 16 Paul emphasizes the kindness of God's patience in the face of pagan idolatry (not unlike the encouragement of Romans 2:4: '...the goodness of God leadeth thee to repentance'): 'who in times past suffered all nations to walk in their own ways.' This means that God had mercifully overlooked their sins of idolatry without passing destructive judgment upon them. As John Calvin comments:

> ...no reason is offered by Paul and Barnabas as to why God allowed the world to wander astray for so long, and surely the will of God alone must be regarded by us as nothing else but the supreme law of equity...We must indeed confess that the world deserved such destruction, but no reason can be adduced as to why God had mercy on one age rather than others, except that it seemed good to Him to do so. Accordingly Paul calls the time divinely appointed for the proclamation of the gospel 'the fulness of the time' (Gal. 4:4), so that some other favourable time might not be looked for.[31]

Paul's emphasis is that the time of 'overlooking' is now past, for God has sent his apostles with a new witness, a full revelation of his mercy. In verse 15, Paul therefore calls them to turn now to the living God, and in verse 7 (the beginning of the healing miracle), he and Barnabas had preached the gospel (which shows the way of salvation in a manner that the witness in nature cannot).[32] Although a very different context and message from Romans 1:18-23, this speech fully agrees in holding mankind outside the covenant community as responsible for a true witness of God in nature, but one they have perverted idolatrously into false religion. The only way to saving knowledge of the true God, therefore, does not come from within the witness of nature, but from the verbal witness of the gospel, now being made known to all nations of the world.

Diognetus on the divine overlooking

Perhaps two generations after the lifetime of the Apostle Paul, the unknown author of the Epistle to Diognetus (c. A.D. 130) conveys some of the crucial

---

[29]I. H. Marshall, op. cit., 239.

[30]Cyril of Alexandria, *Explanatio in Epist. Ad Rom.* I; PG 74, col. 776 A-B.

[31]John Calvin, *The Acts of the Apostles: 14-28*, translated by J. W. Fraser, eds. D. & T. Torrance (Edinburgh: Oliver & Boyd: 1966), 12.

points of this sermon from Acts 14, concerning God's 'overlooking' until Christ came:

> For God, the Lord and Fashioner of all things, who made all things, and assigned them their several positions, proved Himself not merely a friend of mankind, but also longsuffering...He formed in His mind a great and unspeakable conception, which He communicated to His Son alone. As long, then, as He held and preserved His own wise counsel in concealment, He appeared to neglect us, and to have no care over us. But after He revealed and laid open, through His beloved Son, the things which had been prepared from the beginning, He conferred every blessing all at once upon us...He was aware, then, of all things in His own mind, along with His Son, according to the relation subsisting between them.
>
> As long then as the former time endured, He permitted us to be borne along by unruly impulses, being drawn away by the desire of pleasure and various lusts. This was not that He at all delighted in our sins, but that He simply endured them...But when our wickedness had reached its height...and when the time had come which God had before appointed for manifesting His own kindness and power...He Himself took on Him the burden of our iniquities, He gave His own Son as a ransom for us...For what other thing was capable of covering our sins than His righteousness?...O sweet exchange! O unsearchable operation! O benefits surpassing all expectation! that the wickedness of many should be hid in a single righteous One, and that the righteousness of One should justify many transgressors![33]

Acts 17:16-31

The rather larger address to the pagan audience in Athens in Acts 17, though differing in detail from chapter 14, bears essentially the same conclusion:

> 16. Now while Paul waited for them at Athens, his spirit was stirred in him, when he saw the city wholly given to idolatry.
>
> 17. Therefore disputed he in the synagogue with the Jews, and with the devout persons, and in the market daily with them that met with him.
>
> 18. Then certain philosophers of the Epicureans, and of the Stoics, encountered him. And some said, What will this babbler say? other some, He seemeth to be a setter forth of strange gods: because he preached unto them Jesus, and the resurrection.
>
> 19. And they took him, and brought him unto Areopagus, saying, May we know what this new doctrine, whereof thou speakest, is?
>
> 20. For thou bringest certain strange things to our ears: we would know therefore what these things mean.
>
> 21. (For all the Athenians and strangers which were there spent their time in nothing else, but either to tell, or to hear some new thing).

---

[32] '...while the kind of witness mentioned deprived men of excuse, it was, nevertheless, not sufficient for salvation. For the Word of the apostle is true, that it is "by faith that we understand the worlds to have been framed by the Word of God" (Heb. 11:3). But faith is not conceived by the bare observation of heaven and earth, but by the hearing of the Word (*ex verbi auditu*). It follows from that that men cannot be brought to the saving knowledge of God except by the direction of the Word' (Calvin, op. cit., 13).

[33] Epistle to Diognetus, in *The Ante-Nicene Fathers*, Vol. I (Grand Rapids: Eerdmans: 1975 reprint), chs. 8 & 9 (p.28).

> 22. Then Paul stood in the midst of Mars' hill, and said, Ye men of Athens, I perceive that in all things ye are too superstitious.
>
> 23. For as I passed by, and beheld your devotions, I found an altar with this inscription, TO THE UNKNOWN GOD. Whom therefore ye ignorantly worship, him declare I unto you.
>
> 24. God that made the world and all things therein, seeing that he is Lord of heaven and earth, dwelleth not in temples made with hands;
>
> 25. Neither is worshipped with men's hands, as though he needed any thing, seeing he giveth to all life, and breath, and all things;
>
> 26. And hath made of one blood all nations of men for to dwell on all the face of the earth, and hath determined the times before appointed, and the bounds of their habitation;
>
> 27. That they should seek the Lord, if haply they might feel after him, and find him, though he be not far from every one of us:
>
> 28. For in him we live, and move, and have our being; as certain also of your own poets have said, For we are also his offspring.
>
> 29. Forasmuch then as we are the offspring of God, we ought not to think that the Godhead is like unto gold or silver, or stone, graven by art and man's device.
>
> 30. And the times of this ignorance God winked at; but now commandeth all men everywhere to repent:
>
> 31. Because he hath appointed a day, in the which he will judge the world in righteousness by that man whom he hath ordained; whereof he hath given assurance unto all men, in that he hath raised him from the dead.

After his introduction, mentioning the religiosity or superstition of the Athenians (v. 22), the speech seems to fall into three parts: (1) God is the Lord of the world and does not need a temple of human cultic ritual (vv. 24f.); (2) Man is God's creation and needs God (vv. 26f.); (3) God and man are related, therefore idolatry is foolish (vv. 28f.). Paul concludes by calling them to repentance.[34]

Hebrew Scriptures not quoted, though they are followed

Paul typically began where his audience was; in this case, they were surrounded by idolatry,[35] in spite of their sophisticated philosophical systems.[36] In addition to the numerous pagan altars dotted all over Athens, Paul called attention to an altar 'To the Unknown God' (v. 23). Ancient writers indicated the historical existence of such an altar (or altars).[37]

---

[34]I follow the outline of I. Howard Marshall, op. cit., 282.

[35]The abundance of statues in Athens, and in general the evidences of the Athenian religiosity, were remarked by other visitors. Cf. Livy xlv. 27; Pausanias i. 17. 1; Strabo ix. 1. 16; Sophocles, *Oed. Col.* 260 (θεοσεβεστάτας); Josephus, *Contra Ap.* Ii. 11; Lake and Cadbury, op. cit., 209.

[36]The Stoic philosophy has been discussed in Chapter 1 of this work. We simply note here that the Stoic concept of God held him to be something like an impersonal force (λόγος), which was an aspect of nature, rather than transcendent to it. The Epicureans also held god (or gods) to be impersonal forces or causes, rather more remote from the part of nature inhabited by man, and less concerned with it, than in the pantheistic Stoic theory.

[37]e.g. Pausanias, *Description of Greece*, 1. 1. 4; Philostratus, *Life of Apollonius*, 6. 3. 5.

Presumably the Athenians had erected this altar lest they offend some god who might have been left out. In order for Paul to communicate with his Gentile audience, as F. F. Bruce notes:

> Here he does not quote Hebrew scriptures which would have been quite unknown to his hearers; the direct quotations in this speech are quotations from Greek poets. But he does not condescend to his hearers' level by arguing from first principles as one of their own philosophers might do. His argument is firmly based on biblical revelation; it echoes throughout the thought, and at times the very language, of the Old Testament. Like the biblical revelation itself, his argument begins with God the creator of all and ends with God the judge of all.[38]

'Since they acknowledged their ignorance of the divine nature, he would tell them about it.'[39] Paul begins where the Hebrew scriptures begin: with the Creator God, 'who made the world and all things in it' (v. 24). In language similar to King Solomon's prayer at the dedication of the Temple (1 Kings 8:27), he shows that the true God 'dwelleth not in temples made with hands'. Further to indicate the true nature of the one Creator God, Paul states that far from needing anything from the hand of man, God in fact 'gives life and breath and all things unto all' (v. 25). In other words, the Creator both animates all life-forms and exercises providential care over them and all his handiwork. Part of this providential care is to have created all humankind from 'one blood' (i.e. Adam and Eve, according to Genesis 1, Romans 5, and I Corinthians 15), and then to have 'determined the times and places' of their existence in various nations (v. 26). Whatever else this may mean, it certainly indicates that God was not exclusively interested in the descendants of Shem, Abraham and Israel, but also in the other sons and daughters of Adam through the remaining sons of Noah, which of course included the Greeks.

Paul states that the purpose of their times and habitations was not merely for them to experience physical life in his created order, but 'that they should seek and find the Lord', their Creator (v. 27).

> Ever since the creation, he says in Rom. 1:20, the things that God has made have pointed clearly to 'his everlasting power and divinity.' If human beings, beguiled and confused by false worship, have failed to perceive the nature of God in the works of creation, they are without excuse. The attitude expressed in the letter to the Romans is not so widely different from that of the *Areopagitica*... there is no hint in the speech that the Athenians' confessed ignorance of the divine nature was blameless. Even some of their own teachers had realised the folly of trying to represent the divine nature by material images, worship it at material altars, or house it in material temples, and had perceived, however dimly, how near God was to those who truly sought him.[40]

The verb translated 'feel after' [ψηλαφήσειαν] (v. 27) indicates 'groping' in the darkness after God (before the full revelation of the light of the

---

[38]Bruce, op. cit., 335.

[39]Ibid., 336.

[40]F. F. Bruce, op. cit., 338, notes that 'A verbal link has been found in Dio Chrysostom, *Oration* 12.28, where those of primaeval days are described as "not settled separately by themselves far away... from the divine being or outside of him, but...sharing his nature."'

gospel, which Paul is here to announce). 'This groping takes place despite the nearness of God to men, of which Paul goes on to speak, and it may indicate the sinful failure of man to find God to which Romans 1:20f. point. Nevertheless, the main point is that seeking should not be difficult since God *is not far from each one of us*.'[41]

Greek poetry confirms God's nearness

In verse 28, Paul confirms the nearness of God to all humanity by making reference to two pieces of pagan poetry, which he takes as witnesses to the Biblical teaching on the close divine and human relationship. 'In him we live and move and have our being' (v. 28a), may come from an address to Zeus by his son Minos of Crete and/or from Epimenides the Cretan.[42] And 'For we are also his offspring' (v. 28b) comes from the poet Aratus' *Phainomena* 5. In the Stoic context of this Greek poetry, the God referred to was Zeus, who had been reinterpreted by them in a less mythological, and more philosophical direction. Thus, the Stoic philosophers and poets held this Zeus or god to be: 'the λόγος or world principle which animates all things; their language, however, is largely adaptable to the God of revelation. By presenting God as creator and judge, Paul emphasises his personal character as opposed to the pantheistic Zeus of the Stoics.'[43]

The apostle selects these fragments of light from pagan poetry as pointers to the goal for which humankind had been created by God in His own image. Gregory of Nyssa, though not specifically referring here to Acts 17, clearly expresses the basic application Paul would have had in mind for his Greek audience:

> ...God or Word...has been shown by inference to be the maker of the nature of man. He was not urged by any necessity to frame him, but produced such a creature in the activity of his superabundant love...If, therefore, man comes to his birth upon these conditions, namely to be a partaker of the good things in God, necessarily he is framed of such a kind as to be adapted to the participation of such good...so it was needful that a certain affinity with the Divine should be mingled with the nature of man, in order that by means of this correspondence it might aim at that which was native to it...Thus, then, it was needful for man, born for the enjoyment of Divine good, to have something in his nature akin to that in which he is to participate...[44]

Paul shows in verse 29 that such witnesses among the Greeks of who God is (and who mankind are) should have kept the people from their materialistic idolatry, but did not. As regards the infinite offence of pagan idolatry, Paul mentions the great mercy of the true God in having 'overlooked' [ὑπεριδὼν] it in the past, rather like Acts 14:16 ('Who in times past suffered all nations to walk in their own ways'). It is difficult to know just what benefits may be implied in God's 'overlooking' the ignorance of past pagan idolatry. At the very least, God has taken into merciful account their ignorance

---

[41]Marshall, op. cit., 288.

[42]See the discussion in Bruce, op. cit., 384-85.

[43]Bruce, op. cit., 385.

[44]Gregory of Nyssa, *The Great Catechism*, chapter 5.

and previous lack of full revelation (which, with the preaching of Paul, is now being made up to them), and has spared them from final, devastating judgement in view of the historic appearance of Christ.

Diagnosis of pagan idolatry followed by the divine remedy
Now the Gentiles (represented by the Athenians) have reached a crossroads. The full revelation of God's will for them as attested in the historic resurrection of Christ, who has been appointed to raise and judge them and all humankind leaves them with only one legitimate option: repentance [μετανοεῖν]. Earlier sermons in Acts call on the Jews to repent for not having known who God was, in spite of the testimony of their Scriptures (cf. 2:38 and 3:19), and this sermon (and the one in chapter 14) calls on Gentiles to repent for not having known who God was, in spite of the testimony of the created order, as well as that of some of their poets.

Romans 1 and Acts 14 and 17, for all their differences in historical and cultural context, are agreed in ascribing the origins of human religion to the witness of God to Himself in the created order, as well as in the personality of man (God's offspring). And they are agreed in evaluating the results of this divine witness very negatively in light of what mankind has actually done with it. They show that the truth has been perverted into self-serving idolatry by sinful humanity. And this idolatry is destructive to mankind, as well as dishonouring to God, as D. Stăniloae shows us:

> For where there is no faith in the personal God and especially in the incarnate God, the supreme reality is taken to be either an essence which successively absorbs all persons in itself, or a 'god' devoid of or incapable of full love for humankind.[45]

Hence, far from helping them truly reach God, human religion is inevitably idolatrous and destructive, so that mankind's only hope is to repent from it in light of God's fullest revelation of Himself in the gospel of Christ.

B. The Testimony of God within the Conscience of Mankind

Human religion flows, as we have just seen, from God's clear revelation of Himself in the created order, perverted though it is by the rebellious mind of fallen mankind. But there is also a second context (closely related to creation, and indeed, a part of it) from which mankind derives a sense of the divine, and is thus fully responsible for it: the human conscience. This is discussed more fully in chapter two of Romans than anywhere else in Scripture.

---

[45]Dumitru Stăniloae, 'The Faces of our Fellow Human Beings' in *International Review of Missions*, LXXI, 281, Jan. 1982, p. 33.

Romans 2:12-16

In Chapter 1 of Romans (as we have seen), Paul charted the downward devastation of Gentile idolatry, in preparation for showing their desperate need of the gospel. In Chapter Two of this epistle, Paul deals with the more privileged covenant people, the Jews, and shows that they, no less than the pagan Gentiles, also need the gospel. In a word, the pagans did not live up to the knowledge of God they had in nature, whereas the Jews did not live up to the even greater knowledge of God they had in the law. Apart from the gospel, therefore, both Jew and Gentile are under God's judgment. His judgment will equitably take into account their different situations, and will operate on the basis of the usage they made of their conscience, as is described in Romans 2:12-16:

> 12. For as many as have sinned without law shall also perish without law; and as many as have sinned in the law shall be judged by the law.
>
> 13. (For not the hearers of the law are just before God, but the doers of the law shall be justified.
>
> 14. For when the Gentiles, which have not the law, do by nature the things contained in the law, these, having not the law, are a law unto themselves.
>
> 15. Which shew the work of the law written in their hearts, their conscience also bearing witness, and their thoughts the mean while accusing or else excusing one another;)
>
> 16. In the day when God shall judge the secrets of men by Jesus Christ according to my gospel.

These verses contrast those who are 'under' [or 'in'] the law' [ἐν νόμῳ] – v. 12] with those who are 'without the law' [ἀνόμως – v. 12] or, as in verse 14, 'have not the law.' 'Law' here refers to the special revelation of God in Scripture. The Jews had it and the Gentiles did not. In verse 13 Paul shows that merely having the special revelation of the law is not sufficient to be justified (accounted righteous with God). One must actually live by it. In verses 21-25 the apostle argues that the Jews did not live up to their law, and in Romans 3:9, he plainly states that 'both Jews and Gentiles are all under sin.'

Written by nature

Although the Gentiles did not possess the written revelation of the law, they too – like the more privileged Jews – are under sin because they had something to which they did not live up. In the Gentiles' case, it was not the written law, but rather a sense of right and wrong 'written' on their consciences by God, their Creator, as is explained in verses 14 and 15. That is to say, although not possessing the written law (μὴ νόμον ἔχοντα – v.14), the Gentiles nevertheless 'do by nature the things contained in the law' (v. 14). John Murray explains:

> 'By nature' is contrasted with what is derived from external sources and refers to that which is engraven on our natural constitution. What is done 'by nature' is done by native instinct or propension, by spontaneous impulse

> as distinguished from what is induced by forces extraneous to ourselves... 'The things of the law' must mean certain things which the law prescribes and refer to those things practised by pagans which are stipulated in the law, such as the pursuit of lawful vocations, the procreation of offspring, filial and natural affection, the care of the poor and sick, and numerous other natural virtues which are required by the law.[46]

Pierre Viret, sixteenth-century Reformer of Lausanne, had a similar view of the content of this law written in the heart. 'It admonishes us concerning the subjection and obedience we owe to our fathers and mothers.'[47]

John Calvin explicates the societal effects of 'doing by nature the things contained in the law' in terms of 'the general conception of equity' operating in mankind 'by the light of reason':

> ...since man is by nature a social animal, he tends through natural instinct to foster and preserve society. Consequently, we observe that there exists in all men's minds universal impression of a certain civic fair dealing and order. Hence no man is to be found who does not understand that every sort of human organisation must be regulated by laws, and who does not comprehend the principles of those laws. Hence arises that unvarying consent of all nations and of individual mortals with regard to laws. For all their seeds have, without teacher or lawgiver, been implanted in all men...
>
> For while men dispute among themselves about individual sections of the law, they agree on the general conception of equity...Yet the fact remains that some seed of political order has been implanted in all men. And this is ample proof that in the arrangement of this life no man is without the light of reason.[48]

St. Thomas on humankind's natural consciousness of law

Some three centuries before Calvin, St. Thomas discusses equity in light of the precepts of 'natural law' written into the human conscience. He teaches that these precepts are self-evident (or *per se nota*).[49] According to him, humankind has an inbuilt tendency to seek what it self-evidently sees as good for itself. Thus, because of this divine reflection in the conscience, people understand that practical good should be sought and evil avoided. Therefore, 'All things which should be done or which should be shunned pertain to precepts of natural law insofar as practical reason naturally apprehends them to be human goods.'[50]

Their being 'a law unto themselves' (ἑαυτοῖς εἰσι νόμος· – v. 14] means that '...they themselves, by reason of what is implanted in their nature, confront themselves with the law of God. They themselves reveal the law of God to themselves – their persons is the medium of revelation.'[51] As C. K. Barrett says: 'There is then, something, Paul argues, in the very pattern of created existence which should, and sometimes does, lead the Gentiles to an attitude of humble, grateful, dependent creatureliness. When this takes place they are a law for themselves.'[52]

---

[46]John Murray, op. cit., 73.

[47]Pierre Viret, *Instruction Chrestienne en la doctrine de la Loy et de l'Evangile* (Genève, 1564), t. I, 453.

[48]John Calvin, *Institutes of the Christian Religion*, II. 2. 14 (Battles translation).

[49]St. Thomas, *S.T.* IaIIae, q.94.

[50]Ibid., IaIIae, q.94 a.2.

[51]John Murray, op. cit., 73.

[52]C. K. Barrett, *The Epistle to the Romans* (New York: Harper & Row, Publishers: 1957), 52.

Peter Martyr Vermigli, as Richard Muller has shown, taught that:

> All things…show forth 'the eternal power and divinity of God' – but especially human nature which manifests his very likeness and majesty. The soul especially – with its 'justice, wisdom, and many other noble qualities,' with its sense of right and wrong – testifies to the existence of God, as does the conscience with its inward condemnation of wickedness, love of the good, and presentiment of God's future judgment. There is nothing in the created world so vile that it in some way does not give testimony of God.[53]

The difference between the inward, painful recognition of law by nature and the delightful writing of law within the heart by the Holy Spirit

This authoritative and inward, and thus, different sort of law from the written revelation given to the Jews, is clearly not the same as the inward inscribing of God's law on the heart, promised by Jeremiah 31:33 as a benefit of the fullness of the gospel. It is much less than that. It is rather 'the effect [or 'work'] of the law written in their hearts' [νόμου γραπτὸν ἐν ταῖς καρδίαις αὐτῶν].[54] The difference from the promise of Jeremiah seems to be that by means of the gift of the Spirit to those who believe the gospel, they will delight to do God's will from within their innermost being, whereas the mere 'work of the law' on the conscience lacks this inner spontaneity and delight. It is seen as an annoying burden which, unfortunately, cannot be entirely shaken off.[55]

Light of the Gentiles

The obligation of the Gentiles to God's moral order then is owing to 'the effect' or 'the works' of the law on their consciences. The human conscience is a divine endowment placed in all of God's image bearers. W. Pannenburg may well be right in his discussion of how the conscience of an infant gradually develops in its relationship to and then distinction from the mother.[56] Or, as the eighteenth-century Scottish Common Sense philosopher, Thomas Reid suggested:

> Perhaps a child in the womb, or for some short period of its existence, is merely a sentient being: the faculties by which it perceives an external world, by which it reflects on its own thoughts and existence, and relation to other things, as well as its reasoning and moral faculties, unfold themselves by degrees; so that it is inspired with the various principles of common sense, as with the passions of love and resentment, when it has occasion for them.[57]

---

[53]Peter Martyr Vermigli, *Loci communes* (London, 1583), I.ii.1, quoted in Richard A. Muller, *Post-Reformation Reformed Dogmatics: Prolegomena to Theology*, Vol. I (Grand Rapids: Baker Book House, 1987), 171.

[54]Barrett, Ibid.

[55]Paul uses this same expression, 'the works of the law' [ἔργων νόμου] in Galatians 2:16, in a very different context. There he is showing his Jewish adversaries that they cannot be justified by 'the works of the law'.

[56]In his *Systematic Theology*, Vol. I, (Grand Rapids MI: William B. Eerdmans Publishing Co., 1991), 112. But what the Scripture gives us is the completed product of the human conscience and its inexcusable obligation.

[57]Thomas Reid, *An Inquiry into the Human Mind*, V, 7.

We cannot go very far into the dissection of the developing human personality with its conscience, but we rest upon what the Scriptures give us. And that is the 'completed product' of the human conscience (as God's creature, in His image) and its sense of inexcusable obligation to Him.

As C. K. Barrett writes: 'It implies man's ability to detach himself from himself and to view his character and actions independently. He is thus able to act as a witness for or against himself.'[58] Dr. Thomas Reid, again, says it well: 'The sense of guilt makes a man at variance with himself…He sees that he is not what he ought to be…He is conscious of demerit, and cannot avoid the dread of meeting with its reward.'[59]

That is why pagans, who have no access to written revelation, still cannot escape the interior voice of an authoritative moral monitor, which they instinctively recognize to be from above them and therefore obligatory upon them. This interior moral monitor, which cannot be separated from their own mental activities and subsequent decisions, either 'accuses' them, when their actions are consistent with its demands (which they clearly perceive), or 'excuses' them when they obey its voice (which they also clearly perceive). What Reid says here is consonant with Holy Scripture: 'The Supreme Being, who has given us eyes to discern what may be useful and what hurtful to our natural life, hath also given us this light within, to direct our moral conduct.'[60]

St. Paul states that they will be brought into account on the Last Day for what they did with what they had. They will not be judged for what they did not have (the written revelation of God), but for what they did have (the inescapable voice of conscience, calling them to do right). The Last Judgment will involve a searching examination of what mankind did have.

The apostle writes: '…In the day when God shall judge the secrets of men by Jesus Christ according to my gospel.' This day is obviously the Last or Judgment Day. All mankind will be brought into final account on this tremendous day.

Mankind's inescapable responsibility for the light they have

Both Jew and Gentile must finally answer for the light God gave them. The passage immediately following this one (Romans 2:17-29) focuses on the futility of Jewish externalism; to profess the law outwardly while failing to live by it inwardly will on that day be exposed as blasphemy of the name of God (Rom. 2:24). An outward profession of adherence to the written law, unmatched by inner reality, is one of 'the secrets' that will be revealed at that time. By the same token, we may infer from the text that 'the secrets' hidden in the hearts of the Gentiles will also be revealed on that day. They must answer for the light they had, which they suppressed (Rom. 1:18),

---

[58]Barrett, op. cit., 53.

[59]Thomas Reid, *Essays on the Active Powers of Man*, 'Essay III, Part III, Ch. VII, quoted from *The Works of Thomas Reid, D.D.*, preface, etc. by Sir William Hamilton, vol. II (Edinburgh: MacLachlan and Stewart, 1880), 594.

[60]Ibid.

and for not 'liking to retain God in their knowledge' (Rom. 1:28). They did such things, although '...knowing the judgement of God, that they which commit such things are worthy of death, [and] not only [did] the same, but [had] pleasure in them that [did] them' (Rom. 1:32).

It is not reading too much into the text to assume that this includes bringing out into the open before an assembled universe the clear knowledge of God in creation and in 'the works of the law' inscribed on their hearts, that many pagans pretended *not* to possess in order to escape the moral requirements of the God whom they claimed not to exist. For all their profession of atheism or agnosticism, they secretly knew all too well that He existed and had moral rights over them. That secret will be made manifest and their accountability for it will be correctly assessed.

Bertrand Russell once said that if, contrary to his expectations, he should see God after death and be asked why he did not believe in Him, his immediate answer would be: 'Not enough evidence.'[61] Many are the philosophers who have claimed that there is no evidence for God's existence. Others have gone even further (in the line of Richard Dawkins, for instance) and asserted that all of the evidence is entirely contrary to theism. According to St. Paul, the Last Day will reveal the secret they sought to hide; God's divinity and power were constantly manifested to their hearts through creation and conscience.

The one whose august and awesome court will unveil their self-serving secret is the Lord Jesus Christ, agent of creation, redeemer of all believers and judge of all who have ever lived. 'God shall judge the secrets of men by Jesus Christ' (Rom. 2:16). The Lord of gospel grace is also the final judge of the entire universe, as Paul had reminded his Gentile audience in Acts 17:31: 'Because he hath appointed a day, in the which he will judge the world in righteousness by that man whom he hath ordained...' In the light of this inescapable and just judgement of both Jew and Gentile for having violated the light they had, the only hope is to obey God who through the Good News of Jesus Christ 'now commandeth men every where to repent' (Acts 17:30).

C. The Old Testament Witness to the Binding Knowledge of God Held by Pagan Nations

The Psalms

The Old Testament, which largely focuses on the history of Israel, through whose Messianic seed all other nations will be blessed (Gen. 12:3), has no extensive texts comparable to those written by the Apostle to the Gentiles, 'in the fulness of the time' (Gal. 4:4), demonstrating the pagans' knowledge of God in creation and conscience. Yet various portions of the Old Testament seem to assume no less knowledge and obligation on the part of pagans than that taught by Paul in the New Testament. Several of the 'nature Psalms'

[61]Wesley Salmon, 'Religion & Science: A New Look at Hume's Dialogues,' *Philosophical Studies* 33 (1978): 176.

(such as 8, 19 and 29) indicate that the created natural order, 'thy heavens, the work of thy fingers, the moon and the stars, which thou hast ordained' (Ps. 8:3), proclaim the Lord's 'excellent name in all the earth' and his 'glory above the heavens' (v. 1). Psalm 19 teaches that 'the heavens declare the glory of God; and the firmament sheweth his handiwork. Day unto day uttereth speech, and night unto night sheweth knowledge' (vv. 1 & 2). It states that this knowledge of God's glory through the created order and its beauty and regularity is absolutely universal: 'There is no speech nor language, where their voice is not heard. Their line is gone out through all the earth, and their words to the end of the world' (vv. 3 & 4).

These psalms were written by David, within the Covenant of Grace focused in Israel, and include considerable aspects of 'special' or 'written' or 'redemptive' revelation, not yet given to the Gentiles. While there is no indication in any of these psalms that the Gentiles will honor God for His glory which confronts them, still it is clear that they are daily, nightly and universally confronted with that glory in an inescapable way.

The Church Fathers on the testimony of nature

The Church Fathers extensively reflect the Biblical testimony at this point. Athenagoras sees from nature: 'Numerous reasons for worshipping God: the order, complete harmony, colour, form and arrangement of God's invisible power from his works.'[62] Irenaeus makes similar observations in *Adversus Haereses*,[63] as does Cyprian, who states: 'the soul in contemplating the heavens knows their author.'[64] Clement of Alexandria 'sees in the stars that the pagans have worshipped a way given to the heathen to bow themselves before God.'[65] Minucius Felix recognizes (as do the Stoics) God's reality through 'universal harmony'.[66] Tertullian says: 'There is no other sign so manifest of the existence of God than all this work which He has created.'[67] Novatian of Rome mentioned this principle of passing from the works of the creation to their Creator,[68] but denied that pagans actually accepted a true knowledge of God. Rather, he taught that man in his fallen natural surrounding is a 'beast-like, ferocious soul'.[69] In line with the teaching of Romans 1 and Acts 14 and 17, Novatian states that it is only through Christ and 'his apostolic messengers' that mankind truly recognizes its Creator:

> Through Him [i.e. Christ] He willed that we should come to knowledge of Himself, and richly poured out upon us the generous stores of his kindness, by conferring upon the needy and desolate the abundance of his Spirit. His liberality and goodness reach further. In order that the whole world should not dry up in its aversion to the streams of his grace, He willed that through his Son apostolic messengers should be sent into all the world to instruct

---

[62]Athenagoras, *Orat*, iv.
[63]Irenaeus, *Adv. Haer.* Ii. viii. 1; iii. xxix; iv. 4.
[64]Cyprian, *Ad Don.* Xiv – CSEL III, 1, 15, 13–14.
[65]Clement of Alex., *Prot.* 63, 4–5, and *Strom.* Vi. 110, 3–111,1.
[66]Minucius Felix, *Octavius*, xix, 1 and xviii, 11.
[67]Tertullian, Tertullian, *Adv. Marc.* I. 11.
[68]Novatian, *De Trin.* I. 9; III. 20.
[69]Ibid. III. 19.

> our race, that mankind in its condition might recognise its Creator, and if it would then follow Him, could have one whom it might address in its prayers as Father instead of God.[70]

The responsibility of pagan cultures

Both Law and Prophets bear witness against the degrading misuse by pagan nations of the divine glory they perceived in heaven and earth. Deuteronomy 4:19 and 23 warns the covenant people against taking part in degenerate religious worship in the land to which they are going: 'And lest thou lift up thine eyes unto heaven, and when thou seest the sun, and the moon, and the stars, even all the host of heaven, shouldest be driven to worship them, and serve them, which the Lord thy God hath divided unto all nations under the whole heaven…Take heed unto yourselves, lest ye forget the covenant of the Lord your God, which he made with you, and make you a graven image, or the likeness of any thing which the Lord thy God hath forbidden thee.' The Apostle Paul says much the same, when he shows how pagans abuse what they know of God in nature by having 'changed the truth of God into a lie, and worshipped and served the creature more than the Creator, who is blessed for ever…' (Rom. 1:25). Hence Psalm 96:5 says: 'For all the gods of the nations are idols: but the Lord made the heavens.'

Isaiah 17:7 and 8 predicts that it will only be in the future that owing to the mighty work of God, pagan nations such as Syria, will at long last turn from the creaturely idolatry with which they replaced the true Creator to the Lord Himself: 'At that day shall a man look to his Maker, and his eyes shall have respect to the Holy One of Israel. And he shall not look to the altars, the work of his hands, neither shall respect that which his fingers have made, either the groves, or the images.'

Yet at the same time, it is clear that the prophets of Israel, while recognizing the pagan abuse and corruption of what they knew of God, still held them morally responsible both for their idolatry and immorality. Isaiah chapters 13 to 21 teach just as clearly as Paul that judgement is visited on pagan nations and their leaders for their violation of moral standards which they clearly knew. Isaiah and Paul both hold the nations outside Israel to be 'inexcusable'. It is similar with Jeremiah in chapters 46 to 51 and Amos in chapters 1 and 2.

The Wisdom Literature assumes pagan knowledge of divine truth

The 'Wisdom Literature' plainly assumes knowledge of godly ways outside the covenant people, and makes use of it, as with 'the words of Agur' (Prov. 30:1), and it is exhibited in many statements (if not the application they made) of the 'miserable comforters' of Job.[71] One must assume that much of the wisdom and knowledge that non-Israelites enjoyed, outside the covenant community of special revelation, came from God's general revelation in creation and conscience. Yet it is probable that the ancient

---

[70]Ibid. VIII. 42.

nations and their wise men also had at least some access to traditions going back to the common ancestor of all mankind, Noah, as is suggested in the speech of Eliphaz to Job in patriarchal times.[72]

This leads us to the distinction made by classical theology between 'natural' (or 'general') revelation and 'supernatural' (or 'special') revelation, and to the question of how fallen mankind can interpret revelation.

D. Some Traditional Theological Distinctions

From the time of the earliest Church writings in both East and West, as we have already seen, there has always been a recognition of a distinction between a natural knowledge of God (His eternal power and deity seen in creation – cf. Rom. 1:19-20) and the fuller revelation of Himself in Christ and Holy Scripture. In the Latin-speaking West, however, particularly after the great Schism with the Eastern Church in 1054, there were developments concerning 'natural revelation' within Western Scholasticism that were not reflected in the Greek-speaking East.

Western development of natural theology

W. Pannenberg describes this development:

> ...the relation between the biblical revelation of God and the concept of natural theology changed in the Latin Middle Ages. From the 12th century, especially under the influence of Gilbert of Poitiers, the idea increasingly gained ground that only the unity of God, not his trinity, is accessible to rational knowledge. When Aristotle became the normative philosopher of the age instead of Plato, this limitation of philosophical theology came more sharply into focus. Aquinas differentiated what is accessible to rational knowledge very clearly from the articles of faith and put it in preambles to his treatment of the latter (ST 1. 2. Ad 1). Yet even Aquinas could still deal with the doctrine of God, including the Trinity, within an argument presenting God as the first cause of the world, so that he was not yet fully distinguishing between natural and supernatural knowledge. Only later Thomism, Baroque Scholasticism, and Neo-Scholasticism constructed the full two-story theory of natural and supernatural theology which is now judged so critically by Roman Catholic theologians.
>
> When natural theology reappeared in Baroque Scholasticism and older Protestant theology as the opposite of revealed theology, it had undergone a radical change of meaning. 'Natural' no longer meant 'In accordance with the nature of God' but 'in accordance with human nature.'[73]

John Calvin had divided the first half of his *Institutes of the Christian Religion* (published in various editions from 1536 to 1559) into two books: One: The Knowledge of God the Creator, and Two: The Knowledge of God the Redeemer.

---

[71]Derek Kidner, for instance, discusses the 'international' community of wisdom in the ancient Near East in *The Proverbs: An Introduction and Commentary*, ed. D. J. Wiseman, The Tyndale Old Testament Commentaries (Downers Grove: InterVarsity Press, 1964), 16ff.

[72] See Job 22:15-18.

[73]Wolfhart Pannenberg, *Systematic Theology*, Vol. I, translated by Geoffrey W. Bromiley (Grand Rapids: Eerdmans 1991), 81.

The Westminster Confession of Faith (composed in London by 1646, as the Confession for the Churches in the British Isles, during the time that the Calvinists were in control of the British government) mentions in a very balanced way (without using the terms) what Reformed theologians by this time were calling 'natural' and 'supernatural' revelation. This is done in the first paragraph of Chapter 1 – 'Of the Holy Scripture':

> Although the light of nature, and the works of creation and providence, do so far manifest the goodness, wisdom, and power of God, as to leave men inexcusable; yet they are not sufficient to give that knowledge of God, and of his will, which is necessary to salvation; therefore it pleased the Lord at sundry times, and in divers manners, to reveal himself, and to declare that his will unto his church; and afterwards, for the better preserving and propagating of the truth...to commit the same wholly unto writing; which make the holy Scripture to be most necessary; those former ways of God's revealing his will unto his people being now ceased.

Within this background, theologians of the seventeenth century were now using the terms 'natural' and 'supernatural' revelation (or later, 'general' and 'special'). And in this context they dealt with the effects of the Fall of Adam on the minds of his descendants as they interpret revelation.

Natural (or general) revelation

'Natural' revelation refers traditionally to that binding knowledge of God's 'eternal power and Godhead' (Rom. 1:20) viewed by all persons in the created order, as well as to that moral obligation coming from 'the work of the law written in their hearts, their conscience also bearing witness' (Rom. 2:15) within all persons, Jewish or Gentile. The term 'natural' points to the realm where that knowledge is found (creation and conscience), but the source of that obligatory knowledge is definitely 'supernatural' (from the God who chooses thus to 'unveil' Himself). This theological knowledge does not 'inhere in nature' as one of its attributes, but comes from outside it.[74]

'General' revelation implies that the content of these revealed truths are general (such as God's creatorship and the moral force of His law), rather than 'special' (such as the truths of His redemptive action within the Covenant of Grace). As Karl Barth has extensively argued, it is questionable just how clearly these 'general' truths have ever been received by fallen mankind outside the redemptive covenant made manifest in Christ (as Paul seems to say in Acts 17:30 and 31).[75] Nevertheless, the preachers of the evangel make it plain that all pagans who hear the saving message are 'without excuse' for not having honoured the God who has at length come to them in Christ (Rom. 1:20, 32 and 2:12-17).

---

[74]See Hans Urs von Balthasar, *The Theology of Karl Barth* (San Francisco: Communio Books, Ignatius Press, 1991), 143.

[75]cf. Karl Barth *Church Dogmatics* II/1, 117–123.

Universal knowledge of God

St. Thomas summarizes the position in Pauline fashion in stating that 'all knowing beings implicitly know God in any and every thing they know.'[76]

The Psalmist in the Old Testament and Paul in the New take it for granted that this 'general' knowledge of God in the created order and in conscience is of none other than the God of the Covenant, Creator and Redeemer, who reveals Himself most fully in Israel and in the Church. Biblically speaking, natural knowledge of God is therefore always bracketed within supernatural revelation of Him, rather than vice versa.[77]

Novatian accordingly interprets the praise of creation in terms of 'He whom the church knows and worships as God':

> This, then is He whom the church knows and worships as God, rejecting the fables and fictions of heretics. The whole universe of things both visible and invisible ceaselessly bears witness to Him. Angels adore Him, stars marvel at Him, seas bless Him, lands fear Him, even things beneath the earth acknowledge Him. Every human mind feels Him, though it cannot express Him. At His command all things move, springs flow, rivers run their courses, waves arise, all creatures bear their young, winds are compelled to blow, showers descend, seas are stirred, all things overflow with fruitfulness in all places.[78]

Supernatural (or special) revelation

'Supernatural' revelation traditionally refers to the particular communication[79] of the Triune God with His chosen covenant people of Himself and His gracious ways that mark them out for eternal salvation. As far as source is concerned, it is no more 'supernatural' than 'natural' revelation, but it is more particular, more detailed and shines with a clearer, more intense light because of the saving personal communion He establishes with its receivers, thus setting them apart from the recipients of the more general truths proclaimed in nature and conscience (universally abused though these 'general' truths may be).[80] It is often termed 'special' because of its

---

[76]*Quaestiones disputatae de veritae*, qu. 22, art. 2 ad primam.

[77]The Documents of Vatican II reflect well this point in 'The Constitution on the Word of God' (Dei Verbum) ch. 6, by setting natural knowledge of God within redemptive history.

[78]Novatian, *De Trinitate* VIII. 40.

[79]James Barr has written an interesting article arguing for replacing the traditional term 'revelation' with 'communication' (cf. 'The Concepts of History and Revelation' in *Old and New in Interpretation* (London: SCM Press, 1966), 87-92. His point that 'communication comes from one already known' (87) is not sufficient to cover the various biblical instances of revelation, nor does 'communication' carry the strong connotations of 'revelation' (sovereign unveiling with eternally obligatory consequences of 'revelation').

[80]St. Paul shows how fallen mankind turn the witness of the Creator into aspects of the created order, hence replacing Him with things made by Him (Rom. 1:25). This exchange of the holy God for fallen creatures leads to morally abominable practices (cf. Rom. 1:26-32). The Church Fathers commented on this vile exchange at large. Gregory Nazianzus wrote in his Second Theological Oration: 'The pagans are without excuse and even more contemptible than their idols, birds, four-legged beasts and creeping animals, because they prefer the worse to the better even though they have been endowed with a rational nature and are in possession of the grace of God.' Basil the Great said: 'The first knowledge for man is the knowledge of God. But reason can either hand itself over to the deceiving demons and thus fall into servitude to idols, or it can entrust itself to the help of the Holy Spirit and thereby know God' (Epistle 233 to Amphilochius).

specific salvational promises and paternal warnings, and because those who are chosen to receive it are a 'special' or 'peculiar' people (cf. Exod. 19:5 and 1 Pet. 2:9), called into a covenant community with Himself.

The Swiss Reformer, Pierre Viret, considered the distinction between 'natural' and 'supernatural' revelation to be necessary only because of the Fall of man: 'We need another new light to shine upon us from the heavens, which is not natural, like the former, but supernatural.'[81] He later adds: 'There is no doubt that if man had fully retained his original integrity, that light which is now supernatural would have been natural to him in the full knowledge of God which was necessary for the end for which he was created.'[82] Viret does not deal with the question (of interest to some of the Eastern Fathers) as to whether Christ would have still become incarnate, even if man had not fallen, in order to take His bride.[83]

This supernatural revelation is, as we shall see in later chapters, centered in the Lord Jesus Christ, eternal Son of the Father, who is absolute truth in human flesh. The Scriptures of the Old Testament look forward to His coming, and those of the New Testament constitute the inspired record of that advent. The recipients of that revelation of Christ in both Testaments are divinely shaped into a covenant community in which, and only in which, absolute truth can be faithfully discerned by humans.

Hence, Martin Luther exhorts all who would truly know God:

> Begin your search with Christ and stay with Him and cleave to Him, and if your own thoughts and reason, or another man's, would lead you elsewhere, shut your eyes and say: I should and will know of no other God than Christ, my Lord...But if you abandon this clear prospect, and climb up into God's Majesty on high, you must stumble, fear and fall because you have withdrawn yourself from God's grace, and have dared to stare at the Majesty unveiled, which is too high and overpowering for you. For apart from Christ, Nature can neither perceive nor attain the grace and love of God, and apart from Him is nothing but wrath and condemnation.[84]

The noetic effects of sin

Special (or supernatural) revelation (to be discussed in a later chapter) was necessary from man's beginning, because man's finite nature could not of itself grasp the full understanding necessary to please God in all things, and it became even more necessary because of the negative effects the fall of Adam has had on the mind of all his descendants. Adam's fall meant that all

---

[81]Pierre Viret, *Instruction Chréstienne*, t. II, p.279 (My translation).

[82]Ibid., t. II, p. 423 (My translation).

[83]Viret shows the qualitative difference between the light of nature and the light of the gospel: 'Si la lumière naturelle en cette corruption de nature est borne et tant obscure meme qui lui est plus propre et plus naturelle...tu dois entendre qu'elle est du tout aveugle en la connaissance de cette plus haute science révélée en l'Evangile qui ne lui est aucunement naturelle, en laquelle elle n'a pas seulement besoin d'être restaurée, mais aussi qu'on lui en ajoute encore une autre toute nouvelle, comme si Dieu voulait créer des hommes tout nouveaux, autant différents au premier que Jesus' Christ est différent d'icelui' (Ibid., t. II. 429). Compare also John Calvin, *Institutes*, II.12.4-7.

[84]Martin Luther, *Weimarfe Aufgabe* 28, 101-102, quoted in David C. Steinmetz, *Luther in Context* (Grand Rapids: Baker Books, 1995), 27.

of his progeny were born with a fallen nature. The Psalmist summarizes the universal condition accurately: 'Lo, I was shapen in iniquity, and in sin did my mother conceive me' (Ps. 51:5). One of the major effects of this perversion of human nature has been through all ages an unwillingness of heart and mind to accept the clear testimony to God in creation and conscience, for this testimony shows that mankind is not his own Lord, but is absolutely obligated to Another. That, as we have just noted, is asserted by Paul in Romans 1:18: '...Men hold [down] the truth in unrighteousness.'

Bishop Theophilus of Antioch, around the year A.D. 180, explained the noetic effects of sin to his polytheistic adversary:

> God is seen by those who are enabled to see him, when they have the eyes of their soul opened; for all have eyes; but in some they are overspread, and do not see the light of the sun. Yet it does not follow because the blind do not see, that the light of the sun does not shine; but let the blind blame themselves and their own eyes. So you also, O man, have the eyes of your soul overspread by your sins and evil deeds. As a burnished mirror, so ought man to have his soul pure. When there is rust on the mirror, it is not possible that a man's face be seen in the mirror; so also when there is sin in a man, such a man cannot behold God.[85]

Fallen humankind has a vested interest in not seeing what is there and thus in misinterpreting the divine light that shines through creation and conscience. In the words of the Light of the world: '...and men loved darkness rather than light, because their deeds were evil' (John 3:19). Scottish theologian Thomas Halyburton, in his critique of the Deists, captured the sombre results of General Revelation (without special revelation): 'Nature's light is small and our minds are dark,'[86] although he does properly add that general revelation leaves us with no legitimate complaint against God on the final day of judgment.[87] Martin Luther had previously noted that 'there are people like the Epicureans, Pliny and others who deny [God's existence] with their mouths. But they must force themselves to do so; and by trying to extinguish the light in their hearts they act like men who plug their ears and close their eyes so that they may neither see nor hear. This does not solve their problem, however, for their conscience tells them something else.'[88]

The Genevan Reformer, John Calvin, throughout his career held to the unavoidable, objective reality of God's witness to Himself through creation and conscience, and the insufficiency of this 'natural' or 'general' revelation to lead fallen mankind (with its darkened mind) to a right knowledge of God apart from the grace of the 'special' or 'supernatural' revelation of Christ in Holy Scripture.

Developments within Lutheran and Reformed thought on pagan conscience

There appears to have been substantial development and change on this subject in the two German magisterial Reformers: Luther and Melanchthon.

---

[85]Theophilus of Antioch, *Ad Autolycum*, I. 2.

[86]Thomas Halyburton, op. cit., p. 78.

[87]Ibid., 312.

[88]Martin Luther, *Weimare Aufgabe* 19, 206, quoted in Althaus, *The Theology of Martin Luther*, Philadelphia: Fortress Press, 1966), 15.

It has been noted by Lutheran scholars that Luther in his early years accepted the traditional teaching of God's witness to Himself and His law in the conscience. Steinmetz notes that

> '*Synderesis*', for example, functions very much for Luther as the 'sense of divinity' does for John Calvin…Because human reason is blind and the human will is deformed, *synderesis* (which is hailed by Luther at first as a residuum of health in the soul) is a mark of what Paul Tillich called 'unhealthy health,' an apparent health which is only a symptom of a far more serious disease.[89]

Steinmetz points out, however, that Luther later 'drops this concept from his theology', perhaps in reaction to the Occamist anthropology which attributed too much power to the fallen human mind and will, disregarding the serious noetic effects of sin on the human frame.[90] This change (from what he had said regarding the witness to God available to humans through creation and conscience) in his 1515/16 *Commentary on Romans*, had occurred 'By the time of the *Disputation against Scholastic Theology* (1517)' and from what he says in the *Heidelberg Disputation* (1518).[91]

Melanchthon emphasizes the noetic effects of sin more than Luther

Melanchthon, Luther's younger disciple, went in the other direction. Dino Bellucci points out that Melanchthon started out with Luther's (post 1517–18) denial of any significant knowledge of God by humans, except through the gospel (in his 1521 *Didymi Oratio* – CR 1, 303-305).[92] Similarly, in his first *Loci* (1521), he states that there is only one way to know God: '…siquidem hoc est Christum cognoscere beneficia eius cognoscere.'[93] Later, Melanchthon gives much more place to the significance of man's knowledge of God in creation and conscience. Bellucci suggests that this shift was owing to 'new conditions in the cultural world of Wittenberg in view of the necessity to respect the strict distinction between the Law and the gospel.'[94] According to Bellucci:

> In the very beginning of his chapter *de Deo*, Melanchthon prevents all danger of contaminating the knowledge of God in the gospel by 'the physical [natural] knowledge of God'. Having clearly seen that there is a knowledge of God operative in the realm of the Law gave Melanchthon the liberty and desire to study physics. He felt it to be a profound privilege to give himself to the study of the testimonies of God written in nature which surrounds us and in mankind in particular, seeing in this capacity of visible beings to speak of God a particular dignity…[95]

---

89 David Steinmetz, Ibid., 64. He refers to WA 1. 32. 1-8; 1. 36. 11-19; 1. 37. 3-18.

90 Ibid., 65.

91 Ibid., 66.

92 Dino Bellucci, *Science de la Nature et Réformation: La Physique au service de la Réforme dans l'enseignement de Philippe Melanchthon* (Roma: Edizioni Vivere In, 1998), 170ff.

93 *Loci, prima aetas*, StA II, I, 7, 10.

94 Ibid., 177.

95 Ibid.

Melanchthon wrote in his *Initia doctrinae physicae:*

> It is useful to compare the physical [natural] doctrine with that which has been revealed by God, and this comparison gives more light to both types of revelation, and causes us to understand the statement of Paul in the first chapter of Romans, when he says that the Gentiles have held the truth of God captive in unrighteousness, and that one sees the power of God in understanding it at the beginning of his work.[96]

Certainly Melanchthon continued to hold to the noetic effects of sin, even after his new emphasis on the 'natural' knowledge of God in creation and conscience. He states in his *Initia* that:

> The human spirit is conceived as a mirror in which God reflects himself even today, although this mirror is darkened, squalid and the *noticia* or innate idea of God, written within us as in a book, no longer has the power to guide the life of men, who obstinately revolt against it...Even though this light is weakened in its present state, it is not extinguished and thus may still fulfill its function of proving the existence and nature of God.[97]

By the time of his second edition of *Loci Communes* (1535), Melanchthon clearly teaches the importance of making use of the testimony that God has given to Himself in nature. 'The faithful must employ themselves in reviving this knowledge (*noticia*), and in rendering it more powerful by appealing to the signs which God has imprinted in nature. God personally calls us to practice this kind of philosophy. We have no right to neglect it.'[98]

Bellucci notes that the biblical justification given by Melanchthon for seeking to learn of God through nature is found in Romans 1:20, where we are called 'to contemplate God's divinity in nature', and also in Acts 17:27, where we are taught '...that God is so present in nature that we may almost touch Him with our hands. Thus we must think of the entirety of nature as a sort of sacrament by which it gives witness to the existence of God and to his attributes of wisdom, goodness, justice.'[99]

Yet Melanchthon is more positive than Luther or Calvin on 'natural knowledge'

Melanchthon took the implications of the validity of knowledge in nature further than either Luther or Calvin. Kusukawa brings out that 'Proofs (*demonstrationes*) for the existence of God and His Providence, which were explicitly rejected as a matter of human curiosity in the 1521 edition [*sc.* of *Loci*], also appeared in 1535. These proofs had appeared for the first time in Melanchthon's revised commentary on Romans, *Commentarii in Epistolam Pauli ad Romanos,* of 1532. These were the proofs which were subsequently incorporated into the *Initia doctrinae physicae.*'[100] Nevertheless, even after this change of emphasis, Melanchthon always held to the priority of special revelation over natural revelation:

---

[96]CR 13, 198.

[97]Ibid., Quoted in Bellucci, op. cit., 179, 181.

[98]Bellucci, 186.

[99]Bellucci, 188, referring to Melanchthon, *Loci, secunda aetas*, CR 21, 369.

[100]Sachiko Kusukawa, *The Transformation of Natural Philosophy. The Case of Philip Melanchthon* (Cambridge: Cambridge University Press, 1995), 164.

> Mankind must receive confirmation by the Word of the true and correct manner of thinking about God, and must already know Him as Creator, thanks to [written] revelation, before he can devote himself in a 'useful and pleasing manner' to researching the traces of divinity in nature and to gathering arguments for His existence.[101]

Thus, only insofar as Christians are guided by the written Word of God, does Melanchthon 'approve that philosophy which consists in researching the traces of divinity within nature'.[102]

Barth and R. Muller differ on the relationship between Calvin and seventeenth-century Reformed Orthodoxy

The development of thought concerning natural and supernatural theology, its limitations by sin and particularly the place – if any – for proofs of God's existence amongst seventeenth-century orthodox Reformed theologians has been extensively discussed in the twentieth century. Karl Barth has seen in this development of Reformed Scholasticism a discontinuity with Calvin's teaching on the 'duplex' knowledge of God as Creator and Redeemer towards a more rationalistic doctrine of God in which 'natural knowledge of God' forms a basis (or, as with St. Thomas, a 'first treatise') for the revealed knowledge of God (the 'second treatise').[103] T. H. L. Parker has also discussed the increasing attention given to what can be learned by the testimony of nature and conscience by the later Reformed scholars in terms of deviation from Calvin's simpler scriptural and Christocentric stance on the subject towards a more man-centred approach.[104]

Richard Muller in an extensive study of this question admits definite development amongst the seventeenth-century Reformed, as for instance in the series of technical distinctions concerning human knowledge of God in Musculus and Polanus.[105] But, against Barth, Parker, and particularly Otto Weber, he denies

> ...the all-too-frequent and utterly erroneous claim that orthodox or scholastic Protestant theology generally viewed natural revelation and the natural theology drawn from it as a foundation on which supernatural revelation and a supernatural theology can build. Otto Weber makes this mistake when he declares that orthodoxy fashioned its doctrine of special revelation into 'an understanding of the knowledge of God as rational insight into supernatural truths' and thereby came to view special revelation as no more than a completion of our natural knowledge of God and to assume that 'Christian knowledge' fits into "the model of rational knowledge.[106]

---

[101]Bellucci, 188, referring to Melanchthon, *Loci, secunda aetas*, CR 21, 369.

[102]Bellucci, Ibid., referring to Melanchthon, Ibid., CR 21, 370.

[103]e.g. see Karl Barth, *The Knowledge of God and the Service of God According to the Teaching of the Reformation*, translated by J.L.M. Haire and Ian Henderson (London: Hodder and Stoughton, 1938). And also Karl Barth and Emil Brunner, *Natural Theology*, translated by Peter Fraenkel (London: G. Bles, 1946).

[104]e.g. see T. H. L. Parker, *The Doctrine of the Knowledge of God: A Study in Calvin's Theology* (Grand Rapids: Eerdmans, 1959).

[105]Muller, op. cit., refers to distinctions made by Musculus (from his *Loci communes*, lxi) on pages 179-81, and to those made by Polanus (from his *Syntagma, Synopsis Libri IX*, 4. 2 and 5.2) on pages 181-82.

[106]Ibid., 190, quoting Otto Weber, *Foundations*, I: 217.

Muller refers to the important distinction drawn by Heidegger between a *theologia naturalis irregenitorum* and a *theologia naturalis regenitorum*, as does Mastricht in slightly different terms.[107] According to Muller:

> Even though it is not salvific, comments Heidegger, the natural knowledge of God (notitia Dei naturalis) ought not to be dismissed as useless: it leaves the contentious and obstreperous among the unregenerate without excuse before God (Rom. 1:20) and provides those not yet regenerate but searching in nature for God and salvation with the capability of sensing and discovering the presence of God (Acts 17:27).[108]

In summary, Muller seems to be correct in stating that:

> We find no evidence…that the Reformed orthodox recognition of the parallel between the natural law and the Decalogue led to a pagan natural theology (theologia falsa) as a kind of praeparatio evangelica: from Musculus to Polanus and Alsted, to Du Moulin, Charnock, Turretin, and Heidegger, this form of natural theology carries with it only the elenctical or condemnatory function of the Law, not the full usus paedagogicus. It serves only to leave men without excuse…We see here an adumbration of the Puritan and pietist soteriological preparationism, not of any kind of philosophical rationalism.[109]

The concerns of Karl Barth

Even granted Muller's proper correction of several critiques of Reformed orthodoxy as departures from Calvin in the direction of rationalism, it is important to note that Barth has a somewhat different concern, not entirely covered by this correction. In the context of the doctrine of election, for instance, Barth argues against 'a "God in general," as he may be conceived and systematically constructed from the standpoint of sovereignty, of omnipotence, of a first cause, of absolute necessity'.[110] Barth believes that this kind of thinking has been done *by the regenerate* as they contemplated what they found of God by the light of nature, particularly as they did not give sufficient attention to the Scripture's witness to who Christ is and what He has done in this regard.[111]

For instance, Du Moulin, as summarized by Muller, teaches:

> That man has an inherent knowledge of God is demonstrated both by pagan religion and by his general acceptance of the laws deduced from nature. Philosophers, furthermore, have deduced conceptions of God as Unmoved Mover, as first efficient cause, as Creator and Orderer of the world…natural theology contains the idea of God as 'the most perfect Being, from whom flows and on whom depends all entity and perfection.' From this definition follow the attributes of eternity, simplicity, and wisdom.[112]

---

[107]Ibid., 186, quoting Heidegger, *Corpus theol.*, I. 12, and Mastricht, *Theoretico-practica theologia*, I.i.18.

[108]Ibid. 186.

[109]Ibid. 191.

[110]Karl Barth, *Church Dogmatics*, Vol. II, The Doctrine of God, Part 2, 49.

[111]Ibid., 52-55.

[112]Muller, op. cit., 187, referring to Pierre Du Moulin, *A Treatise of the Knowledge of God* (London, 1634), 2.

Rise of Descartes

Precisely, this 'general view of God' (from light of nature, unshaped by God's revelation of Himself in Christ) is thought by Barth to have paved the way for Descartes, fount of the rationalist Enlightenment, which in the intellectual circles of seventeenth and eighteenth-century Europe, effectively undercut Christian orthodoxy.

Discussing Descartes' 'Sixth Meditation', Barth notes:

> The only thing which he knows positively is mathematical truth as such. But he does not know either a real external world corresponding to it, himself a thinking subject, or especially the actual existence of a perfect being who is the basis of, and evinces and demonstrates, the trustworthiness of his own thought, and his own existence, and the reality of an external world ... The God of Descartes is hopelessly enchained within the mind of man ... The God of Descartes does not bear the divine character. His divinity has nothing to do with the fact that He has revealed Himself and is therefore to be believed. This idea of divinity is innate in man. Man can produce it at will from the treasury or deficiency of his mind ... If the case is to be otherwise, I must believe the Word of the God who evinces Himself authoritatively in His revelation, and subject myself to His commands and prohibitions ... By such an attitude I do not merely assert but genuinely recognise the eternal being of the God who transcends me ... Without this subordination, in any other attitude but that of obedience to the divine self-demonstration, there can be no question of any proof of God's existence. And this is the point where Descartes fails.[113]

Barth's concern is that even a 'natural theology of the regenerate' (to use Heidegger's term) will proceed from the basis of general concepts of God, and unless it is corrected by biblical teaching on the Triune being and works of the one true God, will conclude by presenting a God who is different from the biblical one. Thus he writes:

> But the voice which reigns, the voice by which we were taught by God Himself concerning God, was the voice of Jesus Christ...In avoiding the different sources of error, we saw that they had one feature in common: the negligence or arbitrariness with which even in the Church the attempt was made to go past or to go beyond Jesus Christ in the consideration and conception and definition of God ... But when the theology allows itself on any pretext to be jostled away from that name, God is inevitably crowded out by a hypnotised image of man. Theology must begin with Jesus Christ, and not with general principles...Otherwise the highest reality can, and inevitably will, be reduced to the flattest unreality.[114]

Faith is necessary to know the biblical God truly

An illuminating comment of how this works can be found in a homily of St. John Chrysostom in the fifth century, where he shows that without faith (which exists only in the covenant community of grace – the Church – founded on the writings of Prophets and apostles), one cannot properly understand the truths about God that we learn from nature.

---

[113]Karl Barth, *Church Dogmatics*, III. 1, The Doctrine of Creation, 359, 360, 361.

[114]Ibid., *Church Dogmatics*, II. 2, The Doctrine of God, 4, 5.

> For example, God is in no one place and yet is everywhere. Could anything make less sense to reason? And in both of these statements [about where God is or is not] there is much that surpasses our understanding. God does not enclose Himself in one place, and in Him is no space. He did not come into being, nor did He create Himself, nor did He commence to be. What kind of human reasoning [ποῖος λογισμός] would be able to admit this, if it did not have faith? Would this not appear ridiculous? And not to have any limit [τέλος] would this not be the most difficult of enigmas? ... And again, does God limit the universe or does He not? If He does not limit it, then it is the universe which limits Him. But if He limits it – then God is indefinable by nature [ἄπειρος τῇ φύσει]... What obscurity, and how absolutely necessary is faith in all things [πανταχοῦ πίστεως δεῖ]! Faith alone is strong.[115]

Calvin on true knowledge of God

A thousand years later, John Calvin says much the same thing in a very different context, when he is discussing 'what human reason can discern with regard to God's Kingdom and to spiritual insight', which he says 'consists chiefly in three things: (1) knowing God (2) knowing his fatherly favor in our behalf, in which our salvation consists; (3) knowing how to frame our life according to the rule of his law.' His response is this:

> In the first two points – and especially in the second – the greatest geniuses are blinder than moles! Certainly I do not deny that one can read competent and apt statements about God here and there in the philosophers, but these always show a certain giddy imagination...the Lord indeed gave them a slight taste of his divinity in such a way that their seeing did not direct them to the truth, much less enable them to see it...Besides, although they may chance to sprinkle their books with droplets of truth, how many monstrous lies defile them. In short, they never even sensed that assurance of God's benevolence toward us (without which man's understanding can only be filled with boundless confusion). Human reason, therefore, neither approaches, nor strives toward, nor even takes a straight aim at, this truth: to understand who the true God is or what sort of God he wishes to be toward us.[116]

This faith is alone found in that community which is brought into being and sustained by the impact of God's Spirit speaking in the written Word. The centre of that community's life is the incarnate Word, who is the fulfillment of the Holy Scriptures and in whose Person and work we see most clearly who this God is, who 'by faith' we understand to have framed the worlds (Heb. 11:3) by his word. The Church is never asked to stand off this ground in interpreting what can be known by 'the light of nature'. The reality of God's existence and power is witnessed to, but never explicated by nature and conscience themselves, apart from Father, Son and Holy Spirit speaking through the Word.

To attempt to explicate the being and working of God from the light of nature and conscience alone, apart from God's revelation of Himself in Christ through the Holy Spirit, is to fabricate a being who is less than

---

[115]St. John Chrysostom, *Homily on Colossians* 5:3.

[116]Calvin, *Institutes*, II. 2. 18.

and other than the God and Father of our Lord Jesus Christ. That has been the sad story of much of Western thought since the seventeenth-century beginning of the humanistic Enlightenment.

II. Historical Theological Approaches to Knowledge of God from Nature, apart from Scripture (though reverent towards it)

Many outstanding Church theologians, both in medieval times and in the post-Reformation period, have commented on evidences for the existence of God from the light of nature and conscience. In general, what they said was orthodox – in accordance with Scripture and 'the rule of truth' of the Church's central tradition. However, insofar as they attempted to demonstrate that God is and more particularly who He is apart from the Trinitarian witness of Holy Scripture, they unwittingly began a bifurcation between the God of nature and the God of Scripture that would eventually lead to a God of nature who was different from the one of Scripture.

Within their own works, there may have been little evidence of the beginning of this split, since they usually described the God of nature within the context of His triune reality. For the most part their discussions of His qualities (omnipotence, infinity, etc.) quietly assumed the testimony of Scripture, as they described how a 'natural' (or unregenerate) person ought to interpret the powerful evidence of what is trumpeted forth in nature and conscience. But as thought developed, other thinkers would do the very thing St. Chrysostom and Calvin said could not properly be done: attempt to know God prior to or apart from His Triune revelation in Scripture.

The approach of St. Thomas to fallen human reason

We have already noted that St. Thomas in his *Summa Theologiae* placed his fivefold proofs for God's existence within the context of creation by the Triune God. Therefore, although he definitely distinguishes 'preambles to faith' (what can be known about God from nature, apart from the faith of the Church – e.g. 'God exists')[117] from the articles of the faith itself (what can be known only by special revelation to the Church – e.g. the content of the Creed),[118] in his discussion of the preambles, he still assumes the Holy Trinity.

Since St. Thomas's approach to natural theology has been so powerful for over seven hundred years in the West, it is necessary to consider carefully what he said and what he did not say concerning the natural man's ability to know God apart from special revelation. Although he established the structure of 'preambles of faith' (from nature and conscience) and 'the articles of the faith' (the Creed's affirmations of Trinity and redemption), Reformed scholars such as Arvin Vos have shown that he did not in fact state that 'the preambles are a necessary precondition for faith,'[119] nor did

---

[117] *Summa Theologiae*, 11. 2 ad 1m.

[118] Ibid., 2a2ae. 1, 5.

[119] Arvin Vos, *Aquinas, Calvin, & Contemporary Protestant Thought: A Critique of Protestant Views on the Thought of Thomas Aquinas* (Grand Rapids: William B. Eerdmans, 1985), 66.

he hold that the existence of God must be proved before one can believe.[120] Nor did he maintain, as many Protestant scholars have accused him, that the mind of the natural man is unaffected by the fall.

St. Thomas's Theology presupposes Christian faith

On the contrary, Thomas stated that one accepts on faith that which one cannot personally demonstrate:

> The truths about God which St. Paul says we can know by our natural powers of reasoning – that God exists, for example – are not numbered among the articles of faith, but are presupposed by them. For faith presupposes natural knowledge, just as grace does nature and all perfections that which they perfect. However, there is nothing to stop a man accepting on faith some truth which he personally cannot demonstrate, even if that truth in itself is such that demonstration could make it evident.[121]

Elsewhere, he writes:

> The credenda include things that admit of strict philosophical proof, not because these are absolutely speaking objects of faith for everyone, but because they are a prerequisite to the truth of faith; and those who do not have proof of them must at least presuppose them in faith.[122]

Indeed, in the very first Question of his *Summa Theologiae*, Thomas deals with *sacra doctrina*. In working through 'natural theology' in the following questions, he assumes the truth of revelation, and proceeds on the basis of Christian faith, although some of the neo-Thomists of the nineteenth century do not seem to have grasped this.[123]

Certainly he does not put reason above faith. He writes in *Summa Contra Gentiles:* '…it is the acme of stupidity for a man to suspect as false what is divinely revealed through the ministry of angels simply because it cannot be investigated by reason.'[124] Furthermore, St. Thomas taught that man's mind was negatively affected by the Fall, and thus needed grace in order to understand God:

> Human reason is very deficient in things concerning God. A sign of this is that philosophers, in their inquiry into human affairs by natural investigation, have fallen into many errors, and have disagreed among themselves. And consequently, in order that men might have knowledge of God, free of doubt and uncertainty, it was necessary for divine truths to be delivered to them by way of faith, being told to them as it were, by God himself who cannot lie.[125]

Thomas taught that the human mind was damaged by sin and needs grace

St. Thomas placed what later theologians termed 'the noetic effects of sin' in the context of 'the loss of original justice' in Adam's fall (that loss of perfect

---

[120] Ibid., 67.

[121] St. Thomas, *Summa Theologiae*, Ia. 2, 2 ad 1m. Quoted in Vos, op. cit., 70.

[122] Ibid., 2a 2ae. 1, 5 ad 3m.

[123] See Per Erik Persson, *Sacra Doctrina: Reason and Revelation in Aquinas*, translated by Ross MacKenzie (Philadelphia: Fortress Press, 1970), 269.

[124] *Summa Contra Gentiles*, I. 3. 4 (p. 65, Pegis translation).

[125] *Summa Theologiae*, 2a 2ae, 2, 4, reply.

balance amongst all aspects of man's being, in which the bodily appetites were subject to the God-oriented mind). He spoke of this loss of proper order within the human constitution as 'the wounding of nature':

> In so far as reason is deprived of its direction towards truth, we have the 'wound of ignorance'; in so far as the will is deprived of its order toward good, we have the 'wound of malice'; in so far as the irascible appetite is deprived of its ability to face the difficult, we have the 'wound of weakness'; in so far as the concupiscible appetite is deprived of its ability to temper the pleasurable, we have the 'wound of concupiscence'.[126]

Therefore, according to him, humankind needs divine assistance or grace in order to know God rightly (thus, in some measure, beginning to restore the order of 'original justice' within the human frame).[127] The angelic doctor discusses this in a number of citations, as for instance:

> Thus we must say that for the knowledge of any truth, man needs divine assistance so that his intellect may be moved by God to actualise itself. He does not, however, need a new light, supplementing his natural light, in order to know truth in all cases, but only in certain cases which transcend natural knowledge...But the human intellect cannot know more profound intelligible realities unless it is perfected by a stronger light, say the light of faith or prophecy; and this is called the light of grace, in as much as it supplements nature.[128]

Arvin Vos convincingly suggests that Aquinas has been misinterpreted as having maintained that one can reason one's way at least to the 'one God' (or first treatise of theology, or preamble of faith) in terms of 'pure nature' and 'unfallen reason', because he has been read through the lens of post-sixteenth and seventeenth-century Thomism, where the related concepts of pure nature and natural religion made their appearance.[129] These same concepts (in rather different terminology) would become equally influential in European Protestantism by the late seventeenth and early eighteenth centuries, as we shall see. These ideas, however, whether in their Catholic or Protestant forms, were not faithful to the original teaching of St. Thomas.

'Natural theology flourishes only in the soil of historical religion'

Nevertheless, one has to question whether some of the teaching of the true St. Thomas is not seriously problematic in making such a strong structural division between natural knowledge of the One God and supernatural knowledge of the Triune God. It is not that his theological affirmations in both treatises are not, in general, scripturally sound. Rather, the issue is how much he unwittingly assumes as a Trinitarian Christian when he explicates the details of what humankind can know about God and His attributes from creation and conscience.

As A. E. Taylor brought out in his Gifford Lectures, natural theology flourishes only in a soil and atmosphere of historical religion, apart from

---

[126]Ibid., 1a2ae. 85, 3.
[127]See Ibid., 1a2ae. 109, 2.
[128]Ibid., 2a2ae. 2, 4.
[129]A. Vos, op. cit., 152-58.

which it degenerates into naturalism.[130] And W. Pannenberg notes that when the Second Vatican Counsel adopted a statement of Vatican I on the knowledge of God from the works of creation in its Constitution on Revelation (Dei Verbum 6), '...it set the natural knowledge of God in the framework of salvation history according to the divine decree of revelation.'[131]

Philippe Thiry raises the crucial question here:

> This intelligent Being or this ordaining principle is the God of the Christian civilisation of Thomas Aquinas. Various cultural and religious assumptions play their part in giving a certain consistency to a concept otherwise very abstract in content [in French, *fort squelettique*]. How can one be sure that this ordaining principle is a unique, personal subject, creator and providential ruler of the universe? This ordaining principle could be multiple, impersonal, a non-creating architect, like the potter-god of Plato; one who is insensible to the destiny of the universe, like the god of Aristotle. One discerns just how far the arguments of Thomas Aquinas are, in fact, favourable pointers for the believer, which by the way is no small matter.[132]

Thomas had to address 'the integral Aristotle' of Islamic scholars

In the atmosphere of medieval Christendom, Thomas sought to contend with the intellectual onslaught of a naturalistic interpretation of Aristotle, coming from the influence of Islamic scholars such as Averroes (1126–1198). The Aristotelian tradition, as developed in the Arabic Islamic strand, held such ideas (true to the original Aristotle, but incompatible with Christianity) that creation was eternal, that individuals did not have an immortal soul, that there was one intellect for all humanity, that God, 'the unmoved Mover' was essentially a part of (and dependent upon) the created order, and that outside, miraculous intervention by God was impossible. In a word, their God was neither personal nor infinite. Some Christians (such as Siger of Brabant and Boetius of Dacia) were attempting to affirm the rediscovered 'pagan' Aristotle and at the same time hold on to orthodox Christianity by radically separating philosophy and theology. They held that contradictory statements (such as creation is eternal and creation is temporal) can be maintained at the same time as a sort of 'double truth', since one is from philosophy (reason) and the other from theology (revelation).

To follow Averroes' estimate of Aristotle would consequently lead not only to accepting these errors as philosophically necessary, but also to destroying the very possibility of the unity of truth. How, then, could Christianity assimilate philosophy – the philosophy of Aristotle – without destroying either itself or philosophy?[133]

It was St. Thomas's massive achievement convincingly to affirm the unity of truth within the intellectual turmoil of medieval Christian Europe. 'He

---

[130]A. E. Taylor, *The Faith of a Moralist*, London: Macmillan & Co, 1937), Vol.2, 7ff.

[131]W. Pannenberg, op. cit., 76.

[132]Philippe Thiry, *L'Existence de Dieu: Les arguments de l'agnosticism, de l'athéism and du théism* (Namur, Belgium: Presses universitaires de Namur, 1996), 159.

[133]'General Introduction' to *Saint Thomas Aquinas Summa Contra Gentiles: Book One – God*, Translated with an Introduction and Notes by Anton C. Pegis (University of Notre Dame Press, 1975), 22.

believed that truth was one and came from God. He therefore believed that nothing that was philosophically demonstrable could ever contradict or be contradicted by anything taught to man by the Christian Revelation.'[134]

We will not be concerned at this stage with the details of how St. Thomas did this, although it will be well to note, in the words of Etienne Gilson, that he accomplished it 'more by revolution than by evolution'.[135] By commenting on the new translations into Latin of Aristotle's works by his fellow Domincan, William of Moerbeke, and especially in his *Summa Contra Gentiles* (1259–1264), which was written to be a sort of 'missionary' manual of the faith for Christian evangelists in a Spain heavily influenced by Islam, Thomas offered a profoundly Christianized Aristotelianism, one that sought to be compatible with and in some sense preparatory to biblical revelation. Any criticism of particular aspects of his work must never minimize the greatness of his epochal achievement.

The critical question is: how extensive is the knowledge of humankind concerning God from nature and conscience apart from His speaking to them in the context of covenant community? We have seen from the exegeses of such passages as Romans 1, Acts 14 and 17, and references to some of the nature Psalms, that there is true and inescapable knowledge of the living God in the created order and in the conscience of humankind (apart from Scripture), reminding all people of their ethical obligations to a transcendent Power, and leaving them inexcusable for not fulfilling those obligations in their own life. As far as it goes, this is certainly a true revelation from God to all persons created in His image, for otherwise we could make no sense of our own psychology, as Thomas Halyburton pointed out when he noted that 'without revelation we cannot understand on what grounds we condemn ourselves'.[136]

How far can human knowledge take us apart from revelation?

Positively, natural revelation grounds the reality of God's Being and action into the real world of nature and human consciousness. As Henri Bouillard noted, the sort of philosophical reflection carried out by St. Thomas: '...offers to the Christian the means of making explicit the natural knowledge implied in faith and of thus experiencing, through a critical process, the certitude that the God in whom he believes is indeed his God and that this belief is not a dream.'[137] This sort of reflection on what we know about God through our own environment also may assist the believer in removing false 'escape mechanisms' erected by the unbeliever to avoid the theistic reality he would prefer to negate.

As Thomas writes in *Summa Contra Gentiles*: '...the Mohammedans and the pagans do not agree with us in accepting the authority of any Scripture, by which they may be convinced of their error...We must, therefore, have recourse to the natural reason, to which all men are forced to give their assent. However, it is true, in divine matters the natural reason has its

[134]Ibid.

[135]Etienne Gilson, *History of Christian Philosophy in the Middle Ages* (New York: Random House, 1955), 365.

[136]Thomas Halyburton, op. cit., 126.

[137]Henri Bouillard, *Knowledge of God* translated by Samuel D. Femiano, (New York: Herder & Herder, 1968), 61.

failings.'[138] Later he adds: '...whatever arguments are brought forward against the doctrines of faith are conclusions incorrectly derived from the first and self-evident principles imbedded in nature.'[139]

The main point of Thomas's fivefold proof

Without studying the details of St. Thomas's five proofs of God's existence here, we may note that at the very least the main thrust of such arguments as the cosmological one indicate that the intelligibility and reliability of the universe (which have to be assumed even to be argued against) cannot be explained from within the universe itself, but point to something beyond it. The chain of reasoning involved in this substantial matter is of no small help in demonstrating the inexcusability of atheism and in pointing the soul to the source of light and fidelity. St. Thomas showed that empirical reasoning, far from leaving one bound in some sort of closed, materialistic mechanistic framework, actually points beyond sense experience to a reality outside itself, that is necessary to make sense of what one actually feels and knows.

But what or who is the source of this intelligibility and reliability? That is the major question raised by mankind's experience within the created order through means of his senses, intellect and conscience. Humankind generally knows that 'bad' actions are inappropriate because there is pressure upon it from some kind of higher 'good', which gives content to what is bad and what is good. St. Thomas, not inappropriately, reasons that being is good, and that good communicates itself. He rightly holds that it is in the nature of being to communicate its good to others.[140] Thus, God wills other beings than Himself, and this is at the root of the created order with its intelligibility and reliability.[141]

Yet how can we derive this (true) concept from the realm of nature and conscience alone? It is not clear that reworking Aristotle's philosophy (even as powerfully, profoundly and originally as St. Thomas did it) is sufficient to establish the crucial point in and of itself.[142] Although one must keep in mind that, in St. Thomas, nature is seen to be open upwards, not closed in on itself (as in later mechanistic Deism), does not one have to have some kind of relational, verbal communication from a source transcendent to created being to rest upon this foundation? And that is precisely what we find from the very beginning of creation.

III. Knowledge of God From Nature in the Light of Personal, Verbal Revelation

At the end of the first week of creation, God communicated verbally with His image-bearers (cf. Gen. 2:16, 17). After the fall of Adam, God continued

---

[138] *Summa Contra Gentiles*, I. 2. 3.

[139] Ibid., I. 7. 7.

[140] See the discussion in Thomas, S. T., 1a, 19, 2.

[141] S.T., 1a, 19, 2, ad 1.

[142] See the apposite remarks of A. E. Taylor on the brilliance, coherence, and in major respects, originality and independence of St. Thomas 'revolutionary' reworking of Aristotle in A. E. Taylor, *Philosophical Studies* (London: MacMillan and Co., 1934), 233, 237, 246-47.

speaking to his descendants, both bad and good (as to Cain in Gen. 4:7-15 and Enoch in Gen. 5:24). God communicated with Job in pre-Mosiac patriarchal times (cf. Job 42), and called out Abram to become a godly patriarch and father of the faithful (cf. Gen. 12:1-3). After Abraham, the focus of God's communication to the human race was within the community of Israel, established by the Covenant of Grace with them, by means of which they would 'be blessed and made a blessing' (cf. Gen. 12:2), extending to all the families of the earth (cf. Gen. 12:3).

Nature Psalms

Hence, from the very beginning of the world, God's work of creation and His interventions in history have been explained by His verbal communications to particular communities, whom He chose to serve as a sort of lighthouse and universal pulpit to the rest of humankind as providence opens the way in accordance with 'the times before appointed and the bounds of their habitation' (Acts 17:26). How closely the Psalms bind together God's message in nature and in His personal being and activity! Psalm 135 is a vivid illustration of this inseparable connection. Verses 6 and 7 speak of God's continuing control of the forces of nature: 'Whatever the LORD pleased, that did he in heaven, and in earth, in the seas, and all deep places. He causeth vapours to ascend from the ends of the earth; he maketh lightnings for the rain; he bringeth the wind out of his treasuries.' But immediately before these verses, we are told, 'For the LORD hath chosen Jacob unto himself, and Israel for his peculiar treasure.' And immediately afterwards, 'Who smote the firstborn of Egypt, both of man and beast. Who sent tokens and wonders into the midst of thee, O Egypt, upon Pharaoh, and upon all his servants' (vv. 8 and 9).

The intertwining of God's revelation in nature and His supernatural intervention and revelation of Himself to the covenant community is similarly found in many other psalms, as for instance, Psalm 29. Verses 3 to 8 declare God's majestic power in the storms upon the waters and forests. Then verse 9, after describing God's direct intervention in the births of wild animals and the laying waste of forests, directly says: '…and in His temple doth every one speak of his glory.' Psalm 19 devotes the first half (vv. 1-6) to God's revelation of Himself in nature to all humankind, and the second half (vv. 7-14) to the praise of the qualities of His law and the purity of fearing Him. In like fashion, Psalm 8 mingles together God's handiwork in the heavens and in humankind, and the excellence of his name. Psalm 65 interweaves the 'praise of God in Sion' (v. 1), the reality of prayer (v. 2) and forgiveness of sins (v. 3), and the joy of coming into God's temple (v. 4), with the establishing of mountains (v. 6), the stilling of storms at sea (v. 7), the blessing of rain upon the crops (vv. 9-11), and the joy of abundant harvests and rich pastures (vv. 11-13).

Scriptural testimony on divine revelation in nature and in Word

From Genesis 1 and 2, where God creates the heavens and the earth, to Revelation 21 and 22, where 'the holy city, new Jerusalem' comes down from heaven to earth (21:2) so that 'the tabernacle of God is with men' (21:3), and 'the nations of them that are saved walk in the light (of the Lamb)' (21:23, 24), God is always revealing Himself both in His created order of heavens and earth, and in His Word. Prophets and apostles understand these realities of nature and Word together and in light of one another. They do not seem to speak at much length of nature without immediately giving ear to what the Lord of nature is saying, nor do they take us into such abstract spiritual realms that embodied existence would have no material or conceptual tools with which to grasp something of its reality. Thus, Scripture holds together God's revelation in nature and His supernatural revelation in terms of personal, verbal relationship with His covenant people. It seems unlikely that His Church should follow any other procedure in interpreting the reality of the Triune God, who creates the universe, interacts with it and speaks into it through His written Word, and pre-eminently through His incarnate Word.

Not that it could be wrong to distinguish God's revelation in nature and in word, only that it is improper to separate them, as though Israel and the Church did not know what they know.[143] It was not Aquinas's intention to do this, but the methodology of dividing theology into a first treatise on the One God known in nature as a preparation for the second treatise on the Triune God known in Scripture and the Creed, does leave the door open in this direction.

The difficulty of getting a personal God from nature

An illustration of the difficulty here is Aquinas's correct teaching that it is the nature of being to communicate its good (as we just noted).[144] But how definitely could we establish this from nature alone? And even if we could satisfactorily determine that being is not ultimately frustrated in communicating its good by the existence of contagious and destructive evil, how could we then demonstrate that this being is not part of or dependent upon the rest of material reality, and that it has the unique personal qualities of the Triune God? From within nature alone, could one not take the same observations and argue for some of pantheism (whether with the ancient Stoics or a modern scientific philosopher such as Kastler), as Philippe Thiry has suggested?[145]

Even though I believe St. Thomas would get the better of the argument, especially on the basis of his all-important distinction between 'essence' and 'existence' or 'necessary' and 'contingent' being, as Etienne Gilson insightfully pointed out,[146] still it is at best a complicated train of reasoning to pursue within the dark and cloudy halls of nature. And, in that regard, one wonders if the 'I am that I am' of the burning bush (Exod. 3:14), familiar to St. Thomas from earliest years, was not always in the background, casting

---

[143]A. Lecerf, French Reformed scholar, wisely stated that as believers, 'we cannot pretend not to know something we know' (A. Lecerf, *An Introduction to Reformed Dogmatics*, London: Lutterworth Press), 218.

[144]See also St. Thomas, *Summa Contra Gentiles*, I.37.5 and chs. 40, 75, 78.

[145]P. Thiry, op. cit., 156, 157

[146]Etienne Gilson, op. cit., 252-55.

His non-consuming light on the saint's proper teaching that God depends on nothing, while all things depend upon Him?[147] Significantly, the 'subtle Scot', John Duns Scotus begins his complex and difficult proof of God, *De Primo Pincipio* (c. 1303–04) with a prayer to the God who revealed Himself to Moses as 'I am that I am', and prays to 'investigate how much our natural reason can learn about that true being *if we begin with the being which you have predicated of yourself*' (emphasis mine).[148]

In confronting the God upon whom all things depend, who Himself is dependent upon nothing, St. Gregory Nazianzus holds together the One God known through nature and conscience, and the Triune God revealed in creation, incarnation, Pentecost and Scripture:

> No sooner do I conceive of the one than I am illumined by the splendour of the three; no sooner do I distinguish them than I am carried back to the one. When I think of any one of the three, I think of Him as the whole, and my eyes are filled, and the greater part of what I am thinking escapes me.[149]

In another Oration, he stated: 'When I say God, I mean Father, Son and Holy Spirit.'[150] In explicating mankind's knowledge of God through nature, the Church need never hold in abeyance the major part of its knowledge of who the Creator really is. The Church knows the one God from the very start in accordance with His Triune nature.

Taking this approach, the crucial teaching of St. Thomas that the Being of God is supremely good, and it is His nature to communicate good to other beings, has been illuminated in Trinitarian fashion (in closest conjunction with 'natural consciousness') by a Romanian Orthodox theologian, Dumitru Stăniloae:

> But it likewise belongs to our nature – as the only being conscious of itself and the world – to search for a meaning to our own existence and that of the world as well. And only the perspective of the eternity of our existence can give us this meaning. In our consciousness of self, there is implied the will to continue in being forever so that we might deepen the infinite meaning of our own existence and that of the whole of reality.
>
> According to this conception, we have been created for eternity inasmuch as we gasp, like suffocating beings, after eternity, after the absolute. We wish to love and to be loved more and more, striving after a love which is absolute and endless. But this we can only find in relation with a Person who is infinite and absolute, a conscious Person, if we may speak pleonastically. We strive to discover and achieve an ever greater beauty, to know an ever more profound reality, to progress within a continuous newness. In all these ways, we aim at the infinite because we are *person*. Yet all these aspects of an infinite reality we can only find in an infinite Person, or better, in a growing communion with this Personal reality, newer and newer rays of reality, of beauty, and of innovation shine forth in us and – through us – upon all

---

[147]Cf. St. Thomas, *Summa Contra Gentiles*, I. 22. 10. For perceptive remarks on the general influence of Exodus 3:14 on medieval theology, see Etienne Gilson, *The Spirit of Medieval Philosophy*, translated by A. C. Downes (Charles Scribner's Sons: New York, 1940), 51, 433-34.

[148]John Duns Scotus, *A Treatise on God as First Principle*, Translated and Edited with Commentary by Allan B. Wolter (Chicago: Franciscan Herald Press, 1966), I. 2 (p.2).

[149]Gregory Nazianzus, *Oration* 40, 41.

[150]*Oration* 45, 4.

aspects of the world, while more and more dimensions and horizons of reality are being disclosed.[151]

The intelligibility of the universe leads people to look upward to higher levels in order to find meaning

The very intelligibility of the universe leads any thinking person to a higher level above it to give rationality and consciousness their meaning. A rationality enclosed within the life and death cycle of limited nature would finally end in irrationality. Even to argue that life and the world are irrational requires the employment of rationality to frame such arguments. And similarly, to deny the existence of overarching good on the basis of the reality of evil requires the assumption of some supremely good standard by which one calls evil 'evil'. The unique existence of the universe and of man within it cries out for a relationship with the Triune God who created all, in order to give it meaning.

As Stăniloae says:

> According to our faith, the rationality existing in the universe needs to be completed by, and seeks an account of itself within, the rationality of a person. By itself, it does not exhaust all rationality. When the rationality of the world is seen in itself as the only one in existence, it has led many writers and thinkers to go as far as to think of the universe, which draws every person towards death, as one huge graveyard, a universe of the absurd, a place from which meaning is gone and where rationality is irrational. But the rationality of the universe cannot be irrational. It acquires its full meaning, however, only when it is considered to have its source in a rational person who makes it serve an eternal dialogue of love with other persons...Everything which is an object of reason can only be the means for an interpersonal dialogue...
>
> The universe bears the mark given to it by its origin in rational creative Person and by its destiny to be the means for an interpersonal dialogue between that Personal reality and human persons so that these might remain for all eternity in the happiness of that same communion between them. The entire universe bears the stamp of a personal rationality intended for the eternal existence of human persons.[152]

Polanyi: natural science points beyond intelligible nature to a higher realm of personal communion with the Divine

Leading scientists, such as Michael Polanyi, have in their own way seen this same reality; that natural science points beyond intelligible nature to a higher realm of communion with the divine personhood. In an essay on Michael Polanyi's work in this regard, Thomas F. Torrance has summarized the position:

> Now in theological inquiry we are unable to hold apart this intensely personal understanding of God from our understanding of him as the ultimate intelligible Ground of the universe. From the perspective of

---

[151]Dumitru Stăniloae, *Orthodox Dogmatic Theology: The Experience of God*, Vol I – *Revelation and Knowledge of the Triune God*, translated and edited by Ioan Ionita and Robert Barringer (Brookline, Mass: Holy Cross Orthodox Press, 1998), 5, 6.

[152]Ibid., 11.

> theology, therefore, the ultimate intelligible Ground of the universe, which is the sufficient reason for the intelligible states of affairs in the universe disclosed by natural science, is personal. Indeed, he is the one self-sufficient Person who is the Source of all personal being other than himself. How are we to think of this from the perspective of natural science, which has also to face the question as to the ultimate intelligible Ground of the universe and its contingent rational order?...This is not to imply that natural science can answer the question which in some form it is bound to raise, but if it recognises that the universe through its intelligibility points beyond itself to an ultimate self-sufficient Ground, and reckons with Polanyi's reintroduction of the personal model of thought into its epistemological foundations, it must surely go beyond the impersonal conception of Einstein, in entertaining the conception of a personal God as the creative Source of all the meaning and rational order disclosed through its investigations of nature.[153]

Polanyi stated that 'personal knowledge' is profoundly objective 'in the sense of establishing contact with a hidden reality'.[154] Persons cannot be explained merely in terms of their physical bodies and brain cells, but call for contact with something beyond the bounds of the merely physical systems so important to their human frames. In her work on the thought of Polanyi, Drusilla Scott explains:

> A much more real freedom, a much more satisfying recognition of the reality of *persons*, would be open to us if we could accept Polanyi's explanation that life operates by principles *made possible* and *limited* by physical and chemical laws but not *determined by them*.
>
> Yes of course machines and living beings obey the laws of physics and chemistry, but within the operation of these laws there is an area of possible variation left open. Without transgressing the laws of physics and chemistry, machines and living things are also controlled by another set of laws which deal with the areas left open. Thus they harness the laws of inanimate matter by a principle different from those laws for a purpose outside those laws. They impose *boundary conditions* on the laws of the lower level.[155]

The DNA code does not prove chemical determinism of living things

For instance, Polanyi argued that the discovery by Watson and Crick of the 'double helix' DNA chain, which passes on the genetic information by which the cells of offspring are formed as a result of reproduction did *not* prove that living things are physically and chemically determined. Instead, it proved the precise opposite, for 'No arrangement of physical units can be a code and convey information unless the order of its units is *not* fixed by its physical make-up.'[156] That is to say, a relationship to some reality higher up is required for the lower level to function. In the words of Drusilla Scott:

> Polanyi's ideas of tacit knowledge and the many-level world transform the possibilities for recognising persons in their full humanity, without rejecting the scientific knowledge of the physical world. Human thought is the highest

---

[153]T. F. Torrance, 'The Priority of Belief' in *Christian Theology & Scientific Culture*, 71, 72.

[154]Michael Polanyi, *Personal Knowledge* (London: Routledge and Kegan Paul, 1958), viii.

[155]Drusilla Scott, *Everyman Revived: The Common Sense of Michael Polanyi* (Grand Rapids: William B. Eerdmans, 1995), 118, 119.

[156]Michael Polanyi, *Knowing and Being* (Routledge and Kegan Paul: London, 1960), 228.

> level known to us, and all through the range of knowledge of ascending levels of reality we have seen how the higher level is the authoritative level, because only in our perception of the higher level can we see what the items of a lower level really are.[157]

As far as created being is concerned:

> Each level of reality, as we saw, relies on but is not fully determined by the level below it; can be crippled or destroyed by the failure of the lower level, but cannot be explained in its successful working by the laws of the lower level. The higher controls the lower by imposing boundary conditions on the area left undetermined by the lower level laws...
>
> It is the person, the highest level, that gives the particulars of the lower levels their joint meaning and their full reality, which will never be arrived at by focussing on the lower level particulars and then adding up the result...They have to be grasped by a tacit integration, an indwelling knowledge.[158]

This is an illustration of Gödel's Theorem, that a system cannot be closed off to higher levels of reality and remain consistent within itself at the same time. If it is to be consistent, it must be open to a higher level to make sense. In terms of the universe which comes to articulate expressions in persons, we could say that while they function according to (and in that sense are dependent upon) physical and chemical laws of the lower, strictly material level, yet no sense can be made of them unless they are seen as open to a higher level of reality. It is possible that Duns Scotus at the very beginning of the fourteenth century was expressing – in a very philosophical way – something of this openness between various levels, as he reflected on the ordering of causes of nature.[159]

Drusilla Scott's study of Polanyi includes a chapter on 'What is a Person?', where she demonstrates the impersonalist assumptions of such logical positivists as Bertrand Russell, who insist that various level of reality are closed off within themselves without being open to higher levels. With reference to Russell and W. Quine she writes:

> We all in some degree start from our conclusions, as Polanyi said he did. Bertrand Russell started from the conclusion that the rules and methods of the laboratory rule out persons, and was stoically prepared to be ruled out in theory, though in fact he went on illegitimately being there. Quine starts from the same conclusion; the methods of physics are so successful that we must not go outside them; he is prepared to pour mind and meaning down the laboratory sink in order to 'preserve the closed character of the physical world.'[160]

But this philosophical assumption of nature as a closed causal, mechanistic nexus is bad science[161] and hopeless anthropology. On the contrary, in this open universe, natural revelation is 'the music of the spheres' pointing humans upwards to the Maker of spheres and stars, in whose image persons

---

[157]D. Scott, op. cit., 145, 146.

[158]Ibid., 146.

[159]e.g. see Duns Scotus, op. cit., III. 10 and 11 (pp.44-46).

[160]D. Scott, op. cit., 145.

are created, and in whose 'light they see light' (Ps. 36:9). Natural revelation therefore from the beginning requires the illumination and explanation of relational, verbal revelation for its true purposes to be achieved. The key here is person. 'The heavens declare the glory of God' (Ps. 19:1) to persons. The thoughts of consciences 'accuse or excuse' persons (Rom. 2:15). The external 'music' and internal moral assessment comes from the highest personal reality: the God who is a *unique* and undivided community of loving, holy persons (one in essence, and three in person).

As we have seen, Richard of St. Victor brought out that since God is love (1 John 4:8), and that the nature of love is overflowing and outgoing, it requires more than one person for such love to be expressed and returned. Thus, the one God has always existed in three persons – Father, Son and Holy Spirit – One and Three; the ultimate community of love; the fount of life, light and blessing.[162] In the realm of persons, one does not have an 'I' without a 'Thou'. That is to say, personhood is inherently relational. A strictly solitary, individualistic 'person' has never existed and could never exist on its own. It is the infinite, Triune God, an undivided community of Persons within Himself, who reveals Himself in creation and conscience to finite persons, who derive their personhood from His image.

Stăniloae: the personhood of God and the rationality of the universe

D. Stăniloae shows the necessary connection between the personhood of God (and man), and the rationality of the universe, caused by God and perceived by man in nature.

> Persons use reason to communicate with one another and to make their lives a relationship of love. It is not reason that makes use of persons. The person is infinitely more than the circumscribed reason by which he or she imparts himself to other persons...
>
> It is impossible to think of a rational order as existing objectively on its own. It is always a rationality communicated or received by a person...The supreme Person imparts the life-giving mystery of his fulness by means of rational or intelligible forms, and his communications must take on, for non-divine existents, contours defined against the background of his infinity. This is the only way in which he can make himself comprehensible to them. He has conceived the finite rational structures of these existents, and, at the moment which he determined, has given actuality to these mentally discerned existents. Thus in the divine Logos, the living and infinite depth of the Person is likewise the voluntary source of defined, rational thoughts on which the light of their life-giving infinite source is playing.[163]

For that reason, any fruitful understanding of divine truth in the created order must finally be discerned in the light of the triune Creator/Redeemer

---

[161] e.g. see Thomas F. Torrance's chapter on 'Newton, Einstein and Scientific Theology' (chapter 8) in *Transformation & Convergence in the Frame of Knowledge: Explorations in the Interrelations of Scientific and Theological Enterprise* (Grand Rapids: William B. Eerdmans, 1984), 263-283.

[162] See Richard of St. Victor, *De Trinitate* IV. 16, 22, 24.

[163] Dumitru Stăniloae, 'Jesus Christ, Incarnate Logos of God, Source of Freedom and Unity,' in *The Ecumenical Review*, XXVI, Jan.–Oct., 1974, 405, 406.

God; source of all personhood. The intelligibility and reliability of the world are not accidental to it, but have been implanted in it in terms of a supreme personal goal. This goal has been enunciated in human speech, and thus sheds light on the meaning and purpose of all natural revelation. Stăniloae explains:

> Undoubtedly, divine Reason also speaks to men by divine words, whose pattern is embodied in things and in the actions accomplished on them. By such direct speech, the hypostatic Reason which speaks to men through nature gives more explicit contours to the goal towards which it desires to lead men through the circumstances of their life among natural things. This goal is none other than to grow constantly in knowledge of the divine Reason and to be united with Him…
>
> Thus the world is the means of the ordinary dialogue between God and man. All that exists is in the service of this dialogue between the hypostatic [i.e. 'Personal'] Reason of God and the hypostatic ['personal'] reason of man…
>
> All that exists bears the imprint of the person. Everything is permeated by the person, the rational person. Better, let us say that all creation was made for the sake of dialogue between the divine Person and human persons, and to be an expression of the dialogical relationship between these rational persons. Everything bears the actual and virtual imprint of inter-personal dialogue. This provides a personal, mystical basis for the rational order of the world and gives an inexhaustible mystical depth to this rationality itself.[164]

St. Thomas's true teaching: goodness communicates itself

The insight of St. Thomas that being communicates itself, and thus communicates its own goodness, is in this fuller perspective anchored in the very life of the Holy Trinity. From all eternity, the Father, Son and Holy Ghost love one another, give to one another, and receive from one another fulness of personal goodness and joy (e.g. see John 1, 14, 16, 17 and Eph. 1–3). The world itself was created so that a bride could be formed out of it for the Father to give to the Son in the bonds of the Spirit (e.g. see Eph. 5:22-33 and Rev. 21:1-4, 9; 22:17). The central affirmation of the gospel is that 'God so loved the world, that he gave his only begotten Son, that whosoever believeth in him should not perish, but have everlasting life' (John 3:16). This is the ultimate communication of the goodness of being from one level down to the other; a goodness that will not rest until it has elevated the lower back up to the higher.

This world so beloved by God is the very one that He originally created through the joint activity of all three Persons of His own inner life. God the Father created and spoke into existence light, life and structure; God the Son was the agent of this creative work (cf. John 1:3-5; Col. 1:15-17; Rev. 4:11), and God the Spirit 'moved upon the face of the waters' (Gen. 1:2). The created structures of this world therefore from beginning to end can only be ultimately understood and can only reach their appointed purpose as human persons, redeemed by grace and guided by Spirit and Word, engage in devoted reflection upon and live ransomed lives in accordance with the

[164] Ibid., 406, 407.

Triune Personal source and goal of the vast creation and its equally vast redemption.

Creation always to be viewed in light of God's Triune personhood

If it be objected that to view natural revelation from beginning to end in the light of the Trinity of Persons who created it and continue to shine into it is a sort of cheating of the 'natural' person, who has no access to the Word of the Creator/Redeemer, this is to misunderstand the One who created it, why He created and still interacts with it, and to misunderstand the goal of His activity. It is not that God was One and then became Three Persons. For the one true God to exist is to exist in a community of undivided Persons from eternity to eternity. For Him to be is to live in personal relationship within Himself. His creative work must always be viewed in light of who He is as Trinity. Hence, it is not that the Father existed by Himself, and then brought the other two hypostases into being (for in that case, He would not have been the eternal Father), but rather from all eternity He is who He is in continual relationship to the Son and the Holy Spirit. Their co-existence with the Father is part of who He is. As Vladimir Lossky says (in the context of the Eastern Orthodox distinction between essence and energies of the Trinity):[165]

> This is why, in the realm of divine manifestation, it is possible to establish an order of Persons (τάξις) which, strictly speaking, should not be attributed to Trinitarian existence in itself, despite the 'monarchy' and 'causality' of the Father: these confer upon Him no hypostatic primacy over the other two hypostases, since He is a person only because the Son and the Holy Spirit are also.[166]

Near the end of His earthly ministry, our Lord prayed, 'Father, I will that they also, whom thou hast given me, be with me where I am; that they may behold my glory, which thou hast given me: for thou lovedst me before the foundation of the world' (John 17:24). 'The heavens' were framed 'to declare the glory' of *that* Lord (Ps. 19:1), the vision of which glory can only be completed when His saints 'see Him face to face and are like Him, for they shall see Him as He is' (1 John 3:2).

In interpreting faithfully the divine glory in the created realm, the Church can never and need never act as though the source of revelation, whether in nature or in the Word, is other than Who He is. Although the glories of nature and the insistent voice of conscience do lead all rational beings in some inescapable sense up to God (cf. Romans 1 and 2; Acts 14 and 17), from the beginning of the creation of humankind, God has never left the human race without at the same time providing a sort of conceptual lighthouse and verbal pulpit to point to who the Creator and source of revelation is.

---

[165]For a discussion of the Eastern essence/energy distinction, see Appendix I to Chapter 3.

[166]Vladimir Lossky, *In the Image and Likeness of God* (Crestwood, NY: St. Vladimir's Seminary Press, 1974), 92, 93.

God spoke to the first pair both before and after their sin in the Garden of Eden. He gave promises of grace for them and for their descendants even after their fall (cf. Gen. 3:15). He spoke to murderous Cain, walked with holy Enoch ('the seventh from Adam' and a prophet – cf. Jude 14), gave grace to Noah and his family (also 'a preacher of righteousness' cf. 2 Peter 2:5 – to a condemned world that refused to listen), called out Abram from idolatry to be 'the father of all them that believe' (Rom. 4:11), with the universal purpose of being a blessing to 'all the families of the earth' (Gen. 12:3). God made His chosen nation, Israel, not only to be His own peculiar treasure (Exod. 19:5), but also through its Messiah 'a light to lighten the Gentiles' (Luke 2:32) and 'an ensign of the people' to which 'the Gentiles shall seek' (Isa. 11:10). Above all else, 'When the fulness of the time was come, God sent forth his Son, made of a woman, made under the law, to redeem them that were under the law, that we might receive the adoption of sons' (Gal. 4:4).

Jesus Christ and the Holy Spirit are humankind's way back to the Father

This Son of God, Messiah of Israel and Savior of the world revealed the heart of God to humankind in all the being and activities of His Incarnation (cf. John 14:9; 17:6), and stood in their place to give the perfect filial responses required by the divinely instituted Covenant of Grace on behalf of His people (e.g. John 17:19; 2 Cor. 1:20; 5:21) so that in a way appropriate to creatures, they could know the Father as the Son knows the Father (e.g. John 17:19-21, 26; 20:17). The Holy Spirit came out from the Father and the exalted Son to unite believers to their Savior (cf. 1 Cor. 12:13; Eph. 1:3-23) so that they could come into most intimate, direct and filial knowledge of the Father (cf. Rom. 8:14-17; Gal. 4:3-7).

The exalted Lord commissioned His Church: 'Go ye therefore, and teach all nations, baptising them in the name of the Father, and of the Son, and of the Holy Ghost: Teaching them to observe all things whatsoever I have commanded you: and, lo, I am with you always, even unto the end of the world. Amen' (Matt. 28:19, 20). To equip His Church to reach the nations with the saving message, Christ clothed His apostles with unique, supernatural authority so that after His completed work on earth and coronation above, they might accurately interpret His person, work and purposes for Church and world to the end of time in the inspired Scriptures of the New Testament (cf. John 16:12-15), to be as it were, the 'head and eyes' of the body, which is the Old Testament. This completed message is absolutely universal, and yet at the same time individual, for the various tongues are still maintained. Its proclamation in multitudes of languages of humankind on the day of Pentecost is a vivid picture of its universality (cf. Acts 2:1-11).

The chosen community spreads the personal knowledge that God revealed to them

In the long history of redemption, the chosen community which has received the verbal revelation as an aspect of their personal relationship to God, has at times been a smaller and, at other times, a much larger one. It is a bit like putting two funnels together; there is the small neck leading into the wide spout; then another small neck, leading into yet another wide spout, and so on. At the beginning, with Adam and Eve and their children, it was the entire human race who heard God speaking. Then in God's wise way of dealing with sin so as to secure His gracious purposes for humankind in the future, the line of verbal revelation was concentrated in a particular genealogical line: Seth, Noah, Shem and Abraham. The community of personal relationship and verbal revelation begins to broaden significantly with the seed of Abraham, the elect nation of Israel (cf. Micah 4:1, 2).

Then, by the time of the New Testament, it has grown smaller, with the pious remnant of Israel, such as we see in the early chapters of the Gospel of Luke, who welcome the Christ child and John the Baptist. Christ chooses twelve apostles (representing the twelve tribes of Israel), and on the Day of Pentecost, some five thousand are saved. It broadens ever more widely from that point to the end of time, 'when the earth shall be filled with the knowledge of the glory of the LORD, as the waters cover the sea' (Hab. 2:14).

From the beginning of the human story until that glad time, the chosen recipients of verbal revelation are responsible to explain to those outside the enlightened community the meaning of what they dimly see outside and what they confusedly feel inside. They are never called to put themselves on the same grounds as those outside, as though they had neither seen nor heard the vision and Word of the Lord. They are never to act as though the personal God who has brought them into relationship with Himself is anything less than personal (perhaps intimated by the Old Testament concept of 'countenance' as in the Aaronic benediction – Num. 6:26), nor requires anything less of human persons than to walk in humility, justice and love before Him and with others (cf. Micah 6:8).

For reasons known to Himself, God has chosen to reveal His light gradually to the chosen community of grace, and also to convey the verbal message from them to the rest of the world gradually. It is not given to us believers to know all that has or has not transpired between God and the rest of humanity outside the sound of His Word. At the very least, we must say with the Apostle Paul in light of the glorious, universal gospel, 'And the times of this ignorance God winked at; but now commandeth all men everywhere to repent…' (Acts 17:30).

The purpose of verbal revelation

This call to repentance, to turn from the sinful idolatory of serving self and anything less than God, to a new personal relationship of total trust, worship and service with the God who 'is waiting to be gracious unto us' (cf. Isa. 30:18); to make countless multitudes 'his people and the sheep of his pasture' (Ps. 100:3) is the overarching purpose of every aspect of divine revelation.

In the words of Stăniloae:

> This demonstrates that revelation consists not so much in a disclosure of a sum of theoretical information about a God enclosed in his own transcendence, as it consists in God's act of descending to man and of raising man up to himself so that there might be achieved, in Christ, the deepest possible union and that this achievement might be the basis for extending between God and all the people who believe in him this same union…
>
> Hence, revelation occurs through acts and words, through light and power; it is the act that enlightens and the light that transforms the one who believes. It reveals not only what God does for man, but also what man will become through God's action and through his own cooperation; it also reveals the meaning and the final purpose of human existence, or what might be called that final state for which we are destined and which itself constitutes our total fulfillment.[167]

The created order a 'theater' drawing us up to personal knowledge of God's glory

The entire created order with its remarkable rationality and reliability constitutes a sort of 'nursery' (or with Calvin, glorious 'theatre') in which God's own image-bearers, human persons, are prepared to be lifted up into the Son's knowledge of the Father in the bonds of the Spirit, who unites them to the Son. In this sense, as St. Irenaeus once said, the Son (or Word) and the Spirit are like 'the two hands of the Father' to elevate believing image-bearers to behold the heavenly Father.[168] This work of revelation, both in nature and conscience and in Word and Spirit, is anchored deeply within the internal relationships of the Three Persons of the blessed Trinity.

The light of every star, the structure of every cell, the functioning of every organic system, the majesty of every law, the voice of every conscience, the development of every creative potential and 'the change and decay' and renewal of every aspect of nature are all established with their own significance and meaning to be patiently perceived and proclaimed by created persons. And thus all of these created realities being found to be what they are, all of them – even if it be in a mute sort of way – level by level, lift up the eyes of those who behold them in faith to the Triune personal reality, who called everything into being, continually sustains it, and guides it to His appointed purpose. That purpose is personal; an ever-growing, ever-deepening, ever-beautifying communion of life and love between redeemed created persons and the ineffable one, undivided community of Three uncreated Persons, who created them, redeemed them, and will not be without them.

Yet as clear as this upward movement towards the Triune God should be to any of his creatures who are thinking rightly, for some two centuries or more, our powerful and wealthy Western society has rejected this testimony that bears upon it ceaselessly, both internally and externally. We must examine the reasons why in Chapter 3. But first, we must examine the issue of whether or not the God who reveals Himself to all people in creation and conscience, uses non-biblical religions to make Himself known to them. That is considered in the next appendix.

---

[167]D. Stăniloae, *Orthodox Dogmatic Theology*, Vol. I, 34, 35.

[168]Irenaeus, *Adversus Haereses*, V. 1. 3.

Chapter Two
Appendix One

Other Religions as Viewed by the Old Testament

We have addressed the revelation of God in creation and conscience to all persons. We must now consider the question: Does God reveal Himself to people by means of the various world religions?

While the Old Testament definitely speaks of divine salvation reaching nations and multitudes far outside Israel (as in Egypt and Assyria along with Israel in Isaiah 19:19-25), yet this saving knowledge of God comes, not by means of, but by overthrow of their false religions. The prophecy of Jonah gives the classical illustration of this, when the violent and pagan city of Nineveh receives the pardoning mercy of God through repentance, following the preaching of Jonah. Thus, the religions and ethical systems of the pagan nations are not alternative ways to the salvation of God; they are impediments to it; they must be abandoned and forsaken by means of repentance and faith in the true God. God gave this grace to Nineveh, and has probably done so to many another, whose names and times we do not know.

The Exodus and the religions of Egypt

Genesis 1 begins with the Lord creating all reality, both physical and spiritual. In the age when Moses wrote Genesis, many pagan nations considered the sun, the moon and the stars to be deities. But Genesis says that God, after making the sun and the moon, 'made the stars also' (1:16). These luminaries are mere creatures of God; not divinities. An important aspect of the mighty Exodus event which led the children of Israel out of Egypt with a high hand, was the humiliating judgment God visited upon the false gods of Egypt: not least, the Nile River and Pharaoh himself. These false deities were laid low; the Nile was turned into blood and Pharaoh's forces were drowned.

Moses had warned Pharaoh: 'Thus saith the Lord, the God of the Hebrews, Let my people go that they may serve me. For I will at this time send all my plagues upon thy heart ... that thou mayest know that there is none like me in all the earth' (Exod. 9:13-14). On the verge of the Red Sea crossing, God told Moses: 'And I will harden Pharaoh's heart, and he shall follow after them; and I will get me honour upon Pharaoh and upon all his host; and the Egyptians shall know that I am Jehovah' (Exod. 14:4).

After these glorious events, Moses' father-in-law, Jethro, who dwelt in a polytheistic culture, clearly perceived who was God: 'Now I know that the LORD is greater than all gods: for in the thing wherein they dealt proudly he was above them' (Exod. 18:11). This identity of the true God is an appropriate introduction to the first of the ten covenant words (or commandments) given by the Lord to Moses for all the covenant people for all time on Mount Sinai: 'I am the Lord thy God, who hath brought thee out of the land of Egypt, out of the house of bondage. Thou shalt have no other gods before me' (Exod. 20:2,3).

The medieval rabbinical tradition saw very clearly that the Exodus was a judgment upon false gods:

> Rashi interprets verse 12 of Exodus 12: 'I shall render justice upon the gods of Egypt', in showing that God had broken the idols. Other commentators (such as Nahmanides) gave to this verse a more symbolic sense: it was the entire Egyptian religion which had been broken; divine truth had triumphed over the nothingness of idolatry.[1]

In precisely this way Numbers interprets the triumphal exit of the children of Israel out of a devastated Egypt as a judgment upon their gods. 'And they departed from Rameses in the first month, on the fifteenth day of the first month; on the morrow after the Passover the children of Israel went out with an high hand in the sight of all the Egyptians. For the Egyptians buried all their firstborn, which the Lord had smitten among them: upon their gods also the Lord executed judgments' (Num. 33:3-4).

It would be this temptation to be like the other nations in practicing idolatry that would be the chief problem in the history of Israel, and the cause of their deportation to Babylon nearly a thousand years after the Exodus. Pagan religions, with their idolatrous cults, were not seen as possible ways to the Lord. Instead, they were degenerations from the original religion given to Adam and Noah; they were contradictions of God's holy character; they were deadly snares to their votaries; a cause of perverted practices and fearful judgment.

The religions of Canaan

Once the Lord, under Joshua's leadership, successfully got the people of Israel into the promised land of Canaan, the covenant was renewed. One of its major terms was that the people would follow the Lord only, and reject and destroy the surrounding polytheism with its idols and perverted behavior: 'And if it seem evil unto you to serve the Lord, choose ye this day whom ye will serve; whether the gods which your fathers served that were beyond the River, or the gods of the Amorites, in whose land ye dwell: but as for me and my house, we will serve the Lord' (Josh. 24:15).

The Book of Judges shows the long, and frequently unsuccessful struggle of the transplanted twelve tribes to serve the Lord and avoid ancient Middle Eastern idolatry. A significant aspect of the judgeship of Gideon lay in his chopping down the idolatrous grove of Asherah (of the Baal cult) in order

---

[1]André et Renée Neher, *Histoire Biblique du Peuple D'Israel* (Paris: Adrien Maisonneuve, 1988), 126.

to re-institute the worship of the Lord (Judg. 6). He physically showed that Baal had no power to take care of himself (6:31-32). The Lord alone was strong; He alone could remove evil in order to make peace (6:22-24). Thus his altar was called 'Jehovah-shalom' (6:24).

The sole power of the one true God, and the nothingness of idols, was demonstrated again after the Ark of the Covenant was captured by the Philistines and placed in the temple of the fish-god, Dagon. The next morning the priests of Dagon found that Dagon's idol was on its face before the Ark. They stood the idol back up, and on the next day worse had happened: Dagon's head and hands had been cut off, leaving only a mere stump of an idol (1 Sam. 5:1-5). Great plagues then broke out upon the Philistines, so that they decided to send the Ark of the Covenant back to Israel (1 Sam. 5:6–6:18).

The Books of 1 and 2 Chronicles in particular evaluate the reigns of the various kings of Israel (and then of the divided kingdoms of North and South) in terms of whether the king followed the Lord or gave himself to false gods. David was the model of godliness, and there were others who followed 'the man after God's own heart' such as Jehosaphat, Hezekiah and Josiah. Solomon oriented the kingdom in an idolatrous direction, as he allowed his pagan wives to set up idols to their false gods within Jerusalem itself (1 Kings 11:1-12). The kings of the Northern Kingdom from the beginning under Jeroboam went in an idolatrous way by setting up golden calves to be worshipped (as an alternative to going to the Temple in Jerusalem) in Bethel and Dan – (2 Chron. 11:14, 15; 13:8). The nadir of idolatrous Northern kings was under Ahab, whose Sidonian wife, the infamous Jezebel, enforced the religion of Baal throughout the land.

Judgment on the idolatry of the Northern Kingdom

Her enemy, the prophet Elijah, was attended with divine power in showing the futility of Baal's prophets, who could not bring down fire upon their altar, after which he executed the 450 prophets of Baal (1 Kings 18:16-40). But Jezebel did not give up her fight against Jehovah in favor of Baal until she was finally destroyed by Jehu, whom God had told Elijah to anoint as king in place of Ahab (1 Kings 19:15; 2 Kings 9:30-37). Although Jehu instituted a religious reform involving the destruction of the Baal religion (2 Kings 10:18-28), it was not a thoroughgoing return to Jehovah, because it did not entail a change of heart in a faithful, penitent direction. 'But Jehu took no heed to walk in the law of Jehovah, the God of Israel, with all his heart: he departed not from the sins of Jeroboam wherewith he made Israel to sin' (2 Kings 10:31).

Ultimately, the Northern Kingdom sold itself out to idolatry, and as a divine judgment was deported by the Assyrians about 721 B.C. The solemn assessment was that 'they followed vanity [gods of nothingness] and became vain [as empty as their false gods as they 'failed the examination' of a moral universe]' (2 Kings 17:15). It would take until about 586 B.C. before the same judgment against false religion would fall on the Southern Kingdom.

During that period, God raised up mighty prophets, who sought to call the wavering people of Judah back to the Lord from their various idolatries. God had forewarned his people through Moses that the pagan religions of Canaan would draw them down into abominations; unholy, perverted and destructive activities: 'When thou art come into the land which the Lord thy God giveth thee, thou shalt not learn to do after the abominations of those nations. There shall not be found with thee any one that maketh his son or his daughter to pass through the fire, one that useth divination, one that practiseth augury, or an enchanter, or a sorcerer, or a charmer, or a consulter with a familiar spirit, or a wizard, or a necromancer. For whosoever doeth these things is an abomination unto the Lord: and because of these abominations the Lord thy God doth drive them out from before thee' (Deut. 18:9-12).

The prophets such as Isaiah made it plain that a total rejection of both the theologies and the practices of pagan religions was absolutely necessary because of the holiness and truth of God. This necessary rejection of idolatry in order to cleave to the true God was held out not only to Israel, but to such neighboring pagan cultures as Moab, Syria, Ethiopia, Egypt and Babylon (in oracles addressed to them from Isaiah 15–21). The God of Israel had words not only for Israel, but also for their pagan neighbors. They were called to bow before the same one, true God in the same faith and repentance. Damascus, for instance, was called to look away from the altars, Asherim and sun-images which their own hands had made, up to their true Maker, who is the Holy One of Israel (Isa. 17:7,8). That is, God condemns pagan idolatry, while loving and calling the pagans themselves, who are ever on His heart.[2]

It is in the final interest of pagans as well as of believers to demonstrate the nothingness of false gods so as to open the way to the true God. To that end, Isaiah challenged the false gods to predict the future and to control the present; indeed, to do anything! 'Let them bring them forth, and declare unto us what shall happen: declare ye the former things, what they are, that we may consider them, and know the latter end of them; or show us things to come. Declare the things that are to come hereafter, that we may know that ye are gods: yea, do good or do evil, that we may be dismayed, and behold it together. Behold, ye are of nothing, and your work is of naught; an abomination is he that chooseth you' (Isa. 41:22-24).

Hope for the Gentiles

But in the context of His chosen Servant and his Holy Spirit, God has something better for the Gentiles. He will keep working until He establishes righteousness in the earth, while somehow the isles of the Gentiles shall wait for his law (Isa. 42:1-4). God calls Israel from captivity back to their homeland, not in order to exclude the Gentiles from salvation, but to be their light (Isa. 42:6). This salvation for both Israel and the

[2]While ancient (and modern) paganism *substituted* aspects of the creation (and thus, *false gods*) for the true God, modern scientistic materialism holds God to be *a non-entity*. Is not the latter error worse than the first?

Gentiles requires knowing who God is, and thus abandoning empty, powerless idols:

> Thus saith the Lord God, he that created the heavens, and stretched them forth; he that spread abroad the earth and that which cometh out of it; he that giveth breath unto the people upon it, and spirit to them that walk therein: I, the Lord, have called thee in righteousness, and will hold thy hand and will keep thee, and give thee for a covenant of the people, for a light of the Gentiles; to open the blind eyes, to bring out the prisoners from the dungeon, and them that sit in darkness out of the prison house. I am the Lord, that is my name; and my glory will I not give to another, neither my praise unto graven images. Behold, the former things are come to pass, and new things do I declare; before they spring forth I tell you of them (Isa. 42:5-9).

In this spirit, Psalm 96 says: 'For all the gods of the peoples are idols ["nothings"], but the Lord made the heavens... Say among the nations, Jehovah reigneth: the world also is established that it cannot be moved: He will judge the peoples with equity... He will judge the world with righteousness, and the peoples with his truth' (vv. 5, 10, 13).

In summary, we find that the Old Testament while roundly condemning all idolatry with its abominable practices, never forgets that all people are created by God to live within his moral and metaphysical universe. They are still in His image, and as such are called to turn from 'vanities' and from the idols which they have chosen to their own destruction (Hosea 13:9). With Ephraim, they are called to say: 'What have I any more to do with idols?' (Hosea 14:8). The God of Israel Himself will see to this in pouring out His Spirit upon all flesh in days to come: 'And ye shall know that I am in the midst of Israel, and that I am the Lord your God, and there is none else; and my people shall never be put to shame. And it shall come to pass afterward, that I will pour out my Spirit upon all flesh; and your sons and your daughters shall prophesy, your old men shall dream dreams, your young men shall see visions: and also upon the handmaids in those days will I pour out my Spirit... And it shall come to pass that whosoever shall call on the name of the Lord shall be delivered; for in mount Zion and in Jerusalem there shall be those that escape, as the Lord hath said, and among the remnant those whom the Lord doth call' (Joel 2:27-32).

Other Religions as Viewed in the New Testament

The New Testament inaugurates a great change of perspective in regard to the pagan nations, for 'God so loved the world that he gave his only begotten Son, that whosoever believeth in him should not perish, but have everlasting life' (John 3:16). Christ, the Messiah of Israel, is the agent of creation (John 1:3) and is 'the true light that lighteneth every man that cometh into the world' (John 1:9). In His incarnation, life, atoning death, bodily resurrection, outpouring of the Spirit, and coming judgments and glorious cosmic restoration, He involves all humankind. He sends out His disciples with the command: 'Go ye therefore, and make disciples of all the nations, baptizing them in the name of the Father and of the Son and of the Holy Spirit: teaching them to observe all things whatsoever I have commanded you; and lo, I am with you always, even unto the end of the world' (Matt. 28:19, 20). When Christ pours out His Spirit upon the waiting church at Pentecost, they speak in many tongues, from throughout the known world (Acts 2:4-13).[3]

The New Testament calls for repentance from false religions

The very prophecy we just referred to from Joel 2 is quoted by the Apostle Peter on this day of Pentecost (Acts 2:16-21), indicating that the future blessing of universal knowledge of God predicted by Old Testament prophets has now begun its gracious activity. Now that the economy of the Jewish theocracy has been fulfilled and thus surpassed, the entrance into this saving knowledge of God is the same for both Jew and Gentile: faith in Christ, accompanied by repentance from sin (including various sorts of idolatry). Paul commends the Christians of Thessalonica for having 'turned unto God from idols, to serve the living and true God, and to wait for his Son from heaven, whom he raised from the dead, even Jesus, who delivereth us from the wrath to come' (1 Thess. 1:9, 10).

The Lord Jesus preached repentance as the proper response to the coming of the kingdom of God in His Person (Matt. 4:17), even as John the Baptist, his forerunner, had already preached it (cf. Matt. 3:1-12). This repentance required a 'turning away from self-centered thinking and living' (or from being 'idol-centered') and 'a change of mind' (*metanoia*), so that now, one loves God above all and one's neighbor as oneself. Such faith and repentance meant a break with any and every kind of false religion; whether the self-centered works' righteousness of Phariseeism or adherence to the pagan religions of the fallen world system.

After Peter reported the conversion and baptism of the Roman centurion, Cornelius, the Church was able to say: 'Then to the Gentiles also hath God granted repentance unto life' (Acts 11:18). Years later, when Paul stood before King Agrippa, he summarized his preaching this way: '[I] declared both to them of Damascus first, and at Jerusalem, and throughout all the country of Judea, and also to the Gentiles, that they should repent and turn to God, doing works worthy of repentance' (Acts 26:20). Thus, the revelation of God in Christ issues a gracious call to all humanity to repent and believe, and so to leave behind as useless and hopeless every other religion.[4]

As we saw earlier, Paul dealt kindly with the pagans of Lystra and their idolatrous ancestors in calling them to forsake their idols and turn to their Creator and Redeemer now that Jesus has come (cf. Acts 14), but that does not keep him from exposing the real nature of pagan idolatry. In 1 Corinthians 10:14, 20, he states that the sacrificial worship of the Greek cults were a cult of demons. He reminds the believers in Corinth

---

[3]This miracle in principle begins the reparation of the division of tongues at the Tower of Babel.

[4]The work of the victorious Christ removed the ancient power of Satan to keep the nations blinded, and thus the way of missions is opened. See William Hendrickson, *More than Conquerors: An Interpretation of the Book of Revelation* (London: The Tyndale Press, 1973), chapter 14.

that previous to their conversion, they had been led away by dumb idols (1 Cor. 12:2), whose power over them had to be broken by the Holy Spirit in order for them to be able to acknowledge Christ as Lord (1 Cor. 12:3).

At times in the New Testament these pagan idols are shown to be mere 'nothings' (1 Cor. 12:2). In Ephesus a riot was raised by silver merchants, who were enraged that their trade (in making silver idols of Artemis) was destroyed by the preaching of Paul who claimed that these idols were 'no gods' (Acts 19:26). And at other times they are connected to the unclean power of demons behind them (1 Cor. 10:14, 20). Revelation 2:13 speaks to the church at Pergamos as 'dwelling where Satan's throne is' – i.e. possibly the altar of Zeus Soter or the temple of the Emperor Augustus.

The New Testament is thus consistent with the Old Testament; the love of the Creator of all humankind, who redeems sinners from all nations in Christ, extends to the souls of the lost, but not to their false religions. Indeed, because of the universal divine love, all people are called 'to turn to God from idols ... and to wait for his Son from heaven' (1 Thess. 1:9, 10). For in that way alone can they show forth the praises of Him who called them out of darkness into his marvelous light (1 Pet. 2:9). The darkness of paganism and of Phariseeism must be immediately forsaken for one to be translated into the kingdom of God's dear Son (Col. 1:13).

The New Testament therefore gives no positive reading of pagan religions. The idols they engender are either nothings or fronts for demons. The New Testament never even slightly indicates that they might be providential forerunners of the true way to God for pagan nations. Divine revelation does not fulfill them; it contradicts them.[5] And yet glorious hope is offered to the untold millions under their thralldom, for One has come who is stronger than 'the strong man' who has for so long cruelly bound them captive (Luke 11:22). Faith in Christ delivers all who believe from the power of Satan and all the pomps and torments of his false religions.[6]

Hope for the nations

That is to say, the New Testament is suffused with hope for the nations, because God held back final judgment against paganism until 'the fullness of the time' when His eternal Son appeared in the flesh to do something within Israel that would extend its liberating power to all the nations. The speech of Paul in Acts 17 does not end with final condemnation of the pagans. On the contrary, it opens a door of deliverance for them. God, who

---

[5]As Karl Barth says: 'Revelation does not link up with a human religion which is already present and practised. It contradicts it, just as religion previously contradicted revelation. It displaces it, just as religion previously displaced revelation; just as faith cannot link up with a mistaken faith, but must contradict and displace it as unbelief, as an act of contradiction' (*Church Dogmatics* I. 2, 303).

[6]It is difficult not to see the powerful modern *anti-religion* of materialistic naturalism (that seeks to elevate its atheistic presuppositions into the accredited 'findings of science') as, in the end of the day just *another religion* (massively influential and prestigious though it is). Though it would presumably disdain the older, grosser religions of pagan antiquity, could it not actually constitute an illustration of Jesus' parable in Luke 11:14-26: i.e. when one demon is cast out (but the life is not filled with the Spirit of God), then seven other demons come in to fill the vacuum, so that the latter state is worse than the first? In that sense, our apostate modern culture may be in far worse shape than ancient pagan idolatry.

has 'overlooked' the idolatry of their ancestors, did not create them to be finally destroyed. His patient bearing with their suppression of the truth about Himself was for a gracious purpose; it was to preserve them until the fullness of revelation appeared to them in the gospel of Jesus – the Messiah of Israel and Savior of all nations.

Jesus Christ, the eternal Son of God in the flesh, came into an idolatrous culture and acted from within it to save it. That is why repentance must be the next step for idolaters. Repentance is never held out to those who have been totally abandoned and for whom there is no hope. The call to repentance, because Christ's life and death for sinful mankind has been divinely vindicated in His physical resurrection, is the loving call of the heavenly Father to all His image-bearers to come home to the One who 'is waiting to be gracious' to them. This is the only way to be prepared to withstand with confidence and joy the terrors of the final, cosmic judgment.

Other Religions as Viewed by the Church Fathers

The Patristic period (of the Church Fathers) encompasses a vast literature in several languages, from several cultures and nations, over a period of five or six centuries. It would be impossible to summarize even superficially what they all said concerning pagan religions. Nevertheless, it has generally been noted by Patristic scholars that there are two main (and competing) approaches amongst the Fathers to pagan philosophy and religion. We might contrast these differing approaches (especially amongst the Apologists of the first three centuries A.D.), as (1) bridge builders and (2) bridge burners.

1. Bridge builders

From the second century A.D. apologist, Justin Martyr, through the head of the Theological School in Egypt, Clement of Alexandria, to Clement's successor, Origen (c. 185–253), we find the claiming of a sort of 'beach head' in pagan philosophy/religion in terms of their teaching of the Logos. They do not claim that the pagan religions were right or sufficient, but only that somehow the Logos was to a degree shining through them. Or to state it another way, the image of God in mankind was deformed, but not obliterated by the fall. In his *First Apology*, Justin says: 'For not only among the Greeks did reason (Logos) prevail to condemn these things through Socrates [e.g. demons and iniquity], but also among the Barbarians were they condemned by Reason (or the Word, Logos) Himself, who took shape, and became man, and was called Jesus Christ…' (Chapter v). He goes on to assert:

> We have been taught that Christ is the first-born of God, and we have declared that above that He is the Word of whom every race of men were partakers; and those who lived reasonably (*meta logou*) are Christians, even though they have been thought atheists; as, among the Greeks, Socrates and Heraclitus, and men like them; and among the barbarians, Abraham

> and Ananianas and Azarias and Misael and Elias, and many others...So that even they who lived before Christ and lived without reason, were wicked and hostile to Christ, and slew those who lived reasonably... (Chapter xlvi).

In his *Second Apology*, Justin teaches that the Stoics, poets, Heraclitus and others 'were admirable' 'on account of the seed of reason [*logos spermatikos*] implanted in every race of men' (Chapter viii). And yet, the pre-Christian philosophers had only some of the Word, not all of it; for 'the whole Word is Christ' (ibid.). In that way, he explains the mistakes of Socrates and others: 'But since they did not know the whole of the Word, which is Christ, they often contradicted themselves' (Chapter x). He attributes value to Plato's teaching, which he once followed, because of the share he had of the *logos spermatikos*:

> ...not because the teachings of Plato are different from those of Christ, but because they are not in all respects similar, as neither are those of the others, stoics and poets and historians. For each man spoke well in proportion to the share he had of the spermatic word, seeing what was related to it. But they who contradict themselves on the more important points appear not to have possessed the heavenly wisdom, and the knowledge which cannot be spoken against (Chapter xiii).

In his brief *Discourse to the Greeks*, Justin rejects the folly and immorality of Greek mythology and theogony, and calls them to be instructed by the divine Word. But in his longer *Hortatory Address to the Greeks*, he goes to amazing lengths as he attempts at all costs to prove that while Plato and Aristotle are inconsistent, nonetheless, they – insofar as they write truth – depend on Moses.[7] He claims the same for Orpheus, Homer and Solon.[8] He claims that Orpheus testifies to Monotheism,[9] as do the Sibyl,[10] Homer,[11] Sophocles,[12] and Pythagoras.[13] He attempts to demonstrate that Plato teaches the same truth as Exodus 3:14 (i.e. 'I Am The Being').[14] He even claims that Plato derived his theory of forms from Moses (in terms of the pattern of the tabernacle given to Moses on the Mount by God).[15] According to Justin, the Sibyl of Cumae clearly predicted the coming of Christ, and thus calls them to repentance.[16]

But not everyone was impressed with Christians claiming the authority of the Sibyl for having predicted the truths of their religion. Origen notes that the fiercely anti-Christian, Neo-Platonic philosopher, Celsus, called Christians who did this 'Sibyllists'.[17] It is generally accepted that both

---

[7]Justin Martyr, *Hortatory Address to the Greeks*, chs. xii, xxviii.
[8]Ibid.
[9]Ibid., ch. xv.
[10]Ibid., chs. xvi, xxxvii.
[11]Ibid., ch. xvii.
[12]Ibid., ch. xviii.
[13]Ibid., ch. xix.
[14]Ibid., chs. xx, xxi, xxii, xxiii.
[15]Ibid., ch. xxix.
[16]Ibid., ch. xxxvii.
[17]Origen, *Contra Celsum*, V. 61.

Jews and Christians had added portions into the Sibylline Books in order to enhance the historical standing of their own religions.

Clement of Alexandria also saw pagan philosophy as a sort of preparation for the gospel: 'Accordingly, before the advent of the Lord, philosophy was necessary to the Greeks for righteousness... Perchance too, philosophy was given to the Greeks directly and primarily, till the Lord should call the Greeks. For this was a schoolmaster to bring "the Hellenistic mind," as the Law, the Hebrews, "to Christ" (Gal. 3:24). Philosophy, therefore, was a preparation, paving the way for him who is perfected in Christ' (*Stromateis*, Book I, chapter v).

Clement held that the Son of God 'gave philosophy to the Greeks by means of the inferior angels' (Book VII, chapter ii). Yet he trenchantly criticized the immoral rites of the pagans. He held that their philosophy could not finally save them; they would have to wait in limbo for Christ to deliver them (Book VI, 3, 1).

The vast work of Origen (much of it destroyed because of his heterodoxy) also teaches that 'God has implanted in the souls of all men the truths which He taught through the prophets and the Saviour; He did this that every man might be without excuse at the divine judgement, having the requirement of the law written in his heart (Rom. 2:15)...moral ideas have been implanted in men, and ... it was from these that Heraclitus and any other Greek or barbarian conceived the notion of maintaining this doctrine [i.e. against idolatry]' (*Contra Celsum* I.5,6). In *De Principiis* (Book III, Chapter iii), Origen discusses the influence of demons on the religion and occult practices of such as the Egyptians, Chaldeans, Greeks and Indians.

In the Greek portions of Book IV, 23, he seems to be teaching that in accordance with the proportion of sin in one's life (whether Israelite or pagan), one can descend into Hades, and later be gathered by Christ. In a rather difficult passage in *Contra Celsum*, Origen indicates that human nature needs grace to find God: 'But we affirm that human nature is not sufficient in any way to seek for God and to find Him in His pure nature, unless it is helped by the God who is the object of the search. And He is found by those who, after doing what they can,[18] admit that they need Him, and shows Himself to those to whom He judges it right to appear, so far as it is possible for God to be known to man and for the human soul which is still in the body to know God' (VII.42). He writes similarly in VIII.52: 'So also we want to implant a conviction that those who have lived good lives will be happy, seeing that even people alien to the faith make many affirmations about the upright life which are much the same as ours; for one would find that their teachings have not entirely lost the universal notions of good and bad, righteous and unrighteous.'

Because of two major Origenist controversies (in which many of his works were changed so as to appear within orthodoxy and others were destroyed), it is not easy to know for certain what he taught about the fate

[18]See proposed textual emendations for 'do what they can' in Henry Chadwick, *Origen Contra Celsum* (Cambridge: Cambridge University Press, 1980), 430.

of the pagans. But at least he was condemned by the Church as heretical for holding, among other heterodox ideas, that all humans and demons (including Satan) would finally be saved. Origen, therefore, is not a typical representative of the viewpoint of early Christian theology on pagan religion.

2. Bridge burners

A very different opinion on pagan philosophy/religion is found in such early Christian theologians as Tertullian, Theophilus of Antioch and Tatian. Far from 'building bridges', they felt it best to burn them in order to herd the pagans and heretics on to the one way of salvation. Tertullian's words have become classic:

> What indeed has Athens to do with Jerusalem? What concord is there between the Academy and the Church? What between heretics and Christians? Our instruction comes from the porch of Solomon, who himself taught that the Lord should be sought in simplicity of heart. Away with all attempts to produce a mottled Christianity of Stoic, Platonic and Dialectic composition. We want no curious disputation after possessing Christ Jesus, no research after enjoying the Gospel! With our faith we desire no further belief! (*De Presc* 7).

Whereas Justin Martyr spoke of Socrates as a Christian, according to Tertullian, he was 'only a corrupter of youth', not to speak 'of the miserable Aristotle' (Ibid.). He held that the philosophers were 'the patriarchs of heretics' (*De Anima* 3). In this treatise on the soul, Tertullian stated that Socrates' declaration of personal immortality in Plato's *Phaedo* had no value. To know the state of the soul, one must receive divine revelation and not depend on pagan thinkers (Chapters 1–3).

At least Tertullian thought that nature itself bears witness to the reality of God (as in his *The Testimony of the Soul*, chapter 1). Also he admitted that at times pagan philosophers do tell the truth, but he suggests that they really stole their truths from the Old Testament.[19] He was far more concerned about the dangers of idolatry than he was about finding truths in pagan religion. Far from believing that all would be saved, he advocated an excessively strict view as to who – even among church people – could ever attain to forgiveness and eternal life.

Although once a student of broad-minded Justin, Tatian the Syrian (who about A.D.172 founded a strict cult, the Encratites) in his Catholic phase wrote *The Discourse to the Greeks*, which strongly attacks the culture, religion and philosophy of the Greeks (particularly in the Third Book). He (unlike many other Church Fathers) roundly denies that erroneous philosophers such as Diogenes, Plato and Aristotle are 'under the care of providence'.[20] And unlike Justin and Clement, Tatian denies that the Logos has any

---

[19]Certainly Tertullian did, perhaps in spite of himself, make much use of various aspects of pagan philosophy/religion, such as his reliance on Stoic theories of spirit as somehow a material, rational, fiery substance. See Robert H. Ayres, *Language, Logic and Reason in the Church Fathers: A Study of Tertullian, Augustine & Aquinas* (New York: Lubrecht & Cramer, 1979).

[20]Tatian, *Address to the Greeks*, Book I, chapter 2.

relationship to pagans. Although he admits that the Logos created the angels, some of whom fell and became demons (who are behind all pagan religions), the Logos has no fellowship with the devil and his adherents: '...then the power of the Logos excluded the beginner of the folly [i.e. Lucifer/Satan] and his adherents from fellowship with Himself.'[21]

Similar to him (though remaining orthodox) was Theophilus of Antioch, whose work *Ad Autolycum* (c. 180) attacks the absurdities of idolatry (in Book I), and contrasts the foolishness of pagan religion with the truth of the Old Testament (Book II). Finally he shows the immorality of pagan religion, whose gods engendered wickedness in the human race, as opposed to the purity of Christianity (Book III). Theophilus is like most of the Church Fathers in attributing any truth among pagan poets and playwrights to their plundering of the Old Testament. After quoting the Sibyl, Aeschylus, Pindar, Euripides and others, Theophilus concludes: '... they have, willingly or unwillingly, spoken in conformity with the prophets, though they were much more recent, and stole these things from the law and the prophets. The poets corroborate the testimony of the prophets.'[22]

St. Irenaeus, probably the greatest of the second-century theologians, taught that God mercifully put Himself within the grasp of mankind:

> ... because through His love and infinite benignity, He has come within reach of human knowledge (knowledge, however not with regard to His greatness or with regard to His essence – for that has no man measured or handled – but after his sort: that we should know that He who made and formed and breathed in them the breath of life, and nourishes us by means of the creation, establishing all things by His Word and binding them together by His Wisdom – this is He who is the only true God...)[23]

But in this same passage, Irenaeus states:

> For they blaspheme the Creator, Him who is truly God, who also furnishes power to find [the truth]; imagining that they have discovered another God beyond God... Wherefore also the light which is from God does not illumine them, because they have dishonoured and despised God holding Him of small account...[24]

While Irenaeus' main concern here and elsewhere was to refute the Gnostic heresy which was distressing the Church of his time, he also in the same passage mentions 'the god of Epicurus', and what he says in other parts of *Adversus Haereses* indicates that his attribution of some elemental knowledge of God without its illumining the soul would be as true of the rest of mankind as of the heretical Gnostics. He mentions a providential help to the better sort of pagans, who are 'less addicted to [sensual] allurements and voluptuousness, and were not led away to such a degree of superstition with regard to idols...' Thus, this part of fallen mankind: '...being moved, though but slightly, by his providence, were nevertheless convinced that

---

[21]Ibid. I,8.

[22]Theophilus, *To Autolycum*, Book II, chapter 37.

[23]Irenaeus, *Adversus Haereses*, III, xxiv, 2.

[24]Ibid.

they should call the Maker of this universe the Father, who exercises a providence over all things, and arranges the affairs of our world.'[25]

Representative Patristic theologians on pagan religion

Out of the vast congregation of Church Fathers, we select four representative writings which to one degree or another deal with pagan religion and its relationship to the revealed truth of God. These will provide us with a fair survey of the attitude of the Christian religion in their time towards paganism.

(1) Hippolytus of Rome

Though not a great theologian, Hippolytus of Rome (c. 170–235) was widely read in the philosophies, religions and heresies of his day. In 1842 his work that sought to refute all these pagan systems of thought, *Philosophumena* or *Refutation of All Heresies* was rediscovered in a monastery on Mount Athos (books 2 and 3 are still lost). In Book 1, he seeks to show that heresies are only superficially Christian; they are later forms of paganism in religious clothing.

The first major part of *Philosophumena* (books 1 to 4) exposes the various pagan systems of thought and practice, dealing with the history of Greek philosophy and some strands of Hinduism and even Celtic Druidism. Book 4 dissects astrology and magic. The second major part (books 5 to 9) exposes some thirty-three Gnostic sects, and connects them to their ancestral pagan philosophy. The tenth book gives a chronology of Jewish history and an exposition of Christian truth.

Essentially, Hippolytus considers the natural philosophers, pagan religionists and Gnostic heretics to be atheists: '... we may prove them atheists ... they have endeavoured to establish their tenets, taking nothing from the Holy Scriptures... but their doctrines have derived their origin from the wisdom of the Greeks, from the conclusions of those who have formed systems of philosophy, and from would-be mysteries, and the vagaries of astrologers...' (Book 1, The Proemium).

He traces Greek philosophy back to ancient Egyptian lore: 'The origin then, from which Plato derived his theory in the *Timaeus,* is the wisdom of the Egyptians. For from this source, by some ancient and prophetical tradition, Solon [or Solomon?] taught his entire system concerning the generation and destruction of the world, as Plato says, to the Greeks, who were [in knowledge] young children, and were acquainted with no theological doctrine of greater antiquity' (Book VI, chapter 17). Similarly, he traces certain Gnostic heresies back to Egyptian mythology (such as that of Cerinthus),[26] and others (such as that of Marcion and Cerdon) back to the Greek philosopher, Empedocles.[27] Basilides he traces to Aristotle.[28]

Book VIII shows that Hippolytus's goal was not merely negative in refuting the atheism of pagans and heretics: 'Since the great body of [the

---

[25]Ibid., III.25.1.

[26]*Philosophumena* Book VII, (Preliminary) Contents.

[27]Ibid.

[28]Ibid., Book VII, Chapter 2.

heretics] do not employ the counsel of the Lord, by having the beam in the eye (Matt. 7:3, 4), and announce that they see when in reality labouring under blindness, it seems to us expedient in no wise to be silent concerning the tenets of these. Our object is, that by the refutation accomplished by us, the [heretics], being of themselves ashamed, may be brought to know how the Saviour has advised [men] first to take away the beam, then to behold clearly the mote that is in thy brother's eye' (Chapter 1).

Thus, he wishes to show the folly of the origins of philosophy and heresy, so people will scorn them and turn to the saving truth:

> ...to furnish an account and refutation of those heresies that have sprung up in our own day, by which certain ignorant and presumptuous men have attempted to scatter abroad the Church, and have introduced the greatest confusion among all the faithful throughout the entire world. For it seems expedient that we, making an onslaught upon the opinion which constitutes the prime source of [contemporaneous] evils, should prove what are the originating principles of this [opinion], in order that its offshoots, becoming a matter of general notoriety, may be made the object of universal scorn.[29]

His final summary of Greek philosophy is no different from that of St. Paul in Romans 1:

> I consider... that at present it is enough to elucidate those causes of which the Greeks, not being aware, glorified in pompous phraseology, the parts of creation, while they remained ignorant of the Creator.[30]

Having expounded the saving person and work of Christ (the Logos),[31] he calls pagan religionists to repentance:

> Such is the true doctrine in regard of the divine nature, O ye men, Greeks and Barbarians, Chaldeans and Assyrians, Egyptians and Libyans, Indians and Ethiopians, Celts, and ye Latins, who lead your armies, and all ye that inhabit Europe and Asia and Libya. And to you I am become an adviser, inasmuch as I am a disciple of [the] benevolent Logos, and [am myself] humane, in order that you may hasten and by us may be taught who the true God is, and [what] is His well-ordered creation...do not devote your attention to the fallacies of artificial discourses, nor the vain promises of plagiarizing heretics, but to the venerable simplicity of unassuming truth. And by means of this knowledge you shall escape the approaching threat of fire of judgment, and the rayless scenery of gloomy Tartarus, where never shines a beam from the irradiating voice of the Word![32]

(2) Eusebius of Caesarea

About a century after Hippolytus' refutation of pagan religions, Eusebius of Caesarea wrote an influential diagnosis of the pagan religions that had controlled the world of thought up to his time. It was probably written over a period of several years, beginning about A.D. 312, a period before the Constantinian Settlement, when the Christian Church was still liable to

[29]Ibid., Book IX, chapter 1.
[30]Ibid., Book X, chapter 28.
[31]Ibid., Book X, chapters 28 and 29.
[32]Book X, chapter 30.

persecution; a time when the Neo-Platonist, Porphyry, was busily attacking Christian belief and practice from the pagan point of view.

Thus, Eusebius wrote *Praeparatio Evangelica* to defend Christianity and to deconstruct pagan theology in its many forms. In several places, he states the reason for his large volume:

> Let us then begin the *Preparation* by bringing forward the arguments which will probably be used against us both by Greeks and by those of the Circumcision, and by every one who searches with exact inquiry into the opinions held among us.[33]

> All these circumstances then [i.e. particularly fulfilled prophecy] confirm the story of the facts of our religion, and show that it was not contrived from any human impulse, but divinely foreknown, and divinely announced beforehand by the written oracles, and yet far more divinely proffered to all men by our Saviour...[34]

Deliverance of believers from the delusions of devils

Eusebius states many times over that a principal reason for his work is to demonstrate the joy and safety in Christians having renounced and escaped the falsehood and immorality of the pagan religions in which they and their fathers had been ensnared.

> Such then is the character of the theology of the Phoenicians, from which the word of salvation in the gospel teaches us to flee with averted eyes, and earnestly to seek the remedy for this madness of the ancients...[35]

> With good reason then do we avow that we have been freed from all this, and rescued from the long and antiquated delusion as from some terrible and most grievous disease. First, we have been delivered by the grace and beneficence of Almighty God, and secondly by the ineffable power of our Saviour's teaching in the Gospel...[36]

> Moreover, consider all things carefully, and see what blessings God's Christ came to bestow on us, since through His teaching in the Gospel he has redeemed even the souls of Egyptians from such a disease of lasting and long continued blindness, so that now most of the people of Egypt have been freed from this insanity.[37]

> ...how can we have failed to show at the same time, that with sound reason, and without giving ourselves over to folly, we have turned away from the superstition handed down from our fathers, and with just and true judgement have chosen the better part, and become lovers of the inspired and true religion?[38]

In sum, he rejoices in Christ having redeemed His own people (and he clearly counts the ancestors of the Christians among the formerly deluded pagans) from the delusions of devils:

---

[33]Eusebius of Caesarea, *Praeparatio Evangelica*, translator and editor, E. H. Gifford (Oxford: Oxford University Press, 1903), Bk. I, ch. 1.

[34]Ibid., Bk. I, ch. 3.

[35]Ibid., Bk. I, ch. 10.

[36]Ibid., Bk. II, ch. 4.

[37]Ibid., Bk. III, ch. 5.

[38]Ibid., Bk. IV, ch. 4.

> And since no one from the beginning except Jesus our Saviour has ransomed the whole human race from this delusion, we have had good reason for dealing seriously with all the present subjects in the commencement of the *Preparation for the Gospel*, in order that we might learn by facts from what ancestors we are sprung, and by what kind of delusion they were formerly possessed, and from how manifold and great blindness and ungodliness both we ourselves and all men living have emerged, and have found the cure for that long and inveterate daemonical activity in the saving doctrine of the Gospel only.[39]

His diagnosis of the ancestral religions of the ancient world is, like that of Hippolytus, far-ranging in every direction; from the theology of the ancient Egyptians and Phonecians, to Babylonian astrology, Homeric myths, Sybiline Oracles, Indian Brahmanism, Celtic practices of human sacrifice, Dionysian orgies, pre-Socratic philosophers, Plato in particular (with much less on Aristotle), the Sceptics, Epicureans, Stoics and Neo-Platonists (such as Porphyry), to mention only a few of the main ones.

The pagans fell away from the original true religion

He believes that originally mankind had the one, true religion (preserved by the Hebrews), but that they soon fell away from it:[40]

> Before these [i.e. the Phoenicians and Egyptians], it is said, no one made any progress in the knowledge of the celestial phenomena, except the few men mentioned among the Hebrews, who with clearest mental eyes looked beyond all the visible world, and worshipped the Maker and creator of the universe, marvelling much at the greatness of His wisdom and power, which they represented to themselves from His works; and being persuaded that He alone was God, they naturally spoke of Him as God, son from father successively receiving and guarding this as the true, the first and the only religion. The rest of mankind, however, having fallen away from this only true religion, and gazing in awe upon the luminaries of heaven with eyes of flesh, as mere children in mind, proclaimed them gods, and honoured them with sacrifices and acts of worship, though as yet they built no temples, nor formed likenesses of mortal men with statues and carved images, but looked up to the clear sky and to heaven itself, and in their souls reached up unto the things seen there.[41]

It was his theory that 'Orpheus, son of Oeagrus first brought over with him the mysteries of the Egyptians, and imparted them to the Greeks…'[42] For instance, 'Demeter has the same meaning among the Greeks as Isis among the Egyptians: and again, Kore and Dionysus among the Greeks the same as Isis and Osiris among the Egyptians.'[43]

So, from ancient times, mankind worshipped the luminaries:

> It is said [by Diodorus of Sicily] then that the men who dwelled of old in Egypt when they looked up to the cosmos, and were struck with astonishment and

[39]Ibid., Bk. VI, ch. 11.

[40]We will explore the famous research by Wilhelm Schmidt on the universal passing down of patriarchal revelation in Volume II of this *Systematic Theology* under the concept of 'revelation'.

[41]Ibid. Bk. I, ch. 6.

[42]Ibid.

[43]Ibid., Bk. III, ch. 11.

> admiration at the nature of the universe, supposed that the sun and moon were two eternal and primal gods, one of whom they named Osiris, and the other Isis, each name being applied from some true etymology.[44]

Referring to the Egyptians and Phoenicians, he states:

> that the most ancient of the barbarians, and especially the Phoenicians and Egyptians, from whom the rest of mankind received their traditions…applied the names of their kings to the elements of the cosmos…But they knew of no other gods than those of nature, sun and moon, and the rest of the wandering stars, and the elements and things connected with them, so that some of their gods were mortal and some immortal.[45]

In addition to worship of the luminaries, ancient man also deified heroes and kings (the theory of 'Euhemerism). He quotes Diodorus of Sicily:

> The gods they say [i.e. the Egyptians] had originally been mortal men, but gained their immortality on account of wisdom and public benefits to mankind, some of them having also become kings: and some have the same names, when interpreted, with the heavenly deities, while others have received a name of their own, as Helios, and Kronos, and Rhea, and Zeus, who is by some called Ammon; and besides these Hera and Hephaestus, and Hestia, and lastly Hermes. Helios, they say, was the first king of the Egyptians, having the same name with the celestial luminary: some, however, of the priests say that Hephaestus was the first who became king, because he was the discoverer of fire.[46]

Eusebius quotes Euemerus [or Euchemerus] (also referred to by St. Augustine) on the origins of polytheism:

> With regard then to gods the men of old have handed down to their posterity two sets of notions. For some, say they, are eternal and imperishable, as the Sun and moon…Other deities they say were of the earth; but, because of the benefits which they conferred on mankind, they have received immortal honour and glory, as Heracles, Dionysus, Aristaeus, and the others like them…and of the mythologists Homer, Hesiod, Orpheus, and such others as these, have invented very marvellous myths concerning the gods…[47]

Following Plutarch, Eusebius says:

> So then their whole manufacture of gods consists of dead men and their physical explanations are fictitious. For what need was there to model figures of men and women, when without them they could worship the sun and moon and the other elements of the cosmos?[48]

Elsewhere Eusebius writes:

> Here observe, I pray you, how many gods born of women were deified by the Greeks, to be brought forward if ever they attempt to mock at our Saviour's birth…[49]

---

[44]Ibid., Bk. I, ch. 9.
[45]Ibid.
[46]Ibid., Bk. II, Preface.
[47]Ibid., Bk. II, ch. 2.
[48]Ibid., Bk. III, ch. 3.
[49]Ibid., Bk. III, ch. 14.

And in line with Plato's *Timaeus*, Eusebius writes:

> In exhorting us hereby to believe the fables concerning the gods, and the authors also of the fables as being forsooth the children of the gods, in the first place by saying that 'the poets are the offspring of the gods,' it seems to me that he scoffingly implies that the gods also had been men, and of the same nature as their children.[50]

Eusebius' analysis of all this pagan polytheism (whether of luminaries or deified heroes) is essentially the same as that of St. Paul in Romans 1:

> ...why in the world therefore do they not reject the foul and unseemly fables, concerning them, as containing blasphemous and licentious teaching, and celebrate the One and Only and Invisible God openly and purely and without any foul envelopment?... But no one ever yet, barbarian or Greek, began to show all men this truth except only our Saviour; who having proclaimed to all nations an escape from their ancient error, procured abundantly for them all a way of return and of devotion to the one true and only God of the universe. Yet the men perversely wise who boasted of the highest philosophy of life, whereby as the inspired Apostle says, though they knew God, they glorified Him not as God, neither gave thanks; but became vain in their reasonings, and their senseless heart was darkened. They professed indeed to be wise, but became fools...and worshipped and served the creature rather than the Creator, who is blessed for ever (Rom. 1:21, 22, 25).[51]

In other words, except for the Hebrews, mankind universally fell into the folly of idolatry.

> But to understand the sum of the first and greatest benefit of the word of salvation, you must take into consideration the superstitious delusion of the ancient idolatry, whereby the whole human race in times long past was ground down by the constraint of demons...[52]

In common with Christian teaching, Eusebius connected the worship of idols with the presence of demons. 'How we are to regard the powers that lurk in the carved images...'[53] He puts the worship of idols in the context of 'the demons who operate through graven images'.[54] 'But in fact I believe it to be hereby clearly proved that the most ancient and primitive erection of carved images and all the idolatrous creation of gods among the heathen was the work of demons, and of demons who were not even good, but utterly wicked and worthless...'[55]

Eusebius demonstrates at large the immorality that flowed from polytheistic idolatry:

> But that these were the works of worthless and wicked demons would be still more manifest to you, were you to consider their practices of infamous and unbridled fornication still observed in the City of the Sun in Phoenicia, and among many other people. For they say that men ought to practise

[50]Ibid., Bk. XIII, ch. 1.
[51]Ibid., Bk. III, ch. 13.
[52]Ibid., Bk. I, ch. 5.
[53]Ibid., Bk. IV, ch. 1.
[54]Ibid., Bk. IV, ch. 15.
[55]Ibid., Bk. IV, ch. 16.

> adulteries, and seductions, and other unlawful kinds of intercourse in honour of the gods…[56]

> In this way both Greeks and barbarians, wise and simple, falling to the ground and on their belly, worshipped pleasure as a goddess; they cast themselves down on their faces like reptiles; they believed in her as an irresistible and inexorable deity, and were content. In songs also and hymns, and in the festivals of god, and in their public spectacles, they were initiated in the orgies and celebrated the unseemly rites of none other than foul and licentious pleasure; so that this, above all, has been rightly abolished among us. 'For the devising of idols was the beginning of fornication' (Wisdom 14:12).[57]

But polytheism could hold sway only because of the natural sense of God, residing in all his image-bearers. Eusebius writes:

> Now take thou up our argument again from the beginning, and observe the downfall of superstitious error. By nature and by our self-taught ideas, or rather ideas taught by God, there is a something noble and salutary that indicates the name and being of God: for all men had taken this for granted in their common reasonings, since the Creator of all things had implanted this conviction by innate ideas in every rational and intelligent soul.[58]

> For the Creator of all implanted in every soul this natural law as a helper and defender in its actions…[59]

On this point, Eusebius quotes Clement of Alexandria:

> Instinctively, therefore, and without teaching, all things derive from a conception of the Father and Maker of all…And of mankind both Greeks and Barbarians all have this conception…Wherefore every nation of the east, and every one that touches the western shores, the northern also, and all upon the south, have one and the same presentiment of Him who established the government of the world, inasmuch as the most universal of His operations have pervaded all things alike…[60]

Difference between Greek mythology and philosophy

Eusebius makes a strong distinction between the sense of God held by the mythological polytheists, such as Homer and Hesiod, and that of Plato. He discusses Plato's 'demythologization' of the Greek gods and his exclusion of such stories from the ideal state.[61] He approves of Plato in numerous ways, and tries to make, for instance, the creation account found in the *Timaeus* fit with the Genesis account.[62]

He also argues that Plato's doctrine of the immortality of the soul is much the same as Holy Scripture (though he admits differences).[63] Along

[56]Ibid.
[57]Ibid., Bk. VII, ch. 2.
[58]Ibid., Bk. II, ch. 6.
[59]Ibid., Bk. VI, ch. 6.
[60]Ibid., Bk. XIII, ch. 13.
[61]Ibid., Bk. II, chs. 5-7.
[62]Ibid., Bk. XI, chs. 29, 30.
[63]Ibid., Bk. XI, chs. 27,28.

with Clement of Alexandria, he thinks that he finds the Holy Trinity within Plato's teaching.[64]

But, in company with many of the Church Fathers before his time, Eusebius claims that Plato stole his true ideas from the Hebrews, by way of a visit to Egypt, where these writings were supposedly known.[65] '...Plato and his successors have agreed in their philosophy with the Hebrews...'[66] '...Plato is anticipated by Moses...'[67] '...the admirable Plato followed the all-wise Moses and the Hebrew prophets...(since he is proved to have made his studies among the Egyptians at the very time when the Hebrews, having been driven out of their own country, were in the habit of visiting Egypt during the Persian supremacy)...'[68] And quoting the famous line from Numenius, Eusebius exclaims: '... For what is Plato, but Moses speaking in Attic Greek?'[69] This kind of dependency seems to have been generally accepted throughout Christendom until the literary and historical research of the Renaissance was thought to have discredited it.

Yet, more than the earlier Church writers, Clement and Origen, Eusebius also points out the many *mistakes made by Plato*, where he is out of accord with the very Scriptures he is alleged to have plundered. In contrasting Plato with the full truth of the Hebrew Scriptures, he writes:

> But since the philosophy of Plato was shown by us at some length to be in very many things in agreement with the doctrines of the Hebrews (for which we admire the man's wisdom and his candour also in regard to the truth), it is time to consider what the points are in which, as we say, we are no longer so favourably disposed towards him...The oracles of the Hebrews containing prophecies and responses of a divine power beyond that of man and claiming God as their author...are said to be free from all erroneous thought...But not such are the words of Plato...who... superadded to the truth a large mixture of falsehood...[70]

He criticizes Plato for accepting the popular theology of the Greek cities as to the origins of the gods,[71] for claiming that souls are unoriginated,[72] and that souls transmigrate,[73] etc.

Eusebius finally considers most of pagan religion to be functionally in the category of atheism. Such is the account he renders of the pre-Socratic doctrines of the origins of the world (e.g. from water, fire, etc.).[74] He calls the older Greek mythical theology 'the first kind of atheism.'[75] To him, "...the polytheistic delusion of mankind...is no better than atheism.'[76] Quoting

[64]Ibid., Bk. XIII, ch. 13,
[65]Ibid., Bk. X, ch. 4.
[66]Ibid., Bk. X, ch. 14.
[67]Ibid., Bk. XI, ch. 6.
[68]Ibid., Bk. XI, ch. 8.
[69]Ibid., Bk. IX, ch. 6.
[70]Ibid., Bk. XIII, chs. 13, 14.
[71]Ibid., Bk. XIII, ch. 14.
[72]Ibid., Bk. XIII, ch. 15.
[73]Ibid., Bk. XIII, ch. 16.
[74]Ibid., Bk. I, ch. 8.
[75]Ibid., Bk. II, ch. 5.
[76]Ibid., Bk. VII, ch. 16.

Protagoras' statement in *Concerning the gods*, Eusebius writes: 'As to gods I neither know that they exist, nor that they do not exist, nor of what nature they are.'[77] And quoting Plutarch, he writes: 'Some of the philosophers, as Diagoras of Melos and Theodoras of Cyreme, and Eumerus of Tegea, altogether deny that there are any gods.'[78]

Like Clement of Alexandria before him, and St. Augustine and St. Anselm long after his time, Eusebius holds that the starting point of faith in the God who speaks in the Holy Scriptures is the only way to salvation and true thinking:

> With good reason then the Hebrew Scriptures at an earlier time require faith before either the understanding or examination of the sacred writings, where it says, 'If ye will not believe, surely ye shall not understand' (Isa. 7:9), and again 'I believed, and therefore have I spoken' (Ps. 116:10).
>
> For which cause also among us those who are newly admitted and in an immature condition, as if infants in soul, have the reading of the sacred Scriptures imparted to them in a very simple way, with the injunction that they must believe what is brought forward as words of God. But those who are in a more advanced condition, and as it were grown grey in mind, are permitted to dive into the deeps, and test the meaning of the words: and these the Hebrews were wont to name 'Deuterotists,' as being interpreters and expounders of the meaning of the Scriptures.[79]

(3) Basil the Great

Often called 'the second Athanasius', Basil was one of the three Cappadocian Fathers, who successfully guided the fourth-century Church through to victory in its struggle against the Arians, who denied the full deity of Christ. He wrote *Ad Adolescentes* ('How young people may profit from Hellenic Literature') for his own nephews. His concern was not the same as the earlier Hippolytus; to a considerable degree, paganism had already been refuted by the late fourth century, and the Church was triumphing. But the question remained: how may Christians make use of pagan classics (which are largely based on heathen mythology and pagan ethics)? It was no easy question, for the education of that time (for Christians as well as others) was still based on Greek and Roman pagan 'classics.' As Basil answers this question, we see both positive and negative evaluation of pagan philosophy and religion (though the negative clearly predominates).

He counsels his nephews 'not to abandon the rudder of their spirits' to pagan classical writers, nor 'to follow them where they would lead you', but to accept from them what is useful, and to know how to reject the rest.[80] The basic idea for Christians to keep in mind as they seek education is that they are being prepared for another life.[81] Thus, we must make use of what helps us towards that goal, and avoid the rest, like soldiers and athletes.[82]

---

[77]Ibid., Bk. XIV, ch. 3.

[78]Ibid., Bk. XIV, ch. 16.

[79]Ibid., Bk. XII, ch. 1.

[80]Basil, *Aux Jeunes Gens Sur La Manière De Tirer Profit Des Lettres Hélléniques* (Paris: Société d'Edition 'Les Belles Lettres', 1965), I.

[81]Ibid., II.

[82]Ibid.

Moses and Daniel were examples of this process of using pagan learning for higher purposes.[83] The Greek poets gave some examples of virtue, but often portrayed visions and immoral figures. One must avoid such immoral tales, as Ulysses stopped his ears against the song of the Sirens.[84] One must avoid the adulteries of the gods as portrayed in the theatre.[85]

But some have understood the poetry of Homer as the praise of virtue, and so to that degree he deserves attention.[86] One can find the encouragement of virtues (such as sincerity of speech) among such writers as Euripides and Plato.[87] One must seek illustrations of denial of the body to strengthen the life of the soul within the stories of Greek and Persian history and mythology.[88] Basil states in conclusion that the Christian writings are after all better,[89] but still one finds value – if one is very selective – in pagan literature. Basil obviously assumes (without specific discussion in this brief work) that the Christian writings and practice provide the standard of selectivity for those who wish to profit from pagan classics.[90]

(4) St. Augustine

The great doctor of the Latin Church probably gave his fullest evaluation of pagan philosophy and religion contrasted to Christian truth in his *City of God*, composed over a period of years in response to the sack and capture of Rome by Alaric and the Goths in 410. The Neo-Platonists and other non-Christians blamed the Church for the fall of Rome. Some of them thought it was a punishment from the old Roman gods for having been neglected.

Rome fell because of idolatry, not Christianity

Augustine replied at length that Rome's fall was owing to its sin and idolatry, not to its official Christianity. In fact, Rome had never become Christian enough to avert such judgments. Our concern here will be not to trace the logic of Augustine's development of the history of the City of God and the City of man, but merely to look at his central assessment of pagan philosophy and religion as a Christian bishop.

Out of this remarkable thousand-page volume, one can discern certain central theses on pagan religion. Basically, the pagan gods are either empty ('nothings') or unclean (in that case, demons). 'Christian truth proves those "gods" to be useless images or unclean spirits and malignant demons, creatures at any rate, and not the Creator.'[91] Pagans have taken the attributes

---

[83]Ibid., III.

[84]Ibid., IV.

[85]Ibid.

[86]Ibid., V.

[87]Ibid. VI.

[88]Ibid. IX.

[89]Ibid. X.

[90]Jaroslav Pelikan discusses how the Cappadocians, while rejecting the religious foundations of Greek thought, at the same time assimilated much of their logical discoveries in order better to refute biblically the heretics of their time. See *Christianity and Classical Culture: The Metamorphosis of Natural Theology in the Christian Encounter with Hellenism* (New Haven: Yale University Press, 1993).

[91]Augustine, *City of God*, translation by Henry Bettenson (Harmondsworth: Penguin Books, 1972), Book VI, preface (p. 225).

of God and have ascribed them to elements of the creation, as Paul says in Romans 1:

> In fact, all that is attributed to the world by the theology of those 'select' gods, employing ostensibly 'natural' principles of interpretation, should rather be ascribed, without the slightest trace of blasphemy, to the true God, who made the world, who is the creator of every soul and every material substance.[92]

Augustine on Euhemerism

Augustine suggests the theory of 'Euhemerism' (the ancient theory that the gods were deified men)[93] as the foundation of the pagan pantheon. 'What conception of Jupiter was in the minds of those who placed his nurse in the Capitol? Have they not given support to the theory of Euhemerus who, writing as a careful researcher, not as a purveyor of legendary chatter, maintained that all those gods were originally men, mere mortals?'[94] Augustine, like the earlier Fathers, noted the immorality of pagan religious ritual.[95] Following reports of Seneca, Augustine exposes the inhumane cruelty and obscenity of pagan orgiastic worship of false gods.[96] Such gods are evil demons:

> This religion, the one true religion, had the power to prove that the gods of the nations are unclean demons. Those demons seized the chance offered by the souls of the dead, or disguised themselves as creatures of this world, in their desire to be reputed gods; in their arrogance and impurity they took delight in supposed divine honours, a medley of infamy and obscenity, and were full of resentment when human souls were converted to the true God. Man is set free from him who achieved his resurrection by the example of a humility as great as the pride which brought about the fall of the demons.[97]

Higher Platonic philosophy

Yet Augustine, who owed much to pagan Neo-Platonic philosophy himself, saw a certain difference between the straight demonism of popular religion and the higher philosophy of Plato and others. He holds that especially the Platonists went beyond Varro's opinion that God is essentially the World-Soul. 'But these thinkers acknowledge a God who transcends any kind of soul, being the maker not only of this visible world – heaven and earth, in the familiar phrase – but also of every soul whatsoever...These philosophers are called Platonists ...'[98] 'There are none who come nearer to us than the Platonists.'[99] He admits that there may have been others in the world who also held to the supremacy of God:

> There may be others to be found who perceived and taught this truth among those who were esteemed as sages or philosophers in other nations:

---

92 Ibid., VII, 29 (p. 291).
93 Ibid. IV, 27 (p. 169).
94 Ibid. VI, 7 (p. 239).
95 Ibid. II, 26 (p. 82- 85).
96 Ibid., VI, 10 (p. 248-259).
97 Ibid. VII, 33 (p. 294).
98 Ibid., VIII, 1 (298-299).
99 Ibid., VIII, 5 (304).

> Libyans of Atlas, Egyptians, Indians, Persians, Chaldeans, Scythians, Gauls, Spaniards. Whoever they may have been, we rank such thinkers above all others and acknowledge them as representing the closest approximation to our Christian position.[100]

Like other Church Fathers, Augustine holds that Plato by going to Egypt learned his theology from the Jewish Scriptures.[101] Yet he admits that Plato allows polytheism.[102] And even worse, the Platonists 'refuse to recognize the incarnation of the unchanging Son of God, which brings us salvation.'[103]

Platonism insufficient for salvation

Hence, Augustine shows the insufficiency of Platonism for salvation, in the context of arguing against the Neo-Platonist, Porphyry. (Having discussed the necessity of Christ's sacrifice for our sins in the previous section – Book X, 31, Augustine continues):

> This is the religion which contains the universal way for the liberation of the soul, since no soul can be freed by any other way. For this is, one may say, the royal road, which alone leads to the kingdom whose glory is not the tottering grandeur of the temporal, but the secure stability of the eternal.[104]

Relying on Old Testament prophecies such as Isaiah 2:2, Augustine concludes:

> This means that the way does not belong to one people, but is for all nations; and the Law and the Word of God did not stay in Sion and Jerusalem but went out from there so that it might spread through the whole world. Hence the Mediator himself, after his resurrection, said to his trembling disciples, 'What was written about me in the Law, the Prophets, and the Psalms, had to be fulfilled'(Luke 24:44) …
>
> So this is the universal way of liberation for the soul which the holy angels and the holy prophets foretold. They revealed it in former times among a small number of men…the Hebrew people, whose political community was in a manner consecrated for the purposes of prophesying and announcing the City of God which was to be assembled out of all nations…But in the end the Mediator himself came in the flesh, and he and his blessed apostles now revealed the grace of the new covenant and disclosed openly what in previous ages had been indicated by veiled allusions, when hints were given in accordance with the stages of mankind's development, following the plan decided upon by God in his wisdom.[105]

Note on the replacement of other religions and their cultures by Christianity

Since the early twentieth century, most of the 'main-line' (or 'established') Protestant churches of the modern West have become very uneasy about the replacement of non-Christian religions (and major aspects of their culture)

---

[100]Ibid., VIII, 9 (p. 311).
[101]VIII, 11 (314).
[102]VIII, 12 (316).
[103]X, 29 (414).
[104]X, 32 (420).
[105]X, 32 (423, 424).

in non-European lands. A large part of this unease must be owing to these churches having assimilated Enlightenment relativism with its disbelief in any one transcendentally valid revelation. The issue often seems reduced to embarrassment about the colonial and cultural imperialism of the wealthy and powerful West over 'third world' regions (in the past and in the present). While without doubt, the nation states of the West have much to repent for in their mistreatment and immoral exploitation of vast native populations and their environments for reasons of money and power, to say that other religions in these lands should not, therefore, be replaced is surely 'to throw out the baby with the bathwater.' Churches in the West are entirely right to seek to turn their people (and nations) from plunder and abuse of less developed countries and from arrogant denigration of their cultures, but they are failing to show truest love for the welfare of all, if they fail to present to them the revelation of God's grace in Christ as God's final word to them (cf. Heb. 1:1, 2).

To abandon falsehood is no disservice to any culture

We could find no better guide (apart from revelation itself) than the Church Fathers, who lived in centuries of religious pluralism with conflicting moral claims and cultural systems. We find that *negatively* they had to confront and deny the validity of the truth claims of pagan religions (along with the immorality they brought with them), because they had found the liberating cleansing from the falsehood and pollution of idolatry and all false gods. One sees this, for example, in the frequent exclamations of Eusebius of the joy Christians have found in deliverance from the false religious cultures in which they and their fathers had long lived. Hence, Hippolytus, Augustine and the others show the disastrous moral and eternal consequences of following false gods, and confront pagans with a call to faith and repentance; with a call to turn from polluted ways of living and thinking. Not to have done so would have been uncharitable in the highest degree; it would have constituted a failure to help others out of the sordid prison house from which they themselves had been delivered. But they could only do this because they were certain that they had met the one, true living God in His Word and Spirit, and had personally experienced His transforming grace in their lives.

Thus, they were only too glad to have their ancient cultures transformed where called for by His truth. But leaders of churches, (as in so much of the West), whose basic thought is still within the Enlightenment deistic framework, will naturally deny the very possibility of grasping a definitive, divine revelation. So long as they remain within that dualistic framework (that separates God and the real world), they could scarcely be expected to call on others to renounce their prior non-Christian religions and to give up aspects of their ancient cultures that violate the standards of God's Word, for there is no transcendent God to give a final word, nor is there any transcendentally valid standard by which to evaluate any religion or culture. But to say the very least, that was not the position of the apostles and Church Fathers, nor of the medieval Scholastics and Protestant Reformers! They were in no sense hesitant to denounce false religion and immoral cultural practices of any land whatsoever, but always with a very positive and merciful end (the offer of the saving gospel to sinners of every sort and condition).

One need not negate any value or truth from non-Christian cultures

Yet at the same time, the Church Fathers, even those who were most negative against false religions, gratefully assimilated much of truth and value from pre-Christian pagan culture. Eusebius tries to rescue and make use of as much of Plato as he could, as did Augustine in a rather different way. Basil the Great seeks to pass on much of beauty and truth from Homer and others for the development of a Christian education. Even Tertullian, who decried most loudly all pagan philosophy, made more use than he perhaps was aware of, of certain concepts from the physical philosophy of Stoicism (such as the physical constitution of souls).[106]

Scattered, but interesting illustrations of a thoughtful balance between denial of pagan premises and grateful reception of cultural benefits from pre-Christian times (or non-Protestant regions) are to be found in some of the post-Reformational Anglican theologians such as Richard Hooker, Lancelot Andrewes, John Donne and Joseph Hall.[107]

In a sense, what the Church Fathers did might (anachronistically) be termed what the sixteenth-century Reformer, John Calvin, would come to call the appreciative recognition of 'common grace' insights and values from paganism and false religious systems.[108] Calvin writes at large in his *Institutes of the Christian Religion*:

> First, in man's perverted and degenerate nature some sparks [from God] still gleam...Human understanding then possesses some power of perception, since it is by nature captivated by love of truth...Indeed, man's mind, because of its dullness, cannot hold to the right path...Yet its efforts do not always become so worthless as to have no effect, especially when it turns its attention to things below...Yet the fact remains that some seed of political order has been implanted in all men...Then follow the arts, both liberal and manual. The power of human acuteness also appears in learning these because all of us have a certain aptitude...Yet so universal is this good that every man ought to recognize for himself in it the peculiar grace of God...Yet because it is bestowed indiscriminately upon pious and impious, it is rightly counted among natural gifts...Whenever we come upon these matters in secular writers, let that admirable light of truth shining in them teach us that the mind of man, though fallen and perverted from its wholeness, is nevertheless clothed and ornamented with God's excellent gifts. If we regard the Spirit of God as the sole fountain of truth, we shall neither reject the truth itself, nor despise it wherever it shall appear, unless we wish to dishonour the Spirit of God...What then? Shall we deny that the truth shone upon the ancient jurists who established civic order

[106]See Harry A. Wolfson, *The Philosophy of the Church Fathers: Faith, Trinity, Incarnation* (Cambridge, MA: Harvard University Press, 1976), 102-106, and also Roy Kearsley, *Tertullian's Theology of Divine Power* (Carlisle: Rutherford Studies in Historical Theology, Paternoster Press, 1998), chapter two (pp. 4-13).

[107]C. F. Allison, *The Rise of Moralism: The Proclamation of the Gospel from Hooker to Baxter* (London: SPCK, 1966), 1466, discusses helpfully the theology of several of these scholars on justification by faith (though not on cultural issues).

[108]This judicious appreciation is found in Richard Hooker as well. See his *Ecclesiastical Polity* at large; especially vol. V.

> and discipline with such great equity? Shall we say that the philosophers were blind in their fine observation and artful descriptions of nature...Shall we say that they are insane who developed medicine ...What shall we say of all the mathematical sciences...No, we cannot read the writings of the ancients on these subjects without great admiration...But shall we count anything praiseworthy or noble without recognizing at the same time that it comes from God?... Those men whom Scripture [1 Cor. 2:14] calls 'natural men' were, indeed, sharp and penetrating in their investigation of inferior things. Let us, accordingly, learn by their example how many gifts the Lord left to human nature even after it was despoiled of its true good...But if the Lord has willed that we be helped in physics, dialectic, mathematics, and other like disciplines, by the work and ministry of the ungodly, let us use this assistance.[109]

In the sections just quoted, Calvin rightly draws a strong distinction between perceiving inferior things and heavenly things. Unregenerate human nature can certainly be helpful in the former, but not in the latter. Thus, wherever Christianity goes with truth claims that successfully supplant former religions which never could properly reveal the true God and His salvation, one must totally abandon the false gods and false theologies that can only mislead and corrupt. This necessarily does lead to profound changes in the culture (which in some respects is 'religion externalised' as Henry Van Til insightfully said.)[110] But still, major aspects of pagan cultures from which false religion has been exorcized, may well be conveyors of much of God's beauty and truth, and the Christian Church has always been able 'to take on board' these unexpected shinings of God's light from within any culture whatsoever.[111]

Varying approaches of the historic Christian Church to pagan culture

This process, however, is complex and controversial, and it usually takes the Church some generations before she has decided what to accept and what to reject from the former pagan culture of its members. At some periods the Church has gone in a broader direction of accepting a considerable amount of formerly pagan practices, as long as these can be reinterpreted and worked into Christian practices which replace them. An illustration is the famous instruction of Pope Gregory I to the missionary Augustine (in late sixth-century England) to adapt pagan temples and holidays to Christian purposes.[112]

At other times the Church (or part of the Church) has gone in a much stricter direction, such as the English Puritans in the seventeenth-century 'Second Reformation.'[113] In order to reform the worship of the Church of

---

[109]John Calvin, *Institutes*, II.11.12-16. This complex matter of 'common grace' in the thought of John Calvin has been finely discussed by Abraham Kuyper, *De Gemeene Gratie*, 3 vols (Amsterdam: Höveker & Wormser, 1902-04); Herman Kuiper, *Calvin on Common Grace* (Grand Rapids, MI: Oosterbaan & LeCointre, Goes, The Netherlands and Smitter Book Co., 1928); Cornelius Van Til, *Common Grace* (Nutley, NJ: P & R, 1947) and John Murray, *Collected Writings: Systematic Theology 2* (Edinburgh: The Banner of Truth Trust).

[110]Henry Van Til, *The Calvinistic Concept of Culture* (Philadelphia: Presbyterian and Reformed, 1959).

[111]Charles Norris Cochrane's *Christianity and Classical Culture: A Study of Thought and Action From Augustus to Augustine* (London: Oxford University Press, 1940) is an outstanding study of how this process worked out in late Classical and early Medieval Europe.

[112]See Bede, *Ecclesiastical History*, I.30.

[113]The Puritans of Congregationalist convictions (such as John Owen and Thomas Goodwin), and many – though not all – of Presbyterian convictions (such as Walter Travers and George Gillespie) tended

England, they sought to follow the principle that 'what is not required in Scripture (or warranted by it), is forbidden in worship' (whereas Luther had followed a broader principle, that 'what is not forbidden in Scripture, is allowed in worship'). For the Puritans that meant getting rid of the ancient Christian calendar with its dominical and saints' holidays and festivities, as well as much of the symbolism and ceremony in worship that had grown up in the Middle Ages, since these were not required by Scripture (whereas John Calvin had allowed a fuller liturgy of worship, as well as celebration of the 'dominical holidays', such as Christmas, Easter and Pentecost).[114] So, in general, Puritanism was hostile to anything that even smacked of ancient pagan religion and customs, and sought to purge out such influences. Perhaps this strictness in part explains the violent rejection of much of Puritanism and the movement in a libertarian direction by the post-1660 Restoration in Britain.

Almost no Reformed churches for the last century have been so strict as their Puritan forefathers in rejecting anything in the secular culture that may have some kind of pagan religious roots, if one traces them far enough back. After the pendulum swings very far in different directions, the Church probably comes to a point of rest somewhere in between extremes, in the matter of relating Christianity to various aspect of beauty and joy that may come from older, rightly rejected religious cultures.

Sometimes this unspoken principle of legitimate Christian assimilation and reinterpretation of useful pagan art, music, literature, etc. takes place fairly quickly. One can see an illustration of this in the Catacombs of Rome, where the Christians buried their dead from the late second or early third centuries down to the fifth or sixth. In the Catacomb of St. Priscilla on the Via Salaris in Rome (where there are nearly thirteen kilometers of underground burial passages with tombs for some 40,000 persons), one finds some of the very earliest Christian art. There is a painting of the Virgin Mary and Jesus from c. 210–220, which is believed to be the earliest representation in art of the Virgin. Most of the paintings that remain are of biblical or extra-biblical scenes (Daniel in the Lions' Den, the three Hebrew children in the fire, the prophet Balaam speaking to the Virgin Mary, etc.). But there are a small number of paintings that certainly are from classical pagan sources, but definitely adapted to Christian usage (probably third century). One finds Greek-like representations of the four seasons of the year with faces; the phoenix (an ancient pagan symbol going back to Egypt, that Christians used as an illustration of the resurrection), and the peacock (used by Christians to symbolize eternal life), though coming from ancient pagan Rome.

Thus, the early Roman Christians had rejected their own ancestral pagan religion (and many had paid a high price for doing so), but still they were

---

to strictness; while those of Anglican convictions generally took a broader approach (as Richard Hooker, James Ussher, and Lancelot Andrews). See James I. Packer, *Among God's Giants: The Puritan Vision of the Christian Life* (Eastbourne: Kingsway Publications, 1991), and Horton Davies, *Worship and Theology in England from Andrewes to Baxter and Fox, 1603–1690* (Princeton: Princeton University Press, 1975).

[114]Dr. Hughes Old has pointed out that 'The Reformers did not intend to make a choice between "what is not forbidden is allowed" and "what is not commanded is not allowed." ... rather, 'They were determined to find a third principle, the reform of the church according to God's Word'. See his *The Shaping of the Reformed Baptismal Rite in the Sixteenth Century* (Wm. B. Eerdmans: Grand Rapids, 1992), 283, 102, n. 77.

willing to take certain things of beauty from the old pagan context and employ them in a new, purified setting. So, they rejected the false religion in which they had been raised, without negating everything in their ancient culture. In so doing, they enriched the flourishing of Christianity.

Much the same could be said about music. In his *De Doctrina Christiana*, Augustine states that Christians need to learn many things about music and musical instruments from the pagans, if they are to understand and make use of scriptural teaching on music. He writes:

> But whether Varro's story is true or not [about the merely human origin of the statues of the Muses in Apollo's temple], we should not avoid music because of the associated pagan superstitions if there is a possibility of gleaning from it something of value for understanding holy scripture…A person who is a good and a true Christian should realize that truth belongs to his Lord, wherever it is found, gathering and acknowledging it even in pagan literature, but rejecting superstitious vanities and deploring and avoiding those who 'though they knew God did not glorify him as God or give thanks but became enfeebled in their own thoughts and plunged their senseless minds into darkness. Claiming to be wise they became fools, and exchanged the glory of the incorruptible God for the image of corruptible mortals and animals and reptiles'(Rom. 1:21-23).[115]

And the same process is true for literature, as we have already seen in Saint Basil's *Ad Adolescentes*. What Basil said (in Greek) was fairly similar to what Augustine said shortly afterwards in Latin. Augustine defends using a pagan rhetorician such as Cicero with the Biblical illustration of Moses having listened to his non-Jewish father-in-law, Jethro:

> Is it not true that God spake with Moses, and yet Moses accepted advice about guiding and governing such a great people from his father-in-law, a man actually of another race, with an abundance of foresight and an absence of pride [Exod. 18]? He was well aware that true advice, from whatever mind it came, should be ascribed not to man but to the unchangeable God who is the truth.[116]

As non-Christian religions are still being rejected in favor of Christianity in large and populous areas of the world (as in Africa, East Asia and South America), those who are liberated from falsehood into the glorious freedom in Christ, will be just as keen as the early Roman, Greek and Celtic Christians to draw a line between light and darkness, truth and lies, holy living and immorality. Western Christians who do not applaud their doing so are out of accord with both Holy Scripture and the best in their own ancestral tradition.

But at the same time, we may look with glad anticipation on valuable aspects of beauty and creativity that will survive the collapse of paganism in those regions, and 'come out of the fire like gold', thus enriching the whole of world Christianity in days to come. Perhaps this process is a foretaste of

---

[115]Augustine, *On Christian Teaching*, translated by R. P. H. Green (Oxford: Oxford University Press, 1997), Book Two, 71-72 (p. 47).

[116]Ibid., Preface, 15 (p. 6).

what Revelation 21 says will happen when at last there is a new heaven and a new earth, and the dwelling place of God is with men. Then the gates of the celestial New Jerusalem will ever be open, and according to verse 26, 'They shall bring the glory and honour of the nations into it.'

Chapter Two
Appendix Two

Theologoumenon: Are the Pagans, who Lived Before the Gospel of Christ Came to their Culture, Condemned to Destruction, Since their Religions were Not True Bearers of the Salvation of God in Christ?

We have seen that the Old and New Testaments and the Church Fathers consider pagan religions not to be true bearers of the saving revelation of God in Christ. Rather, they are contradictions of it and impediments to its reception by their votaries. True orthodoxy is agreed that only some kind of contact with the saving mercies of the Triune God in the Covenant of Grace can ever be sufficient for salvation of the lost. Could any such contact ever have occurred in the experience of the multitudes who have lived outside conscious knowledge of the gospel?

In terms of the time-bound and space-bound limitations of our human life and knowledge, the simple answer would seem to be 'no'. If lost mankind were finally dependent upon the various world religions as the way to God, Holy Scripture and the ancient Church would preclude the possibility. The orthodox verdict would have to be that of St. Cyprian: '*extra ecclesiam, nulla salus*'. Apart from the grace of the God of the covenant, the good intentions of fallen humanity have been accurately assessed by the Westminster Confession of Faith (from the 1640s in Britain): '…much less can men not professing the Christian religion be saved in any other way whatsoever, be they ever so diligent to frame their lives according to the light of nature and the law of that religion they do profess…' (Chapter X, 'Of Effectual Calling', par. 4).

While it would probably be wisest to leave the issue here (especially since I do not in general favor theological speculation), still, many years of reflection on this matter have made me willing at last to speculate, albeit hesitantly and humbly – always *under* Scripture and the Creeds. Thus I append these reflections as a sort of 'theologoumenon'; a personal opinion, *not* an authoritative teaching clearly based on exegesis of Scripture or on generally received Church Confessions.

I believe that there are two grounds (closely involved in one another) to suggest a tentative 'yes' to the possibility of the eternal salvation of multitudes who have lived before the gospel came to their culture. These two grounds are God's relationship to the time and space in which He created His image-bearers to dwell.

1. God's relationship to time

As St. Augustine reminds us, time is as much a creature of God as is matter and space, for it was only with the creation of the cosmos that time began its flight.[1] Hence, time and space are God's servants, not His masters. Justin Martyr said in the second century A.D.: 'God, the Creator of all things is superior to the things that are to be changed'[2]

God is not subject to time

Augustine stated: 'For God made the creatures that were to be in the future in such a way that without Himself being subject to time, He made them subject to time.'[3]

These Fathers thus indicate that God's eternal plan of redemption unfolds within the passing of temporal history, yet without God's being limited in what He can accomplish by the time series of past, present and future. The great turning point of that divine plan of salvation history is located in the coming of God in Christ. We saw previously that Joel's prediction near the end of the Old Testament period, of the Holy Spirit being poured out upon all flesh (thereby profoundly changing the relationship of people outside the Covenant to the God of Israel) was taken up by the Apostle Peter and applied to the events on the day of Pentecost (cf. Joel 2 and Acts 2).

After the Father's vindication of His Son's holy life and sacrificial death for Adam's fallen race, by means of His resurrection from the dead (cf. Rom. 1:4; 1 Cor. 15:12-19; Rom. 4:24, 25), the Holy Spirit was poured out upon representatives of many tongues and nations – indicating that the salvation of Christ was now to be extended to those many nations. Those representatives were, of course, Jewish; nevertheless, the tongues in which they were given supernatural utterance represented the tribes and nations who spoke those languages (and not just the Jewish diaspora). This pouring out of the Spirit after the divine blood was shed was surely the fulfillment of the Levitical ceremony of the oil (symbolizing the Holy Spirit) being poured upon the sacrifices on the Old Testament altar.

The great turning point in the working out of the plan of salvation came according to the divine schedule: 'In the fullness of the time, God sent forth his Son…' (Gal. 4:4). 'The lamb of God slain from the foundation of the world' (Rev. 13:8) knew when the exact moment was come to glorify His Father by His death on the cross (John 12:27-32; John 17:1). His death on that cross was a one-time, definite historical event: *eph-hapax* (Heb. 10:10), but its power of application was in no sense limited to the time when it took place. It was the defining moment for all other moments, past, present and future.

The 'eternal Spirit' applies Christ's historic redemption in all times

This is to a degree explained by Hebrews 9:14: 'How much more shall the blood of Christ, who through the eternal Spirit offered himself without spot

---

[1]Augustine, *The Literal Meaning of Genesis*, Vol. I: *Ancient Christian Writers*, No. 41, Quasten et al. editors, John H. Taylor, translator (New York: Newman Press, 1982), Book 5, chapter 5 (153, 154).

[2]Justin Martyr, *First Apology*, ch. xx.

[3]Augustine, *op. cit.*, Book 4, chapter 35 (145).

unto God, cleanse your conscience from dead works to serve the living God?' The adjective 'eternal' (rather than the more normal 'Holy') modifying 'Spirit' tells us something of massive significance here. That is, Christ's blood is shed for sinners in the very presence and working of 'the eternal Spirit'. Eternal means eternal; not bound by time, as we creatures are.

From this perspective, the eternal Spirit is able, as it were, to put us who believe in Christ (those of us who love Him without having seen Him – cf. John 20:29) under the arms of the cross, so that His saving blood falls upon the totality of our souls and bodies. On this premise, the Church was commissioned by her Lord to offer this gospel to all nations to the end of time. The power of the blood still avails, no matter how many centuries ago it was shed. As Calvin suggests, it is as though the blood of Christ were constantly distilling in the presence of the Father so as to consecrate the way for all who come to God by Him.[4] If this perpetual working of Christ through the eternal Spirit did not suffice to overleap the bonds of time, then the Christian Church could have lasted for barely one generation.

The eternal One applies Christ's once-for-all salvation both forwards and backwards in time

But the eternal Spirit applies the saving life, atoning blood and powerful resurrection of the incarnate Lord *backwards* in time, as well as *forward* in time. That is how Abraham was saved, who somehow 'saw Christ's day' (John 8:56). That is how penitent David was saved when he begged, 'Purge me with hyssop, and I shall be clean; wash me and I shall be whiter than snow' (Ps. 51:7). That is how God answered the confessions and petitions of Daniel for the Hebrew people in captivity, when demonic powers were resisting in unseen places their going home after the seventy years of bondage (cf. Dan. 10:10–11:1). That is how God spared the rebellious Israelites in the wilderness, as they were being bitten as a divine punishment by fiery serpents. God answered Moses' intercessions for them by telling him to put a brass serpent high on a pole, so the bitten ones could look to it and live (Num. 21:1-9). Jesus shows Nicodemus that His own lifting up on the cross (as a curse, like those who die on a tree in Deuteronomy 21:23 quoted in Galatians 3:13, and as a curse like the serpent in Genesis 3) is the only way to eternal pardon appropriated in the new birth (John 3:1-21).

Adam was saved by Christ

The Scots' Confession of 1560 rightly teaches that Adam is saved and thus part of the one Church, and how else could our first parents have come into the blessings brought by Christ's salvation other than through the eternal Spirit overleaping the created bonds of time with the triumphant grace of God?[5] But to have noted all of this, is to have said nothing new, for orthodox

---

[4]John Calvin, *Commentary on the Epistle to the Hebrews*, (Grand Rapids, MI: Baker Books, 1979) at 10:19.

[5]'We most surely believe that God preserved, instructed, multiplied, honoured, adorned, and called from death to life his Kirk in all ages since Adam until the coming of Christ Jesus in the flesh' (*The Scots Confession*, Chapter V – 'The Continuance, Increase and Preservation of the Kirk').

Christians have always understood that somehow the eternal Spirit applied *backwards* in time the benefits of the Christ event to the Old Testament people of God. St. Irenaeus in the late second century condemned Tatian for his opinion that Adam was not saved![6] All are agreed that the Old Testament saints were saved; though none understands how it worked.

St. Symeon the New Theologian (d. 1022) graphically expresses the salvation of the First Adam in terms of the Last Adam:

> But this was allowed [*sc.* the Fall] so that there might be performed a certain great and fearful mystery, namely, so that Christ, the Sinless One, should suffer, and through this Adam, who had sinned, might receive forgiveness. For this also, in place of the tree of knowledge, there was the Cross; in place of the stepping of the feet by which our first ancestors walked to the forbidden tree, and in place of their stretching out of their hands in order to take of the fruit of the tree, there were nailed to the Cross the innocent feet and hands of Christ; in place of the tasting of the fruit, there was the tasting of gall and vinegar, and in place of the death of Adam, the death of Christ.[7]

About the same time as St. Symeon in the East, St. Anselm in the West also held to the salvation of our first parents. Speaking of the application of the atoning death of Christ, Anselm writes:

> ...that it [His death] was not intended to benefit those only who were present, is hence easily to be understood, since not so many could be present at His death as are needed for the formation of the celestial city; nor even though all who were living at the time of His death, wherever they were, should be admitted to that redemption; for there are more devils, than there were living at that time men from whom their number is to be replaced.[8]

St. Anselm then adds:

> ...it is necessary that something belonging to the predicted reconciliation should always have existed. Whence it cannot be doubted that Adam and Eve partook of that redemption, although divine authority does not expressly assert it.[9]

Martin Luther makes reference to Anselm, and agrees that Adam and Eve were saved:

> Elsewhere Anselm draws the conclusion that Adam and Eve were Christians and that they were called back to life immediately after the fall; they were shattered by the law and the fall. Then their sin was repaid because when they fled from God they were not displeasing to God; instead, he brought them back even after the fall. Thus he [Anselm] says that they had to be justified so that the church could remain...[10]

But would it not also follow by the same token, that chosen individuals *outside* the covenant of the Lord with His chosen people, Israel, were also

---

[6]Irenaeus, *Adversus Haereses*, III.23.

[7]St. Symeon the New Theologian, *The First Created Man: Seven Homilies*, Selected and translated by Fr. Seraphim Rose, (Platina, CA: St. Herman of Alaska Brotherhood, 2001), 46.

[8]Anselm follows the theory of St. Augustine that the number of the elect will be the same as the number of the angels who fell. In *Cur deus homo* II.xvi.

[9]Ibid.

[10]Martin Luther, 'Lecture on Psalm 90, 1534–1535, *LW* 13, 90.

somehow in saving contact with the redemptive being and activities of the Triune God? Must they not have been included in the applicatory work of Christ by the eternal Spirit, generations before Christ's incarnation and sacrifice?

What about elect persons outside the known covenant community?
We cannot go very far here. All that can be safely said is that in the Old Testament from time to time we 'overhear' the voices and catch a glimpse of the activities of a few individuals who knew the one true God of Israel, and yet lived outside the visible bonds of the Covenant of Grace with Israel. To know God is to be saved (cf. John 17:3), so a number outside of Israel were obviously saved, without – so far as we know – any relationship to Torah and Tabernacle.

Melchizedek, Job and Balaam. Melchizedek, the mysterious priest/king of ancient Salem was part of the Canaanite culture, and yet truly knew God and conveyed divine blessing to Abraham, who was father of all the faithful (cf. Gen. 14; Ps. 110; Heb. 6 and 7), so that 'the less is blessed of the better' (Heb. 7:7). Job, who appears to have lived during the times of the Patriarchs, was not an Abrahamite of Ur or of Palestine. Job lived in pagan Edom. Yet he was righteous in God's sight and inherited eternal blessing. The Moabite prophet Balaam, whose willingness to curse Israel for personal gain was turned by God into future blessings for His people, clearly knew the same Lord that Israel knew, and spoke true words from Him that are preserved in Holy Scripture (cf. Num. 22–25). But he was no Israelite and had no access to the Tabernacle, and – one assumes – had no copy of the five books of the Moses whose people the king wanted him to curse. But he knew God.[11] His very knowledge of God is what made his 'error' (as Jude 11 calls it) so severe.

The Wise Men. It is the same with the wise men in the New Testament (cf. Matt. 2:1-18). They came from the East; clearly they were not part of Israel. Maybe they were from Sheba, but we cannot be sure. These 'magi' could somehow read the stars accurately enough to find their way to the land where the Son of the Star-Maker was born! They, like the others just referred to, were outside the visible bounds of the covenant with Israel, but that did not prevent them from knowing some of the crucial blessings of that Covenant of Grace, which involves a certain saving contact with the Triune God.

Lancelot Andrewes dealt with this question in a sermon on Matthew 2:1-2. He suggests that they may have had access as scholars to parts of the Old Testament, such as Numbers 24.[12]

---

[11]A rediscovered fragment of St. Irenaeus (c. early third century), while accepting that Balaam knew God, shows that he sinned by not continuing in that knowledge: '"And Balaam the son of Beor they slew with the sword" (Num. 31:8). For, speaking no longer by the Spirit of God, but setting up another law of fornication contrary to the law of God (Rev. 2:14), this man shall no longer be reckoned as a prophet, but as a soothsayer. For, as he did not continue in the commandment of God, he received the just reward of his evil desires' (*Ante-Nicene Christian Library*, Vol. IX [Edinburgh: T. & T. Clark, 1871], 179).

[12]Lancelot Andrewes, *Sermon 15 'On the Nativity'* (on Matthew 2:1, 2 – preached in 1622) in *Ninety-Six Sermons, vol. I* (Oxford: John Henry Parker, 1841), 254.

St. Augustine taught that in the Old Testament era, there were people who were entirely outside the covenant community of salvation, and yet they knew God. He gives Job as an illustration, and believes that there are such persons in his day.[13] He does not think that their salvation was based on their own good works as practiced in some pagan religion, but that somehow they received a personal revelation of God in Christ. Commenting on Job, Augustine writes:

> I have no doubt that it was the design of God's providence that from this one instance we should know that there could also be those among other nations who lived by God's standards and were pleasing to God, as belonging to the spiritual Jerusalem. But it must not be believed that this was granted to anyone unless he had received a divine revelation of 'the one Mediator between God and men, the man Christ Jesus' (1 Tim. 2:5) whose future coming in a material body was fore-announced to the saints of antiquity, just as his coming has been announced to us as something achieved, so that one and the same faith may lead to God, through him, all who are predestined for the City of God, which is God's house and God's temple.[14]

People outside the visible covenant have been divinely blessed

Granted, as we must if we take Old and New Testaments seriously, that such non-Israelite (and non-Church) persons, who had neither Torah nor Temple, were in a saving relationship with God, is it not most likely that others – who are not named in Scripture; others from pagan, non-covenantal backgrounds – may also have been touched by the benefits of Christ through the eternal Spirit? As Augustine wrote: '…there is nothing far-fetched in the belief that among other peoples besides the Jews there existed men to whom this mystery was revealed, and who were compelled to go on to proclaim what they knew.'[15]

This may or may not be a possible referent of the words of Jesus to the Pharisees: 'And I say unto you, that many shall come from the East and the West, and shall sit down at table with Abraham, and Isaac, and Jacob, in the kingdom of heaven' (Matt. 8:11). If so, it would be consistent with the inspired Psalmist, who testifies that 'The Lord is good to all and his tender mercies are over all his works' (Ps. 145:9). Mankind is the crown of creation; the chief wonder of the handiwork of God. The same holy God whose character must punish sin wherever it is found, has provided a way in His infinite love to extend His tender love and saving mercies to vast multitudes of sinners, through pouring out His eternal Spirit upon all flesh so as to turn the eyes of the blind to see Christ and to open their hearts to trust in Him and to repent of rebellion from Him.

Even so, is it not stretching credibility to think that lost people could somehow come into contact with the blessings provided for sinners in the gospel, if they live in times before that gospel comes to be announced in their culture? Once again we must contemplate the mysterious relationship between God's eternity and man's experience of time to get the right approach.

---

[13]Augustine, *City of God*, Book XVIII, 47-50.

[14]Ibid., XVIII, 47.

[15]Ibid.

Boethius' understanding of eternity

The sixth-century Italian Christian philosopher, Boethius, may offer us time-bound thinkers some assistance here in grasping the forward and backward application across time of Christ's person and work over all generations. He suggests in Book 5 of his most famous work, *On the Consolation of Philosophy*, that because of His own eternity, God is not limited or bound by the succession of time: past, present or future. Rather, past, present and future are always, and all at once, and constantly, spread out at His feet, as it were, for Him to work with and control as He deems best.

In that light, the life and work of Christ are just as available to be applied by the eternal Spirit to any part of that 'all flesh' on whom, according to Joel 2 and Acts, the Spirit will be poured out. Historically, the pouring out is only subsequent to the divine acceptance and vindication of Christ's atoning work for sinners, but with the God who inhabits eternity and created time as His servant, the concepts of 'previous', 'contemporary' and 'subsequent' are not a hindering reality as they are for us mere humans. The cross was in God's heart before the world was made (cf. Rev. 13:8), and His eternal Spirit is well able to apply it at any and every point of rolling time to whomsoever He will, whatever their privileges or lack of them at any one 'time'. The same eternal One who catches the tears of His saints in a bottle to use them later as mightily availing prayers (Ps. 56:8, 9), can take account of tears of repentance long before they are shed, and cries of true faith long before they are heaved upwards from the tender soul of a new creation in Christ!

Past and future are one vibrant present with God

Maybe it would (or would not) be reading too much into Acts 17:30 to attempt to relate God's 'overlooking the times of pagan ignorance' with the spreading out in one vibrant present at God's feet what seems to us past, present and future, in which the eternal Spirit applies as He will to the fallen sons and daughters of Adam the infinitely powerful blessings of the gospel. In doing so He is not hindered by when they lived, where they lived, nor what privileges they had or did not have at that period.

The Westminster Confession teaches that some who are incapable of responding to preaching are yet saved

The Westminster Confession of Faith states that 'God in his ordinary providence maketh use of means, yet is free to work without, above and against them, at his pleasure' (Chapter V, par. 3). And similarly in its discussion of the salvation of elect infants and others who are incapable of responding to the preaching of the gospel, it affirms: 'Elect infants, dying in infancy, are regenerated and saved by Christ through the Spirit, who worketh when, and where, and how he pleaseth. So also are all other elect persons, who are incapable of being outwardly called by the ministry of the word' (Chapter X, par. 3).

This first set of reflections on the implications of the relationship of God's eternity to historical time for the possible salvation of some (or many) of the pagans seems to me to be responsible inferences from Holy Scripture, though not in the front rank of its clearly taught doctrines. In all doctrinal matters, it is only proper to put emphasis where God speaking in Scripture puts the emphasis. And that emphasis is never on 'the secret things which belong unto the Lord our God, but the things that are revealed belong unto us and unto our children that we may do them' (Deut. 29:29). For example, the mysterious heights of God's holy and sovereign election of sinners to salvation in Romans 9 is concluded by a quotation from Isaiah 8:14 (in Rom. 9:33), thus reminding the Church of the place of faith in the matter of sovereign salvation. This ninth chapter is then followed up by the tenth chapter with its great emphasis on the preaching of the Word, the sending of the preacher and the efficacy of 'confessing with the mouth that Jesus is Lord and believing with the heart that God has raised him from the dead' (Rom 10:9).

Obedience to the Great Commission, rather than speculation, is commanded
Revelation of God's sovereign working and contemplation of it by His people are in these chapters seen to encourage the necessary going out to the lost with the preaching of the good news. Similarly, although we have sought to draw out some possible implications of God's eternity on the salvation of temporally disadvantaged pagans by referring to Christ, Peter and Paul, we must conclude this first grounds of discussion by putting the emphasis where they put it. While never hiding the mysteries of divine sovereignty and never swallowing up eternity into temporality, still the Lord and His apostles place the weight of their teaching upon the arrival of the kingdom of God and the necessity of mankind to believe and repent; to be baptized and to spread the good news to the ends of the earth. Obedience in evangelism and mission, not speculation, will show us to be in the company of the Lord and His apostles.

2. God's relationship to space

While the first set of reflections dealt with the relationship of the eternal God to created time, here we must particularly think of the relationship of the Logos (the eternal Christ; second Person of the Holy Trinity) to space. And all that is said of Him is ever in the context of *perichoresis* (the mutual indwelling and co-working of Father, Son and Holy Spirit). There are consequences of the relationship of the Logos to space for the situations of the heathen nations, and that is our main concern here at present.

Significance of 'extra-Calvinisticum'
The crux of the issue is found in what is meant by the 'extra-Calvinisticum' (a term coined by sixteenth-century Lutheran theologians to criticize the Calvinists for leaving something of the Logos (hence, 'Calvinist *extra*') outside Christ's incarnation in the body and soul of the Lord Jesus Christ. In the *Institutes of the Christian Religion*, Calvin wrote: 'Although the boundless essence of the Word [Logos] was united with human nature, nevertheless we do not imagine there to be any enclosing of the Word in it. The Son of God descended miraculously from heaven, yet without abandoning heaven; was pleased to be conceived miraculously in the Virgin's womb, to live on earth, to hang on the cross, in such a way that He always filled the world

as from the beginning.'[16] The late-sixteenth-century Anglican theologian, Richard Hooker, taught essentially the same thing.[17]

Basically, Calvin and Hooker were saying that the Son of God (the Logos), while fully incarnate, is not *contained* by the body of Jesus. Because of His Godness, although truly within space, He remains transcendent to it. That is, Christ remained truly God when He became truly man; He did not lose His transcendence. As Archbishop William Temple wisely asked, if the Logos lost His transcendence when He became man, then what happened to the cosmic functions of Christ, who holds the universe together? (cf. Col. 1:15-17).[18]

This kind of thinking was certainly in line with the Fathers of Eastern Orthodoxy. G. V. Florovsky notes that Athanasius strongly distinguishes between the transcendence of the Logos and His creative activities: 'The Logos is present in the world, but only "dynamically", that is, by His "powers." In His own "substance" He is outside of the world.'[19] Or as Duncan Reid comments: '…we can distinguish this [i.e. the incarnation] from the inner being of the Logos which remains within the being of the trinity even during the earthly life of Christ.'[20] We shall see immediately below more detailed description of Athanasius' thought on this matter.

God is not spatially related to space

In his *Space, Time, and Incarnation*, T. F. Torrance showed that what was happening (not only with Calvin, but long before in some of the Church Fathers) was the rejection of a container (or receptacle) notion of space, in accordance with which notion God Himself would have to be contained and limited.[21] On the contrary, the Logos was not subordinated to the flesh it assumed; its transcendent nature was not thereby altered. That is, God is not spatially related to space, but rather is related to it in terms of omnipotent power.

It is difficult to express such things in our human language, but St. Athanasius pioneered the way for theologians to seek to deal accurately with the relationship of the Logos to space. Commenting on Athanasius' *Contra Arianos* (1.23f; 4.27; *De Synodis* 42; *Ad Serapionem* 1.8-9, 16-20), Torrance noted:

> Hence Athanasius insisted that when our ordinary terms are applied to God they must be *stretched* beyond their natural sense and reference and must be employed in such a way that they indicate more than the actual terms can naturally specify. Theological terms, therefore, which by function and use are deployed to refer to God in his relation to the world, in the nature of the case must have an elastic quality, terminating on God himself at one end and upon the world or man at the other end. To use modern scientific

---

[16] II.13.4.

[17] Richard Hooker, *Ecclesiastical Polity*, Book V, chapters lii-lvi.

[18] William Temple, *Christus Veritas* (London: Macmilan Co., 1934), 42 ff.

[19] G. V. Florovsky, 'Idea of Creation in Christian Philosophy,' *Eastern Churches Quarterly* 8 (1949; Supplementary Issue: Nature and Grace), 46.

[20] Duncan Reid, *Energies of the Spirit: Trinitarian Models in Eastern Orthodoxy and Western Theology* (Atlanta, GA: Scholars Press, 1997), 77.

[21] (Oxford: Oxford University Press, 1969).

language, theological terms inevitably embody a relation of differentiality like the variational principles of physics, conformable to the precise nature and force of the realities to which they are used to refer. Indeed, in developing a theological understanding of space in respect of the dynamic relation between 'the place' (*topos*) of God which is to be understood strictly in accordance with the nature of man as man, Athanasius projected something rather like what we now call topological language.[22]

The Logos remained Transcendent during the Incarnation

For instance, Athanasius wrote of what would later be called 'the extra-Calvinisticum' in *De Incarnatione*:

> For he was not shut up in the body. And he was not in the body in such a way as not to be elsewhere, nor did he move the body in such a way that the universe was left void of his activity and providence. But the most unexpected thing is that Word [Logos] though he is, he was not contained by anything but he himself rather contains all things. And just as while he is present *in* the whole of creation, he is 'outside' everything in respect of his essential being but is 'in' all things in respect of his own powers, giving order to the universe, extending his providence to all and in all things without being contained, but being wholly and in every respect in his Father alone – so also while being present in a human body and giving life to it himself, he was quite consistently giving life to the universe as well: He was 'in' every event and yet 'outside' the universe. Moreover while he made himself known from the body through his works he was not unmanifest through his activity in the universe (17).

The Holy Scriptures maintain a holy reserve as to what the being and activities of the Logos may mean for humankind outside Israel and the Church. At least we could conclude that the divine Logos (in consubstantial fellowship with Father and Spirit) is no more limited by space than He is by time, in overseeing the providential affairs of the lives of every descendant of Adam and Eve. But that does not take us very far in speculating on what these spatially transcendent relations of the Logos to all humankind might imply for those outside the covenant people of God.

Presumably if the Holy Spirit speaking in Scripture had wanted us to know more, then He would have told us more. The Logos is able temporally and spatially to do whatever He deems to be in accordance with the divine character of holiness, love and power, and in accordance with the eternal Triune purposes for each member of creation. The eternal Spirit is able to apply all the benefits of the incarnation, atonement and resurrection whenever and wherever the Father and Son so ordain (without being hindered by location in time or space). The constant emphasis of Scripture is that that application is in the context of the preaching of the Word by the Spirit-endowed community in their mission to all the world. It is best for piety to leave it at that.

Universalism is against the Holy Scriptures

One concluding remark is called for here. Theories of universal salvation cannot be justly traced to the biblical teaching on the *logos asarkos* [Word

[22]Thomas F. Torrance, *Divine Meaning: Studies in Patristic Hermeneutics* (Edinburgh: T & T Clark, 1995), 204, 205.

apart from the flesh] and *logos ensarkos* [enfleshed Word]. These are not two different Words. They are the same Word, looked at in two different, but complementary perspectives. Thus, they are never contradictory. That is important to keep in mind when responding to universalism. The incarnate Word clearly and solemnly warned against the horrendous consequences of the refusal of sinners to repent and believe the gospel (e.g. Matthew chapters 24 and 25). What He says on this matter (as Word incarnate) could not be contradicted by what He is considered in His transcendent relations to time and space (as *Logos Asarkos*).

Karl Rahner's 'anonymous Christian' theory

That, in my view, raises serious problems with the theory of Karl Rahner on 'the anonymous Christian'. Rahner wrote: 'Christianity does not simply confront the member of an extra-Christian religion as a mere non-Christian but as someone who can and must already be regarded in this or that respect as an anonymous Christian. It would be wrong to regard the pagan as someone who has not yet been touched in any way by God's grace and truth.'[23]

But to accuse Rahner's 'anonymous Christian' theory of not being biblical, would not – I assume – have worried unduly this prolific Roman Catholic theologian. For elsewhere he wrote critically concerning the teaching of St. Paul on human religions as being 'pessimist'.[24] Miikka Ruokanen showed that Rahner's theory not only was not based on the Scriptures, it was also out of accord with Church tradition, including the Second Vatican Council.[25] The Council addressed this issue in section 16 of 'Dogmatic Constitution on the Church' ('Lumen Gentium').[26] The development within Roman Catholicism on the salvation of the lost outside the Church has been addressed by Hendrik Nys[27] and more recently by Jorge Ruiz Ortiz.[28]

---

[23]Karl Rahner, *Theological Investigations* (New York: Seabury, 1966), vol. 5, 131.

[24]Karl Rahner, *Mission and grace* translated by Cecily Hastings, (London: Sheed & Ward, 1966), vol. III, 6.

[25]Miika Ruokanen, *The Catholic Doctrine of non-Christian Religions according to the Second Vatican Council* (Leiden, New York: E. J. Brill, 1992), 115-19.

[26]*The Documents of Vatican II*, Walter M. Abbott, S. J. General Editor (New York: Guild Press, 1966), 35: 'Those also can attain to everlasting salvation who through no fault of their own do not know the gospel of Christ or his Church, yet sincerely seek God and moved by grace strive by their deeds to do his will as it is known to them through the dictates of conscience. Nor does divine Providence deny the help necessary for salvation to those who without blame on their part, have not yet arrived at an explicit knowledge of God, but who strive to live a good life, thanks to his grace. Whatever goodness or truth is found among them is looked upon by the Church as a preparation for the gospel. She regards such qualities as given by Him who enlightens all men so that they may finally have life.

'But rather often men, deceived by the Evil One, have become caught up in futile reasoning and have exchanged the truth of God for a lie, serving the creature rather than the Creator (cf. Rom. 1:21-25). Or some there are who, living and dying in a world without God, are subject to utter hopelessness. Consequently, to promote the glory of God and procure the salvation of all such men, and mindful of the command of the Lord, "Preach the gospel to every creature" (Mark. 16:15), the Church painstakingly fosters her missionary work.'

[27]Hendrik Nys, *Le Salut sans l' Evangile. Etude historique et critique du problème du 'salut des juifs fidèles' dans la littérature théologique récente (1912-1964)* (Paris: Cerf, 1966).

[28]Jorge Ruiz Ortiz, *L'Ancienne Alliance est-elle révoquée? L'élection du people juif selon la 'nouvelle théologie' catholique* (Doctoral Thesis: Aix-en-Provence, 2005).

John Donne, the great Anglican preacher of the seventeenth century, addressed this question of the salvation of those outside the known Church in one of his sermons:

> To me, to whom God hath revealed his Son, in a Gospel, by a Church, there can be no way of salvation, but by applying that Son of God, by that Gospel, in that Church. Nor is there any other foundation for any, nor any other name by which any can be saved, but the name of Jesus. But how this foundation is presented, and how this name of Jesus is notified to them, amongst whom there is no Gospel preached, no Church established, I am not curious in inquiring. I know God can be as merciful as those tender [Church] Fathers present him to be; and I would be as charitable as they are. And therefore humbly embracing that manifestation of the Son, which he hath afforded me, I leave God, to his unsearchable ways of working upon others, without further inquisition.[29]

[29]John Donne, *Sermons* (Ten Volumes), edited by George R. Potter and Evelyn M. Simpson, Volume IV, 77-78 (Berkeley: University of California Press, 1953–1962).

Chapter Three

Western Rejection of God's Testimony to Himself in Creation and Conscience (The Continuing Heritage of the Enlightenment)

We have seen in Chapter 2 that the inescapable voice of the Triune God speaks to all His image-bearers of His reality and of their obligation to Him through both creation and conscience. Yet most of the once-Christian West has for nearly three centuries largely turned a deaf, recalcitrant ear to divine messages that constitute its only hope for temporal significance and for eternal salvation. Such apostasy could not have occurred without a sheer revolution in world-view.

There is a wide and deep gap that divides the history of Western Christian culture into two parts as far as its theology, underlying value system and intellectual procedures are concerned; that cavernous divide is the Enlightenment, which began about 1650, and in many respects (as far as its critical assumptions) continues today. The Enlightenment has been spoken of by one of its best historians, Peter Gay, as *The Rise of Modern Paganism*.[1] But 'the modern paganism' of seventeenth and eighteenth century Europe was very different from ancient, pre-Christian paganism in that 'the modern pagans' represented apostasy: a willful rejection of their own Christian heritage, although this occurred in stages.

The secularism of the Enlightenment had been prepared for by the fifteenth-century Renaissance, with its turn of attention from God and grace to man and nature. Alexander Solzhenitsyn attributes to this brusque change of focus the beginnings of 'a world split apart.'[2]

The Church Fathers, as we have seen, dealt with the false religions of pagan idolatry in the first four centuries of Christianity. In the thirteenth century, St. Thomas sought to answer the resurgence of pagan Hellenism (that is, 'integral Aristotelianism', shorn of its medieval, Christian glosses) which came in with the rediscovery of original texts of Aristotle, previously unknown in the West, especially through Arabic Islamic philosophy, mediated through the Moors of Spain. (This development will be discussed later in this systematic theology).

---

[1]Peter Gay, *The Enlightenment: An Interpretation*, vol. I, *The Rise of Modern Paganism* (New York: Alfred A. Knopf, 1967).

[2]Alexander Solzhenitsyn, 'A World Split Apart,' Commencement Address given at Harvard University in May 1978 and published in *National Review*, July 7, 1978.

Less than two hundred years after Thomas, yet another religion began to emerge with the Italian Renaissance, and became fully developed in the European Enlightenment of the seventeenth and eighteenth centuries. This religion was perhaps all the more powerful for parading as non-religion, anti-superstition, as an objective approach to truth. But religion it was; it was a powerful and aggressive alternative to historic Christianity, which it was determined to replace. It was religion in the sense of being based on improvable faith axioms, on inuring these basic axioms from criticism, on requiring total commitment, and on establishing a foundational set of ultimate values that caused it to oppose all other religions (especially Christianity).

The Renaissance and Enlightenment as alternatives to Christianity

The Renaissance, which came into its own only in the Enlightenment, worked a far deeper split within Western Christendom than did the sixteenth-century Protestant Reformation. It alienated much of the West, especially its intellectual leadership, from the anciently accepted theological and moral beliefs of the recently divided Roman Catholic and Protestant churches. Both Protestant and Catholic populations were inundated by this new form of pagan secularism, and their most basic beliefs and practices came under heavy attack from this new religion which said it was not a religion. The new pagan philosophy offered a thoroughly different programme that required the overturning of Christian doctrine at nearly every point. So far as I know, no alternative religion ever had such success in debilitating Christianity and in replacing it. Thus, we must consider this anti-Christian religious philosophy, particularly as it proceeds on a necessarily different understanding of knowledge of God and His will in nature.

However, by no means were all (or even the majority) of those in the Renaissance against Christianity. Devout scholars such as Erasmus and Lefèvre d'Etaples thought within a Christian framework. Yet others hoped to find salvation for man, not so much in terms of Holy Scripture and the means of grace of the Catholic Church, but in a return to Classical Antiquity. As Jean Brun writes:

> Thus they thought it possible to arrive at a *restitutio* of antiquity, that is a *renovatio* of man that would perhaps permit a restoration of humanity in its state of primitive innocence, and that all the more since the joachimite dream was still alive.[3]

Christian scholars in the Renaissance, such as Jacques Lefèvre d'Etaples[4] and Erasmus, structured their programme for renewal within a still Catholic context.[5] A return to classical, biblical and Patristic sources:

---

[3]Jean Brun, *L'Europe Philosophe: 25 siècles de pensée occidentale* (Paris: Clefs de l'Histoire, Stock, 1997), 140 (my translation).

[4]See the biography by Philip Edgecombe Hughes, *Lefèvre: Pioneer of Ecclesiastical Renewal in France* (Grand Rapids, MI: Wm. B. Eerdmans Publ. Co., 1984).

[5]See the biography by Roland H. Bainton, *Erasmus of Christendom* (New York: Charles Scribner's Sons, 1969).

ad fontes, was no denial of revelation and grace, but rather a sort of purification. In the train of Lorenzo Valla's *Annotations on the New Testament* (1449) and John Colet's *An Exposition of the Epistle to the Romans* (1496), Erasmus issued his Greek New Testament in 1516 (correcting the errors of the Latin Vulgate), in which 'he expressed his desire to "summon all men, as with a trumpet blast, to the most sacred and life-giving study of Christian philosophy"...'[6]

On the other hand, more pagan scholars such as Machiavelli, rejected the Christian world-view with its teaching of the sinfulness of man, the necessity of God's grace and the control of providence, in order to pursue the innate possibilities of man's own genius, especially under the strong leadership of the secular prince.[7] They tended to replace divine providence with the pagan concept of *fortuna*.[8]

Invention of the concept of 'Middle Ages'

Indeed, it was this group of paganizing thinkers who invented the concept of 'the Middle Ages' as a time of darkness, between the light of pagan Classical culture and the return to it in the Renaissance:

> They first of all invented the concept of the 'middle' ages – which they also thought of as the 'dark' ages – to describe the period lying between the achievements of classical antiquity and the restoration of its grandeur in their own time.[9]

For instance, Pico della Mirandola's *Oration on the Dignity of Man* holds that: 'Man alone is "constrained by no limits" and endowed with his "own free will". And the reason God gives for having placed humanity "at the world's centre" in this way is the desire that men should be able "with freedom of choice" to create and mould their own characters.'[10] As Skinner rightly remarks, this new approach 'involved a direct attack on the assumptions of Augustinian Christianity'.[11]

Leading Renaissance Humanists started a trend that the later Enlightenment would follow: use the classical past to criticize the more recent (Christian, medieval past), so as to weaken the thousand-year-old Catholic synthesis. '... the Humanists' recovery of the ancients was more of an intellectual than a physical exploration...Renaissance scholarship, like its rhetoric, had public purposes and political consequences. To reconstruct the real Plato or the real Aristotle, to rescue them from the incrustations of Christian interpretations, was to gain firm philosophical ground from which to criticize medieval systems of thought.'[12] The Renaissance set sail

---

[6]Quentin Skinner, *The Foundations of Modern Political Thought: Volume One: The Renaissance* (Cambridge: Cambridge University Press, 1978), 212.

[7]See Ernst Cassirer on the anti-mythical (i.e. anti-Christian) scope of Machiavelli in *The Myth of the State* (New Haven: Yale University Press, 1946).

[8]See Machiavelli, *The Prince*, translated by Luigi Ricci, pp. 106, 143 on fortune 'as the significant concept, rather than providence', (London: Oxford University Press, 1935).

[9]Quentin Skinner, op. cit, 110.

[10]Ibid., 97.

[11]Ibid., 98.

[12]Ibid., 263.

in a direction that could only be taken to its destined course some 150 years later by the Enlightenment:

> The Humanists saw themselves as men at work rescuing a maltreated past for the sake of perfecting their own civilization, and their metaphysical ... and theological speculations stood in the service of their impatience. The affinity between Renaissance and Enlightenment, therefore, is quite fundamental: the same dialectic characterizes them both. Both appealed to antiquity, developed tensions with Christianity, and launched themselves on the sea of modernity.[13]

Politically and culturally, the anti-Christian pagan stream of the Renaissance (which tended to predominate in Southern Europe, while Christian Humanism held the field in most of Northern Europe) was set back for over a century by the outbreak of the sixteenth-century Protestant Reformation and the opposing Roman Catholic Counter-Reformation, both of which – in spite of their vigorous differences in detail – were God-centered rather than man-centered. The best minds of Europe for the next century functioned in the atmosphere of a renewed, Reformed Christianity (with the Protestants) or an anti-Reformational, integral Christianity (with the Roman Catholics, especially after the Council of Trent [1545–1563]).

Division of the Church and rise of dualist scientific theories

The gaping hiatus in Western thought came, not at the time of the Renaissance, but at that of the Enlightenment. The mighty Western Catholic Church was badly divided as a result of the sixteenth-century Protestant Reformation (and it had already weakened itself as a result of the theological decline found in Nominalism, not to mention significant immoralism within much of both clergy and laity, along with never-absent aspirations for political power and widespread economic venality). The ever stronger dualism of Western culture (an axiomatic assumption of a disjunction between God and the world) rendered the biblical world-view less credible, especially after Galileo and Newton.[14] The seventeenth century, in so many aspects, profoundly theocentric, saw a serious weakening of the power of both Catholic and Protestant churches, partly because of the all-European revulsion at the horrific devastations caused by various religious wars,

---

[13]Ibid., 268.

[14]T. F. Torrance writes: 'However, when the Aristotelian network of science, metaphysics, and psychology that underpinned the medieval synthesis succumbed to the critical attacks of Reformation theology and Galilean science, the old radical dualism reappeared and was considerably reinforced through Renaissance Neoplatonism and Reformation Augustinianism, as also indeed through Galileo's far-reaching distinction between primary and secondary qualities, or geometry and appearance. Hence, even while the Ptolemaic cosmological outlook gave way before the Copernican revolution, the new era ushered in with Galileo continued to be characterized by an inveterate dualism that was given in philosophical expression by Descartes and Locke and its scientific expression by Isaac Newton – who built into his great system of the world the massive dualism between absolute mathematical time and space and relative apparent time and space that was to become paradigmatic for all modern science and cosmology up to Einstein. This development gave rise to the deistic disjunction between God and the universe that has so deeply plagued modern theology and to the conception of the mechanistic universe, which closed the universe to any interaction with it on the part of the Creator' (in *The Ground and Grammar of Theology* (Charlottesville: University Press of Virginia, 1980), 22, 23.

but also partly because of the previous growth of the theory and practice of absolute monarchy.

Even as many serious thinkers were becoming more sceptical concerning the truth claims of warring Christian churches, new forms of statist absolutism were coming in to fill the gap left by a broken Christendom. Such monarchs as Henry VIII of England, Philip II of Spain, Francis I of France, and Charles V of the Holy Roman Empire, while still loyal sons of the Church (until Henry VIII split with the Pope over his divorce), were busy consolidating their state power as the church was in increasing tumult.

By the early seventeenth century in Great Britain, for instance, King James VI (of Scotland), now James I (of England), held to the absolute rights of monarchs, beyond any restraint of law (and this was *before* the worst of the wars of religion). In his great study, *Concerning Power: the Natural History of its Growth*, Bertrand de Jouvenel addresses the development of monarchical absolutism in England, and shows how it split with the historic teachings of the Church.[15] He discusses the writings of James I, which asserted absolute monarchy[16] He notes that Pope Paul V had the theologian Suarez to draw up a refutation of James' volume. King James, in turn, had Suarez' refutation publically burned before the Church of St. Paul's in London.[17] The intransigence of James on absolute monarchy would elicit a reply from the famous theologian, Cardinal Bellarmin:

> James I had claimed that even if a royal order was unjust, 'the people can do nothing but flee the fury of the king without resistance. Their only proper response to him is with tears and sighs. Only God can be called in to help them.' Bellarmin replied:[18] 'The people have never delegated their power to such a degree that they no longer potentially hold it. In certain cases, they may actively take it back.'[19]

It is interesting to note that some of the arguments of Suarez and Bellarmin against absolute monarchy were soon taken up by the Reformed theologian of Scotland (who was part of the Westminster Assembly in the 1640s), Samuel Rutherford. He refers to both of them in his pivotal work against absolute monarchy and in favour of popular liberty: *Lex Rex*.[20]

Note on religious wars

In addition to the growth of absolute monarchy on its own, it is certainly true that the religious wars of the sixteenth and seventeenth centuries alienated the affections of multitudes in Western Europe; turning them from Christianity, and opening the way for a secularism, which claimed to be the solution to the battle between the hostile confessional groups. But

---

[15]Bertrand de Jouvenel, *Du Pouvoir: Histoire Naturelle de sa Croissance* (Paris: Librairie Hachette, 1972).

[16]In James' *Basilikon Doron*.

[17]De Jouvenel, op. cit., 46.

[18]Bellarmin, 'Réponse à Jacques Ier d'Angleterre,' *Oeuvres*, t. xii, pp. 184 et suiv.

[19]Ibid., 46.

[20]See Samuel Rutherford, *Lex, Rex*, 1644 [reprint Harrisonburg, VA: Sprinkle Publications, 1980, pp. 3, 4, etc. See also, Douglas F. Kelly, *The Emergence of Liberty in the Modern World* (Phillipsburg, NJ: P&R Publishing, 1992), ch. 2.

the situation leading to these terrible wars is more complex than a simple decision of the opposing religious leaders to wipe out the opposition. Augusto Del Noce points out that these wars actually were carried out as an instrument of state policy during the period of the growth of absolutism in the emerging nation states.[21]

Wars engendered by religion

Nonetheless, religious leaders were all too ready to take the sword and torch to those of different theological persuasion (especially in tandem with aggressive states), and thus the various churches are to a degree culpable for the devastation of these inter-confessional wars. At the same time, it must also be noted that absolute monarchs were only too glad to exploit the weakness of the now-divided churches in Europe. Even so, the churches bear some definite blame for this; their unrestrained aggression against each other was, to say the least, a bad testimony for Christ and cost them deeply in the wide and deep cultural influence they soon lost to secularism.

In his *La Crise de la conscience européene*, Paul Hazard discusses the vain attempt of the famous German Protestant philosopher, Leibniz, to seek a reunion of the Protestant and Catholic churches.[22] He corresponded with the equally famous Bishop Bossuet of the Roman Catholic Church in France. But nothing came of these discussions (in the late seventeenth century). Even in face of the anti-Christian onslaught of the developing Enlightenment, the Protestants and Catholics could not stand together, without feeling that they would have been seriously violating their own principles. Hazard summarizes the sad position:

> Catholics and Protestants could not agree with one another; the time to have done so had now passed, and the most able and charitable of men [Leibniz] had failed in the task he had assumed. How the enemies of Christianity rejoiced and triumphed! What destruction! What ruins![23]

Wars engendered by anti-religious philosophy

But if the churches are to some degree culpable for wars, is it not true to say that the Enlightenment is also, to a degree its early exponents did not intend, culpable for even worse wars, such as the French Revolution of 1789 and the Russian Revolution of 1917? From that perspective, if the Thirty Years' War came out of Protestant and Catholic rivalries of the seventeenth century (manipulated as it was by competing political entities), is not the 1789 French Revolution even more directly the daughter of the philosophy of the Enlightenment? It seems strange that many of the *philosophes* who condemned the wars of religion would, at least indirectly by their call

---

[21]Augusto Del Noce, *L'irréligion occidentale*, translated into French by Philippe Baillet from the Italian original, *Il problema dell' atheismo* (Paris: FAC-editions, 1995): '... les guerres de réligion sont une erreur, car comme l'histoire l'enseigne, elles ont conduit a l'idée de la réligion comme *instrumentum regni* et à la victoire, au xviie siècle, du machiavélisme et de la "raison d'Etat". Elles ne doivent pas être confondues avec le combat réligieux sur le plan de la culture, qui est chose bien différente' (p. 244 n).

[22]Part II, Chapter V – 'Leibniz et la faillite de l'union des eglises' (206-222).

[23]Hazard, op. cit., 221.

radically to abandon the Christian past, bring about wars that were more violent and more widespread than those of the seventeenth century.[24]

In the play, *Les Miserables*, taken from Victor Hugo's novel of that name, one of the heroes of the failed 1848 Revolution, Gavroche, sings that he must die behind the barricades:

> Je suis tombé par terre,
> C'est la faute à Voltaire,
> Le Nez dans le ruisseau,
> C'est la faute à Rousseau.[25]

A contemporary of the 1789 Revolution, the ex-pastor, Rabaut dit Saint-Etienne, wrote in his *Histoire de la Révolution Française*:

> One man, more than all the others, advanced the progress of reason in France. It was he who united all the talents, who combated all the abuses, who took charge of defending all the oppressed, and who, during sixty years, led or commanded public opinion ... all the principles of liberty; all the seeds of the Revolution are found in the writings of Voltaire. He predicted it and caused it.[26]

Auguste Cochin in his *L'Esprit du Jacobinisme* (and elsewhere) showed the importance of 'thought societies' ('Societés de Pensée') in conveying the revolutionary premises of the Enlightenment to the broader French public (and especially to its potential leadership).[27] These 'thought societies' '...were of several sorts: lecture halls, salons, masonic lodges, literary societies, provincial academies...Philosophism [i.e. of the Enlightenment] was à la mode...all of this stellar world had only mockery for the detested Faith and Christian practice. They constantly employed such words about Christianity as "superstition", "obscurantism", and "fanaticism".'[28] Cochin

---

[24]In *Le Génocide Franco-Francais: La Vendée-Vengé* (Paris: Presses Universitaires de France, 1986), Reynald Secher states that 'This war was the most atrocious of the wars of religion and the first ideological genocide' (p. 24). He refers to the systematic slaughtering of 'la Vendée militaire' (formed out of parts of Normandie, Brittany, Anjou, Vendee and the Loire) in 1793 because of their refusal *on religious grounds* to support the revolutionary decisions against Christianity and the Church. The statistics of this genocide of a significant part of France (detested because it stoutly held on to the Faith) are as follows: 'Concerning human loss, a comparison of parish records with those of the civil state give a minimum of 15% (115 to 120,000 dead). This minimum is collaborated by other ways of research: 120,000 dead over a fifth of the territory in about eighteen months. Think of the massacres at Lyon, Toulon, Bordeaux, Marseilles, in several sections of West Chouanèrie...add the guillotine at Paris and you will pass half a million. To this one must add the losses brought about by a war foolishly started, carried on against all good sense and you will reach more than a million dead, victims, according to Andre Corvisier, of the revolutionary follies from 1792 to 1800. Out of a population of 27 million, this many casualties is a higher percentage than the War of 1914-1918' (p. 23).

[25]'I am fallen onto the ground, It is Voltaire's fault, My nose is in the gutter, It is Rousseau's fault.' I owe this reference to the article by Pierre Courthial, 'L'Idéologie antichrétienne de la Révolution Francaise' in *Révolution et Christianisme: Une Appréciation Chrétienne de la Révolution Francaise* (Lausanne: L'Age d'Homme, 1992), 59.

[26]Quoted in Courthial, op. cit., 59, 60.

[27]Augustin Cochin, *L'esprit du jacobinisme* (Paris: Presses Universitaires de France, 1979, from a work written before his death in 1916). Other – posthumous – works on this subject had been published much earlier: *Les Sociétés de pensée et la démocratie* (1921); *La Révolution et la libre-pensée* (1924), and *Les Sociétés de pensée et la Révolution en Bretagne* (1925).

[28]Courthial, op. cit., 61.

traced this readiness to abandon the ancient faith on the part of the thought societies to the decay of the traditional Christian order in eighteenth-century France.[29]

A nineteenth-century German adversary of the philosophy of the Enlightenment, which lay behind the French Revolution, Friedrich Julius Stahl (1802–1861), characterized the relationship between the two (in 1852):

> The revolution is rationalism exteriorised; rationalism is the revolution internalised. Both the one and the other are the mortal disease of our century. Some say that rationalism is unbelief. This is false; it believes in man. Some say that the revolution is the denigration of authority. This is false; it understands simply that mankind is the unique source of power and the only goal of society. Both one and the other set mankind free from God. One necessarily leads to the emancipation of the flesh and to communism; the other to the apotheosis of human reason. Both together lead to the man of sin predicted by Saint Paul.[30]

Development of the Enlightenment

As the power of official structures of once united Western Christendom gradually declined, and as the power of nation-states began coming into their own, it became somewhat safer to speak against Christianity and in favour of some kind of paganism (though it would take until the end of the eighteenth century for this sort of 'free speech' to be completely safe). This changing environment of early seventeenth-century Europe made the pagan Enlightenment possible (though it did not cause it).

Here I can attempt no summarization of the history of Enlightenment philosophy; it would require several volumes, for which I would not be competent, nor would space permit it, even if I were competent. All that can be done here is to take a very basic survey (brief, but I hope fair to the complex sources) of those crucial principles or assumptions of Enlightenment thought which are directly relevant to how they understood religion and specifically – the Christian religion – in which they had been brought up and which they rejected and sought to replace.

In his famous study of the sudden change from a Christian world-view to an anti-Christian, secularist one from about 1680 to 1715, Paul Hazard notes both the suddenness of this revolution in thought and practice, and its intensely anti-Christian character. From the seventeenth century to the eighteenth century in France, he indicates the astounding differences of attitude: 'The majority of Frenchmen thought like Bousset; all of a sudden, the French thought like Voltaire. It was a revolution.'[31] Hazard adds: 'The first [of the seventeenth century] are Christians, and the others [of the eighteenth century] anti-Christians: the first believe in divine law, and the others in natural law; the first live easily in a society which is divided into unequal classes, the second think only of equality.'[32]

---

[29]Cochin, *L'esprit du Jacobinism*, 31.

[30]From F. J. Stahl, *Was is die Revolution*? (1852), quoted by Jean-Marc Berthoud, 'La Révolution Francaise et les Révolutions' in *Révolution et Christianisme* (1992), 114.

[31]Paul Hazard, *La Crise de la conscience européenne* (Paris: Librairie Antheme Fayard, 1981), 7.

[32]Ibid.

A move from Unitarianism to Atheism

Even to speak of 'the principles of the Enlightenment' or the assumptions of seventeenth and eighteenth-century Humanism may be to raise more questions than one could answer. The Enlightenment was a long-lasting movement of thought (from at least the 1640s to about 1800, or perhaps till the present day); it involved many sophisticated minds (who often disagreed with one another on important points);[33] it was international, with writings in several languages, and saw much development and change of position from one stage of its life to another.[34] It tended to move from the Unitarian God of the 'religion of nature' to open atheism.[35] It is also complex, because frequently 'the philosophes' had to cover over, and indeed, prevaricate about what they meant, for reasons of personal and political safety in an age of powerful censors, backed by church and state.

In spite of great differences within the Enlightenment from the early phases of optimistic Cartesianism and English Deism of the classical 'Age of Reason' to the scepticism of Hume and atheism of Holbach, we can nonetheless find certain basic presuppositions (or starting points) that are generally true of 'the new paganism' all through its long development. We note a denial of the orthodox Christian doctrine of God as Trinity; a denial of the biblical teaching of creation; a denial of revelation – with the concomitant necessity of 'criticism', and a rejection of the fall of man and the noetic effects of sin upon his mind and will. In other words, the Enlightenment opposed at all significant points the traditional Christian teaching on God, nature and true religion. That is why there is such a wide and deep gap theologically, philosophically, morally and culturally between the 'pre-critical' and 'critical' periods; between 'the Age of Faith' and 'the Age of Reason'. We must look at these foundational axioms, which are the unprovable 'faith assumptions' of modern secularism.

A denial of God as Holy Trinity

From early English Deism down to Voltaire and Rousseau, most of the Enlightenment thinkers assumed a Unitarian view of God, as found in 'the

---

[33]The criticisms of Diderot, Voltaire and Hume against Rousseau are well known: see, F. C, Green, *Jean-Jacques Rousseau: A Study of His Life and Writings* (Cambridge: Cambridge University Press, 1955), and 'Deux Frères: Diderot et Jean-Jacques' (*Diderot Studies*, III (1962), 155-213); Diderot, *Réfutation suivie de l'ouvrage d'Helvétius intitulé l'Homme, Oeuvres Philosophiques*, (Amsterdam: S.N., 1772), 619; also, Voltaire, *Du contrat social, Oeuvres* III, (Paris: Societe litteraire typographique, 1784), 468-9, and George R. Havens, *Voltaire's Marginalia on the Pages of Rousseau: A Comprehensive Study of Ideas* (Columbus: Ohio State University, 1933), and David Hume, *Treatise of Human Nature*, A.D. Lindsay, ed. (London: Everyman's Library, 1964), 493.

[34]For instance, the idealistic theory of innate ideas in Descartes was thoroughly rejected by the later Enlightenment philosophers such as Isaac Newton. As Gay writes: 'Hence Newton could not – or at any rate did not –acknowledge, even to himself, the great debt he owed to Descartes: "*Error, error, non est Geom*" he scribbled over and over again in the margins of his copy of Descartes's *Geometry*, while in public, in the *Principia*, he scolded Descartes for his mistakes and passed over his contributions to the new science in silence' – Peter Gay, *The Enlightenment*, Vol. II, 147. Voltaire critiqued the dogmatic, idealistic nature of Descartes' philosophy at large in his *Eléments de la Philosophie de Newton* (1739), and John Locke's *Essay on the Human Understanding* replaced Descartes' 'innate ideas' with the theory of a human mind as a blank, 'tabula rasa', ready to receive sense impressions, and then to reflect on them.

[35]The English Deists in the middle and late 1600s posited a sort of Unitarian deity, who had set the world going, and then left it to run on its own, without divine interference. Supposedly, this god

religion of nature', and opposed strenuously Trinitarianism as 'irrational and superstitious'. Given the desire of the new paganism to submit all teaching (particularly Christianity) to the criticism of the human mind, their attack against the Trinity is no surprise. Even for devout believers, the doctrine that God is one substance (or reality) in three persons is mind-stretching. But for those who think that their human minds are the limits of what God can be, then Trinitarianism is a great offence, for it demands the submission of faith to a supremely high reality. In this respect, the Deists had philosophical/theological forerunners in the Arians of the fourth century, who worked on the principle that what they could not understand about God simply could not be true. Basil the Great, for instance, rebuked Eunomius for holding that human comprehension was the measure of divine reality.[36]

An axiomatic gap between God and the world

As far as the particular use of the Enlightenment mind to measure what God could be, no doubt their axiomatic assumption of a deep dualism or gap between God and the world, precluded their taking seriously the incarnation of Christ and outpouring of the Holy Spirit. Hence their denial of the Trinity to a large degree came from 'a faith axiom' of their own philosophy; a dualistic disjunction between God and the natural world of space and time.

It is never easy to discern people's motives, but from their general position, one would assume that many in the Enlightenment wished to escape the Holy Trinity of the last millennium and a half of both Catholic and Protestant teaching, which they took to be oppressive. The Trinity was the foundation of the Church, with its fairly strict moral and intellectual teaching. The Enlightenment, following many in the Southern European Renaissance, looked longingly back to the permissive god or gods of classicism, leaving open many areas of life and thought that true Christianity closed. In addition to that, there was the widespread revulsion against the sixteenth and seventeenth-century wars between the competing Christian confessions; peace might be assured by a vague kind of Unitarianism, and certainly the intellectual and moral realms would be left far more fluid.

---

could be deduced from nature itself, without the need of supernatural revelation. A representative thinker, in most respects, would be John Toland (a follower of John Locke, who went much further from orthodoxy than Locke). In his *Christianity Not Mysterious* (1696), he claims that his form of Christianity includes nothing beyond that which is acceptable to unaided human reason. Thus, he excludes the essence of Biblical Christianity: the Holy Trinity, the incarnation of Christ and the miracles. In fact, Toland taught a sort of pantheism (and in this was unrepresentative of Deism). Tindal's *Christianity as Old as Creation* (1730) was similar (though not pantheistic). The Scottish theologian and professor at St. Andrews University, Thomas Halyburton, gave a brilliant refutation of Deism in *Natural Religion Insufficient and Revealed Necessary to Man's Happiness in his Present State* (Edinburgh: Heirs of Andrew Anderson, 1714), from a Christian perspective. Later in the century, David Hume (an unbelieving Scot) destroyed the Deist position in his *Dialogues Concerning Natural Religion* (published posthumously in 1779). As Stanley Jaki properly pointed out in his Gifford Lectures, the God of nature whom Hume refutes is, in fact, the God of Descartes (*The Road of Science and the Ways of God* (Edinburgh, 1978), pp. 103, 106, 107. In the later phase of the Enlightenment, Holbach was openly atheist, as in his sequel to Lucretius, *Système de la Nature* (1770). This movement from Deism to atheism confirms what Lecerf once said, 'A Deist has not yet had time to become an atheist', in *An Introduction to Reformed Dogmatics* (Lutterworth Press: London, 1949), 125.

[36]Basil, *Contra Eunomium*, 2.24.

English Deism dissected

The attempts of various English Deists to derive – apart from divine revelation – a God of nature, owed much to their wishful thinking, and to a surreptitious and eclectic borrowing from revelation such elements of divinity as they deemed non-threatening to their programme for reform. None demonstrated more clearly their procedure here than Thomas Halyburton in his *Natural Religion Insufficient and Revealed Necessary to Man's Happiness in his Present State.*[37] He wrote: 'None are more credulous than they who set up for rational religion.'[38] He notes that 'Deists beg the question by prescribing what was fit for God.'[39] He shows that the Deists 'bootleg' the Scriptures, taking – without acknowledgment – elements that they find acceptable.[40] But to do this (and to claim that they derived these elements from classical religion), they must take the natural theology of the pagans out of its proper context.[41]

He lucidly discusses Herbert's 'five articles of religion'[42] and shows that Herbert fails to prove that 'piety and virtue' were principal parts of pagan worship[43] and that he reads his own glosses into their practices.[44] He easily overthrows 'the five articles',[45] and shows that the real history of religion undercuts the popular Deist 'five articles.'[46] Halyburton believed that the real reason why the Deists attempted to construct a religion of nature was simply in order to facilitate their rejection of Christianity:

> ...of the design or rather tendency of his [Herbert's] books, we may safely judge. And as to this I say, that if it is granted, that the *Scriptures* are the only Standard of the *Christian Religion*, which cannot modestly be denied; I shall upon this supposition undertake to maintain against any who will defend him, that his books aim at the *utter subversion of the Christian Religion*, that his *principles* overthrow entirely the *authority of the Scriptures*, and are not only inconsistent with, but destructive to the *essentials of Christianity*. And I further add, that this is every where so obvious in his writings, that it will require a strange stretch of charity to believe our author could be ignorant of it.[47]

English Deism, even within the Enlightenment, was fairly short-lived. John Locke wrote against Herbert's mythical ideas of pagan piety and showed instead, pagan ignorance of God, and criticized the Deists' importations of

---

[37]Evidently Halyburton owed some of his critique against Deism (published in 1714) to the earlier work of John Locke, *The Reasonableness of Christianity* (1690).

[38]Thomas Halyburton, *Natural Religion Insufficient, and Revealed Necessary, to Man's Happiness in his Present State: or a Rational Inquiry into the Principles of the Modern Deists* (Albany, N.Y.: H. C. Southwick, 1812), p. 38.

[39]Ibid., 69.

[40]Ibid., 71, 76, 216, 237.

[41]Ibid., 75, 76.

[42]Ibid.,Chapter xiv. These 'five articles' are: 1. There is one supreme God; 2. This one God is to be worshipped; 3. That virtue and piety are the principal parts of the worship of this one true God; 4. We must repent when we do amiss; 5. There are rewards and punishments after this life.

[43]Ibid., 238ff.

[44]Ibid., 247, 250, 257, 263, 270, 281.

[45]Ibid., 254ff.1

[46]Ibid., 280.

[47]Ibid., 300.

moral law into the religion of nature (without referring to the name of any particular Deist).[48] And later, David Hume gave the finishing blow to Deism, and in so doing, sought to deny any real relation between Transcendence and the created order.[49]

Insofar as asserting that the Trinity is a contradiction of reason, they were better at making this claim than in proving it. It is not that the *philosophes* were ignorant on the traditional teaching of the Church of the Trinity. Most of them had been to school to the Jesuits (and a few to the Jansenists). For instance, the article in Diderot's and d'Alembert's *Encyclopedie* on the Trinity is certainly competent.[50] But their underlying dualism between God and the world made it impossible to accept.

Sir Isaac Newton

The work of Sir Isaac Newton is more complex, though still dualistic in a rather similar sense. His form of Unitarianism was part and parcel of his metaphysical views of cosmic reality.[51] He held that absolute space and time are actually part of 'the sensorium' of God, and thus limitations to his interaction with the world.[52] As T. F. Torrance explains:

> It was important for Newton's theoretic system of the world that time and space should constitute an isotropic, necessary and unchanging frame of reference for the orderly reduction of all bodies in motion to patterns which were amenable to mathematico-mechanical calculation and to formalisation in immutable laws. He achieved that by relating time and space not only to the eternity and infinity of God but to his immutability and impassibility, which allowed him to think of absolute time and space as containing all bodies in the universe and controlling their behaviour without being changed in themselves by what they contained and controlled – that is what he meant by the term 'absolute'. Time and space thus identified with the unchanging presence and reality of God constituted an independent cause or inertial system in the whole geometrico-causal structure of Newtonian physics and mechanics.[53]

For example, Newton connects God physically (or substantially) to space and time, as in his 'General Scholium' following Book III of *Principia Mathematica*:

> He [God] is not eternity and infinity, but eternal and infinite. He endures forever, and is everywhere present, and by existing always and everywhere, he constitutes duration and space....He is omnipresent not *virtually* only, but also *substantially*; for virtue cannot subsist without substance. In him are all things contained and moved; yet neither affects the other: God

---

[48]John Locke, *Essay* 1.1.5; *The Reasonableness of Christianity*, ed. by I. T. Ramsey (London: Adam & Charles Black, 1958), sections 238, 241, 242, 243 (pp. 57-58, 60-67).

[49]David Hume, *The Natural History of Religion* (1757).

[50]Diderot et d'Alembert, *L'Encyclopédie ou Dictionnaire Raisonné des Sciences, des Arts et des Métiers* (Fairview, Elmsford, NY: Pergamon Press, reprint of 1775 edition), Vol. III (Tome 16, pp. 645-649).

[51]See Richard Westfall, *Life of Isaac Newton* (Cambridge: Cambridge University Press, 1993).

[52]Isaac Newton, *Principia Mathematica* (1686-87), p. 6.

[53]Thomas F. Torrance, *Christian Theology & Scientific Culture* (New York: Oxford University Press, 1981), 18,19.

suffers nothing from the motion of bodies; bodies find no resistance from the omnipresence of God.[54]

Newtonian dualism

This imported a dualism between God and the world, so that God could not enter into the world by means of the Incarnation of Christ. Hence, Christ is not fully God (thus, the Trinity could not be true). A similar sort of dualism (though rather closer to traditional orthodoxy) is found in John Locke's contradistinction between reason and faith.[55] Locke follows Newton in limiting the personal interaction of God with the creation, and yet he is closer to Christianity than Newton (and far closer than the French *philosophes*), for while never affirming the Trinity (nor denying it),[56] Locke does teach the Virgin birth and divine sonship and Messiahship of Christ.[57] The latter realities were generally unacceptable to most of the Enlightenment. At first, most of them assumed a vague sort of Unitarianism (as Montesquieu and Voltaire), and later several of them moved on to atheism (as Diderot and Holbach).

In the end of the day, whether Unitarian or atheistic, the Enlightenment wished to get rid of the God confessed by the Church and witnessed to in the Scriptures: they wished to rid themselves of the Holy Trinity. Much of Western society had been focused on Him for over a millennium, and the new pagans realized that to reshape their society, they had to replace this God, and they left no stone unturned to do so. Presumably one of the important stages of replacing the Triune God would be to grade Him down to a vague, Unitarian Deity; a sort of abstract, limiting concept, who would, in later hands, more readily be dethroned.

A denial of creation

With a few exceptions, the Enlightenment, especially in its middle and later phases, denied divine creation of all things 'out of nothing.' As for the exceptions, Sir Isaac Newton certainly believed in divine creation. Yet he assumes it rather than discussing it. He regularly speaks of God as the Creator, but in his *Principia Mathematica*, he nowhere discusses it. He would have had an opportunity to have done so in his *Chronology of Ancient Kingdoms*, but does not do so.[58] Whether he had before him Archbishop James Ussher's *The Annals of the World*, which had been published well before his time (1658), I do not know.[59] But Ussher begins with the creation

---

[54]Isaac Newton, *Mathematical Principles of Natural Theology and his System of the World* (translated into English by Andrew Motte in 1729; the translation revised by Florian Cajori (Berkeley, CA: University of California Press, 1946), 545.

[55]John Locke, *Essay*. IV. Chs. 17 & 18.

[56]John Locke, *A Paraphrase and Notes on the Epistles of St. Paul*, ed. By Arthur W. Wainwright, Vol. I (Oxford: Clarendon Press, 1987): '... his failure to assert the traditional Christian doctrines about Christ and the Trinity...while Locke protested that he never denied the doctrine of the Trinity, he never took the trouble to affirm it' (pp. 37, 38).

[57]John Locke, *The Reasonableness of Christianity*, p. 45.

[58]Isaac Newton, *The Chronology of Ancient Kingdoms* (London: J. Tomson, MDCCXXVIII).

[59]James Ussher, *Annals of the World*, first published in Latin (1650–1654), and then in English (1658); recently reprinted: Revised and Updated by Larry and Marion Pierce – Master Books, Inc., PO Box 726, Green Forest, AR 72638.

of the world (computed by him to have been in 4004 B.C.), and traces the various kingdoms from Adam, and then from Noah's sons. Instead, Newton begins with the lineages of ancient kingdoms. Certainly he mentions Japheth,[60] Peleg and Noah,[61] thus assuming as true the Old Testament genealogies. He also says that 'mankind could not be much older than is recorded in Scripture'.[62] But creation is passed over in silence.

John Locke also affirms the God of the Bible to be the Creator and Governor of all.[63] Yet, beyond that, he avoids any discussion of creation. He had a good opportunity to expand on creation and its consequences in his paraphrase of Romans 1:20 and 21, but failed to do so, other than (correctly) to paraphrase it, with a view to rebuking idolatry.[64] What he says is thoroughly orthodox, yet – as with Newton – the weighty implications of creation are left untouched. Actually the article on 'creation' in Diderot's secularist *Encyclopedie* comes closer to some of the significant consequences of this doctrine for human thought, although not too close, for about two-thirds of the article interacts with pagan alternatives to creation, with considerable sympathy for the alternatives.[65]

Denial of the influence of the fall on humanity

What is of importance in the development of secularist thought, is that even the Enlightenment thinkers who are closer to traditional orthodoxy do *not* place the natural and human history of the world in the biblical context of creation out of nothing, fall, redemption and consummation. Locke specifically denies the effects of the fall on the human mind and constitution. He affirms that Adam's Fall brought death upon us, but denies imputed or heredity guilt and denies our sinful nature and biased minds.[66] Thus, even in the less radical men of the Enlightenment, creation is taken out of its biblical context, and becomes more of a limiting, intellectual concept, focused on mankind, than an open reality (with the constant 'back and forth' of creation, redemption and providence) focused on God.

---

[60]Newton, *Chronology*, 184.

[61]Ibid., 186.

[62]Ibid., 190.

[63]Especially in *The Reasonableness of Christianity*, section 1, where he affirms Adam's fall, and in *Essay*, book IV, chapters 18 and 19, as well as in *A Discourse of Miracles*, where he teaches the superiority of divine power.

[64]John Locke, *A Paraphrase and Notes on the Epistles of St Paul*, ed. Arthur W. Wainwright, vol. 2 (Oxford: Clarendon Press, 1987 edition of 1707 (posthumous) original. On Romans 1:20, 21, he comments: '… so that what is to be known of his invisible Being, might be clearly discovered and understood in the visible beauty, order and operations observable in the constitution and parts of the universe by all those who would cast their regards and apply their minds that way in so much that they are utterly without excuse, for that when the Deity was soe plainly discovered to them, yet they glorified him not as was suitable to the excellency of his divine nature: nor did they with due thankfulness acknowledge him as the author of the Being, and the giver of all the good they enjoyed: but following the vain phansies of their own vain minds set up to them selves fictitious noe gods and their foolish understandings were darkened…' (pp. 494,495).

[65]Diderot et d'Alembert, *L'Encyclopédie ou Dictionaire Raisonné des Sciences, des Arts et des Métiers* (reprint of 1754 edition by Pergamon Press: Fairview, Elmsford, NY) on 'Creation' in Vol. I (tome 4).

[66]John Locke, *The Reasonableness of Christianity*, 25, 26, 28, and *Paraphrases* (op. cit.), where he specifically denies original sin (p. 35).

A return to ancient theories of materialism

Both the men of the Renaissance and of the Enlightenment were well acquainted with pagan Greek and Roman theories of origins. They knew of Democritus' and Leucippus' atomic and evolutionary theories, and gave close attention to Lucretius' materialism (especially Voltaire, Diderot and Holbach).

A striking illustration of the difference between the thought of the sixteenth-century Reformation and the eighteenth-century Enlightenment is seen in their very different evaluations of Lucretius (in particular, his materialistic and immoralist *De Rerum Natura*). John Calvin speaks of him as 'the filthy dog Lucretius',[67] whereas Voltaire in his *Epitre à Uranie* '... poses as a modern Lucretius who defies a cruel God and all His horrible mysteries and explicitly abandons Christianity so that he may be free to love the deist deity...'[68]

Some of them (such as Montesquieu) leaned towards Stoic theories of an eternal god/world synthesis. All of these pagan cosmogonies agreed in positing an eternal world (or its component parts), thus making 'god' at least as dependent upon the world as the world was upon him. None of them worked with the biblical Creator/creature distinction as basic to all reality and thought.

Yet it took some time for the Enlightenment to be able effectively to focus its energies against biblical creation, much as it was antithetical to their man-exalting and materialist philosophy. Peter Gay fairly summarizes their general position before the early nineteenth century:

> But it was not until the nineteenth century, when Danish archaeologists applied a periodic scheme to prehistoric remains, that prehistory became, if not precisely transparent, at least a subject of informed study...These spectacular advances were accompanied, and partly caused, by advances in geology and biology which ruined, for all but fundamentalists, the Christian view that the world had been created six thousand years earlier. The intellectual atmosphere and even some of the scientific presuppositions that were to govern Lyell's and Darwin's work were the creation of the Enlightenment: returning to antique teachings of an eternal, or at least a very ancient universe, philosophes like Buffon and Diderot, La Mettrie and Hume, Holbach and Kant, postulated a course of cosmic and terrestrial development wholly incompatible with Archbishop Ussher's date for the creation in 4004 B.C., or other, similar Christian dates.[69]

It would take until about 1749 with Buffon's *Histoire Naturelle* seriously to attempt to replace the Genesis account of creation with a naturalistic alternative. 'He encompassed the history of the earth from the moment it had first been shaken loose from the sun by a comet, blazing hot, to a time of universal death on a frozen planet...'[70] He intended his ideas to be a clear alternative to the creation as taught by Judaism and Christianity: 'He

---

[67]John Calvin, *Institutes of the Christian Religion*, I.5.5.
[68]Peter Gay, op. cit., vol 1, 387.
[69]Ibid., 88, 89.
[70]Ibid., 152.

was convinced that to account for the palpable facts of geology, the earth must be assigned an age, not of thousands, but of millions of years. In the same way, his geological speculations offered alternatives to the Christian creation myth, his biological speculations alternatives to the Christian view of man ...'[71]

But well before the time of Darwin, David Hume had probably delivered the heaviest blow against the biblical doctrine of creation in his denial of causation (i.e. according to traditional theology, the world is an effect which is caused by God; but if cause and effect are only imaginary associations of ideas in the human mind, there are no valid grounds for assuming creation).[72] Thomas Reid's response to Hume's argument against creation (and causation) has been discussed in Appendix II to Chapter 1.

Darwin's influence

It is clear that by the time Charles Darwin published his *Origin of Species* in 1859, the Western world had been prepared to receive this apparently convincing alternative to divine creation by the previous two hundred years of controversy against the traditional Christian view of God, man and the cosmos by the Enlightenment. Looking back at this time, George Bernard Shaw in the early twentieth century noted that the issue had been between Calvin's God and Darwin's evolution, and that 'the world jumped at Darwin.'[73] As R. J. Rushdoony noted: 'The first edition of Darwin's *On the Origin of Species* appeared on November 24, 1859, and all 1,250 copies sold out on the day of publication. It continued to sell at an amazing rate. Its influence in every area of life was rapid and far-reaching.'[74]

This radical alternative to creation, that the Enlightenment itself had not been able convincingly to work out, was an effective way to accomplish two purposes that lay deep in the programme of most (though not all) of its proponents: (1) get rid of God, and (2) set free man to be part of the plastic 'system of nature', which can be reworked by those with knowledge and power.

(1) The glory of the Triune God was felt to denigrate the glory of His image-bearer, mankind. If He could be reduced or even removed, then mankind could shine the more brightly. In his article on 'Man' in *The Encyclopedia*, Diderot wrote:

> If we banish man, the thinking or contemplating being, from the face of the earth, this moving and sublime spectacle of nature will be nothing more than a sad and mute scene. The universe will cease to speak; silence and night will seize it. Everything will be changed into a vast solitude where unobserved phenomena take place obscurely, unobserved. It is the presence of man which makes the existence of beings meaningful.

---

[71]Ibid., 156.

[72]E.g. see David Hume, *Treatise of Human Nature*, I.iii.14.

[73]Quoted in Arnold Lunn, ed. in intro., p. 4 of Douglas Dewar and H. S. Shelton: *Is Evolution Proved?* (London: Hollis and Carter, 1947).

[74]R. J. Rushdoony, *The Mythology of Science* (Nutley, NJ: The Craig Press, 1978), 14. In one sense, Darwin could be thought of as having applied Hegelian dialectical philosophy to biology, though without saying so.

This enthusiastic turning from God to man had been a major strand of the Florentine Renaissance (although at that stage, the Christian context was still not yet generally rejected). Quentin Skinner writes:

> But by far the most important consequence of adopting the ideal of the *uomo universale* was that it prompted the humanists to reject the entire Augustinian picture of human nature [as sinful and needing the constant grace of God to accomplish anything praiseworthy]...This anti-Augustinian view of man's nature and capacities recurs even more markedly among the humanists of early *quattrocento* Florence. They start by insisting that men do in fact have the power to attain the highest excellence...The most famous example is of course the oration on this theme composed by Pico della Mirandola in 1484... The recovery of this classical dramatisation of the human condition again represents an almost Pelagian departure from the prevailing assumptions of Augustinian Christianity...Pico [in his *Oration on the Dignity of Man*] says that [of all other beings] 'Man alone is "constrained by no limits" and endowed with his "own free will." And the reason God gives for having placed humanity "at the world's centre" in this way is the desire that men should be able "with freedom of choice" to create and mould their own characters...'[75]

(2) The undesirability of God's creation to the Enlightenment lay in the way they understood it to 'hem in' mankind from change because of the divine sovereignty operating through fixed creational orders and forms of existence, and through divine purposes and divine providence for the created realm. The creational orders of marriage and family, reproductive order within the basic 'kinds', and of covenantally limited structures of church and state (as in the book of Genesis) were taken by the *philosophes* to be entirely restrictive of human possibilities. Perhaps more than anything else, they wished to be out from under the restraints of the medieval Scholastic teachings on the four forms of created life (by which Aristotles' four causes has been given a Christian interpretation[76]). That is to say, the denial of creation 'ex nihilo' brought with it the denial of a divinely established created order.

It would be shortly after the French Revolution that the consequences of the Enlightenment's deracination of man as God's image-bearer would shine most clearly. Xavier Martin's *Nature Humanine et Révolution Francaise: Du Siècle des Lumières au Code Napoléon* traces the legal consequences of the anthropology of secularism. He finds that :

> The anthropology of the Enlightenment ... propagates in effect, under the sign of science, the idea of a human interiority, a pure and simple passivity, which it would thus be possible to manipulate as needed without trouble, and technically – supposedly – without great difficulty ... towards social felicity...the foundation of such a conception is mechanist, sensualist, and thus, doubly materialist... The application to man is based on sensualism: that is, the belief that human interiority is nothing but a pure chemical reaction to sensual experience...[This means] a logical tendency to deny to man every aspect of his being that is non material; to deny every decisive

---

[75]Quentin Skinner, op. cit., vol. I, 91, 93, 95, 97.

[76]An appreciative Protestant Reformed critique of the way Thomism developed Aristotle's four causes is found in Jean-Marc Berthoud's *Les Différentes Formes de Causalité et la Pensée de La Bible* (Positions Créationnistes, No. 25, Septembre 1996, Case postale 4, CH 1001 Lausanne).

> distinction between man and beast; in a word, a decided negation of all human will and of free will and of all responsibility, and thus of human dignity...This weapon is one of the major ways where progressivism of that time managed to outdate and discredit the catholic tradition, whose anthropology...taught the exact reverse. For it postulated an active principle in every man, which gave grounds to all that was denied by the age of Enlightenment.[77]

Bernardino Casadei, in an article on the thought of Augusto Del Noce, suggests as regard this second point, that man must be taken out of the context of God's creation and image-bearing, in order to remove limitations on the utilization of politics to remake society in its desired image: 'The very existence of a transcendent reality founded on the principle of non-contradiction is always a limit on political power which one cannot abuse in practice in a too evident manner without losing its source of popular legitimacy.'[78]

Modern Gnosticism seeks to escape the fixity of divine creation

Eric Vogelin explored what the intellectual wrenching of mankind out of God's created order, which began in earnest in the Renaissance and Enlightenment, would come to mean in the totalitarian movements of the twentieth century. He calls these modern movements 'Gnostic', deliberately taking the name from the early pagan heretical movements that threatened Christianity during the first three or four centuries of its existence.[79] Ancient Gnosticism dealt with 'the loss of meaning that resulted from the breakdown of institutions, civilizations, and ethnic cohesion in the Hellenistic culture of the first three centuries, and attempted to regain an understanding of the meaning of human existence in the given conditions of the world.'[80] The early Gnostics explained the world as 'an alien place'; 'creation' (which they explained as 'aeons' or extrusions from an impersonal, unknowable god) was a sort of prison from which one should employ Gnostic knowledge and practice in order to escape to one's other world of origin.[81]

They divided man into 'soul' (psyche) and 'spirit' (pneuma). '...gnostic man must carry on the work of salvation himself. Now, through his psyche ("soul") he belongs to the order, the nomos, of the world; what impels him toward deliverance is the pneuma ("spirit"). The labor of salvation, therefore, entails the dissolution of the worldly constitution of the psyche and at the same time the gathering and freeing of the powers of the pneuma.'[82] The lifting up of the spirit of man through secret 'gnosis'

---

[77]Xavier Martin, *Nature Humaine et Révolution Francaise: Du Siècle des Lumières au Code Napoléon* (France: Dominique Martin Morin, 1994), 11, 12.

[78]Bernardino Casadei, 'Genèse et Signification du problème de l'athéisme: le lacisime' in *Del Noce Interprète du XXe siecle: Une Introduction* (Paris: Catholica, 2002), 93.

[79] See his 'Introduction' in Eric Vogelin, *Science, Politics & Gnosticism* (Wilmington, DE: ISI Books, 2004 reprint [1968]), 3-10.

[80]Vogelin, op. cit., 7.

[81]Ibid.

[82]Ibid., 9.

(knowledge) provided by these sects, would show the Gnostic man 'the way out of the prison of the evil [Creator] God of this world (be he Zeus or Yahweh or one of the other ancient father gods)'[83] up to the non-creating, 'hidden' (or '*Buthus*' – 'depth') god, who has no contact with the nasty (inherently evil) material of this created realm.

In the late second century, Irenaeus of Lyon summarized what salvation meant for the Valentinian sect of the Gnostics of his time:

> Perfect salvation consists in the cognition, as such, of the Ineffable Greatness. For since sin and affliction resulted from ignorance (*agnoia*), this whole system originating in ignorance is dissolved through knowledge (*gnosis*). Hence, gnosis is the salvation of the inner man ... Gnosis redeems the inner, pneumatic man; he finds his satisfaction in the knowledge of the Whole. And this is the true salvation.[84]

Eric Vogelin then seeks to trace profoundly motivating Gnostic concerns in such modern movements as 'progressivism, positivism, Marxism, psychoanalysis, communism, fascism, and national socialism.'[85] He believes that such 'gnostic movements' (whether of the intellectual or political variety) 'have shaped the thinking of millions of people in the Western world, very often without their being aware of it.'[86] These Gnostic movements, he suggests, came about at the time of the Enlightenment, and especially the time of German Idealism, a later offspring of the Enlightenment.[87]

Hostility to the order of created being

Gnosticism, whether ancient or modern, is *not* the philosophy of the Enlightenment, but both of them share a hostility to creation by God, and – by definition – to the God who created. Vogelin writes:

> The aim of parousiastic [i.e. the modern, revolutionary form of Gnosticism] is to destroy the order of being, which is experienced as defective and unjust, and through man's creative power to replace it with a perfect and just order. Now, however the order of being may be understood – as a world dominated by cosmic-divine powers in the civilizations of the Near and Far East, or as the creation of a world-transcendent God in Judaeo-Christian symbolism, or as an essential order of being in philosophical contemplation – it remains something that is given, that is not under man's control. In order, therefore, that the attempt to create a new world may seem to make sense, the givenness of the order of being must be obliterated; the order of being must be interpreted, rather, as essentially under man's control. And taking control of being further requires that the transcendent origin of being be obliterated: it requires the decapitation of being – the murder of God.[88]

Vogelin quotes many passages from the writings of Marx, Nietzsche, Feuerbach and others to show how central this was to their program. Among six characteristics that he argues 'taken together, reveal the nature

---

[83]Ibid.
[84]St. Irenaeus, *Adversus Haereses*, quoted in Vogelin, op. cit., 10.
[85]Vogelin, op. cit., 61.
[86]Ibid., 62.
[87]Ibid., 3,4.
[88]Ibid., 39, 40.

of the Gnostic attitude', and are found in the twentieth-century modern Gnostic movements,[89] let us look at two of them that show why creation, with its divinely ordained structures for human and animal life, has to be at all costs rejected:

> 4) ...the belief that the order of being will have to be changed in an historical process. From a wretched world a good one must evolve historically. This assumption is not altogether self-evident, because the Christian solution might also be considered – namely, that the world throughout history will remain as it is and that man's salvational fulfilment is brought about through grace in death.
>
> 5) With this fifth point we come to the Gnostic trait in the narrower sense – the belief that a change in the order of being lies in the realm of human action, that this salvational act is possible through man's own effort.[90]

But to accomplish this, mankind must avoid – and deny the existence – of the transcendent origin of Being: the Triune God. Vogelin reflects on Heidegger's concept that 'man is to be understood historically as an existence that can either open or shut itself to the domination of being...The construct of the closed process of being; the shutting off of immanent from world-transcendent being; the refusal to acknowledge the experience ... of ontic events wherein the soul participates in transcendent being and allows itself to be ordered by it...and finally, the refusal to permit the very idea of a construct of a closed process of being to be called into question...was to be found in the speculative Gnostics of the nineteenth century.'[91]

And, in several respects, they prepared the way for the world-destroying 'gnostic mass movements' of the twentieth century, just as the Enlightenment had prepared the way for the renewal of Gnosticism. A high price would be paid for denying supernatural creation with its divinely ordained structures of life and society.

Dooyeweerd on modern statism's rejection of the structures of creation

The Dutch Reformed philosopher, Herman Dooyeweerd, analyzed modern 'statism' in terms of a rejection of God's ordering of the various 'spheres' of creation in order to re-work society, as though men were numbers or chemical elements, which could be recomposed by a scientifically driven state. This is not far from what Vogelin meant by 'modern Gnosticism'. Dooyeweerd writes:

> As long as this mathematical science-ideal had the primacy in modern philosophy, even human society was constructed after its pattern. The given societal order, which still showed many remnants of the medieval feudal regime, did not satisfy the Humanist view of human autonomy. Thus,

---

[89]Ibid., 64, 65.

[90]Ibid.

[91]Ibid., 35, 36.

> this societal order, too, was subjected to a methodological destruction by theoretical thought. It was dissolved into its supposed elemental components, the free and equal individuals who were assumed to have existed in a pre-societal state of nature. From these elements philosophical thought could freely create a theoretical image of human society, corresponding to the Humanist mathematical science-ideal, which aims at complete control over the temporal world.
>
> The first concern was to construct a body politic, provided with absolute power over all other societal relationships, in order to dissolve all connection with medieval society. To this end, the state was defined as an artificial body characterized by its absolute sovereignty, excluding any internal sphere sovereignty of non-political institutions such as the family and the church.[92]

Elsewhere, Dooyeweerd showed that secular statism, and the philosophy behind it, functionally denied the reality of the divinely given laws written into the created order; laws and structures which restrain political tyranny in light of the sovereign rights of the transcendent Creator as expressed in His revealed will.[93] Thus, the thinking begotten by the Enlightenment had the strongest interests in excluding from its universe: God, the truth of His creation of all things out of nothing, and the written revelation of His creation and His will in Holy Scripture. Such concepts would have to go in order to create a new, humanist paradise.

A Christian alternative to statism

In the aftermath of the French Revolution and the years of European war and turmoil following it, Dutch Calvinists sought a better way; a way to renew Christian faith and Western society. Groen Van Prinsterer (a disciple of F. Stahl and Merle d'Aubigné) gave influential lectures on *Unbelief and Revolution* in early nineteenth century Holland, in which he traces the French Revolution to the unbelief of the Enlightenment, to its rejection of Christianity. He saw that the issue leading up to the revolution was a deliberate denial of God, so as to remove his control over and law-structure for the creation; especially for man, society and the nations.

Groen founded the Christian 'Anti-Revolutionary Party' with the design of replacing the Enlightenment both philosophically and politically. The most famous person to join that party was Abraham Kuyper (a Dutch Reformed minister) who in due time, started an effective newspaper, a university, and became Prime Minister of the Netherlands.

Abraham Kuyper on Calvinism

In a famous series of lectures given at Princeton University in 1898, Kuyper spoke on 'Calvinism and Politics'.[94] He spoke of the dominating principle of Calvinism as 'cosmological': *'the Sovereignty of the Triune God over the whole*

---

[92]Herman Dooyeweerd, *In the Twilight of Western Thought* (Philadelphia: Presbyterian and Reformed, 1960), 69.

[93]Herman Dooyeweerd, *A New Critique of Theoretical Thought* (Philadelphia: Presbyterian and Reformed, 1953), vol. I, 108.

[94]Lecture 3 of Abraham Kuyper, *Lectures on Calvinism* (Grand Rapids: Wm. B. Eerdmans, 1978 reprint [1898]), 78-109.

cosmos, in all its spheres and kingdoms, visible and invisible. A *primordial* Sovereignty which eradiates in mankind in a threefold deduced supremacy, *viz*., 1. The Sovereignty in the *State*; 2. The Sovereignty in *Society*; and 3. The Sovereignty in the *Church*.'[95]

The divinely given division of powers amongst the various sovereign spheres comes from the Creator God; is written into the structures of created nature and human life, and is always the source of human liberty and productive (in principle) of happiness. Of particular interest to the Dutch Calvinist thinkers of the nineteenth century was the connection between the direct and continuing authority of the Creator with legitimate (and thus limited) human authority in the various social spheres:

> In a Calvinistic sense we understand hereby, that the family, the business, science, art and so forth are all social spheres, which do not owe their existence to the state, but obey a high authority *within* their own bosom; an authority which rules, by the grace of God, just as the sovereignty of the State does...
>
> In this independent character a special *higher authority* is of necessity involved and this highest authority we intentionally call – *sovereignty in the individual social spheres*, in order that it may be sharply and decidedly expressed that these different developments of social life have *nothing above themselves but God*, and that the State cannot intrude here, and has nothing to command in their domain. As you feel at once, this is the deeply interesting question of our civil liberties.[96]

Kuyper's ideal is profoundly unlike the Enlightenment theory, which attempted to dissolve the restraints of creation-based law structures, reflected in the somewhat independent social orders and institutions of late medieval society, so as to strengthen the hands of the secular state to reform man and society towards a paradisiacal condition (that wound up with vast wars and totalitarian tyranny in many places). Instead, he returns to the biblical doctrine of creation, which lies behind 'constitutional government' with its ordered structure of various spheres, all directly under the Law of God, so that no one sphere (let us say, either church or state) can dominate and remove the liberty of the other. Unlike Enlightenment thinking, this kind of respect for creation and its law-ordered structures seeks to keep the state from temptations towards totalitarian power.

> It [Calvinism] demanded for both independence in their own sphere and regulation of the relation between both, not by the executive, but *under the law*. And by this stern demand, Calvinism may be said to have generated constitutional public law, from its own fundamental idea.[97]

> ...there exists, side by side with this personal sovereignty, the sovereignty of *the sphere*. The University exercises scientific dominion; the Academy of fine arts is possessed of art-power; the guild exercised a technical dominion; the trades-union rules over labor – and each of these spheres or corporations is conscious of the power of exclusive independent judgment and authoritative action, within its proper sphere of operation. Behind these organic spheres,

[95]Kuyper, op. cit., 79.

[96]Ibid., 90, 91. Kuyper refers to his work of 1880: *Sovereignty in the Sphere of Society*.

[97]Ibid., 94.

> with intellectual, aesthetical and technical sovereignty, the sphere of the family opens itself, with its right of marriage, domestic peace, education and possession; and in this sphere also the natural head is conscious of exercising an inherent authority – not because the government allows it, but because God has imposed it. Paternal authority roots itself in the very life-blood and is proclaimed in the fifth Commandment. And so also finally it may be remarked that the social life of cities and villages forms a sphere of existence, which arises from the very necessities of life, and which therefore must be autonomous.[98]

Pope Leo XIII on 'The Condition of Labor' ('Rerum Novarum')

During the same period when Kuyper was seeking to formulate a Christian alternative to the various forms of statist socialism that had grown in power in Europe since the French Revolution, Pope Leo XIII published one of the most influential of all papal encyclicals, Rerum Novarum ('The Condition of Labor') on May 15, 1891.[99] In it he dealt with the same issues involved in what Abraham Kuyper called 'the social question' (or the problem of poverty[100]).

Leo XIII, no less than Kuyper, teaches that personal, religious and social rights do not come from the state, but directly from God, whose image we bear (cf. par. 6, 9, 32). The Pope rejects state socialism (par. 11), especially as it seeks to replace parents (ibid.). He teaches the God-given right of private property (cf. par. 4-8, 35). He rejects the Marxist (without naming Marx) theory of 'conflict of interest' in favor of 'harmony of interest' (par. 15-17, 21). Along with this, he rejects socialist levelling (par. 13), based on the political manipulation of class envy (par. 3).

At the same time, he reflects the biblical concern for just laws (par. 25-27), for equal protection of all (par. 27-30), and decries unrestrained economic competition, rapacious usury and oppressive monopolies [so characteristic of debt capitalism – though he does not employ this term] (par. 2). He explains the necessity of the Church for society to function in a wholesome manner. The holy life and teaching of the Church leavens all of society (par. 13). It teaches the truth and practices love (par. 22).

Rerum Novarum looks to the Christian diaconal ministry for large scale uplift of the poor, rather than to state-administered welfare (par. 24). Yet it gives the state a restrained, but real place in dealing with the problems of the poor (par. 25-32). This encyclical teaches the necessity of humane working conditions (cf. par. 31-34), and the right of labor to organize (par. 36-43) and take group action to achieve just goals. It places human economy and culture in the light of the eternal goal to which we are called (cf. par. 18, 42).

---

[98] Ibid., 95, 96.

[99] I am using the text of 'Rerum Novarum' found in William J. Gibbons, S. J., ed., *Seven Great Encyclicals* (Glen Rock, NJ: Paulist Press, 1963).

[100] See James W. Skillen, ed. *The Problem of Poverty* (English tr. Of Abraham Kuyper, *Het Sociale Vraagstuk en de Christelijke Religie* (Amsterdam: J. A. Wormser, 1891), Grand Rapids: Baker Book House, 1991.

Hence we see that both Roman Catholic and Calvinist leaders of the late nineteenth century offered serious alternatives to Enlightenment statism. In this early third millennium, various forms of the Enlightenment program hold the vast majority of political power, East and West, with relatively little thought given (even by the churches) to either the teaching of Leo XIII or Kuyper. But as Christianity continues to grow at exponential rates in much of 'the South' (i.e. Africa, South America and East Asia),[101] this teaching may be once again taken seriously by multitudes of both Protestants and Catholics, whose sheer numbers may make them impossible to ignore.

A denial of revelation and its replacement with criticism

Peter Gay summarizes the arguments of Voltaire's *Dictionnaire philosophique*, where – following the arguments of earlier English and French deists – he holds that

> ...The Old and New Testaments are alike a collection of childish absurdities and irreconcilable contradictions – hence the prophecies of the Jews and the claims of the Apostles are either primitive allegories or manifest deceptions. The morality of the 'Chosen People', exemplified by the conduct of King David, is abhorrent, and the history of the Church is a sanguinary compilation of stupid wrangles ending in civil war and mass murder – hence the fathers of Christianity, and Christians through history, are with their conduct conclusive arguments against the Christian religion. Revealed religion is an infectious disease: 'Fanaticism is to superstition what delirium is to fever and rage to anger' [article on 'Fanaticism', I, 267]. The infection inevitably leads to virulent manifestations: 'The superstitious man is ruled by the fanatic, and turns into one' [article on 'Superstition', II, 475]. And Voltaire defines superstition broadly: 'Almost everything that goes beyond the worship of a supreme Being, and the submission of one's heart to his eternal commands, is superstition' [Ibid., 473]. And that 'almost' was a last concession to prudence.[102]

Paul Hazard shows how crucial it was to the program of the Enlightenment to negate the authority of Holy Scripture: 'How could the Holy Scripture have been spared? Since it represented the supreme authority, it was logical that when one came to examine it, one would criticize it. When they could show that it contradicted itself, the libertines rejoiced.'[103]

Enlightenment hostility to divine revelation

David Hume held the same antipathy to revelation. As Gay notes: '"There is only one relation to revealed truth: believing it" – thus Kierkegaard epitomized in one striking sentence the essential characteristic of the Christian, and many centuries of apologetic effort. For Hume, of course, the appropriate reaction to what passed for revealed truth was not believing it, and his own critical task was to find the reasons why it was unbelievable.'[104]

---

[101]Cf. Phillip Jenkins, *The Next Christendom: The Coming of Global Christianity* (Oxford: Oxford University Press, 2002).

[102]Peter Gay, op. cit., I, 396.

[103]Paul Hazard, op. cit., 171.

[104]Ibid., 404.

Certainly two of the greatest minds of the Enlightenment, Isaac Newton and John Locke, accepted in some measure the validity of divine revelation. In his *Paraphrases*, Locke actually states that revelation is superior to reason.[105] Yet when it comes to describing the real world of humanity, Locke obviously feels free to deny major points of revelation, as for instance its teaching on original sin. Isaac Newton similarly holds to the truth of prophecy, and spent much effort, for instance, trying to understand the prophecies of Daniel. Yet he freely denied the scriptural teaching on the incarnate deity of Christ and on God's independence from and constant interaction with the world. We cannot doubt their sincere belief in certain aspects of divine revelation, but they interpreted it in the context of the human right to criticize, ignore or reverse its most crucial teachings; especially on the relationship of God, man and the world. Most of the Enlightenment, however, would have a far less respectful approach to divine revelation, and would be more consistently hostile to all aspects of it, and indeed to the very possibility of it, as we have seen in Voltaire.

Paul Hazard devotes an entire chapter to tracing the powerful influence of Richard Simon on Biblical exegesis.[106] He introduces the skeptical theories of what came to be known as 'Higher Criticism': *a priori* assumptions which, if accepted as valid scholarship, undercut the inspiration and authority of Holy Scripture. Hazard quotes Baron de Lahontan, who as early as 1703 reported the influence of the 'Higher Criticism' on the European masses:

> What a treasure was [Simon's 'Higher Criticism'] for the unbelievers! They are not able to examine the sacred texts for themselves, but they are disposed to believe anything that would undercut their authority. And they enthusiastically say: 'How would you think that I could accept the sincerity of these Bibles, written so many centuries ago, translated out of many languages by ignorant persons who had no conception of their true meaning, or by liars who may have changed them by adding to or taking away the words which are found in them today?'[107]

The great Italian philosopher of modern atheism, Augusto Del Noce, believes that the root cause of hostility of the Enlightenment (and its contemporary heirs) to the very possibility of divine revelation is owing to their aversion to absolute truth, which holds them back from the kind of societal progress they so desire. He writes:

> From this point of view, [humanistic] progress can make progress if we desire, that is, if the advance of science and its applications is not impeded by forces hostile to the rationalisation of the world. In practice, if it is not held back by the resentment of classes which are opposed to the movement of history; decadent classes who, not unexpectedly, speak in the name of absolute truths.[108]

---

[105]Locke, *Paraphrases*, op. cit., 32.

[106]Paul Hazard, op. cit., Part II, chapter III (pp. 171-86).

[107]Baron de Lahontan, *Dialogues curieux*, 1703, p. 163, de l' ed. G. Chinard, quoted by Hazard, op. cit., 186.

[108]Augusto Del Noce, *L'Irréligion Occidentale* (Paris: FAC-editions, 1995), 263.

Elsewhere, Del Noce showed how Marxism (a bastard heir of the Enlightenment) had carried out its work on this basis:

> Does not the Marxist critique of ideologies repose on the principle according to which everything which surpasses immediate verification, everything which in sum is metaphysical, is explained as the expression of the historico-social situation of a group, thus by means of the sensible, since this which considers itself to confer the maximum extension, winds up enclosing the entire human world itself? Does not Marxism claim that it is a conception of thought, an expression and instrument of it, precisely the opposite of every metaphysical form of thinking?[109]

In other words, Marxism is the *replacement* of the Christian metaphysic by a materialist one. The thought of the Enlightenment prepared the way for this substitution.

With this denial of the absolute truths of divine revelation (both general and special), came its replacement:

The absolute authority of human criticism of reality

The Enlightenment is particularly marked by its spirit of criticism of the received authority statements of Christianity above all else. It functionally replaces the absolute truths of divine revelation by the absolute authority of the critical capacities of the human mind. This critical spirit characterized the Enlightenment from the beginning to the present day. Its fountainhead was Descartes (1596–1650), the inventor of co-ordinate geometry, and prime author of the spirit of doubt and criticism.

In his famous *Discourse on Method* (1637), Descartes speaks of how he determined 'never to accept anything for true which I did not clearly know to be such.'[110] He sought to model his method of obtaining truth on mathematics and upon reliable thought based on the workings of his own mind. That is, rather than taking an empirical approach (which looks at the specifics of reality), which he held to be too unreliable, he took a rationalist approach, and sought to discern truth by 'clear and distinct ideas' found in his mind. Thus, his own consciousness becomes the measure of truth.

But as Wittgenstein argued in his later writings, to have ideas in one's own mind and to formulate them in language assumes that one has been brought up as part of a speaking community with particular customs and shared grammatical practices: 'And hence also "obeying a rule" is a practice. And to *think* one is obeying a rule is not to obey a rule. Hence it is not possible to obey a rule "privately": otherwise thinking one was obeying a rule would be the same thing as obeying it.'[111] This raises severe problems with the theory of Descartes of an isolated, self-derived 'private knowledge' and 'private language' that are the source of 'clear and distinct ideas', supposedly superior to and apart from the historical teachings of the

---

[109]A. Del Noce, *L'Epoque de la Sécularisation*, with preface by Bernard Dumont and translation by Philippe Baillet (Paris: Editions des Syrtes, 2001), 127, 128.

[110]*Discourse*, Part ii, p. 15.

[111]Ludwig Wittgenstein, *Philosophical Investigations*, translated by G. E. M. Anscombe (Oxford: Blackwell Publishing, 2001), section 202 (p. 69).

community in which he had been reared. Indeed, the very words Descartes had to use to express his 'clear and distinct ideas' were dependent for their meaning on the general usage of the language of his community, and were not independent from it.[112] And that historical community certainly involved the teachings of the Catholic Church.

Descartes, unlike later *philosophes*, did not, in general, directly attack Christian doctrine, but rather offered an approach to truth which would be followed by others to dethrone divine revelation and God Himself, and replace them by the autonomous reasoning of man.[113] From that point of view, some of the Cambridge Platonists (More and Cudworth), who had first followed Descartes, later denounced his philosophy '...as an invitation to godless atheism'.[114] Voltaire wrote that Descartes prepared the way for atheism: 'I have known many persons whom Cartesianism has led to admit no God other than the immensity of things.'[115] In Descartes' own lifetime, the Reformed theologian of Holland, Gisbertius Voetius (1589–1687), carried on a hot debate with him, accusing him of a philosophy that would lead to atheism.[116] Voetius stated that 'doubt can never and in no way be the right method for finding the truth.'[117]

Ernst Bizer summarizes the large writing of Voetius against Descartes (quoting from Voetius' *Disputationes Selectae*).[118] Particularly as to Voetius' charge of atheism against the Cartesians, Bizer notes:

> In other respects, also, the new method [i.e. Cartesianism] offers a great deal that is offensive to orthodox understanding. The way of doubt in itself is sinful, because even when it is meant to be only experimental it intends to put man in a state of unbelief. The summons to doubt is a manifest summons to disobedience against the first commandment, and therefore a further, direct contradiction of the holy Spirit.[119] Man thereby runs the danger of not finding his way back to knowledge, the more so as the way to it is admittedly difficult in the first place. The assertion that seekers of truth must pass through the state of doubt for the sake of truth is to be rejected, because one is not supposed to do evil in order to attain to the good.[120] The

---

[112]Ibid., section 43. See also Anthony Kenny, *Wittgenstein* (London: Penguin Books, 1975), and O. R. Jones (ed.), *The Private Language Argument* (London: Macmillan, 1971).

[113]Descartes claims that he did not submit theology to his method of analytical geometry so as not to impair revealed truths: *Discourse on Method*, Part II, (Everyman Edition) 7f. But it would not be long before his method did in fact exclude the truths of revelation.

[114]P. Gay, op. cit., II, 147.

[115]Voltaire, *Eléments de la Philosophie de Newton*, in *Oeuvres*, XXII, 404.

[116]See Voetius, *Selectae Disputationes Theologicae* (Utrecht, 1648-1669).

[117]Quoted in Heinrich Heppe, *Die Dogmatik der evangelisch-reformierten Kirche*, edited by Ernst Bizer, second edition (Neukirchen: Neukirchener Verlag, 1958), lxiii.

[118]Ernst Bizer, 'Reformed Orthodoxy and Cartesianism', translated by Chalmers MacCormick in Rudolf Bultmann et al., *Translating Theology into the Modern Age*, vol. two of 'Journal for Theology and Church', Robert W. Funk and Gerhard Ebeling, eds. (New York: Harper & Row, 1965).

[119]Bizer refers to Voetius's *Disputationes Selectae*: 'Atqui homo adultus non potest absque peccato vel ad momentum esse in statu *agnosias* Dei et cultus divini, hoc est in statu atheismi; non potest veritatem detinere in iniustitia, no potest dubitationibus suis aut affectata purae negationis ignorantia communes notiones de Deo et rebus divinis inducere aut obfuscare. Vera Dei cognitio primo decalogi praecepto nobis praescribitur, ut docent communiter omnes interpretes. Et quis ille vermis qui obloquatur Spiritui Sancto?' in ibid., 176.

[120]Bizer quotes ibid. (p. 179): 'Atqui talis affectation ignorantiae et sequestration omnis cognitionis et oblivio veritatis, quam diximus est malum, peccatum *sc.* Contra primum decalogi praeceptum et

> onset of a new hermeneutic is likewise rejected: those 'who are suspicious of the authority of Holy Scripture because they find in it many things which do not suit their carnal mind, and who so little esteem the Mosaic and Scriptural physics, which after all is dictated by the Holy Spirit, that they prefer their own theories of the world and of the nature of things,' render themselves suspect. 'They dispute the divinity of Scripture, accuse *implicite* the Holy Spirit of stupidity, and thereby further atheism.'[121]

But as Bizer notes: 'One can understand Descartes' agitation over the defamatory charge…'[122] And Bizer defends Cartesianism against the fierce attack of the orthodox scholastic, Voetius:

> The charge of scepticism against Cartesianism is unjustified not only on formal grounds; it fails to recognize the optimism regarding knowledge which is integral to this philosophy. It confuses methodological with sceptical doubt, and has no feeling for the fact that this doubt has broken in upon the age with a kind of elementary force, so that the customary procedures could no longer be effective against it.[123]

I would answer that although Voetius may have been fierce against Descartes, and may have certainly evaluated his teaching in a very negative light, yet he did correctly see that the underlying attitude which starts with human doubt, rather than Holy Scripture, means that philosophy, theology and life itself have been put on a very different basis than the 1500-year-old Christian tradition had inculcated. And I would say that Voetius *did* understand that his age had been 'broken in upon by doubt as a kind of elementary force'. That sense of widespread intellectual change with its threat to Christianity helps explain the vehemence of Voetius' reaction against it, and his determination to cut down to the roots of the problem (whether or not his approach was widely accepted).

It was not only the conservative Calvinist, Voetius, who warned against the tendency of Cartesianism to erode the basis of Christianity. Some traditional Roman Catholic scholars and some English Unitarians (generally hiding as Anglicans) also did so. Someone wrote from the traditional Catholic viewpoint: '… But let a little time pass: and you will see just how far the effects of Cartesian thought will go: "You would be quite astonished if Descartes were now to come back to this world. I think that you would find him to be the greatest enemy of Christianity."'[124]

---

contra John 17:3, Phil. 1: 9f., Prov. 4: 5, 23f. Videntur hi hominess similes illi fatuo philosopho, qui amore sapientiae oculos sibi eruebat, ut tanto liberius philosophari posset. Sensus enim exterenos abnegant et in impietatis abysso versari eos proclamant, qui ad cognitionem Dei sensum auxilio utuntur. Insuper lumen internum principiorum naturalium ad tempus extinguere conantur, ut *sc.* Lumen affectatae et admirandae suae cognitionis accendant. In utroque tacite accusare mihi videntur Spiritum Sanctum Rom. 1: 19f., 2 Thess. 1:8; James 2:19.

[121]Bizer quotes ibid. (p. 177): 'qui Scripturae autoritatem suspectam habent propter nonnulla, quae ibi occurrent carnali ipsorum sensui minime congruentia, … qui physicam Mosaicam et scripturariam a Spiritu Sancto dictatam tam parvi faciunt, ut suos conceptus de universo et rerum natura illi longe praeferre videantur … quique pseudographematis in probatione Deitatis tacite insimulant et sic manus atheorum atque infidelium confirmant.'

[122]Bizer, art. cit., 35.

[123]Bizer, art. cit., 38.

[124]Paul Hazard, *La Crise de la Conscience européenne*, 129.

The close friend of Sir Isaac Newton (and like him, a tacit Unitarian, though remaining in the established Church of England), Dr. Samuel Clarke, stated in his 1704 Boyle lectures that Cartesianism leads to atheism.[125] The criticism of Descartes by the Jansenist scholar, Antoine Arnauld, is very different in spirit from the previous opponents, for Arnauld accepts the genuine piety of Descartes.[126] Yet at the same time, he sees the potentially destructive fallacies of Descartes' methodology.

In a restrained and careful, but incisive fashion, Arnauld critiques the critical methodology of one who undertook the criticism of the entire Western, Christian tradition. Rather than condemning Descartes 'en masse', he penetrates to the heart of his philosophical assumptions (in his 'Objections,' dans une 'Lettre de M. Arnauld au R. P. Mersenne').[127] He notes that in his proof of God (as in his 'Sixth Meditation'), Descartes thinks that a *formal* distinction rather than a *real* one is sufficient to establish his points (that is, one assumes that what one formulates in the mind does not need external, objective reference for its establishment).[128] Arnauld then shows that to claim that an idea is 'clear and distinct' to one's mind does *not* constitute an objective proof of it.[129] Indeed, he suggests that Descartes' proof of God by means of his clear and distinct ideas is in fact 'arguing in a circle.'[130] And finally, he shows the deleterious, and ultimately impossible procedure of establishing one's philosophy by doubting all things.[131]

Methodological doubt not the same as true scientific questioning

Descartes starts his philosophical program with methodological doubt. That is, he can only be certain of himself, and needs to doubt everything else, until it is proven by 'clear and distinct' ideas properly utilized by his own mind. T. F. Torrance has shown how this methodology of doubt is the opposite of modern science:

> Scientific questioning is not the same thing as *doubt*. Doubt rests upon a form of self-certainty, whereas scientific questioning rests upon the certainty of the object before which we are open to question in ourselves. That is very apparent in the programme of Descartes where the dualism already posited in the Platonic method of inquiry becomes so extreme in the division between the ego and the world, mind and matter, that the halting of sophisticated doubt upon self-certainty (*cogito, ergo sum*), makes self-certainty the starting point and basis for methodological doubt. That is the very reverse of scientific procedure. There is always a deep-seated element of false subjectivity in doubt, so that doubting questions are fundamentally unreal for they are posed in self-isolation from the object, whereas scientific questions are

[125]Alexandre Koyré, *Du monde clos à l'univers infini* (Paris: Gallimard: Presses universitaries de France, 1973), 279.

[126]*Oeuvres philosophiques D'Antoine Arnauld*, par M. Jules Simon (Paris: Charpentier, 1843), 24.

[127]Found in ibid., 3-24.

[128]Ibid., 7.

[129]Ibid.

[130]Ibid., 20.

[131]Ibid., 21.

directed toward objectivity in which we open ourselves up to face whatever the object may disclose to us.[132]

Mechanistic view of the world

Underlying Descartes' methodological doubt was an axiomatic disjunction between God and the world, which became integral to the Enlightenment, even as it had been part and parcel of Platonism in a somewhat different way. This gave rise to the mechanistic view of the world, which of course excluded God and His revelation:

> If man is considered only as 'thinking thing' poised upon himself over against the world out there (*res cogitans* over against *res extensa*), then the world can be brought within the knowledge of the detached subject only through determining phenomena... Thus the 'world' is that which is constructed out of the states of man's consciousness...It was of course this way of thinking that gave rise to the mechanistic view of the universe within which man has found his personal existence threatened through the tyranny of rigid, impersonal concepts, but that result was implied in the assumptions of its starting point.
>
> It is evident that a Cartesian, observationalist and abstractive way of thought inevitably detaches any thought of God from the world...so that on this model of thought we cannot arrive at, or we inevitably exclude from our thought, any idea of God as interacting with the world and interacting with man in his personal and historical existence.[133]

Colin Gunton has helpfully contrasted the Cartesian (and Enlightenment) starting point with that of traditional Christianity at this point:

> Augustine had taught that 'unless you believe you will not understand', a view that was both developed and criticised by different thinkers in the centuries after him. In the Enlightenment, it was reversed. 'If you believe you will not understand' has some claim to represent one of its chief mottoes. The Enlightenment was right to attack credulity and superstition. But in the process it produced a view of the human mind that falsified its relation to the world, especially in suggesting that there could be attained an absolute objectivity and impartiality: a God's-eye-view, so to speak.[134]

Polanyi: doubt is not the way modern science works

Yet this is not the way modern science has progressed, as Michael Polanyi has pointed out:

> We must now recognize belief once more as the source of all knowledge. Tacit assent and intellectual passions, the sharing of an idiom and of a cultural heritage, affiliation to a like-minded community: such are the impulses

---

[132]Torrance, *Theological Science*, 122, 123. Torrance refers to Michael Polanyi, *Science, Faith, and Society*, p. 62, 'where he shows that complete methodological doubt would destroy all belief in natural science and lead to metaphysical nihilism.' Cartesian skepticism as a scientific method had already been brilliantly examined and refuted by Bolzano, *Wissenschaftslehre*, 1, sections 34-44, and *Lehrbuch der Religionswissenschaft*, 1, section 62. See the analysis of his argument by H. Scholz, *Mathesis Universalis*, pp. 236 ff (Quoted in Torrance, op. cit., 122).

[133]Torrance, *Reality and Scientific Theology*, 57.

[134]Colin Gunton, *Enlightenment & Alienation: An Essay towards a Trinitarian Theology* (Grand Rapids: Wm. B. Eerdmans, 1985), 3, 4.

> which shape our vision of the nature of things on which we can rely for our mastery of things. No intelligence, however critical or original, can operate outside such a fiduciary framework.[135]

As we have already seen, Descartes was strongly critiqued and in major respects surpassed within the Enlightenment itself. That is, Newton, Locke, Voltaire, Hume and others did not accept his rationalistic idealism, but worked within a framework closer to empiricism. Newton, for instance, believed in looking at facts rather than hypotheses; as he famously said in his motto: 'hypotheses non fingo.'[136] And later, David Hume wrote: 'When we run over libraries, persuaded of these principles [i.e. metaphysics], what havoc must we make? If we take in our hand any volume; of divinity or school metaphysics, for instance; let us ask, *Does it contain any abstract reasoning concerning quantity or number?* No. *Does it contain any experimental reasoning concerning matters of fact and existence?* No. Commit it then to the flames: For it can contain nothing but sophistry and illusion.'[137]

Continuing influence of the dualistic disjunction in Western thought

Yet while rejecting Descartes' theory of 'innate ideas' with its world-building system of idealistic rationalism, the Enlightenment never left his assumption of a dualist disjunction between God and the world; between subject and object. They, in their own rather different way, continued to exercise his right to doubt and criticize everything except man's self. Thus, many (including Hume) gladly followed the seventeenth-century French, ex-Huguenot, rationalist, Pierre Bayle, whose *Dictionnaire historique et critique* (1697) was based on the method of doubt and criticism – particularly of religious authorities.

Gibbon said of Bayle:

> … In reviewing the controversies of the times, he turned against each other the arguments of the disputants; successively wielding the arms of the Catholics and Protestants, he proves that neither the say of authority nor the say of examination can afford the multitude any test of religious truth; and dexterously concludes that custom and education must be the sole grounds of popular belief. The ancient paradox of Plutarch, that atheism is less pernicious than superstition, acquires a tenfold vigour when it is adorned with the colours of his wit, and pointed with the acuteness of his logic. His critical dictionary is a vast repository of facts and opinions; and he balances the *false* religion in his sceptical scales, till the opposite quantities (if I may use the language of algebra) annihilate each other.[138]

---

[135]Michael Polanyi, *Personal Knowledge. Towards a Post-Critical Philosophy* (London: Routledge and Kegan Paul, 1962), 266. See T. F. Torrance's discussion of Polanyi's work on the fiduciary framework of science in *Christian Theology & Scientific Culture* (New York: Oxford University Press, 1981), 62-72, and also in *Transformation & Convergence in the Frame of Knowledge*, Chapter 3: 'The Place of Michael Polanyi in the Modern Philosophy of Science.'

[136]Isaac Newton, *Principia Mathematica*, edited by F. Cajori (Berkeley & Los Angeles: University of California, 1966 reprint), vol. 2, 547, 'The General Scholium'.

[137]David Hume, *Enquiry Concerning Human Understanding*, 135.

[138]Edward Gibbon, *Autobiography*, (London: J. Murray, 1897), 89.

And the atheistic philosophe, Baron Holbach, spoke of Bayle as the celebrated man 'who teaches so well how to doubt.'[139] Thus, the universal authority of the critical human spirit continued its sway, and in so doing sought to excise all testimony to God and His moral law in creation and conscience. Throughout the various stages of the Enlightenment, it would continue to be assumed that this critical human spirit is not disabled by the fall of Adam from reasoning properly concerning God and His revelation in creation and in Scripture.

No doubt, the philosophy of Immanuel Kant represented the most effective means of criticism of God and divine revelation, by placing the organizing forms of making sense of phenomenal reality within the categories of the human mind. But we must postpone discussion of this 'critical triumph' until a later chapter.

Denial of man's fall and the noetic effects of sin

John Calvin, sixteenth-century Reformer, noted that the fall of Adam entailed the darkening and skewing of man's mind, so that humans could not and would not properly interpret God's revelation in conscience, creation and Scripture. Thus, corrective 'spectacles' were needed in order to understand aright, and these were provided in the Holy Scriptures.[140] What St. Thomas Aquinas had taught in the thirteenth century was not dissimilar to this, for he spoke of Adam's fall as 'the wounding of nature' with negative effects upon the human understanding (i.e. 'the wound of ignorance').[141] That is, the effects of sin in biasing the human mind was the traditional understanding of all orthodox Christian anthropology.

The Enlightenment, however, was characterized throughout by its denial of the effects of sin upon the powers of man's mind. Peter Gay summarizes their attitude: 'The philosophy of the Enlightenment insisted on man's essential autonomy: man is responsible to himself, to his own rational interests, to his self-development, and, by an inescapable extension, to the welfare of his fellow man. For the *philosophes*, man was not a sinner, at least not by nature; human nature – and this argument was subversive, in fact revolutionary, in their day – is by origin good, or at least neutral.'[142]

Arnaud-Aaron Upinsky with much insight noted that by the late seventeenth century in Europe, '… the noble savage – this model of the first man – was imagined by the philosophers in order to replace Adam and Eve …'[143] Upinsky goes on to quote Paul Hazard:

> As the old cartographers drew plants, animals and men upon the continents, so we notice the place and the importance of the noble savage upon the intellectual map of the world. Not that he was new, but that during the time we are studying [the turn of the seventeenth to the eighteenth century],

---

[139]Holbach, *Système de la nature*, (Amsterdam: S.N., 1770), II, 356 n.

[140]John Calvin, *Institutes of the Christian Religion*, I.vi.1.

[141]Thomas Aquinas, *Summa Theologiae*, 1a2ae. 85, 3.

[142]Peter Gay, op. cit., II, 398.

[143]Arnaud-Aaron Upinsky, *La Tête Coupée: Le Secret du pouvoir*, 53.

between one century and the other, he took on his definitive form and became aggressive.[144]

Descartes: 'Augustinianism without a soul'

Commenting on Del Noce's analysis of Descartes' denial of original sin in his idealistic system, Danilo Castellano quotes Del Noce as considering Cartesianism to be 'an Augustinianism, reworked by means of a necessity of philosophical essences, but fixed under the form of a thought which is in radical and unreconcilable conflict with Thomism.'[145] Castellano adds: 'In Descartes, Del Noce sees a thinker who reworked the theme of subjectivity, but in doing so mutilated it away from its fundamental aspect, the dogma of original sin: St. Augustine affirmed subjectivity, but Descartes tore it out of its context in the antipelagian controversy. Thus Cartesianism became a sort of Augustinianism without soul.'[146]

Much as later Enlightenment figures such as John Locke rejected Descartes' theory of innate ideas and idealistic rationalism, they continued his rejection of original sin. According to J. A. Passmore, 'The crucial importance of Locke's *Some Thoughts Concerning Education* lies not so much in its rejection of innate ideas as in its rejection of original sin.'[147] Rousseau spoke for many when he uttered the famous lines: 'Man is born free, and everywhere he is in chains.'[148] In other words, there is no original sin; man's problem is society. As Diderot explained to his mistress: 'No, dear friend, nature has not made us evil; it is bad education, bad models, bad legislation that corrupt us.'[149]

No sin: no need of grace

Thus, fallen humanity's need of the grace of God and the enlightenment of the Holy Spirit were roundly denied in the interests of man's saving himself and perfecting his society, unaided or untrammelled by any divinity. To that end, it was necessary to deny the witness of human conscience within and the created order without, and above all, it was necessary to deny the very possibility of divine revelation in Scripture, if man were to be free to pursue the Enlightenment program of replacing God with man.

That is why Augusto Del Noce in his *Il Problema dell' ateismo* saw the origins of Enlightenment thought (which in this sense continue to control modern secular theory) as coming from a denial of man's original fall.[150] This necessitated a strong rejection of Christianity, and particularly of any true revelation. Danilo Castellano comments on this central thesis of Del Noce:

---

[144]Paul Hazard, *La crise de la conscience européenne, 1680-1715* (Paris: Fayard, 1961), 12.

[145]Del Noce, *Reforma cattolica e filosofia moderna* (Bologne: Il Mulino, 1965), p. x; quoted in *L'irréligion occidentale*, 15.

[146]*Augusto Del Noce: L'Irréligion Occidentale* (Paris: FAC-éditions, 1995), 15.

[147]J. A. Passmore, 'The Malleability of Man in Eighteenth-Century Thought,' in Earl R. Wasserman ed.: *Aspects of the Eighteenth Century* (1965), 22, quoted in Peter Gay, op. cit., II, 511.

[148]J.-J. Rousseau, *Contrat Social* in *Oeuvres*, III, 351.

[149]Diderot to Sophie Volland (November 2 to 6 or 8, 1760), *Correspondence*, III, 226, quoted in Peter Gay, op. cit., II, 170.

[150]Augusto Del Noce, *Il Problema dell' ateismo*, 65, 89.

> Modern philosophy is characterized by *separation*, which in reality is *opposition* to theology and thus to Revelation. Stated in other words, it has been a thought *against* Christianity...[Thus] 'modern philosophy' is characterized by its atheism or radical immanence...[151]

So the antipathy of the Enlightenment to divine revelation seems not to lie so much in the difficulties of revelation, but in its very possibility, as a transcendent threat to and humiliation of human independence and glory. Jean Brun traces how this antipathy to divine revelation had developed on the European intellectual scene by the late seventeenth and early eighteenth centuries:

> The reading of 'the Book of Nature' was founded upon human reason, which was glorified by Cartesianism, and upon experience, which was put in first place by anglo-saxon empiricism. Thus, it was increasingly thought that because of the resources of 'natural light' one no longer needed recourse to the revelation in Scripture, so that the world would become self-explanatory for those who would be capable of interpreting scientifically what it was saying...
>
> This cult of reason and of experience carried on in the new ideal that man was perfectible and that history may and should open the way for progress. From there came the conviction that sin does not inexorably mark the human condition, but that man is capable himself of *doing good*; this *doing good* would allow everyone to be assured a life where pleasure would be substituted for contrition...[152]

Denial of the fall necessary for the creation of a humanist paradise

Del Noce states it clearly: 'The ultimate achievement of rationalism, that is, atheism, demonstrates the choice which underlies it: that is, the refusal of *status naturae lapsae* which constitutes the first stage of the rejection of all transcendence in any vertical sense.'[153] Hence, man hopes to be left in his own secular paradise, undisturbed by the transcendent voices of revelation in nature and Scripture. But this unfallen nature of humanity is, as Del Noce frequently points out, 'a postulate without any proof', and one that cannot make sense of the world or the human condition.[154] Del Noce traces relentlessly the tragic consequences of this denial of the Fall and of divine revelation in the failed Marxism of the East and in the continuing technological dehumanization of mankind in the opulent West. He notes that the opulent society of the West finally reduces man to an animal:

> When one makes the goal of society 'well-being', philosophy as such must be abolished. What remains is science...Out of that, one finds once again a new life from the worst rubbish of the end of the 19th century, the myth of Science and that of Evolution. In effect, that Science, or better, modern Science, which

[151]D. Castellano, 'Introduction' to A. Del Noce, *L'Irréligion occidentale*, op. cit., 13,14, n.14.

[152]Jean Brun, *L'Europe philosophe*, 212.

[153]A. Del Noce, *L'Epoque de la Sécularisation*, op. cit., 23.

[154]Del Noce, ibid.: 'In the absence of a direct proof, atheism can only present itself as the result of an irreversible historical process, understood as the process of secularization...'

> can only study man as an animal...the *qualitative* difference between man and animal are necessarily lost... Furthermore, the society of well-being is intrinsically *totalitarian*, in the sense that culture is completely submerged in politics...The process of the abolition of the sacred is a constituent of the opulent society.[155]

Similarly, Arnaud-Aaron Upinsky interprets much of the thought leading up to the French Revolution as an abolition of the sacred in order to replace it with human happiness in this world. He shows an important *change of language* in the French Revolutionary vocabulary:

> But to invert the mind and the senses requires substituting the search for *bourgeois happiness* in place of the *medieval quest for salvation*. And *happiness* in the revolutionary language would take the place formerly held by *paradise* in Christian language. Even Saint-Just would proclaim in the midst of the (French Revolutionary) Reign of Terror that 'Happiness is a new idea in Europe'.[156]

It would take over a century for the somewhat inchoate atheism lying behind the French Revolution to become a 'clear and distinct' controlling idea; a legislated foundational principle of an even larger revolution: the Marxist take-over of Russia in 1917. Speaking of the atheism of Karl Marx, James Billington contrasts it to Hegel, who in so many ways shaped Marx:

> Whereas Hegel had identified God with the totality of history, his [*sc*. Marx] followers took God totally out of it. In a sense, Hegel had prepared the way by placing philosophy above religion, and by subordinating all Gods to his own concept of an all-controlling 'world spirit.' Contemporaries viewed this as tantamount to atheism...
>
> Feuerbach prepared the way for revolutionary atheism by inverting the Hegelian belief that God created man out of his spiritual need to overcome divine alienation. Feuerbach suggested that, on the contrary, man had created God out of *his* material need to overcome human alienation. To Marx, this suggested that alienation was to be solved not by spiritual, but by material forces. Both the source and the cure lay in political economy...[157]

The victory of the Enlightenment in the twentieth century

If Del Noce is right, the Enlightenment, with its evacuation of transcendence, did not reach its full force in the West until after World War II. He writes:

> But why did this choice [i.e. between religious revival and radical atheism] have to be made *after* Hitler? For older people, the end of fascism should have been a sort of waking up after a terrible nightmare; after the 'parenthesis', they should have found again the path marked by the 'religion of liberty' of the 19th century. For the youth, the issue was to follow the phenomenon of the Resistance [i.e. to the Nazi occupation of World War II France], to the point of digging down to the ultimate roots of Nazism and to tearing them out. The spirit of the Resistance thus rested upon a confidence in an admirable mechanism by means of which utilisation of force in the sphere of human

---

[155]Del Noce, op. cit., 49, 51, 52, 55.

[156]Arnaud-Aaron Upinsky, *La Tête coupée: Le Secret du pouvoir*, 298.

[157]James H. Billington, *Fire in the Minds of Men: Origins of the Revolutionary Faith* (New York: Basic Books, Inc., 1980), 268.

> action should automatically produce justice; it in fact acquired the same error with which Simone Weil reproached Marxism and economic Liberalism. Moreover, the equation between value and the spirit of modernity, in sum, the acceptance of the spirit of the Enlightenment, was favoured by the ideology of the coalition of forces against Nazism, which necessarily had to be adopted…One could not find another name for this value than 'democracy', and since among the forces of the Resistance there was also ranged the USSR and communism – certainly difficult to include under the normal meaning of democracy – it was necessary to add the term 'progress.' From that point of view, it became almost inevitable to move from an insistence on the political value of democracy to a 'spirit of democracy' elevated to the rank of myth, and which would have to be introduced into all human activities in order radically to reform them…the issue between totalitarian Marxism and totalitarian Nazism represented the two faces of the political drama of Germany, in the moment when this drama encountered reality.[158]

Widespread atheism in Europe before World War I

Bernardino Casadei comments on this analysis of Del Noce that the confusion that led to World War I was directly related to the problem of widespread atheism in Western Europe, under the influence of the Enlightenment.[159] He explains:

> Once the insufficiency of the resistance offered by Kantian morality to the [totally humanist] sociologisms demonstrated their ancillary character and the inevitable nihilist development of every philosophy founded on human reason alone, only a new ethic founded on a truth, no longer in any sense revealed, in which man could participate, but created by man himself; this alone could save humanity. In place of the Totality which is not of this world, celebrated by Catholicism, it became convenient to substitute another reality which is of terrestrial origin…This process made its appearance at the beginning of the 20th century…[160]

But now at the beginning of the twenty-first century, Nazism is happily long gone, and Marxism was largely surpassed by 1989, apart from China. Marxism with its centralist state planning was economically inefficient, and the economically freer West outstripped it, partly by forcing the Soviet Union to go bankrupt as it spent billions attempting to catch up with the missile defence system of the United States developed in the 1980s; not to mention the powerfully effective anti-communist leaders of the 1980s and 1990s: Pope John Paul II, Prime Minister Margaret Thatcher of Great Britain, and U. S. President Ronald Reagan, in addition to the literary and personal witness of Russian writer, Alexander Solzhenitsyn, and others, as well as the sufferings and prayers of the persecuted Church in the East.

Triumphant capitalism denies the Transcendent

Yet, even in the triumphant West, the Enlightenment heritage of denial of the Transcendent (including divine revelation, whether in creation or Scripture) with its gathering of values from humanity alone, lives on.

---

158 A. Del Noce, *L'Epoque de la Sécularisation*, 212, 213, 215.

159 *Del Noce: interprète du 20e siècle* (Paris: Catholica, 2002), 84.

160 Ibid., 85.

One could say that this denial of the Transcendent took two different streams after the 1917 Revolution in Russia: that of Marxism in the East and of materialist debt capitalism in the West. As Solzhenitsyn pointed out, both were descendants of the anthropology of the Renaissance and Enlightenment. After the collapse of Euro-Communism, only materialist debt capitalism remained as an effective force. It powerfully – and effectively – disagreed with the means of organizing society for human happiness, but not with the underlying premise of no transcendence. It is not only the left-wing thinkers, such as Noam Chomsky, who have pointed out the immoralism of the massively influential multinational companies with their sway over many national governments.[161] Those on the right wing, such as the Roman Catholic, Eric Von Kuehnelt-Leddihn,[162] and the Reformed, nineteenth-century Robert L. Dabney,[163] as well as the twentieth century Eugene Rosenstock-Huessy[164] and R. J. Rushdoony,[165] have seen it too. One does not have to agree with either left wing or right wing to perceive deadly serious problems for the entire world in this area.

Bernard Dumont, speaking of the dissipation of the revolutionary spirit in the industrial bureaucracy of today's Western technological society says:

> This society accepts all the negations of Marxism concerning contemplative thought in regard to religion or metaphysics, but it refuses the messianic revolutionism of Marxism; in other words, it rejects the religious aspect of Marxism. Whence it results that the new materialistic society of the West truly represents a pure form of the bourgeois spirit, victorious over its two traditional adversaries: transcendent religion and the Marxist Revolution.[166]

Thus, the original Enlightenment hostility to any transcendent revelation from God continues in the controlling powers of today's world. The form that this hostility to the divine takes in the United States of America has been examined by Claes Ryn in *America the Virtuous*.[167] His chapter on 'Jacobin Capitalism' is particularly apposite here.[168] And the parent form of it was seen, analyzed and denounced by the Virginia Calvinist theologian and political philosopher, Robert L. Dabney in the late nineteenth century.[169]

---

[161]E.g., see his 2004/05 Gifford Lectures at the University of Edinburgh, of which the last was 'Illegal but Legitimate: a dubious doctrine for the times.'

[162]Eric Von Kuehnelt-Leddihn, *Leftism Revisited: From de Sade and Marx to Hitler and Pol Pot* (Washington, DC: Regnery Gateway, 1990).

[163]See Douglas F. Kelly, 'Robert L. Dabney: "The Cassandra of Yankeedom",' a chapter in Joseph A. Pipa and C.N. Willborn, *Confessing Our Hope: Essays in Honor of Morton Howison Smith on His Eightieth Birthday* (Taylors, SC: Southern Presbyterian Press, 2004), or in French: Douglas F. Kelly, 'Robert L. Dabney ou Cassandre chez les Yankees' in *Catholica*, no. 79, Printemps 2003, Bernard Dumont, red. (Paris), 101-113.

[164]Eugene Rosenstock-Huessy, *Out of Revolution* (Norwich: Argo Books, 1969).

[165]E.g., R. J. Rushdoony, *The Politics of Guilt and Pity* (Nutley, NJ: Presbyterian and Reformed Publishing Co., 1970).

[166]Bernard Dumont in *Augusto Del Noce: L'Epoque de la Sécularisation*, Preface, 21.

[167]Claes G. Ryn, *America the Virtuous: The Crisis of Democracy and the Quest for Empire* (New Brunswick and London: Transaction Publications, 2003).

[168]Ibid., ch. 14, 145-54.

[169]See Douglas F. Kelly, 'Robert Lewis Dabney' chapter 2 in *Southern Reformed Theology: Reformed Theology in America*, edited by David F. Wells (Grand Rapids, MI: Baker Book House, 1989), 37-60.

Del Noce: the society of opulence requires atheism

Indeed,

> ...The society of well-being has attained a degree of impiety greater than that of Marxism. Because while rigorously atheistic in denying all revelation and all supernatural, Marxism in its communist version was, in effect, a religion, with the Future replacing Eternity and the Totality substituting for the Absolute and the City of God. Inversely, the society of well-being is the only one in the history of the world which does not draw its origin from a religion, but which was born essentially against a religion; even if the paradox remain that this religion was the Marxist religion (successively, the critique against Transcendence certainly extended to every other form of religion). It is not by accident if the point of view of the intellectuals of the society of well-being can be resumed in the two following affirmations: acceptance of the Death of God and a critical posture towards Marxism in what remained of its religious aspect...History experienced a definitive chasm, represented by the Second World War; not only were Fascism and Nazism vanquished, but along with them the entire ancient tradition of Europe...By virtue of this judgement, anyone who refers to this tradition is always...a 'reactionary' or a 'fascist' (the two terms being foolishly confounded together).[170]

The life-work of Del Noce demonstrated that 'The consumer society served (and serves) to rout communism, but not atheism and materialism. The consummation of consumerism serves permissive capitalism in today's "radical" society, but leads to the total de-humanisation of mankind ... Its relativism makes it impossible to derive valid a priori behaviours and values.'[171] In this opulent society, 'every value is reduced to pure efficacious sensibility. In the society of well-being, men are reduced to a pure economic dimension as simple instruments of an activity which exists for nothing but itself ...' [quoting Franco Rodano, Del Noce adds]: 'the opulent society ... is the society of "empty men": beings who have no more purpose, no more values; the height of salvation can only be [freedom from] material suffering; beings who can only feel themselves alive in the abstract excitement of sex, or in the sudden and unforeseeable ups and downs of a sporadic and vain anarchy.'[172] From that point of view, one can understand why Del Noce proclaimed that it was necessary to oppose the Enlightenment in order to save civilization.[173]

The two greatest and most valuable realities are negated by the Enlightenment

The Lord Jesus Christ summarized the Ten Commandments as 'loving the Lord our God with all our heart...and our neighbour as ourselves' (Matt. 22:37-40). These two heart-felt attitudes and outgoing actions, which together make life worth living, are precisely what are lost by the 'full-fledged Enlightenment'.

---

[170]A. Del Noce in *L'Epoque de la Sécularisation*, 51.

[171]Del Noce, *L'Epoque de la Sécularisation*, 23, 24.

[172]Rodano, 'Il pensiero cattolico di fronte alla societa opulenta', quoted by Del Noce in *L'irréligion occidentale*, 277, 278.

[173]Ibid, 24.

First, commitment to the 'full-fledged Enlightenment'[174] *precludes a love relationship with the Triune God, thus missing the supreme peace and joy of that relationship, a relationship which transforms the self and opens one up to love others.*[175] No one has explained better than Stăniloae why the assumption of a vague, absentee, Unitarian god (not to mention the atheism that usually follows Unitarianism) destroys fullest joy and meaning in human life:

> The revelation of the Trinity, occasioned by the incarnation and earthly activity of the Son, has no other purpose than to draw us after grace, to draw us through the Holy Spirit into the filial relationship the Son has with the Father. The Trinitarian acts of revelation are acts that save and deify, acts that raise us up into communion with the persons of the Holy Trinity ... A unipersonal god would not have within himself that eternal love or communion into which he would wish to introduce us too...In Christ, however, we are saved because in him we have a relationship to God which is at once correct and intimate. We are saved in Christ because in him and from him we possess the fullness of humility; we experience the total warmth of communion and yet are maintained eternally each in his own personal reality...An incarnate god who was not the Son of a Father would not remain as person through relationship with another person equal to himself. The humanity such a god had assumed would sink down within him as into some impersonal abyss and have no share in the love of the Son for the Father ...[176]

Or, to state the same thing in other words, the Westminster Shorter Catechism (written in England in the 1640s) asks in its first question: 'What is the chief end of man?' It wisely answers: 'Man's chief end is to glorify God and to enjoy Him forever.' But with its willful apostasy from the Triune God, the Enlightenment precludes its followers from ever achieving the chief end (or supreme purpose) of their lives.

Secondly, a commitment to the full-fledged Enlightenment empties human life of its personal meaning, and thus keeps us 'from loving our neighbour as ourselves.' Again, we must hear Stăniloae:

> Properly speaking, both pantheism and individualism represent a falling away into nature from the plane of a personal existence which is genuinely spiritual. That is why the passage from individualism to pantheism is an

[174]By the term 'full-fledged Enlightenment', I am making a strong distinction between those hundreds of millions who are influenced by various aspects of the Enlightenment (who are not 'full-fledged') and those who knowingly accept the later phases of Enlightenment commitment to atheism and materialism (a much smaller number, even today). Thus, it is important to note that I am *not* suggesting that all of us (which would include nearly all members of the Christian churches in the Western world) who have been educationally and culturally shaped by strands of Enlightenment assumptions are necessarily not involved in loving God and neighbour. For, some tools of the Enlightenment would remain even under a Christian world view (such as an awareness of historical development; careful sifting of documentary sources, respectful attention to other cultures, and resistance to authoritarianism [but not to valid authority]). Positive contributions of the Enlightenment such as these to Western civilization are, as John Calvin would have said, results of 'the common grace of God.' Such attitudes and practices do not constitute 'full-fledged Enlightenment.' But atheism and resultant materialism (with their hatred of true spiritual authority) do constitute a 'full-fledged' development of Western secularism, which – for the love of God and the love of mankind – must be resisted and in due season replaced.

[175]E.g., see John chapter 17; Romans 5:5; I John 3:1-3, 10-24.

[176]Dumitru Staniloae, *Orthodox Dogmatic Theology: The Experience of God*, 249.

> easy one, for the individual tends to melt down into himself. By themselves, however, persons cannot escape from this falling away into nature; they must have help from the personal – that is to say, Trinitarian – mode of existence which belongs to the transcendent reality, to God. The holy Trinity alone assures our existence as persons.[177]

From a rather different perspective, but one that also shows the danger of the Enlightenment for human well-being, Wolfhart Pannenberg writes:

> … in the cultural tradition which has its roots in the faith of Israel and the thought of Greece, the idea of the unity of humanity is grounded in the concept of the one God. Today, in the process of the secularization of modern culture, the idea of the unity of humanity has been severed from its religious roots. It first remained tied to the one God of natural religion, but finally it became itself the basis of the idea of the unity of religion irrespective of its varying cultural manifestations … The alternative is not polytheistic religion but an atheistic version of the idea of human unity on the basis of our equality by nature. On this view the plurality of gods would simply be the product of human imagination…But is it really possible to establish human unity and equality atheistically? Can we simply presuppose unity and equality as simple facts?[178]

For these two good reasons, therefore, Del Noce is right to have said that the Enlightenment must be opposed and overturned in its dehumanizing aspects by a return to the Holy Trinity and His transcendent revelation of grace and truth to the human race. And that is one of the central themes of this *Systematic Theology*.

So, as our contemporary culture still groans under the influence of the finally atheistic Enlightenment, with its 'abolition of the sacred', there is no one present to speak to mankind transcendentally, whether in conscience, nature or Holy Scripture. In that sense, the later philosophy of the West has gone far beyond the native paganism and false religion (of its own past and of the non-European countries at present). Presumably then, there would be a profound moral difference between wilful philosophical/theological denial of truth one once had and of pagan ignorance, before it received that truth. That issue has been addressed in a previous 'appendix.'[179]

The depressing darkness of 'the Enlightenment' is scattered only by the healing and transforming light of the Triune God, the One Lord who 'dwells in light unapproachable' (I Tim. 6:16). But He is also the LORD who 'by the appearing of our Saviour Jesus Christ…hath abolished death and hath brought life and immortality to light through the gospel…' (2 Tim. 1:10). In light of the Holy Scriptures and the Church tradition, we seek His face in the next chapter.

---

[177]Ibid., 276.
[178]Wolfhart Pannenberg, *Systematic Theology*, Vol. 1, 150,151.
[179]Appendix 2 to Chapter 2.

Chapter Three Appendix One

Testimony of Dostoevsky

Creative personalities, especially artists, poets and novelists, are often more sensitive than most of us in discerning the underlying roots of a culture, and at times see very clearly which way it is going. That was certainly the case with the superb nineteenth-century Russian novelist, Fyodor Dostoevsky. In many remarkable ways, he foresaw what would happen in a Europe which was turning its back in his lifetime on Christianity, in order to follow the secularist Enlightenment with its replacement of the Triune God with either individual man or the central state. Dostoevsky understood – and conveyed in his novels – the profoundly different view of human happiness offered by the Enlightenment from that offered in Christianity. Largely by means of dialogues between his various characters, he shows some of the tragic consequences of rejection of God in order to enthrone self. From that perspective, Dostoevsky's novels are as accurate a commentary on the underlying meaning of the secular Enlightenment as are the official histories of it. More than once, he has been referred to as 'a prophet.'[1]

Here I simply abstract some of his insights in this direction, without any comment, for his dialogues are sufficient to convey their own message.

Dostoevsky, *Demons* translated by Richard Pevear & Larissa Volokhonsky (New York: Vintage Classics: Knopf, 1991)

115 **They shall be as gods: the new man; nihilism; proud and fearless apathy**: "Life is pain, life is fear, and man is unhappy. Now all is pain and fear. Now man loves life because he loves pain and fear. That's how they've made it. Life now is given in exchange for pain and fear, and that is the whole deceit. Man now is not yet the right man. *There will be a new man, happy and proud. He for whom it will make no difference whether he lives or does not live, he will be the new man. He who overcomes pain and fear will himself be God.* And this God will not be."

"So this God exists, in your opinion?"

[1]E.g. see Joseph Frank, *Dostoevsky: The Mantle of the Prophet, 1871-1881* (Princeton and Oxford: Princeton University Press, 2002).

"He doesn't, yet he does. There is no pain in the stone, but there is pain in the fear of the stone. God is the pain of the fear of death. He who overcomes pain and fear will himself become God. Then there will be divided into two parts: from the gorilla to the destruction of God, and from the destruction of God to …"

"To the gorilla?"

"… to the physical changing of the earth and man. Man will change physically. And the world will change, and deeds will change, and thoughts, and all feelings…"

"It makes no difference whether one lives or does not live, then everyone will kill himself, and perhaps that will be the change."

"It makes no difference. They will kill the deceit. Whoever wants the main freedom must dare to kill himself. He who dares to kill himself knows the secret of the deceit. There is no further freedom; here is everything; and there is nothing further. He who dares to kill himself, is God … He who kills himself to kill fear, will at once become God."

238 **Intro to man-god** (vv. God-man): "They're not good, because they don't know they're good…They must find out that they're good, then they'll all become good at once, all, to a man."

"Well, you did find out, so you must be good?"

"I am good."

"With that I agree, incidentally."

"He who teaches that all are good, will end the world."

"He who taught it was crucified."

"He will come, and his name is the man-god."

"The God-man?"

"The man-god—that's the whole difference."

"Can it be you who lights the icon lamp?

"Yes, I lit it… "

"You've become a believer? … but you don't pray yet?"

"I pray to everything …"

"I bet when I come the next time you'll already believe in God…"

"Why?"

"If you found out that you believe in God, you would believe; but since you don't know yet that you believe in God, you don't believe…"

250: **Socialism as 'scientific' atheism**: Not one nation has ever set itself up on the principles of science and reason; there has never been an example of it, unless perhaps only for a moment, out of foolishness. Socialism by its very nature must be atheism, because it has precisely declared, from the very first line, that it is an atheistic order, and intends to set itself up on the principles of science and reason exclusively. *Reason and science always, now, and from the beginning of the ages, have performed only a secondary and auxiliary task in the life of nations; and so they will to the end of the ages.*

403-04 **Primeval paradise**: "He suggests a final solution of the question, the division of mankind into two unequal parts. One tenth is granted freedom of person and unlimited rights over the remaining nine tenths. These must lose their person and turn into something like a herd, and in unlimited obedience, through a series of regenerations, attain to primeval innocence, something like a primeval paradise—though, by the way, they will have to work. The measures proposed by the author for removing the will from nine tenths of mankind and remaking them, by means of re-educating of entire generations—are quite remarkable, based on natural facts, *and extremely logical*. One may disagree with certain conclusions, but it is difficult to doubt the author's intelligence and knowledge"

"… to work for the aristocrats and obey them as if they were gods is vileness!"

"What I propose is not vileness but paradise, earthly paradise, and there can be no other on earth."

417-18 **Dehumanizing equality; Shigalyovism**: "He got spying. He's got each member of society watching the others and obliged to inform. Each belongs to all, and all to each. *They're all slaves and equal in their slavery*. Slander and murder in extreme cases, but above all—equality. First, the level of education, science, and talents is lowered. A high level of science and talents is accessible to higher abilities—no need for higher abilities! Higher abilities have always seized power and become despots. Higher abilities cannot fail to be despots and have always corrupted rather than been of use; they are to be banished or executed. Cicero's tongue is cut off, Copernicus' eyes are put out, Shakespeare is stoned—this is Shigalyovism! Slaves must be equal: there has never yet been either freedom or equality without despotism, but within a herd there must be equality, and this is Shigalyovism."

Unquestioning obedience, hatred, envy, paranoia, immorality and, finally, impersonality as necessary preconditions:

"I'm for Shigalyovism! No need for education, enough of science! There's sufficient material even without science for a thousand years to come, but obedience must be set up. Only one thing is lacking in the world: obedience. The thirst for education is already an aristocratic thirst. As soon as there's just a tiny bit of family or love, there's a desire for property. *We'll extinguish desire: we'll get drinking, gossip, denunciation going; we'll get unheard-of depravity going*; we'll stifle every genius in infancy. Everything reduced to a common denominator, complete equality. 'We've learned a trade, and we're honest people, we don't need anything else'—that was the recent response of the English workers. Only the necessary is necessary—henceforth that is the motto of the whole globe. But there is also a need for convulsion; this will be taken care of by us, the rulers. Slaves must have rulers. Complete obedience, complete impersonality, but once every thirty years Shigalyov gets a convulsion going, and they all suddenly start devouring each other, up to a certain point, simply so as not to be bored. Boredom is an aristocratic sensation; in Shigalyovism there will be no desires. Desire and suffering are for us; and for the slaves—Shigalyovism."

420-21 **Socialist recruitment; creation of a new race of depraved, 'emancipated' free-thinkers**: I've already told you: we'll penetrate among the people themselves. Do you know that we're already terribly strong now? Ours aren't only the ones who knife and burn, or perform classic pistol shots, or bite people. That kind only gets in the way. I can conceive of nothing without discipline. I'm a crook, really, not a socialist, ha, ha! Listen, I've counted them all up: the teacher who laughs with children at their God and at their cradle, is already ours. The lawyer who defends an educated murderer by saying that he's more developed than his victims and couldn't help killing to get money, is already ours. Schoolboys who kill a peasant just to see how it feels, are ours. Jurors who acquit criminals right and left, are ours. The prosecutor who trembles in court for fear of being insufficiently liberal, is ours, ours. Administrators, writers—oh, a lot of them, an awful lot of them are ours, and they don't know it themselves! On the other hand, the docility of schoolboys and little fools has reached the highest point; their mentors have burst gallbladders; everywhere there is vanity in immeasurable measure, appetites beastly, unheard-of …

Do you know, do you know how much we can achieve with little ready-made ideas alone? When I left, Littre's thesis that crime is insanity was raging. I come back—crime is no longer insanity but precisely common sense itself, almost a duty, at any rate a noble protest. And this is just the fruit. The Russian God has already folded in the face of 'rotgut.' The people are drunk, mothers are drunk, children are drunk, the churches are empty…Oh, just let this generation grow up! Only it's a pity there's no time to wait, otherwise they could get themselves drunker … *But one or two generations of depravity are necessary now, an unheard-of, mean little depravity, that turns men into vile, cowardly, cruel, self-loving slime—that's what's needed*! And with a bit of 'fresh blood' to boot, for the sake of habit.

617 **Suicidal atheism (i.e. suicide as the only logical response to atheism); self-will as divinity**: "If there is no God, then I am God."

"Now, there's the one point of yours that I could never understand: why are you God then?"

"If there is God, then the will is all his, and I cannot get out of his will. If not, the will is all mine, and it is my duty to proclaim self-will."

"Self-will? And why is it your duty?"

"Because the will has all become mine. Can it be that no one on the whole planet, having ended God and believed in self-will, dares to proclaim self-will to the fullest point? It's as if a poor man received an inheritance, got scared, and doesn't dare go near the bag, thinking he's too weak to win it. I want to proclaim self-will. I may be the only one, but I'll do it … It is my duty to proclaim unbelief. For me no idea is higher than that there is no God. The history of mankind is on my side. Man has done nothing but invent God, so as to live without killing himself; in that lies the whole of world history up to now. I alone for the first time in world history did not want to invent God. Let them know once and for all … There is nothing hid that shall not be revealed. *He* said that."

"So you still believe in *Him*, and keep the little lamp lit; what is it, 'just in case' or something?... You know what, I think you believe maybe even more than any priest."

"In whom? In *Him*? Listen to a big idea: There was one day on earth, and in the middle of the earth stood three crosses. One on a cross believed so much that he said to another: 'This day you will be with me in paradise.' The day ended, they both died, went, and did not find paradise or resurrection. What had been said would not prove true. Listen: this man was the highest on all the earth, he constituted what it was to live for. Without this man the whole planet with everything on it is—madness only. There has not been one like *Him* before or since, not ever, even to the point of miracle. This is the miracle, that there has not been and never will be such a one. And if so, if the laws of nature did not pity even *This One*, did not pity even their own miracle, but made *Him*, too, live amidst a lie and die for a lie, then the whole planet is a lie, and stands upon a lie and a stupid mockery. Then the very laws of the planet are a lie and a devil's vaudeville. Why live then, answer me, if you're a man?"

"That's another turn of affairs. It seems to me you have two different causes mixed up here; and that is highly untrustworthy. But, excuse me, what if you are a God? If the lie ended and you realized that the whole lie was because there had been this former God?"

"You've finally understood! So it can be understood, if even someone like you understands! You understand now that the whole salvation for everyone is to prove this thought to them all. Who will prove it? I! I don't understand how, up to now, an atheist could know there is no God and not kill himself at once. To recognize that there is no God, and not to recognize at the same time that you've become God, is an absurdity, otherwise you must necessarily kill yourself. Once you recognize it, you are king, and you will not kill yourself but will live in the chiefest glory. But one, the one who is first, must necessarily kill himself, otherwise who will begin and prove it? It is I who will necessarily kill myself in order to begin and prove it. I am still God against my will, and I am unhappy, because it is my *duty* to proclaim self-will. Everyone is unhappy, because everyone is afraid to proclaim self-will…For three years I have been searching for the attribute of my divinity, and I have found it: the attribute of my divinity is—Self-will.

664 **Necessity of the immeasurably great**: The one constant thought that there exists something immeasurably more just and happy than I, fills the whole of me with immeasurable tenderness and—glory—oh, whoever I am, whatever I do! Far more than his own happiness, it is necessary for a man to know and believe *every moment* that there is somewhere a perfect and peaceful happiness, for everyone and for everything … *The whole law of human existence consists in nothing other than a man's always being able to bow before the immeasurably great.* If people are deprived of the immeasurably great, they will not live and will die in despair. The immeasurable and infinite is as necessary for man as the small planet he inhabits.

Dostoyevsky, *Brothers Karamazov* (New York: Bantam Classics, Translated by Andrew R. MacAndrew, 1984)

70 **Secular, evolutionary view of the Church's fate**: "Which means, to sum up briefly," said Father P., stressing every word, "that, according to certain theories of which *the point has become only too clear in our nineteenth century, the Church is to evolve into a state, the way a lower order of life evolves into a higher one, and eventually is to disappear altogether as a religious institution, being superseded by science, technical progress, and secularism.* And if the Church refuses to accept that fate and resists, it is to be rewarded for its pains by being allotted a corner in the preserve of the State, and even that would be under the supervision of the State. This is the situation today in every European country. But, according to the Russian idea and hope, it is not the Church that is to be transformed into the State, as an inferior form into a superior one; it is rather the State that eventually must become part of the Church. So it shall be and so be it!"

80 **Atheistic 'natural' law (taken to its logical progression)**: If there is any natural law, it is precisely this: *Destroy a man's belief in immortality and not only will his ability to love wither away within him but, along with it, the force that impels him to continue his existence on earth.* Moreover, nothing would be immoral then, everything would be permitted, even cannibalism…for every individual—people like us now, for instance—who do not believe in God or immortality, the natural moral law immediately becomes the opposite of religious law and that *absolute egotism*, even carried to the extent of crime, must not only be tolerated but even recognized as the wisest and perhaps the noblest course.

365-66 **Brotherhood vs. Individuality; materialism as suicide**: "In order to change the world, man's way of thinking must be changed. Thus, there can be no brotherhood of men before all men become each other's brother. There is no science, no order based on the pursuit of material gain, that will enable men to share their goods fairly and to respect each other's rights. There will never be enough to satisfy everyone; men will always be envious of their neighbors and will always destroy one another. So to your question when heaven on earth will come about, I can only promise you that it will come without fail, but first the period of man's isolation must come to an end."

"Isolation?"

"The isolation that you find everywhere, particularly in our age. But it won't come to an end right now, because the time has not yet come. Today everyone asserts his own personality and strives to live a full life as an individual. But these efforts lead not to a full life but to suicide, because, instead of realizing his personality, man only slips into total isolation. *For in our age mankind has been broken up into self-contained individuals, each of whom retreats into his lair, trying to stay away from the rest of mankind, and finally isolating himself from people and people from him. And, while he accumulates material wealth in his isolation, he thinks with satisfaction how mighty and secure he has become, because he is mad and cannot see that the more goods he accumulates, the deeper he sinks into suicidal impotence. The reason for this is that he has become accustomed to relying only on himself; he has split off from the whole and become an isolated unit; he has trained his soul not to rely on human help, not to believe in men and mankind, and only to worry that the wealth and privileges he has accumulated may be lost.* Everywhere men today are turning scornfully away from the truth that the security of the individual cannot be achieved by his isolated efforts but only by mankind as a whole."

378-79 **Worldly view of freedom; immediate satisfaction of impulses**: Look at the worldly, at those who set themselves above the people of God—have they not distorted the image of God and His truth? They have science, but science contains nothing that does not come through the senses. *The spiritual world, the nobler side of man's being, has been rejected altogether, banned as it were triumphantly*, perhaps even with hatred. The world has proclaimed freedom, now more loudly than ever; but what do we find in that freedom of theirs? Nothing but enslavement and suicide! The world says: "*You have needs—satisfy them. You have as much right as the rich and the mighty. Don't hesitate to satisfy your needs; indeed, expand your needs and demand more.*" This is the worldly doctrine of today. And they believe that this is freedom. The result for the rich is isolation and suicide; for the poor, envy and murder; for while the poor have been handed all these rights, they have not been given the means to enjoy them. Some claim that the world is gradually becoming united, that it will grow into a brotherly community as distances shrink and ideas are transmitted through the air. Alas, you must not believe that men can be united in this way. *To consider freedom as directly dependent on the number of man's requirements and the extent of their immediate satisfaction shows a twisted understanding of human nature*, for such an interpretation only breeds in men a multitude of senseless, stupid desires and habits and endless preposterous inventions. People are more and more moved by envy now, by the desires to satisfy their material greed, and by vanity. Giving dinners, riding in private carriages, occupying high social positions, and having myriads of servants—those are considered so important by some that they devote their whole lives to acquiring them and sacrificing for their sake their love of their fellow men, and *sometimes even kill themselves if they cannot obtain what they believe they must have*. It is the same with those who are not rich. And, as to the poor, who cannot satisfy their needs at all, they just drown their envy of others in alcohol. But the way they are being aroused now, it will soon be blood rather than liquor on which they will get drunk. Now let me ask you: Do you really think that such men are free?...

379 **Inverse correlation between materialism and happiness**: So it is not surprising that, instead of freedom, they lapse into slavery, that, instead of promoting unity and brotherhood, they encourage division and isolation… That is how the idea of service to mankind and brotherly love has been dying out in the world; indeed, now it is often sneered at, for what can a man do who has become the slave of the innumerable needs and habits *he*

has invented for himself? He lives in his separate little world and does not care about the great world outside. The result of all this is that, today, when more material goods have been accumulated than ever, there is less joy.

708 **Atheism, 'chemistry' and self-determination**: "Science is wonderful, Alyosha—it will produce a *new man*. I understand that very well. But I am unhappy about God—I miss Him!"

"That's something at least. I'm thankful for that," Alyosha said.

"You think it's good that I miss God? Why, if I feel like that, *it's just chemistry*. Yes, everything's chemistry! It's no use, my holy brother, you'll just have to move out of the way a bit, to make room for chemistry. Rakitin now—he doesn't like him, God is a sore spot. But they hide it, they lie, they pretend…But tell me," I asked him, "what will happen to men? If there's no God and no life beyond the grave, doesn't that mean that men will be allowed to do whatever they want?" "Didn't you know that already?" he said and laughed again. "An intelligent man can do anything he likes so long as he's clever enough to get away with it …"

712 **Atheism as proposed antidote to doubt; man as replacement of God and social service as replacement of religion**: You see, I never had any doubts before, but these were all hidden inside me. And perhaps it was because all those ideas were raging within me without my even being aware of their existence that I drank, behaved wildly, and beat people up; without knowing it, I was trying to drown out silence and doubts. But Ivan is no Rakitin. There's an idea hidden inside Ivan. Our brother Ivan is a sphinx. He doesn't speak. He won't open up. But God torments me. And what if there is no God? What if Rakitin is really right and God is just a fiction created by men? *Then, if there is no God, man becomes master of the earth and of the universe. That's great. But then, how can a man be virtuous without God*? That's the snag, and I always come back to it. For whom will man love then? Whom will he be grateful to? Whom will he praise in hymns? Rakitin just laughs and says that one can love mankind without God. But I feel you have to be a piece of slime to say that. I can't see it at all. Solving the problem of existence is easy for Rakitin: 'If you wanted to do something useful today, you could, for instance, fight for people's civil rights or even maintain the price of beef at a reasonable level; *that would be simpler than playing with all kinds of philosophical theories*.' So I said to him: 'But if there's no God, you'd jerk up the price of beef yourself if you knew how to, and if you had a chance, if you could, you'd fleece people to make a ruble of profit on each kopek.' That made him angry. But what's virtue then?

781-82: **Destruction of God and the birth of the fleeting man-god**: *You*—kill *me*? Oh no, you'll just have to excuse me and hear me out. This is a treat for me and that's why I came. Oh, I love the aspirations of my ardent young friends, trembling with eagerness to live! When you were about to come here last spring, you thought to yourself: 'There are new people there who plan to destroy everything and start once again with cannibalism. Ah, the stupid fools, they ought to consult me first, *for I don't believe they have to destroy anything, except man's idea of God—that would be the way to start.* Then the blind fools would achieve their goal! Once every member of the human race discards the idea of God (and I believe that such an era will come, like some *new geological age*), the old world-view will collapse by itself without recourse to cannibalism. *And the first thing to disintegrate will be the old morality, for everything will be different.* Men will unite their efforts to get everything out of life that it can offer them, but only for joy and happiness in *this* world. *Man will be exalted spiritually with a divine, titanic pride and the man-god will come into being.* Extending his conquest over nature beyond all bounds through his will and his science, man will constantly experience such great joy that it will replace for him his former anticipation of the pleasures that await him in heaven. Everyone will know that he is mortal, that there is no resurrection for him, and will accept his death with calm and dignity, like a god. He will understand, out of sheer pride, that there is no point in protesting that life lasts only a fleeting moment and he will love his brother without expecting any reward for it. Love will satisfy only a moment in life, but the very awareness of its momentary nature will concentrate its flames, which before were diffused and made pale by the anticipation of eternal life beyond the grave...' And so on and so forth. Very sweet!

782 **Victory over the man-slave**: The whole question, my thinker thought, was whether such a time would ever come. If it did come, then everything would be solved and mankind would be all right. But since, because human stupidity is so deeply ingrained, it could not come to pass for at least for a thousand years, *every thinking man who already recognized the truth could arrange his life as he pleased in accordance with the new principles, without waiting*. In that sense, 'everything was permitted' to him. Furthermore, even if such a time never did come, since God and immortality still would not exist, the new man might become the man-god, even if he were the only one in the whole world, and, of course, in that new capacity, he might if the need arise, jump without scruple over every barrier of the only moral code devised for the man-slave. *There is no law for God, for whatever stand God takes is right. Wherever I stand thereby becomes the most important spot...So everything is permitted and that's all there is to it*! That is all very nice. But if you have made up your mind to break the rules, why do you still need the stamp of righteousness?

Chapter Four

The God Who Is: the Holy Trinity as One Lord

The one God has always existed in a communion of love amongst three co-equal Persons. The eternal divine love is perfected in three Persons, not one, two or four (or otherwise). The being of this Triune God is absolutely basic to all reality, and needs no proof beyond being what it eternally is. God's being as the eternal 'I am' is the proof of everything else, and constitutes the ground of His sole sovereignty over creation and law-giving in the context of the Covenant of Grace (see chapter 6).

In this chapter, we must discuss *the oneness of God*, but it is impossible to do so without some immediate reference to the threeness of His personhood (because the one Lord is always three in Person). It is theologically impossible to separate completely the oneness and the threeness, for it is part of the essential character of *the one Lord* that for Him to be is to be in relationship within Himself. Then in Chapter 5, we shall think in a more detailed way about *the three Persons* of the one God.

Holy Scripture presents us with one God who exists from all eternity as three Persons, as we shall see in detail presently. But before we enter into the necessary details, let us think briefly and summarily of *why* the one God has always existed as three co-equal persons. It is primarily because the very nature of God is love, as 1 John 4:8 tells us, and the Father sending the Son to save us shows us (John 3:16), and the love of the Spirit demonstrates by inwardly warming and transforming us (Rom. 15:30; Rom. 5:5; Gal. 5:22, 23). The high priestly prayer of Christ encompasses all His saving work for the lost human race in terms of the eternal love and glory between Father and Son that are conveyed from the very heart of the Father to them:

> And the glory which thou gavest me, I have given them; that they may be one, even as we are one: I in them, and thou in me, that they may be made perfect in one; and that the world may know that thou hast sent me, and hast loved them, as thou hast loved me. Father, I will that they also, whom thou hast given me, be with me where I am; that they may behold my glory, which thou hast given me: for thou lovedst me before the foundation of the world (John 17:22-24).

Why God exists as three Persons rather than as one Person

Richard of St. Victor, a Scottish theologian in twelfth-century France, meditated on why the one God would exist in three Persons rather than one Person. He saw that it was because of the nature of love. For love to exist, more than one Person is required so that the love may be shared. 'One never says that someone properly possesses love if he only loves himself; for it to be true love, it must go out towards another. Consequently, where a plurality of persons is lacking, it is impossible for there to be love.'[1]

That is to say, the true God has never existed as a single, solitary individual, 'cut-off' as it were, in lonely isolation within Himself. But rather, the inner being of the one true God has always consisted in a rich, personal diversity within that profound unity: for God 'to be' is 'to be in relationship' within Himself, an eternal relationship of three co-equal Persons within the one divine reality. As John Zizioulas has written, in the context of the Father/ Son relationship: 'To say that the Son belongs to God's substance implies that substance *possesses almost by definition a relational character*.'[2] Or, using analogies from the first and last books of the Bible (Genesis and Revelation), one could say 'anthropomorphically' that 'rivers of living water'– fountains of life, light and love – are constantly flowing amongst the three blessed Persons of the Holy Trinity. Or again, the relationship of the three divine Persons within the Godhead constitutes the benediction and supreme 'happiness' of God, as God; the one who is 'the blessed [or "happy" – *makarios*] and only Potentate, the King of kings and Lord of lords…' (1 Tim. 6:15).

As T. F. Torrance stated it:

> The Father is in himself the whole divine nature, but this is true also of the Son and of the Spirit. The Father is not Father apart from the Son, and the Son is not Son apart from the Father, nor are they what they are as Father and Son apart from the Spirit, while the Holy Spirit is not what he is as Holy Spirit apart from the Father and the Son, for they all coinhere consubstantially and inseparably in the one Being of God. The Godhead is intrinsically Trinitarian, and the Trinity is essentially one, a Unity in Trinity and a Trinity in Unity.[3]

Stăniloae says:

> A subject who was unique in an absolute sense would lack the joy and hence the meaning of existence. He would be doubtful even of his own existence which would become something mingled with dreams. According to our Christian teaching, if a subject and an object are together, or if a subject is even confronted with a whole world of objects, that subject is kept within a loneliness devoid of all joy and meaning to existence. 'What will it profit a man if he gains the whole world and forfeits his life?' (Matt. 16:26).[4]

[1]Richard of St. Victor, *De Trinitate*, III. 2; my translation from *Richard de Saint-Victor, La Trinité* (G. Salet, ed., Paris: Sources Chrétiennes, 1959), p. 168. Richard seems to be directly following Gregory the Great, who had written centuries before: 'Minus quam inter duos caritas haberi non potest. Nemo enim proprie ad semetipsum habere caritatem dicitur, se dilectio in alterum tendit ut caritas esse posit' (*In Evang.*, 17, 1 (76, 1139).

[2]John Zizioulas, *Being as Communion* (Crestwood, NY: St. Vladimir's Press, 1993), 95.

[3]T. F. Torrance, *The Trinitarian Faith*, 224.

[4]Stăniloae, op. cit., 266.

Thus, true love and the fullness of personal relationship, which is an expression of that divine and eternal love, precludes the thought of God ever having been either impersonal or unipersonal. Stăniloae explains:

> A lone 'I' cannot experience the fullness of existence proper to the divine being, a fullness on which depend that complete joy and happiness found only in the form of pure subjectivity. The joy of the lone 'I' is not a complete joy and, therefore, not the fullness of existence. And the joy of existence communicated by one 'I' to another 'I' must be just as full in the one who receives as in the one who gives. Hence there is also fullness of existence. But this implies the complete self-giving of one 'I' to another 'I', not merely the giving of something from oneself or from what one possesses. There must be a correlation of total giving and receiving between two 'I's' who nevertheless remain distinct within this very possession.
>
> In perfect love persons do not merely engage in a reciprocal exchange of self; they also affirm themselves reciprocally and personally, and establish themselves in existence through giving and receiving. But the divine love is all efficacious. The Father therefore establishes the Son in existence from all eternity by his integral self-giving, while the Son continually affirms the Father as Father from all eternity by the fact that he both accepts his own coming into existence through the Father and also gives himself to the Father as Son. The acts through which the divine persons, in their distinction and through perfect love, affirm one another reciprocally in existence are eternal acts and have a totally personal character, although they are acts in which the divine persons are active together.
>
> If love belongs essentially to God, then the reciprocal relationship in which the love of the persons manifests itself must also have an essential basis, even though the positions occupied by the persons in this relationship do not change among themselves. In God there must be Father, Son and Holy Spirit. But the persons do not change these positions among themselves. On the other hand, since the being is one and is perfect love, the relationship is that of equal to equal, not that of superior to inferior or stranger to stranger. If God needed to relate to something outside himself, this would imply that he lacked something distinct from himself. Divine relations must take place in God himself, although between distinct 'I's', so that the relation and hence the love may be real.[5]

Why God is three in Person, rather than two

Stăniloae explains why neither one Person, nor two Persons, can constitute the loving fullness of the being of God:

> A single person might be taken to be merely a process of intellection; two persons immersed in their exclusive communion can have the impression that they have departed from reality. Only a third person assures them that they are within an objective reality and that in this reality they surpass their own dual subjectivity … The third fulfils the role of 'object' or horizon, assuring the sense of objectivity for the two by the fact that he keeps the two from becoming confused within an indistinct unity because of the exclusiveness of their love, an exclusiveness which can flow from the conviction of each that nothing worthy of love exists outside the other …

---

[5]Stăniloae, op. cit., 257, 258.

> In the case of human beings, the third can have the role of keeping the other two not only from immersing themselves in each other, but also from falling into a lethal boredom because their finite character makes it impossible for them to keep up their reciprocal interest in one another permanently. With men, therefore, the third person has the role of offering ... the newness of another communion from which they can return, with interest refreshed and enriched, to the communion that exists between themselves.
>
> In the case of God there can be no question of the third person playing a role in rekindling the love between the other two, but only in preserving them in their personal distinction, accompanied by the enduring love that persists in them by reason of their infinite character ... In the three persons there is fully confirmed the 'truth' of God's existence, a truth which, in the case of the two, would be confirmed only in part, and in the case of one alone would remain uncertain. Hence in a special way the Holy Spirit is named 'the Spirit of truth' (John 15:26; 16:13), and has as his task to strengthen in truth.[6]

We see then why the essential nature of God which is love, requires more than one Person, and not an impersonal or unipersonal existence of God. But why three Persons, rather than two Persons, or four Persons, or more? Richard of St. Victor seeks to answer this question in Book III of *De Trinitate*. He suggests that without a Trinity of Persons, there would be no communication of the delights of love, which would be contrary to the perfection of love in each of the two Persons.[7] The full sharing of love requires 'condilection'[something like 'delightful sharing'] and thus the third Person of the Trinity, so that this love is 'social' and harmonious, never self-centered or exclusive.[8]

Why God is three in Person rather than four

In Book V, Richard explains why four Persons (or a 'quaternity') is not possible within the one God, because of the giving and receiving amongst the three Persons (which is constitutive of who they are, as unbegotten, begotten and proceeding): the hypothesis of a fourth property (i.e. subsistent Person) is excluded because such a one would possess without having received; furthermore, such a supposed Person, neither receiving nor giving, would remain solitary, which is contradictory to God's Triune Being.[9]

Or, as Stăniloae writes:

> They [i.e. the two persons] must have an awareness of a horizon which extends beyond themselves though it is linked with both of them. Nor can this horizon be constituted by an object or a world of objects, for that would not deliver the two from the monotony of a limited vision or of a loneliness *à deux*. Only the third subject – and one who can be a partner in communion and does not stand over against them as object – takes the two out of their uninterrupted loneliness as couple.[10]

---

[6] Ibid., 268, 269.
[7] Richard of St. Victor, op. cit., III, xv.
[8] Ibid., III, xvi-xx.
[9] Ibid., V. xiv, xv.
[10] Stăniloae, op. cit., 266, 267.

> In God this relation [i.e. 'I' and 'Thou'] is perfect and permanent, since no one is third in the strict sense, that is, in the sense that he would be outside the direct 'I – Thou' relation. This is all the more true as each person sees the other through each person, or sees the others as himself. In God the 'we – thou' or 'I – you' relations all obtain simultaneously with the 'I – thou' relation. Each divine subject is capable of this simultaneous attentiveness to the others, whether seen as distinct or in pairs. To make the fullness of existence something actual and to confirm the two in existence, a 'fourth' is not a further necessity. The third represents all that can exist over and above the two, the entire reality in which the two can be confirmed. A fourth in God would disperse and limit the third and diminish his importance. The existence of a fourth would mean that the whole of the objective horizon in which the two are found is no longer concentrated within one person.[11]

We must now consider in some detail, in this fourth chapter, (1) the being of God as the one Lord God Almighty. In the next chapter we shall consider more fully (2) the Being of God as a communion of three co-inherent Persons in that one eternal Being.

(1) The Being of God as One Lord God Almighty

The Being of God: (a) we think of the Being of God, and then (b) how His Being involves eternal lordship.

(a) God's Being comes first, and our knowing of it follows. That is, in scholastic terms, the *ordo essendi* must always go before the *ordo cognoscendi*.

God is. The profound truth expressed by this simple sentence is the source and meaning of every kind of reality. It is the basis of all theology; it is that which gives meaning to every aspect of life and the world; it is the potential illumination 'of all things, visible and invisible.'

God's existence is its own explanation (and the explanation of everything else); thus, it can have no explanation outside it or above it, as though His existence were dependent on some other kind of authority. As Richard Swinburne wrote: 'To say that "God exists" is necessary, is, I believe, to say that the existence of God is a brute fact that is inexplicable – not in the sense that we do not know its explanation, but in the sense that it does not have one…if God's essence is an eternal essence, any complete explanation of phenomena in terms of God bringing them about is also an ultimate explanation.'[12]

God is His own proof

In the context of affirming the self-authentication of Holy Scripture, John Calvin takes us back to the most certain of certainties; to the basis of all true reasoning, which is God's eloquent existence pressing upon us:

> We seek no proofs, no marks of genuineness upon which our judgment may lean; but we subject our judgment and wit to it as to a thing far beyond

[11] Stăniloae, op. cit., 270.

[12] Richard Swinburne, *The Existence of God* (1979), 96.

> any guesswork! This we do, not as persons accustomed to seize upon some unknown thing, which, under closer scrutiny, displeases them, but fully conscious that we hold the unassailable truth!... By this power we are drawn and inflamed, knowingly and willingly, to obey him, yet also more vitally and more effectively than by mere human willing or knowing!
>
> God, therefore, very rightly proclaims through Isaiah that the prophets, together with the whole people, are witnesses to him; for they, instructed by prophecies, unhesitatingly held that God has spoken without deceit or ambiguity [Isa. 43:10]. Such, then, is a conviction that requires no reasons; such, a knowledge with which the best reason agrees – in which the mind truly reposes more securely and constantly than in any reasons; such, finally, a feeling that can be born only of heavenly revelation. I speak of nothing other than what each believer experiences within himself – though my words fall far beneath a just explanation of the matter.[13]

A. Lecerf, following Calvin, shows how 'God is' is the one and only ground on which we can make sense of everything else:

> When we say 'God is', we affirm a fact which is forced on us by the consciousness that we have of our own existence, of our own mind, and in fact of the meaning which we attach to such expressions as 'to be' and 'to be true'. The existence of God and the affirmation of this existence can only be in the nature of a principle, a principle supreme in all orders of truth. It would not be worthy of His majesty if one could approach Him like any other object. The existence of God is implied in all affirmation, all negation, all thought … The supremely real Being, the foundation of all necessity, ontological as well as noetic, He can only become a problem for certain minds as to His existence and the divinity of His revelation, as a result of a spiritual rupture of the moral nature, impairing the moral judgment.[14]

Calvin and Lecerf were certainly in line on this point with the early Church Fathers, such as Clement of Alexandria and Athanasius. Clement writes: 'If to provide a proof means a kind of knowledge that requires a principle more profound than He whom we wish to demonstrate, then there is no proof for God.'[15] Athanasius said: 'The Deity does not submit to logical demonstrations, but to the faith and the piety of reason.'[16]

The first verse of the Holy Scriptures starts with God creating 'the heavens and the earth' (a Hebraic 'merism', meaning absolutely all things). God is, and – at a certain point in eternity – He brings into being everything else in the universe. He needs no proof for His existence, for everything that exists points upwards to Him who created all (unless one's mind is confounded by the darkness of sin).

Similarly, the Prologue to John's Gospel begins the same way that Genesis 1:1 begins: with the God who is, who creates and who reveals Himself. 'In the beginning was the Word [Logos], and the Word was with God and the Word was God. All things were made through Him, and without Him was not anything made that was made' (John 1:1-3).[17]

---

[13]John Calvin, *Institutes*, I. vii. 5.

[14]Auguste Lecerf, *An Introduction to Reformed Dogmatics* (London: Lutterworth Press, 1949), 211, 212.

[15]Clement of Alexandria, *Stromateis* V.6.

[16]Athanasius, *Letters to Serapion*, I. 20 (PG 26, 577A).

[17]We shall return to this passage later in some detail.

The significance of the divine name: 'I Am'

Scripture has no philosophical proof of God (beyond His reality itself), nor does it offer a philosophical discussion of God's Being (beyond the inescapable fact that He is and that He acts sovereignly). But the God who is does name Himself in various ways in His written Word. All of His revealed names are of highest importance, but Christian theologians from early centuries have been right to have seen the redemptive, covenant name that God gave to Moses at the burning bush as central to any understanding of God's existence.

Moses was, to say the least, concerned that he, a nobody, should – at God's command – go to the Hebrew nation of slaves to announce their coming deliverance (and then into Pharaoh's court itself and demand the liberation of the Hebrews). So Moses asks God a question:

> And Moses said unto God, behold, when I come unto the children of Israel and shall say unto them, The God of your fathers hath sent me unto you; and they shall say to me, What is his name? what shall I say unto them? And God said unto Moses, I AM THAT I AM: and he said, Thus shalt thou say unto the children of Israel, I AM hath sent me unto you (Exod. 3:13, 14).

'I AM THAT I AM' [JHVH] is taken from the four consonants that form the Hebrew verb for 'to be.'[18] We are uncertain of how these consonants were pointed (with vowels), so the right translation is probably 'I am that I am', or it could be 'I will be what I will be.' The holy name is generally rendered in our Bibles as 'Yahveh' or 'Jehovah' (which takes the four original consonants, and points them with the vowels from *'adonay* the word for 'Lord', which is regularly employed in the Synagogue in place of the ineffably holy name: JHVH).[19]

In the immediate context, it is clear that God is saying to Moses, 'I will be present with you in this humanly impossible task.'[20] Geerhardus Vos rightly saw a close connection between Exodus 3:14 and 33:19, when God is speaking to Moses at a later time:

> And he said, I will make all my goodness pass before thee, and I will proclaim the name of the LORD before thee; and will be gracious to whom I will be gracious, and will shew mercy on whom I will shew mercy.

Vos suggests that this connection (where Hebrew imperfect verbs for 'to be' and 'to have mercy [or compassion]' are connected with the relative pronoun *'asher'*) shows both the sovereignty of God's being and of his actions.[21]

---

[18]Geerhardus Vos, *Biblical theology: Old and New Testaments* (Grand Rapids: Wm. B. Eerdmans, 1984), 132, writes: 'God says to Moses: "Ehyeh esher Ehyeh." Then this is abbreviated to "Ehyeh", and finally turned from the first into the third person "Yehveh".'

[19]Vos, ibid., 129, writes: 'With this feature of the sovereignty shown in redemption is connected the specifically Mosaic name of God, Jehovah. This form is a pronunciation in which the vowels of Adonai were given to the consonants of the name in question [i.e. *yhvh*]. The writing of these vowels sprang originally from the Jewish scrupulousness refraining from the utterance of this most sacred name altogether. Because Adonai was always read in place of it, therefore, when vowels were added, for convenience' sake the vowels required for the reading of Adonai were simply attached…This was first done in Christian reading, when the old Jewish scrupulosity was no longer felt, and thus the hybrid form *Jehovah* arose. It has been in use since the sixteenth century.'

[20]Cf. Martin Buber, *The Kingship of God* (London: Allen and Unwin, 1967), 105.

[21]Op. cit. Vos, 132-34.

'I AM THAT I AM' means that God depends on nothing, while everything else depends on Him. God needs no explanation and no origin, but everything less than God needs an explanation and an origin. With this in mind, Pharaoh and the deliverance of the Hebrew slaves can well be handled.[22] And the organization of the life of Israel on a holy basis can well be handled. And every other redemptive action necessary to restore in its totality a broken creation can well be handled by 'Him who is.'

As the French Jewish scholars, André and Renée Neher, explain:

> Then Moses gives another reason for refusing [i.e. to heed the divine call to liberate the Hebrews from Egypt]: if he speaks to the Hebrews, they will not listen to him. If he speaks in the name of the God of the ancestors to a people of whom so many have been assimilated into Egypt, and have lost the memory of their traditions, they will not listen. A God who only has a name with respect to the past will find no credit before a people whose grief obliges them to think only of the future. God responds to this objection. In verses 14 and 15 of Exodus 3, God gives his name to Moses, this time oriented towards the future, as much as towards the past of the patriarchs; this name is more or less untranslatable into French. For in it God names himself at the same time by forms of the verb 'to be' (is He not 'the Being' – 'ὁ ὤν' – *par excellence;* the Being in every tense of the verb?) So by the Tetragrammaton he constructs His reality upon the verb 'to be.' And thereby, God sets forth, by describing his programme to Moses, all that he will have to do in order to deliver his people from Egypt.[23]

The Church Fathers comment on 'I Am'

For the most part, the Christian Church (until the sixteenth-century Reformation) used the Septuagint [Greek] translation of the Hebrew Old Testament, which rendered JHVH as 'ἐγω εἰμι ὁ ὤν, and the Latin Vulgate translation of the Western branch of the Church rendered it as *'ego sum qui sum'*.

The Fathers of the Church of course understood that the name 'I AM' means that God is the ultimate, transcendent and Triune Being, yet sovereignly present with His people. Athanasius cannot speak of the Being of God (as given in Exod. 3:14) without immediately referring to the Triune nature of God:

> "When you hear it said 'I am who I am', and 'In the beginning God created the heaven and the earth', and 'Hear, O Israel, the Lord our God is one Lord', and 'Thus says the Lord Almighty', we understand nothing else than the very simple and blessed and incomprehensible Being of him who is, for although we are unable to grasp what he is, yet on hearing 'Father' and 'God' and 'Almighty' we understand nothing else to be signified than the very Being of him who is. And if you have said of Christ that 'he is the Son of God', you have thereby said that 'he is from the Being of the Father'. And since the Scriptures have anticipated you in declaring that the Lord is the Son of the Father, and the Father himself has already said 'This is my beloved Son' – and a son is no other than the offspring of his father – is it

[22]Cf. Gerhard Von Rad, *Old Testament Theology*, translated by D.M.G. Stalker (Edinburgh: Oliver & Boyd, 1962) vol. I, 179-82.

[23]André and Renée Neher, *Histoire Biblique du Peuple d'Israel*, (Paris: Adrien Maisonneuve, 1988), 112.

> not evident that the Fathers of Nicaea were right to have said that the Son is from the Being of the Father?"[24]

Thus, Athanasius does not use Exodus 3:14 to formulate a doctrine of the Being of God in a Greek philosophical, abstract or impersonal manner (as many have accused the Church Fathers). On the contrary, he shows that for God 'to be' is 'to be in personal relationship within himself'. 'To name God Father is to signify his very Being.'[25] And Gregory Nazianzus spoke similarly of God's Being as exhibited by the Son in His identity with the Father in His Being. He says that while 'ὁ ὤν' applies to the Father as unoriginate, yet the nature of the Father is perfectly exhibited by the Son in His identity with the Father's Being and as *homoousios* with Him.[26]

Torrance expands on the significance of Athanasius' statement:

> This is a particularly significant argument...since in it Athanasius shows that the word *ousia* (οὐσία), derived from the verb εἰναι, to be, with the quite straightforward meaning of be-ing (ὤν), is to be understood in terms of the divine 'I am' (ἐγω εἰμι); and at the same time he relates it to the fact that Jesus Christ is of one and the same being as God the Father...Thus the 'I am' of God and the 'I am' of Christ in their bearing upon one another determined for Athanasius...the Christian understanding of the divine Being or *ousia* as living self-revealing and self-affirming personal Being. The repeated 'I am' of Christ in the Gospel confirms the intensely personal nature of the 'I am who I am' of *Yahweh*, while the 'I am who I am' of *Yahweh* discloses the ontological ground of the 'I am' of Christ in God.[27]

The meditation of St. Hilary (c. A.D. 350) on the meaning of the name of God given in Exodus 3:14 is, I think, a model of pious faith thinking through the fuller ramifications of the central fact that God is Being:

> While my mind was dwelling on these and on many like thoughts, I chanced upon the books which, according to the tradition of the Hebrew faith, were written by Moses and the prophets, and found in them words spoken by God the Creator testifying of Himself 'I AM THAT I AM, and again, HE THAT IS *hath sent me unto you*' (Exod. 3:14). I confess that I was amazed to find in them an indication concerning God so exact that it expressed in the terms best adapted to human understanding an unattainable insight into the mystery of the Divine nature. For no property of God which the mind can grasp is more characteristic of Him than existence, since existence, in the absolute sense, cannot be predicated of that which shall come to an end, or of that which has had a beginning, and He who now joins continuity of being with the possession of perfect felicity could not in the past, nor can in the future, be non-existent; for whatsoever is divine can neither be originated nor destroyed. Wherefore, since God's eternity is inseparable from Himself, it was worthy of Him to reveal this one thing, that He is, as the assurance of His absolute eternity.[28]

---

[24]Athanasius, *De Synodis*, 34.

[25]Ibid., 35.

[26]Gregory Nazianzus, Oration, 30. 19.

[27]T. F. Torrance, *The Christian Doctrine of God*, 118, 119.

[28]Hilary, *De Trinitate*, I.5.

Gregory of Nazianzus, likewise in the fourth century, also saw the name God gave of Himself to Moses as absolute Being:

> ... and Moses asked what his name was, this was what he called himself, bidding him say to the people 'I Am hath sent me'...But we are enquiring into a Nature whose Being is absolute and not into Being bound up with something else. But Being is in its proper sense peculiar to God, and belongs to him entirely, and is not limited or cut short by and before or after, for indeed in him there is no past or future.[29]

A century later, St. Augustine took the name of God as 'Being' to indicate that because the supreme reality is Being and is good, therefore, even lesser (created) realities are also good:

> How gloriously then and divinely did our God say to his servant: *Ego sum qui sum*, and then: *Dices filiis Israel, Qui est misit me ad vos*. For He Himself most truly is because He is altogether immutable. For this in fact is always the result of change: that what once was, is no more; that, therefore, can truly be said to be which is immutable: but as to other things which have been made by him, it is from him that each in its own way has received its being. Since therefore He is being *par excellence* He has no contrary save that which is not, and, consequently, as all that is good exists by Him so everything in nature exists by him, for everything in nature is good. In one word, every nature is good, now all that is good comes from God, therefore every nature comes from God.[30]

Medieval theological reflections on 'I Am'

By the thirteenth century, St. Thomas Aquinas took the theological understanding of the 'God who is' of Exodus 3:14 to a new conceptual level. As Etienne Gilson said: '[Thomism] did not come out of Aristotelianism by way of evolution, but of revolution ... It is a revolution in the history of the metaphysical interpretation of the first principle, which is "being".'[31] The crucial point made by St. Thomas is that of the distinction between 'essence' and 'existence'.

Taking seriously the crucial biblical distinction between uncreated Being and created being (or between the Creator and the creation), Thomas states that in the Being of God alone is 'essence' (or what He is as God) and is precisely the same reality as 'existence' – that is, God cannot *not* exist, whereas all created being can either exist or not exist – it can be brought into being or cease to live. Only of the *jhvh* who reveals His name at the burning bush to Moses is it the case that He eternally exists; everything less than God (the various orders of creation) were brought into being by Him, and are thus totally dependent upon Him for their continued life.

St. Thomas seeks to state (in a philosophical/theological) way the foundational distinction between Creator (or uncreated Being) and creature (or created being). To do so he takes us back to the burning bush. In *Summa Contra Gentiles* (Book I) he tells us:

---

[29] Gregory of Nazianzus, *The Fourth Theological Oration*, xviii.

[30] Augustine, *De Natura Boni*, ch. xix.

[31] Etienne Gilson, *History of Christian Philosophy in the Middle Ages* (New York: Random House, 1955), 365.

> [9] Everything, furthermore, exists because it has being. A thing whose essence is not its being, consequently, is not through its essence but by participation in something, namely, being itself. But that which is through participation in something cannot be the first being, because prior to it is the being in which it participates in order to be. But God is the first being, with nothing prior to Him. His essence is, therefore, His being.
>
> [10] This sublime truth Moses was taught by our Lord. When Moses asked our Lord: 'If the children of Israel say to me: what is His name? What shall I say to them?' The Lord replied: 'I AM WHO AM ... Thou shalt say to the children of Israel: HE WHO IS hath sent me to you' (Exod. 3:13,14). By this our Lord showed that His own proper name is HE WHO IS. Now, names have been devised to signify the natures or essences of things. It remains, then, that the divine being is God's essence or nature.
>
> [11] Catholic teachers have likewise professed this truth. For Hilary writes in his book *De Trinitate*: 'Being is not an accident in God but subsisting truth, the abiding cause and the natural property of His nature' (Hilary, *De Trin.*, Bk. VII, 11). Boethius also says in his own work *De Trinitate*: 'The divine substance is being itself, and from it comes being' (Boethius, *De Trin.*, II).[32]

Thomas writes in *On Being and Essence*:

> Whatever does not enter into the understanding of an essence or quiddity [i.e. 'what it is' or 'whatness'] comes to it from without and enters into composition with the essence, since no essence could be understood without the parts that make it up. Every essence or quiddity, however, can be understood without its being understood that it exists in fact; for I can understand what a man or a phoenix is and yet not know whether they are given in reality. Therefore, it is clear that existence is other than essence or quiddity, unless indeed there should be some thing whose quiddity is its existence; and such a thing could only be unique and first.[33]

Ralph McInerny comments: 'The upshot of this teaching is quite clear. God alone is a being for whom to be is *what* he is; God alone is such that he cannot not be. He is, in short, a necessary being. Whatever other than God exists does so, not because it is of its nature to exist, a definitional necessity, as it were, but because it has received existence.'[34]

Again, Etienne Gilson explains:

> In order to know what God is, Moses turns to God. He asks His name, and straightway comes the answer: *Ego sum qui sum, Ait: sic dices filiis Israel; qui est misit me ad vos* (Exod. iii. 14). No hint of metaphysics, but God speaks, *causa finita est*, and Exodus lays down the principle from which henceforth the whole of Christian philosophy will be suspended. From this moment it is understood once and for all that the proper name of God is Being and that, according to the word of St. Ephrem, taken up again later by St. Bonaventure, this name denotes His very essence. Now to say that the word *being* designates the essence of God, and the essence of no other being but God, is to say that in God alone essence and existence are identical. That

---

[32]St. Thomas, *Summa Contra Gentiles*, op. cit., I.22. 9-11.

[33]St. Thomas, *On Being and Essence*, ch. 5, n. 3.

[34]Ralph McInerny, *St. Thomas Aquinas* (Notre Dame and London: University of Notre Dame Press, 1977), 97.

> is why St. Thomas Aquinas, referring expressly to this text of Exodus, will declare that among all divine names there is one that is eminently proper to God, namely *Qui est*, precisely because this *Qui est* signifies nothing other than being itself: *non significat formam aliquam sed ipsum esse.*[35] In this principle lies an inexhaustible metaphysical fecundity; all the studies that follow here will be merely studies of its results. There is but one God and this God is Being, that is the corner-stone of all Christian philosophy, and it was not Plato, it was not even Aristotle, it was Moses who put it in position.[36]

This distinction between essence and existence did not have the key importance in Eastern Orthodoxy that it had in the West. But it is carefully discussed by an Eastern theologian, C. Yannaras, who certainly sees its central significance for the Western understanding of God.[37]

In the century following St. Thomas Aquinas, John Duns Scotus properly placed any understanding of the name of God in the context of prayer:

> O Lord our God, true teacher that you are, when Moses your servant asked for your name that he might proclaim it to the children of Israel, you, knowing what the mind of mortals could grasp of you, replied: 'I am who am,' thus disclosing your blessed name. You are truly what it means to be, you are the whole of what it means to exist. This, if it be possible for me, I should like to know by way of demonstration. Help me then, O Lord, as I investigate how much our natural reason can learn about that true being which you are if we begin with the being which you have predicated of yourself.[38]

The prayer of Duns Scotus (a necessary prayer for all who will ever have some true understanding of God) is the proper response of limited, created being to the One who is infinite and eternal; the fount of our own created being. Hans Urs Von Balthasar (1905–1988) explores with insight just what Thomas's distinction – in some sense, going back to Exodus 3:14 – between essence and existence (which Von Balthasar calls 'the ontological difference' or 'the real distinction') may mean for human life today in a limited and fallen world; a world that needs to enter into this prayer. In his *TheoDrama: The Dramatic Theory, vol. II: The Dramatis Personae: Man in God*, he uses this distinction to show that 'man exists as a limited being in a limited world, but his reason is open to the unlimited, to all of Being,' and in particular that man does not have in himself the foundation of his own being.[39] That recognition which Moses knew in his own way, is the basis of true theology and true life. It is the basis for valid philosophy and culture in every sphere.

---

[35]St. Thomas, *Sum. Theol.*, I.13,11.

[36]Etienne Gilson, *Spirit of Medieval Philosophy* (Notre Dame and London: University of Notre Dame Press, 1936 [1991]), 51.

[37]C. Yannaras, *De l'absence et de l'inconnassance de Dieu d'après les écrits aréopagitiques et Martin Heidegger* (Paris: Editions du Cerf, 1971).

[38]John Duns Scotus, *A Treatise on God as First Principle*, Translated and Edited with Commentary by Allan B. Wolter O. F. M. (Chicago, IL: Franciscan Herald Press, 1966), I.2.

[39]Hans Urs Von Balthasar, *Theodrama: The Dramatic Theory, vol. II: The Dramatis Personae: Man in God*, translated by Graham Harrison, (San Francisco: Ignatius Press, 1988), 189-190.

While Duns Scotus was active in the West, Gregory Palamas in the East dealt with some of the same issues, though from a necessarily different point of view. The surpassing importance of God as the absolute 'I AM' seems to be reflected in Chapter 89 of his *The One Hundred and Fifty Chapters* (though he does not make direct reference to Exodus 3:14). He describes the absoluteness of God as the 'I Am' in terms of 'absolute existence' which does not participate in anything else:

> If someone should claim that absolute existence is a participation since it alone does not participate but is only an object of participation, for the other participations participate in it, he should know that his notion regarding the other participations is devoid of understanding. That which is living, holy and good is said to be living, holy and good by participation, not because of absolute being and participation in absolute existence, but because they participate in absolute life, holiness and goodness. Absolute life and other such things do not become absolute life by participation in another absolute life. And so, as absolute life, it belongs among the objects of participation but not among the things which participate ...[40]

If I have read him correctly, V. N. Lossky expresses this point of Palamas by speaking of the Triune God as an 'absolute stability'.[41] That is a way of saying that the 'I AM' is (in Palamas' terms) 'absolute existence' that does not 'participate' in anything else to be who it is.

Having looked at **(a) God's Being**, we now consider:

(b) God as one sovereign Lord. For God to be, involves His being in relationship within Himself as Holy Trinity (which we shall discuss later in this chapter more carefully), and it involves His being one sovereign Lord. Genesis 1:1 begins with God speaking worlds into existence, creating all things ('the heavens and the earth') out of nothing by the word of His power. That is the sovereign, utterly miraculous action of the one Lord; none less than He could do such a thing, 'For he spake, and it was done; he commanded, and it stood fast' (Ps. 33:9). Isaiah shows God's sovereignty by a number of rhetorical questions:

Divine sovereignty in creation

> Who hath measured the waters in the hollow of his hand, and meted out heaven with the span, and comprehended the dust of the earth in a measure, and weighed the mountains in scales, and the hills in a balance? Who hath directed the Spirit of the Lord, or being his counsellor hath taught him? With whom took he counsel, and who instructed him, and taught him in the path of judgment, and taught him knowledge, and shewed to him the way of understanding? Behold, the nations are as a drop of a bucket, and are counted as the small dust of the balance: behold, he taketh up the isles as a very little thing...All nations before him are as nothing; and they are counted as less than nothing, and vanity (Isa. 40:12-15, 17).

---

[40]St. Gregory of Palamas, *The One Hundred and Fifty Chapters*, edited and translated by Robert E. Sinkewicz, C. S. B. (Toronto: Pontifical Institute of Medieval Studies, 1988), 188,189.

[41]V. N. Lossky, *The Mystical Theology of the Eastern Church* (New York: St. Vladimir's Seminary Press, 1978), 45.

In a humanly impossible situation, Jeremiah cries out the sovereignty of God: 'Ah Lord God! Behold, thou hast made the heaven and the earth by thy great power and stretched out arm, and there is nothing too hard for thee' (Jer. 32:17). 'Creation ... is depicted [*sc.* in Genesis 1 and 2] as the result of the dynamic word of God. To call forth the world in direct response to His word was to act as Jesus of Nazareth did when in response to His word men were healed. Said the centurion, "Only speak the word, and my servant will be healed" (Matt. 8:8). So the word was likewise spoken here [Gen. 1 and 2], and the world came into being.'[42]

Divine sovereignty in law-giving

The basis of the ten commandments given by God through Moses to the liberated people of Israel on Mount Sinai is the first commandment (called by Jesus, 'the first and great commandment' – Matt. 22:38,39). It is briefly prefaced by mention of the sovereignly wrought deliverance by God: 'I am the Lord thy God, which have brought thee out of the land of Egypt, out of the house of bondage. Thou shalt have no other gods before me' (Exod. 20:2,3).[43] This is the foundation of biblical monotheism, as the French Jewish scholars, André and Renée Neher, have explained:

> God is unique, righteous and good; he is the God of every human; he is the God of human history: such are the fundamental theological affirmations of the Torah. They define Biblical monotheism, which is not simply a belief in the unity of the divine person, but faith in a moral God, and one who, despite his transcendent majesty, is very near to men and watches over their actions and destinies. These definitions cut across all that antiquity was able to elaborate in this domain. The monotheisms which were sketched out elsewhere, particularly in Egypt, under Amenophis IV, lift up a divinity among others, without conceding the moral basis that the Bible finds in the Unity of God. The 'good and just' gods, known in certain ancient philosophical doctrines, are very far from men. They carry, in some way, their equity within themselves, without causing it to shine out; men adore divine justice, without taking part in it, whereas the Bible presents the goodness and justice of God as values which men may and should force themselves to imitate and realize upon earth. Finally, no philosophical or religious doctrine of antiquity knows a God who, like the God of the Bible, has created humanity and the world with a precise goal, oriented towards the accomplishment of a certain plan, which cannot be carried out apart from the cooperation by means of the covenant between God and man, in a history which includes at the same time both divine and human elements.[44]

Or as Vos notes: 'The most striking feature of the Decalogue is its specifically religious character. It is not an ethical code in and by itself, resting, as it were, on the bare imperative of God. The preamble brings the affection to Jehovah, in view of what He has redemptively done for the people, to bear through a responsive affection upon their conduct.'[45]

---

[42]Walter C. Kaiser, *Toward an Old Testament Theology* (Grand Rapids, MI: Zondervan, 1991), 72.

[43]These are covenant words and must be interpreted within a covenant context, which – for convenience' sake – is postponed for a few pages, immediately after this section.

[44]André and Renée Neher, op. cit., 151, 152.

[45]G. Vos, op. cit., 147, 148.

The central confession of faith in Judaism from the time of Moses has come from the Shema of Deuteronomy 6:4-5: 'Hear, O Israel: The LORD our God is one LORD: And thou shalt love the LORD thy God with all thine heart, and with all thy soul, and with all thy might.'

This confession gives absolute loyalty to the One Sovereign Lord. The names used for Him are *jhvh* and *elohim*. Thus, the God who revealed Himself to Moses at the burning bush (Exodus 3:14) by his name 'I AM THAT I AM' (*jhvh*), the God who created all things out of nothing in Genesis 1 (*elohim*), the God who revealed the ten commandments to His redeemed people in the wilderness of Sinai in Exodus 20 as 'the LORD thy God' (*jhvh elohimkah* – v. 2), is the one sovereign God of creation, redemption and revelation. He therefore deserves our total love and total obedience.

Isaiah connects the sovereign power of God the Lord who 'created the heavens and stretched them out; he that spread forth the earth, and that which cometh out of it; he that giveth breath to the people upon it and spirit to them that walk therein' (Isa. 42:5) with his Covenant of Grace to His people, and the redemption that will be brought to pass by the terms of that covenant: 'I the LORD (*jhvh*) have called thee in righteousness, and will hold thine right hand, and will keep thee and give thee for a covenant of the people, for a light of the Gentiles; To open the blind eyes, to bring out the prisoners from the prison, and them that sit in darkness out of the prison house' (Isa. 42:6, 7).

Then immediately Isaiah speaks of His unique sovereign glory, which can be given to no other being: 'I am the LORD, that is my name: and my glory will I not give to another, neither my praise to graven images' Isa. 42:8). Only the one true God is competent to create, to redeem and to reveal truth; therefore, He deserves the absolute loyalty of all his rational creation.

As Walter Kaiser notes, 'The context of God's moral demands was twofold: "I am Yahweh your God" and "I brought you out of the land of Egypt, out of the house of slavery"' (Exod. 20:2). Kaiser goes on to state:

> Consequently, the standard of moral measurement in deciding what was right or wrong, good or evil, was fixed in the unwavering and impeccably holy character of Yahweh, Israel's God. His nature, attributes, character, and qualities provided the measuring stick for all ethical decisions. But there was, by the same token, an environment of grace – the free loving act of deliverance from Egypt. Israel did not need to keep the law in order to be released from Egypt. On the contrary, since she was so dramatically redeemed, the lever of obligation could not be easily removed.[46]

Divine sovereignty precludes polytheism

The uniqueness of the Sovereign God in creation was one of the major truths by which the Church Fathers defeated the irrationality of the polytheism of their culture. Tertullian, for example, about the year A.D. 207, argues that good sense excludes more than one supreme Being: 'In short, we feel that reason herself expressly forbids the belief in more gods than one, because

[46]Walter C. Kaiser, op. cit., 114.

the self-same rule lays down one God and not two, which declares that God must be a Being to which nothing is equal; he must moreover be unique.'[47]

Novatian of Rome (c. 250) carries these thoughts further:

> And over all these things He Himself, containing all things, having nothing vacant beyond Himself, has left room for no superior God, such as some people conceive. Since, indeed, He Himself has included all things in the bosom of perfect greatness and power, He is always intent upon His own work, and pervading all things, and moving all things, and quickening all things, and beholding all things, and so linking together discordant materials into the concord of all elements, that out of these unlike principles one world is so established by a conspiring union, that it can by no force be dissolved, save when He alone who made it commands it to be dissolved, for the purpose of bestowing other and greater things upon us. For we read that He contains all things, and therefore that there could have been nothing beyond Himself. Because, since He has not any beginning, so consequently He is not conscious of an ending; unless perchance – and far from us be the thought – He at some time began to be, and is not above all things, but as He began to be after something else, He would be beneath that which was before Himself, and would so be found to be of less power, in that He is designated as subsequent even in time itself. For this reason, therefore, He is always unbounded, because nothing is greater than He; always eternal, because nothing is more ancient than He. For that which is without beginning can be preceded by none, in that He has no time ... Concerning Him, therefore, and concerning those things which are of Himself, and are in Him, neither can the mind of man worthily conceive what they are, and what they are like; nor does the eloquence of human discourse set forth a power that approaches the level of His majesty. For to conceive and to speak of His majesty, as well all eloquence is with reason mute, as all mind poor. For He is greater than mind itself; nor can it be conceived how great He is, seeing that, if He could be conceived, He would be smaller than the human mind wherein He could be conceived ... For He is above all that can be said.[48]

The fourth-century theologian, Epiphanius, Bishop of Salamis, showed how the then popular Gnostic theory of dualism (an Old Testament Creator God, who is evil, and a New Testament God of love; both of whom oppose each other) is senseless and impossible, given the plain meaning of biblical lordship. In arguing against one sect of the Gnostics – the followers of Cerdo – he writes:

> ... I shall begin the refutation of Cerdo from the very things he says. For that there cannot be two first principles at once is obvious. Either the two principles are derived from some one; or the one is a second principle, while the other is the cause and principle of the second. So we shall either need to find a cause for the two or find which of them is the principle of the other and therefore [its cause], as I said. And thus our reasoning leads inevitably to the one, the actual first principle, the source either of the second or both, as I have shown.

---

[47]Terrtullian, *Adversus Marcionem*, I.v.

[48]Novatian, *De Trinitate*, ch. II.

But the two first principles cannot exist at once, nor can the one be different from the other. For if they are different, there are two of them; but by being two, they have become more than one. But since the one, first number is required, 'two' is implied by the number which is "one", and comes before it, and is the cause of 'two.' For 'two,' which comes after the number 'one' – or, after the single, first principle – cannot be its own cause. The unit, which comes first of all, is always required.

For if the two turn out to be of one accord and to have a mutual complaisance and agreement, in that the one remains in existence with the consent of the other while the other enjoys its partnership with the first, what conflict is there between them? But if they are in conflict, and each is just as strong as the other, then, although Christ came to do away with the one, he will no longer be capable of destroying its tyranny. It will stand its ground and have the ability to struggle with the invisible, unnameable power on high and hold out, and can never be destroyed.

The fool says that both the Law and the prophets belong to the inferior and contrary principle, whereas Christ belongs to the good one ...[49]

Universal harmony requires one sovereignty over the universe

A generation before Epiphanius, St. Athanasius had shown that the harmony of the order of nature and the unity of God are correlative truths:

> Since then, there is everywhere not disorder, but order, proportion and not disproportion, not disarray but arrangement, and that in an order perfectly harmonious, we must needs infer and be led to perceive the Master that put together and compacted all things, and produced harmony in them. For though He be not seen with the eyes, yet from the order and harmony of things contrary it is possible to perceive their Ruler, Arranger, and King...the inference surely follows that the presence of a ruler enforces concord, even if we do not see him; (for disorder is a sign of absence of rule, while order shews the governing authority: for when we see the mutual harmony of the members in the body...that each accomplishes its service without variance, we perceive from this that certainly there is a soul in the body that governs these members, though we see it not); so in the order and harmony of the universe, we must needs perceive God, the governor of it all, and that He is one and not many ...[50]

> For we must not think there is more than one ruler and maker of Creation: but it belongs to correct and true religion to believe that its Artificer is one, while creation herself clearly points to this. For the fact that there is one universe only and not more is a conclusive proof that its Maker is one. For if there were a plurality of gods, there would necessarily be also more universes than one. For neither were it reasonable for more than one God to make a single universe, nor for the one universe to be made by more than one, because of the absurdities which would result from this ...[51]

---

[49]Epiphanius, *The Panarion*, translated by Frank Williams in 'Nag Hammadi and Manichaean Studies', J. M. Robinson & H. J. Klimkeit, eds., XXXV (Leiden: Brill, 1997), Bk. I, Sect. 41, pp. 270-71.

[50]Athanasius, *Contra Gentes*, 38.

[51]Ibid., 39.

In the eighth century, John of Damascus writes similarly, though in a different context:

> … But that God is one and not many is no matter of doubt to those who believe in the Holy Scriptures. For the Lord says in the beginning of the Law: *I am the Lord thy God, which have brought thee out of the land of Egypt. Thou shalt have no other Gods before me* (Exod. 20:2, 3). And again He says, *Hear, O Israel, the Lord our God is one Lord* (Deut. 6:4). And in Isaiah the prophet we read, *For I am the first God and I am the last, and beside me there is no God. Before me, there was not any God, nor after me will there be any God, and beside me there is no God* (Isa. 43:10). And the Lord, too, in the holy gospels speaketh these words to His Father, *And this is life eternal, that they may know thee the only true God* (John 17:3). But with those that do not believe in the Holy Scriptures we will reason thus.
>
> The Deity is perfect, and without blemish in goodness, and wisdom, and power, without beginning, without end, everlasting, uncircumscribed, and in short, perfect in all things. Should we say, then, that there are many gods, we must recognize difference among the many. For if there is no difference among them, they are one rather than many. But if there is difference among them, what becomes of the perfectness? For that which comes short of perfection, whether it be in goodness, or power, or wisdom, or time, or place, could not be God. But it is this very identity in all respects that shews that the Deity is one and not many.
>
> Again, if there are many gods, how can one maintain that God is uncircumscribed? For where the one would be, the other could not be.
>
> Further how could the world be governed by many and saved from dissolution and destruction, while strife is seen to rage between the rulers? For difference introduces strife. And if any one should say that each rules over a part, what of that which established this order and gave to each his particular realm? For this would the rather be God. Therefore God is one, perfect, uncircumscribed, maker of the universe, and its preserver and governor, exceeding and preceding all perfection …[52]

Richard of St. Victor (in the twelfth century) wrote concerning God's unique oneness in divine lordship:

> Furthermore, it is impossible for several all-powerful Beings to exist. Because He who is really all-powerful would be able easily to reduce all the others to impotency; otherwise, he would not really be all powerful. But what are these 'all-powerful ones' who are so easily reduced into totally impotent beings? Ah, how easy it is to demonstrate that even the nature of things precludes the existence of more than one Omnipotent!... Consequently, since there can be only one Omnipotent, there can be only one God.[53]
>
> Besides what we have already said concerning the singular unity of the divinity, how many more ways there are of proving that there is only one God! One sole uncreated one, one sole eternal one, one sole immense one; every one of these affirmations manifestly prove that there is only one God. If you think about it carefully, you would be able to find another argument in the consideration of what his unity means. For, if one pretends that there are several gods, this consideration will be able to demonstrate that no matter

---

[52]John of Damascus, *De Fide Orthodoxa*, I.v.

[53]Richard of St. Victor, *De Trinitate*, I.xxv.

> which one of them derives his being from another one, he therefore lacks the property of existing out of himself...[54]
>
> It is therefore necessary that the sovereign Good be sovereignly one and not only sovereignly one, but sovereignly unique. For there cannot exist two sovereign goods, any more than two totally sovereign perfections...If indeed God is truly the sovereign Good, just as there cannot be but one sovereign good, there can truly be but one God, according to the affirmation of our Faith.[55]

Divine names indicate God's sovereignty

Elohim and Jahveh

The LORD (*jhvh*) is named something like 6,800 times in the Old Testament, and is used 'in every book but Esther, Ecclesiastes and Song of Solomon'.[56] Elohim is used 2,570 times ('sometimes used for other gods – Exodus 20:3 – when it also may take the definite article – Exodus 18:11, plural adjectives and plural verbs – Psalm 97:7').[57]

> The OT begins with reference to Elohim rather than Yahweh (Gen. 1:1); this may indicate that it more readily carried a universal sense for that audience than the personal name Yahweh. The addition of Yahweh to Elohim, 'LORD God,' in Gen. 2:4–3:23 may be meant to claim that this universal creator God is none other than Israel's personal God. That the name Yahweh was invoked from earliest times (Gen. 4:26), and this by non-Israelites in a setting that has all of humankind in view, may reflect a comparable universal intention related to worship. Yahweh is a God for all people and may be prayed to and worshiped by all (see 1 Kings 8:41-43). The constant interchange between Yahweh and Elohim in the subsequent Genesis narratives, particularly with their lively interest in the interaction between the chosen family and the surrounding peoples, may carry this universal intention forward. That this carries a missional interest may be seen in the repeated word that Abraham has been chosen for the sake of 'all peoples of the earth' (Gen. 12:3 and par.). Election is for mission.[58]

Heinrich Bullinger pointed out long ago that *Elohim* could take in Scripture either the plural or singular number of the verb. He believed that this was an indication of the difference of persons in the Holy Trinity:

> And although the word *Elohim* be of the plural number, yet is it set before verbs in the singular number; as in the first of Genesis we find, 'In the beginning,' *Bara Elohim*, *Creavit Dii*, 'God created' (for *Bara*, *created*, is the singular number) heaven and earth. In that phrase of speech is shewed unto us the mystery of the reverend Trinity; for Moses seemeth to have said in effect, In the beginning that God in the Trinity created heaven and earth. In the seventh chapter of the second book of Samuel, *Elohim* in the plural

---

[54]Ibid., II. xiv.

[55]Ibid., II. xix.

[56]William Van Gemeren, gen. ed., *New International Dictionary of Old Testament Theology & Exegesis* (Grand Rapids: Zondervan, 1997), vol. 4, 1295.

[57]Ibid., vol. 1, 405.

[58]Ibid., vol. 1, 406.

number is joined with verbs of the plural number, to declare that there is a difference of persons in the blessed Trinity.[59]

Baal

'There are two words for "lord" and "master" in Hebrew just as there are two in English, and both these words were applied to God as well as to man.'[60] The first word *baal* was used of the false gods of the Canaanite fertility cults. 'Originally *baal* meant nothing more nor less than master,' and its usage for heathen deities 'is really a developed use of the word.'[61] '... the early Hebrews ... called their God Jahweh a *baal* too in early times (cf. 2 Sam. 6:2)... Even David calls Jahweh *baal* in 2 Sam. 5:20.'[62]

But there is a second, and far more widely used word in the Old Testament for Lord:

Adhonai and Kyrios

> In its place there was used another and corresponding word for 'lord', viz., the word *Adhonai*. To this day the Jew, when he has to utter the sacred Tetragrammaton which records the divine name in the MT, instead of reading it as Jahweh, reads it as *Adhonai*. In other words, all down the centuries the thought of both Jews and Christians in this matter has been dominated by the conception of God as Lord. The LXX translated *Adhonai* as *kyrios*, and so the NT uses *kyrios* as a title for God, just as does the Jew.[63]

> In the LXX *kyrios* occurs over 9,000 times. It is used to translate *'adon*, lord, and as such refers 190 times to men. It is used only 15 times for *ba'al*, lord...In the overwhelming majority of cases (some 6,156), however, *kyrios* replaces the Heb. Proper name of God, the tetragrammaton YHWH. The LXX thus strengthened the tendency to avoid the utterance of the name of God, and finally to avoid its use altogether. The substitution of the title *adonay* for the proper name Yahweh was a result of Israel's development from a national religion in the pre-exilic period to an international one in the period of Alexander (356–323 B.C.). Where originally the exodus was the theological focal point, after the exile the emphasis fell on the creation of the world. Where *kyrios* stands for *'adon* or *'adonay* there has been genuine translation, but where, on the other hand, it stands for Yahweh it is an interpretative circumlocution for all the Heb. Text implied by the use of the divine name: Yahweh is Creator and Lord of the whole universe, of men, Lord of life and death. Above all he is God of Israel, his covenant people.[64]

> Of the 717 passages in which *kyrios* occurs in the NT, the majority are to be found in the Lucan writings (210) and in Paul's letters (275). This one-sidedness can be explained by the fact that Luke wrote for, and Paul to, people who lived in areas dominated by Gk. Culture and language. On the other hand, the Gospel of Mark, more firmly based in Jewish Christian

---

[59]Heinrich Bullinger, *The Decades: The Fourth Decade* (Cambridge at the University Press: Parker Society, 1851), 'The Third Sermon,' 134,135.

[60]George A. F. Knight, *A Biblical Approach to the Doctrine of the Trinity* in 'Scottish Journal of Theology Occasional Papers, No. 1 (Edinburgh: Oliver & Boyd, 1953), 18.

[61]Ibid.

[62]Ibid., 19.

[63]Ibid.

[64]*New International Dictionary of New Testament Theology*, Colin Brown, gen. ed. (Grand Rapids: Zondervan, 1986), vol. 2, pp. 511, 512.

> tradition, uses the *kyrios*-title only 18 times, and these mostly in quotations. The remaining occurrences of *kyrios* are spread over the other NT books: Matt. 80; John 52; Heb. 16; James 14; 1 Pet. 8; 2 Pet. 14; Jude 17; and Rev. 23. The fact that *kyrios* is one of the most frequently used words in the NT is in accordance with its varied use in the LXX.[65]

The New Testament uses *kyrios* of God:

> In accordance with the usage of the Hellenistic synagogues God is frequently called *kyrios*, especially in the numerous quotations from the OT in which *kyrios* stands for Yahweh, corresponding to the custom of pronouncing the title *kyrios* instead of the tetragrammaton in public reading (e.g. Rom. 4:8 = Ps. 32:2; 9:28f. = Isa. 10:22; 10:16 = Isa. 53:1; 11:3 = Luke 19:10; 11:34 = Isa. 40:13; 14:11 = Isa. 45:23; 15:11 = Ps. 94:11; 14:21 = Isa. 45:23; 15:11 = Ps. 117:1; 1 Cor. 3:20 = Ps. 94:11; 14:21 = Isa. 28:11f.). *kyrios* frequently denotes God in the Lucan birth narratives (e.g. Luke 1:32; 2:9); *kyrios* in the gen. accompanying another word corresponds to OT usage: the hand of the *kyrios* (Luke 1:66; Acts 11:21 … The formula 'says the *kyrios*' (Rom. 12:19 = Deut. 32:35; 2 Cor. 6:17 = Isa. 52:11; Rev. 1:8 cf. Exod. 3:14) also comes from the OT. To the OT phrase *kyrios ho theos* the author of Rev. sometimes adds an emphatic, solemn *pantokrator*, All-Sovereign (Rev. 1:8; 4:8; 11:17; 16:7; 19:6; 21:22 …) … By addressing and acknowledging God as *kyrios*, the NT expresses particularly his creatorship, his power revealed in history and his just dominion over the universe, and at the same time confesses the continuity of its belief with that of the OT.[66]

Jesus was addressed as *kyrios* during his earthly life. Sometimes it was a polite form of address, related to a rabbi. But it was more, for he was '*kyrios* of the Sabbath' (Mark 2:28f.).

After his exaltation, Jesus was widely confessed as *kyrios*.

> The confessional cry used in worship, *kyrios Iesous*, Jesus (is) Lord, no doubt originated in the pre-Pauline Hellenistic Christian community. This confession is one of the oldest Christian creeds, if not the oldest. With this call the NT community submitted itself to its Lord, but at the same time it also confessed him as ruler of the world (Rom. 10:9a; 1 Cor. 12:3; Phil. 2:11 …). God has raised Jesus from the dead and exalted him to the position of universal *kyrios*. Moreover, he has 'bestowed on him the name which is above every name' (Phil. 2:9ff; cf. Isa. 45:23f.), i.e. his own name of Lord and with it the position corresponding to the name…The exalted *kyrios*, Christ, rules over mankind (Rom. 14:9). All powers and being in the universe must bow the knee before him. When that happens, God the Father will be worshipped (cf. Eph. 1:20f.; 1 Pet. 3:22) …[67]

Kyrios, Elohim, Jahveh and Shaddai

Kittel summarizes the evidence of the many passages of Scripture bearing on *kyrios* (*jhvh*):

> 'In the religious sphere, then, *kyrios* or *ho kyrios* is reserved for the true God, and apart from unimportant periphrases of the name in figurative speech,

---

[65] Ibid., 513.
[66] Ibid., 513, 514.
[67] Ibid., 514.

> it is used regularly, i.e. some 6,156 times, for the proper name (*Yahweh*) in all its pointings and in the combination (*Yahweh Tsabaot*) or in the short form (*Ya*). Only by way of exception is *kyrios* used for the other terms for God (*Elohim*, etc.)... Thus *kyrios* is best understood by looking at the original name, *Yahweh*.
>
> The God to whom the canon bears witness is called 'Lord' because He is there shown to be the exclusive holder of power over the cosmos and all men, the creator of the world, and the master of life and death...*Yahweh* is used with a strong sense of its significance as the confession of a specific experience of the divine', especially in the age of Moses, and as in Exod. 3:14, has redemptive connotations.[68]

Heinrich Bullinger faithfully summarizes the evidences on the names of the Lord as *Shaddai* and *Jahveh* ('*Jehovah*'):

> The Lord himself, in the sixth chapter of Exodus, putteth these two names together, *Schaddai* and *Jehovah*, as two of the most excellent names that he hath, and saith: 'I am Jehovah. And I appeared to Abraham, Isaac, and Jacob, as God Schaddai; but in my name Jehovah I was not known unto them.' Not that the patriarchs had not heard or known the name Jehovah: for that name began to be called upon in the time of Seth, immediately after the beginning of the world. Therefore it seemeth that the Lord meant thus in effect: 'I opened myself unto the patriarchs as God Schaddai, who am able in all things sufficiently to fill them with all goodness; and therefore I promised them a land that floweth with milk and honey: but in my name Jehovah I was not yet known unto them, that is, I did not perform unto them that which I promised.' For we have heard already, that he is called Jehovah of that which he maketh to be; and therefore he bringeth his promise to performance. 'Now therefore' (saith he) 'I will indeed fulfil my promise, and shew myself to be, not only *Deus Schaddai*, an all-sufficient or almighty God, but also to be Jehovah, an essence or being eternal, immutable, true, and in all things like myself, or standing to my promise.'[69]

The One God, therefore, the great 'I AM' always exists as three co-equal, loving Persons, as His Old Testament names indicate, and as crucial New Testament passages make clear. His unique, divine Being exercises sole sovereignty in creation and law-giving in the context of the Covenant of Grace.

---

[68]*Theological Dictionary of the New Testament*, edited by Gerhard Kittel; trans. and ed. G. W. Bromiley (Grand Rapids: Wm. B. Eerdmans, 1965), vol. 3, pp. 1059, 1062, 1063.

[69]H. Bullinger, op. cit., 136.

Chapter Four
Appendix One

The Distinction in Eastern Orthodox Theology Between God's Essence and His Energies

An important theological distinction was made in medieval Eastern Orthodoxy by St. Gregory Palamas between God's inner being (*ousios*) – essence or substance – and his energies or operations (*energeiai*) – including His attributes (*idiomata*) and names (*onomata*). Duncan Reid has written an illuminating work on this distinction: *Energies of the Spirit: Trinitarian Models in Eastern Orthodox and Western Theology*.[1] I make grateful use of it in this appendix.

Although this distinction was not fully developed until the fourteenth-century, it seems in some sense to go back to 'the patristic distinction between *theologia* and *economia*.'[2] This distinction was made especially in the context of the theology of 'deification' of believers, who thereby participate in the divine nature (I Peter 1:4). 'We are destined, according to Maximus the Confessor, to become 'everything that God is, except for *essential* identity.'[3] This, in turn, is related to '... the Biblical experience of God as the one who is both *Deus revelatus* and *Deus absconditus*. This God is encountered at the burning bush, in the liberation of the Hebrew slaves from captivity in Egypt, and in the death and resurrection of Jesus Christ. But the witnesses to these events are always aware that there is more to God than is revealed in the events themselves...One type of discourse relates to God in relation to us (*pro nobis*); the other relates to God in Godself (*a se*).'[4]

St. Photios may have had in mind some such distinction in his late ninth-century *On the Mystagogy of the Holy Spirit*, where in the context of the mutual glorification of the three Persons of the Trinity, he writes: '... In the superessential Trinity, above all glory, the ineffable and mutual glorification of the Three Persons is a common attribute.'[5] If so, this would be consistent with the later teaching that the essence of God is above the energies.

---

[1]With a foreword by Jürgen Moltmann (Atlanta, GA: Scholars Press, 1997).

[2]Ibid., 1.

[3]Ibid.

[4]Ibid., 7.

[5]Chapter 27 in St. Photios, *La Mystagogie du Saint Esprit: Oeuvres Trinitaires II* (Paris: Fraternité Orthodoxe Saint Grégoire Palamas, 1991), 98.

But a more direct influence than Photios upon the later Palamite distinction between essence and energies was that of the Patriarch of Constantinople, Gregory of Cyprus (1283–1289). Gregory restored the traditional Eastern Orthodox understanding of the Son proceeding only from the Father, after the Council of Lyon in 1274 had forced the few Greek Orthodox delegates to agree to the Filioque clause. Gregory led the Council of Blachernae (1285), which repudiated the forced Lyon settlement of 1274. Gregory II surveyed what occurred before and during the Council in his official *Tomus*, soon afterwards. There he makes a strong distinction between the one essence and the three Persons.[6]

Aristeides Papadakis shows that Gregory

> ... differentiates between the hypostasis of the Spirit and the energy, between the person of the Spirit and the eternal gifts received at Pentecost ... Pentecost is not an incarnation of the Spirit, but the communication or the bestowing of the gifts of divine or uncreated grace ... for the divine, as Gregory emphasizes, is alone participable through its *eternal* (and therefore, uncreated) energies. God is not limited solely to His essence, but interacts with creation through the eternal and uncreated character of His radiance or manifestation.[7]

Papadakis then notes:

> ... the striking similarity between the above exposition and the subsequent fourteenth-century Palamite conception of God. Patriarch Gregory's unwillingness to limit God to his essence, and his insistence that it is through the energy that God is made manifest, are the main threads from which the theological fabric of Palamas is woven.[8]

A difference between East and West on essence and attributes of God

Generally, in the West, on the basis of the simplicity of God, essence and attributes are understood to be identical. As M. Schmaus writes:

> It is the hallmark of the Augustinian notion of God that God is absolutely simple being. He allows no real distinction between substance and accidence, between accidence and accidence, between being and being-active, between activity and activity. Augustine never tires of emphasizing this simplicity.[9]

But in the East, a distinction developed between essence and energy. 'It is the distinction that we come across in John of Damascus, between the divine 'nature' (φύσις) and 'that which surrounds the nature' (τὰ περὶ τὴν φύσιν) [John of Damascus, *Exposito Fidei*, I.1,4,8, etc.], or between 'according to the essence' (κατ̓ οὐσίαν and 'according to the energy' (κατ̓ ἐνέργειαν) [Ibid., I.9].'[10]

---

[6]See Aristeides Papadakis, *Crisis in Byzantium: The Filioque Controversy in the Patriarchate of Gregory II of Cyprus (1283-1289)* (Crestwood, NY: St. Vladimir's Seminary Press, 1997), 117.

[7]Ibid., 128.

[8]Ibid.

[9]M. Schmaus, *Die Psychologische Trinitätslehre des Heiligen Augustinus* (Munster, 1967), 86; cited in Reid, op. cit., 11.

[10]Reid, op. cit., 15.

Distinction developed by St. Gregory Palamas

Palamas expands this distinction in the context of his mystical theology, in which believers become united with God's uncreated light or energy, but *not* with His substance. He writes:

> This very radiance and divinizing energy of God, by which the beings that participate are divinized, is a certain divine grace but not the nature of God... The divine energy and grace of the Spirit, while it is everywhere present and is inseparable from him, remains imparticipable ...[11]

> The light of the sun is inseparable from its ray and the heat produced by it, but among those who enjoy the sun's rays the light is imparticipable to those who have not acquired eyes... So too, and much more, will there be no participation in the substance of the Creator by any of those who enjoy the divine resplendence, for there is not, nor does there exist any creature who has a power capable of perceiving the nature of the Creator.[12]

> ... neither is the participated energy created nor is it the substance of God ... Chrysostom, the Church Father, goes on to point out still another difference of the uncreated substance with respect to the uncreated energy, when he says, 'If the energy of the Spirit is without measure, much more is the substance' [John Chrysostom, *Homilia in Ioannem* 30.2, PG 59.174].[13]

> ... creation will become divine, and God will share his rank with creatures. For this reason the divine Cyril pointed out the distinction between the substance and energy of God when he said that 'begetting belongs to the divine nature but creating to his divine energy,' adding the wise statement, 'Nature and energy are not identical' [Cyril of Alexandria, *Thesaurus* 18, PG 75: 312c].[14]

Gregory Palamas and Karl Barth

We Christians of the Western churches might be able to grasp something of what underlies this distinction that is foreign to our tradition by considering the possible connection our concern to uphold the transcendence and incomprehensibility of God may have with the Eastern essence/energies distinction. The great twentieth-century Romanian Orthodox theologian, to whom I frequently refer, Dumitru Stăniloae, perceived a connection between this Palamite distinction and Karl Barth's emphasis on God as 'Totally Other':

> Stăniloae continued an intellectual dialogue with [Karl Barth] for many years. He deeply considered the Barthian idea of *Diastasis* (Totally Other), in which the Protestant theologian sought to underline the total transcendence of God and his incomprehensibility...Already studying the theology of Gregory Palamas, he sought to build a bridge between that which in God is communicable and that which is incommunicable in His relation to the

---

[11]St. Gregory Palamas, *The One Hundred and Fifty Chapters*, ch. 93, p. 193.
[12]Ibid., ch. 94, p. 195.
[13]Ibid., ch. 95, p. 196, 197.
[14]Ibid., ch. 96, p. 197.

world. According to Stăniloae's intuition, the Palamite divine essence is comparable to the Barthian *diastasis*.[15]

Later, Stăniloae wrote of his preference for the Palamite over the Barthian approach:

> Both the dialectical theology and the theology of Saint Gregory Palamas made me see a living, personal God; but, while in the dialectical one God was separated from man because he could not free himself from his own sins, in the Palamitical theology God moved towards man called by prayer. In the dialectical theology I found an image of a separate and distant God, while in the Palamitical one I met a God who comes towards man, opens Himself to him like light through prayer. He fills him with His energies, yet remaining uncommunicable with respect to His essence, incomprehensible, apophatic.[16]

East and West both hold to the Creator/creature distinction

Another way to find a similar underlying concern between the Eastern distinction and Western theology (whether Catholic or Protestant) is to think of the all-important distinction made by all biblical Christians between the Creator and the creature. With reference to Florovsky's 'The Idea of Creation in Christian Philosophy', Reid states that:

> The world does not have to exist. In fact the creation finds its basis in the *will* of God, not the nature or essence of God [Florovsky, op. cit., 48]. This distinction between nature/essence and will becomes the basis, for Florovsky, for a defense of the distinction between essence and energy. That which is of God by nature, or essence (e.g. the generation of the second person of the trinity) is necessary; that which is in accordance with God's will (viz. the creation of the world) is contingent. The former *must* be; the second *may* be, but need not...The distinction between essence and energy *is* in fact the distinction between necessity (or nature – as Florovsky would prefer to call it) and will. This in turn becomes the foundation for a proper ontological differentiation between God and the creation.[17]

Does the Palamite theology make God finally unknowable?

All of classical Western theology is agreed on this point. But for us in the West it becomes rather more difficult when the Palamite theology appears to make such a strong distinction between the substance or essence of God and His energies or operations that all we actually know and experience of the Triune God pertains to His energies, and not to His substance. By that token, the substance of God is finally unknowable. Palamas writes:

> The transcendent, supremely living, divine and good nature, in that it is supremely good and divine and suchlike, is neither spoken of, nor conceived, nor contemplated in any way at all because it transcends all things and is supremely unknowable and established beyond the supercelestial minds

[15] Maciej Bielawski, *The Philokalical Vision of the World in the Theology of Dumitru Stăniloae* (Dissertatio ad Lauream in Facultate S. Theologiae apud Pontificiam Universitatem S. Thomae in Urbe: Romae, 1997), 23.

[16] Ibid., 27.

[17] Reid, op. cit., 34, 37, 38.

> by an incomprehensible power and is always utterly inapprehensible and ineffable for all ...[18]

What we know and do not know in 'deification', according to Palamas

The aspect of God that we can truly know (and be united with in 'deification') therefore is not His substance or nature, but His energies. 'In view of the gifts bestowed by illumination and the Patristic and scriptural witness to it, Palamas concluded that it must be an uncreated reality, distinct from the divine substance.'[19] Palamas writes:

> Thus [Dionysius the Areopagite] clearly shows that there is another distinction alongside that of the hypostases and a distinction belonging to the Godhead, for the distinction of the hypostases is not a distinction belonging to the Godhead. And he says that according to the divine processions and energies God is multiplied and enters multiplicity and at this point he says that the same procession is also processions; but at another point the Divinity does not enter multiplicity – certainly not! – nor as God is he subject to distinction. For us God is a Trinity but he is not threefold. Dionysius demonstrates also the uncreated character of these processions and energies, for he calls them divine and says that they are distinctions belonging to the whole Godhead; he mentions also that the very thearchy itself is compounded and multiplied in these divine processions and energies while it does not assume anything external – certainly not!...'[20]

Where are the attributes of God 'located'?

This seems to entail the conception that God's attributes are actually 'located' in His uncreated energies, but not in His substance. That is profoundly different from the West, where it is understood that God *is* His attributes; that they are His substance. Particularly is this true of the hypostatic relations: God *is* in His very substance Father, Son and Holy Spirit. The uncreated energies (including the attributes of God) are said to be 'around His essence', but not His essence or nature.[21]

In reference to Florovsky's 'Creation and Creaturehood,' Reid explains that Florovsky

> ... begins by distinguishing two types of attributes or names of God ['Creation and Creaturehood,' 62], both of which have their basis in activities. First there are the inner attributes, viz. Father, Son, and Holy Spirit, who receive their being from the inner acts of generation and procession. Second, there are the outer attributes, which receive their being from outer acts of the entire trinity. Thus we have the distinction between divine nature or essence on the one hand, and the divine will, which is located 'beyond the essence' [Ibid., 63]. This distinction (Florovsky insists that it is not a separation) is, of course, that which underlines all Palamite theology.[22]

---

[18]St. Gregory Palamas, *The One Hundred and Fifty Chapters*, ch. 106, pp. 201, 203.
[19]Ibid., 40.
[20]Ibid., ch. 85, pp. 183, 185.
[21]See Reid, op. cit., 15
[22]Ibid., 39.

Thus, it would appear that the persons of the Trinity are in the nature of God, but not the attributes (or energies), into which latter we are brought by grace and adoption into union. At times it sounds (at least to Western ears) that Palamas has so strictly isolated the unknown essence of God, that the divine hypostases are actually energies or attributes, rather than constituents of the divine substance. He writes for instance:

> Nor indeed does everything predicated of him denote the substance, for relation is predicated of him, which is relative and refers to relationships with another but is not indicative of substance. Such also is the divine energy in God, for it is neither substance nor accident, even though it is called a quasi-accident by some theologians who are indicating solely that it is in God but is not the substance.[23]

The divine hypostases are in the substance and operate through the energies

So does that mean that the Trinitarian persons, since they are relationships, are not in the very substance of God? Answering his opponents (such as Barlaam and Akindynos), who either denied the distinction between essence and energies, or held that the energies were created, St. Gregory replies:

> For they do not understand that just as God the Father is called Father in relation to his own Son, and being Father belongs to him as an uncreated reality even though 'Father' does not denote the substance, so too God possesses the energy as an uncreated reality even though the energy is distinct from the substance. And when we speak of one Godhead we speak of everything that God is, namely, both the substance and the energy. Therefore, they are the ones who are impiously splitting the one divinity of God into created and uncreated.[24]

John Meyendorff follows in this Palamite line by referring to the sixth-century Pseudo-Dionysius:

> God, therefore, is absolutely transcendent and above existence, and – as long as one remains in the categories of existence – can be described only in negative terms [Pseudo-Dionysius, *Mystical Theology*, V; PG 3: 1045b-1048a]. God does, however, make Himself known outside of His transcendent nature: 'God is manifested by His 'powers' in all beings, is multiplied without abandoning His unity' [Vladimir Lossky, *Vision of God* (London: Faith Press, 1963), 102]. Thus, the concepts of beauty, being, goodness, and the like, reflect God, but not His essence, only His 'powers' and 'energies' [Pseudo-Dionysius, *On the Divine Names*, II; PG 3: 165a] – which are not, however, a diminished form of deity, or mere emanations, but themselves full God, in whom created beings can participate in the proportion and analogy proper to each.[25]

Christos Yannaras explains this as: '...the coming into appearance, the coming out of hiddenness' and 'out of absence into presence'.[26]

---

[23]Palamas, op. cit., ch. 127, 231.

[24]Ibid., ch. 126, 231.

[25]Meyendorff, *Byzantine Theology*, 27,28.

[26]*Person und Eros: Eine Gegenüberstellung der Ontologie der grieschischen Kirchenväter und der Existenzphilosophie des Westens* (Göttingen, 1982): Vandenhoeck and Ruprecht, 21].

The 'superessential' Trinity makes Himself available in the energies
Reid comments:

> This, according to Yannaras, is precisely the intention of the Palamite doctrine of energies. In mystical experience God is experienced in a sensible or aesthetic (in contrast to an intellectual or noetic) way, precisely because God makes Godself available to us in the energies, while remaining at the same time essentially inaccessible to us.[27]

Objections from the West to the essence/energy distinction of Palamism

Theologians of the West have raised a number of problems about the tenability of this distinction. We need not deal with all of them, but only with what I would consider to be the most important one. Karl Barth raises this crucial objection from the vantage point of Western Trinitarian theology to the distinction between God's essence and God's energies. This distinction seems to leave us in a position where we do not really know who God is in his inner reality; it seems to leave us with an unknowable, faceless God; perhaps, an impersonal God.

Reid summarizes Barth's main objections:

> It is in his critique of nominalist reductionism in relation to the attributes of God that Barth attacks the Palamite distinction between essence and energies, on the grounds that the energies are identified in Palamite theology with the names or activities of God [Barth, *Church Dogmatics* 2/1, 325ff.] ... The concept of energies is rather condescendingly characterized as 'a middle-level of the divinity', and Barth endorses the criticism made originally by Nicephorus Gregoras that the doctrine of energies means either a fourth hypostasis or else an impersonal manner (that is, not belonging specifically to any one of the trinitarian hypostases) of God's action in and dealing with the world...The result of this [fourteenth-century Palamite] victory was, according to Barth, a separation of being from attributes in God, so that the being becomes formless and God's form becomes insubstantial. The fundamental question for Barth is the possibility – and its apparent realization in Palamism – of a hidden, faceless God who is in reality quite other than what God outwardly pretends to be.[28]

Duncan Reid defends this Palamite distinction from Barth's accusation of its being a form of nominalism, leaving us finally ignorant of God Himself:

> Considered a form of nominalism (or seminominalism), Palamism appears to restrict the names of God to a purely creaturely level. The energies are an uncreated, therefore eternal reality that also acts in relation to the creation. *Speech about the energies remains speech whose subject matter is God.* We are dealing here not with a merely created manifestation of God. This, in fact, is the common thread that runs through all Palamite writings, the affirmation that the energies are uncreated.[29]

---

[27]Reid, op. cit., 86.
[28]Ibid., 95.
[29]Ibid., 96.

Particularly, Reid suggest that the West needs to keep in mind the inseparability of being and act (or energies) in God:

> ... in our experience of God, act and being are not separate. It is equally clear, though, that God is more than we experience ... The significance of the problem of act and being for the issue under discussion can be summarized in this way. Being, for Palamism, denotes more than act. God is both being *and* act, or rather, superessentiality and act. This superessentiality of God is indeed distinguished from the activity of God in this model, but the 'being' of God in the more general sense encompasses both. This distinction is exactly the same as that made by Barth between 'being as such' (*Wesen als Solches*) and 'acts' (*Wirken*), which both come under the larger heading of the 'reality of God' (*Wirklichkeit Gottes*) ... The doctrine of energies demands no static concept of God, nor does it introduce any 'middle-level' of divinity into the doctrine of creation. It offers a way of avoiding both these problem areas.[30]

The West agrees that we cannot penetrate the essence of God

Let us note here, that even from the Western viewpoint, it is profoundly biblical to say that there is more about the Being or substance of God than we can know. While we rightly believe that the Being of God is the three Persons, and the three Persons are the Being of God, yet that does not imply that we can penetrate the essence of God as though we know what makes God God.

Let us briefly mention a few main witnesses from the Western tradition on this point: St. Thomas Aquinas, Martin Luther, Melanchthon, John Calvin and Heinrich Bullinger.

St. Thomas Aquinas

In *Summa Theologiae*, St. Thomas writes:

> *Reply Objection 2. To be* can mean either of two things. It may mean the act of essence, or it may mean the composition of a proposition effected by the mind in joining a predicate to a subject. Taking *to be* in the first sense, we cannot understand God's existence nor His essence; but only in the second sense. We know that this proposition which we form about God when we say *God is*, is true; and this we know from His effects (Q. 2, A. 2).[31]

He writes similarly in *Summa Contra Gentiles*:

> [4] Now, the mode of supereminence in which the above-mentioned perfections are found in God can be signified by names used by us only through negation, as when we say that God is *eternal* or *infinite*, or also through a relation of God to other things, as when He is called the *first cause* or the *highest good*. For we cannot grasp what God is, but only what He is not and how other things are related to Him, as is clear from what we said above.[32]

---

[30] Ibid., 99.

[31] St. Thomas Aquinas, *Summa Theologiae* I. 3. 4.

[32] St. Thomas Aquinas, *Summa Contra Gentiles* Book One, ch. 30, sec. 4 (p. 141 of Pegis edition).

Martin Luther

Martin Luther constantly made a distinction between the transcendent essence of God and our knowledge of Him in His works and words. 'God also does not manifest himself except through his works and word, because the meaning of these is understood in some measure. Whatever else belongs essentially to the Divinity cannot be grasped and understood.'[33]

Philip Melanchthon

Luther's assistant, and 'the preceptor of Germany,' Philip Melanchthon, certainly followed Luther and the entire Christian tradition in teaching the mysteriousness and ineffability of the divine essence. But Melanchthon's consistent emphasis on the Christocentric nature of our knowledge of God follows from his foundational insight in his 1521 *Loci Communes*, that 'to know God is to know Christ, and to know Christ is to know his benefits.'[34]

John Calvin

The theology of John Calvin is not essentially different at this point. In his *Institutes of the Christian Religion*, he writes:

> For the Lord manifests himself by his powers, the force of which we feel within ourselves and the benefits of which we enjoy. We must therefore be much more profoundly affected by this knowledge than if we were to imagine a God of whom no perception came to us. Consequently, we know the most perfect way of seeking God, and the most suitable order, is not for us to attempt with bold curiosity to penetrate to the investigation of his essence, which we ought more to adore than meticulously to search out, but for us to contemplate him in his works whereby he renders himself near and familiar to us, and in some manner communicates himself.[35]

Reflecting on Exodus 34:6-7 ['Jehovah, Jehovah, a merciful and gracious God, patient and of much compassion, and true, who keepest mercy for thousands, who takest away iniquity and transgression ... in whose presence the innocent will not be innocent, who visitest the iniquity of the fathers upon the children and the children's children'], Calvin states:

> Here let us observe that his eternity and his self-existence are announced by that wonderful name twice repeated. Thereupon his powers are mentioned, by which he is shown to us not as he is in himself, but as he is toward us; so that this recognition of him consists more in living experience than in vain and high-flown speculation.[36]

Calvin regularly warns against trying to pry into the mysteries of God's being:

---

[33]Luther, *WA* 2, 9, cited in Paul Althaus, *The Theology of Martin Luther*, translated by Robert C. Schultz (Philadelphia: Fortress Press, 1966), 20. See chapter 4 – 'God in Himself and God as He Reveals Himself' in Althaus, op. cit., 20-24.

[34]'... siquidem hoc est Christum cognoscere beneficia eius cognoscere', *Loci communes rerum theologicarum seu hypotyposes theologicae*, 1521, StA, II, I, 7, 10.

[35]Calvin, *Institutes* I.v.9.

[36]Ibid., I.x.2.

> But all the signs that he ever gave forth aptly conformed to his plan of teaching and at the same time clearly told men of his incomprehensible essence. For clouds and smoke and flame {Deut. 4:11], although they were symbols of heavenly glory, restrained the minds of all, like a bridle placed on them, from attempting to penetrate too deeply.[37]

> But even if God to keep us sober speaks sparingly of his essence, yet by those two titles that I have used [*sc.* 'infinite and spiritual essence'] he both banishes stupid imaginings and restrains the boldness of the human mind. Surely, his infinity ought to make us afraid to try to measure him by our own senses.[38]

In the same passage, Calvin – in answer to the literalist Anthropomorphites – makes it clear that in speaking to us, God massively lowers himself: 'For who even of slight intelligence does not understand that, as nurses commonly do with infants, God is wont in a measure to 'lisp' [Latin: *balbutire* – to 'prattle'] in speaking to us? Thus such forms of speaking do not so much express clearly what God is like as accommodate the knowledge of him to our slight capacity. To do this he must descend far beneath his loftiness.'[39]

In his *Commentary on Exodus*, chapter 34, Calvin works with a distinction between *essence* and *nature* that in some sense may approximate the Eastern distinction between *essence* and *energy*.

Heinrich Bullinger

Heinrich Bullinger, the great Reformation preacher of sixteenth-century Zurich, and successor of Zwingli, said much the same:

> ... no tongue either of angels or of men can fully express what, who, and of what manner God is, seeing that his majesty is incomprehensible and unspeakable; yet the scripture, which is the word of God, attempering itself to our imbecility, doth minister unto us some means, forms, and phrases of speech, by them to bring us to some such knowledge of God as may at leastwise suffice us while we live in this world: so yet notwithstanding that still we should think that the thing that is incomprehensible cannot be defined, but that by those phrases as occasion is only given, by which we are to be brought to greater things through the illumination of the Spirit... Therefore let no man go beyond the limited bounds, or prevent the time appointed, nor yet presume by wicked boldness and curiosity in this life to behold the face, that is, the very essence or being of God. Let that revelation of God suffice every one which God himself voucheth safe in his word to open unto us, namely, so much as he of his goodness thinketh necessary and profitable for us to know. And I do here with warrant say, that that wisdom is the true wisdom, which will not in this matter go about to know or savour more than the eternal wisdom doth teach to know.[40]

Calvin and Hilary on the poverty of our language

In line with Bullinger, Calvin notes that the names used to express God are beyond our human understanding:

---

[37]Ibid., I.xi.3.
[38]Ibid., I.xiii.1.
[39]Ibid.
[40]Heinrich Bullinger, *The Decades, The Fourth Decade,* 129, 130.

> A little later he [referring to St. Hilary's *De Trinitate* II.2] excuses himself at length for daring to put forward new terms; for when he has set forth the natural names – Father, Son, and Spirit – he adds that whatever is sought beside these is beyond the meaning of language, above the reach of sense, above the capacity of understanding...And Augustine's excuse [*De Trinitate* VII.iv. 7,9] is similar: on account of the poverty of human speech in so great a matter, the word 'hypostasis' had been forced upon us by necessity, not to express what it is, but only not to be silent on how Father, Son, and Spirit are three.[41]

This same awareness may be a major factor behind Palamism

It appears to me that it may be an awareness of this poverty of our human language, and its inability to reach the realities of transcendent infinity, which to a large degree lies behind the Eastern reliance upon 'apophatic' (or negative) theology – that is, one can say nothing about God's substance, only about His energies. Is that why Palamas (following Pseudo-Dionysius) gives God's superessentiality such a large place in his theology? That is to say, he claims that God is 'beyond being.' From the Western point of view, there could be no problem with that, *if* one follows St. Athanasius in stating that God is 'beyond *created* being.'[42]

How St. Thomas interprets 'superessential'

St. Thomas appears to interpret 'superessential' in this way. He quotes Dionysius and comments:

> There is in Dionysius this remark: 'The being of all things is the superessential divinity' [Pseudo-Dionysius, *De caelesti hierarchia*, IV, 1 – PG 3, col. 177D]...For if the divinity is the formal being of all things, it will not be over all but among all, indeed a part of all. Now, since Dionysius said that the divinity was above all things, he showed that according to its nature it was distinct from all things and raised above all things ...[43]

In that sense ('beyond created being'), we do not know the essence of Him who is above all things. Therefore, an 'apophatic' or negative approach is called for concerning His transcendent essence.

The seventeenth-century English Puritan, John Owen, says something along these lines, after he has mentioned the mystery of three distinct persons in the one divine essence:

> That infinite and inconceivable distance that is between him and us keeps us in the dark as to any sight of his face or clear apprehension of his perfections. We know him rather by what he does than by what he is – by his doing us good than by his essential goodness; and how little a portion of him, as Job speaks, is hereby discovered![44]

So, there is no difficulty in affirming that the essence of God is transcendent, mysterious, and incomprehensible to us. Both East and West are agreed on

---

[41]*Institutes*, I.xiii.5.

[42]Athanasius, *Contra Gentes* 2.2; 40.2.

[43]St. Thomas, *Summa Contra Gentiles*, translated by Anton C. Pegis (Notre Dame and London: University of Notre Dame Press, 1975), Book One, ch. 26, 10 (p. 131 of Pegis edition).

[44]John Owen, *Works*, vol. VI, 67.

this. But the far more difficult issue is whether or not the Eastern, Palamite distinction between essence and energies is so strongly drawn that it places the hypostases (or triune persons) within the energies rather than the essence?

Are the divine hypostases only in the energies, according to Palamism?

If I have understood them correctly, this is *not* the case; they do not go so far as to deny that the substance of God is the Triune Persons. They do not place the three hypostases only within the uncreated energies, 'without remainder.' St. Gregory Palamas himself writes: 'And when we speak of one Godhead we speak of everything that God is, namely, both the substance and the energy.'[45] He goes on to make it clear that the Trinity is indeed in the very substance of God: 'The trihypostatic character of the Godhead is eliminated if relation is not observed in God's substance. And one who is not trihypostatic nor master of the universe is not even God.'[46]

Palamas then sees God as being triune both in His substance and in his energies. 'According to the orthodoxy of God's Church which we hold by his grace, God possesses a natural energy which makes him manifest and in this respect is distinct from his substance…And so he is shown to possess individual subsistence, rather than being solely a substance without such individual subsistence. And since all such energies are contemplated in not one but three persons, God is known to us as being one substance in three hypostases.'[47]

The doctrine of energies speaks of the Trinitarian essence of God

Duncan Reid believes that 'The doctrine of energies speaks of the *trinitarian essence* of God, which of itself is inaccessible, while God is at the same time accessible in the energies.'[48] He admits a danger in some of the statements of Vladimir Lossky, but finally defends what Lossky is attempting to establish:

> This much we can concede, that there is a danger in Lossky[49] that the doctrine of the Trinity may be lost, especially – as Wendebourg emphasizes[50] – when the distinction between being and act, or between inner-trinitarian processions and outer missions, is polemically asserted. But we also have to say just as emphatically that the energy doctrine does not necessarily bring this danger in its train. A distinction between the trinitarian persons on the one hand and the common trinitarian energy on the other can be held without losing an effective doctrine of the trinity. The doctrine of energies need not replace the doctrine of the trinity.[51]

Stăniloae: we do not penetrate the essence, but we do know the Triune God

Dumitru Stăniloae, who certainly followed in the train of Dionysius and Palamas, nonetheless interacted carefully with the Western tradition (both

---

[45]St. Gregory Palamas, op. cit., ch. 126 (p. 231).

[46]Ibid., ch. 134 (pp. 239,241).

[47]Ibid., ch. 137 (p. 243).

[48]Reid, op. cit., 82.

[49]As for instance in Lossky, *The Mystical Theology of the Eastern Church*, translated by the Fellowshop of St. Alban's and St. Sergius (Cambridge: Cambridge University Press, 1957)

[50]Wendebourg, *Geist oder Energie*, 79.

[51]Reid, op. cit., 78.

critically and appreciatively). Perhaps that is why I find his exposition of the essence/energy distinction most helpful. He is at pains to show that whom we meet in 'the economy' or the going forth of 'the energies of God' is the personal, Triune God Himself, not something less than God. He writes: 'We experience nothing from God, in content, other than his varied operations that have to do with the world, which is to say, in relation to us. Beyond this we know that at their basis is the personally subsistent essence, but how it is, we do not know, for it is an essence beyond all essences.'[52]

Following Palamas, Stăniloae writes that '[God] is above all his acts and above all the divine attributes which he manifests through them ...'[53] But in the same passage, a few lines earlier he gives the other side of the truth of God's self-revelation:

> On the other hand, the same God in his entirety makes himself known to us and frequently enough, causes us to experience him through each operation and, through them, the same God in his entirety makes himself known to us as bearer of a number of general attributes...Through his attributes God makes something of his being evident to us, but this something is made specific within one vast and uninterrupted symphony of continually new acts that guide creation and each element of it separately towards the final goal of full union with him. Through all of these God pursues the fulfillment of this plan.[54]

Stăniloae shows that the 'superexistence' – or 'hyperessence' – of God is personal (and thus, Triune), and therefore, that what He communicates to us in 'the economy' (or energies) is Himself.

> Thus God indicates himself as the truly or existent or superexistent one and manifests himself as personal reality: 'I.' He is 'I' *par excellence*. Self-existence can only have a personal character. Impersonal essence is not superexistent; in all respects it would fall within a system of references ...
>
> The threefold supreme hypostasis creates, sustains, and perfects all things through inexhaustible acts, because it is the threefold hypostasis of the superessence. Our reality as subject is the hypostatization of a nature whose fundamental part is the spirit, and among all the essences created by God the spirit is the image of the superessence hypostatized by the trinitarian persons. Only for this reason can our reality as subject have the character of being person and for this reason is it endowed with an eternal stability which other essences do not have, though the angels too are similar essences.'[55]

One Western response to the Palamite essence/energy distinction

It is not for me, a lowly member of one of the churches in the West, to suggest that the Eastern churches should not hold the distinction they draw between God's essence and his energies. Nor do I know enough to say that such a distinction is necessarily out of accord with God's truth. Perhaps our traditional Western distinction between 'the ontological Trinity' and 'the economic Trinity' has been a way to deal with some of the

---

[52]Stăniloae, *The Experience of God*, 126.
[53]Ibid., 128.
[54]Ibid.
[55]Ibid., 135, 136.

same underlying concerns. But what I will say without hesitation is that the churches of the West have no good reason to bring this aspect of the Dionysian and Palamite theology into their doctrine. Insofar as we follow our own sound scriptural and ecclesiastical traditions, we already have in place exactly the same blessings of redemption in Christ that are spoken of in the East as 'deification.'

Western uneasiness over the term 'deification'

It would appear that the cruciality of 'deification' to the theology and practice of the East is what requires something like the energy/essence distinction. But we do not speak of 'deification', although what we affirm about redemption reaches the same goal. Since we are so certain that the Persons of the Trinity *are* the very essence of God (in spite of the infinite mysteriousness of it), we are most hesitant to call our redemption 'deification', lest it be thought that we expect to be transmuted into the substance of God. Of course, we fully understand that this is *not* what the Eastern Orthodox mean by the doctrine. But in order to avoid any suspicion of pantheism, we are uneasy to employ such a term (even when it is carefully and fairly defined, as it is in all good Orthodox theology).

What the West has in place of deification: order of salvation

Instead of 'deification' (and the consequently necessary distinction of essence/energy), our tradition has held to various forms of 'the order of salvation'. Although the Roman Catholics have placed considerably more emphasis on the place of the redeemed in the sacramental system of the Church than some (though not all[56]) of the Protestants,[57] still they hold to their own understanding of 'the order of salvation, which is not exactly the same as deification.'[58]

But on the classical Protestant side, the Reformed in particular have held that by the sheer grace of God we are elected and called into union with Christ. That spiritual union involves such things as effectual calling, regeneration, conversion and faith, justification, adoption, sanctification and glorification (cf. Rom. 8 and Eph. 1 and 2).[59]

---

[56]Much of classical Protestantism has been very Church-centered in its teaching on the appropriation of salvation. From the Reformed viewpoint, see John Calvin, *Institutes of the Christian Religion* II. xv.6 and IV.1.11-29; also, Hughes Old, *The Shaping of the Reformed Baptismal Rite in the Sixteenth Century*. From the Lutheran side, see Martin Luther, *Large Catechism*, 'Third Article' [WA 30-1], and Robert W. Jensen, 'The Church as Communio' in *The Catholicity of the Reformation*, Carl E. Braaten and Robert W. Jenson, eds. (Grand Rapids, MI: Wm. B. Eerdmans, 1996), and also Bjarne W. Teigen, *The Lord's Supper in the Theology of Martin Chemnitz (1522–1586)* (Brewster, MA: Trinity Lutheran Press, 1986).

[57]See for instance, *The Documents of Vatican II*, 'Dogmatic Constitution on the Church, II. 11; and *Catechism of the Catholic Church*, Part II, Article I: 'The Sacrament of Baptism'.

[58]See St. Thomas Aquinas, *Summa Contra Gentiles*, Book Four: Salvation, especially chapters 39-97; and more recently, *Catechism of the Catholic Church*, Part I, Article II: 'The Church's Origin, Foundation, and Mission', and Part II, Articles II – XI: 'The Seven Sacraments of the Church.'

[59]John Murray gives an exegetical survey of 'the order of salvation' (from the conservative Reformed perspective) in *Redemption Accomplished and Applied* (Wm. B. Eerdmans: Grand Rapids, MI, 1955).

Classical Lutheranism tended to focus the order of salvation on its inception in baptism. Luther wrote in his *Small Catechism* that water baptism signified 'that the old Adam in us together with all sins and evil lusts, should by daily sorrow and repentance be put to death, and be drowned, and that the new man should come forth daily and rise up, cleansed and righteous to live forever in God's presence.'[60] It viewed sanctification as '...nothing else than a completion of baptism,'[61] as Luther says in *The Holy and Blessed Sacrament of Baptism of 1519*.[62]

In his famous Treatise of 1520, 'The Freedom of the Christian', Luther shows how salvation is life in union with Christ. 'From Christ the good things have flowed and are flowing into us...We conclude, therefore, that a Christian lives not in himself, but in Christ and in his neighbor. Otherwise he is not a Christian. He lives in Christ through faith; in his neighbor through love. By faith he is caught up beyond himself into God. By love he descends beneath himself into his neighbor. Yet he always remains in God and in his love, as Christ says in John 1: 51: "Truly, truly, I say to you, you will see heaven opened, and the angels of God ascending and descending upon the Son of man."'[63]

For all their considerable differences in emphasis,[64] we are taught in our various churches that our union with Christ is both real and spiritual. The Holy Spirit brings it to pass in time and maintains it to eternity. His mighty, invisible presence 'evacuates' the bonds of space and time, and mysteriously – but truly – works a personal, spiritual union with Almighty God – 'from the Father, through the Son, and in the Holy Spirit.' We are thus united to the Lord Himself, thereby avoiding a deistic separation from the one, whom to know is eternal life (John 17:3), and at the same time avoiding any implication of pantheism, or transgression of the Creator/creature distinction, since we hold that it is spiritually real without any transmutation into the substance of God (just as our brethren in the East also hold).

It is a personal union by grace and adoption that enters into the closest and dearest relationship with the Triune God Himself, so that we can say with the Apostle Paul: 'I am crucified with Christ: nevertheless I live; yet not I, but Christ liveth in me; and the life which I now live in the flesh I live by the faith of the Son of God, who loved me, and gave himself for me' (Gal. 2:20).

With much respect to the East, the West does not need to adopt this distinction

In summary, in various places of this *Systematic Theology*, I have gently suggested that we would do well to appropriate some ways of looking at God's truth from our fellow Christians in the East. It is our great loss that we in the West (particularly Protestants) functionally lost most of our

---

[60]Cited in Paul Althaus, op. cit., 355.

[61]Ibid..

[62]*WA* 2, 727-737.

[63]Martin Luther, *Three Treatises* (Philadelphia: Fortress Press, 1960), 309.

[64]We will discuss these differences in Volume Three of this *Systematic Theology*, Chapter Two.

Patristic heritage by the eighteenth century, owing perhaps to the influence of the secularistic Enlightenment. If we seriously seek to regain our heritage from the Church Fathers, then we shall be following in the good steps of the best theologians of the West, such as Peter Lombard, Anselm, Thomas Aquinas, Henry Bullinger, John Calvin, Pierre Viret, Richard Hooker, Lancelot Andrewes, John Owen and Francis Turretin. A movement in this direction started in the twentieth century among theologians of the West. But here, I think, we do not need to follow the East, in spite of our great regard and affection for them and for all that they have taught us. Rather, what we do need to do is to reappropriate the best of our own traditional, biblically faithful teaching on who the Triune God is and what our union with Him entails for lives of joy, love and service to God and neighbor. I fear that we are still far from doing so.

The churches of the West need to take seriously again our union with Christ in the Holy Spirit

Hence, given the relative deadness and lack of holy zeal in the churches of the West, instead of worrying over our terminological (or otherwise) differences with the East, we as the people of God in the West need humbly and earnestly to seek to experience the full reality of holy life in an unholy and needy world, by means of a fresh and constant awareness of our union with Christ in and through the Holy Spirit. That reality alone can cause 'streams of living water' to flow through our 'innermost beings' to the thirsty, secular society around us, who need nothing so much as God.

With desperate need – and limitless opportunity – in mind, we must take to heart the words of Robert Bruce, minister and theologian of the Church of Scotland (and successor of John Knox), addressed to his congregation in the High Kirk of St. Giles' in Edinburgh in 1589. In his sermon on 'The Lord's Supper in Particular – 1' ['For I have received of the Lord that which also I delivered unto you, that the Lord Jesus, the night in which he was betrayed, took bread' – 1 Cor. 11:23], he shows that '…by the presence of Christ in my soul, I see a blessed life, I feel a blessed life, and that life daily increases in me, more and more.'[65] The union of Christ with the soul, is, as Bruce says, 'a spiritual conjunction, hard and difficult to be acquired or procured.'[66] He states that there are 'means' to be used 'in this conjunction' both on the part of God, and the part of man:

Robert Bruce on the 'means' of our union with Christ

> There is one means employed on God's part – God helps us to get Christ; and another means employed on our part. On the part of God, there is the Holy Spirit, who offers the Body and Blood of Christ to us. On our part there must also be a means employed, or else when He offers, we will not be able to receive.[67]

[65]Robert Bruce, *The Mystery of the Lord's Supper: Sermons on the Sacrament preached in the Kirk of Edinburgh in A. D. 1589*, translated and edited by Thomas F. Torrance (Edinburgh and Fearn: Rutherford House & Christian Focus, 2005 reprint of 1958), 91.

[66]Ibid.

[67]Ibid.

Bruce then explains what these two means are:

> Therefore there must be faith in our souls to receive what the Holy Spirit offers, to receive the heavenly food of the Body and Blood of Christ. *Thus faith and the Holy Spirit are the two means employed in this spiritual and heavenly conjunction.* By these two means, by faith and the Holy Spirit, I receive the Body of Christ – the Body of Christ is mine, and He is given to my soul.[68]

In line with Bernard of Clairvaux[69] and John Calvin,[70] Bruce states that in spite of the fact that the body of Christ is sitting now at the right hand of the Father, while I am on earth:

> ... Christ's Body is really given to me...I am made to possess His Body and Blood. The distance of place does not hurt my title or right ... no distance, however great it may be, can make any difference to my possession of Him.[71]
>
> Do you not know that the Spirit who joins us and Christ is infinite, so that it is as easy for the Spirit to join Christ and us, no matter how distant we may be, as it is for our soul to link our head and the feet of our body, though they are separated from one another?[72]

The *invisibility* of the Holy Spirit's work in bringing about and sustaining this union is why Bruce lays such emphasis upon the importance and necessity of the *visibility* of the sacrament of the Lord's Supper, and the *audibility* of the preached Word of God. He said earlier in another sermon:

> Thus it is chiefly because the Lord has appointed the Sacraments as hands to deliver and exhibit the things signified, that they are called signs ... Because he has appointed them as instruments whereby He will deliver His own Son to us; for this is certain, that no one has power to deliver Christ Jesus to us, but God Himself, and His Holy Spirit ... God by His Word, and God by His Spirit, delivers Christ Jesus to you. I call them signs, then, because God has made them potent instruments to deliver the same thing that they signify.[73]

What the sacraments signify, is, Bruce explains by referring to St. Irenaeus, '*the whole Christ with His whole gifts, benefits and graces*, applied and given to my soul.'[74] This reality determines the way in which we should come to the Lord's Table:

> And therefore he goes to the Table to get strength in his misery, to lay hold upon mercy at the throne of grace, to get remission and forgiveness of his

---

[68]Ibid., 91, 92.

[69]E.g. Bernard of Clairvaux, *On the Love of God* and *Sermons on the Song of Songs*, as in *Late Medieval Mysticism*, Vo. XIII of 'The Library of Christian Classics', Ray C. Petry, ed. (London: SCM Press, 1957), 66-78; and *Saint Bernard on the Love of God*, translated by Terence L. Connolly (Techny, Il: Mission Press, S.V.D., 1943).

[70]John Calvin, *Institutes* III. Chapters vi – x. See also the study by Dennis E. Tamburello, *Union with Christ: John Calvin and the Mysticism of St. Bernard* (Louisville, KY: Westminster John Knox Press, 1994).

[71]Bruce, op. cit., 92, 93.

[72]Bruce, op. cit., 95.

[73]Sermon on 'The Sacraments in General', ibid., 36, 37.

[74]Ibid., 37.

> sins, to get the gift of repentance, that more and more he may seek to live uprightly, holily and soberly all his days.[75]

The supernatural work of the Spirit through Word and Sacrament
The humble and believing receiver of Word and Sacrament is lifted up by the Holy Spirit from a 'general knowledge' of God's existence, to a particular and saving knowledge of the gracious God in Christ. God thereby works a supernatural and substantial change within the human personality:

> Whereas before I knew not God, now I see Him, not only with a general knowledge that He is God, but I know that He is God in Christ. What else does the Holy Spirit do? He opens the heart as well as the mind….He makes me love God better than anything else. He changes the affections of my soul. He changes their faculties and qualities. But although the substance of our hearts and minds is not changed, they are made new to such an extent that we are called new creatures.[76]

The necessary human response of faith: 'This secret conjunction, then, is brought about by faith and by the Holy Spirit. By faith we lay hold upon the Body and Blood of Christ, and though we are as far distant as heaven and earth are, the Spirit serves as a ladder to conjoin us with Christ, like the ladder of Jacob, which reached from the ground to the heavens.'[77]

The necessary consent of our heart and will: 'If you do not seek to get faith in your hearts as well as in your minds, your faith will not avail. What does faith avail which only floats in the imagination, and brings a naked knowledge without opening up the heart and involving the consent of the will.'[78]

The necessity of diligent receiving of Word and Sacraments: 'Then seek to get faith in your heart and mind, and in so doing, you do what Christians should do. This is not done without the diligent hearing of the Word, and diligent receiving of the Sacraments. Therefore be diligent in these exercises, and be diligent in prayer, praying in the Holy Spirit that He may nourish your souls inwardly with the Body and Blood of Christ, that He may increase faith in your hearts and minds, and make it grow up daily more and more, until you come to the full fruition of that blessed immortality.'[79]

Robert Bruce's teaching on the powerful reality of our union with Christ conveys (in my inevitably circumscribed opinion) at least as much strength for godly living and hope for a joyous eternity for the people of God, as the Eastern Orthodox understanding of deification (and behind that, the distinction between God's essence and His energies).

Two prayers follow:

---

[75]Ibid., 42.
[76]Ibid., 96.
[77]Ibid.
[78]Ibid., 96, 97.
[79]Ibid., 97.

A Prayer for Grace by Lancelot Andrewes (1555–1626), Bishop of Winchester

May thy strong hand, O Lord,
be ever my defence;
Thy mercy in Christ
my salvation;
Thy word of truth
my instructor;
the grace of Thy life-giving Spirit
my consolation,
all along, and at last.
The soul of Christ hallow me,
and the body strengthen me,
and the blood ransom me,
and the water wash me,
and the bruises heal me,
and the sweat refresh me,
and the wound hide me.
The peace of God
which passeth all understanding,
keep my heart and mind
in the knowledge and the love of God.[80]

A hymnic prayer for the Holy Spirit:

Eternal Spirit, by whose breath
The soul is saved from sin and death,
Before thy throne we sinners bend;
To us Thy quickening power extend.[81]

---

[80]Taken from 'Prayer for the Week', Sixth Day, in Alexander Whyte, *Lancelot Andrewes: And His Private Devotions* (Edinburgh and London: Oliphant Anderson and Ferrier, 1896), 116.

[81]A verse from 'Father of heaven, whose love profound' by Edward Cooper (1770–1833).

Chapter Five

What Kind of Lord He Is: His Transcendence, Beauty and Majesty mean that His Sovereign Control is 'Good News'

The vast number of texts where the holy Name is used (often in conjunction with Elohim, Adonai or other divinely revealed names) indicate (i) God's transcendent Being and absolute priority as Creator of all; (ii) His majestic authority over all that he has created; (iii) His universal personal control of all reality. The lordship of the Triune God is marked by beauty and majesty, and is the source of strength for our earthly journey and the successful facing of every trial, and it is the ground of endless thankfulness. And it will be noted in Chapter 6 that we know God's lordship truly only to the degree that we participate in the saving knowledge He provides in a divinely constituted community in the context of the Covenant of Grace.

(i) God's transcendent Being and absolute priority as Creator of all

Lordship in creation

The sheer lordship of God nowhere shines more brightly than in the miracle of miracles: His creation of all things out of nothing.[1] Genesis 1:1 teaches that 'In the beginning, God created the heavens and the earth…'[2] The world had not existed before the first moment of divine creation (nor had anything else outside God, including the angelic orders). God neither had nor needed any pre-existing material out of which to make the cosmos. His bare word, speaking into reality the desire of His will, was fully sufficient to create, order and control a universe of marvelous complexity and harmony; a stunning world of vastness, order and beauty. Never was miracle like this! Creation is a standing testimony to the sovereign lordship of the Triune God (and no doubt, that is one of the reasons it is so resisted in the secular culture).

Who could do something like that: bring into being solar systems 'by the breath of his mouth'? For, 'By the word of the Lord were the heavens

---

[1]Of equal, or perhaps, surpassing wonder, is the other miracle of miracles: the incarnation of the eternal Son of God, to be discussed a little later.

[2]A later chapter will be devoted to the doctrine of creation, so it will not be developed here, but only insofar as it is a primary witness to God's lordship.

made; and all the host of them by the breath of his mouth' (Ps. 33:6). 'I am the LORD that maketh all things; that stretcheth forth the heavens alone; that spreadeth abroad the earth by myself' (Isa. 44:24). 'I have made the earth, and created man upon it; I, even my hands, have stretched out the heavens' (Isa. 45:12).

Only the sovereign Lord can do such wonders: 'Thou art the God that doest wonders' (Ps. 77:14). 'Blessed be the LORD God, the God of Israel, who only doeth wondrous things' (Ps. 72:18). Powers less than God, non-sovereign beings, non-eternal powers could never create anything 'out of nothing.'[3] It takes full lordship to do so.

Jeremiah says concerning the folly of idolatry: 'Thus shall ye say unto them, The gods that have not made the heavens and the earth, even they shall perish from the earth...He hath made the earth by his power, he hath established the world by his wisdom, and hath stretched out the heavens by his discretion' (Jer. 10:11,12). 'For all the gods of the nations are idols: but the LORD made the heavens' (Ps. 96:5). Good King Hezekiah encouraged himself against the deadly threats of the powerful Assyrian empire, by calling to mind the difference between the God of Israel and the gods of Assyria; the basis of that difference was that God was the Lord of creation, and the others were not:

> O Lord of hosts, God of Israel, that dwellest between the cherubims, thou art the God, even thou alone, of all the kingdoms of the earth: thou hast made heaven and earth. Incline thine ear, O Lord, and hear; open thine eyes, O LORD, and see: and hear all the words of Sennacherib, which hath sent to reproach the living God. Of a truth, LORD, the kings of Assyria have laid waste all the nations...And have cast their gods into the fire: for they were no gods, but the work of men's hands, wood and stone: therefore they have destroyed them. Now therefore, O Lord our God, save us from his hand that all the kingdoms of the earth may know that thou art the LORD, even thou only (Isa. 37:16-20).

Lordship in providence

Thus, the lordship of having created all things out of nothing, directly entails the lordship of sovereign control over that creation, including its nations and their history. Only one who is Lord can perform the utter miracle of creating out of nothing. Francis Turretin of Geneva (1623–1687) rightly says:

> Nothing can come from nothing: (1) not naturally through a finite and created power; (2) not from a subject as the principle and intrinsically constitutive material; (3) not by way of generations. On the contrary, all things are properly said to be from nothing supernaturally through infinite power (as from the terminus a quo and by the way of creation.)[4]

[3]As we shall see in chapter 7, the Hebrew word used in Genesis 1:1 for 'create' – bara – when employed (as here) in the Qal stem of the verb, is used only of God, and never of men or angels. That is, *bara* means 'absolute creation' – i.e. 'out of nothing' (with no pre-existing material). There are other verbs in Hebrew that are also rendered in our versions as 'to create', but these refer to 'secondary creation' (or 'relative creation'), that can be attributed to men or angels. In these cases, the 'relative creator' has pre-existing material to be fashioned, shaped and re-worked 'creatively.' But only the sovereign Lord can start with nothing and speak reality into existence.

[4]Francis Turretin, *Institutes of Elenctic Theology*, translated by George M. Giger (Phillipsburg, NJ: P & R Publishing: , 1992), Vol. I, 432.

Only the sovereign Lord has the power to do so, as Wilhelmus à Brakel of Rotterdam (1635–1711) explains:

> The creation of the world came to pass (1) by the exercise of omnipotent power, merely by a singular verbal command of God's omnipotent will, all of which occurred without the least exertion. 'Let there be light,' etc. 'Hast thou not known? Hast thou not heard, that the everlasting God, the LORD, the Creator of the ends of the earth, fainteth not, neither is weary?' (Isa. 40:28). (2) by virtue of his absolute sovereignty. God was able to create the world, and He could have also refrained from doing so. He could have created prior to 5,750 years ago, at a later date, or also could have brought forth several worlds. He only made this one world, however, brought forth at the precise moment according to his volitional decree.[5]

In twentieth-century philosophical language, Richard Swinburne states that 'The existence of a complex physical universe over finite or infinite time is something "too big" for science to explain...Like Leibniz, I conclude that the existence of the universe over finite or infinite time would be, if only scientific explanation is allowed, a brute inexplicable fact. And, as Leibniz also did, I conclude that there is the possibility of an explanation of that existence in personal terms. The existence of the (physical) universe over time comes into my category of things too big for science to explain. If the existence of the universe is to be explained, personal explanation must be brought in...'[6]

The Scots Confession (1560) explicates God's lordship in terms of His eternal Being, His creation and His providential control of all He created, and of our necessary trust in Him:

> We confess and acknowledge one God alone, to whom alone we must cleave, whom alone we must serve, whom only we must worship, and in whom alone we put our trust. Who is eternal, infinite, immeasurable, incomprehensible, omnipotent, invisible; one in substance and yet distinct in three persons, the Father, the Son and the Holy Ghost. By whom we confess and believe all things in heaven and earth, visible and invisible, to have been created, to be retained in their being, and to be ruled and guided by his inscrutable providence for such end as his eternal wisdom, goodness, and justice have appointed, and to the manifestation of his own glory.[7]

God's universal, personal control of all reality and its denial

Legitimate authority gives the right of legitimate control; unbounded authority gives the right of unbounded control, and such is the authority of the Triune God, and of Him alone. Thus, the full authority of the Lord is used by Him to fulfill all His glorious purposes for His creation. We must postpone the exposition of how this authoritative and total control of all specifically works out.[8] All we shall do here is to note that full control flows from fully present lordship.

---

[5]Wilhelmus à Brakel, *The Christian's Reasonable Service*, translated by Bartel Elshout (Grand Rapids, MI: Reformation Heritage Books, 1999), 270, 271.

[6]Richard Swinburne, *The Existence of God* (Oxford: Clarendon Press, 1979), 142, 143.

[7]'Scots Confession', chapter I.

[8]Until our chapter on 'Providence'. At that point we shall discuss (but of course, not explain!) how the sovereign control of God over all events does not lessen human responsibility, nor remove

No Deistic gap between God and the world

Above all, it means that God is constantly present with His creation to work out His purposes. Unlike the dualism of the Deistic Enlightenment, there is not a gap between God's ever-present control and the world of nature and science. He is not a distant clockmaker, who leaves the world to run on its own. He is always with it, superintending every aspect of its reality, both seen and unseen.

But when we creatures of finite minds begin to speak of infinite Being with its infinite authority to control, we are immediately faced with mystery, because we face transcendent Being. Even where God comes closest to us (and most 'immanent'), as in the incarnate Christ, we can often hear him say to us, as he did to Simon Peter, who protested at his feet being washed by the Lord: 'What I do thou knowest not now; but thou shalt know hereafter' (John 13:7). The Psalmist speaks for us: 'Clouds and darkness are round about him: righteousness and judgment are the habitation of his throne' (Ps. 97:2). Even when we sometimes get through much of the darkness of mysterious and painful events, we must still, with Job, 'lay our hand upon our mouth' (Job 40:4). Or as St. Paul says, in the context of believers having to face persecution and physical death now, in light of the certain glory to come: 'For we walk by faith, not by sight' (2 Cor. 5:7). Faith, even weak and faltering faith, shows us that Jehovah (Yahweh) is present immediately, instead of being absent, in all our concerns – even the most desperate ones.

Much of the Old Testament shows how Israel over and over, through darkness and struggle, found this present control of God to be the case. In Exodus 3, where the major definition of who God is is given (v. 14 – 'I AM THAT I AM), the passage goes on to show the beneficent nature of His personal control for His people:

> And God said moreover unto Moses, Thou shalt say unto the children of Israel, the LORD God of your fathers, the God of Abraham, the God of Isaac, and the God of Jacob, hath sent me unto you: this is my name forever, and this is my memorial unto all generations. Go, and gather the elders of Israel unto them, The LORD God of your fathers, the God of Abraham, of Isaac, and of Jacob, appeared unto me, saying I have surely visited you, and seen that which is done to you in Egypt: And I have said, I will bring you up out of the affliction of Egypt unto the land of the Canaanites, and the Hittites, and the Amorites, and the Perizzites, and the Hivites, and the Jebusites, unto a land flowing with milk and honey. And they shall hearken to thy voice and thou shalt come, thou and the elders of Israel, unto the king of Egypt, and ye shall say unto him, 'The LORD God of the Hebrews hath met with us: and now let us go, we beseech thee, three days' journey into the wilderness, that we may sacrifice to the LORD our God' (Exod. 3:15-18).

---

inner spontaneity of human choice. But rather, as the Westminster Confession of Faith affirms, God's sovereign will is the very basis of real human choice; not its antithesis: 'God from all eternity did by the most wise and holy counsel of his own will freely and unchangeably ordain whatsoever comes to pass: yet so as thereby neither is God the author of sin, nor is violence offered to the will of the creatures, nor is the liberty or contingency of second causes taken away, but rather established' (Chapter III.1).

The ten plagues that devastated the economy of Egypt, and the miraculous crossing of the Red Sea shortly afterwards, that destroyed its Pharaoh and much of his army, were the results of the direct control of the Lord over all elements of nature and the minds of men to accomplish His gracious purposes of deliverance for His people. By the way, there is not a shred of empirical scientific evidence to indicate that the God of creation and redemption could not have been present to orchestrate all of these events, so supernatural in their timing and effects. The problem for the Enlightenment is not what happened, but with the interpretation of it. They axiomatically assume that God could not have been present in such wonders, because of their philosophical dualism between the divine and the human. But this is not science; it is philosophy, and a particular kind of philosophy, which rules out facts before it considers their reality and meaning (if such things go contrary to their deeply rooted presuppositions). That is not how modern science advanced, and it is not how the Bible can be credibly interpreted.

The God of the Bible is present; not absent. Thus, David writes in Psalm 139: 'Whither shall I go from thy spirit? Or whither shall I flee from thy presence? If I ascend up into heaven, thou art there: if I make my bed in hell, behold, thou art there. If I take the wings of the morning, and dwell in the uttermost parts of the sea; Even there shall thy hand lead me, and thy right hand shall hold me' (vv. 7-10).

N. T. Wright correctly says that '...the Jews did not conceive of their one true God as a long way away, either from them or from the world at large. He was, of course, transcendent; he couldn't be contained within the world. But he was not detached. When he acted within the world, he didn't intervene from a great distance. He was always present, always active.'[9]

God's immanence guarantees His purposes

This God carries through His purposes of grace for His people, by His personal presence with them and control of all that concerns them:

> Though the LORD be high, yet hath he respect unto the lowly: but the proud he knoweth afar off. Though I walk in the midst of trouble, thou wilt revive me: thou shalt stretch forth thine hand against the wrath of mine enemies, and thy right hand shall save me. The LORD will perfect that which concerneth me: thy mercy, O LORD, endureth forever: forsake not the works of thine own hands' (Ps. 138:6-8).

Indeed, one of the most basic names of the Messiah is 'Immanuel': God (is) with us. 'Therefore the Lord himself shall give you a sign: Behold, a virgin shall conceive, and bear a son, and shall call his name Immanuel' (Isa. 7:14). John 1:14 shows how God's personal presence in the incarnate Word is 'God with us' in its supreme manifestation: 'And the Word was made flesh, and dwelt among us, (and we beheld his glory, the glory as of the only begotten of the Father,) full of grace and truth.'

---

[9]N. T. Wright, *What Saint Paul Really Said* (Grand Rapids, MI: Wm. B. Eerdmans, 1997), 64.

The incarnate presence of Immanuel changes, in principle, the world order from brokenness to wholeness, thus putting the governance of all upon His shoulders:

> For unto us a child is born, unto us a son is given: and the government shall be upon his shoulder: and his name shall be called Wonderful Counselor, the Mighty God, the everlasting Father, the Prince of Peace. Of the increase of his government and peace there shall be no end, upon the throne of David, and upon his kingdom, to order it, and to establish it with judgment, and with justice from henceforth even for ever. The zeal of the LORD of hosts will perform this (Isa. 9:6, 7).

In union with the victorious Christ, His Church shall be granted final triumph over the nations, and victory over death:

> And when I saw him [i.e. the Apostle John on Patmos sees the risen Lord], I fell at his feet as dead. And he laid his right hand upon me, saying unto me, Fear not; I am the first and the last: I am he that liveth, and was dead; and, behold, I am alive forevermore, Amen; and have the keys of hell and of death… (Rev. 1:17, 18).

> And he that overcometh, and keepeth my works unto the end, to him will I give power over the nations: And he shall rule them with a rod of iron; as the vessels of a potter shall they be broken to shivers: even as I received of my Father (Rev. 2:26, 27).

Power over all things without exception

To accomplish this requires complete power over all things without exception, as both Cyril of Jerusalem in the fourth century and John Calvin in the sixteenth century show:

> Nothing then is withdrawn from the power of God; for the Scripture says of Him, for all things are Thy servants (Ps. 119:91). All things alike are His servants, but from all these One, His only Son and One, His Holy Spirit, are excepted; and all the things which are His servants serve the Lord through the One Son and in the Holy Spirit. God then rules all, and of His long-suffering endures even murderers and robbers and fornicators, having appointed a set time for recompensing every one, that if they who have had long warning are still impenitent in heart, they may receive the greater condemnation. They are kings of men who reign upon earth, but not without the power from above: and this Nebuchadnezzar once learned by experience, when he said: For His kingdom is an everlasting kingdom, and His power from generation to generation (Dan. 4:34).[10]

And Calvin writes similarly:

> And truly God claims, and would have us grant him, omnipotence – not the empty, idle, and almost unconscious sort that the Sophists imagine, but a watchful, effective, active sort, engaged in ceaseless activity. Not, indeed, an omnipotence that is only a general principle of confused motion, as if he were to command a river to flow through its once-appointed channels, but one that is directed toward individual and particular motions. For he is deemed omnipotent, not because he can indeed act, yet sometimes

[10]Cyril of Jerusalem, *Catechetical Lectures*, VIII.5.

> ceases and sits in idleness, or continues by a general impulse that order of nature which he previously appointed; but because governing heaven and earth by his providence, he so regulates all things that nothing takes place without his deliberation. For when in The Psalms it is said that 'he does whatever he wills' [Ps. 115:3; Cf. Ps. 113:3 –Vulgate], a certain and deliberate will is meant. For it would be senseless to interpret the words of the prophet after the manner of the philosophers, that God is the first agent because he is the beginning and the cause of all motion; for in times of adversity believers comfort themselves with the solace that they suffer nothing except by God's ordinance and command, for they are under his hand.[11]

In Scripture, God's omnipotent control of all events is always directly related to His personal presence with the creation (though He is always distinguished from it), and to His sovereign freedom to be near it, as well as to the infinite love of His Triune Being, behind all His actions within and without Himself. Karl Barth has expounded the lordship of His presence with creation:

> God's presence includes His lordship. How can He be present without being Lord?... And if nothing exists without Him, this means that everything is subject to Him. And that it is subject to Him means that it can and must serve His glory...The presupposition of all divine sovereignty is based on the fact that for God nothing exists which is remote, i.e. which is not near even as it is remote, so that there is no remoteness beside and outside Him which is remoteness without His proximity. There is remoteness as there is proximity. Otherwise there would be no creation. And because creation is God's creation, there is also a divine remoteness and proximity. But in God Himself remoteness and proximity are one ... But the divine remoteness and proximity rest on the wealth of the divine perfections. And God is One in this wealth of perfections. Therefore God is Lord over these antitheses. He is Himself distant and near in one being ...
>
> All that God is in His relationship to His creation, and therefore His omnipresence too, is simply an outward manifestation and realisation of what He is previously in Himself apart from this relationship and therefore apart from his creation...It is in the fact that there is in God proximity and remoteness in irresolvable unity...it is in this fact – that we recall anew His triune essence – that God is love...But above all there exists in the very unity of this wealth of His the triunity of His essence. Thus there exists a divine proximity and remoteness, real in Him from all eternity, as the basis and presupposition of the essence and existence of creation, and therefore of created proximity and remoteness. God can be present to another. This is His freedom. For He is present to Himself. This is His love in its internal and external range. God in Himself is not only existent. He is co-existent...This co-existence, of course, can be only one which is posited, limited, conditioned and circumscribed by His own essence. It will be characterised by the unlimited priority of His, the divine existence of the other which co-exists with Him. Yet under these presuppositions and in this order this co-existence has both its basis and its possibility in God. God is love in Himself...[12]

---

[11]John Calvin, *Institutes*, I.xvi.3.

[12]Karl Barth, *Church Dogmatics*, II/1, p. 461, 462, 463.

Moltmann's limitation of the divine lordship over creation

Jürgen Moltmann finds this section in Karl Barth's writings problematical. In Moltmann's fascinating *The Trinity and the Kingdom of God* he refers to Barth's teaching of God as 'the one who loves in freedom.'[13] But Moltmann argues that the sovereign freedom of God is akin to the late medieval concepts of Western Catholic Nominalism, and thus '...only have a very limited value for our understanding of God's freedom.'[14]

For Moltmann, this traditional concept of sovereign freedom means that 'The people he is master of are not free.'[15] He wishes to replace the traditional 'freedom' of the sovereign God with 'friendship'. 'This freedom consists of the mutual and common participation in life, and a communication in which there is neither lordship nor servitude...'[16]

The divine love is not deficient without human love

In an otherwise fine chapter on 'God is love', Moltmann seems to limit God's lordship in yet another way, when he says that: 'In this sense God "needs" the world and man. If God is love, then he neither will nor can be without the one who is his beloved.'[17] But this is to neglect the foundational truth that within the Trinity there is the fullest, most satisfying, and complete interchange of love amongst the three holy Persons, so that God does not stand in need of anything from His creatures. It is profoundly and encouragingly true that 'God will not be without us', but that is based on the generosity of His grace, not His need. As Barth says in another context: 'There is total sovereignty and grace on the part of God, but total dependence and need on the part of man.'[18]

And as Stăniloae has shown, the fully sufficient divine love within the Trinity does not stand in need of, nor is it somehow made complete by created human love. Instead, it is the foundation of all human love:

> From eternity the divine persons remain perfect, for their love is that perfection of love which is not able to increase the communion among them. Were this not the case, the origin of all things would have begun from utmost separation, from absence of love. Love, however, presupposes a common being in three persons, as Christian teaching tells us...This unperfected love [i.e. of humans] between us presupposes, however, the perfect love between divine persons with a common being. Our love finds its explanation in the fact that we are created in the image of the Holy Trinity, the origin of our love. From supernatural revelation we know that God is essence subsisting in three persons. But nothing like this exists in the created order, and even if it did exist, it would differ wholly from the tripersonal subsistence of the infinite and uncreated essence. Hence, even expressed in this way, it remains a mystery.[19]

---

[13]Ibid., section 28 (pp. 257ff), in Moltmann, *The Trinity and the Kingdom of God* (London: SCM Press, 1989), 55.

[14]Ibid., 56.

[15]Ibid.

[16]Ibid.

[17]Ibid., 58.

[18]K. Barth, *Church Dogmatics* III/2, 219.

[19]Stăniloae, op. cit., 245, 246.

To say, as Moltmann does, that God 'will not be without us', who are His beloved, is profoundly true, and should be grounds for much rejoicing.[20] But His creation of us and His determination not to be without us, are the overflow of His infinitely generous love. They do not point to a defect in the God who has always existed in the most joyful and fulfilling inner-personal relationships within the one divine Being.

Jonathan Edwards (about 1722) expressed well the perfect eternal joy and beatitude in God, apart from and prior to the creation. To some degree, he uses the Idealist language of his century to do so, but his content is biblically faithful to who God always is:

> The image of God which God infinitely loves and has his chief delight in, is the perfect idea of God. It has always been said that God's infinite delight consists in reflecting on himself and viewing his own perfections or, which is the same thing, in his own perfect idea of himself, so that 'tis acknowledged that God's infinite love is to and his infinite delight [is] in the perfect image of himself. But the Scriptures tell us that the Son of God is that image...
>
> The perfect act of God must be a substantial act...The perfect delights of reasonable creatures are substantial delights, but the delight of God is [much more] properly a substance, yea, an infinitely perfect substance, even the essence.
>
> The Holy Spirit is the act of God between the Father and the Son, infinitely loving and delighting in each other: If the Father and the Son do infinitely delight in each other, there must be an infinitely pure and perfect act between them, an infinitely sweet energy which we call delight. This is certainly distinct from the other two...It is distinct from each of the other two, and yet it is God. It is in the Spirit that God is eternal and pure act.[21]

Father Justin Popovitch (1894–1979) has expounded the eternal beatitude and perfectly fulfilled love within the Godhead, prior to any of His external works:

> 1) *Beatitude* [*makariotes*] is, ceaselessly and immutably, the eternal sensation that God has of Himself. It comes from His living of all the divine perfections as the essence of His Being. It is because He possesses an absolute plenitude of all the perfections which are His, *ipso facto* perfect blessedness. The perfect and immutable harmony of all the properties of the divine Being means that God is perfectly and immutably happy. This is why God is the only Blessed One, the Sole Potentate, the King of kings and Lord of lords (1 Tim. 6:15). As the divine beatitude is a permanent, uninterrupted state – since it does not come to God from anything outside Himself – it cannot either diminish or increase, or alter. Having always possessed in their perfect plenitude all eternal blessings, God is ever happy in equal measure, whether men worship Him or not...
>
> 2) *Love* [*'agape*] is that property of the divine sensibility by which God lives in Himself and faces the world outside Himself. According to the teaching of divine revelation, not only does God love, but *He is* love. In Him, being and love are one and the same thing. On that is founded the good news of the Gospel of Christ: *God is love* [*'o theos agape estin*] (1 John 4:8)...It is also

[20] Moltmann, op. cit., 58.

[21] Jonathan Edwards, *Miscellany*, quoted in John H. Gerstner, *Jonathan Edwards: A Mini-Theology* (Morgan, PA: Soli Deo Gloria Publications, 1996), 30, 33, 34 .

> love that led God to create the world, to His providence over the world and to the salvation of the world. Motivated by love, God created the world in order to give His creatures participation in His divine perfections, but in the measure in which they would be capable to receive and assimilate them [as creatures] (Eph. 1:5, 9; John 14:23; Matt. 25:34) ...[22]

Shared lordship within the Trinity

The one sovereign Lord who created, did so as a communion of infinite being, love and power amongst the three co-equal persons in that one substance of His Godness, as the Westminster Confession of Faith (1647) states: 'It pleased God the Father, Son and Holy Ghost, for the manifestation of the glory of his eternal power, wisdom and goodness, in the beginning, to create, or make of nothing, the world, and all things therein, whether visible or invisible, in the space of six days, and all very good.[23]

Similarly, the Second Helvetic Confession (written by Heinrich Bullinger in 1561 for the Swiss cantons): 'GOD CREATED ALL THINGS. This good and almighty God created all things, both visible and invisible, by his co-eternal Word, and preserves them by his co-eternal Spirit, as David testified when he said: "By the word of the Lord the heavens were made, and all their host by the breath of his mouth"' (Ps. 33:6).[24]

In other words, the Confessions of the Church affirm the biblical teaching that the lordship of the one God in creation is shared equally (though in their own appropriate ways) by the three co-eternal persons: Father, Son and Holy Spirit. (Here we focus attention only upon the Triune lordship in creation; other important Trinitarian questions will be dealt with later).

As we shall see later in some detail, the Hebrew word for the God who created the heavens and the earth is Elohim (in Gen. 1:1). It is essentially a plural noun, regularly employed for the one God. But it implies a diversity with the one divine Being. As George A. F. Knight writes:

> We must just accept the fact of the word's [i.e. *Adhonai*] being a plural and in consequence a manifest parallel in usage to the common word for God in Hebrew, viz. *Elohim*. There are, indeed, singular words for God. *Elohah* is said to occur 57 times, almost always in poetry or very late prose. However, in the great majority of occurrences it is coupled with an attribute, such as *Gabhor* or *ki* or *shada*, and consequently is used descriptively of some aspect of divinity. It is true that not every case of the use of *El* (and of *Elohah*) is thus accounted for. But even if we could do so, the fact is not altered that *Elohim* is used most peculiarly (from our point of view) to cover an aspect of the Godhead which is specifically Hebraic, viz., the conception that God is both singular EL and plural *Elohim* at one and the same time...As for the LXX rendering of this peculiar singular-cum-plural word, *Elohim*, we are to

[22]Justin Popovitch, *Philosophie Orthodoxe de la Verité: Dogmatique de l'Eglise Orthodoxe*, translated [into French] from Serbian by Jean-Louis Palierne (Paris: Collection La Lumière du Thabor, L'Age d'Homme, 1992), tome I, 150, 151.

[23]Westmimster Confession of Faith, ch. IV.

[24]The Second Helvetic Confession, ch. VII.

> remember that the Greek language had no word to express a belief in mere polytheism…the LXX was unable to appreciate the need for a word that is both singular and plural at the same time.[25]

The doctrine of the Holy Trinity was not clearly revealed in the Old Testament. That would have to wait for the incarnation of the Son and the outpouring of the Holy Spirit at Pentecost. But the Church Fathers and Reformers were right to have seen intimations of the existence and work of the Trinity in the Old Testament. Looked at from the vantage point of the New Testament, we can see that many key passages of the Old Testament definitely intimate a rich personal diversity in the one God that is fully consistent with what is later revealed after the coming of Christ.

Even within the creation account of Genesis 1, we find the Trinity alluded to in the employment of the plural noun – *Elohim* – and the 'executive divine counsel' within the Godhead: 'Let us make man in our image' (Gen. 1:26). W. à Brakel appropriately summarizes the evidence:

> The Son has created the world. 'All things were made by him (that is, the Word, the Son of God); and without him was not anything made that was made' (John 1:3). 'For by him were all things created' (Col. 1:16). In doing so He did not assist, nor did it occur through Him as a means, but He is the moving cause Himself, for the word 'by' refers to the original cause. '…Through Him … are all things' (Rom. 11:36). 'God is faithful, by whom ye were called' (1 Cor. 1:9).
>
> Creation is also attributed to the Holy Spirit. 'And the Spirit of God (*Merachepheth*) moved (in a forming, creating, and generating manner) upon the face of the waters' (Gen. 1:2). 'By the word of the LORD were the heavens made; and all the host of them by the breath of his mouth' (Ps. 33:6). Since creation is the work of the Holy Trinity, it is stated in Genesis 1:26, 'Let us (*Na'aseh*, plural) make man.' 'Remember thy (*Boreecha*), *Creators* (Eccles. 12:1); (*Bo'alaich 'osaich*), thy *Makers* is thine *Husbands*' (Isa. 54:5).'[26]

Some scholars have sought to deny any inter-Trinitarian plurality in the phrase 'Let us make' by calling it 'an expression of majesty' which would be made by only one royal person. But George A. F. Knight gives a proper answer:

> Let us dismiss out of hand some of the 'explanations' of this peculiar phenomenon of a plural word for God made by exegetes whose premises were consciously or unconsciously firmly planted on the speculative approach of the Greeks. Some have suggested, for example, that the word is a plural of majesty. But that is surely to read into Hebrew speech a modern way of thinking. The kings of Israel and Judah are all addressed in the singular in our biblical records. Or again, I have seen the suggestion that here we have the 'we' of the newspaper editor![27]

N. T. Wright suggests that evidence indicates that it was not until after the rise of Christianity that Judaism began to interpret monotheism as an absolute numerical oneness of God's being:

---

[25]George A. F. Knight, *A Biblical Approach to the Doctrine of the Trinity* in 'Scottish Journal of Theology Occasional Papers, No. 1 (Edinburgh: Oliver & Boyd Ltd., 1953), 19, 20.

[26]W. à Brakel, op. cit., 267, 268.

[27]G. A. F. Knight, op. cit., 20.

> Within the most fiercely monotheistic circles throughout our period – from the Maccabean revolt to Bar-Kochba – there is no suggestion that 'monotheism', or praying the *Shema*, had anything to do with the numerical analysis of the inner being of Israel's God himself. It had everything to do with the two-pronged fight against paganism and dualism. Indeed, we find strong evidence during this period of Jewish groups and individuals who, speculating on the meaning of some difficult passages in scripture (Daniel 7, for example, or Genesis 1), suggested that the divine being might encompass a plurality [He refers to Alan F. Segal, *Two Powers in Heaven: Early Rabbinic Reports About Christianity and Gnosticism* (Leiden: Brill, 1977), and Lapide and Moltmann, *Jewish Monotheism and Christian Trinitarian Doctrine: A Dialogue* (Philadelphia: Fortress, 1981), 34ff.] Philo could speculate about the Logos as, effectively, a second divine being [*de Som*.1.229]; the Similitudes of Enoch might portray the Son of Man/Messiah as an eternal divine being [1 Enoch 48:2f; cf. 61:8; 69:29]; but none of these show any awareness that they are transgressing normal Jewish monotheism. Nor are they. The oneness of Israel's God, the creator, was never an analysis of this God's inner existence, but always a polemical doctrine over against paganism and dualism. It was only with the rise of Christianity, and arguably under the influence both of polemical constraint and Hellenizing philosophy, that Jews in the second and subsequent centuries reinterpreted 'monotheism' as 'the numerical oneness of the divine being.'[28]

Richard Bauckham has discussed with insight several contemporary renditions of supposed Old Testament monotheism, which by definition would exclude any rich diversity within God. Some of these renditions would present the One God as a sort of impoverished monad, but Bauckham demonstrates that these deviate from a close reading of the Old Testament witness.[29]

The lordship of the Triune God in creation is celebrated in Revelation 4:11: 'Thou art worthy, O Lord, to receive glory and honour and power: for thou hast created all things, and for thy pleasure they are and were created.' The uniqueness of the sovereign lordship that brought forth the creation was revealed to Job:

> Where wast thou when I laid the foundations of the earth? Declare, if thou hast understanding. Who laid the measures thereof, if thou knowest? Or who hath stretched the line upon it? Whereupon are the foundations thereof fastened? Or who laid the corner stone thereof; when the morning stars sang together, and all the sons of God shouted for joy? (Job 38:4-7).

God's word to Job shows that the human mind, even a pious one, cannot comprehend the miracle of divine creation of all things out of nothing. If we cannot understand how any miracle happens, then certainly we cannot understand how God brings to pass the miracle of miracles. Thus, we begin and end with faith: 'Through faith we understand that the worlds were framed by the Word of God, so that things which are seen were not made of things which do appear.' In the apposite words of W. a Brakel: 'Natural

---

[28]N. T. Wright, *The New Testament and the People of God*, (Minneapolis: Fortress Press, 1992), 259.

[29]Richard Bauckham, 'Biblical Theology and the Problems of Monotheism', in Craig Bartholomew et al. (eds.), *Out of Egypt: Biblical Theology and Biblical Interpretation* (Grand Rapids, MI: Zondervan, 2006).

reason teaches that by virtue of causal relationships one ultimately must come to God as the original cause of all things.[30] Natural reason, however, cannot understand the "how"; that is, how something can come into existence out of nothing, how God with one word and with one single command has caused everything to come into existence. All this we accept by faith.'[31]

The beauty of creation reflects the beauty of the Lord God

Even those who refuse to exercise faith (and thus can never understand until they do so) have a difficult time denying the majesty and power of God's splendid work of creation; a majesty and splendor that speaks eloquently of his sovereign lordship over all. Solomon wrote: 'He hath made every thing beautiful in his time; also he hath set the world in their heart, so that no man can find out the work that God maketh from the beginning to the end' (Eccles. 3:11).

His father, David, wrote many a Psalm about the beauty and splendor of the creation, and its testimony to its Lord:

> O LORD our Lord, how excellent is thy name in all the earth! Who hast set thy glory above the heavens. Out of the mouth of babes and sucklings hast thou ordained strength because of thine enemies, that thou mightest still the enemy and the avenger. When I consider thy heavens, the work of thy fingers, the moon and the stars, which thou hast ordained; What is man, that thou art mindful of him? And the son of man, that thou visitest him? (Ps. 8:1-4).

> The heavens declare the glory of God; and the firmament sheweth his handywork. Day unto day uttereth speech, and night unto night sheweth knowledge. There is no speech nor language, where their voice is not heard. Their line is gone out through all the earth, and their words to the end of the world. In them hath he set a tabernacle for the sun, which is as a bridegroom coming out of his chamber, and rejoiceth as a strong man to run a race. His going forth is from the end of the heaven, and his circuit unto the ends of it: and there is nothing hid from the heat thereof (Ps. 19:1-6).

Another psalmist connects the creative lordship of God with his redemptive lordship. He does so in antiphonal style, no doubt suitable for responsive singing in the Temple:

> O give thanks to the Lord of lords: for his mercy endureth forever. To him who alone doeth great wonders: for his mercy endureth forever. To him that by wisdom made the heavens: for his mercy endureth forever. To him that stretched out the earth above the waters: for his mercy endureth forever. To him that made great lights: for his mercy endureth forever: The sun to rule by day: for his mercy endureth forever: The moon and stars to rule by night: for his mercy endureth forever. To him that smote Egypt in their firstborn: for his mercy endureth forever… (Ps. 136:3-10).

---

[30] I have sought to address David Hume's denial of cause and effect in Appendix II to Chapter 1. By denying causation, he hoped that he had denied creation.

[31] W. à Brakel, op. cit., 270.

The same juncture of lordship over creation and over redemption is found in Psalm 146. 'Happy is he that hath the God of Jacob for his help, whose hope is in the LORD his God: Which made heaven and earth, the sea, and all that therein is: which keepeth truth forever: Which executeth judgment for the oppressed...' (vv. 5-7).

The response of faith for God's wonderful lordship in creation (and redemption) is praise: '

> Praise ye the LORD. Praise ye the LORD from the heavens: praise him in the heights. Praise ye him, all his angels: praise ye him, all his hosts. Praise ye him, sun and moon: praise him all ye stars of light. Praise him, ye heavens of heavens, and ye waters that be above the heavens. Let them praise the name of the LORD: for he commanded, and they were created. He hath also stablished them for ever and ever: he hath made a decree which shall not pass... Let them praise the name of the LORD: for his name alone is excellent; his glory is above the earth and heaven.' (Ps. 148:1-6, 13).

Paul in Romans 1, as we saw earlier, shows that the glory of creation points to the glory of its sovereign Creator, and demands that He be honored:

> 'Because that which may be known of God is manifest in them; for God hath shewed it unto them. For the invisible things of him from the creation of the world are clearly seen, being understood by the things that are made, even his eternal power and Godhead; so that they are without excuse...' (Rom. 1:19-21).

The beauty and splendor of the creation always point to the beautiful lordship of the triune God who brought it all into being, preserves it and redeems it. One could easily devote an entire volume to this beauty of God's lordship in creation. Indeed, the Roman Catholic theologian of Switzerland, Hans Urs Von Balthasar (1905–1988), devotes several remarkable volumes to this theme.[32]

The beauty of the heavens

Let us take an illustration of the beauty of the Lordship of the Trinity in creation from the stars. Genesis 1:16 tells us: 'he made the stars also.' The contemporary British mechanical engineer and professor (of Bristol University), Stuart Burgess, has helped us appreciate just how beautiful the arrangement of the stars is.

> The Solar System is positioned about two-thirds of the way out from the centre of the Galaxy, which is far enough away from the galactic bulge to keep the night sky dark ... if the Earth were located in the galactic bulge, the night sky would be 'ablaze' with light ... Big Bang cosmologists are fully aware that the Earth has an ideal location. However, this remarkable fact is not considered to be significant because secular astronomers assume that the Earth's position was determined by chance ...[33]
>
> If stars were uniformly spaced with the same distance between each one, there would be no distinctive star patterns in the sky and the sky would

[32]*The Glory of the Lord: A Theological Aesthetics* in seven volumes, translated by Erasmo Leiva-Merikakis (San Francisco: Ignatius Press, 1982).

[33]Stuart Burgess, *He Made the Stars Also: What the Bible Says About the Stars* (Epsom, Surrey: Day One Publications, 2002), 78.

look monotonous in every direction. However, the actual spacing is very non-uniform and this produces varied and beautiful patterns in the sky such as the Bear, Orion and the Pleiades ...[34]

The book of Job describes how God has 'adorned the heavens 'by His Spirit' (Job 26:13). Modern telescopes have revealed the astounding degree to which God has indeed adorned the heavens with beauty. When we look up at the stars and galaxies with powerful telescopes, there are countless beautiful colours, shapes and patterns to behold ... Despite the great evidence of design, secular astronomers totally reject the idea that God has deliberately put beauty in the stars. They do not deny that the stars are beautiful but they insist that the beauty has appeared by chance ... [but] the beauty of the Universe is so striking and so co-ordinated that it provides great evidence of supremely intelligent design.[35]

One of the beautiful aspects of the Solar System is the great variety of colours, shapes and patterns amongst the planets and moons. The planet Mars is commonly known as the 'red planet' because of its red appearance when viewed from the Earth. In contrast, Uranus is green-blue and Saturn is yellow ...[36]

One reason why stars are beautiful is that they come in a great range of sizes. Right across the night sky there is a great variation in brightness of the stars. The variation in brightness is mentioned in the Bible where we read: 'There is one glory of the sun, another glory of the moon, and another glory of the stars; for one star differs from another star in glory' (1 Cor. 15:41) ... The colour of a star is determined mainly by its temperature: a red star is relatively cool; a yellow star is slightly hotter; a white star is hotter still; and a blue star is very hot. When God created the stars on the fourth day of creation, He deliberately created each star with a specific temperature that would produce the colour that He wanted. God made the temperature of most stars such they that would give a white-yellow colour...the range of colours that we see today presents great evidence of design ...[37]

It is very easy to take the colours of the Earth, the sky and the stars for granted. However, in reality the colour scheme of the Universe is amazingly well designed for man...One reason why the colour scheme is perfect is that the colours which dominate in each part of creation are 'restful' colours. Studies have shown that green is very easy on the eyes and reduces eyestrain. Blue is a restful colour because it slows down the heart rate. The night sky is also restful because it is so dark. In contrast to these colours, red is quite a stressful colour which raises the blood pressure. If either the land or sky were dominated by red, then life would be very stressful!

A second reason why the colour scheme is perfect is that there is a different dominating colour in each part of creation. The blue sky contrasts with the green land and with the white stars. If the sky and land were both blue or both green, life would be very strange. A third reason why the colour scheme is perfect is that all three primary colours can be seen in each part of creation. Even though red does not appear as a dominating colour in any of the environments, this is made up for by the fact that it appears as a

[34]Ibid., 79.
[35]Ibid., 92.
[36]Ibid., 93.
[37]Ibid., 95, 96.

> common secondary colour in each case … The perfect colour scheme in the Universe presents astounding evidence of design.[38]

God's own beauty

> The truth is that colours, shapes and patterns have been deliberately put in place to produce a beautiful sight and to declare God's glory…How we need to follow the advice of Elihu who said: '…stand still and consider the wondrous works of God (Job 37:14).[39]

St. Augustine on beauty

Yet St. Augustine shows that, psychologically and spiritually, the relationship between our perception of creational beauty and the original personal beauty of God is a very complex one; often involving those who come to faith in intense and long struggles.

> But what do I love when I love my God? Not material beauty or beauty of a temporal order; not the brilliance of earthly light, so welcome to our eyes; not the sweet melody of harmony and song; not the fragrance of flowers, perfumes and spices; not manna or honey; not limbs such as the body delights to embrace. It is not these that I love when I love my God. And yet, when I love him, it is true that I love a light of a certain kind, a voice, a perfume, a food, an embrace; but they are of the kind that I love in my inner self, when my soul is bathed in light that is not bound by space; when it listens to sound that never dies away; when it breathes fragrance that is not borne away on the wind; when it tastes food that is never consumed by the eating; when it clings to an embrace from which it is not severed by fulfilment of desire. This is what I love when I love my God.
>
> But what is my God? I put my question to the earth. It answered, 'I am not God', and all things on earth declared the same. I asked the sea, and the chasms of the deep and the living things that creep in them, but they answered, 'We are not your God. Seek what is above us.' I spoke to the winds that blow, and the whole air and all that lives in it replied, 'Anaximenes is wrong. I am not God.'[40] I asked the sky, the sun, the moon, and the stars, but they told me, 'Neither are we the God whom you seek.' I spoke to all the things that are about me, all that can be admitted by the door of the senses, and I said, 'Since you are not my God, tell me about him. Tell me something of my God.' Clear and loud they answered, 'God is he who made us.' I asked these questions simply by gazing at those things, and their beauty was all the answer they gave.[41]

But then, Augustine was converted in Milan, and found the source of beauty in a Person:

> I have learnt to love you late, O Beauty at once so ancient and so new! I have learnt to love you late! You were within me, and I was in the world outside myself. I searched for you outside myself. I searched for you outside myself

---

[38]Ibid., 102, 103.

[39]Ibid. 104.

[40]Anaximenes of Miletus, a pre-Socratic philosopher of the sixth century B.C., held that air is the first cause of all things.

[41]St. Augustine, *Confessions*, translated by R. S. Pine-Coffin (Harmondsworth: Penguin Books, 1961), Bk. X, 6.

> and, disfigured as I was, I fell upon the lovely things of your creation. You were with me, but I was not with you. The beautiful things of this world kept me far from you and yet, if they had not been in you, they would have had no being at all. You called me; you cried aloud to me; you broke my barrier of deafness. You shone upon me; your radiance enveloped me; you put my blindness to flight. You shed your fragrance about me; I drew breath and now I gasp for your sweet odour. I tasted you, and now I hunger and thirst for you. You touched me, and I am inflamed with love of your peace.[42]

What happened to Augustine, and to all believers who are drawn by beauty out of themselves and into touch with God, is something like this. Von Balthasar quotes 'Dionysius the Areopagite' (from *The Divine Names*, Book IV, section 13): 'And the divine Eros also brings rapture, not allowing them that are touched by it to belong to themselves, but only to the objects of their love ...'[43] Edward T. Oakes comments on this phrase: 'Not allowing them that are touched by it to belong to themselves.'

Von Balthasar on beauty

> Here perhaps is the key that unlocks the whole point of the Aesthetics [i.e. of Von Balthasar], for beauty is inherently attractive, meaning that it draws contemplators out of themselves and into a direct encounter with the phenomenon manifesting itself, and this beauty, the contemplator knows, testifies to itself in a way that the Good and the True cannot do. Although all three transcendentals, the Beautiful, the Good, and the True, in the traditional Platonic understanding, are all inherent aspects of the nature of Being, nonetheless we may doubt, and often do, the inherent goodness and truth of the being of the world. But this, Balthasar maintains we cannot do with beauty, once experienced ...[44]

The various forms of beauty are created precisely in order to point beyond themselves. Von Balthasar says: 'The form as it appears to us is beautiful only because the delight it arouses in us is founded upon the fact that in it, the truth and goodness of the depths of reality itself are manifested and bestowed, and this manifestation and bestowal reveal themselves to us as being something infinitely and inexhaustively valuable and fascinating.'[45] He adds:

> In the luminous form of the beautiful the being of the existent becomes perceivable as nowhere else, and this is why an aesthetic element must be associated with all spiritual perception as with all spiritual striving. The quality of 'being-in-itself' which belongs to the beautiful, the demand the beautiful itself makes to be allowed to be what it is, the demand, therefore, that we renounce our attempts to control and manipulate it, in order truly to be able to be happy by enjoying it: all of this is, in the natural realm, the foundation and foreshadowing of what in the realm of revelation and grace will be the attitude of faith.[46]

---

[42]Ibid., Bk. X, 27.

[43]Von Balthasar, *The Glory of the Lord*, Vol. I, 122.

[44]Edward T. Oakes, *Pattern of Redemption: The Theology of Hans Urs Von Balthasar* (New York: Continuum, 1994), 143, 144.

[45]Von Balthasar, *The Glory of the Lord*, vol. I, 118.

[46]Ibid., 153.

Patrick Sherry shows that for Von Balthasar, the mutual love shared by the Father, the Son and the Holy Spirit is the very source of the beauty of God.[47]

Pierre Viret on beauty

Pierre Viret, the sixteenth-century Reformer of Lausanne, and friend of John Calvin, wrote in his own way, though somewhat similarly, concerning beauty and how it leads us to God:

> God has not only provided in these things [i.e. the lovely streams, hills, trees and flowers, with the animals and birds that inhabit them] for the necessities of mankind, but also for their desires and pleasures, and has desired to join together an excellent beauty with profit and usefulness. For how beautiful He has made these lovely isles between the waters of the seas to appear, and the beautiful and clear fountains and the beautiful streaming currents issuing from the rocks and caves of the earth, running down among the mountains and valleys and plains, and among the forests and the fields and the prairies, and the beautiful branches of the trees which are around them, along with so many various types of species, and then the lovely little birds walking about, flying and singing in the midst of them, with a great melody and natural music![48]

Viret goes on to show that these beauties of nature are given to point us upward to the beauty of the Creator who made them. In a very similar way, the twentieth-century poet laureate of South Carolina, Archibald Rutledge of Hampton Plantation, shows the same connection.

The poet had just visited a simple mountain woman, the sister of a man who had recently been arrested for murder. Rutledge noticed that she had placed a red flowering branch in a jar on the rough mantle of her remote log cabin:

> As I went up the old gullied mountain road toward the home of the first [of the two mountain men who had been involved in a murderous altercation], I noticed in the wild glen, down which a white stream gurgled and spurted, incessant, vehement, and joyous, that the rhododendrons were in blossom. There may be a more beautiful flower, but I have not seen it – taking it all in all, and considering the wildwood setting in which it invariably grows. To look at this wondrous flower and not to feel that God exquisitely designed it, and did it not merely as a vagrant artist but with precision and nobility of purpose is to me incredible. Ere long I reached the cabin, and one of the man's sisters greeted me and talked with me. Over the humble mantle I saw a crude little photograph of him [the murderer] in his [World War I] uniform; and beside it, in a small bottle that functioned as a vase, I saw a sprig of rhododendron blossom. I looked at the picture; then I said something casual about the flower.

---

[47]Patrick Sherry, *Spirit and Beauty: An Introduction to Theological Aesthetics* (Oxford: Clarendon Press, 1992), 85-109.

[48]Pierre Viret, from *Instruction Chrétienne*, 1564, II, p. 161, reproduced in *Pierre Viret D'Après Lui-Même: Pages extraites des oeuvres du Réformateur à l'occasion du quatrième centenaire de sa naissance* par C. Schnetzler et al. (Lausanne: Georges Bridel & Cie, 1911), 269.

> 'I don't know why,' my hostess said, 'but to have it there helps me. It 'minds me of God...' I never see a rhododendron without remembering that. And are not all of life's extras reminders of the love and the yearning compassion of God?[49]

Like the scientist, Stuart Burgess (quoted earlier), Rutledge suggests that the very colors of nature point to the beauty of God's purposes and Being:

> I mentioned sunsets and sunrises as extras. Almost the whole complex and wonderful matter of color in the world seems as extra. The color of the sky might have been a dingy gray, or a painful yellow, or a plum-colored purple. But it is sapphire; and my philosophy makes me believe that such a color for the sky is by no means the result of mere chance. Granted that it is the result of the operation of certain laws, forces, and conditions; yet behind it all, back of the realized dream, is the mighty intelligence of the Creator, the vast amplitude of the dreamer's comprehension. And let us not forget that the two colors at which we can gaze longest are blue and green. There is about them a coolness, a serenity, a spirit of fragrant peace. And as the blue prevails in the sky, the green does upon the earth.[50]

Jonathan Edwards on beauty

The eighteenth-century New England theologian, Jonathan Edwards, also found the beauties of the creation lifting him upwards to the Triune God (in this case, to Jesus Christ), the source of all beauty:

> When we are delighted with flowery meadows and gentle breezes of wind, we may consider that we only see the emanations of the sweet benevolence of Jesus Christ; when we behold the fragrant rose and lily, we see his love and purity. So the green trees and fields, and singing of birds, are the emanations of his infinite joy and benignity; the easiness and naturalness of trees and vines [are] shadows of his infinite beauty and loveliness; the crystal rivers and murmuring streams have the footsteps of his sweet grace and bounty...That beauteous light with which the world is filled in a clear day is a lively shadow of his spotless holiness and happiness, and delight in communicating himself.[51]

Edwards, in some respects like St. Augustine, writes of how the beauties of the created order were – after his conversion – constantly lifting his heart up to the glorious God; the Creator and Redeemer. After having spoken to his ministerial father about certain passages in Holy Scripture (i.e. 1 Tim. 1:17: 'Now unto the King eternal, immortal, invisible, the only wise God, be honour and glory, for ever and ever. Amen' and Song of Solomon 2:1: 'I am the rose of Sharon, and the lily of the valleys.'), he writes in his 'Memoirs':

> Not long after I first began to experience these things, I gave an account to my father of some things that had passed in my mind. I was pretty much affected by the discourse we had together; and when the discourse was ended, I walked abroad alone, in a solitary place in my father's pasture, for contemplation. And as I was walking there, and looking upon the sky and clouds, there came into my mind so sweet a sense of the glorious majesty

---

[49]Archibald Rutledge, *Life's Extras* (New York and London: Fleming H. Revell Company, 1928), 11, 12.

[50]Ibid., 12,13.

[51]Quotation from George M. Marsden, *Jonathan Edwards: A Life* (New Haven and London: Yale University Press, 2003), 100.

> and grace of God, as I know not how to express. – I seemed to see them both in a sweet conjunction; majesty and meekness joined together…
>
> After this my sense of divine things gradually increased, and became more and more lively, and had more of that inward sweetness. The appearance of every thing was altered; there seemed to be, as it were, a calm, sweet cast or appearance of divine glory, in almost every thing. God's excellency, his wisdom, his purity and love, seemed to appear in every thing; in the sun, moon and stars; in the clouds and blue sky; in the grass, flowers, trees; in the water and all nature; which used greatly to fix my mind. I often used to sit and view the moon for a long time; and in the day, spent much time in viewing the clouds and sky, to behold the sweet glory of God in these things: in the mean time singing forth, with a low voice, my contemplations of the Creator and Redeemer. And scarce any thing, among all the works of nature, was so sweet to me as thunder and lightning: formerly nothing had been so terrible to me. Before, I used to be uncommonly terrified with thunder, and to be struck with terror when I saw a thunder-storm rising; not now, on the contrary, it rejoiced me. I felt God, if I may so speak, at the first appearance of a thunder-storm; and used to take the opportunity, at such times, to fix myself in order to view the clouds, and see the lightnings play, and hear the majestic and awful voice of God's thunders, which oftentimes was exceedingly entertaining, leading me to sweet contemplations of my great and glorious God. While thus engaged, it always seemed natural for me to sing or chant forth my meditations; or, to speak my thoughts in soliloquies with a singing voice.[52]

So the eyes of faith, and the regenerated heart behind them, delight in the created beauties of God's handiwork, and realize with calm confidence that creation is the miracle of miracles; that if God is powerful enough to bring all things into existence by His mere word, then every other miracle spoken of by the divine revelation follows.

The beauty of God's creation which is given both to delight God and man, and to point man up to God, is an objective reality. But without faith, man will ignore – or misinterpret – the source of that beauty, so as to deny the Lordship behind it, in order to escape the Lord's claims upon him. Hebrews 11:6 says: 'But without faith it is impossible to please him: for he that cometh to God must believe that he is, and that he is a rewarder of them that diligently seek him.'

An illustration of the power of beauty from a German-Swiss novel

The beauties of creation not only can lead us up to their (and our) Creator, but once experienced can play a part in reconciling us to our fellow humans. They have a way of pointing past the ugliness of our relationships upwards to the beauty of the divine and human love intended by the triune God in their very shining in our darkness. The German-Swiss novelist of the nineteenth century, Jeremias Gotthelf, gives a poignant illustration of how this transpires in one of his stories about an unhappy marriage that through the grieved wife's perception of the beauty of the natural and

[52]Jonathan Edwards, 'Memoirs' in *The Works of Jonathan Edwards* (Edinburgh: The Banner of Truth Trust, 1974), vol. I, xiii.

animal creation, found it possible to seek true reconciliation with her cold husband.

For this remarkable story of ordinary peasant folk, who found the grace of God through the beauties of the ordinary realm around them, so that their love was restored to one another, we extract a few pages from Gottfelf's *L'Argent et l'Esprit*, a French translation of the German original.[53]

> But sadness was already coming back, just like the heaviest downpours of rain after each ray of sunshine. 'How appropriate is this darkness for us, she kept muttering; as if we could be happy, and yet what a life we are now living! We are in worse shape than the poor merchants of dishes or cheap buckles; not because of poverty, for what we have would be more than enough for us and possibly for our children, but the evil resides inside of us. That is where trouble has always done its worst work.'
>
> Anneli sat down, and while she let her eyes wander all along the rich countryside which was shining with abundance, from the valley to the summits of the pre-alps, she saw, as far as her sight could go, the immense celestial vault lowering itself towards the peaks. She noticed a circle taking shape before her eyes, as she saw heaven uniting itself to earth. It was from that union that the rich benediction was coming from the sunshine, from the rain, from the mysterious rosy colours, from the amazing power which created life in the bosom of the earth. Anneli felt a strange emotion while becoming aware of this alliance of heaven and earth which confirmed exactly how everything was so beautiful and magnificent to contemplate, because peace reigned between heaven and earth; that heaven was dispensing its fullness, and that earth was praising heaven. She wondered if ultimately heaven ought to encompass, not only the earth, but also the life of men, in such a way that when life would push them to their final limits on earth, the heavens would not open themselves before them.
>
> Now that is why all the events of our life ought to lift us up like a mountain on which the heaven is coming down, by which we would be able to gain heaven. Yes, every day we live is a sort of little life in itself; ought it not to be the beginning of heaven, and when after our long march in the heat of the day, and the evening arrives with sleep weighing down our weary eyelids, ought we not to be refreshed there where little angels ascend and descend upon the pilgrim who is sleeping in the peace of the Lord, so that at daybreak, he may awaken, strengthened by this celestial calm, in order to take up once again his earthly tasks? And did it not used to be this way with us in past years, Anneli wondered.
>
> When the night used to come as the day was waning, did we not used to lift up our souls to seek God and His peace and rest, leaving behind us earthly miseries, drowning in the sea of forgetfulness all our bad thoughts and bitter experiences? In those times we woke up with things feeling right every morning, and we carried the blessing of God with us all day long, and every night we would wash away all the dirty spots with which life on earth had soiled us. But now, at evening, we no longer wash away anything; we go to bed, wrapped up in our misery and distress, in sadness and hatred, and with evil spirits coming during the night to make it worse with awful

[53]Jeremias Gotthelf, *L'Argent et l'Esprit* (Lausanne: L'Age d'Homme, 2000), pp. 93-98. I owe this reference to my friend, Jean-Marc Berthoud of Lausanne.

nightmares. And in the morning, there is no longer any bright sunshine to lighten our souls, no more blessing to carry with us throughout the new day, but on the contrary, the same old misery, the same old distress which never let up during the night, and only gets worse during the day so that it swallows up every day of our lives, and our eyes no longer see heaven, like on rainy days when the skies are so black with storms that the mountains are shrouded with dark clouds that keep us from being able to see the sky.

It was precisely then that Anneli understood for the very first time what a sin she had committed in ceasing to pray, and thus from that moment allowing anger and resentment to take deep root in her spirit. Things which formerly would have been taken care of each night became a permanent state. Of course she had continued to pray in silence, but her prayers slipped away without finding any resonance in the soul of Cristen [her husband], and without removing all the offences, and even more, growing further and further away from God. Hence these lifeless prayers left her soul in the darkness of her own misery, and they became nothing more than meaningless words rolling off her tongue like rocks washed down a riverbed. The light from on high no longer purified her soul, but earth darkened her spirit more every day.

Understanding at last precisely what her sin was, she no longer sought to explain her misery by the loss of the five thousand pounds of money that weighed more heavily upon her husband than on her. But on the contrary, she saw that it lay in the rupture of the spiritual bond that had so long once held their souls united together in faithfulness and love, and that she felt herself guilty for this rupture. This revelation shot through her soul like a bolt of lightening, and shook Anneli profoundly. And that had been the very problem that she had been unable to see or understand; yet she could have touched it with her finger! And she almost took this sin with her into the next life, along with the cries of her children whose lives, and maybe even whose hearts she had poisoned with it. But now she recognized how easy it was to see the speck of dust in our neighbour's eye, while ignoring the log in our own eye! Oh, if God had judged her in the same way she had so often judged her own husband!

An infinite humility took hold of her when she saw how far down she had fallen; no punishment seemed sufficient to her; far from refusing to be punished, on the contrary, she desperately hoped for it. To go through punishment would give her a certain kind of joy. She had the impression that she would not feel at ease until the moment when God chastised her soundly; that only then would she be able to recognize the Face of God which she had for so long ignored, once again resting upon her. Only then would His hand be opened once more upon her. But she also felt at the same time that she ought to make restitution for her wrongs, to confess her sins, clearly understanding in the depths of her soul that pardon can only be granted to someone who admits his sins with all his heart, and not to someone who mentions them superficially and as a whole, in hopes of having them pardoned and washed away all at once. She understood that it is necessary to confess one's sins in an act of love that does not let itself become embittered, which acknowledges its sin every day, without waiting for reconciliation; which perseveres in this confession, even when one's neighbour abuses one's intention by refusing not only to recognize his wrongs, but even piling up more of them day by day. She now knew that in spite of it all, everything depended on her; that she was the pivot

> around which turned the destiny of her family; that she must lose no time in getting herself courageously to work, for will not the Master come as a thief in the night to require an account of his servant for what he did on his estate? She knew that it was her responsibility to mend the broken tie; that was her great and holy task.[…]
>
> When Anneli reached the brow of the hill, after waging victorious battle against the spirit of pride and bitterness, she opened her eyes and all around her everything was far more beautiful than ordinary. The sky not only seemed to her to circumscribe the earth, but she saw it reach down upon her, as if she were merged with it so as to be only one with it. Up until that moment, Anneli had not noticed that when heaven has come down into our soul and dwells in us, we sanctify the very places our feet walk on, transforming them into heaven.
>
> Strengthened and, as it were, reborn to a new life, she went back down towards the house. The pigeons and chickens bid her a friendly welcome; they followed her to the door of the kitchen, where they stopped and waited for her to bring them their feed, and she noticed them gaily and gently putter around the grain. And then it was the dog who showed up, passing through the pigeons and chickens, wagging his tail without scattering them, and laying his head on Anneli's knees, without disturbing the cat, who was already resting on the same place. The cat touched the dog with his paw, once he had drawn in his claws, for he loved to play with his old comrade.
>
> Experiencing a real joy in seeing this concord and mutual confidence, Anneli in her own turn played the role of the dog and then of the cat in caressing one after the other. But this harmony so touched her heart that it caused tears to well up in her eyes. If even a dog and a cat, who are old acquaintances, can live together in perfect concord and peace, how could it be that a man and a woman, created for one another, could so torture and torment each other by continuing to live in an ever-increasing mutual hostility?

This touchingly illustrates that the beauties of nature, including life in the animal kingdom, speak to us of the beauty of God. But in so doing, they are also intended to play a part in dissolving the bitternesses that inevitably develop in the relationships of life in a fallen world. Thereby, the simple beauties in nature around us, by reminding us of a higher beauty, have a hand in transmuting our own ugliness into the beauty God intended for us.

(ii) God's majestic authority as King over all that He has created

God as King

Holy Scripture presents God both as Creator and sovereign King or Lord of that creation. His kingship is majestic, involving the most proper and 'deserved' royal authority over absolutely all things. '… Yahweh occurs as subject of the verb מלך [Hebrew for "to rule"] 13 times and *melek* ["king"] is used as an epithet of Yahweh. He is 'king' of the world, the gods, the nations, and Israel.'[54]

---

[54] *New International Dictionary of OT Theology & Exegesis*, W. Van Gemeren, gen. ed., vol. 2, p. 960.

> The kingship of Yahweh is an aspect of faith found neither in the wisdom literature,[55] the oral teaching of many of the prophets, nor in a considerable number of historical narratives. It is frequent, on the other hand, in the hymns of the Psalter (the so-called enthronement Psalms), later prophetic writings including the prophecies to the nations in Jeremiah (e.g. Jer. 46:18; 48:15; 51:57), and in the narrative parts of the book of Daniel. Thus it tends to feature in the later parts of the OT.[56]

But one must say, that although the word 'king' is not used of the LORD in Genesis 1 and 2, the creation accounts assume his ultra-lordship, for He speaks worlds into being. Exodus 20 does not use the word 'king' of 'I AM THAT I AM', but the suzerainty-treaty form of the ten covenant words given to Moses by God on Sinai are the authoritative instructions, promises and threats made by an ancient Middle Eastern monarch. The God who had shortly before the Sinai revelation brought His people out of the house of bondage in Egypt, had thereby 'got glory over Pharaoh' (Exod. 14:17,18). Pharaoh was the world's most powerful monarch, but was drowned with his army in one of the smallest seas of the Lord of Hosts. All of this is to say, that the concept of majestic kingship is in view throughout the Old Testament (and New), even when the term is not there.

A number of Old Testament passages reflect the universal nature of Yahweh as king. He is creator of the world:

> The earth is the LORD's and the fullness thereof; the world, and they that dwell therein.' (Ps. 24:1)

> The LORD reigneth, he is clothed with majesty; the LORD is clothed with strength, wherewith he hath girded himself: the world also is stablished that it cannot be moved. Thy throne is established of old: thou art from everlasting. (Ps. 93:1, 2)

> For the LORD is a great God, and a great King above all gods. In his hand are the deep places of the earth; the strength of the hills is his also. The sea is his, and he hath made it: and his hands formed the dry land. O come, let us worship and bow down: let us kneel before the LORD our maker. (Ps. 95:3-6)

God's kingdom rules over all:

> For the LORD most high is terrible; he is a great King over all the earth…For God is the King of all the earth: sing ye praises with understanding. God reigneth over the heavens: God sitteth upon the throne of his holiness. (Ps. 47:2, 7-8)

> The LORD is great in Zion; and he is high above all the people…Exalt the LORD our God, and worship at his holy hill; for the LORD our God is holy. (Ps. 99:2, 9)

> Who would not fear thee, O King of nations? For to thee doth it appertain: forasmuch as among all the wise men of the nations, and in all their

---

[55]But what about Proverbs 21:1 ('The king's heart is in the hand of the LORD, as the rivers of water: he turneth it withersoever he will'), which in the very context of human kingship, affirms God's superior and total control. What is this but divine Kingship?

[56]*New International Dictionary of NT Theology*, C. Brown, gen ed., vol. 2, pp.374, 375.

> kingdoms, there is none like unto thee ... But the LORD is the true God, he is the living God, and an everlasting king: at his wrath the earth shall tremble, and the nations shall not be able to abide his indignation. Thus shall ye say unto them, The gods that have not made the heavens and the earth, even they shall perish from under these heavens. He hath made the earth by his power, he hath established the world by his wisdom, and hath stretched out the heavens by his discretion. (Jer. 10:7, 10-12)

God rules the future:

> ... That they may see, and know, and consider, and understand together, that the hand of the LORD hath done this, and the Holy One of Israel hath created it [i.e. future blessings of return and restoration for deported Israel]. Produce your cause, saith the LORD; bring forth your strong reasons, saith the King of Jacob. Let them [i.e. idols/false gods] bring them forth, and shew us what shall happen: let them shew the former things, what they be, that we may consider them, and know the latter end of them; or declare us things for to come. Shew the things that are to come hereafter, that we may know that ye are gods: yea, do good, or do evil, that we may be dismayed, and behold it together. Behold, ye are of nothing, and your work of nought: an abomination is he that chooseth you.' (Isa. 41:20-24)

> Thus saith the LORD the King of Israel, and his redeemer the LORD of hosts; I am the first, and I am the last; and beside me there is no God. And who, as I, shall call, and shall declare it, and set it in order for me, since I appointed the ancient people? And the things that are coming, and shall come, let them shew unto you. Fear ye not, neither be afraid: have not I told thee from that time, and have declared it? Ye are even my witnesses. Is there a God beside me? Yea, there is no God; I know not any. (Isa. 44:6-8)

> How beautiful upon the mountains are the feet of him that bringeth good tidings, that publisheth peace; that bringeth good tidings of good, that publisheth salvation; that saith unto Zion, Thy God reigneth! (Isa. 52:7)

The New Testament continues the exaltation of God as King in the same way as the Old Testament. The Hebrew noun for king – *mlk* – is translated as *basileus* in the LXX, and this translation continues in the New Testament. 'The NT follows closely the precedent set by the OT and Judaism in giving to God and Christ alone the full right to the title king. Human kings, by contrast, are generally regarded as of limited importance...Just as the OT is at variance with oriental views of divine kingship, so the NT is opposed to Hellenistic and Roman ideas of this kind: the earthly king is not an incarnation of the deity, since no one but God or the Messiah can occupy such a position. Thus in Revelation, in sharp contrast to the presumptuous claims to divinity of Domitian, only God is recognized as king of the nations *basileus ton ethnon* (Rev. 15:3), and only Christ as the king of kings, *basileus basileon* (Rev. 19:16; 17:14), The OT attitude to the great kings is found again in the NT with regard to the 'kings of the east' (Rev. 16:12): the supremacy of God is asserted by making them a rod in his hand, only to destroy them at the last day if they do not submit to him in obedience (Rev. 17:2 ff.; 18:3 ff.; 19:18 ff.; 21:24).'[57]

Lordship of Messiah

Psalm 2, a major Messianic Psalm, contrasts the rebellious 'kings of the earth' with the LORD [THE KING], who sets up his Son as King on Zion (v. 6). His Son is made king not only of the people of God, but also of the rest of the heathen people of the earth (v. 8). Thus, the kings of the earth are told to submit to Him and to kiss His feet in humble subjection, lest they be destroyed by the true King (9-12). This Psalm is (next to Psalm 110) the most quoted Psalm in the New Testament. Psalm 2 is quoted in Matthew 3:17; 17:5; Mark 1:11; 9:7; Luke 3:22; 9:35; John 1:49; Acts 4:25-26; 13:33; Philippians 2:12; Hebrews 1:2, 5; 5:5; Revelation 2:26-27; 11:18; 12:5; 19:15, 19.

The portion of the Old Testament most frequently quoted in the New is Psalm 110, probably the leading Messianic Psalm of them all. It is a Psalm of lordship, of kingly rule, in which the Lord establishes His Son as victorious Captain, who 'shall strike through kings in the day of his wrath' (v. 5). This Lord who sits at His Father's right hand (v. 1) is also a priest; not Levitical, but 'after the order of Melchizedek'; one who accomplishes in fullness the priestly work for all his people that Aaron and his descendants could never perfect (v. 4; cf. Hebrews, Chapters 6-10). Jesus referred to this Psalm in order to confound the Pharisees, who were 'astonished at his doctrine' (Matt. 22:33), but wished to deny who He was as Messiah and King:

> While the Pharisees were gathered together, Jesus asked them, Saying, What think ye of Christ [i.e. 'Messiah']? Whose son is he? They say unto him, the son of David. He saith unto them, How then doth David in spirit call him Lord, saying, 'The Lord said unto my Lord, Sit thou on my right hand, till I make thine enemies thy footstool'? If David then call him Lord, how is he his son?' (Matt. 22:41-45). See also the other references to Psalm 110 in the New Testament: Matthew 26:64; Mark 12:36; 14:62; 16:19; Luke 20:42-43; 22:69; John 12:34; Acts 2:34-35; Romans 8:34; 1 Corinthians 15:25; Ephesians 1:20; Colossians 3:1; Hebrews 1:3, 13; 5:6, 10; 6:20; 7:3, 17, 21; 8:1; 10:12-13; 12:2.

Lordship of the Spirit

The Person of the Holy Spirit, and thus His royal rule, is usually hidden behind that of the Father and the Son, for, as Jesus said of this blessed Person, '... He shall not speak of himself ... He shall glorify me: for he shall receive of mine, and shall shew it unto you' (John 16:13, 14). Yet from time to time the kingly rule of the Holy Spirit comes above the surface, as in the rather complex passage in 2 Corinthians 3:17, 18: 'Now the Lord is that Spirit: and where the Spirit of the Lord is, there is liberty. But we all, with open face beholding as in a glass the glory of the Lord, are changed into the same image, from glory to glory, even as by the Spirit of the Lord.'

---

[57] Ibid., vol. 2, 378.

N. T. Wright notes that '... The early Christians ... maintained the Jewish insistence on monotheism over against paganism and dualism, while bringing the unique and striking claim of Judaism to a new focal point: this creator God had acted specifically and climactically in Jesus, and was now acting through his own Spirit in a new, Jesus-related way.'[58] Elsewhere he writes, in the context of Galatians 4:

> ... the story comes out this time in a threefold form. The one true God sent his Son; then he sent the Spirit of his Son. The result (verses 8-11) is that these redeemed people now truly know the true God, or rather have been known by him; in other words, this Father-Son-Spirit combination is the true revelation of who the one true God is...The Spirit is not a being other than the one true God; to speak of God acting through his Spirit is to speak of God himself acting.[59]

Particularly, the phrase 'where the Spirit of the Lord is', as John Calvin aptly notes, 'means the Holy Spirit, that Christ himself confers upon his people.'[60] And this passage, as many another, puts the Holy Spirit in the context of the kingly operation of the lordship of Christ. It is similar with the central confession of Christianity, that Jesus is Lord; it can only be made with the help of the Holy Spirit: 'Wherefore I give you to understand, that no man speaking by the Spirit of God calleth Jesus accursed: and that no man can say that Jesus is the Lord but by the Holy Ghost' (1 Cor. 12:3).

Similarly, in the opening of the Apocalypse, the Holy Spirit (spoken of under the symbol of perfection and completeness – 'the Seven Spirits')[61] is placed in the context of the exalted Christ, 'ruler of the kings of the earth': '... Grace be unto you, and peace, from him which is, and which was, and which is to come; and from the Seven Spirits which are before his throne; and from Jesus Christ, who is the faithful witness, and the first begotten of the dead, and the prince of the kings of the earth ...' (Rev. 1:4, 5).

Athanasius shows the supreme and regal authority of the Holy Spirit in making believers partakers in the divine nature (2 Pet. 1:4),[62] as well as his sharing in the lordly tasks of creation and redemption:

> For there is nothing that is not originated and actuated through the Word in the Spirit. That is sung in the Psalms: 'By the Word of the Lord the heavens were established, and all their might by the Spirit of his mouth' (Ps. 33:6)...We were justified, as the Apostle says: 'in the name of our Lord Jesus Christ and in the Spirit of our God' (1 Cor. 6:11).[63]

---

[58]N. T. Wright, *The New Testament and the People of God* (Mineapolis: Fortress Press, 1992), 457.

[59]N. T. Wright, *What Saint Paul Really Said*, 73.

[60]John Calvin, *Commentary on the Second Epistle to the Corinthians*, ch. iii. 17 (Pringle translation, p. 12).

[61]As John Owen writes on this verse: 'The seven Spirits before the throne, are the Holy Spirit of God, considered as the perfect fountain of every perfect gift and dispensation. All are here joined together, and yet all mentioned as distinguished in their communication of grace and peace unto the saints' (*Works of John Owen*, 'Of Communion with God' in vol. II, p. 15).

[62]St. Athanasius, *Letters Concerning the Holy Spirit*, trans. by C. Shapland (London: The Epworth Press, 1951), I.24 (pp. 125,126).

[63]Ibid., I.31 (p. 143).

> … it is clear that the Spirit is not a creature, but takes part in the act of creation. The Father creates all things through the Word in the Spirit; for where the Word is, there is the Spirit also, and the things which are created through the Word have their vital strength out of the Spirit from the Word.[64]

Thomas G. Weinandy comments:

> Our resurrection in the Spirit then becomes an icon of Jesus' resurrection in the Spirit, but because of this we see more closely that his own resurrection is then the supreme icon of the inner Trinitarian life. If our sonship is established in the Holy Spirit and finds its resurrected completion in the Holy Spirit, mirroring the work of the Spirit in Jesus' own resurrection, we have a transparent window into the work of the Spirit within the Trinity. Reversing the argument, if the Father raises both Jesus and us to glory by the Holy Spirit, and our resurrection is founded on our being adopted as sons by the Holy Spirit, then Jesus' resurrection not only establishes him as Son in power in the Spirit, but equally manifests (in a manner analogous to our own adopted Sonship) his being Son by nature in the Spirit.[65]

Gregory of Nazianzus in his 'Oration on Pentecost' calls the Holy Spirit the Princely Spirit,[66] and lists some of His authoritative attributes and activities:

> invisible, eternal, incomprehensible, unchangeable, without quality, without quantity, without form, impalpable, self-moving, eternally moving, with free-will, self-powerful, All-powerful (even though all that is of the Spirit is referable to the First-Cause, just as is all that is of the only-begotten), Life and Lifegiver, Light and Lightgiver; absolute Good and Spring of Goodness; the Right, the Princely Spirit; the Lord, the Sender, the Separator; Builder of his own temple; leading, working as he wills; distributing his own gifts; the Spirit of adoption, of truth, of wisdom, of understanding, of knowledge, of godliness, of counsel, of Fear (which are ascribed to Him [i.e. by Isaiah]) by whom the Father is known and the Son is glorified …[67]

Thus, this incomparably majestic Creator and reigning King has the inherent authority; the true, moral right, to control absolutely everything. This is no small part of His majesty, as compared to false gods and merely human kings and nations. His authority and majesty are very closely connected. Highest authority is found only in the highest majesty; lesser authority has lesser majesty, and false authority has no majesty, but instead, shame. The majesty of the one God, Father, Son and Holy Spirit jointly and severally, is directly involved in His moral propriety to control absolutely all things as their King.

There is such a thing as human majesty, and there is such a thing as divine majesty. With C. S. Lewis, I tend to think that earthly majesty was ordained by God primarily in order to bear witness to that ineffable, heavenly majesty that is infinitely above it. In other words, earthly kings

---

[64]Ibid., Epistle II.3.5 (p. 174).

[65]Thomas G. Weinandy, *The Father's Spirit of Sonship: Recovering the Trinity* (Edinburgh: T & T Clark, 1995), 38.

[66]Gregory Nazianzus, 'Oration on Pentecost' in *Nicene and Post-Nicene Fathers* (Grand Rapids: Wm. B. Eerdmans, 1989 reprint), vol. VII, ix (p. 382).

[67]Ibid.

and queens certainly have served important governmental purposes in history, but the most important thing about them (at their very best) is that they are frail testimonies to the Majesty above.

Biblical references to God's majesty

The Holy Bible is full of passages witnessing to the majesty of the Triune God. And yet a closer look will show that in the original biblical languages (Hebrew, Aramaic and Greek) there is really not any one particular word for majesty. The Bible literally shines with God's majesty, but seven different Hebrew words and two different Greek words are used for the glorious concept of majesty. Our English translators therefore rendered nine different words in the original biblical languages with the grand anglicized Latin term 'majesty'.

In several Old Testament passages we find references to the Hebrew word גָּאוֹן, meaning something like 'excellency.' In Job, for instance, this word refers to such awe-inspiring sights as the height of tremendous waves (perhaps like a mighty tidal wave – Job 38:11); or to the eminence of extremely high mountain peaks (perhaps like the Rockies or Alps or Himalayas). These massive forms in nature humble us with our smallness before them, and inspire us with thoughts of higher things. God's majesty is something like that. Isa. 24:14 uses this word and says, 'They shall sing for the majesty of the LORD.' Earth's greatest grandeur is a frail pointer to the excellent majesty of our mighty Creator God, and indeed, it sets the saved soul singing! The well-loved hymn, 'How great thou art,' expresses it appropriately.

A closely related word, גֵּאוּת means almost the same idea of excellent splendor. It is used in Psalm 93:1: 'The LORD reigneth; he is clothed with majesty.' The concept is something like the twinkling beauty of the hosts of stars in early evening, or the roseate hues of the dawn in the Eastern skies; or maybe the sparkling colors of the twelve splendid jewels in the breastplate of the Jewish High Priest; 'clothed in majesty.'

Yet another term for majesty is used in several Old Testament passages – הָדָר something close to 'honor and majestic beauty.' It is the thought of being adorned in splendor and majesty. In Daniel 4, King Nebuchadnezzar, after he was brought low and lived like an animal for his pride, regained his reason and greatly honored the true God, who alone is clothed in honor and beauty of this kind. Psalm 90:16 prays that God's deeds 'be shown to thy servants; thy splendour (or eminence) unto their children.' Probably the idea of magnificence is conveyed here, as the same word is used in Psalm 29:4, for the magnificent sound as the Lord rolls mighty thunder across the heavens, and in Psalm 96:6, for the splendor of the glory of his majesty. A related word in Proverbs 14:28 speaks of the splendor of a king, who rules multitudes of people. Part of his majesty lies in the wide range of his control.[68]

As Christian people, we realize that God's majestic control over myriads of myriads of sentient beings (and, indeed, over every aspect of all reality) is vastly good news. But some do not see it that way. The late

[68]See W. Van Gemeren, *New International Dictionary of OT Theology and Exegesis*, vol. I, pp. 1013-1015 (article by C. John Collins).

nineteenth-century liberal American theologian, Walter Rauschenbusch, denied this aspect of the majesty of God in his book *A Theology for the Social Gospel*. Verging on blasphemy, Rauschenbusch literally says: '... the worst thing that could happen to God would be to remain an autocrat while the world is moving to democracy... It is not enough for theology to eliminate this or that autocratic trait. Its God must join the social movement.'

About a century later (i.e. in the 1990s) the 'Openness of God Theism' has accepted Rauschenbusch's invitation to denude God of His Godness, in order to make Him more acceptable to proud, secular humanists, who are uncomfortable with the Almighty One in their universe. These 'Openness of God' theologians (or 'Free Will Theists') deny that God even knows the future, on the grounds that either He is too weak to control it, or would not think it is fair to do so, so that the future lies in the hands of proud, corrupt mankind.

Another Hebrew word רִבּוֹא speaks of the thousands of thousands, the immense numbers of men and angels directly under God's sovereign control (Ps. 68:17, 18). And that text (quoted in Ephesians 4:8) says that God uses His majestic control over things in heaven and things in earth to send down mighty blessings upon His Church as a result of the ascension of the crucified, risen Christ.[69]

Similarly, the term הוֹד (hod) tells of God covering the very skies with his majesty in Habakkuk 3:3, and this word in Psalm 111:3 expresses God's work as 'majestic' (or honorable) and glorious; that is, His work both of creation and also the covenant of redemption. That is, God is majestic both in creation (where 'the heavens declare the glory of God and the firmament showeth forth His handiwork') and also in redemption, where the Son of His glory restores the beauty of a lost and ruined creation by His atoning work and resurrection. Only someone as great as the Creator could restore a sinful creation, and that is none other than 'the Word through whom all things were made' (John 1:3).[70]

This leads us briefly to the two Greek words employed for majesty in the New Testament. There, most appropriately these words for majesty are applied directly to our Lord Jesus Christ, who is the fullest manifestation of God in all the universe. In Hebrews 1:3 and 8:1 the risen Jesus is in closest contact with the supreme majesty: 'Who being the brightness of his glory and the express image of his person, and upholding all things by the word of his power, when he had by himself purged our sins, sat down on the right hand of the majesty μεγαλωσύνη (*megalosune*) on High.' And 2 Peter 1:16 uses a word rather like this one μεγαλειότης (*megaleiotes*) for the majestic transfiguration of the Savior's countenance on the Mount, to which Peter was an eyewitness.[71]

Theological reflections on God's majesty

In summary, the majesty of God involves vastness of Being, infinite, sovereign power, outrayed splendor and glory, absolute perfection of beauty

[69]Ibid., vol. III, 1036-1037. Article by P. P. Jenson.

[70]Ibid., vol. I, 1016-1017. Article by C. John Collins.

[71]Colin Brown, *New International Dictionary of NT Theology*, vol. II, 424-27. Article by F. Thiele.

in His Triune personhood, and – perhaps to our surprise – that surpassingly wondrous beauty is especially found in the self-sacrificial divine love (as John 3:16 tells us). Let us say a word here about the beauty of God. In his wonderful book on 1 Corinthians 13, *Charity and its Fruits*, Jonathan Edwards pointed out that the devils themselves are not atheists. According to James, 'the devils believe and tremble' (James 2:19). But Edwards rightly shows that the evil one and his minions see only the massive power of God, and they hate and fear Him for it. But the saints, while never denying the infinite power, also see something else: the irresistibly alluring beauty of God; and they love and praise Him for it.

Twentieth-century dictators such as Hitler, Stalin, Mao and others had immense power over millions of lives, but no one ever accused them of majesty. It takes beauty of personhood and character for that. On a very personal level, this is what Jonathan Edwards says in his 'Memoirs'[72] about the majestic beauty of God that he discovered during the great revival known as 'The First Great Awakening':

> Sometimes, only mentioning a single word caused my heart to burn within me; or only seeing the name of Christ, or the name of some attribute of God. And God has appeared glorious to me, on account of the Trinity... The sweetest joys and delights I have experienced, have not been those that have arisen from a hope of my own good estate; but a direct view of the glorious things of the gospel... I felt an ardency of soul to be, what I know not otherwise how to express, emptied and annihilated; to lie in the dust and to be full of Christ alone; to love him with a holy and pure love; to trust in him; to serve and follow him; and to be perfectly sanctified and made pure with a divine and heavenly purity...
>
> I have, many times, had a sense of the glory of the Third Person in the Trinity, and his office as Sanctifier; in his holy operations, communicating divine light and life to the soul. God in the communications of his Holy Spirit, has appeared as an infinite fountain of divine glory and sweetness; being full, and sufficient to fill and satisfy the soul; pouring forth itself in sweet communications; like the sun in its glory, sweetly and pleasantly diffusing light and life...

This majestic self-sufficiency of our glorious God is expressed with superb clarity in Chapter II, par. 2 of the Westminster Confession of Faith:

> God hath all life, glory, goodness, blessedness, in and of himself; and is alone in and unto himself all-sufficient, not standing in need of any creatures which he hath made, not deriving any glory from them, but only manifesting his own glory in, by, unto and upon them; he is the alone fountain of all being, of whom, through whom, and to whom, are all things; and hath most sovereign dominion over them, to do by them, for them, or upon them, whatsoever himself pleaseth.

Divine majesty and utter humiliation

The self-sufficient name of God, revealed to Moses at the burning bush in Exodus 3:14 (YHWH), is applied to the Lord Jesus Christ in the New Testament. In Greek it comes across as 'I am' (εἰμι) (and at other times as

[72] *The Works of Jonathan Edwards*, Vol. I, p. xlvii

κυρίος). Here we may note particularly his name as 'I am' (ειμι): Jesus as the eternal God in the flesh; the fullest expression of the one 'I am' forms the very structure of the Gospel of John. In John chapter 18, Jesus has been going through unspeakable agony in the Garden of Gethsemane, as He contemplates being blackened with our sins and being separated from His holy Father as He endures hell in our place on the cross of Calvary. What depths of the most abject, shameful humiliation, as Isaiah 52:14 cries out: '... his face was more marred than any man, and his form more than the sons of men...'

But John 18 shows us that we must go down to the low point of the horrid shame of the suffering Redeemer to find the supreme majesty of God. Yes, His majesty is in the highest heavens and streams from the farthest star of the most distant solar system, as Psalm 8 tells us; but that very same majesty is also here, and is directly accessible to me, a sinner. In other words, the majestic heart of God is revealed to us in the infinite sufferings of Christ, as much as – and indeed, even more than – the spangled light from ten million twinkling stars in all their heavenly array! The sufferings of Jesus show who God is in a different way, but one equally majestic, as the construction of awesome solar systems by the word of His power! Let us never forget that the Incarnate Christ is 'the express image of God's person' (or in the Greek word in Heb. 1:3, he is the 'character' of God Himself). And He says in John 5:17: 'My Father worketh hitherto, and I work.' Thus, what Jesus is doing, the Father is doing.

And how we see His majesty (hidden though it seemed to be just then) as the massed soldiers surround the humble Mediator who has been betrayed by Judas and forsaken by all human help! At that low point, an officer demands to know His name. Jesus utters to them the same name that God gave Moses: 'I am'. When He does that something supernatural happens. It is as though a surge of divinity goes through the humanity of our Lord; a beam of the uncreated light breaks through the thick darkness of the Judean night; this poor broken one is none less than He who sits enthroned with Deity; the one before whom the cherubim veil their faces. And the whole army is knocked flat on their faces to the ground before Him whom they would arrest!

Elsewhere in John, Jesus speaks of the final work of the cross as being 'the glory of God.' Strangely (to our inadequate human way of thinking), because the majestically holy God is who He is, when His eternal Son is lifted up to die for the sins of His people on Calvary, thus magnifying the holiness of the Father and securing the salvation of the Church, Almighty God is glorified beyond measure. And how gladly did the Father vindicate the supreme sacrifice, 'declaring him to be the Son of God with power, according to the Spirit of holiness, by the resurrection from the dead' (Rom. 1:4). And how 'the gates lifted up their heads on high', the Father welcomed Him, and the archangels praised Him as the Risen One took His seat on the Throne of Majesty, from there to bless His Church and bring us all safely home!

A Welsh hymn says:

> Mighty was He in heaven's purpose,
> Mighty, in the pledge to save,
> Mighty, from His birth to Calv'ry,
> Mighty, bursting from the grave.
> Still will He
> Mighty be
> When things hidden now we see.[73]

That is who God is: majesty indeed! You will find God's truest majesty at the cross as a repentant sinner, or you will find it nowhere. But once you meet Him there by faith, all the splendour and majesty of beauteous worlds unseen will begin to open before you (the sharing of realms of resurrection in union with your Risen Lord), and there will be no end to the wonder and joy of it all, for as the Westminster Shorter Catechism instructs us from childhood: 'Man's chief end is to glorify God and to enjoy Him forever.' It will be so for all who trust in Him, for He is determined to share His majesty with His elect. For God will answer Jesus' prayer in John 17:24: 'Father, I will that they also, whom thou hast given me, be with me where I am; that they may behold my glory, which thou hast given me: for thou lovedst me before the foundation of the world.' The humiliation and then exaltation of the eternally majestic One leads to the endless bliss of consummated and ever fresh glory for all who will ever be in Him.

Majesty and the right of universal control

We must constantly keep in mind this serene and costly majesty of the Triune God as we think of His rightful authority to control all things. Sheer power without majestic character can be brutal, ugly and immoral. But the majestic character of the 'Kings of Kings and Lord of Lords' means that nothing can be more uplifting and beautiful than to know that He is in charge of all that can ever happen under His lordship (which includes absolutely every aspect of reality, visible and invisible).

His majestic lordship gives Him the moral right to total control of everything. He who created all things out of nothing had the proper right to command mankind, created in His image, to obey Him from the heart in every area of life, through the words of the ten commandments (Exod. 20). It gives Him the authority to set the moral standards for the world in terms of His own holy character, and not to be questioned for it, as Isaiah says:

> Woe unto him that striveth with his Maker! Let the potsherd strive with the potsherds of the earth. Shall the clay say to him that fashioneth it, What makest thou? Or thy work, He hath no hands? Woe unto him that saith unto his father, What begettest thou? Or to the woman, What hast thou brought forth? Thus saith the LORD, the Holy One of Israel, and his Maker, Ask of me of things to come, concerning my sons, and concerning the work of my hands command ye me. I have made the earth, and created man upon it:

---

[73] An anonymous stanza from the hymn by Titus Lewis (1773–1811), 'Mighty Christ from time eternal' in *Christian Hymns* (Bridgend, Evangelical Movement of Wales, 1977), number 117.

> I, even my hands, have stretched out the heavens, and all their host have I commanded (Isa. 45:9-12).

And Jeremiah:

> O house of Israel, cannot I do with you as this potter? saith the LORD. Behold, as the clay is in the potter's hand, so are ye in mine hand, O house of Israel. At what instant I shall speak concerning a nation, and concerning a kingdom, to pluck up, and to pull down, and to destroy it; If that nation, against whom I have pronounced, turn from their evil, I will repent of the evil that I thought to do unto them … (Jer. 18:6-8)

The Apostle Paul makes the same point in Romans 9, quoting the passage in Malachi 1:2, 3 ('Yet I loved Jacob and I hated Esau'):

> As it is written, Jacob have I loved, but Esau have I hated. What shall we say then? Is there unrighteousness with God? God forbid. For he saith to Moses, I will have mercy on whom I will have mercy, and I will have compassion on whom I will have compassion. So then it is not of him that willeth, nor of him that runneth, but of God that sheweth mercy…Thou wilt say then unto me, Why doth he yet find fault? For who hath resisted his will? Nay but, O man, who art thou that repliest against God? Shall the thing formed say to him that formed it, Why hast thou made me thus? Hath not the potter power over the clay, of the same lump to make one vessel unto honour, and another unto dishonour? What if God, willing to shew his wrath, and to make his power known, endured with much longsuffering the vessels of wrath fitted to destruction: And that he might make known the riches of his glory on the vessels of mercy, which he had afore prepared unto glory. Even us, whom he hath called, not of the Jews only, but also of the Gentiles? (Rom. 9:13-16, 19-24).[74]

The majestic lordship of God should answer the ancient question, going back at least to Plato: does God command something because it is right, or is it right because God commands it? Romans 9:19-21 clearly indicates that the standard of ultimate right is in the character and will of God Himself; it is a personal standard, not an impersonal standard outside of God or somehow above God. He who is good; He who is light; He who is holy; He who is all-wise is the standard. And thus, what He wills is always in accordance with who He is as good, light, holy and wise. What He wills is right because the King of all majesty is right.

In a suffering world, this is not always easy to see. Job had many excruciating struggles before he reached this serene understanding:

> Moreover the LORD answered Job, and said, Shall he that contendeth with the Almighty instruct him? He that reproveth God, let him answer it. Then Job answered the LORD and said, Behold, I am vile; what shall I answer thee? I will lay mine hand upon my mouth. Once have I spoken; but I will not answer: yea, twice; but I will proceed no further … (Job 40:1, 2)

> Then Job answered the LORD, and said, I know that thou canst do every thing, and that no thought can be withholden from thee. Who is he that hideth counsel without knowledge? Therefore have I uttered that I

[74] I shall seek to deal with this passage more fully in the chapter on election.

understood not; things too wonderful for me, which I knew not. Hear, I beseech thee, and I will speak: I will demand of thee, and declare thou unto me. I have heard of thee by the hearing of the ear: but now mine eye seeth thee. Wherefore I abhor myself, and repent in dust and ashes (Job 42:1-6).

In Job's Lord and Savior, and in our Lord and Savior, is lodged this absolute authority to control all that will occur. As the Risen Lord commissions His Church, He does so on the basis of this majestic authority: 'All power [ἐξουσία = authority] is given unto me in heaven and in earth ...' (Matt. 28:18). He is the same one seen in His divine, now enfleshed glory in the visions given to the Apostle John on the Isle of Patmos. After a conveyance of grace and peace from God the Father and from the Holy Spirit (Rev. 1:4), the apostle adds this description of the majestic authority of Christ:

And from Jesus Christ, who is the faithful witness, and the first begotten of the dead, and the prince of the kings of the earth. Unto him that loved us, and washed us from our sins in his own blood, And hath made us kings and priests unto God and his Father; to him be glory and dominion for ever and ever. Amen. Behold, he cometh with clouds; and every eye shall see him, and they also which pierced him: and all kindreds of the earth shall wail because of him. Even so, Amen. I am Alpha and Omega, the beginning and the ending, saith the Lord, which is, and which was, and which is to come, the Almighty (Rev. 1:5-8).

Thus, the final judgment of all who have ever lived in the universe – humans, as well as angelic and demonic beings – is directly, fully and finally committed into the hands of this Christ. 'Because he hath appointed a day, in the which he will judge the world in righteousness by that man whom he hath ordained; whereof he hath given assurance unto all men, in that he hath raised him from the dead' (Acts 17:31). The one who has this sort of supreme authority over the final destiny of every person in the cosmos is the one who was the agent of creation; the Redeemer of that creation through His incarnation, death for sinners, bodily resurrection and enthronement. It is entirely proper that such a one should have such infinite authority, as He alone deserves it and could use it as it should be used.

My times are in thy hands;
Jesus, the crucified,
Those hands my cruel sins had pierced
Are now my guard and guide.[75]

One Lord, one empire all secures,
He reigns and life and death are yours;
And He is at the Father's side,
The man of love, the Crucified.[76]

---

[75]'My times are in Thy hand' by William Freeman Lloyd (1791–1853), from *The Church Hymnary: Revised Edition* (Oxford: Oxford University Press, 1930), number 551.

[76]'The Lord is King, Lift up thy voice!' by Josiah Conder (1789–1855), from ibid., number 25.

God's rightful authority is the strength of the martyrs

These truths have sustained many Christian martyrs. The Scottish Covenanter and martyr, Alan Cameron, put to death in 1680 by the government of the restored king of Great Britain, Charles II (which wanted to stamp out the Scottish Presbyterian resistance to the Episcopalianism at that time imposed on the state church), was imprisoned in Edinburgh before his execution (not long after his son, Richard's execution). Richard Cameron's head and hands had been cut off, and brought in a sack into the presence of his soon-to-be executed father, Alan. Jock Purves tells the true story of the father's triumphant faith in the Lord's authority and control of all things, this included:

> On reaching Edinburgh, the dragoons put the heads upon halberds with the cry, 'there are the heads of traitors, rebels!' One who was there said that he 'saw them take Mr. Cameron's head out of the sack; he knew it, being formerly his hearer – a man of fair complexion with his own hair, and his face very little altered, and they put a halberd in his blessed mouth out of which had proceeded many gracious words …
>
> Before the hangman set head and hands on the bloodstained Netherbow Port, the fingers pointing grimly upwards on either side of the head, a hero saint lying in prison was shown them. He was Alan Cameron, Covenanter. The cruel question was asked him. 'Do you know them?' His son's head and hands which were very fair, being a man of fair complexion like himself.' He kissed them saying, 'I know them, I know them. They are my son's, my own dear son's. It is the Lord. Good is the will of the Lord, who cannot wrong me nor mine, but has made goodness and mercy to follow us all our days.'[77]

The spirit of thankful acknowledgment of God's good and wise authority over absolutely everything, even in face of death, has given triumphant constancy and joy to Christian martyrs through all the ages. The distinguished jurist of Carthage, Tertullian seems to have been moved towards conversion (about A.D. 193) by just this spirit that he saw in the Christian martyrs: 'everyone in the face of such prodigious endurance feels himself, as it were, struck by some doubt, and ardently desires to find out what there is at the bottom of this matter; from the moment that he discovers the truth he forthwith embraces it himself.'[78]

The massive spread of Christianity through the nineteenth century, continuing now into the twenty-first, especially in parts of Africa, East Asia and South America, owes a great deal to this victorious trust in the divine authority amongst the many martyrs of our own time. What philosophers and theologians debate and, in some cases, resist (i.e. the rightful authority of God over all) is believed by ordinary Christians, and it is their testimony (not the wranglings of the hesitant intellectuals of the church) that wins multitudes to Christ and changes the world.

William Law on thankfulness for God's beneficent authority

The right response – once we realize whose authority lies behind all our destinies, and all the events that enter into those destinies – is thankfulness.

---

[77]Jock Purves, *Fair Sunshine: Character Studies of the Scottish Covenanters* (Edinburgh: The Banner of Truth Trust, 2003), 37, 38.

[78]Tertullian, *Ad Scapulam* 5.

What Paul enjoined us in 1 Thessalonians 5:18 ('in every thing give thanks: for this is the will of God in Christ Jesus concerning you') is explained in terms of everyday life and thought by the English devotional writer, William Law (1686–1761):

> I have been the longer upon this head [i.e. Thankfulness] because of its great importance to true religion. For there is no state of mind so holy, so excellent, and so truly perfect as that of thankfulness to God, and consequently nothing is of more importance in religion than that which exercises and improves this habit of mind. A dull, uneasy, complaining spirit, which is sometimes the spirit of those that seem careful of religion, is yet of all tempers the most contrary to religion, for it disowns that God which it pretends to adore. For he sufficiently disowns God who does not adore Him as a Being of infinite goodness. If a man does not believe that all the world is as God's family, where nothing happens by chance, but all is guided and directed by the care and providence of a Being that is all love and goodness to all His creatures, if a man do not believe this from his heart, he cannot be said truly to believe in God. And yet, he that has this faith, has faith enough to overcome the world, and always be thankful to God. For he that believes that everything happens to him for the best, cannot possibly complain for the want of something that is better. If, therefore, you live in murmurings and complaints, accusing all the accidents of life, it is not because you are a weak, infirm creature, but it is because you want the first principle of religion, a right belief in God. For as thankfulness is an express acknowledgment of the goodness of God towards you, so repinings and complaints are as plain accusations of God's want of goodness towards you. On the other hand, would you know who is the greatest saint in the world? It is not he who prays most or fasts most; it is not he who gives most alms, or is most eminent for temperance, chastity or justice; but it is he who is always thankful to God, who wills everything that God willeth, who receives everything as an instance of God's goodness, and has a heart always ready to praise God for it. All prayer and devotion, fastings and repentance, meditation and retirement, all sacraments and ordinances, are but so many means to render the soul thus divine and conformable to the will of God, and to fill it with thankfulness and praise for everything that comes from God. This is the perfection of all virtues; and all virtues that do not tend to it, or proceed from it, are but so many false ornaments of a soul not converted unto God. You need not, therefore, now wonder that I lay so much stress upon singing a psalm at all your devotions, since you see it is to form your spirit to such joy and thankfulness to God as is the highest perfection of a divine and holy life. If any one would tell you the shortest, surest way to all happiness and all perfection, he must tell you to make a rule to yourself, to thank and praise God for everything that happens to you. For it is certain that, whatever seeming calamity happens to you, if you thank and praise God for it, you turn it into a blessing. Could you, therefore, work miracles, you could not do more for yourself than by this thankful spirit; for it heals with a word speaking, and turns all that it touches into happiness. If, therefore, you would be so true to your eternal interest as to propose this thankfulness as the end of all your religion; if you would but settle it in your mind that this was the state you was to aim at by all your devotions, you would then have something plain and visible to walk by in all your actions; you would then easily see the effect of your virtues, and might safely judge of your improvements in piety. For so far as

> you renounce all selfish tempers and motions of your own will, and seek for no other happiness but in the thankful reception of everything that happens to you, so far you may be safely reckoned to have advanced in piety. And although this be the highest temper that you can aim at, though it be the noblest sacrifice that the greatest saint can offer unto God, yet it is not tied to any time, or place, or great occasion, but is always in your power, and may be the exercise of every day. For the common events of every day are sufficient to discover and exercise this temper, and may plainly show you how far you are governed in all your actions by this thankful spirit.[79]

Strength to suffer and thankfulness in all things are, therefore, the proper response to the good news of the transcendent, beautiful and majestic Lordship of the One Triune God over all things.

[79]William Law, *A Serious Call to a Devout and Holy Life* (London: Tenth edition, 1772), 277.

Chapter Five
Appendix One

Contemporary Challenges to God's Lordship

I. THE DARWINIAN CHALLENGE TO GOD'S LORDSHIP

Enlightenment denial of God's lordship over creation

So far as I know, the chief attack upon the lordship of the Triune God has come in the denial of creation out of nothing. The earlier Enlightenment had sought to remove God as far as possible from his creation, and the later Enlightenment, as in David Hume, actually denied 'cause and effect' so as to negate the very concept of creation as being caused by God. Immanuel Kant, as we shall later see, although accepting some idea of 'creation', placed divine creation into the unknowable class of the 'noumenal', while placing our 'phenomenal' understanding of natural phenomena into the subjective categories within the human mind, which in a sense themselves were 'creative' of the constructs with which we try to make sense of external reality.

Darwinian denial of God's creation

But it was with Darwinian evolutionary theory in the mid-nineteenth century that secularism found its escape from any necessity of divine creation. The idea was that within the matter and energy of the world, there were innate potencies which somehow were able to develop themselves in an upwardly, more organized direction, thus giving substance to various 'evolved' life-forms. A divine Creator was not only not necessary to account for the origin of the world, He was, in fact, excluded (at least for the atheistic strand of evolutionary theory); although God, of course, remained a reality for the theistic evolutionists.

Rapid accommodation of the churches to evolutionary theory

It is surprising how quickly the Christian churches of the West accommodated their teaching to what they came to consider the irrefutable fact of evolution! Dr. Nigel Cameron showed how nearly all Protestant Bible commentators had accommodated Genesis 1–11 to evolution by the last third of the

[1]Nigel Cameron, *Evolution and the Authority of the Bible* (Exeter: The Paternoster Press, 1983), Chapter 6: 'Genesis and the Commentators: an historical perspective'.

nineteenth century; almost without a fight for the primal doctrine of the Holy Scriptures![1] And Phillip Johnson has noted that clergymen were more ready to adopt Darwin's theory than were fossil experts:

> ... Darwinism so fitted the spirit of its age that the theory attracted a surprising amount of support from religious leaders. Many of Darwin's early supporters were either clergymen or devout laymen, including his most prominent American advocate, the Congregationalist Harvard Professor Asa Gray. Supporters of 'evolution' included not just persons we would think of as religious liberals, but conservative Evangelicals such as Princeton Theological Seminary Professor Benjamin Warfield.[2]

So from that time till now in the third millennium, most Christian commentators and theologians have functionally given up on the biblical teaching on creation, as found in Genesis 1–11 and elsewhere. Of course they say that they accept creation in some ultimate sense (and no doubt they are sincere), but in order to allow the secularist chronology of billions of years of cosmic history, as well as of chemical and biological evolution, they must disregard the plain teaching of Holy Scripture on a fairly recent creation, directly superintended by the Trinity, with the specific creation of 'kinds' which pro-create in accordance with the 'seed' placed in them, so that there is no crossing-over of one basic kind to another, and hence no evolution of one species into another.

Undoubtedly, the intellectuals of the Western Church feared that the rest of their teaching would be considered incredible by the secular culture unless they abandoned the Biblical doctrine of divine creation, since it ran at such radical cross-purposes to the very foundations of the secular intellectual framework for science and every aspect of culture: evolution. In order to accomplish this feat – of separating what God's Word says on creation from what secularist scientism says about it – they have tended to employ a highly symbolical or even 'equivocal' mode of interpretation for Genesis 1–11, and a more historic-literal hermeneutic for most of the rest of Holy Scripture. No doubt, in doing so they have sincerely intended to save the message of the parts of Scripture following Genesis 12, and felt that the first 11 chapters of Genesis must not be taken as they are written in order to maintain historical and scientific credibility for the rest.

Equivocal predication to avoid creation

Frequently commentators who have felt it necessary to affirm some form of evolution in their understanding of origins have used what the medieval scholastics would have called 'equivocal' reasoning in order to avoid the embarrassingly different account of creation given in Genesis 1 and 2. That is, instead of using traditional 'analogical' reasoning, which does not separate the divine and the human, they took refuge in equivocal predication, which does separate them.[3] Biblical statements affirming the

---

[2]Phillip Johnson, *Darwin on Trial* (Downers Grove, ILL: Inter Varsity Press, 2nd ed., 1993), 45.

[3]Traditional Christianity rejected 'univocal' predication (or '*unus vox*' – 'one sound' or the same reality) which assumes that God's words and actions are on exactly the same level as those of man, so that God is limited in what He can accomplish, just as mankind is limited. It also rejected

direct (and relatively 'recent') actions of God in creation (as in a plain reading of Genesis 1 and 2) are placed into an 'upper register' that has very little, if any, real connection with the 'scientific', physical state of affairs, or the 'lower register.'

This kind of equivocal predication in effect tends to abandon the real world of creation to what man can understand and hypothesize. Thus, the Church must get its teaching on 'what really happened' with the origins of the world from the secular textbooks, as the liberal Old Testament scholar from nineteenth-century Edinburgh, Marcus Dods, famously said.[4]

Nothing has done more to remove God's true lordship from the Western mind than this craven abandonment of creation by the Christian churches in the nineteenth century. In a sense, the natural order itself becomes ultimate, rather than the personal God who made it and controls it; thus, it tends to be understood in an impersonal framework, rather than the expression of the sovereign will of the Holy Trinity. Nature becomes Lord in place of the true Lord (although theistic evolutionists have worked hard to maintain a personal framework, as best they can).

A good illustration of this is seen when there is a conflict between plain biblical teaching on reality and the claims of anti-theistic science (and vast areas of science are in no sense anti-theistic; never more so than today). In that case, most Church scholars hasten to adapt the Scriptures to secularist scientific claims, rather than vice versa; as in accounts of the age of the earth and biological fixity of the kinds as opposed to evolutionary development from one species into another. Whose word then is sovereign? This sort of thinking lay behind much of the German 'higher critical' methodology, which cut the Scriptures into disparate parts and imposed an evolutionary model on their supposed production (as we shall see later in the chapter on biblical criticism).

When creation is denied, God is seen as unreal

If God's sovereign lordship over creation is functionally denied in this way (including the authoritatively binding account He gives of creation in His written Word), then important components of His lordship tend to be eclipsed! His eternal plan, with its predestinated purposes for the creation, cannot consistently co-exist with an impersonal, chance-based universe, 'running on its own steam'. His lordship over providence, which lies behind the fall of every sparrow, the rustling of every leaf, the dash of every wave, the numbers of hair on every head, the allotted number of days of every life-

---

'equivocal' predication, which so radically separates human words or things from divine words or realities, that all they have in common is the sound of the same word – i.e. *'equus vox'* ('same sound'). Equivocal reasoning leaves us with a sort of agnosticism concerning what God says or does in the real world, since He and His doings are so different from ours. Instead the Church worked with 'analogical reasoning' in which there are both similarities and differences (so that the word or sound points upwards to higher reality, without exhaustively describing that reality), depending on the type of analogy (such as 'analogy of proportionality'). All of this was carefully discussed by Thomas Aquinas, and will be dealt with in our later chapter on Christian epistemology. But for the present, see: E. L. Mascall, *Existence and Analogy* (London: Libra Books, 1966), chapter 5 – 'The Doctrine of Analogy', and Thomas Aquinas, *Summa Theologiae*, I, xiii, 5c.

[4]Marcus Dods, *Expositor's Bible, Genesis* (Edinburgh: T. & T. Clark, 1888), 1.

span, not to mention the rise and fall of kingdoms, tends to be discounted *as to the real world* (though in accordance with the equivocal philosophy, many will put predestination and providence into 'a higher register' that seems scarcely to touch 'the lower register' of the real world).

If the great miracle of miracles – creation of all things out of nothing, and the equally great miracle of miracles (maybe even greater than the first?) – the incarnation of the eternal Son of God, whereby the agent of creation becomes a creature *without ceasing to be the Creator God* – are discounted as to the real world, then all 'lesser miracles' of Holy Scripture (not that any true miracle – requiring as it does the direct intervention of God – could ever be thought small!) become rather more problematic for one's explanation of reality.

Any recovery of a Christian world-view and a Christian culture must be based in a renewed assertion of God's direct, sovereign lordship over creation. The placing of real creation into a 'higher register' must be profoundly rethought and replaced by a glad submission to scriptural truth that 'In the beginning, the Lord created the heavens and the earth ...' Then, and only then, will the Church have the solid foundations and motivation from which the diseased, relativistic culture can begin to be renewed for the glory of God. To speak of God's lordship and to avoid dealing with creation is potentially to empty that lordship of serious meaning for the real world.

Unintended consequences of theistic evolution

The point to be noted here is not that theistic evolutionists ever intentionally desire to weaken the lordship of God over creation; on the contrary, they believe that only by reinterpreting Genesis 1–11 through the prism of evolution can they render the biblical testimony to the Lordship of God credible for the modern culture. But the *unintended consequence* of using one sort of hermeneutical procedure to explain the first eleven chapters of Genesis, and a very different one to explain the rest of Scripture, raises very serious problems for accepting the historical and theological claims of the other parts. Its very employment leaves the Church with the temptation to take refuge in symbolical or equivocal modes of interpretation whenever the clear teaching of the rest of Holy Scripture cuts across currently accepted views of the world as far as the reigning scientific and historical theories are concerned. Those who keep abandoning the field of battle against unbelief may be truest Christians, but – even to unbelievers – they may appear to be less than convinced of the full Lordship over all things of their Captain.

However, this separation of scriptural truth from the world of history and science is only a tendency, and the tendency varies greatly depending on the basic theological stance of the particular commentator or theologian. For the most part, it must be noted that the large company of theologians who were firmly committed to biblical authority and also felt it necessary to accommodate in some fashion theistic evolution, were in general, very faithful to the Christian tradition and thus turned out fine work in nearly all areas of the theological curriculum. Major conservative theologians such as A. H. Strong, W. Shedd, B. B. Warfield, J. G. Machen and many others, certainly did not evacuate the authority of their Lord over the world, even though they accepted to some degree evolutionary theory. Their strong biblical stance kept them from carrying through the implications of evolution into other areas of theology.

But with a less committed biblical viewpoint, this tendency does assert itself throughout theological work. Some extreme examples would be Teilhard de Chardin of France and the process theologians, such as Charles Hartshorne of the United States, and more recently the 'Openness of God' theists in America (led by Clark Pinnock). They rework everything – including the Being of God Himself – through the process of evolution, and end up with someone far less than the eternal and sovereign God; far less than the transcendent Lord of heaven and earth. But happily, such have so far remained in a minority.

2. Other contemporary denials of divine lordship over creation

We look briefly at two other denials of the divine lordship over creation: (1) 'The Openness of God' theologians, and (2) Marcus Borg of the 'Jesus Seminar.'

(1) The 'Openness of God' reduction of God's lordship

The Openness of God: A Biblical Challenge to the Traditional Understanding of God by Clark Pinnock, Richard Rice, John Sanders, William Hasker and David Basinger was published in 1994.[5] Its authors claim to be 'Free Will Theists' as well as evangelical Protestants. They oppose traditional Catholic and Protestant teaching of the full lordship of God. They seem to think that God cannot be infinite and personal at the same time. To deal with us personally, rather than harshly and mechanically (which is how they seem to see 'sovereignty' – as on pp. 90, 143, 151), God must either be finite, or at least, refrain from employing such infinitude as He may actually possess. Some of the authors evidently hold that God really is not infinite (e.g. God literally does not know what is future – pp. 36, 37, 128), or perhaps some of them hold that He must voluntarily refuse to use His infinite abilities as the price of humankind's being guaranteed personal significance (e.g. pp. 104, 113, 115). As the results of a selective biblical exegesis (that looks only at the human limitations implied in a word, such as 'repent' [e.g. pp. 26-35] and strangely fails to consider the word in the light of the infinite Subject to whom it refers) and a (presumed) failure actually to read the Church Fathers, these writers attempt to get rid of God's infinity by ascribing it to classical theology's being the illegitimate offspring of the cohabitation of biblical concepts with pagan, Hellenistic philosophy (e.g. pp. 59, 80, 97, 107, 140).

---

[5]Downers Grove, IL: InterVarsity Press.

This idea seems to come from Adolph Von Harnack's *History of Dogma*.[6] But careful reading of the Fathers of the Church (such as Athanasius, for instance) would indicate the profound Christianization of Hellenistic terms and concepts, so that the culture of the ancient Mediteranean world was transformed by the gospel, rather than the gospel being dominated and perverted by Greek philosophy. Such concepts as creation, being, logos, providence and person (though originally Greek terms conveying pagan content) were thoroughly transformed during the first four or five centuries of the Christian Era in the light of Old Testament prophecy and the apostolic testimony to Christ in the New Testament.

The Patristic scholarship of this book leaves much to be desired. For instance, the authors dismiss out of hand the entire classical Christian doctrinal tradition as being Neo-Platonic for having said that God is 'beyond being' (p. 85). But they fail to note the fact that when Athanasius quotes this passage from Plato's *Republic*, he changes it to state that God is 'beyond all created being' – which is precisely what Holy Scripture teaches.[7] This lays open the heart of their problem, as interpreters of who God is and what His lordship means in this world.

Univocal epistemology

These 'Openness' writers have failed to consider seriously the profound implications of the difference between created (finite) being and uncreated (infinite) Being. This failure to think clearly on a major issue is demonstrated in their impoverished grasp of the relationship of language to being (i.e. epistemology). They seem to work on the assumption of the univocal validity of language for both God and man. That is, a word must mean for God exactly the same thing it does for a human. For instance, 'before' and 'after' impose in God's experience the same limitations they do in that of humankind (e.g. pp. 120, 128).

One wonders how, as scholars, they could have neglected the Church's pivotal teaching on the analogical usage of language (i.e. that there are both similarities and differences when the same word is applied to created and to uncreated being)? A brief reading of a few sections of St. Thomas Aquinas's *Summa Theologiae* or perhaps chapter 5 of E.L. Mascall's *Existence and Analogy* might have prevented their fatal misunderstanding of the biblical and centuries-old Christian theological tradition. And long before Aquinas or Mascall, St. Hilary of Poitiers (fourth century) wisely remarked in *De Trinitate* (4.14) that human words are subject to God, rather than God subjected to human words (in the sense of being comprehensively defined by and thus limited by them).

The reminder of Hilary in *De Trinitate* (1.17) that the true believer 'must take his stand upon the ground (*substantia*) of God, as holy Jeremiah says, that since he is to hear about that nature (*substantia*) he may expand his thoughts till they are worthy of the theme, not fixing some arbitrary standard for himself, but judging of infinity.' Then Hilary adds that the

---

[6]Harnack, *History of Dogma*, translated by James Millar (London: Williams & Norgate, 1897), III, 194.

[7]Athanasius, *Contra Gentes*, 2.2; 40.2.

human mind 'must not measure the divine nature by the limitations of his own, but must gauge God's assertions concerning himself by the scale of his own glorious self-revelation ... Since we are to discourse of the things of God, let us assume that God has full knowledge of himself, and bow with humble reverence to his words.'

In other words, the reason why the five authors of *The Openness of God* deny the infinitude of nearly all the attributes of God which they discuss – and in particular, His sovereign lordship – is their failure to have heard what Hilary, and the whole orthodox Christian tradition, could have said to them. That is, we must not attempt to project our creaturely limitations onto the God who made us (as though we had made Him!). That would be a violation of the second commandment, not to make graven images of God. Theologians can make conceptual, as well as graven, images of God; both are prohibited.

Piety and analogy

Rather, true piety is to understand with the Apostle Paul that the analogy (and glorious reality to which it takes us) of God as our Father makes sense because fatherhood is from God (Eph. 3:14, 15), as the incarnate Christ and outpoured Holy Spirit have shown us. Hence, as Athanasius says, 'God does not make man his pattern, but rather, since God alone is properly and truly Father, we men are called fathers of our own children, for of him every fatherhood in heaven and earth is named.'[8]

Human reason, therefore, must adjust itself to God's Being, and not the reverse. Such statements in this book as '... God knows all propositions such that God's knowing them at that time is logically possible' (p. 136; also see pp. 148, 150, 162) are univocally limiting the infinite God by what the authors of the book are able to understand in terms of the Enlightenment philosophy they follow. This short-sighted procedure causes them throughout the book to deny one side of clear biblical teaching (particularly, the sovereign Lordship of God over all reality, past, present and future) in order to affirm the other side (such as human responsibility).[9]

An example of this one-sided methodology is seen in Pinnock's contrasting God as either 'an aloof monarch' or 'a caring parent':

> We may think of God primarily as an aloof monarch, removed from the contingencies of the world, unchangeable in every aspect of being, as an all-determining and irresistible power, aware of everything that will ever happen and never taking risks. Or we may understand God as a caring parent with qualities of love, and responsiveness, generosity and sensitivity, openness and vulnerability, a person (rather than a metaphysical principle) who experiences the world, responds to what happens, relates to us and interacts dynamically with humans.[10]

But Pinnock seriously misrepresents the Christian doctrine of God as supreme monarch in order to make credible his replacement of true

[8] Athanasius, *Contra Arianos* 1. 23.
[9] Much that I say here comes from a review published in *Christianity Today*, October, 1994.
[10] *The Openness of God*, 103.

Lordship with God as 'caring parent.' Anyone who reads Scripture and the Christian theological tradition, whether Eastern Orthodox, Roman Catholic or historic Protestant, will immediately know that the supreme and eternal and unhindered Lord of Lords is also supreme in His tender love and self-sacrifice for all who are His children by grace. Never was there such 'a caring parent' as the Father who 'so loved the world that He gave His only-begotten Son that whosoever believeth in him should not perish but have everlasting life' (John 3:16). God did not need to deny or reduce the full authority and control of His lordship over absolutely everything in order to do so. Instead, the sending of the Son and the outpouring of the Holy Spirit was based on the fullness of that authority and control. Otherwise, the ancient Old Testament prophecies about both events could not have been so perfectly and completely fulfilled 'in the fullness of the time' (Gal. 4:4), if God did not have in His personal, ever-present control all times and everything that is in them.

Theologians such as these five authors split what should not and cannot be split: God's infinite love and infinite power; God's Fatherhood and God's full lordship. In so doing, they present us with a different God, and – without meaning to – lose the true gospel.

(2) The non-interventionist 'Lord' of Marcus Borg

Marcus Borg, a member of 'the Jesus Seminar' (which will be discussed under the chapter on Christology) in 2000 at a seminar at Oregon State University presented 'Seeing God Again: What's at Stake.'[11] While Borg has written a number of books which are much larger than this brief chapter (and I will deal with some of them later in this volume), the advantage of this brief work is the clarity of its testimony as to how he lost faith in the lordship of the God whom we meet in Holy Scripture and in the historic Christian tradition.

He grew up as a Lutheran, and thus originally believed in the exclusivity of God's Lordship and of the Christian religion.[12] But 'this older way of seeing God has made the notion of God incredible or doubtful.'[13] 'Indeed, if I thought that being a Christian meant believing that Christianity is the only true religion, I could not be one...A major task for Christians in the twentieth-first century is grateful and enthusiastic affirmation of religious pluralism.'[14]

He states his sad experience: 'The God of supernatural theism became harder and harder to believe in. And because it was the only way of thinking about God – the only form of theism – that I knew of, I experienced my difficulties with it as creeping atheism. Indeed, by my twenties my creeping atheism had become full-blown closet atheism. Supernatural theism had turned me into an atheist.'[15] But in order to come back to some species of

[11]As chapter 1 of *God at 2000*, edited by Marcus Borg and Ross MacKenzie (Harrisburg, PA: Morehouse Publishing, 2000), pp. 1-26.

[12]Ibid., 2, 4-5.

[13]Ibid., 3.

[14]Ibid., 4.

[15]Ibid., 8.

religious belief, Borg felt it first of all necessary specifically to reject 'the monarchical model' of God[16] in favor of the 'divine lover' model.[17] Thus, he would now have a God who is compassionate[18] and is 'passionate about social justice.'[19]

Enlightenment presuppositions

This newly found God is the antiquated God of Deism: he does not intervene in the real world, for he says that 'the events of the 20th century make utterly impossible the belief in an interventionist God.'[20] Borg has a hard time answering the question raised by a listener: 'If God is non-interventionist, what is the purpose of prayer? Does God respond?'[21] Although unwilling totally to abandon intercessory prayer, he replies that 'There may well be non-interventionist ways in which God is involved in the process. I think paranormal healings happen...'[22]

Here again, not unlike the 'Openness of God' theists (who claim to be evangelicals), Borg (a definite liberal) makes the same fatal mistake (although he goes considerably further with it than the 'Openness' theologians). He (and they) split what should never be split: God's sovereign lordship and His infinite love; His infinite power and His fatherhood. They do this, I assume, because they have accepted the premises of the Enlightenment (and indeed, of Arianism, long before the Enlightenment). Especially, they presuppose that if God has sovereign control over all reality, then mankind will be oppressed and in bondage. Thus, they posit a 'non-interventionist' deity, in Enlightenment fashion, who leaves the world to its own. They make God absent, and not present. They reduce His lordship to the practical vanishing point, and thereby – probably without realizing it – denude mankind of his only hope. The Church must pray for such theologians, that the God, who – according to the teaching of Borg – does not intervene in the real world, will, in fact, intervene in their souls in such a way that, with the Psalmist, 'In God's light, they shall see light' (Ps. 36:9).

In sum, the fairly large number of twentieth-century theologians who have wished to accommodate the full authority and control of the divine lordship to the sensibilities of the Enlightenment, would do well to heed the advice given in the fourth century by Cyril of Jerusalem:

> To thee, poor little feeble man, India is far from the land of the Goths, and Spain from Persia; but to God who holds the whole *earth in the hollow of his hand* (Isa. 40:12), all things are near at hand. Impute not then weakness to God, from a comparison of thy feebleness, but rather dwell on his power. Does then the sun, a small work of God, by one glance of his beams give warmth to the whole world; does the atmosphere, which God has made, encompass all things in the world; and is God, who is the Creator both of

[16]Ibid., 13.
[17]Ibid., 14-16.
[18]Ibid., 15.
[19]Ibid., 16.
[20]Ibid., 20.
[21]Ibid., 25.
[22]Ibid., 25.

the sun and of the atmosphere, far off from the world? Imagine a mixture of seeds of different plants (for as thou art weak concerning the faith, the examples which I allege are weak also), and that these different seeds are contained in thy single hand; is it then to thee who art a man, a difficult or an easy matter to separate what is in thine hand, and to collect each according to its nature, and restore it to its own kind? Canst thou then separate the things in thine hand, and cannot God separate the things contained in his hand, and restore them to their proper place? Consider what I say, whether it is not impious to deny it?[23]

[23]Cyril of Jerusalem, *Catechetical Lectures*, XVIII.3.

CHAPTER FIVE APPENDIX TWO

Attempts to Know the Lord outside the Community of Faith: (1) How the Jesus Seminar and (2) Ancient and Modern Gnosticism both Remove God's Lordship

(1) Note on how 'the Jesus Seminar' knows God and Removes His lordship

'The Jesus Seminar' was started in 1985 by Robert W. Funk, at that time a professor in the University of Montana. In some respects it is an extension of the older 'Quest for the Historical Jesus'. Several North American liberal scholars have taken part in it, with the particular purpose of deciding the authenticity of what Jesus did nor did not say in the Gospels.[1] It is not my purpose here to interact with the *details* of the findings of the Seminar; I shall do that in the chapter on Christology with some care. All I wish to do here is briefly to look at their basic *methodology*, for it is the contrary of how Holy Scripture and the historic Christian tradition have understood God to make Himself known. Their underlying methodology contradicts at every major point how the truth of God has always been found by believers: that is, (1) in a particular faith community; (2) historically, and (3) through reconciliation with 'the Truth.'

Robert W. Funk and Roy W. Hoover in *The Five Gospels: The Search for the Authentic Words of Jesus* make it clear that their work is *not* under the authority of the Church, but that their 'Scholars Version is authorized by scholars'.[2] Thus it would appear that scholars in their group have functionally replaced the historic Christian apostolate. An illustration of their putting themselves outside the nearly two thousand years' old apostolate is that they included the Gnostic 'Gospel of Thomas' along with the other four Gospels. In *The Five Gospels*, Funk and Hoover state among their 'premises' as 'premise 24', 'Thomas represents an earlier stage of the tradition than do the canonical gospels.'[3]

The Jesus they give us is largely disconnected from Old Testament Judaism, and in that sense is more like the anti-Old Testament Gnostic Jesus. Particularly the Seminar member, Burton Mack, denies 'a direct

---

[1]See Robert W. Funk, Bernard B. Scott, and James R. Butts, eds. *The Parables of Jesus: Red Letter Edition. A Report of the Jesus Seminar* (Sonoma, CA: Polebridge Press, 1988).

[2]Robert W. Funk and Roy W. Hoover in *The Five Gospels: The Search for the Authentic Words of Jesus*, (New York: Macmillan), 1993, xviii.

[3]Ibid., 11.

engagement of specifically Jewish concerns...Jewish institutional issues... Jewish concepts and authorities...'[4] Marcus Borg, however, does hold to a certain Jewishness of Jesus, but clearly denies his deity.[5] Seminar member Mack also denies the deity of Christ. For him, Jesus is not God, but is more of a cynic philosopher.[6]

For a Seminar member such as John Dominic Crossan, what the canonical Gospels say about the events of Jesus' life fulfilling the Old Testament Scriptures cannot be taken as historically true, but is more like a 'vaticinium ex eventu': '... hide the prophecy, tell the narrative and invent the history.'[7] Burton Mack probably reflects most of the Jesus Seminar scholars in denying the central beliefs of historic Christianity (whether Protestant, Roman Catholic or Eastern Orthodox): the incarnation of God in the flesh, the redeeming atonement of Christ, his bodily resurrection, the validity of the sacraments and the authority of the Church.[8]

We can leave the important details of their varying portrayals of Jesus until later. But it is obviously impossible to be reconciled with the Truth if one denies that 'the Truth' is who He says He is. Two methodological points must be raised here as to how these 'Seminar' scholars know God.

(1) They discount the authoritative truth of the Scriptures of the Old and New Testaments, especially when the sacred texts go contrary to the Enlightenment philosophy of these scholars, such as a Deistic disjunction between God and nature/history. The 'Jesus Seminar' is not alone in this, for it comes out of the late eighteenth and early nineteenth century 'Higher Critical' movement, which itself was a direct product of the Enlightenment mentality.[9] This mentality, which axiomatically shuts off Jesus as a man in Deistic fashion from the eternal reality of God, is the crux of the problem of the various 'Quests for the Historical Jesus,' and of the more recent Jesus Seminar, which is subsidiary to them.

T. F. Torrance has shown how this presuppositional shutting off of Jesus from God the Father works in modern scholarship of this sort:

> A signal instance of the impasse we can reach when we neglect the auditory aspect of theological concepts is the attempt made by many people in modern times to interpret the life and person of Jesus only within the field of the observable and perceptible; that is the attempt to look at the life of Jesus 'in the flat', as it were, without attention to the dimension of depth behind it, in the Word of God become flesh, so that even the teachings of Jesus are ironed out flat into static ideas. When this is done consistently the portrait of Christ breaks down again and again until the foolish cry is raised that it is impossible to give an account of the historical Jesus Christ at all. Jesus will always prove intractably enigmatic, indeed an impossible subject for plastic representation of any kind, precisely because He is a Subject who by

---

[4] *A Myth of Innocence: Mark and Christian Origins* (Philadelphia: Fortress, 1988), 73.

[5] Marcus Borg, *Meeting Jesus Again for the First Time: The Historical Jesus & the Heart of Contemporary Faith* (San Francisco, CA: Harper San Francisco, 1994).

[6] Ibid., 68.

[7] John Dominic Crossan, *The Historical Jesus: The Life of a Mediterranean Jewish Peasant* (San Francisco: HarperCollins, 1991), 372.

[8] See Burton Mack, op. cit., 365ff.

[9] I shall discuss 'Higher Criticism' in a later chapter devoted to it.

> His very nature resists being subjected to what we deem to be observable or being interpreted exclusively in terms of cosmic perceptibility.[10]

But sadly, this procedure cuts off its practitioners from really knowing and participating in the truth, because by definition, one has to be reconciled to the personal Truth in order to know it (i.e. the Triune God). What Tertullian said about the heretics of his time having no spiritual right to use the Scriptures must be said to the Jesus Seminar members; not uncharitably, but as an earnest call to faith and repentance (the only way that any of us sinners come to God).

> Now this heresy of yours does not receive certain Scriptures; and whichever of them it does receive, it perverts by means of additions and diminutions, for the accomplishment of its own purpose; and such as it does receive, it receives not in their entirety; but even when it does receive any up to a certain point as entire, it nevertheless perverts even these by the contrivance of diverse interpretations. Truth is just as much opposed by an adulteration of its meaning as it is by a corruption of its text. Their vain presumptions must needs refuse to acknowledge the [writings] whereby they are refuted. They rely on those which they have falsely put together, and which they have selected, because of their ambiguity. Though skilled in the Scriptures, you will make no progress, when everything which you deny is [by them] maintained. As for yourself, indeed, you will lose nothing but your breath, [and] gain nothing but vexation from their blasphemy.[11]

Tertullian goes on to show that morally and spiritually speaking, no one can properly discuss the true meaning of the Holy Scriptures unless 'they have the faith to which the Scriptures belong':

> But even if a discussion from the Scriptures should not turn out in such a way as to place both sides on a par, [yet] the natural order of things would require that this point should be first proposed, which is not the only one which we must discuss: 'With whom lies that very faith to which the Scriptures belong? From what [original Giver], and through whom, and when, and to whom, has been handed down that rule, by which men become Christians?' For wherever it shall be manifest that the true Christian rule and faith shall be, *there* will likewise be the true Scripture and expositions thereof, and [indeed] all the Christian traditions.[12]

(2) They introduce into the historic New Testament canon books that the ecumenical Church rejected as heretical from early centuries.[13] An illustration is the Gnostic Gospel of Thomas. The thorough rejection of Gnosticism *and its writings* is found on hundreds of pages in such Church Fathers as Justin Martyr, Irenaeus, Tertullian (technically, a Church writer, not a Church Father), Hippolytus, Athanasius, Epiphanius, etc. If – as the scholars of the Jesus Seminar wish – one takes seriously as truth the Gnostic writings, anciently excluded by the Church, then one in effect *displaces* the four canonical Gospels, and most of the New Testament as well.

---

[10]T. F. Torrance, *Theological Science*, 23.

[11]Tertullian, *De Prescriptionibus Haereticorum* xvii.

[12]Ibid., xix.

[13]Of course, the Jesus Seminar is *not* to be blamed for carefully studying the rediscovered Gnostic texts. All Christian scholars should study all ancient sources in any way related to Christianity,

Philip Jenkins has described this process:

> Though the controversial 'Quest for Jesus' has been widely publicized, no less significant for contemporary Christians is the equally subversive Quest for the Earliest Church, a search which depends entirely on insights from the hidden gospels...The true Jesus tradition was not primarily found within the Great Church, but was rather preserved within the dismissively named heretics ... For Elaine Pagels, perhaps the most important of these submerged early traditions was Gnosticism, the followers of *gnosis* or spiritual knowledge, who were most active in the second and third centuries, and whose ideas permeate the Nag Hammadi writings. Viewed through her wistful account, Gnosticism was a glorious historical might-have-been, which is both relevant and attractive to a modern audience ... dense mystical texts written 1800 years ago by obscure Syrian and Egyptian heretics have demonstrated real appeal for a modern mass audience. The alternate gospels play a central role in the 'Jesus books' published by the major commercial publishing houses, which give the impression that *Thomas*, *Peter*, and the rest do in fact represent gospel truth, that they even predate the famous four evangelists. The picture of early Christianities described here has been popularized not just through academic books and articles but through many popular presentations, in television documentaries such as the PBS series *From Jesus to Christ*, broadcast in 1998... As one orthodoxy is established, so older ideas are relabelled as deviant or marginal: in terms of understanding early Christianity, the heretical has virtually become orthodox, and vice versa.[14]

One might note here, as far as popular Western culture is concerned, that the widely read novel (which many take as truth, in spite of the disclaimers of its author), *The DaVinci Code* of Dan Brown (which makes Jesus a mere man, who secretly married Mary Magdalene and engendered a long line of descendants), was followed up by a Hollywood film in 2006. Although it is technically fiction, its 'theology' of Jesus seems to be based on the Jesus of the modern advocates of Gnosticism and of the Jesus Seminar (although the Seminar is not to be blamed directly for it).

A few years before the Jesus Seminar was organized, Elaine Pagels in order to establish as truth the Gnostic writings, followed the nineteenth-century liberal Protestant scholar, von Harnack, who falsely claimed that historic Christianity was 'the acute Hellenizing of Christianity', and

---

whether orthodox or heretical. Much light is cast on the past in this way. But the point here is that no group of modern scholars has the proper authority to add to or take away from the anciently established canon of the Old and New Testament Scriptures, particularly when what they are adding was knowingly rejected by the Church Fathers and Councils. And the early Church leadership rejected the Gnostic writings (such as the Gospel of Thomas) simply because these writings were contrary to the clear teachings of Old and New Testaments. In particular, the Gnostics presented a different Jesus and a different God; with a different way of salvation. One has only to read Irenaeus *Adversus Haereses* to see how very different! Or, indeed, to read James M. Robinson or Elaine Pagels... The Gnostic gospels cannot be true if the Bible is true, and vice versa. One cannot have both types of writing in the *same* canon, for they are mutually contradictory! In effect, to canonize the Gospel of Thomas is to de-canonize the four Gospels (and the rest of Holy Scripture). One's final authority then becomes some form of Gnosticism, to the exclusion of historic Christianity.

[14]Philip Jenkins, *Hidden Gospels: How the Search for Jesus Lost its Way* (Oxford: Oxford University Press, 2003), 10, 11.

incredibly put in the place of the Church Fathers the Gnostics as 'the first Christian theologians.'[15] She argues that 'the fifty-two writings discovered at Nag Hammadi offer only a glimpse of the complexity of the early Christian movement. We now begin to see that what we call Christianity – and what we identify as Christian tradition – actually represents only a small selection of specific sources, chosen from among dozens of others. Who made that selection, and for what reasons...'[16]

To turn back the ecumenical Christian consensus concerning the canon of Scripture for well over a millennium and a half is for all practical purposes to replace the ancient apostolate with modern, Enlightenment scholars, who do not hold the faith of the Scriptures. It is easy enough to do this in the secularized modern West, but if persisted in, it will bring ultimate spiritual disaster, as wilful rejection of light for darkness always does.

This kind of thing is far more than a merely scholarly exercise. It is deliberate rebellion against the Lord, in which one dares to use as weapons against His truth the very Scriptures which He inspired. St. Hilary described the treacherous procedure employed by certain Gnostics, out of whose circles came the very 'Gospel of Thomas' which the Jesus Seminar elevates to canonical status. The ancient Gnostic procedure has certain affinities with that of the modern Jesus Seminar:

> The Lord said that the nations were to be baptized *in the name of the Father, and of the Son, and of the Holy Ghost* (Matt. 28:19). The words of the faith are clear; the heretics do their utmost to involve the meaning in doubt. We may not on this account add to the appointed form, yet we must set a limit to their license of interpretation. Since their malice, inspired by the devil's cunning, empties the doctrine of its meaning while it retains the Names which convey the truth, we must emphasize the truth which those Names convey. We must proclaim, exactly as we shall find them in the words of Scripture, the majesty and functions of Father, Son and Holy Spirit, and so debar the heretics from robbing these Names of their connotation of Divine character, and compel them by means of these very Names to confine their use of terms to their proper meaning. I cannot conceive what manner of mind our opponents have, who pervert the truth, darken the light, divide the indivisible, rend the scatheless, dissolve the perfect unity. It may seem to them a light thing to tear up Perfection, to make laws for Omnipotence, to limit Infinity; as for me, the task of answering them fills me with anxiety; my brain whirls, my intellect is stunned, my very words must be a confession, not that I am weak of utterance, but that I am dumb. Yet a wish to undertake the task forces itself upon me; it means withstanding the proud, guiding the wanderer, warning the ignorant ... Language is exhausted by the magnitude of the theme, the splendour of its effulgence blinds the gazing eye, the intellect cannot compass its boundless extend.[17]

(2) Note on how Gnosticism – ancient and modern – knows 'God' outside His Word and removes His lordship

The reappearance of Gnosticism in modern form, after some 1,700 years, is certainly an illustration of the principle that the evil one has few tricks:

---

[15]Elaine Pagels, *The Gnostic Gospels* (New York: Vintage Books of Random House, 1981), xxxi.
[16]Ibid., xxxviii.
[17]Hilary, *De Trinitate* II.5.

he simply brings out the old errors in new forms, time after time, and usually gains a hearing. During the latter half of the second century A.D., probably the greatest threat to the spread of the gospel, and indeed to the very life of the Church, was not external persecution by the civil government (though thousands did seal their testimonies with their blood, rather than acknowledge Caesar as Lord): the greatest danger was internal – a rampaging heresy that was striking at the vital organs of Christian truth and life. Unchecked, Gnosticism would have leeched the life out of apostolic Christianity, and transformed its remains out of all recognition to the scriptural religion of redemption.[18]

Gnosticism was a hydra-headed movement in both Eastern and Western areas of the Roman Empire. Irenaeus and Hippolytus and other Church writers said that its origins lay in pagan Greek philosophy and in Greek mystery religions.[19] Probably the various Eastern religions, such as Hinduism and Parseeism, as well as some aspects of late Judaism, entered into this strange conglomeration of religious philosophy, superstition and practice.[20]

The various groups of 'Gnostics' (from Greek *Gnosis* – knowledge or 'enlightened ones'), while disagreeing on particular details, were united in their dualism: holding that the 'spiritual' is good, while the material creation is utterly evil. They posited a radical disjunction between the supreme God (*Buthus* – depth) and the natural world. In order to solve the problem of evil as they saw it (essentially the existence of material reality and man's alienation because of it), they imagined a whole series of gods (or *aeons*) between the supreme God and the world; each *aeon* somehow extruding from the higher God and then producing a lower and inferior god. Creation, they held, was made by one of these inferior gods: the Demiurge, who was the same as the God of the Old Testament. Furthermore, Christ was one of these emanating *aeons*. The Gnostics, especially Marcion of the Valentinian School, radically rejected the Old Testament as harsh, materialist, and from an inferior God. They of course denied the incarnation of the Son of God as well as his bodily resurrection because of their hostility to material reality.

Although to the Gnostics creation was a disaster, still they believed that a certain spark of divinity was implanted in some men. There were three

---

[18]Harnack's theory of the Gnostics as merely differing in detail, but not in essence from the early Church, and his praise of them as 'the first Christian theologians' is certainly not how the Church Fathers assessed the situation – Adolph Harnack, *History of Dogma* (English Translation), vol. II (London: Williams & Norgate, 1896), 230-318. But see on the other side: James Orr, *The Progress of Dogma* (London: James Clarke & Co. Ltd., 1901), 55; and Geoffrey W. Bromiley, *Historical Theology, An Introduction* (Grand Rapids: Wm. B. Eerdmans, 1978), 19.

[19]Irenaeus, *Adv. Haer.*, 2.14.1-6; Tertullian, *De Praesc. Haer.*, 7; Hippolytus, *Philosoph.*, Books 1; 4; 5; 6; 9; 16-24; 32; 47; etc.

[20]See Hans Jonas, *Gnosis und spätantiker Geist: Teil I: Die Mythologische Gnosis, 3 Auflage* (FRLANT, Neue Folge, 33 Heft, Göttingen: Van den Hoect & Ruprecht, 1965), and A. D. Nock and A. J. Festugière, *Hermes Trismégiste: Corpus Hermeticum*, Tomes I–IV (Paris: Societe d'Edition "Les Belles Lettres", 1954-60), 1954-60); also, J. Daniélou, *Théologie du Judéo-Christianisme* (Paris: Desclée, 1958); James M. Robinson, ed., *The Nag Hammadi Library* (Harper & Row: San Francisco, 1977); Robert Grant, *Gnosticism and Early Christianity* (New York: Harper and Row, 1959); and Gershom Scholem, *Jewish Gnosticism, Merkabah Mysticism, and Talmudic Tradition*, second edition (New York: Jewish Theological Seminary of America, 1965).

classes of men: the spiritual (who had a bright spark of divinity) and thus would be definitely saved; the soulish (who had only a little spark) and could go either way, depending on their use of 'knowledge' (or the *gnosis* offered by the Gnostics), and the animal men (devoid of the spark), who could only be lost. To be saved meant to escape the material creation and rise up through the series of aeons back to the supreme God by the proper use of knowledge, including secret passwords and other practices.

Though Gnosticism was largely a matter of knowledge and religious theory, it did involve practice. The Gnostics took two different approaches to the despised physical body. In order to deny the body, some of them were ascetic. Others, however, were quite licentious, acting on the theory that since the body is hopelessly bad, what one does with it is of no consequence.[21] The remarkable discovery of a large library of ancient Gnostic writings at Chenoboskion in Upper Egypt in 1945/46 has greatly increased our knowledge of this movement, which previously had been largely restricted to quotations in the Church Fathers. It appears that the understanding of the Fathers of Gnosticism is fairly close to these original writings.[22]

Without entering into further details of the Gnostic teachings, we may note certain of their cardinal principles, which run contrary to the scriptural world-view. First, they confused morals and metaphysics: that is, they thought that man's problem is physical limitation rather than sin. In this they had some affinities with Hinduism, Buddhism, certain aspects of Christian Neo-Platonism, as well as twentieth-century Existentialism. Second, as Bernard Lonergan points out, the Gnostics rejected propositional truth.[23] That meant that they had to describe reality by means of myth making. Third, as contemporary authorities on Gnosticism have noted, this movement rejected 'the usefulness and meaningfulness of historical events.'[24] Having rejected history, they turned to an extreme form of 'Idealism', in which the human imagination supplants reality.

These cardinal principles of Gnosticism would have effectively subverted the good news of God's actions in Christ and the Holy Spirit. Thus, Church Fathers such as Irenaeus and many others waged successful battle against this side-stepping of the reality of the Triune God and of His creation, redemption and revelation. We shall take some brief excerpts from the writing of St. Irenaeus as a representative sample of how Gnosticism was overcome by the Church. In his *Adversus Haereses*, we find a clear answer to the three main Gnostic principles:

---

[21]See Morton Smith, *Clement of Alexandria and a Secret Gospel of Mark* (Cambridge, MA: Harvard University Press, 1973), 82, 185, 295ff., concerning Gnostic license.

[22]See W. F. Albright, 'Recent Discoveries in Palestine and the Gospel of John,' in *The Background of the New Testament and its Escatology in Honour of C. H. Dodd*, edited by Davies and Daube (Cambridge: The University Press, 1956), and also James M. Robinson, op. cit., 4-10, 37, 207, 308, 329, 417, 435.

[23]Bernard Lonergan, *The Way to Nicea*, A translation by C. O'Donovan of the first part of *De Deo Trino* (Philadelphia: The Westminster Press, 1964), 8.

[24]Malcolm Lee Peel, *The Epistle to Rheginos, A Valentinian Letter on the Resurrection* (Philadelphia: The Westminster Press, 1969), 151, note 156, which refers to Peuch and Laeuchli.

(1) The confusion between morals and metaphysics

Irenaeus reaffirmed the biblical doctrine that man's problem is not primarily and originally metaphysical, but moral. His alienation derives neither from his materiality nor finiteness, but rather from sin; from his disobedience to God's command. To establish this point, Irenaeus brings forward these historical facts: God is the creator of material reality; God in Christ entered the physical creation in order to save it; the creation needs atonement, reconciliation and restoration, not because it is physical or limited, but because it disobeyed its creator.

The Gnostics taught that since material reality is unworthy of the Supreme God (*Buthus*), without his knowledge an inferior power created it: 'And hence they declare material substance had its beginning from ignorance and grief, and fear and bewilderment.'[25] Irenaeus showed the foolishness of thinking that there can be a supreme God who is ignorant of what a lesser god does, and the impossibility of there being a supreme God who does not contain all things in His own power: 'For how can there be any other Fulness (*Pleroma*), or principle or power or God above him, since it is matter of necessity that God, the Pleroma (Fulness) of all these, should contain all things in his immensity, and should be contained by no one?'[26]

> For it must be either that there is one Being who contains all things, and formed in his own territory all those things which have been created, according to his own will; or again, that there are numerous unlimited creators or gods, who begin from each and end in each other on every side; and it will then be necessary to allow that all the rest are contained from without by someone who is greater...[27]

> That God is the creator of the world is accepted...all men, in fact consenting to this truth: the ancients on their part preserved with special care, from the tradition of the first-formed man...while the very heathen learned it from creation itself.[28]

The Gnostics posited an impassable gap between God and (inherently evil) material creation. Man's only hope for redemption was to escape material reality by crossing over the gap. But far from avoiding the material world, Irenaeus shows on the contrary that God truly entered physical creation in order to atone for it and thus redeem it. He teaches that the material realm can be redeemed: 'For if the flesh were not in a position to be saved, the Word of God would in no wise have become flesh.'[29]

> But flesh is that which was of old formed for Adam by God out of the dust, and it is this that John has declared the Word of God became.[30]

> But the thing which had perished possessed flesh and blood. For the Lord, taking dust from the earth, moulded man; and it was upon his behalf that all

[25]Irenaeus, *Adv. Haer.*, I.2.3.
[26]Ibid., II.1.2.
[27]Ibid., II.1.5.
[28]Ibid., II.9.1.
[29]Ibid., V.14.1.
[30]Ibid., I.9.3.

> the dispensation of the Lord's advent took place. He had himself, therefore, flesh and blood, recapitulating in himself not a certain other, but that original handiwork of the Father, seeking out the thing which had perished.[31]

Closely related to this abhorrence of God in the flesh was their hostility to the Old Testament. A Gnostic such as Marcion claimed that a degenerate, inferior god, who had made the material creation, was the god of the Old Testament. Hence the Old Testament law was said to be harsh and evil, whereas the New Testament (or at least some parts of it) was said to be good.[32] But with all of the Church, Irenaeus holds together Old and New Testaments as the Word of the same Creator, Redeemer God:

> For all the apostles taught that there were indeed two testaments among the two peoples; but that it was one and the same God who appointed both ...[33]

> ... The Lord did not abrogate the natural [precepts] of the Law...but he extended and fulfilled them...[The Sermon on the Mount] does not contain or imply an opposition to and an overthrowing of the [precepts] of the past, as Marcion's followers do strenuously maintain; but [they exhibit] a fulfilling and an extension of them [as Matt. 5:20 shows]...Now he did not teach us these things (i.e. not to lust) as being opposed to the law, but as fulfilling the law, and implanting in us the varied righteousness of the law...[34]

> Preparing man for this life, the Lord himself did speak in his own person to all alike the words of the Decalogue; and therefore, in like manner, do they remain permanently with us, receiving by means of his advent in the flesh, extension and increase, but not abrogation.[35]

Having demonstrated that the problem of man and the world is not metaphysical, for the material creation is good, not evil; he shows that evil, alienation and death spring from a moral disorder. That is, creation needs redemption, not because it is material and limited, but because it disobeyed its Creator: 'Because of the sin of disobedience, infirmities have come upon men.'[36]

Hence the solution to evil is not to escape material reality (so as to get across a metaphysical gap) by means of secret knowledge (*gnosis*), but it is a moral renewal of the entire created order through the coming of the agent of creation into it to pay for its sins and renew it from within by raising it from the dead, in Christ who is 'the first-fruits of them that sleep' (1 Cor. 15:20). Thus, the need to redeem the created order leads us to examine Irenaeus' refutation of another major Gnostic principle:

(2) The Gnostic rejection of history as meaningless and useless

The position of Irenaeus is that God created the world – thus bringing history into being; that man fell in history, that God made atonement in

---

[31]Ibid., V.14.2.
[32]For Marcion's canon, see *Adv. Haer.*, I.27.2.
[33]Ibid., IV.32.2.
[34]Ibid., IV.13.1.
[35]Ibid., IV.16.4.
[36]Ibid., V.15.2.

history, raised His Son in history, poured out His Spirit in history, and thus history is in principle redeemed. History, then, is the locus of God's creative, redemptive activities, thus excluding the imaginary realms of the myth-making Gnostics.

T. F. Torrance has clarified the reason beneath the essential difference between Judeo-Christian history and Gnostic mythology:

> Hellenistic thought operated with a radical dichotomy between a realm of ideas and a realm of events, and it took its stand within the realm of ideas as the realm of the ultimately real. From this perspective it could only regard the Christian doctrines of God at work in history, of the coming of the Son of God into human and creaturely existence, of the Eternal entering the world of space and time, as unreal, or at best as a 'mythological' way of expressing certain timeless truths. Various attempts were made to solve this question, by Christian 'mythology' and so developed a highly intellectual system in which *gnosis* and ritual, the conceptual and the symbolic, while sharply distinguished, were religiously correlated; and by some early apologists who sought to 'demythologize' the Christian Gospel by subjecting the crudities of faith (*pistis*) to scientific treatment (*episteme*) and so producing a Christian understanding (*gnosis*) acceptable to the world of culture and science. Both these attempts failed, although they have been revived from time to time, as in our own day, and of course with different thought-forms, by thinkers like Tillich and Bultmann.[37]

A vivid illustration of the unhistorical, almost Buddhistic relativism of the ancient Gnostics is found in the tractate, 'The Thunder, Perfect Mind.'[38] Few writings could illustrate so well the wild Gnostic mythology that Irenaeus had to cut through in order to safeguard the gospel. Irenaeus sought to awaken the Gnostics from their self-absorbed dream world by confronting them with the solid, historical reality of the creation, fall and redemption of mankind, exemplified and accomplished in Adam and in Christ, 'the last Adam.' His central use of the Pauline First/Last Adam schema demonstrates his insistence on the whole course of biblical history as the true explanation of reality and the fount of redemption, over against all humanly invented dreams, theories and systems:

> For it is thus that thou wilt both controvert them in a legitimate manner, and wilt be prepared to receive the proofs brought forward against them, casting away their doctrines as filth by means of celestial faith; but following the only true and stedfast Teacher, the Word of God, our Lord Jesus Christ, who did, through his transcendent love, become what we are that he might bring us to be even what he is in himself.[39]

In sum, Irenaeus teaches – with St. Paul in Romans 5:12-21 – that the Last Adam 'recapitulates' the First Adam; restoring all he lost: '...when he became incarnate...He commenced afresh the long line of human beings, and furnished us ... with salvation; so that what we had lost in Adam – namely to be according to the image and likeness of God – that we might

[37]T. F. Torrance, *Theological Science*, 17,18.
[38]James M. Robinson, op. cit., 271-77.
[39]Irenaeus, op. cit., V. prf.

recover in Christ Jesus.' [40] 'Wherefore also he passed through every stage of life, restoring all to communion with God.'[41]

Irenaeus taught that we are saved not only by the incarnation of Christ in our flesh, but also by the shedding of His blood for our sins. He writes that Christ redeemed us by blood 'from the apostasy';[42] that He 'purified the Gentiles by his blood';[43] that He 'died and was buried for the human race.'[44] After quoting Matthew 23:35,[45] [Christ] thus points out the recapitulation that should take place in His own person of the effusion of blood from the beginning, of all the righteous men and of the prophets, and that by means of Himself there should be a requisition of their blood.[46] The death of Christ removed our condemnation,[47] redeemed the fallen race from captivity and brought it to communion with God and to immortality.[48] '... in order that God also might be pleased to offer up for all his seed his own beloved and only-begotten Son, as a sacrifice for our redemption.'[49] '... having become "the mediator between God and men"; propitiating indeed for us the Father against whom we had sinned, and cancelling our disobedience by his own obedience ...'[50]

In accordance with the Scriptures (cf. 1 Cor.15), Irenaeus also teaches that our salvation is brought to victory by the resurrection of the Christ who lived to restore our flesh and died to forgive our sins:

> ... as our species went down to death through a vanquished man, so we may ascend to life again through a victorious one; and as through a man death received the palm [of victory] against us, so again by a man we may receive the palm against death.[51]
>
> Now Adam had been conquered, all life had been taken away from him; wherefore, when the foe was conquered in his turn, Adam received new life; and the last enemy, death, is destroyed, which at the first had taken possession of man ... For his salvation is death's destruction. When therefore the Lord vivifies man, that is Adam, death is at the same time destroyed.[52]

(3) The denial of the significance of propositional truth

Not only did the Gnostics reject the Church's *regula veritatis*, but they even denied the ability of propositions to indicate correctly ultimate truth. In this denial, they were not really consistent, for at least they thought that they could explain reality by means of their mythology, for which they had to

---

[40]Ibid., III.18.1.
[41]Ibid., III.18.7.
[42]Ibid., III.5.3.
[43]Ibid., III.12.6.
[44]Ibid., III.9.2.
[45]'That upon you may come all the righteous blood shed upon the earth, from the blood of righteous Abel unto the blood of Zacharias son of Barachias, whom ye slew between the temple and the altar.'
[46]Irenaeus, op. cit., V.14.1.
[47]Ibid., IV.8.2.
[48]Ibid., V.1.1.
[49]Ibid., IV.5.4.
[50]Ibid., IV.17.1.
[51]Ibid., V.21.1.
[52]Ibid., III.23.7.

use words in propositional statements. Still, their emphasis was not on faith in Christ and his truth, but on a sort of metaphysical salvation by entering into a kind of 'spirituality' which escapes the material.

Irenaeus replies to this false position by emphasizing faith in God and his truth: 'For if nature and substance are the means of salvation, then all souls shall be saved; but if righteousness and faith, why should these not save those bodies, which equally with the souls, will enter into immortality?'[53] Referring to John the Baptist's preaching, he states: 'This knowledge of salvation, therefore, did John impart to those repenting and believing in the Lamb of God who taketh away the sin of the world.'[54]

After quoting Proverbs 1:7,[55] Irenaeus says: 'The sense of sin leads to repentance, and God bestows his compassion upon those who are penitent.'[56] Elsewhere, defending the evangelical character of the Old Testament law, Irenaeus explains: '... Men can be saved in no other way from the old wound of the serpent than by believing in him who in the likeness of sinful flesh is lifted up from the earth upon the tree of martyrdom, and draws all things to himself, and vivifies the dead.'[57] 'If then, those who do believe in him through the preaching of his apostles throughout the east and west shall recline with Abraham, Isaac and Jacob...one and the same God is set forth ...'[58] In sum, faith in what is set before us by the truths of Scripture is the way to salvation, for Christ was to bring himself 'within the capacity of those who believe, that he might vivify those who receive and behold him through faith.'[59]

Faith in the One who became incarnate in space/time history, shed His blood in the dust of His own created world, and was bodily resurrected in history was the exact antithesis of the Gnostic rejection of creation, history and revelation of truth in Scripture in favor of their idealist mythology as the way of salvation. The faith in God's revealed truth and the repentance of mind and morals called for by Christ's victorious sacrifice ends all confusion between morals and metaphysics, all escaping of the realities of history, and all denial of the revealed truths of God. It is clear that the voluminous writings of the Gnostics soon passed into oblivion, so little were they valued now that their false nature was revealed by Irenaeus and other Church writers.[60]

---

[53]Ibid., II.29.1.

[54]Ibid., III.10.1.

[55]'The fear of the LORD is the beginning of knowledge: but fools despise wisdom and instruction.'

[56]Irenaeus, op. cit., III.34.5.

[57]Ibid., IV.2.7.

[58]Ibid., IV.36.8.

[59]Ibid., IV.20.5.

[60]James M. Robinson has a different interpretation of the disappearance of the Gnostic writings in Robinson, op. cit., 20. His interpretation is not convincing to me.

Chapter Five Appendix Three

Feminist Theology and the Fatherhood of God

Any volume on theology that seeks to speak intelligibly of God in our twenty-first century Western culture would be incomplete if it failed to address some of the crucial issues concerning the identity of God as Father and King, raised since the 1960s by the various strands of feminist theology. Let us say a word first, about feminist theology, and secondly, about the single and most pressing issue within Christian feminism that we shall discuss in this appendix.

Many types of feminist theology

(1) Feminist theology exists along a very broad front, taking many different forms. Some of the main ones are: Liberal Protestant,[1] Evangelical Protestant,[2] relatively traditional Roman Catholic, though with strong feminist critique of the tradition,[3] Roman Catholics with radical proposals,[4] Ex-Christian[5] and Neo-pagan.[6] It has gone through complex development during the approximately forty years of its existence as a serious force. I do not wish to paint with such a broad brush that I confound any of these differing positions with one another, or misrepresent any of them. However, it is not my purpose here to trace all of this development. Its growth is substantial and is still increasing in influence in most of the churches and in the culture in general. But as a general survey, you are referred to 'The

[1]E.g., see Mary Kassian, *The Feminist Mistake*, rev. ed. (Wheaton, IL: Crossway, 2005).

[2]A substantial bibliography on different sorts of evangelical feminism is provided by Wayne Grudem in *Evangelical Feminism & Biblical Truth: An analysis of 118 disputed questions* (Leicester: Apollos, Intervarsity Press, 2005), pp. 767-781. He also interacts with them critically in his *Evangelical Feminism: A New Path to Liberalism?* (Wheaton, IL: Crossway Books, 2006).

[3]E.g., see Elizabeth A. Johnson, *She Who Is: The Mystery of God in Feminist Discourse* (New York: Herder & Herder, The Crossroad Publishing Company, 2003).

[4]E.g., see Rebecca S. Chopp, *The Power to Speak: Feminism, Language, God* (New York: Crossroad, 1989), and Rosemary Radford Ruether, *Women-Church: Theology and Practice of Feminist Liturgical Communities* (San Francisco: Harper & Row, 1985).

[5]Cf. Mary Daly, *The Church and the Second Sex: With the Feminist Postchristian Introduction and New Archaic Afterwords by the Author* (Boston: Beacon Press, 1985).

[6]See Rosemary Radford Ruether, *Gaia and God: An Ecofeminist Theology of Earth-Healing* (San Francisco: Harper San Francisco, 1992). For a critique of this Goddess religion from within the Roman Catholic Church by one who holds some feminist ideas, see Mary Jo Weaver, *Springs of Water in a Dry Land* (Boston: Beacon Press, 1992).

New Vision of Feminist Theology' by Anne E. Carr, in which she follows the typology of feminism suggested by Carolyn Osick, as follows:[7]

Osick speaks of 'the rejectionist' position, which 'simply refuses to acknowledge any authority or usefulness in the Bible or in the entire religious tradition it represents'.[8] There are the 'loyalists', who 'insist that the Bible, as the Word of God, cannot be oppressive, but is the source of a divine plan of true human freedom.'[9] The 'revisionist' position 'holds that the patriarchal framework of the Jewish and Christian traditions is a historical fact but is not theologically necessary. The male supremacist, androcentric and sexist elements of the Bible are not intrinsic to its message but can be sifted from it by means of exegetical method and analysis of cultural context.'[10]

> The sublimationist option is based on the 'otherness' of the feminine as witnessed in the imagery and symbolism of culture. Either the feminine is seen as innately superior to the masculine, or the life-giving and nurturing qualities of woman are considered to be of such a different order that any crossing of sex roles runs counter to nature itself. In this option the typically feminine characteristics of Jesus and the Spirit are emphasized.[11]

> The liberationist alternative proposes that the central message of the Bible is human salvation as liberation, either as found in the prophetic tradition (freed from its patriarchal contexts) or in those texts that transcend androcentrism and patriarchy and point to the conversion and transformation of society today and in the future.[12]

Feminist theology questions the exclusive fatherhood of God

(2) We restrict ourselves in this brief appendix to the discussion of only one central concept of most feminist theology; one that enters profoundly into our understanding of the Holy Trinity: that is, is God to be spoken of exclusively as Father, or could He also with propriety be called Mother? Should our Bible translations be changed[13] and our liturgies adjusted accordingly?[14] For the present, we will not discuss here the very significant issues of male and female roles and relationships, marriage, and ordination within the Church. These will be approached in Volume Two.

Feminist theologians, from a variety of perspectives, have generally agreed in opposing the continued exclusive usage of addressing God as

---

[7]Chapter 1 in *Freeing Theology: The Essentials of Theology in Feminist Perspective*, edited by Catherine Mowry LaCugna (San Francisco: Harper San Francisco, 1993), 5-29.

[8]Ibid., 12.

[9]Ibid.

[10]Ibid.

[11]Ibid.

[12]Ibid., 12,13.

[13]D. A. Carson, from the conservative Protestant viewpoint, offers a very careful study of the whole issue of how we should translate the Bible in light of feminist concerns, in *The Inclusive Language Debate: A Plea for Realism* (Leicester: Intervarsity Press: , 1998).

[14]Paul Wells points out that the Methodist Church in England has introduced into its liturgy the option of addressing God as 'Our Father and/or Mother in heaven …' in P. Wells, *God and Gender*, an unpublished paper by Dr Paul Wells (written c. 2005, p.1). He is Professor of Theology at the Reformed Seminary in Aix-en-Provence (France). Also see a brief discussion of addressing God in public prayer ('Trinity and God-language') in Catherine Mowry Lacugna's 'God in Communion with us', a chapter in *Freeing Theology*, Lacugna, ed., 99-100.

our heavenly Father. They give a number of reasons for this opposition. Some of the main ones are:

The fatherhood of God comes from a sociological, cultural phenomenon

(1) To think and speak of God exclusively as Father is largely a result of the patriarchal societies in which the biblical writers (and the people who later formed the Church tradition) lived, with negative consequences for women ever after.

Sandra M. Schneiders writes: 'The biblical text, like most texts in world history, arose in a patriarchal setting, that is, in a society and culture in which ruling males owned and dominated other people and most property and used them with impunity for their purposes. *Patriarchy* is the term that refers to the ideology and social system of "father rule," which was the virtually universal pattern of social organization in the world of the Bible…The legitimation of patriarchy in family and society follows logically from this theological premise …'[15]

Catherine Mowry LaCugna adds: 'The divine monarchy was used to justify different types of hierarchy: religious, sexual, political. This was clearly the triumph of a patriarchal understanding of God, despite the theoretical possibility to the contrary contained in the doctrine of the Trinity.'[16]

Elizabeth A. Johnson sees these patriarchal concepts as a sort of violence against women: 'Psychologically, exclusive, patriarchal imagery for the divine functions as a tool of symbolic violence against the full self-identity of female persons, blocking their identity as images of God and curtailing their access to divine power … What needs to be shattered according to feminist theological critique is the stranglehold on religious language of God-He. Normative imagination and conceptualization of God on the model of ruling men alone is theologically the equivalent of the graven image …'[17]

The exclusive fatherhood of God is not based on theological reasons

(2) To state it somewhat differently, patriarchy (involving God as Father) is said finally to be based on sociological reasons, not theological ones. Daphne Hampson has spoken for many feminists when she argues that the fatherhood of God and sonship of Christ are essentially sociologically conditioned constructs (imposed by an androcentric, sexist culture), not divinely revealed expressions of who God really is.[18] Elizabeth A. Johnson, though very respectful and highly learned concerning the doctrine of the Trinity, appears – if I have read her aright – to find its basis (or much of its basis) in human cultural experiences: '… over time the triune symbol has been divorced from the original multifaceted, life-giving experiences that gave it birth in human understanding.'[19]

---

[15]Sandra M. Schneiders, 'The Bible and Feminism' in *Freeing Theology*, edited by Catherine Mowry LaCugna, p. 34.

[16]In ibid., 94.

[17]Elizabeth A. Johnson, op. cit., 39,40.

[18]Daphne Hampson, *Theology and Feminism* (Oxford: Blackwell, 1990).

[19] E. A. Johnson, op. cit., 192.

In fairness to Johnson, however, she certainly does not wish to deny some kind of revelation, nor to explain away sociologically the entire mystery of the Trinity[20]. She clearly teaches that theology is more than a sociological construct.[21] Yet the way she phrases her teaching makes it very difficult to sort out what is sociologically conceived, and what may be considered truly divine revelation. And, in my limited knowledge, she appears to be the most knowledgeable, scholarly and careful of the large company of feminist theologians (many of whom are very able).

God's fatherhood is a projecting of male gender into God

(3) If, as several of the feminist theologians argue, the fatherhood of God largely (though not necessarily exclusively) comes primarily from the constructs of patriarchal societies, then His fatherhood appears in considerable measure to be the projecting of male gender into God. Or at least, as Elizabeth Johnson maintains (in an insightful discussion of analogy and paternity), an emphasis on God the Father has eclipsed 'in some ways the even more appropriate symbol of God as mother.'[22]

A Response to the Claim that God's fatherhood is largely sociological

To the credit of several of the feminist theologians, they have correctly understood in line with the historic Church, that Christian theology has not claimed that God is a male; i.e. the Church has not projected literal maleness into God.

Some feminist theologians rightly see that there is no gender in God. Catherine Lacugna's summary of the fourth-century Cappadocian teaching is accurate:

> The Cappadocians flat-out denied any comparisons between divine and human begetting. For example, Gregory of Nazianzus wrote that God is not male because God is called Father, nor is deity female because of the word, nor does God's fatherhood have anything to do with marriage, pregnancy, midwifery, or the danger of miscarriage.[23] In effect the Cappadocians challenged the Christian imagination to renounce biological, cultural, and commonsense notions of fatherhood, including the patriarchal idea of the self-sufficient father.[24]

Along the same lines, Elizabeth Johnson properly follows the teaching of St. Thomas Aquinas that 'God is not in any genus' (ST I, q. 3, a.5): 'God who is pure being transcends any genus, any concept, even being itself if that be considered an overarching category. The horizon itself cannot be present within the horizon; the limit by which everything is defined cannot itself be defined by a still more ultimate limit: "God is not in any genus."'[25]

---

[20]As we see at large in her book, and especially in Chapter 10 – 'Triune God: Mystery of Relation.'

[21]'According to the witness of Scripture, Jesus is a genuine Spirit-phenomenon, conceived, inspired, sent … risen from the dead by her [Sic] power' in ibid., 150.

[22]E. A. Johnson, op. cit., 173.

[23]Gregory of Nazianzus, *Oration* 31.8 (*Patrologia Graeca* 36. 142).

[24]Catherine Lacugna, 'God in Communion with us' in *Freeing Theology*, C. Lacugna, ed., 93. 94.

[25]E. A. Johnson, op. cit., 239.

God is not the projection of a male image into infinity. James B. Torrance fills out what St. Thomas's crucial insight, *'Deus non est in genere'*, means in accurately distinguishing the fatherhood of God from human ideas of sexuality:

> God has commandeered human language to reveal himself. We only know human fathers. For us the word 'father' is a human class concept, which we predicate of creaturely male parents. How then can a word which is a human class concept, be used to denote God who is not a member of that class? How can we use a word with sexual connotations to denote God who is beyond gender? How can fatherhood then be predicated of God and man? Clearly not univocally, with identity of mean. That would certainly imply gender in God.[26] If the human word 'father' is to be used of God, there must be a shift of meaning to denote God the Creator who is the only true Father, after whom all earthly fatherhood is named (Eph. 3:15). In the order of being, God's Fatherhood is prior to ours, as the Creator is prior to the creature. However, in the order of knowing, we know earthly fathers before we know God as Father.[27]

In other words, we are in God's image; He is not a projection of our image. The *Catechism of the Catholic Church* faithfully summarizes the Christian tradition on this point (based on John 4:24 – 'God is spirit'): 'In no way is God in man's image. He is neither man nor woman. God is pure spirit in which there is no place for the difference between the sexes. But the respective "perfections" of man and woman reflect something of the infinite perfection of God: those of a mother and those of a father and husband.'[28]

Feminine qualities in God, according to Scripture

One can raise no objection to the feminists pointing out that in Scripture there are certain passages which speak of qualities in God's Being that we normally think of as feminine. Some of these texts are:

> Of the Rock that begat thee thou art unmindful, and thou hast forgotten God that formed thee. (Deut. 32:18)

> The LORD shall go forth as a mighty man … now will I cry like a travailing woman; I will destroy and devour at once. (Isa. 42:13, 14)

> Woe unto him that striveth with his Maker! Let the potsherd strive with the potsherds of the earth… Woe unto him that saith unto his father, What begettest thou? Or to the woman, What hast thou brought forth? (Isa. 45:9, 10)

> But Zion said, The LORD hath forsaken me, and my Lord hath forgotten me. Can a woman forget her sucking child, that she should not have compassion on the son of her womb? Yea, they may forget, yet will I not forget thee. (Isa. 49:14, 15)

---

[26]He refers to Battista Mondin, *The Principle of Analogy in Protestant and Catholic Theology* (The Hague: Martinus Nijhoff, 1963).

[27]James B. Torrance, op. cit., 113, 114.

[28]Par. 370.

> As one whom his mother comforteth, so will I comfort you; and ye shall be comforted in Jerusalem. (Isa. 66:13)
>
> O Jerusalem, Jerusalem, thou that killest the prophets, and stonest them which are sent unto thee, how often would I have gathered thy children together, even as a hen gathereth her chickens under her wings, and ye would not! (Matt. 23:37)
>
> Either what woman having ten pieces of silver, if she lose one piece, doth not light a candle, and sweep the house, and seek diligently till she find it? (Luke 15:8)

Yet Scripture teaches God's fatherhood, not His motherhood

One can only rejoice in these 'motherly' characteristics of the Living God towards us, His often erring children! Without failing to appreciate these qualities, we must note that the Bible clearly and directly speaks of God as our Father, but never as our mother; it teaches the divine paternity, but never the divine maternity. I believe that James B. Torrance is right when he points out that texts speaking of motherly qualities of God (such as those immediately previous) are 'similes, not metaphors':

> These are similes, not metaphors. There is no assertion of any motherhood in God, but certain attributes of a woman are used to speak about the attributes of love and compassion in God. In similar fashion, the word *Sophia* (wisdom) is used to describe an attribute in God, or the wise purposes of God. There is a certain personification of wisdom in Proverbs 8. But *Sophia* is not literally a person to be personally addressed.
>
> What then about the word 'Father' when God is addressed as Father? Is this just another metaphor for God, like 'shepherd'? Clearly God is not really a shepherd, although it is a meaningful word. Do we then say that God is not really Father, but this is a meaningful form of address? **Is not God more truly Father than we human fathers are?** [29]

Why does Scripture refer to God exclusively as Father, but not mother?

Since, as the entire Christian theological tradition agrees, God is spirit, beyond gender (which is an aspect of the created order, not of the Creator Himself), then why does the Bible, and why does the orthodox Christian Church always speak of God as He? Why should we not agree with the very able feminist theologian, Elizabeth A. Johnson, in calling God *She Who Is*?

God calls Himself 'He' and 'Father'

(1) God identifies Himself throughout His written Word as 'He', as Father, Son and Holy Spirit. Although God is spirit and thus not characterized by the sexuality belonging to created bodies, and in that sense, is not literally a male, yet He has chosen generally masculine metaphors and pronouns through which to reveal to us who He is. Why should this be the case?

---

[29] J. B. Torrance, op. cit., 112; emphasis mine.

I believe that Denis Ramelet is right when he suggests that these masculine terms are 'more adequate *for us*.'[30] In stating the obvious truth that the divine revelation is *for us*, Ramelet takes into account the classical work of John Calvin on God's *accommodating* Himself to us in the language He uses (already discussed earlier in this volume). In other words, the names He chooses through which to reveal Himself to us are more adequate to convey who He truly is and the blessings of relationship to Him than names He does not choose. No name in finite language could ever be fully and exhaustively adequate to infinite being, but God has provided certain ones that are more adequate than others. In particular, that most adequate of all names is Father; specifically, Father of the eternal Son.

Names exceed metaphors

James B. Torrance has briefly and perceptively shown that 'Father' is not merely a metaphor, but even more, a divinely chosen *name*:

> Clearly much depends on how we interpret metaphor. There have been many discussions about this, some saying that Father, unlike rock or shepherd, is a 'reality depicting metaphor'.[31] The word denotes personal identity in God , not just certain fatherly attributes, in virtue of which we can address him as 'Father'.
>
> Perhaps it is better to talk about *analogy*. The word 'father' is truly predicated of God and of creatures, but analogically. God has revealed himself to us as Father. He has not left himself to be unknown. But the word is not just a model, a metaphor which *we* use to describe God – 'reality depicting' as such a metaphor might be. A name is more than a metaphor. In naming himself, God has commandeered human language to reveal himself.[32]

In naming Himself as *Father*, God shows us, as the *Catechism of the Catholic Church* explains, his original creation of all reality, his transcendent authority over all, and his goodness and solicitude over his children.[33] And above all else, the name Father shows that while he was not always Creator, yet He always had a Son (as Athanasius said and as, for example, John chapters 1 and 17 clearly teach). Thereby we see that even prior to creation, God is a relational being of loving communion and speech (*Logos*).

Paul Wells shows how the Father/Son relationship although metaphorical or analogical to our creaturely, human experience transcends metaphor as a revealed proposition:

> To illustrate, we say 'God is a rock' meaning God is *like* a rock, but we would not say 'God is like a Father' or 'Jesus is like a son'. We say 'God is Father' and 'Jesus is Son' ... Even if these expressions are metaphorically *andromorphic* as well as anthropomorphic, in this case metaphor is transcended as we are dealing with a revealed proposition...

---

[30]Denis Ramelet, 'Pourquoi Dieu est-il Père et non mere?' in *Contre-poisons: Cahiers de la renaissance Vaudoise*, no. cxlv, (Lausanne, 2006), 90.

[31]Torrance refers to Janet Martin Soskice, *Metaphor and Religious Language* (Oxford: Clarendon, 1985), and Sallie McFague, *Metaphorical Theology, Models of God in Religious Language* (London: SCM Press, 1982).

[32]J. B. Torrance, op. cit., 112, 113.

[33]'By calling God "Father," the language of faith indicates two main things: that God is the first origin of everything and transcendent authority; and that he is at the same time goodness

> The relation between the Father and the Son is transcendent and absolute, and therefore mysterious and unfathomable. However, because Jesus reveals himself as being one with the Father – 'I and my Father are one', 'if you had known me you would have known the Father' – we can know that a similar personal relationship and order of being pertains in eternity as is revealed in the incarnation. Father and Son are not andromorphic symbols projected by man into eternity, but anthropmorphisms selected in the divine wisdom as appropriate to God's historical self-revelation because they correspond in a certain way to realities, to certain functions and orders, existing in the immanent Trinity.[34]

Why not God as mother, who has a son or daughter?

But why could not God as mother and Christ as Son or daughter be equally adequate to speak of the inner communication within the life of the Triune God? Paul Wells believes that the reason why God identifies Himself as Father and not mother is related to God's transcendence over all He has created:

> Divine fatherhood implies separation and the ultimate qualitative distinction between God and the world … Only the trinitarian language of Fatherhood and Sonship is adequate to portray anthropomorphically the fact that God is transcendent, but also personal … What can be said about maternity and motherhood? Goddess-talk in relation to material reality would affirm that it is formed and borne in the womb of the divinity, given birth by it, nurtured and supported by it. The theological consequence of this is that the world is formed out of the same substance and nature as the divinity as a partaker in the divine spirit … The world is a product of divine fecundity. A feminine goddess who gives birth to the world from her womb infuses material reality with the substance and life of divinity. Here we are in the realm of fusion and participation … This could well be the key to why God is not called 'mother-divine' in the Scriptures … Therefore it was not out of anti-feminism or patriarchy that in Israel the idolatry of goddess worship was proscribed. God's people were to understand that God is not comparable to the goddesses of the fertility cults which give birth to a natural cycle of productivity. God alone is creator and his election establishes his people through his will …[35]

Wells's final point is that

> Biblical creation takes place outside God, not as the result of divine fecundity. Ultimately the distinction between God as Father and a mother-god comes down to the difference between biblical theism and paganism … The biblical

---

and loving care for all his children. God's parental tenderness can also be expressed by the image of motherhood, which emphasizes God's immanence, the intimacy between Creator and creature. The language of faith thus draws on the human experience of parents, who are in a way the first representatives of God for man. But this experience also tells us that human parents are fallible and can disfigure the face of fatherhood and motherhood. We ought therefore to recall that God transcends the human distinction between the sexes. He is neither man nor woman: he is God. He also transcends human fatherhood and motherhood, although he is their origin and standard: no one is father as God is Father' (par. 239).

[34]Paul Wells, op. cit., 4, 5.

[35]Ibid., 7, 8.

> world view presents a different God, who is not linked to the nature of creation, which is passing away, is not caught up in the cyclical movement of myth, and who is "God the Father almighty – Creator of heaven and earth", directing history in a linear way to its consummation.[36]

For this reason, we cannot as faithful Church people replace in our various liturgies, the Holy Trinity with female or creaturely images. J. B. Torrance has clearly answered the question now being raised in 'the worship wars' of many churches: 'why we cannot use female images for God, to express his love and compassion.'[37] He writes:

> Some have suggested that instead of talking about 'Father, Son and Holy Spirit', we talk about God as 'Creator, Redeemer, Sanctifier'. But this would be a new form of modalism or Sabellianism, a job description of the one God at work. It would not do justice to the personal communion between the persons of the triune God.[38]

Underlying concerns of feminist theology

Having read many of their books (some of which impressed me profoundly for their erudite scholarship and ability to communicate), it is my opinion that most of the feminist theologians will still not be satisfied with this traditional discussion of the exclusive fatherhood of God. Presumably the reason why they wish to change the entire tradition away from masculine concepts and terms to feminine ones is not primarily because the scriptural and ecclesiastical traditions have been unclear as to what God as Father really means.

Rather, their books often exhibit a cry of outrage for abuses committed against women in the name of the authority of God the Father. Sheer honesty and openness to historical and contemporary facts mean that their loud protests are generally valid. Who among us does not know all too many instances of brutal husbands and unresponsive institutions and bureaucracies that severely mistreat women and children in the name of divinely granted authority? Who could deny that many in the Church (contrary to the Holy Scriptures and to the example of Christ) have considered women to be inferior to males?

It is the presupposition of feminist theology that a large part of the problem of abuse of women, and of denying them access to corridors of privilege and power, as well as their own healthy personal development comes directly from the assumptions and structures of patriarchal society, and lying behind that, patriarchal assumptions about God and his will for our lives. Mary Daly is known for the famous remark that 'if God is male, then males are God.' No doubt, male headship can be used as a cover for arrogance and viciousness: denials of that tender, self-sacrificial love which Christ gave to His Church, and holds forth as the model for the husband's relationship to his wife (cf. Eph. 5).

I am entirely unable to disprove these suggested connections between the widespread (biblical) belief in the fatherhood of God, and how this

---

[36] Ibid., 8.

[37] J. B. Torrance, op. cit., 97.

[38] Ibid., 97,98.

has worked out in patriarchal societies and the hierarchical structure of the churches, and in the tragically broken lives of less powerful people. But I do make these preliminary responses, to open the way for further discussion.

Have not all societies been patriarchal?

(1) Has there ever been a society that was not patriarchal? I am no social anthropologist, and thus cannot know how valid is the statement of Steven Goldberg that 'patriarchy is universal. For all the variety different societies have demonstrated in developing different types of political, economic, religious, and social systems, there has never been a society that has failed to associate authority and leadership in these areas with men. No anthropologist contests the fact that patriarchy is universal.'[39]

But if he is right, the problem in abuse and holding down of women and others is both personal and social sin, rather than specifically patriarchal structures of the society. An interesting question is: would matriarchal societies (if such should ever exist) be any less characterized by broken lives and abused persons? Would people who held views of God as feminine be kinder and more holy than those who believe in God as Father? That leads to the next point:

Many societies have indeed worshipped feminine and androgynous deities

(2) While there may have been few (or no?) cultures that were matriarchal or strictly egalitarian, there have indeed been many that worshipped female and androgynous deities. It is not at all clear that these pagan societies gave any better treatment to women than did those who worshipped God as Father (nor, in fact, as good a treatment). James B. Torrance asks the right question here:

> Would this approach really help the feminist cause? The ancient world was full of goddesses like Astarte or Aphrodite, or the female deities in Canaanite religion. But did it help women? Tragically the deifying of sex led too often to temple prostitution as a celebration of sexuality. The Old Testament prophets of Israel were very well aware of this, and although they could use beautiful similes of God being 'like a mother' they never addressed God as 'Mother'. I do not think this can be dismissed on the basis that they were too patriarchal! They were well aware of the danger of the fertility cults.[40]

The true way ahead for women

(3) The way ahead for women – and for all people – is not to deny whom God has named Himself to be, but rather to 'allow Jesus Christ to interpret true fatherhood for us, both human and divine.'[41] James B. Torrance says it well:

> It seems to me that the right approach for the Church to adopt in seeking women's liberation is to take a stand on the incarnation. To hold out Jesus

---

[39]Steven Goldberg, *The Inevitablity of Patriarchy* (New York: William Morrow and Company, 1973), 31-32.

[40]J. B. Torrance, op. cit., 98,99.

[41]Ibid., 92.

> Christ to the world is not only to hold out personal salvation and eternal life in our evangelism, but it is also to give all people their humanity. Whatever else the incarnation means, it is that all people and all races – Jew or Gentile, black or white, male or female – are meant to see their humanity assumed by Christ, sanctified by his life in the Spirit of unbroken communion with the Father, by his death and resurrection, offered to the Father 'without spot or wrinkle', and given back to them in the mission of the Church ... Women are meant to find in Christ and receive from the Church the full dignity and beauty of their humanity, equally with men. Tragically the Church has been so often 'moulded', not by Jesus Christ, but by the patterns of a patriarchal culture.[42]

It would be disingenuous to pretend that the Church has always been faithful to hold forth to women their true humanity in Christ. I shall seek to discuss the equality of women with men in terms of the image of God, and their authentic position as 'Christ-bearers', as much as males, in the second volume of this work. The Church always has much to repent of, and she is 'always reforming.' But in the meantime, it is necessary to say that the true interest of women as a constituent part of the pilgrim people of God lies in affirming from the heart the fatherhood of God, the sonship of Christ and the co-equality of the Holy Spirit, the Comforter, rather than turning from the scriptural testimony to His identity in favor of humanly devised views of deity.

---

[42]Ibid., 93.

Chapter Six

The Triune God Makes Himself Known in the Covenant of Grace

We know this LORD and His truth only in and through the Covenant of Grace that He establishes, which is revealed to a community of faith. That saving community has defined itself in terms of the 'rule of truth' revealed to it by God in the sending of His Son and Spirit; a rule laid down in the Holy Scriptures and always safeguarded by the true Church. Heretical approaches to God deviate from this 'rule of truth' and cannot know God truly.

We know the LORD only in and through the Covenant of Grace that He establishes

The created order and our own consciences witness in their appointed ways to the reality of Almighty God, as we have seen. But relational knowledge of God is the basis of salvation, as Jesus said: 'And this is life eternal, that they might know thee the only true God, and Jesus Christ, whom thou hast sent' (John 17:3). This statement is in the context of Jesus' high priestly prayer for all who would ever be His; all who would be saved in His Church: 'Neither pray I for these alone, but for them also which shall believe on me through their word…' (John 17:20). We know God in this saving, relational way only in a God-ordained community; first, in Old Testament Israel, and then in the New Testament Christian Church. Christ prays that His people be 'sanctified through thy truth; thy word is truth' (John 17:17). God's saving, sanctifying truth is always given to a divinely constituted community of faith. We do not know God savingly outside the community of faith that He has appointed; a community constituted by divine covenant.

We look (a) at covenant, and then at (b) how we can know God and His truth only in the covenant community appointed by Him.

(a) Covenant

The divinely appointed community of faith is established on the basis of *covenant*. The Old Testament Hebrew word is *berith*. As Dumbrell noted:

> The task of determining the etymology of *berit* is made more difficult by the fact that there is no final consensus as to the origin of the word. However, the derivation which has most commended itself and probably ought to be

> adopted[1] is that which takes its meaning back to the Middle Assyrian noun *biritu*, a word whose sense is 'bond' or 'fetter'. This is the more probable, since in the Old Testament, *berit* when used in contexts where relationships are established or confirmed, seems usually to carry with it the note of obligation, whatever else may be implied at the same time.[2]

The concept of covenant is employed throughout Scripture, and enables a great deal of its massive content to be coherently organized. The Hebrew word for covenant, *berith*, is generally translated in the LXX as *diatheke*.

> ... while covenant is found almost 300 times in the OT, it occurs only 33 times in the NT. Almost half of these instances come in quotations from the OT, and another 5 clearly look back to OT statements ... If the term covenant (*diatheke*) does not appear as often as one might expect, the reason is that the underlying thought has been taken over in the sayings about the kingdom of God. Linguistically we can see this perhaps most clearly in Luke 22:29 in the phrase *diatithemai ... basileian*, appoint a kingdom, which exactly expresses the formula *diatithemai diatheken*. The new covenant and the kingdom of God are correlated concepts.[3]

Covenant theologians in the Reformed tradition have generally seen the many different covenants of redemptive history as falling into two major types: 'law covenants' and 'promise covenants'.[4] Michael Horton shows that Pope Benedict XVI has seen the same distinction.[5] Sometimes these two different types of covenants have been referred to as 'Covenant of Works' and 'Covenant of Grace' (though not without considerable exegetical and theological challenges, as we shall see).[6]

'Law covenants' (or 'suzerainty treaties')

G. E. Mendenhall some fifty years ago pointed out the similarity of covenant concepts between Hittite suzerainty treaties and the Old Testament.[7] Mendenhall finds that the Hittite suzerainty treaty ('in which the stipulations of the treaty are binding only upon the vassal, and only the vassal took an oath of obedience'[8]), are paralleled 'in three different bodies of material in the books of Exodus, Deuteronomy, and Joshua... directly connected with this legal tradition.'[9] He states that 'The covenant of Moses...imposes specific obligations upon the tribes or clans without binding Yahweh to specific obligations, though it goes without saying that

[1]Dumbrell refers to the 'survey of the possible etymologies of *berit* offered by E. Kütsch, *Verheissung und Gesetz*, BZAW 131 (Berlin: De Gruyter, 1973), 28-30 in W. J. Dumbrell, *Covenant and Creation: A Theology of the Old Testament Covenants* (Carlisle: Paternoster Press: , 1984), 36.

[2] Dumbrell, op. cit., 36.

[3] Colin Brown, *New International Dictionary of New Testament Theology*, op. cit., vol. 1, 369.

[4] See Michael Horton, *Lord and Servant: A Covenant Christology* (Louisville, KY: Westminster John Knox, 2005).

[5] Benedict XVI (Joseph Cardinal Ratzinger), *Many Religions – One Covenant: Israel, the Church and the World* (San Francisco: Ignatius Press, 1999), 55, quoted in Horton, op. cit., 26,27.

[6] See *The Westminster Confession of Faith* (of the 1640s), chapter VII, referring to 'the first covenant' as 'a covenant of works', and 'a second covenant, the covenant of grace.'

[7] George E. Mendenhall, *Law and Covenant in Israel and the Ancient Near East* (Pittsburg, PA: The Biblical Colloquium, 1955).

[8] Ibid., 30.

[9] Ibid.

the covenant relationship itself presupposed the protection and support of Yahweh to Israel.'[10] But Mendenhall notes that the Old Testament includes a different kind of covenant from the suzerainty treaty:

'Promise covenants' or 'royal grants'

He distinguishes the Decalogue and the narrative in Joshua 24 as being obedience covenants, like the Hittite suzerainty treaties, from the covenants with Abraham and Noah, which are of 'a completely different form:'[11]

> Both in the narrative of Genesis 15 and 17, and in the later references to this covenant, it is clearly stated or implied that it is Yahweh Himself who swears to certain promises to be carried out in the future. It is not often enough seen that no obligations are imposed upon Abraham. Circumcision is not originally an obligation, but a *sign* of the covenant, like the rainbow in Genesis 9. It serves to identify the recipient(s) of the covenant, as well as to give a concrete indication that a covenant exists.[12]

The contemporary Jewish scholar, Moses Weinfeld, speaks of this other type of covenant as a 'royal grant', and found parallels to it in the records of Ugarit.[13] While the law covenants (like the suzerainty treaties) are conditioned on obedience, the covenants of promise (like the royal grant) depend directly on the kind, undeserved action of the sovereign. Michael Horton distinguishes these two types of covenant by contrasting the Sinaitic and Davidic Covenants '...in terms of their conditional versus promissory character.'[14]

Several years earlier, the Reformed Old Testament scholar, Meredith Kline, had also sharply distinguished between these two types of covenants as 'inheritance by law' and 'inheritance by works' (in terms of Paul's critique of works' righteousness in Gal. 3:18): 'In contrast to his classification of the Sinaitic Covenant as law, Paul placed God's covenantal dealings with Abraham in the category of promise ...'[15]

Two different viewpoints on how the covenants of Scripture are related

This proper distinction made by biblical scholars between two types of covenant: suzerainty and grant; law and promise, has given rise to two very different interpretations of how the many and varied covenant administrations found in Holy Scripture can be related. Many traditional Reformed scholars follow the Westminster Confession of Faith tradition in rather sharply distinguishing the 'Covenant of Works' from the 'covenant

[10] Ibid.

[11] Ibid., 36.

[12] Ibid.

[13] Moses Weinfeld, 'The Covenant of Grant in the Old Testament and the Ancient Near East,' *Journal of the American Oriental Society* 90 (1970), 185-186.

[14] Michael S. Horton, *Covenant and Salvation* (Louisville, London: Westminster John Knox Press, 2007), 18.

[15] Meredith Kline, *By Oath Consigned: A Reinterpretation of the Covenant Signs of Circumcision and Baptism* (Grand Rapids: Wm. B. Eerdmans, 1968), 24.

of grace.' Some of them place the Mosaic Covenant and the Palestinian Covenant in the category of the covenant of works,[16] and oppose this very strongly *as a different type of covenant* to the unconditional covenant of promise to Noah and Abraham. Michael Horton, for instance, after a judicious review of the comments of Paul in Romans 4, Galatians 4, etc. summarizes the position: 'There are two covenants, not one: a covenant of law (Sinai) and a covenant of promise (Abraham and his Seed) (Gal. 4:21-31).'[17]

Other Reformed scholars, however, understand all of the covenants of Scripture (including the Adamic, Mosaic and Palestinian) as progressive aspects of the one overarching Covenant of Grace. John Murray,[18] O. Palmer Robertson[19] and Pierre Courthial[20] are among many others in interpreting the Mosaic Covenant as one stage in the unfolding redemptive story of the Covenant of Grace (although as we shall soon see, John Murray does not hold Adam to have been in a covenant, but rather speaks of 'the Adamic Administration,' whereas Pierre Courthial does consider Adam to have been specifically in covenant with God). And O. Palmer Robertson also understands all the covenants of Scripture, including the Adamic and Mosaic, to be aspects of the one Covenant of Grace.[21] Pope Benedict XVI has rightly stated that 'The one Covenant is realized in the plurality of covenants.'[22]

The first covenant theologian within the Reformation, Heinrich Bullinger of Zurich, taught five points about the covenant in his major work on this subject (1534), and all of these points affirm the oneness of the covenants of Holy Scripture: (1) There is only one covenant in history. It was first made with Adam, renewed with Abraham, and throughout the entire Old Testament, and was fulfilled and thus renewed by Christ. (2) This covenant is bilateral, although sovereignly administered. But its obligations are fulfilled for us in Christ. This renewed covenant requires of us faith and love. (3) This one covenant is found all through the Scriptures, and constitutes the scope of the Scriptures. (4) The Old Testament phase of the covenant had two sacraments: circumcision and Passover, and these were fulfilled and replaced by Christ with baptism and the Lord's Supper. (5) The substance of the covenant with Adam is found in the Christian gospel. Bullinger saw the Protestant Reformation as a renewal of the covenant after many years of apostasy.[23]

---

[16] Meredith Kline, who does so, is still very careful as to terminology, and thus, notes 'The weakness of the traditional designation, "Covenant of Works" for the pre-redemptive covenant is that it fails to take account of the continuity of the law principle in redemptive revelation and therefore is not a sufficiently distinctive term' (Ibid., 32).

[17] M. Horton, op. cit., 69.

[18] John Murray, *The Covenant of Grace* (Phillipsburg, NJ: Presbyterian and Reformed, 1988).

[19] O. Palmer Robertson, *The Christ of the Covenants* (Phillipsburg, NJ: Presbyterian and Reformed, 1980).

[20] Pierre Courthial, *Le Jour des Petits Recommencements: Essai sur l'Actualite de la Parole (Evangile-Loi) de Dieu* (Lausanne: Messages: L'Age d'Homme, 1996).

[21] O. Palmer Robertson, *The Christ of the Covenants* (Phillipsburg, NJ: Presbyterian and Reformed, 1980).

[22] Benedict XVI, *Many Religions – One Covenant: Israel, the Church and the World*, 56, quoted in Horton, op. cit., 27.

[23] H. Bullinger, *De Testamento seu foedere Dei unico & aeterno Heinrychi Bullingeri brevis exposition* (1534).

Unlike Bullinger, Murray, Robertson and others, Drs. Kline and Horton do not consider all the covenants of Scripture to be within the one Covenant of Grace. In fairness, it must be noted here that these able scholars, while denying that the Adamic and Mosaic are parts of the Covenant of Grace, are still careful to affirm that both of these 'covenants of law' play an important role in redemptive history, and in no sense undercut the 'covenants of promise' such as the Abrahamic, Davidic and new covenants. And they also affirm that recipients of these legal covenants were often touched by the grace of God.[24] Before we can further explore the consequences of these differing interpretations of the covenants, let us briefly look at the major biblical covenants themselves.

The Adamic Covenant?

It has long been recognized that the actual word for covenant (*berith*) does not appear in Genesis prior to the Covenant with Noah (Gen. 6–9). Therefore, the *word* for covenant is not used with God's relationship with Adam in the Genesis text. For that reason, the consummate Reformed, Biblical theologian, John Murray, declined to speak of 'the Covenant of Works', but rather called it 'the Adamic Administration.'[25] Yet in the end of the day, Murray is still *theologically* very close to chapter VII of the Westminster Confession of Faith, in that he holds to the 'federal headship' of Adam as the representative in whom all humankind fell.[26] (The same would have to be said of John Calvin, whom the Westminster Assembly followed in so many ways. Calvin never spoke of 'the Covenant of Works',[27] but he firmly taught the solidarity of all mankind in fallen Adam.[28])

Yet the absence of the word, *berith*, from Genesis 2 and 3, significant as it is, may not finally be sufficient to exclude our thinking of Adam (at least by analogy with Rom. 5:12-21) from having been in a covenantal-like relationship with his Maker. As the famous German Old Testament scholar, Walter Eichrodt, whose work so emphasizes the covenant, brought out (in his 'Preface to the English Edition' of his *Theology of the Old Testament*):

> The crucial point is not – as an all too naïve criticism sometimes seems to think – the occurrence or absence of the Hebrew word *berit*, but the fact that

---

[24] E.g., M. Kline, op. cit., 25 and M. Horton, op. cit., 19-21, 25.

[25] John Murray, *Collected Writings*, vol. 2, (Edinburgh: The Banner of Truth Trust, 1977), 'The Adamic Administration' (ch. 5), 47-66. In addition to the problem of *berith* not being applied to Adam, Murray feels that 'works' fails to convey the elements of grace in this administration (p. 22).

[26] John Murray, op. cit., 49.

[27] In his *Institutes* II. X, where Calvin discusses the relationship and differences between the covenants with the Patriarchs and with us, he has no concept of a covenant of works, nor does he in his *Commentary on Genesis* and *The Harmony of the Pentateuch*. This would be developed in the next century. For a positive exposition of this sixteenth-century development, see Donald MacLeod, 'Covenant Theology', art. in *Dictionary of Scottish Church History & Theology*, N. Cameron, ed. (Downers Grove, IL: InterVarsity Press, 1993), 214-218, and for a negative evaluation, see James B. Torrance, 'The Covenant Concept in Scottish Theology and Politics and its Legacy', *Scottish Journal of Theology* 34. no. 3 (1981), 225-240. Of great interest here is the sound recording (three cassette tapes) by Rutherford House in Edinburgh (1996) of a review by Donald MacLeod of Thomas F. Torrance's *Scottish Theology* (Edinburgh: T & T Clark, 1996), and a response by Torrance, along with a dialogue between the two scholars. Many of the crucial questions in these tapes deal with covenant concepts in the Bible and in Reformed theology.

[28] E.g. see John Calvin, *Commentary on Romans*, 5:12-21.

> all the crucial statements of faith in the OT rest on the assumption, explicit or not, that a free act of God in history raised Israel to the unique dignity of the People of God… The actual term 'covenant' is, therefore, so to speak, only the code-word for a more far-reaching certainty, which formed the very deepest layer of the foundations of Israel's faith, and without which indeed Israel would not have been Israel at all.[29]

Along these lines, numerous theologians and biblical exegetes have long held that God had a covenant with creation (although the specific word *berith* is not used of creation in Scripture). We will glance at a few of them.

Covenant with Creation

Karl Barth for instance expounded 'creation as the external basis of the covenant', and 'the covenant as the internal basis of the creation'.[30] Pierre Courthial understands the Covenant of Grace to have existed even before the fall of Adam, partly on the basis that the Hebrew form of the verb (i.e. the *hiphil*) is used with *qum*, and is more likely to signify 'to confirm' rather than 'to establish.'

> … in chapters 6, 9, and 17 of Genesis, as in Exodus 6, each time the text deals with the covenant, it is necessary to choose the translation 'to confirm' rather than 'to establish'. Why? Simply because the general context that precedes reveals … that the covenant of grace already existed since (and even before) Adam fell! … Genesis 6:18 says: 'Noah found grace in the eyes of the Lord …' Now, no one can obtain the grace of the Lord, no one can be upright and just, no one can walk with God, unless he does so *in* the covenant of grace, this covenant that God calls *my covenant*.[31]

O. Palmer Robertson, while noting the absence of the word *covenant* before Noah's time in Genesis 9, also finds reasons to believe that the reality of covenant was already in existence from the time of creation. Commenting on Jeremiah 33:20,21 ('Thus saith the LORD; If ye can break my covenant of the day, and my covenant of the night, and that there should not be day and night in their seasons; Then may also my covenant be broken with David my servant …'), Robertson asks: 'When did God establish a "covenant" with "day and night"?'[32] He suggests that it may refer 'to the ordinances of the third day of creation'. According to Genesis 1:14 God said: 'Let there be lights in the expanse of the heaven, to divide between the day and the night.'

But does Jeremiah 33:20 refer to God's covenant with Noah, '… or is he alluding to a covenantal relationship that has existed since creation?'[33] Another passage from Jeremiah (31:35, 36 – 'Thus saith the LORD, which giveth the sun for a light by day, and the ordinances of the moon and stars for a light by night, which divideth the sea when the waves thereof roar;

---

[29] Walter Eichrodt, *Theology of the Old Testament*, vol. 1, English Translation, (Philadelphia: The Westminster Press, 1961), 17,18.

[30] Karl Barth, *Church Dogmatics*, III/1. section 41. Although affirming a covenant of creation, Barth strongly rejected the concept of 'Covenant of Works.'

[31] Pierre Courthial, *Le Jour des Petits Recommencements*, 6.

[32] Robertson, op. cit., 19.

[33] Ibid., 20.

The LORD of hosts is his name: If those ordinances depart from before me, saith the LORD, then the seed of Israel also shall cease from being a nation before me for ever') indicates that it refers to creation and not to Noah. Robertson comments:

> Quite interestingly, the reference to the sun and moon specifically as light-bearers for day and night is found in the creation narrative but not in the narrative describing God's covenant with Noah. Furthermore, the narrative of the creation-activity of the third day refers to the stars as well as to the moon (Gen. 1:16), as does Jeremiah 31:35. The record of God's covenant with Noah makes no mention of the stars. For these reasons, it seems likely that Jeremiah 31 alludes to the Genesis narrative of creation rather than to the establishment of God's covenant with Noah. His reference seems to be to the 'statutes' of God's creation ordinances.[34]

Dumbrell also holds that Genesis 6:18 ('But with thee will I establish my covenant') refers not to the setting up of a new covenant (for the technical term for that – 'to cut a covenant' – is notably missing in this verse), but rather to the *confirming* of a covenant already in existence:

> Evidence of this character makes it more than likely that in contexts where *heqim berit* stands (Gen. 6:18; 9:9, 11, 17; 17:7, 19, 21; Exod. 6:4; Lev. 26:9; Deut. 8:18; 2 Kings 23:3) the institution of a covenant is not being referred to but rather its perpetuation ... what is being referred to in Genesis 6:18 is some existing arrangement presumably imposed by God without human concurrence, since it is referred to as 'my covenant'. Despite the human sinful condition, he is determined to maintain it. The nature and details of this arrangement are not clear from Genesis 6:18, though they might with some probability have been inferred from the course of the Genesis narrative to that point.'[35]

Dumbrell adds: 'Until the end of time the continued existence of the created order will thus be grounded simply in the gracious nature of the divine character.'[36]

But does God's covenant with creation involve a covenant with Adam? At the very least, God establishes a sovereign relationship with the first man and his progeny. As far back as the late second century, St. Irenaeus spoke of 'the covenant with Adam' as one of the four 'principal' (or 'catholic') covenants.[37] Francis Turretin speaks of 'the Covenant of Nature', and by this term specifically means a covenant with Adam.[38] While the Genesis text does not call it 'covenant', yet many theologians have considered it to be such by analogy of the covenant with the 'Last Adam' in terms of Romans 5:12-21. There, all humanity is represented by the First and Last Adam. The First Adam disobeys God, and the Last Adam obeys God. From the Pauline point of view, all the difference between condemnation

---

[34] Ibid., 20, 21.

[35] W. J. Dumbrell, op. cit., 26.

[36] Ibid., 27.

[37] Irenaeus, *Adversus Haereses*, III.11.8. He mentions the four as being with Adam, Noah, Moses, and the Gospel.

[38] Francis Turretin, *Institutes of Elenctic Theology*, translated by G. M. Giger (Phillipsburg, NJ: P & R Publishing, 1992), vol. 1, Third Question ('The Covenant of Nature'), 574, 575.

and salvation turns on this question: are we in the First Adam or the Last Adam? Both of these arrangements (or, by analogy, 'covenants') involve (1) the sovereign initiative of God in setting up the administration, and (2) in structuring it to function by means of the principle of representation, which entails obedience with stipulations issuing in blessing or cursing.

Adam: grace/law/grace

In biblical terms, one can properly speak of the original sovereign arrangement (or 'covenant') with Adam, the representative head of humanity,[39] as *gracious* on the part of God though it required obedience, with severe stipulations for disobedience (called by some 'a law covenant'). Jean-Marc Berthoud has helpfully noted that:

> The word *grace* has two meanings in the Bible. First, it can have the sense of benefit [or undeserved favour]. Then secondly, grace can be considered as divine pardon, in which God out of His mercy shows grace to those who, because of their sin, are bound to eternal condemnation. When we speak of the grace shown to unfallen Adam in the arrangement or covenant God sovereignly established with him, grace is being used *in the first sense*, that of benefit or favour. Grace as pardon has no place before the fall, because no sin had yet been committed. Before the fall, everything was very good, and the good creation of God contained no wrong whatsoever, and furthermore, man himself knew not the slightest shadow of sin.[40]

Pierre Courthial argues that the 'covenant' with Adam is gracious on the part of God to Adam, in the relationship established between superior and inferior, in the perfect environment provided, and even in its requirements with their promises and threats to the representative head and his progeny:

> In addition to the benediction ('Gospel'!) accorded to the human creature of creation in God's image, God adds requirements ('Law'!) which are inseparable from the divine benefit of sharing God's image. Insofar as the human partner to the covenant is faithful and gives thanks for such grace, he has access to 'the tree of life' which is in the midst of the garden. If he inexplicably becomes unfaithful, if he no longer recognizes and serves God as God; if, in a hard-hearted manner, he seeks to be autonomous; if he wishes to become 'like God', a law to himself, then he will die. He will be chased out of the garden. He will be cut off from the pathway to 'the tree of life', now guarded by the Cherubim with the flaming sword. The death of [fallen] man has two 'moments': first, spiritual death, because man is no longer in communion with God, and secondly, at a later time, physical death. If he becomes born again, his resurrection will also have two moments: first, an immediate spiritual resurrection, for he will find himself to be again in communion with God; and then, at the very end of time, the resurrection of his body.[41]

---

[39] For a classical theological discussion of many of the ramifications of Adam's 'federal headship' over humanity, see Scottish theologian, Thomas Boston, *Human Nature in its Fourfold State* (Edinburgh: The Banner of Truth, 1989 reprint) , 254-320, where he contrasts union with Adam and union with Christ. The exegetical questions involved in the principle of representation are postponed to our volume dealing with anthropology.

[40] Jean-Marc Berthoud, "Le traité d'alliance et son histoire dans la Bible", second lecture in the series *Cours de Formation Biblique* (unpublished: Lausanne, 2007).

[41] P. Courthial, op. cit., 4.

St. Augustine seems to have thought of God's grace to unfallen Adam in a similar sense of something like grace (which we might call 'beneficence'), *before* grace as 'pardon' became necessary. In his *De Correptione et Gratia* (*On Admonition and Grace*), he maintains that even before the fall, Adam had need of an *adiutorium* of grace from God, without which he could not avoid falling into sin.[42] Along this line of thought, Augustine explains the shame that our first parents felt at realizing that they were naked, because they had been stripped of the grace that had been upon their bodies and minds previously.[43] Francis Turretin, however, argues against the need of unfallen Adam for a supernatural gift of grace to maintain his 'original righteousness', but Turretin's concern is the direction in which this concept had been taken by Bellarmine (no doubt, following Thomas Aquinas). Turretin does not mention Augustine, whose point was not so much the later Medieval theory of the supernatural gift of 'original righteousness', as more simply a reflection on the necessary condescension (or 'beneficence') of an infinitely holy Person to a finitely holy person.[44]

Although founded in grace (in the first sense of 'benefit' or 'unmerited favour'), the covenant with Adam and his progeny has been described as taking the form of what Meredith Kline calls 'a law covenant'.[45] Of course, to draw the distinction as early as unfallen Adam between 'law covenant' and 'promise covenant' is in a sense anachronistic, although perhaps it is inevitable that we read back post-lapsarian distinctions into a perfect created order with perfect relationships (not least, that between God and man). It might be most accurate to state that this was simply a divine administration (or by analogy with Rom. 5, 'a covenant') with Adam, founded in the infinitely kind condescension of God's beneficent grace, and bearing responsible stipulations with serious consequences. Especially in light of what happened almost immediately after the fall (cf. the unconditional promise of Gen. 3:15), one might say that the 'covenantal' relationship with Adam actually had elements of both kinds of covenant, as they come to be defined after the fall, and thus not exactly like either one of them. For that matter, in Holy Scripture no covenant ever seems to be strictly and only grace or strictly and only obligation or law. In grace there is obligation, and in obligation there is grace.

The seventeenth-century Dutch theologian, Witsius, is certainly right when he says that 'Moses is ... sparing on the particulars of that [Adamic] covenant ...'[46] But developments in twentieth-century research

---

[42] Augustine, *De Correptione et Gratia* (Migne's *Patrologia Latina*, vol. 44, xi. 29), where he says: 'Istam gratiam non habuit homo prius, qua nunquam vellet esse malus: sed sane habuit, in qua si permanere vellet, nunquam malus esset, et sine qua etiam cum libero arbitrio bonus esse non posset, sed eam tamen per liberum arbitrium deserere posset.'

[43] Augustine, *City of God*, XIV, 17.

44 Francis Turretin, op. cit., vol. 1, First Through Tenth Topics, Fifth Topic ('Creation'), Eleventh Question ('Was Original Righteousness natural or supernatural?'), 470-73, interacting with Bellarmine's 'De gratia primi hominis,' 5, 6 in *Opera* [1858], 4:23-29.

[45] Kline, op. cit., 26.

[46] Herman Witsius, *The Economy of the Covenants Between God and Man: Comprehending A Complete Body of Divinity* (London: R. Baynes, English translation and reprint, 1822 of 1677 Dutch original), 75.

in the Ancient Middle East have helped us to see (at least, by looking backwards to a very different situation, where there cannot be a one-to-one relationship) that the Adamic Arrangement (or Covenant) is closer to the Hittite suzerainty treaty (with a heavier emphasis on law), rather than to the royal grant (with a heavier emphasis on promise).

Kline explains:

> Our claim is not that the literary structure of these opening chapters of Genesis [*sc.*, ch. 1 & 2] is patterned after the legal form exhibited in the ancient treaties, but simply that the various components of the relationship between God and man found in these chapters correspond to the more significant aspects of the lord-servant relationship attested to by the treaties…a revelation of law, including both service obligations and dual sanctions.[47]

Our task here is not to expound the immense significance of Adam's disobedience (that awaits a later volume), but more simply to note what kind of relationship God originally established with Adam. We could call it: grace/law/grace. For if the first arrangement (or covenant) with Adam came out of divine beneficence (or grace in the first sense), still the form of it was more in the category of a law covenant (conditional suzerainty treaty) rather than an unconditional promise covenant (or 'royal grant'). In that sense, we can speak of God's covenant with Adam in terms of grace and then law. As Michael Horton writes: 'The form and content are those of a suzerainty covenant …evident also in the covenant between God and Adam (Gen. 2:16-17). Like Adam, Israel has a mission to undertake, a task to perform, a destiny to realize not only for itself but also for the whole world, and this vocation was Israel's to either keep or lose.'[48]

Yet, Genesis 3 shows us that Adam's disastrous breaking of the graciously given law covenant was followed by grace! Of course, the text shows that God fulfilled His righteous threat; that 'sin brought death.' But that was not God's last word. Indeed, even the judgment of physical death itself, which was assured by barring access to the tree of life, was in fact a mercy, as Hebrews 2:14-17 explains:

> Forasmuch then as the children are partakers of flesh and blood, he also himself took part of the same; that through death he might destroy him that had the power of death, that is, the devil; And deliver them who through fear of death were all their lifetime subject to bondage. For verily he took not on him the nature of angels; but he took on him the seed of Abraham. Wherefore in all things it behoved him to be made like unto his brethren, that he might be a merciful and faithful high priest in things pertaining to God, to make reconciliation for the sins of the people.

St. Irenaeus showed that God removed Adam from Paradise with its tree of life out of pure grace, not out of 'envy':

> Wherefore also He drove him out of Paradise, and removed him far from the tree of life, not because He envied him the tree of life, as some venture

---

[47] Kline, op. cit., 27.

[48] Horton, op. cit., 15.

> to assert, but because He pitied him, [and did not desire] that he should continue a sinner for ever, nor that the sin which surrounded him should be immortal, and evil interminable and irremediable. But He set a bound to his [state of sin] by interposing death, and thus causing sin to cease, putting an end to it by the dissolution of the flesh, so that man, ceasing at length to live to sin, and dying to it, might begin to live to God.[49]

In Genesis 3:15, God promises our first mother, Eve, that she will in due time have 'a seed', who would reverse all the consequences brought about by her having given in to the Satanic tempter. God Himself will do this (as Paul shows in Gal. 3:16). Adam and Eve are not asked to do it. Therefore, this is grace in the second sense: that of pardon (and reversal of all the deleterious consequences of disobedience).

This 'first promise of the gospel' of Genesis 3:15, is to be considered in the class of covenant of promise, or 'royal grant.' According to Michael Horton (after speaking of the rediscovery of the Book of the Law in the time of King Josiah) (2 Kings 22:13):

> The point is this: *The deepest distinction in Scripture is not between the Old and New Testaments, but between the covenants of law and the covenants of promise that run throughout both.* The two covenant traditions are distinguished both in form and content. There is a covenant of law (the prelapsarian covenant with humanity in Adam as well as the Sinai covenant), according to which each and every person swears to personally fulfil the stipulations. There is also a covenant of promise made to Adam and Eve after the fall, to Abraham and Sarah, Noah, David and the new covenant), according to which God swears to bring redemption through the promised heir (seed). These two covenant traditions are united by many bonds, yet always remain distinguished ...[50]

From this point of view, we can properly think of Adam as – within the grace of creation – having been obligated by 'covenant relationship' to fulfil the requirements which God had endued him with the power to carry out. But Adam willfully disobeys God and undergoes the just penalty against his sin. Blessedly for us all, just punishment against the human sinner (who was head of the whole race) was *not* God's last word. For God then intervened with a word of gracious, indefectible promise, as He spoke to Eve in Genesis 3:15. Thus, the first pair can be thought of as surrounded by grace on both sides of their earthly existence: grace, *in the first sense* of beneficence, and then, after they willfully broke God's law to them, grace *in the second sense* of divine forgiveness upon the guilty couple (and their progeny) . Hence, Adam's 'covenanted' relationship to his Maker could be characterized as *grace* (beneficence), *law*, *grace* (forgiveness).

Or (by analogy with other biblical passages), to apply covenantal concepts to these arrangements (which, as we have seen, are *not* specifically found in the text of Genesis), we could say that within a context of beneficent grace, Adam was placed in a conditional law covenant (like a suzerainty treaty) – which he broke, and then was placed in an unconditional promise

---

[49] Irenaeus, *Adversus Haereses* III.23.5 (*The Ante-Nicene Fathers*, vol. I, 457).

[50] Michael Horton, *Covenant and Salvation* (Louisville, London: Westminster John Knox Press, 2007), 17,18.

covenant (like a royal grant) – which God Himself kept. We will find reason to believe that any divinely initiated law covenant has grace before it and grace after it. This is not only true with Adam (*if* we call the Adamic Administration 'covenant'), but also with Moses (which Scripture *does* call 'covenant'), as we shall soon note.

There are good reasons for this general context of grace (in *both* of its senses) even in the law covenants within Holy Scripture. More than any other reason, the gracious context of both promissory and law covenants lies in the nature of the Triune God. In a word, the God who is love (cf. 1 John 4:8) has for that reason caused His grace in His relationships with His created order 'much more to abound where sin abounded' (Rom. 5:20).

Pre-temporal aspects of the Covenant of Grace

No reader of Scripture can fail to see that the fall of Adam (under the 'law covenant') and disobedience and deportation of the Israelites (under the Mosaic Covenant) came as no surprise to the eternal God, who arranges every covenant with His sovereign and gracious purposes always in view. That is why even in law covenants, there is an overarching context of divine grace on both sides of them: in their being given and after they have been broken. God foresaw it all and planned it all in terms of His purposes of grace for the cosmos. Not to take this reality of the pre-temporal aspects of the Covenant of Grace into account as we look at law covenants, will cause us to see them outside a context of divine grace, and thereby to miss their larger background and bearings.

Strictly speaking, Scripture never speaks of a pre-temporal economy as 'a covenant'. As John Murray writes: '… the term "covenant" in Scripture refers to temporal administration, and it is not strictly proper to use a biblical term to designate something to which it is not applied in the Scripture itself.'[51] Yet as Murray and virtually all orthodox Reformed scholars believe, God's *eternal plan* included the various covenants with creation, with mankind, and with Israel and the Church; all of which are finally subservient to the kind purposes of His grace. John Murray calls this pre-temporal background of redemptive history 'the inter-trinitarian economy of salvation.'[52]

Rather similarly, the Dutch Reformed theologian, Herman Bavinck draws various terms from Scripture to refer to this same pre-temporal aspect of what will be worked out in space/time history as an overarching Covenant of Grace:

> There is mention made at various points of Scripture of a counsel which precedes things (Isa. 46:10), which works all things (Eph. 1:11), and which has as its content especially the work of redemption (Luke 7:30 and Acts 20:27). This counsel is not a counsel of His mind only but also of His almighty will (Eph. 1:5, 11), is unbreakable (Isa. 14:27 and 26:10), immutable (Heb. 6:17), and will stand forever (Ps. 33:11 and Prov. 19:21). Other names are also used, and shed further light on the matter; besides *counsel*, we read of a *good pleasure* which God has manifested to men in Christ (Luke 2:14),

---

[51] John Murray, *Collected Writings*, vol. 2, 130.

[52] Ibid.

> and which delights in their being brought in and accepted as children of God (Eph. 1:5 and 9). We read of a *purpose* which goes about the work of election (Rom. 9:11 and Eph. 1:9), which is purposed in Christ Jesus (Eph. 3:11), and which realizes itself in the calling of those who love God (Rom. 8:28). We read, further, of an *election* and *foreknowledge* which has its source in grace (Rom. 11:5) and which has Christ as its center (Eph. 1:4), particular persons as its object (Rom. 8:29), and their salvation as its purpose (Eph. 1:4). And finally, we read of an *ordination* or *foreordination* which by means of the proclaiming of the wisdom of God (1 Cor. 2:7) culminates in the adoption of children by Jesus Christ to Himself and in eternal life.[53]

Many of the seventeenth-century Puritans in Britain and orthodox Reformed on the continent referred to this pre-temporal reality as 'the Covenant of Redemption'. It is notable that the 1640s' Westminster Confession of Faith refrains from using this terminology, no doubt considering it as speculative (as to its *term* as a covenant before history, but not as to its *contents*). John Owen describes this as God's 'eternal counsel' at length, in Trinitarian fashion in his *The Death of Death in the Death of Christ*.[54] The Scottish theologian Thomas Boston (in 1734) also dealt with the pre-temporal aspect of the Covenant of Grace, not as 'the Covenant of Redemption', but rather as a 'covenant completely made from eternity.'[55] Herman Witsius speaks of this pre-temporal plan as a covenant or compact between the Father and the Son as Mediator (as its basis), and between God and the elect (as its outworking). Both of these eternal aspects are called by Witsius 'the Covenant of Grace.'[56] Seventeenth-century Scottish theologians David Dickson[57] and Samuel Rutherford[58] both spoke of 'the Covenant of Redemption,' as did the famous 'Sum of Saving Knowledge', so frequently bound with editions of the Westminster Confession of Faith in Scotland.[59]

Apart from valid issues of terminology (e.g. even if this is not 'a *Covenant* of Redemption'), the point is that the same Scriptures which trace so much of redemption through the historical development of various covenants, clearly teach that these covenants are part of the larger plan of the grace of the Triune God for His creation in general and for His people in particular. That is why we must view even law covenants in a larger context of grace, in which the very legal requirements, which (after the fall) will not be met by mankind (except for One divine/human substitute), actually hasten the purposes of grace. That is, 'royal grants' or 'promise covenants' on their very surface make grace a reality, but also 'suzerainty treaties' or 'law covenants', in a very different form and different mode, subserve the purposes of divine grace to the undeserving, although on first glance they

---

53 Herman Bavinck, *Our Reasonable Faith: A Survey of Christian Doctrine*, English translation (Grand Rapids, MI: Baker, 1977 reprint), 266.

54 John Owen, *The Death of Death in the Death of Christ*, in *Works*, vol. 10, chapters 3, 4, 5 (163-179).

55 Thomas Boston, *A View of the Covenant of Grace* (Choteau, MT: Old Paths Gospel Press, 1990 reprint of 1734 edition), 11.

56 Witsius, op. cit., 165.

57 David Dickson, *Therapeutica Sacra*, English translation (Edinburgh, 1664).

58 Samuel Rutherford, *The Tryal & Triumph of Faith* (London, 1645).

59 'Head II.'

seem to do the contrary. We shall later see that it is the Apostle Paul who most lucidly shows just how this works, and how it does *not* work.

The Noahic Covenant

As we have seen, 'covenant' is not specifically used of pre-temporal arrangements in Scripture. Its first usage is found in Genesis chapters 6 to 9, when God promised Noah and all his descendants (which includes the entire human race after him) to maintain the stability of nature, and specifically not to send another flood. As Michael Horton notes, 'The Noachian covenant too was a one-sided promise on God's part, with no conditions attached...'[60] The covenant with Noah is therefore in the form of a promise covenant, or an unconditional royal grant; not a law (or conditional) covenant.

Francis Turretin rightly emphasizes the unconditional promise aspect of this covenant:

> Covenant is sometimes taken more broadly for a simple promise of God without the stipulation of any obedience on the part of the creature – such as is the covenant he made with men and living things of the earth, not to destroy them anymore by a flood (which was also sealed by the rainbow, Gen. 9:9-11) – and that mentioned in Jeremiah 31:35 and 33:25 which disposes and preserves the changes of day and night and the ordinances of heaven and earth (called moreover one-sided [*monopleuron*] because it consists in the disposition of promise of one party only).[61]

Pierre Courthial sees the Covenant with Noah as a renewal and confirmation of the Covenant of Grace.[62] He relates the animal sacrifices offered by Noah after he came out of the Ark to the animals sacrificed by Abel (Gen. 4:4).[63] Courthial, following many church fathers, also relates the blood sacrifices by Noah to the coats of animal skins given by God to fallen Adam and Eve:

> God's grace is signified and sealed by God's providing Adam and Eve with coats of skin (Gen. 3:20-21). These coats of skin speak sacramentally ahead of time of redemption, prefigured by the blood of provisional sacrifices, which were repeated throughout the ancient disposition of the Covenant, and finally accomplished once for all in the unique and perfect sacrifice of Christ Jesus.[64]

Thus, the Covenant with Noah is a clear illustration of the definition of covenant given by O. Palmer Robertson: 'a bond in blood, sovereignly administered.'[65] John Murray notes five characteristics of the covenant with Noah:

> 1. It is God's covenant in that it is conceived, devised, determined, established, confirmed and dispensed by God Himself (Gen. 9:9).

---

[60] M. Horton, op. cit., 17.

[61] Turretin, op. cit., vol. 1, Eighth Topic, 574.

[62] Courthial, op. cit., 11.

[63] Ibid.

[64] Ibid., 10.

[65] Robertson, op. cit., 56. Robertson points out however that the usual phrase 'to cut a covenant' is not used in the covenant with Moses. According to Dumbrell, the lack of this phrase indicates that this is a *renewal* of the covenant, not the *initiation* of a new one (cf. p. 6 of this chapter, n. 33).

> 2. It is universal in its scope, a covenant not only with Noah but with his seed after him and with every living creature (verses 9, 10). This places in obvious relief the fact that it affects for good even those who do not have any intelligent understanding of its meaning... It is a covenant with all flesh.
>
> 3. It is an unconditional covenant... And there is not the slightest suggestion to the effect that the covenant could be annulled by human unfaithfulness or its blessings forfeited by unbelief; the thought of breaking the covenant is inconceivable. The confirmation given is to the opposite effect. In a word, the promise is unconditional.
>
> 4. The covenant is intensively and pervasively monergistic (Gen. 9:16)...
>
> 5. It is an everlasting covenant. (Gen. 9:11)... Perpetuity and divinity are complementary and mutually interdependent... We may think of Noah as co-operating with God in carrying out the provisions of the covenant but the co-operation is quite foreign to that of pact or convention. It is the co-operation of response which the grace of the covenant constrains and demands.[66]

The Covenant with Abraham

God's sovereign, unconditional Covenant with Abraham is the very heart of the Covenant of Grace in Holy Scripture. It is a high exemplification of the type of covenant known as 'the royal grant.' Michael Horton calls it 'purely promissory' and contrasts it to the Sinaitic Covenant, which 'is certainly represented as conditioning Israel's national status by the works of the law...'[67]

John Murray finds new features in the Abrahamic Covenant:

> First, (Gen. 15:8-18) is 'the solemn sanction by which the Lord confirmed to Abraham the certainty that he would inherit the land of Canaan ... a self-maledictory oath in which, anthropomorphically, God calls upon Himself the curse of dismemberment if He does not fulfil to Abraham the promise of possessing the land...
>
> Second, 'The distinctiveness of the sanction and the added solemnity which it involves are correlative with the intimacy and spirituality of the blessing which the covenant imparts. The essence of the blessing is that God will be the God of Abraham and of his seed, the characteristic promise of the Old Testament, "I will be your God, and ye shall be my people." In a word, this consists in union and communion with the Lord.'[68]

Abraham gave the God-ordained response to the 'purely promissory' covenant: faith. 'Abraham believed in the Lord and he counted it to him for righteousness' (Gen. 15:6, also cited in Rom. 4:3; Gal. 3:6; and James 2:23). Abraham demonstrated his faith in the promises of God for his seed by the rite of circumcision.

God at this point instituted circumcision as a sacramental sign of this phase of the Covenant of Grace. 'This sacrament (cf. Gen. 17:9-14 and 23-27)

---

[66] John Murray, *The Covenant of Grace* (Phillipsburg, NJ: Presbyterian and Reformed, 1988), 12-16.

[67] Horton, op. cit., 100.

[68] Murray, op. cit., 16,17.

sealed the triple promise made by the Lord to the father of the faithful; a promise inscribed as it were in the very bodies of the male members of the Covenant of Grace.'[69]

In this Abrahamic Covenant, 'The grace bestowed and the relation established do not wait for the fulfilment of certain conditions on the part of those to whom the grace is dispensed. Grace is bestowed and the relation established by sovereign divine administration…'[70] Or as Murray says, regarding the requirement of exercising faith within the promise-type covenant, '… keeping the covenant presupposes the covenant relation as established rather than the condition upon which its establishment is contingent.'[71]

That is why the Apostle Paul so frequently harks back to Abraham and the promissory, faith covenant that God established with him and his seed, as the essence of true Judaism, and a prime illustration of the gospel of grace in which we are saved through faith in God's promise, and not by works of the law (e.g. Rom. 4 and Gal. 3). We must presently return in some detail to the Pauline interpretation of the Covenant with Abraham.

The Mosaic (Sinaitic) Covenant

Meredith Kline develops in more detail the connection drawn by George Mendenhall between *the form* (though *not* content or spirit) of fourteenth and thirteenth century B.C. Hittite suzerainty treaties and the Mosaic Covenant. '…"covenant" in these divine-human transactions denoted a law covenant…'[72] Michael Horton more recently shows the similarities:

> The covenant at Sinai certainly bears the marks of a suzerainty treaty. In fact, the exact form is followed in Exodus 19 and 20 as well as in Deuteronomy 5: Yahweh identifies himself as the suzerain (preamble), with a brief historical prologue citing his deliverance of the people from Egypt, followed by the Ten Commandments (stipulations), with clear warnings (sanctions) about violating the treaty to which they have sworn their allegiance. The covenant of Joshua 24 follows this pattern as well.[73]

A characteristic of a covenant that is primarily a law covenant is its conditionality. Obedience to God's Law given at Sinai is the condition for Israel's remaining in the Promised Land, as we see particularly in Deuteronomy, chapters 8 and 28, and in Joshua 24. As Horton says: 'Remaining in the land is therefore conditional on Israel's personal performance of the stipulations that the people swore at Sinai.'[74] However, I would add that God's unconditional love relationship to the sinning people continues, even after they have broken the conditional covenant, and have been put out of the land.

---

[69] Courthial, op. cit., 17,18.
[70] Murray, *The Covenant of Grace*, 19.
[71] Ibid.
[72] Kline, op. cit., 21.
[73] Horton, op. cit., 13.
[74] Ibid., 15.

Thus, in traditional theological terms, one must say that while the primary form of the Mosaic Covenant is legal and conditional, still it is preceded by grace and followed by grace. As Alec Vidler wrote: 'Notice that in the Old Testament story this [the giving of the law at Sinai] comes after the deliverance of the Israelites from bondage in Egypt. It is to a people whom He has already redeemed and blessed that God declares His commandments and promulgates His Law. He gives His Law in its sternness and rigour to enable His people to respond to a deliverance which He has already wrought.'[75]

There is therefore a profound sense in which the Mosaic Covenant, though in primary form a law covenant, is bounded within the gracious promises of an earlier covenant: the Abrahamic, and indeed, exemplifies important elements of grace within itself. David L. Baker correctly notes that:

> ... the Mosaic covenant is a confirmation and elaboration of that made with Abraham, not something new or different... Thus 'the covenant at Sinai is a specific covenant within the context of the Abrahamic covenant' [quoting Terence E. Freitheim, *Exodus* (Interpretation: Louisville: John Knox, 1991)], made with an already existing covenant community.[76]

And in the very heart of this law covenant are the divine provisions of grace: the sprinkling of the blood of animal substitutes – 'the blood of the covenant' (Exod. 24:8), and the mediatorship of Moses, who regularly 'stood in the gap' (in terms of Ezek. 22:30) for a disobedient people, and by his intercession saved them from destruction (cf. Exod. 32 and Deut. 9). The law covenant with Moses was never legalistic, for these provisions of sacrifice and intercession are provisions of an overarching Covenant of Grace, in which the Mosaic covenant played its own part in advancing redemption.

One of the major ways the Mosaic Covenant (following the Exodus event) advanced the history of redemption from the time of Abraham was its constitution of Israel as a people out of clans and families.[77] Courthial shows that the constitution of this holy nation in Moses' time was actually a specific fulfillment of God's promise of grace to Abraham to make of him a great people.

> ... Here are the people of the first promise made to Abraham, and now accomplished: *the people of Israel*. After Genesis 50:20, and in the rest of the Torah, God will say 'my people' as he was already saying 'my covenant'; 'I have surely seen the misery of my people in Egypt' (Exod. 3:7); 'I will take you to be my people' (Exod. 6:7). And Moses will say later to Israel: 'The Lord has taken you and brought you out of the furnace of iron in Egypt so

---

[75] Alec R. Vidler, *Christ's Strange Work* (London: Longmans, Green and Co, 1944), 6.

[76] *The God of Covenant: Biblical, Theological and Contemporary Perspectives*, Edited by Jamie A. Grant and Alistair I. Wilson (Leicester: Apollos: Intervarsity Press, 2005), 25,26.

[77] Even more significant than the constitution of Israel as a people in the Mosaic economy, was – as Paul shows us – its revealing the horrendous nature of sin and of one's need of a Saviour, who saves us by sheer grace. In that way the Mosaic economy powerfully advanced redemption (cf. 2 Cor. 3 and Gal. 3). And of course, basic to this revelation of sin and grace, is the primary message of Sinai: the unveiling of the holy character of God as summarized in the moral law.

> that you might be a people of his heritage' (Deut. 4:20). 'Thou art a holy people for the Lord thy God, and the Lord has chosen you to be a people of his possession from among all the peoples who are on the face of the earth (Deut. 14:2).'[78]

When at length the people arrogantly and continually across many generations broke this law covenant 'with a high hand' by giving themselves over to idolatry, they were indeed removed from the land into Babylonian captivity, for not having fulfilled its central condition of loyalty to the Lord. But deportation was not God's last word to them. Here again we find, as we did with Adam, the movement of grace/law/grace.

The fuller historical revelation of divine covenantal grace is advanced in the next major covenant that follows the one with Moses: the Davidic Covenant. This one partakes of the promissory character of the Covenant with Abraham, and does not have the conditionality of that with Moses.

The Davidic Covenant

G. Mendenhall properly pointed out that the covenant with David was unlike that with Moses, but instead, like that with Abraham:

> ... in the time of David, the tradition of the covenant with Abraham became the pattern of a covenant between Yahweh and David, whereby Yahweh promised to maintain the Davidic line on the throne (2 Sam. 23:5). Yahweh bound Himself, exactly as in the Abrahamic and Noachite covenant, and therefore Israel could not escape responsibility to the king. The covenant with Abraham was the 'prophecy' and that with David the 'fulfilment.'[79]

Psalm 89:3, 4 speaks of the promise made by God to David (in 2 Sam. 7:12-17) as a covenant: 'I have made a covenant with my chosen, I have sworn unto David my servant: thy seed will I establish for ever, and build up thy throne to all generations.' Its unconditionality is shown in Psalm 89:34: 'My covenant will I not break, nor alter the thing that is gone out of my lips.' And David gladly responds to this promise that depends on the Lord, not on himself: 'Verily my house is not so with God; yet he hath made with me an everlasting covenant, ordered in all things, and sure: for it is all my salvation, and all my desire, although he maketh it not to grow' (2 Sam. 23:5).

Horton shows the close connection of the Davidic to the Abrahamic:

> In 2 Samuel 7 the pure divine condescension (promissory covenant) is underscored (esp. v. 5, with the emphatic 'you'). David wants to build a house for God, but the Davidic covenant is a unilateral promise from God to build a house for David... The Abrahamic covenant will not be realized in history if it is in any way dependent on the zeal of his sinful people. If the promise is going to become a reality, it is Yahweh himself who will have to make it happen. 'It is this promise of an eternal royal line that essentially constitutes the covenant with David,' [Steven] McKenzie notes.[80]

---

[78] Courthial, op. cit., 21, 22.

[79] Mendenhall, op. cit., 46.

[80] Steven L. McKenzie, *Covenant* (St. Louis: Chalice Press, 2000), 66, quoted in Horton, op. cit., 18.

The promissory covenant to David, with its unconditional provision of an eternal royal line, advances the 'seed' of Eve and the 'seed' of Abraham, as it reaches forward to the New Covenant in which, according to the most quoted Old Testament passage in the New Testament (messianic Ps. 110): 'The LORD said unto my Lord, Sit thou at my right hand, until I make thine enemies thy footstool. The LORD shall send the rod of thy strength out of Zion: rule thou in the midst of thine enemies' (vv. 1, 2). This shows us that the main focus of the Davidic phase of the one Covenant of Grace is God's unconditional promise of a Messiah, 'great David's greater Son', as the hymn writer phrased it. John Murray shows the nature of this bright Messianic focus in the promises to David:

> These Davidic promises are, of course, messianic; it is in Christ that David's seed is established for ever and his throne built up to all generations. In this connection we cannot overlook the relevance of those passages in Isaiah in which the servant of the Lord is said to be given for a covenant of the people. The prophet introduces this messianic personage with the words, 'Behold, my servant, whom I uphold; mine elect in whom my soul delighteth' (Isa. xlii. 1)... The co-ordination of Isa. lv. 3,4 is equally significant: 'Incline your ear, and come unto me; hear, and your soul shall live; and I will make an everlasting covenant with you, even the sure mercies of David. Behold, I have given him for a witness to the peoples, a leader and a commander to the peoples' (R.V.).[81]

This Messianic development in the Covenant of Grace brings us to:

The New Covenant

The New Covenant is described at length in Jeremiah 31, and quoted and amplified in Hebrews 8 and 10. The content of both 'Old' (or Mosaic) and 'New' is much the same: love to God and neighbour (hence, the fulfilling of God's immutable moral law), but the difference lies in the spirit by which it is accomplished. In the New Covenant, God by the supernatural efficacy of His Holy Spirit so changes the human heart that His divine law is actually written upon a renewed heart of flesh, not external tables of stone:

> ... After those days, saith the LORD, I will put my law in their inward parts, and write it in their hearts; and will be their God, and they shall be my people. And they shall teach no more every man his neighbour, and every man his brother, saying, Know the LORD: for they shall all know me, from the least of them unto the greatest of them, saith the LORD: for I will forgive their iniquity, and I will remember their sin no more (Jer. 31:33,34; cf. Heb. 8:1-7; 10:16,17).

John Murray shows how the New Testament interprets the other covenants of the Old Testament as leading up to the New Covenant:

> ...the new covenant is the fulfilment of the covenant made with Abraham (Luke 1:72; Gal. 3:15ff.)... We can express the fact that the new covenant is the expansion and fulfilment of the Abrahamic by saying that it was just because the promise to Abraham had the bonded and oath-bound character

[81] Murray, op. cit., 23, 24.

> of a covenant that its realization in the fullness of the time was inviolably certain…the features of the covenant [in the New Testament] are the same as those we found in connection with covenant in the Old Testament…When we turn to the Epistle to the Hebrews and particularly to those passages in which the contrast is drawn between the inferiority of the Mosaic covenant and the transcendent excellence of the new and better covenant we find that the conception of covenant which we have already found is applied to the highest degree…For it is the new covenant *par excellence* which brings to realization the promise 'I will be to them a God, and they shall be to me a people' (Heb. 8:6). In other words, the spiritual relationship which lay at the centre of the covenant grace disclosed in both the Abrahamic and Mosaic covenants reaches its ripest fruition in the new covenant…The superiority of the new does not consist in the abrogation of that law but in its being brought into more intimate relation to us and more effective fulfilment in us. 'I will put my laws into their mind, and upon their hearts will I write them' (Heb. 8:10).[82]

Murray concludes:

> Preponderantly in the usage of Scripture covenant refers to grace and promise specifically redemptive. The successive covenants are coeval with the successive epochs in the unfolding and accomplishment of God's redemptive will ... the epochal strides in the unfolding of redemptive revelation are at the same time epochal advances in the disclosure of the riches of covenant grace… At the centre of covenant redemption as its constant refrain is the assurance 'I will be your God, and ye shall be my people'… The mediator of the new covenant is none other than God's own Son, the effulgence of the Father's glory and the express image of His substance, the heir of all things… Grace and truth, promise and fulfilment, have in this covenant received their *pleroma*, and it is in terms of the new covenant that it will be said, 'Behold, the tabernacle of God is with men, and he will dwell with them, and they shall be his people, and God himself shall be with them' (Rev. 21:3).[83]

Only one covenant

Dumbrell agrees with the seventeenth-century Reformed theologians that, although many covenants are spoken of in Holy Scripture, ultimately there is only *one* covenant:

> It would follow from our analysis of Gen. 1–9 that there can be only one divine covenant, and also that any theology of covenant must begin with Genesis 1:1. All else in covenant theology which progressively occurs in the Old Testament will be deducible from this basic relationship, and we shall have occasion to note the chain of connection which having moved from creation to Noah, leads us from Noah to Abraham, from Abraham to Sinai, to David, to the Jeremianic new covenant and thence to Jesus its fulfiller. In postulating a unity for biblical theology in covenant, the older reformed theologians were entirely correct.[84]

The establishment and confirmation of the one Covenant of Grace underlying the whole of the history of creation and redemption given

---

[82] John Murray, op. cit., 27, 28.
[83] Ibid., 31,32.
[84] Dumbrell, op. cit., 42.

us in the Scriptures is a sign of the royal lordship of God our King: 'The presupposition of covenant is the present kingship of God.'[85] God sovereignly created the world and placed mankind, His image-bearers, in it, so they might know Him in a community of love, shared life and obedience. That is, God arranged covenant conditions for them, so that they might know Him within the believing, obeying community which He sets up by virtue of His gracious covenant. It is to this covenant community that He reveals Himself; first, to its original parents, Adam and Eve, and then to their descendants: particularly Noah (who represents all mankind) and then Abraham (who represents the community of saving faith, both Israel and the Church). All of these covenantal administrations lead up to the New Covenant, as Robertson demonstrates:

> The primary covenants in Scripture are those made with Noah, Abraham, Moses, David, and the new covenant. In addition, strong evidence favors viewing the original creation relationship between God and man, as well as the first bond established by God with man after the fall, as covenantal.[86]

Robertson goes on to trace the unity of these covenants from two perspectives: (1) *structural unity* and (2) *thematic unity*.

(1) Structural unity of the covenants.

'The Abrahamic, Mosaic and Davidic covenants do not present themselves as self-contained entities. Instead, each successive covenant builds on the previous relationship, continuing the basic emphasis which had been established earlier. The unity of these three covenants is seen particularly in the historical experience of Israel, and in the genealogical emphasis of Scripture.'[87]

Robertson finds this *structural unity* expressed in three different ways:

> (a) This unity is seen in how each of the covenants is *inaugurated*. 'To set aside a people to himself, God established his covenant with Abraham. Subsequently Abraham's descendants lived also under the Mosaic and Davidic covenants. At those points in history in which God initiated the new covenantal relationships under Moses and David, evidence indicates that God was intending to bring to a further stage of development the same redemption that had been promised earlier. Instead of "wiping clean the slate" and beginning anew, each successive covenant with Abraham's descendants advanced the original purposes of God to a higher level of realization.'[88]

> (b) This unity is displayed in *the history of life under the covenants*. 'Once the Mosaic covenant has been inaugurated, it is not as though the Abrahamic covenant were "shelved" for the duration. Much to the contrary, the history after Sinai continues to center on the old original promises to the patriarchs… The Mosaic covenant did not annul or interrupt the Abrahamic covenant. The Abrahamic covenant continued to function actively after the institution

---

[85] Ibid.
[86] Robertson, op. cit., 27.
[87] Ibid., 28.
[88] Ibid., 29.

> of the Mosaic covenant...the Davidic covenant in its turn did not annul or interrupt the Mosaic covenant. Each of the basic triumphs and tragedies of David and his sons may be seen as the outworking of the stipulations of the Mosaic covenant.'[89]

In sum, 'The Abrahamic, Mosaic, and Davidic covenants do not supplant one another; they supplement one another. A basic unity binds them together.'[90]

> (c) This unity of the covenants is also seen in *genealogical administration*. 'When God determined to relate to a people covenantally, he made his arrangement a genealogical one...present in the Abrahamic, the Mosaic, and the Davidic covenants. It is manifested specifically in the reference to the "seed"-concept (cf. Gen. 15:18; Exod. 20:5,6; Deut. 7:9; 2 Sam. 7:12). David's son is not simply heir of the covenant promise made to David. He is heir also of the covenant promises made to Moses and Abraham. The genealogical promises of God's covenants assure his participation in the blessings of the Abrahamic and the Mosaic as well as in the Davidic covenant.'[91]

Crucial covenant texts in Scripture emphasize this genealogical unity running through the various covenants. Deuteronomy 5:2,3: 'The LORD our God made a covenant with us in Horeb. The LORD made not this covenant with our fathers, but with us, even us, who are all of us here alive this day.' Many of those alive in the plains of Moab when Moses was speaking, had not been born when God gave His Law on Sinai. Yet because of solidarity with their ancestors, they had indeed been present – even before their birth. This same concept is used in Hebrews 7:5-10 to state that the Aaronic priestly line had paid tithes to Melchizedek, mysterious priest-king of Salem, to whom their ancestor, Abraham, had given tithes (in Genesis 14). Aaron 'was yet in the loins of his father, when Melchizedek met Abraham.'

This genealogical unity of the covenants is further demonstrated in Deuteronomy and the Psalms. In Deuteronomy 29:13-14: 'That he may establish thee today for a people unto himself, and that he may be unto thee a God, as he hath said unto thee, and as he hath sworn unto thy fathers, to Abraham, to Isaac, and to Jacob. Neither with you only do I make this covenant and this oath...' Psalm 105:8-10 shows God's faithful remembrance over the generations of his covenant promise to Abraham: 'He hath remembered His covenant for ever, the word which he commanded to a thousand generations. Which covenant he made with Abraham, and his oath unto Isaac. And confirmed the same unto Jacob for a law, and to Israel for an everlasting covenant.'

The same genealogical faithfulness of the Lord to His servants' descendants is shown in Deuteronomy 7:9 and Isaiah 59:21: 'Know therefore that the LORD thy God, he is God, the faithful God, which keepeth covenant and mercy with them that love him, and keep his commandments to a thousand generations' (Deut. 7:9). 'As for me, this is my covenant with

---

[89] Robertson, op. cit., 32, 33.
[90] Ibid., 34.
[91] Ibid., 35.

them, saith the LORD; my spirit that is upon thee, and my words which I have put in thy mouth, shall not depart out of thy mouth, nor out of the mouth of thy seed, nor out of the mouth of thy seed's seed, saith the LORD, from henceforth and for ever' (Isa. 59:21).

The apostles Peter and Paul both counted on God's faithful remembrance over the generations to the remote seed of Abraham. Peter said in his sermon to the Jewish people after the crucifixion and resurrection of Christ: 'Ye are the children of the prophets, and of the covenant which God made with our fathers, saying unto Abraham, And in thy seed shall all the kindreds of the earth be blessed' (Acts 3:25). Paul sees the gift of the Spirit to believing Gentiles as a fulfillment of the covenant promises to Abraham: 'That the blessing of Abraham might come on the Gentiles through Jesus Christ: that we might receive the promise of the Spirit through faith' (Gal. 3:14).

Involved in this expansion of the blessings of the Abrahamic Covenant to the Gentiles is the principle of engrafting. By it, people of all nations become part of the people of God; that is, true Israelites (Gal. 3:29). Paul in Romans 11 shows that believing Gentiles are grafted in to the ancient stock of the true Israel: 'For if the firstfruit be holy, the lump is also holy: and if the root be holy, so are the branches. And if some of the branches be broken off, and thou, being a wild olive tree, wert grafted in among them, and with them partakest of the root and fatness of the olive tree; Boast not against the branches. But if thou boast, thou bearest not the root, but the root thee' (Rom. 11:16-18).

Superiority of the New Covenant within the one Covenant of Grace

The greatest development within the various covenants is that envisaged in Jeremiah 31 and Hebrews chapters 7, 8, 9 and 10, where we are shown the contrast between the old and the new covenants. Hebrews 7–10 seems to have in mind as 'old covenant' the Mosaic Covenant, and contrasts it sharply in emphasis (though not in essential content) to the New Covenant. As John Murray has pointed out, the chief difference between old and new covenants here is not between works and grace, or between law and promise, but between two different orders of priesthood.[92]

The inferiority of the old order reposes in the fact that its Aaronic priests had continually to renew their sacrifices, and to be replaced by other priests after their own deaths (Heb. 7:23). But Jesus, the final and great High Priest 'continueth ever, having an unchangeable priesthood' (Heb. 7:24). The animal sacrifices offered by the Aaronic priest could only *cover* sins temporarily (Heb. 10:4), whereas the once-for-all sacrifice of Christ (the priest after the order of Melchizedek) forever *removes* all sin (Heb. 10:10, 14). Our great High Priest, unlike the order of Aaron, which had daily to minister sacrifices that could finally never take away sins (Heb. 9:25; 10:11), 'after he had offered one sacrifice for sin for ever, sat down on the right hand of God' (Heb. 10:12), having by his own precious blood 'entered in once into

[92] John Murray, class notes (unpublished), 1962–1963.

the holy place, having obtained eternal redemption for us' (Heb. 9:12). That 'holy place' is the heavenly sanctuary, of which the holy place of tabernacle and temple were but earthly and temporary copies (Heb. 9:23, 24).

The New Covenant excels the Old (or Mosaic) because its final and perfect sacrifice conveys the blessing of the Holy Spirit in a new and fuller way into the hearts of believers, so that as Jeremiah 31:33, 34 promises (taken up and explicated in Hebrews):

> For this is the covenant that I will make with the house of Israel after those days, saith the Lord: I will put my laws into their mind, and write them in their hearts: and I will be to them a God, and they shall be to me a people: And they shall not teach every man his neighbour, and every man his brother, saying, Know the Lord: for all shall know me, from the least to the greatest. For I will be merciful to their unrighteousness, and their sins and their iniquities will I remember no more. In that he saith, A new covenant, he hath made the first old. Now that which decayeth and waxeth old is ready to vanish away (Heb. 8:10-13).

Thus, the New Covenant surpasses the Old in its perfect and final sacrifice, and therefore in its conveyance of the Spirit to the hearts of believers. But it does not contradict the Old, for both were based on faith in the promises of God (as Hebrews 11 shows to be the case with the Old Testament saints), and both have as 'their sum and substance' God as our God, and we as his people. Thus, from creational, to Noahic, to Abrahamic, to Mosaic to New, there is a profound unity underlying the development and distinctions between all the covenants.

David L. Baker isolates the central element of the New Covenant (i.e. its *new* characteristic) which makes it superior to all the others:

> One important characteristic of the new covenant, according to Jeremiah 31:34a, is *personal knowledge of God*… The great commandment of Deuteronomy 6:4-9 makes love of God the prime responsibility of his people, and a relationship of love surely presupposes personal knowledge, but this is implicit rather than explicit. So the explicitness and universality in Jeremiah's prophecy is new. Just as God knows his people intimately (Exod. 33:17; Jer. 1:5) and loves them passionately (Exod. 34:6-7; Deut. 7:6-9; Ps. 103:13; Isa. 43:1-4), the prophets make clear that he longs for them to know and love him (Jer. 9:24; Hosea 6:4, 6; 11:1-11). In the new covenant such unmediated knowledge of God will be a daily reality for every member of the community… Knowledge of God will no longer be restricted to a few privileged individuals but will become a reality for all (Jeremiah 31:34). And at last God's passionate love for his people will be reciprocated (Hosea 2:14-23).[93]

As Robertson reminds us: 'Because of this continuing relationship of creature to Creator, it may be said also of the original bond of God to man that it continues to have abiding significance. The covenantal relation established by creation permeates the whole history of God's forming a people for himself.'[94]

---

[93] Baker, 'Covenant: An Old Testament Study', in Grant and Wilson, op. cit., 48, 49.

[94] Robertson, op. cit., 45.

In addition to (1) the *Structural Unity of the Covenants*, Robertson has also pointed out (2) the *Thematic Unity of the Covenants*. This unity also leads up to the climax of all the administrations within the Covenant of Grace, consisting in personal knowledge of the Triune God, beyond which there is nothing greater.

(2) Thematic unity of the covenants

'This unity of theme is the heart of the covenant as it relates God to his people. Throughout the biblical record of God's administration of the covenant, a single phrase recurs as the summation of the covenant relationship: "I shall be your God, and you shall be my people..." This phrase may be designated as the "Immanuel principle" of the covenant. The heart of the covenant is the declaration that "God is with us."'[95]

Robertson notes three main points about 'the Immanuel principle':

> (a) *This theme appears explicitly in connection with the Abrahamic, the Mosaic, the Davidic, and the new covenant.*[96] In the Old Testament, one can compare Genesis 17:7; Exodus 6:6, 7; 19:4, 5; Leviticus 11:45; Deuteronomy 4:20; 29:13; 2 Kings 11:17; 2 Chronicles 23:16; Jeremiah 24:7; 31:33; 32:37f.; Ezekiel 34:24; Zechariah 2:11; 8:8. In the New Testament, one can compare 2 Corinthians 6:16; Hebrews 8:10; and Revelation 21:3.
>
> (b) *This theme* 'I shall be your God and you shall be my people' *is developed particularly in association with God's actually dwelling in the midst of his people.*[97] Ezekiel 37:26-28 says: 'Moreover I will make a covenant of peace with them; it shall be an everlasting covenant with them: and I will place them, and multiply them, and will set my sanctuary in the midst of them for evermore. My tabernacle also shall be with them; yea, I will be their God, and they shall be my people. And the heathen shall know that I the LORD do sanctify Israel, when my sanctuary shall be in the midst of them for evermore.'
>
> This is taken up in the prologue to John's Gospel: 'And the Word was made flesh, and dwelt among us, (and we beheld his glory, the glory as of the only begotten of the Father,) full of grace and truth' (John 1:14). Because of the incarnation, holy life, crucifixion and resurrection of the Word (the eternal Son of God), the Holy Spirit is poured out, and unites all believers to this incarnate Word in His death and resurrection (cf. Rom. 6; Gal. 2:20). God's people are thereby the temple of the Lord (Eph. 2:21f.).
>
> (c) *The theme* 'I shall be your God and you shall be my people' *reaches its climax through its embodiment in a single person.* Not in the tabernacle, but in Christ the covenant theme finds consummate fulfilment.[98]

Isaiah focuses on this person, who is chosen to suffer for His people (cf. Isa. 52:13–53:12), and is appointed to be 'a covenant to the people, and a light to the nations' (Isa. 42:6; cf. Isa. 49:8; 55:3,4).

> It is not 'the' blood of the covenant that he administers, as does Moses (Exod. 24:8). Instead he solemnly declares 'this is *my* blood of the covenant...' (Matt. 26:28; cf. Luke 22:20)... In the person of Jesus Christ, the covenants

[95] Ibid., 45, 46.

[96] Ibid., 46.

[97] Ibid., 49.

[98] Ibid., 51.

> of God achieve incarnational unity. Because Jesus, as the Son of God and mediator of the covenant, cannot be divided, the covenants cannot be divided. He himself guarantees the unity of the covenants, because he himself is the heart of each of the various covenantal administrations.[99]

Tertullian clearly caught sight of the central focus of the New Covenant in the early third century as true personal knowledge of the Triune God: 'It was God's will to make a new covenant for the very purpose that in a new way His unity might be believed in, through the Son and the Spirit, so that God who had aforetime been preached through the Son and the Spirit without being understood might now be known in His own proper names and persons.'[100]

'Lumen Gentium' ('The Light of the Gentiles' – 'The Mystery of the Church'), which is the first chapter of the Documents of the Second Vatican Council, shows the oneness of the Covenant of Grace throughout the Scriptures, as it comes to focus in Christ and His Church:

> The Church is a tract of land to be cultivated, the field of God (1 Cor. 3:9). On that land grows the ancient olive tree whose holy roots were the patriarchs and in which the reconciliation of Jew and Gentile has been brought about and will be brought about (Rom. 11:13-26). The Church has been cultivated by the heavenly Vinedresser as His choice vineyard (Matt. 21:33-43 par.; cf. Isa. 5:1ff.). The true Vine is Christ who gives life and fruitfulness to the branches, that is, to us. Through the Church, we abide in Christ, without whom we can do nothing (John 15:1-5).
>
> The Church has more often been called the edifice of God (1 Cor. 3:9). Even the Lord likened himself to the stone which the builders rejected, but which became the cornerstone (Matt. 21:42 par.; cf. Acts 4:11; 1 Pet. 2:7; Ps. 118:22). On this foundation the Church is built by the apostles (cf. 1 Cor. 3:11), and from it the Church receives durability and solidity… As living stones we here on earth are being built up along with this City (1 Pet. 2:5). John contemplates this Holy City, coming down out of heaven from God when the world is made anew, and prepared like a bride adorned for her husband (Apoc. 21:1f.).[101]

The New Perspective on Paul and the one covenant

Scholars in general sympathy with 'The New Perspective on Paul' base much of their program on the oneness of the covenant in Judaism, and at first glance this seems not far from the traditional Reformed interpretation. Yet Michael S. Horton has recently (2007) argued that they take the concept of 'one covenant' so far that, in consequence, they fail to distinguish between 'law covenant' and 'promise covenant', and thereby offer problematic interpretations of both true Judaism and true Pauline theology.[102]

The New Perspective on Paul is a broad and deep and voluminous phenomenon, and it would require several volumes to convey fairly what

---

[99] Ibid., 51, 52.

[100] Tertullian, *Adversus Praxean*, xxxi.

[101] *The Documents of Vatican II*, Walter M. Abbott, S.J., General Editor (New York: Guild Press, 1966), 18, 19.

[102] Michael S. Horton, *Covenant and Salvation: Union with Christ* (Louisville: Westminster John Knox, 2007).

they have to say. And in addition to the sheer number of their writings, in spite of important commonalities, there are considerable differences among the major proponents of this 'school' of thought (such as James D.G. Dunn,[103] W. D. Davies,[104] E. P. Sanders[105] and N. T. Wright). N. T. Wright's *What Saint Paul Really Said: Was Paul of Tarsus the Real Founder of Christianity* is a useful introduction to their similarities and differences, as is his *The Climax of the Covenant: Christ and the Law in Pauline Theology*.[106] Also, Guy P. Waters has provided a judicious critique of leading members of this influential school of thought.[107]

For the modest purposes of this sub-section on the covenant, I wish merely to summarize some of the central findings of Michael Horton on problematic interpretations of Judaic and Pauline teaching on the covenant by a few of the leading 'New Perspective' scholars. But first, let us note a crucial claim made by most of the NPP proponents. Commenting on E. P. Sanders' work, *Paul and Palestinian Judaism*, N. T. Wright states:

> His major point ... can be quite simply stated. Judaism in Paul's day was not, as has regularly been supposed, a religion of legalistic works-righteousness... Most Protestant exegetes had read Paul and Judaism as if Judaism was a form of the old heresy Pelagianism, according to which humans must pull themselves up by their bootstraps and thereby earn justification... No, said Sanders. Keeping the law within Judaism always functioned within a covenantal scheme. God took the initiative, when he made a covenant with Judaism; God's grace thus precedes everything that people (specifically, Jews) do in response. The Jew keeps the law out of gratitude ... not, in other words, in order to *get into* the covenant people, but to *stay in*. Being 'in' in the first place was God's gift. This scheme Sanders famously labelled as 'covenantal nomism' (from Greek, *nomos*, law). Keeping the Jewish law was the human response to God's covenantal initiative. Sanders thus, at a stroke, cut the ground from under the majority reading of Paul, especially in mainline Protestantism.[108]

He writes that

> Covenantal nomism is the view that one's place in God's plan is established on the basis of the covenant and that the covenant requires as the proper response of man his obedience to its commandments, while providing means of atonement for transgression... Obedience maintains one's position in the covenant, but it does not earn God's grace as such... Righteousness in Judaism is a term which implies the maintenance of status among the group of the elect.[109]

---

[103] E.g. cf. James D. G. Dunn, *Jesus, Paul and the Law: Studies in Mark and Galatians* (Louisville, KY: Westminster/John Knox, 1990).

[104] Cf. W. D. Davies, *Paul and Rabbinic Judaism*, with a Foreword by E. P. Sanders (Mifflintown, PA: Sigler Press: , 1998 reprint of 1948 edition).

[105] Cf. E. P. Sanders, *Paul, the Law, and the Jewish People* (Minneapolis: Fortress Press, 1983), and more briefly, his *Paul: A Very Short Introduction* (Oxford: Oxford University Press, 2001).

[106] N. T. Wright, *What St. Paul Really Taught* (Grand Rapids, MI: Wm. B. Eerdmans, 1997), and his *The Climax of the Covenant* (Minneapolis: Fortress Press, 1992).

[107] Guy Prentiss Waters, *Justification and the New Perspectives on Paul: A Review and Response* (Phillipsburg, NJ: P & R Publishing, 2004).

[108] N. T. Wright, *What St. Paul Really Said*, 18, 19.

[109] Sanders, *Paul*, 75, 420, 544, quoted in J. Dunn, 'The New Perspective on Paul' in *Jesus, Paul and the Law*, 186.

On this basis, Dunn later proffers a very different interpretation of 'works of the law':

> 'Work of law,' 'works of the law' are nowhere understood here, either by his Jewish interlocutors or by Paul himself, as works which earn God's favour, as merit-amassing observances. They are rather seen as badges: they are simply what membership of the covenant people involves, what mark out the Jews as God's people, given by God for precisely that reason, they serve to demonstrate covenant status... In other words, Paul has in view precisely what Sanders calls 'covenantal nomism'...[110]

N. T. Wright agrees that justification is not about getting saved, but about 'signs' that one is already in the covenant community. He states:

> Justification ...is not a matter of how someone enters the community of the true people of God, but of how you tell who belongs to that community... In standard Christian theological language, it wasn't so much about Soteriology as about ecclesiology; not so much about salvation as about the church... What Paul means by justification, in this context, should therefore be clear. It is not 'how you become a Christian', so much as 'how you can tell who is a member of the covenant family'.[111]

The failure to make a necessary covenant distinction

It is clear that the NPP view of the covenant profoundly shapes their understanding of justification (a central doctrine for Christianity) in a contrary direction to that taken by the Reformation.[112] Michael Horton sees a major component of the new assessment of Judaism, Paul and justification in NPP thought as lying in their failure to distinguish the two types of covenant within the redemptive history of Judaism: promise covenants and law covenants. Horton agrees with the NPP that there is certainly such a thing as 'covenant nomism' in historic Judaism. But to take 'covenant nomism' as the norm for salvation (or justification) within the covenant is to ignore one whole line of covenant administration: the promissory, so that one interprets the law covenant as the true issue between 'second Temple Judaism' and the Apostle Paul. Horton states this point:

> To embrace covenantal nomism as an appropriate system for the national covenant of Israel is, I have argued, properly to interpret the old covenant history. However, to embrace it as an appropriate system for answering the question as to how an individual is rightly related to God remains, as it has always been, a confusion of Abraham with Moses, which Paul relates as a confusion of Sarah with Hagar, freedom with bondage, Sinai with Zion, and law with gospel. To put it differently, it is appropriate to treat the earthly promises (land, temple, kingdom) as conditioned upon the covenant people's personal obedience to the law, but fatal in Paul's view to treat the heavenly promises (the new creation, Christ, and his everlasting Davidic reign) as conditioned on the obedience of anyone other than Christ himself.[113]

---

[110] Dunn, op. cit., 194.

[111] Wright, op. cit., 119, 122.

[112] See particularly chapters 4 and 8 of Guy Waters, *Justification and the New Perspectives on Paul*, 35-58; 151-90.

[113] Horton, op. cit., 50.

Horton argues at large that while 'covenantal nomism' was indeed a major aspect of law covenants (such as the Mosaic and Palestinian), it was never the true hope of Israel, for that lay in the promissory covenants: particularly that of Abraham. 'Far different from such covenantal nomism is the expectation that comes from the new covenant, in fulfilment of the royal promises of the Abrahamic and Davidic covenants…'[114] He states that 'Paul distinguishes between *two covenants*, not between *covenant* and *law*. The entire argument of Galatians 3-4 rests on the legal basis for inheriting the Abrahamic promise: it is a covenant "ratified by God," just as was the Sinai covenant 430 years later (Gal. 3:17).'[115]

In a word, Horton believes that

> … Dunn, like the NPP generally, has room for only a single covenant. Since it must be primarily gracious, elements that seem to suggest a different kind of covenant (a conditional law-covenant) must be assimilated. I do not doubt that this approach generally fits Second Temple Judaism. In fact, the conflation of these two covenants (and therefore of law and gospel) is precisely the focus of the Pauline critique.[116]

Horton refers along these lines to C. K. Barrett, as quoted by Graham Stanton:

> As C. K. Barrett notes, 'They probably took the view that the Abrahamic covenant had been redefined by the Sinaitic.' Paul will have none of this. God's covenant with Abraham was based on faith; it was not set aside, supplemented or reinterpreted by the law, given 430 years later… In Paul's re-interpretation of the traditions concerning Abraham's two sons, those who belong to Christ trace their line of descent directly back to Abraham, by-passing completely Mount Sinai and the law.[117]

According to Horton, the NPP's failure to affirm the relevance of two different covenants (law covenant and promise covenant) leads to a sort of reductionism, in which the conditional Sinaitic Covenant submerges the unconditional Abrahamic Covenant, and thus makes it impossible to appreciate the main point of Paul's controversy against the Jews of his day with their insistence on conditional works righteousness, over against Paul's insistence on the sheer faith that accepts the promise of the promissory/grace covenant.

> By contrast [with N. T. Wright who holds monocovenantalism, and explains the difference between law and promise as consisting of different *mediators*, not different *covenants*][118], I would argue that according to Paul (as well as Hebrews), there are more radical reasons why Moses cannot mediate the promised blessing to the world. It is not simply because the Sinai covenant is exclusively concerned with Israel, but also because Christ is the mediator of a better covenant, founded on better promises. Paul's target is

---

114 Ibid., 51.

115 Ibid., 121.

116 Ibid., 82.

117 Ibid.

118 Horton (ibid., 84) refers to N. T. Wright's discussion of Galatians 3:15-18 in Wright's *Climax of the Covenant*, 166.

> the monocovenantalism (covenantal nomism) that, for all their differences, Sanders, Dunn, and Wright seem largely to affirm. The single covenant may undergo ecclesiological redefinition (inclusion of Gentiles), thereby modifying its doctrine of election, but there are not two covenants with distinct foundations (law and promise).
>
> By contrast, when we distinguish these covenants, the Abrahamic/new covenant promises are seen to be better not merely because they include Gentiles, but because they are unconditional, sworn by God himself, with a better ministry (conducted in the heavenly sanctuary), high priest, and sacrifices (in addition to Galatians, see Heb. Esp. 7–10). As the prophets promised, something more radical has appeared with Christ than the renewal of the Sinai covenant and restoration of Israel, only this time ethnically diverse. John's Gospel expresses the decisiveness of the event that Paul elaborates: 'From [Christ's] fullness we have all received, grace upon grace. The law indeed was given through Moses; grace and truth came through Jesus Christ' (John 1:16-17).[119]

Thus, if Horton is right, the NPP is characterized by a sort of reductionism of two kinds of covenants into one, in which it is primarily the Mosaic (or conditional law covenant) which is seen as being the central focus of the renewal that came through Christ, rather than the unconditional royal grant or grace covenant of Abraham.[120] This perspective certainly seems to make much more sense of the arguments against works righteousness raised by St. Paul in Galatians 3 and 4, and by the similar contrasts raised by the writer of Hebrews (in ch. 7 to 10, and 12:18-29). And it helps us understand why the NPP seems to teach a sort of merger between works and grace as concerns one's standing in the covenant, rather than salvation by grace alone through faith alone.

Horton leaves us with the right question:

> This question [is grace subsumed under 'covenantal nomism' of the Mosaic covenant] lies at the heart of the debates over justification. Is the promissory covenant subsumed under (or absorbed into) the covenant of law, resulting in a covenantal nomism? Or are these two covenants always distinguished and, on the point of justification, to be treated as antithetical means of inheriting eternal life?[121]

In sum, although the necessary exegetical work on these issues must wait for the third volume in this systematic theology (where justification is dealt with in detail), we can note here in anticipation that the unconditional, promissory nature of the Abrahamic, Davidic and New covenants is what the Apostle Paul takes as the background of the gospel of salvation by grace through faith in Christ (e.g. as in Rom. 4:1-25; Gal. 3:6-29). Certainly he shows that the Mosaic Covenant is harmonious with the Abrahamic Covenant of promise in that 'it shuts up all under sin, that the promise by faith of Jesus Christ might be given to them that believe' (Gal. 3:22); and even though the glory of the Mosaic is exceedingly surpassed by the

---

[119] Horton, op. cit., 84.

[120] Horton affirms the fact that the Mosaic covenant, conditional and legal though it was, clearly pointed to Christ, op. cit., 19.

[121] Ibid., 29.

glory revealed in Christ (2 Cor. 3:6-18), still it was true glory even in its ministration of death for law-breaking in terms of the concentrated purity of God. It makes sense of the progress of redemption that the focus of the ten commandments on God's holiness, thus showing up our human sinfulness, should come before God's final revelation of grace in Jesus Christ. In that sense, for all its conditionality and condemnatory function, the Mosaic covenant must be seen as playing a grand part in the Covenant of Grace. That is, after the unconditional promise of the Abrahamic Covenant, 'the law was added on account of the transgression until the seed [Christ] should come' (Gal. 3:19). It was an addition; not a suspension or change of principle. In that sense too, the Mosaic Covenant furthered the reign of grace. It also provided salvation for sinners (even before 'the seed came') through blood sacrifices and mediatorship. So, in a very real sense, the Mosaic is part of the overarching Covenant of Grace.

But it appears to me that Horton is right in suggesting that the NPP has failed to make clear that John (as in John 1:16, 17), Paul (as in Gal. 3:6-29), and the writer to the Hebrews (as in Heb. 12:18-29) preach the gospel as calling for faith, like that of Abraham (cf. Rom. 4:13; Gal. 2:16; 3:6-8); not the works of the law (revealed through Moses) as the way to put oneself in the right with God (cf. Gal. 3:10, 11). The apostles therefore indicate that the gospel takes us primarily back to the promise to Abraham. The New Covenant in Christ is a renewal of the Abrahamic covenant, not of the Sinaitic.

Horton writes:

> To see the new covenant about which Paul is speaking as a renewed Sinai covenant is to miss the central point the apostle makes. In fact it is to miss the explicit point in Jeremiah 31, where Yahweh pledges that the new covenant 'will not be like the covenant that I made with their ancestors' at Sinai, which they broke (v. 32).[122]

It appears that 'Second Temple Judaism' had, in focusing only upon the renewal of the Mosaic form, rather than the Abrahamic form of the covenant, forgotten – as Paul vehemently reminds them – that the inheritance of covenant salvation is by promise and grace, not by law and works (Gal. 3:18). On this distinction – left rather unclear in the NPP – Paul rested the entire good news of Christ.

The two main types of covenant in Scripture are to be distinguished, not separated

That is why the two forms of covenant must always be *distinguished*, so as *to preserve the gospel*. But at the same time, we must not *separate* the two forms of covenant, so as *to encourage godly lives and to structure society wholesomely with a view to its reformation* in terms of who God is.[123] In other words, the promise covenant and law covenant are not to be thought of as though

---

[122] Horton, op.cit., 82, 83.

[123] We can think of the relationship of the differing covenants on the analogy of the relationship of the two natures in the one person of Christ, as presented by the Council of Chalcedon: distinct, but not separate.

they are mutually contradictory. In the truest sense, grace provides for the fulfilling of the law, and law is given within the context of grace.

The nineteenth-century devotional writer and theologian, Andrew Murray, helps us avoid the typically human 'logical' mistake of strictly separating God's law from God's grace, or fear of God from love of God, so as to evacuate one or the other in terms of our poor 'logical consistency' that thereby fails to adapt itself to the reality of who God is. Commenting on Psalm 33:18-22 (especially, v. 18 – 'Behold, the eye of the Lord is upon them that fear him, upon them that hope in his mercy'), Murray writes:

> 'The eye of the Lord is on them that *fear* Him, on them that *hope* in His mercy.' Fear and hope are generally thought to be in conflict with each other; in the presence and worship of God they are found side by side in perfect and beautiful harmony. And this because in God Himself all apparent contradictions are reconciled. Righteousness and peace, judgment and mercy, holiness and love, infinite power and infinite gentleness, a majesty that is exalted above all heaven, and a condescension that bows very low, meet and kiss each other. There is indeed a fear that hath torment, that is cast out entirely by perfect love. But there is a fear that is found in the very heavens. In the song of Moses and the Lamb they sing, 'Who shall not fear Thee, O Lord, and glorify Thy name?' And out of the very throne the voice came, 'Praise our God, all ye His servants, and ye that fear Him.' ...The deeper we bow before His holiness in holy fear and adoring awe, in deep reverence and humble self-abasement, even as the angels veil their faces before the throne, the more will His holiness rest upon us, and the soul be fitted to have God reveal Himself... 'The eye of the Lord is on them that fear Him.'[124]

From this perspective, it is to be kept in mind that in the promissory, gracious New Covenant, the law of God given through Moses, rather than being denied, is fully honored by the perfect obedience of Christ to all its precepts in word and spirit (cf. Matt. 5:17; John 8:29, and 46); by His vicarious death to pay its penalty (cf. Rom. 4:25), and then by His sending down the Holy Spirit to regenerate believers (cf. John 3:3-8), whom He forthwith inhabits and sanctifies (cf. Rom. 8:1-10), so as to remake them into the holy image of God, thus at last fulfilling the moral law codified in Moses (cf. 2 Cor. 3:18; 1 John 3:2), and accomplishing the purposes of God for the entire created order (cf. Rom. 8:18-23).

The prayer of a covenant theologian

All the covenants of Scripture finally terminate in the Mediator of the New Covenant, namely, the Lord Jesus Christ, so that all the promises of grace and blessing which are included in these covenants are conveyed to us through Him. Thus, the Apostle Paul says: 'For all the promises of God in him are yea, and in him Amen, unto the glory of God by us' (2 Cor. 1:20). Across the centuries, covenant theologians have seen that the many covenants of redemptive history find their meaning within the one Covenant of Grace, whose chief focus is on Him who is 'the one mediator between God and men, the man Jesus Christ, who gave himself a ransom

---

[124] Andrew Murray, *Waiting on God* (James Nisbet & Co.: London, 1901), 55,56.

for all to be testified in due time' (1 Tim. 2:5, 6). Since the covenants lead us to the One who gave Himself for us, then the only proper response is praise of Him and prayer to Him!

That is the direction in which the seventeenth-century covenant theologian, Herman Witsius, leads us, when he asks us:

> How calmly does conscience, overwhelmed with the burden of its sins, acquiesce in such a Surety, and in such a suretyship; when here at length, apprised of a method of reconciliation, both worthy of God, and safe for man? Who, on contemplating these things in the light of the Spirit, would not break out into the praises of the most holy, the most righteous, the most true, the most gracious, and the most high God?

Then, Witsius leads us in a covenant prayer:

> O! the depth of the wisdom and knowledge of God! O the height of mysteries, which angels desire to look into! Glory to the Father, who raised up, accepted, and gave us such a Surety! Glory to the Son, who clothing himself in human flesh, so willingly, so patiently, and so constantly performed such an engagement for us. Glory to the Holy Ghost, the revealed, the witness, and the earnest of so great happiness for us. All hail! O Christ Jesus, true and eternal God, and true and holy man, all in one, who retains the properties of both natures in the unity of thy person. Thee we acknowledge, thee we worship, to thee we betake ourselves, at thy feet we fall down, from thy hand alone we look for salvation. Thou art the only Saviour; we desire to be thy peculiar property, we are so by thy grace, and shall remain such for ever. Let the whole world of thine elect, with us, acknowledge and adore thee, and thus at length be saved by thee. This is the sum of our faith, and hope, and this the top of all our wishes. *Amen.*[125]

(b) We know God and His Truth only in the Covenant Community Appointed by Him

The boy, Samuel, as we saw in Chapter 1, could not understand the Word of the Lord without the help of the older prophet, Eli. This is the case with all of God's people in all ages: one must live in the community of faith in order to hear God and to know Him and His truth.

This is the opposite of the Enlightenment theory of Descartes, who fondly thought that by going inside of his own consciousness and deriving 'clear and distinct ideas' he could thereby know the ultimate truth. Although the Enlightenment soon rejected Descartes' theory of 'innate ideas', still they followed him in seeking knowledge of God apart from Church and Holy Scripture, as though the unaided mind of the individual were sufficient to determine who God is and what He requires. Those who seek to know God and His truth outside Israel and the Church are always doomed to failure. The decline of Western culture since that time is the bitter fruit of such willful presumption.

On the contrary, T. F. Torrance has shown the necessity of the common faith and life of Old Testament Israel as a background and context to the

---

[125] Witsius, op. cit., 201.

true knowledge of God.[126] He explains the significance of the history of Israel as the prehistory of the incarnate Word of God, which was forming in Israel a womb for the birth of Christ. Torrance suggests three lines of thought: (1) If one is to make a thing, one needs tools to give it shape; (2) A community of reciprocity is necessary; and (3) An organic relationship is essential.

(1) If one is to make a thing, one needs tools to give it shape

By 'tools' he means analogies or categories to shape the apprehending of the knowledge of God in the human mind. God's infinity does not preclude the finite mind from knowing its Creator and Redeemer. He finds a mode of entry into our mortality and mode of existence, in order to build us up to an appropriate apprehension of His being and of our fellowship with Him.

Thus, God elected a small instrument; a small race of unimpressive people to demonstrate His grace and purpose. This race often resisted God's salvational purposes. Yet God held on to them, to mold them as instruments through which He could reveal himself. Israel was the lump of clay molded by the Potter, using their obedience and disobedience to teach them truth; to make them the womb for Christ's birth. The prophecies of Simeon and Anna in Luke chapter 2 point in this direction. Christ was the culmination of the preparatory Old Testament history.

Without the history of Israel, we have no conceptual tools with which to grasp the meaning of the incarnate Son of God and His work. One cannot truly understand Christ and His salvation without some grasp of the whole Levitical system, the story of Abraham and Isaac and Jacob, and the prophets and wisdom literature. Without the Levitical system, one could not understand the cross of Christ. Without the Old Testament the New Testament would be bodiless; without the New Testament the Old Testament would be headless.

For instance, Hosea 11 and Matthew 2:15 speak of the 'Son called out of Egypt'. Matthew means that Israel was a forerunner of God's only-begotten Son. Christ was called out of Egypt, just as Israel had been called out generations earlier. The slavery of Egypt was solved by the Exodus, but a greater Exodus occurred in Christ's cross and resurrection, when He called sinners out of their slavery to sin. At the transfiguration of Christ, not long before His passion, we find Moses and Elijah discussing with Christ 'the decease' (literally – 'the *Exodus*') which He should accomplish at Jerusalem. Presumably, they knew that the earlier Exodus under Moses, and the prophetical renewal of the covenant under Elijah, finally depended for their validity upon what Christ would accomplish once and for all 'in the fullness of the times' (Gal. 4:4); in 'the last days' (Heb. 1:2).

(2) A community of reciprocity is necessary for understanding God

God was working in Old Testament Israel to create a community of reciprocity: His Word evoked a response back to God, which helped make

[126] T. F. Torrance, unpublished handout notes to his Dogmatics classes at Edinburgh University in the 1960s. These notes are being prepared for publication by his nephew, Robert Walker.

that Word apprehensible to His people. That community of reciprocity is in some ways like a marriage, in which one person comes to know the other at the deepest level (and not merely 'about' the other). God chose a people to whom He could speak His word, and then could give a response. In His infinitely powerful providence, He used even the bad responses of Israel to penetrate their life more deeply, so that the Word would come to them – and eventually to all of mankind – more clearly.

Corporate Israel was the antitype of which Christ is the reality. The experience of Israel as a community of reciprocity with God gave concreteness to that fuller knowledge believers have of their Lord in His life, death and resurrection. Even though the inner knowledge of Spirit-filled believers of God and His will far surpasses the knowledge granted to the people in the old covenant (cf. Jer. 31 and Heb. 8, already discussed), still the fuller knowledge would not be apprehensible without the prior (although poorer) knowledge of the first community of reciprocity. Without the previous history of the community of Israel, we in the Church could not really grasp what it is to live in union and communion with the Lord.

(3) An organic relationship is necessary for knowing God truly

This 'knowing' relationship between God and Israel is not only conceptual or intellectual, but it is also an organic relationship, binding Israel integrally into God's Being. This was a covenanted relationship, so that the people of God were radically different from other nations. God created 'a peculiar people.'

Through the Word, the covenant and the cult, God worked into their very existence a knowledge of the way of response that He would ultimately provide in the one whom He elected to fulfill that covenant; in a way that Israel never did, nor ever could do (as we see in Hebrews chapter 8–10). The communal, organic experience of Israel with the Lord – both positive and negative – provides the structure and pointers to the organic relationship of believers with the incarnate Christ, and through Him in the bonds of the Spirit, with the heavenly Father. Without the organic relationship between God and Israel, the Church would have never had the eyes 'in God's light to see light' (Ps. 36:9). The New Covenant with its fullness of blessing could only make sense in light of the Old Covenant, which – though by no means bereft of blessing – was only a pointer to something far greater. But without a pointer, no one can find the goal; and the organic relationship of Israel to God is essential to the Church's resting in the bosom of her – and Israel's – Lord.

God and His truth have always been revealed within a believing community

In the beginning, God created and entered into fellowship with his image-bearers, Adam and Eve. He condescended to spend time with them, verbally giving them tasks, a gracious promise of life, and a solemn threat of death (for disobedience) – Genesis 2:15-25. After their fall into sin, meriting judgment and death, the gracious God gave them 'the first promise of the gospel' (Gen 3:15), and removed them from the Garden of Eden, thereby keeping them from eating of 'the tree of life', lest they be confirmed in a state of irrevocable deathly separation from God (Gen. 3:22-24).

The Lord continued his grace to the Patriarchs, giving them a son, Seth, through whom the seed of promise would come (Gen. 4:25). God spoke to Seth's descendant, Noah, who 'found grace in the eyes of the Lord' (Gen. 6:8), and hence with his family was delivered from the world-wide Flood, which destroyed all flesh. Of Noah's three sons, God appointed Shem to be the bearer of the promised seed through whom deliverance from sin and death would be brought to mankind (Gen. 9:26-27).

Abram (later Abraham), a descendant of Shem, was elected by God as the bearer of the Messianic seed, to reconstitute a believing community of grace in fellowship with the Lord (Gen. ch. 12, 17, 21). From the descendants of this one chosen family would come the salvation of the world, for God promised Abraham that 'in thee shall all the families of the earth be blessed' (Gen. 12:3). God's gracious presence and word constituted this family, and in turn this family (i.e. believing community) became the recipients of divine revelation for the rest of the world. The divine pressure upon them and the divine Word to and through them gave rise to the Holy Scriptures of the Old Testament. The Holy Scriptures arose within a believing community; they were not given to the minds of dissociated individuals, as Enlightenment philosophy would have it.

Thus, Moses, a descendant of Abraham through Levi, was chosen by God to be the deliverer of the now-embondaged children of Israel out of slavery in Egypt. Moses, among his other multifarious tasks of leadership to the reconstituted people of God, wrote the first five books of the Old Testament. Much that he wrote reflected and guided the community within which he lived and wrote. Hence, the earliest Scriptures did not come out of the mind of an individual philosopher or wise man, living on his own and thinking his own thoughts; they came from God to a chosen community of faith in fellowship with God Himself.

The rest of the Old Testament also was given by God to chosen vessels within the community of Israel. 'Thus saith the Lord' unto the many prophets. Through them He rebuked the community, chastened it, had it taken into captivity for idolatry, in seventy years restored it to its homeland, and gave it gracious promises of a Messiah, in whom 'the Lord whom ye seek, shall suddenly come to his temple, even the messenger of the covenant, whom ye delight in: behold, he shall come, saith the LORD of hosts' (Mal. 3:1).

Out of the heart of this community, God from time to time raised up psalmists and singers of life and truth, not least, David – shepherd and king – descendant of Abraham through the Patriarch Judah. The life of David was so crucial to this believing community to whom God's revelation was given, that he himself becomes a 'type' and foreshadow of the promised seed of Eve (cf. Ps. 110). Some of his inspired words were taken into the lips of Christ on the cross (e.g. Ps. 22:1) as the deepest expression of the significance of His atoning work (in that Christ was separated from the

Father so that the believing community of all times and places could be reunited to Him).

Historical books ('the *ketubim*' or 'the writings') are divinely inspired commentaries of the life of this chosen community, and come from within it by divine pressure, resulting in a transcendently given word. These histories (e.g. 1 and 2 Samuel, 1 and 2 Kings, 1 and 2 Chronicles) were not penned by self-appointed individualist scholars of the world. Their writers (not always known to us) were appointed to their tasks by God (we do not know exactly how), and they always came from within the believing community, speaking directly to its concerns, and yet delivering truth for all others, far beyond their known concerns and mental horizons.

So it was with the 'wisdom literature'. Certainly this literature often made use of wisdom garnered from non-Israelites, such as 'the words of Agur, the son of Jakeh' (Prov. 30:1) and various sayings (often true, though often misapplied) of the various 'miserable comforters' of Job, who came from lands outside the believing community. But they became 'Holy Scripture' by virtue of passing through the hands and minds of divinely chosen editors from within that believing community. One of them was King Solomon, son of David (Prov. 1:1; Eccl. 1:1), and some of his own wise words were copied out 'by the men of Hezekiah, King of Judah' (Prov. 25:1). The words of divine wisdom, whether coming directly into the minds of the wise within Israel from the Spirit of God (Prov. 8:22-36), or mediated through non-Israelites of other cultures (as Agur – see directly above), were all of them ultimately aspects of 'the fear of the LORD; the beginning of wisdom, and the knowledge of the holy, which is understanding' (Prov. 9:10). They were collected and assimilated within the divinely chosen, believing community, and though in one sense, thoroughly immanent within it, were at the same time from a transcendent source – from God, the fount of light and wisdom Himself.

God does not reveal exactly how it is that immanent words are also transcendent words; nor how the reflections from within one limited and imperfect human culture are universally true and eternally binding. What He does is to give us the results of a process that surpasses our understanding. He gives us the completed revelation of His word to and through the believing community of Israel, with which the Church of God is in continuity. Thus we know God from our fellowship with Israel in and through its divinely given revelation. God does not give Himself to be known apart from that chosen community of faith. As Blaise Pascal said, 'He is the God of Abraham, Isaac and Jacob; He is not the God of the philosophers.' The gods of the philosophers tend to be figments of the human imagination (no doubt, with sprinklings of true light at times). They lead astray, and if followed to the willful exclusion of the divine revelation given from within Israel and the Church, they lead down into death, for '... he that sinneth against me [i.e. the divinely revealed wisdom] wrongeth his own soul: all they that hate me love death' (Prov. 8:36).

Church in the New Testament

The principle is the same with the New Testament Church. The Lord of the Church is none less than the seed of the woman, Eve; the seed of Shem, Abraham, Judah, David, and that prophet promised by God through Moses: 'The LORD thy God will raise up unto thee a Prophet from the midst of thee, of thy brethren, like unto me; unto him ye shall hearken' (Deut. 18:15). The Gospels (and Matthew in particular) show Him extensively fulfilling the prophetic promises made concerning the coming Messiah. The twelve apostles are the counterpart of the twelve Old Testament patriarchs. The sacraments of the Church are the counterpart of the signs and seals of the Old Testament phase of the one Covenant of Grace (i.e. baptism and Lord's Supper fulfil circumcision and Passover). The representative government of the Church is largely based on patriarchal eldership and the eldership developed in the synagogue. As Israel's coming into existence and continuance in existence depended upon the divine election, so does that of her fulfilment, the Church (cf. John 17; Rom. 9 and 11; and Eph. 1 and 2). As Israel was God's covenant community, so is the Church (cf. Rom. 3 and 4; 2 Cor. 3; Gal. 3; Rev. 21 and 22).

God's Word, both incarnate and verbal, constituted the Church as it had constituted Israel. From within the 'new Israel' came the divine revelation for the purpose of leading to restored, eternal fellowship with God. The apostles and 'apostolic men' (such as Luke and Mark) were divinely inspired as true interpreters of the Christ event, so that when they spoke and wrote, the Lord Himself spoke and wrote (cf. John 14:16-26; 16:7-16). Their words were thus God's words. Therefore, the risen Christ commissioned His Church to the very end of time to spread this true revelation to all the world: 'Go ye therefore, and teach all nations, baptizing them in the name of the Father, and of the Son, and of the Holy Ghost: Teaching them to observe all things whatsoever I have commanded you: and lo, I am with you alway, even unto the end of the world. Amen' (Matt. 28:19,20).

God's truth which shows us the way to a saving knowledge of God and how to live on this earth comes, therefore, from within the written records of the covenant communities of Old Testament Israel and New Testament Church. It is not a matter of human-based, individualist philosophy from outside these divinely appointed communities. For the Apostle Paul warns us: 'Beware lest any man spoil you through philosophy and vain deceit, after the tradition of men, after the rudiments of the world, and not after Christ' (Col. 2:8). Merely human thoughts and systems darken the mind and lead the soul astray, whereas 'the entrance of thy words giveth light' (Ps. 119:130); for 'thy word is a lamp unto my feet, and a light unto my path' (Ps. 119:105).

The divine revelation, first given to Israel and the Church, is intended to lead us home to God. Thus, with the Psalmist we may pray expectantly: 'O send out thy light and thy truth: let them lead me; let them bring me unto thy holy hill, and to thy tabernacles. Then will I go unto the altar of God, unto God my exceeding joy: yea, upon the harp will I praise thee, O God my God' (Ps. 43:3,4).

God gives Himself to be known only in the Church

In the late second century, St. Irenaeus of Lyon, in opposition to the multitude of Gnostic heretics of his time, who offered *gnosis* ('knowledge') of a God apart from the truth divinely revealed to Israel and the Church, clearly stated that God is known truly only in the Christian Church:

> True knowledge is [that which consists in] the doctrine of the apostles, and the ancient constitution (*sustema*) of the church throughout all the world, and the distinctive manifestation of the body of Christ according to the successions of the bishops, by which they have handed down that church which exists in every place, and has come even unto us, being guarded and preserved, without any forging of Scripture, by a very complete system ('tractatione' or 'tractatio') of doctrine, and neither receiving addition nor [suffering] curtailment [in the truths which she believes]; and [it consists in] reading [the word of God] without falsification, and a lawful and diligent exposition in harmony with the Scriptures, both without danger and without blasphemy; and [above all, it consists in] the pre-eminent gift of love, which is more precious than knowledge, more glorious than prophecy, and which excels all the other gifts [of God].'[127]

Novatian of Rome (c. 250) showed that the true God is the One whom the Church knows:

> This God, then, setting aside the fables and figments of heretics, the Church knows and worships, to whom the universal and entire nature of things as well visible as invisible gives witness...He instructed the prophets by His Spirit, and by all of them He promised his Son Christ; and that at the time at which He had covenanted that He would give Him, He sent Him, and through Him He desired to come into our knowledge, and shed forth upon us the liberal stores of His mercy, by conferring His abundant Spirit on the poor and abject. And, because He of His own free-will is both liberal and kind, lest the whole of this globe, being turned away from the streams of His grace, should wither, He willed the apostles, as founders of our family, to be sent by His Son into the whole world, that the condition of the human race might be conscious of its Founder; and if it should choose to follow Him, might have One whom even in its supplications it might now call Father instead of God.[128]

The Scriptures are rightly interpreted in the Church

Tertullian (early third century) stated that only where true Christian faith is found can there be true interpretation of God's revelation:

> 'With whom lies that very faith to which the Scriptures belong? From what [original Giver], and through whom, and when, and to whom, has been handed down that rule, by which men become Christians?' 'For wherever it shall be manifest that the true Christian rule and faith shall be, *there* will likewise be the true Scriptures and expositions thereof, and [indeed] all the Christian traditions.'[129]

---

[127] Irenaeus, *Adversus Haereses* IV.33.8.

[128] Novatian, *De Trinitate* ch. VIII.

[129] Tertullian, *De Praescriptionibus Haereticorum* xix.

Tertullian had already shown that the Holy Scriptures and their accurate interpretation had first come through the Jews and then to the apostles:

> For it is clear that the next words also apply to the Jews: 'Knock and it shall be opened unto you' (Matt. 7:7). The Jews had formerly been in covenant with God; but being afterwards cast off on account of their sins, they began to be without God. The Gentiles, on the contrary, had never been in covenant with God; they were only as 'a drop from a bucket,' and 'as dust from the threshing-floor' (Isa. 40:15), and were ever outside the door...Therefore it was to Israel that He spake when He said: 'I am not sent but to the lost sheep of the house of Israel' (Matt. 15:24) ... It is only at the last that He instructs them to 'go and teach all nations, and baptize them' (Matt. 28:19), when they were so soon to receive 'the Holy Ghost, the Comforter who should guide them into all the truth' (John 16:13) ... the apostles, who were ordained to be teachers to the Gentiles, were themselves to have the Comforter for their teacher... All the Lord's sayings, indeed, are set forth for all men; through the ears of the Jews have they passed on to us...[130]

Epiphanius, Bishop of Salamis (fourth century) wrote that the Church is needed for true interpretation of God's revealed Word:

> The Church, as I said, has received this message and this faith. Though it is dispersed all over the world it guards them as carefully as if it lived in one house. It believes in accordance with them, as though it had one soul and the same heart. It preaches, teaches and transmits them in unison, as though with one mouth. Even if the languages of the world are different, the meaning of the tradition is one and the same. The Churches founded in Germany have not believed differently or transmitted the tradition differently – or the ones founded among the Iberians, the Celts, in the east, in Libya, or in the center of the earth ... the proclamation of the truth, shines everywhere and illumines all who are willing to come to a knowledge of truth. The ablest speaker of the church's leaders will say nothing different from these things, for no man is above his master (Matt. 10:24). Nor will the feeblest speaker diminish the tradition. For as faith is one and the same, someone with much to say of it does not enlarge it, or someone with little to say does not diminish it.[131]

Epiphanius also stated that 'If I reject the Old Testament, I am not a Catholic' (II. 408). This should have raised the most serious questions about the validity of the reinterpretation of Christianity by the nineteenth-century German scholar, Adolph Von Harnack, who functionally rejected the authority of the Old Testament in order to found a 'humanistic' religion, based on the fatherhood of God, the brotherhood of man and the infinite value of the human soul (in such famous books as *Marcion* and *What Is Christianity*).[132]

Note on 'regula veritatis'

The whole vast community of Christian apologists and Church Fathers of the first five centuries were agreed in stating that a right understanding of

---

[130] Ibid. viii.

[131] Epiphanius, *The Panarion* II. 31. 1-4 (p. 187).

[132] Karl Barth comments with clarity on Harnack's bias against the Old Testament in *Church Dogmatics* I/2 (E.T.), 79, 127, 367.

God and His truth is to be found only within the orthodox Christian Church; that outside the community of faith, amongst heretical groups and pagan thinkers, were (as Paul had warned the Ephesian elders) 'grievous wolves, entering in among you, not sparing the flock…' (Acts 20:29).

These early Christian writers told their people that they would recognize a true Church, which alone could lead them to a saving knowledge of God, by discerning whether or not the *regula veritatis* ('rule of truth') were taught in it. In both the New Testament and in the Apologists and Church Fathers, what came to be called the 'rule of truth' (or 'rule of faith') is closely connected with baptism. This *regula* is essentially the threefold formula which comes directly from the command of Christ in Matthew 28:19: 'Go ye, therefore, and teach all nations, baptising them in the name of the Father, and of the Son, and of the Holy Ghost…' This Trinitarian concept (at least, its reality, though not its later theological elaboration) is an integral part of the entire structure of the New Testament revelation.

The baptismal formula

While the Trinitarian name is given explicitly only at the end of the Gospel of Matthew and also of Luke (24:49), the concept is implicit in the beginning of all four Gospels in the baptism of Jesus. As St. Augustine pointed out, at the Jordan River one will find the Trinity: for there the Father speaks, the Holy Ghost is seen, and the Son is baptised.[133]

As we gather together the multiple strands that relate to baptism in the New Testament, we find that the name and nature of God are revealed in this transaction because it is specifically dealing with our passing into the family and life of the Triune God as represented in this sacramental action. Thus, the revelation of God's name (and through His name, His nature) as the foundation of the redemption and constitution of His people into one body is exhibited in this sacramental reality.

Hence the baptismal formula became the symbol and safeguard of the Church's faith. This was a natural development because converts who were to be admitted to the Church through baptism into the name of the Trinity, were asked if in fact they believed in the Persons signified by the names. From subapostolic days onward, a brief summary statement of the redemptive work of each of the three Persons began to be attached to the confession of the name. This was already so around the year A.D. 130, at the baptism of Justin Martyr in Ephesus.[134] This baptismal 'question and answer' is the source of what became known in the Western Church as the 'Apostles' Creed' early in the second century.

This threefold formula was useful not only as a symbol for entrance into the household of faith, but it also served as a safeguard for orthodox belief against the alternative teachings of heretics within the Church, and the polemics of contemporary Judaism. From the subapostolic age down to the Council of Nicea, the 'rule of truth' is widely expounded by the Church

---

[133] Augustine, *On the Gospel of Saint John*, VI.6.

[134] Sanday, 'Recent Research on the Origin of the Creed,' *Journal of Theological Studies*, Vol. I, 1899, p.9.

Fathers as a witness to God's revelation of Himself as Father, Son and Holy Spirit in His creative and redeeming activities.

The Rule of Truth in the Church Fathers

In the writings of the Fathers, this *regula* usually involves three basic elements: (1) a brief historical exposition of the self-revelation of the Persons and activity of the Triune God; (2) the apostolic, scriptural basis of this tradition; (3) the ecclesiastical unity produced and maintained by this articulated belief.

St. Irenaeus

St. Irenaeus of Lyon gives a rather full discussion of these three points, as he expounds the *regula* in *Adversus Haereses* (c. 180):

> The Church, though dispersed throughout the whole world, even to the ends of the earth, has received from the apostles and their disciples this faith: in one God, the Father Almighty, Maker of heaven and earth, and the sea and all things that are in them; and in one Christ Jesus, the Son of God, who became incarnated for our salvation; and in the Holy Spirit, who proclaimed through the prophets the dispensations of God, and the advents, and the birth from a Virgin; and the passion and the resurrection from the dead, and the ascension into heaven in the flesh of the beloved Christ Jesus our Lord and God and Saviour and King, according to the will of the invisible Father, 'every knee should bow, of things in heaven and things in earth, and things under the earth, and that every tongue should confess to him'; and that he should execute just judgment towards all; that he may send 'spiritual wickedness' and the angels who transgressed and became apostates, together with the ungodly and unrighteous … among men, into everlasting fire; but may, in the exercise of his grace, confer immortality on the righteous, and holy … and may surround them with everlasting glory.
>
> As I have already observed, the church, having received this preaching and this faith, although scattered throughout the whole world, yet as if occupying but one house, carefully preserves it. She also believes these points just as if she had but one soul, and one and the same heart; and she proclaims them and teaches them, and hands them down with perfect harmony, as if she possessed only one mouth. For although the languages of the world are dissimilar, yet the import of the tradition is one and the same. For the churches which have been planted in Germany do not believe or hand down anything different, nor do those in Spain… But as the sun, that creature of God, is one and the same throughout the whole world, so also the preaching of the truth shineth everywhere, and enlightens all men that are willing to come to a knowledge of the truth. For will anyone of the rulers in the churches, however highly gifted he may be in point of eloquence, teach doctrines different from these (for none is greater than the Master). Nor will he on the other hand, who is deficient in power of expression inflict injury on the tradition. For the faith being ever one and the same, neither does one who is able at great length to discourse regarding it make any addition to it, nor does one who can say but little, diminish it.[135]

[135] Irenaeus, *Adv. Haer.* I.X.1,2.

Aristides and Diognetus

Some fifty years earlier than *Adversus Haereses*, Aristides, a 'Christian philosopher of Athens', wrote an apology to the Emperor Hadrian (c. 130–140), in which he expounded the substance of the 'rule of truth' (though without using the name *regula*). His exposition seems to be an expansion of 1 Timothy 3:16, and looks very like a proto-form of what became known as 'The Apostles' Creed'. It involves the three Persons of the Trinity, much like the other Apologists and Fathers. Around the year 150–152, Justin Martyr in his *First Apology to Antoninus Pius*, in a similar manner reproduces the main substance of the rule of truth (without employing the technical term *regula*), though in a rather disjoined way.

The anonymous *Epistle to Diognetus* (perhaps c. 140–180), seems to contain a reference to the substance of the rule of truth, particularly as regards the handing down of the tradition from the apostles, concerning the incarnation of Christ and 'mystery of the Father'. Diognetus sees the Church as the guardian of the 'traditio apostolorum'.[136] These two elements of the Godhead (incarnation and fatherhood) are presented as 'the truth', which it is the task of the Church to safeguard. This truth includes what became the *regula veritatis*, although the form of it found in *Diognetus* is early and hence lacking in the completeness of the later formulations.

Theophilus of Antioch

Theophilus of Antioch, and Eastern contemporary of Irenaeus of Gaul, wrote *Ad Autolycum* around A.D. 181. This work was written, he says: 'That you may have a *symbolon* [σύμβαλον] or pledge of the truth.'[137] Presumably, the words 'pledge of truth' actually refer to the book that Theophilus had written, but the term seems to reflect a knowledge of the concept of *regula veritatis* which is expounded in substance in his book. Though separated by a great geographical distance from Lyon in Gaul, this *symbolon* [σύμβαλον] contains the same elements as the *regula* (or 'deposit of faith') of Irenaeus.

Recognitions of Clement

This 'rule of truth' is also witnessed to by the pseudonymous *Recognitions of Clement*. Both the author and date of this material are unknown. It appears to be a composite work that was added to and re-edited over a period of years, probably from the early third century down to the fifth century. Some sections of the source material, particularly concerning doctrine and morality in the 'Preaching of Peter', appear to have been taken from antecedent works of the late second century, or possibly earlier – though this is still unclear. In this doctrinal material which may be from an early source, one finds reference in two different places to 'an entire and firm rule of truth from the Scriptures ... handed down from the fathers.'[138] Here, the author is more concerned with the use of this rule than with its

---

[136] *Epistle to Diognetus*, chapter XI.

[137] Theophilus, *Ad Autolycum*, III.30.

[138] *Recognitions of Clement*, X.42, and X.51.

content. Therefore, he does not in these places specify what it contains, but rather stresses the fact that it is to be used as a means of establishing the true sense of Scripture.

In the works of Irenaeus of Lyon, the rule of truth is fully expounded and extensively quoted. Along with the *Recognitions of Clement*, he sees it as useful in establishing the true meaning of the Holy Scriptures.[139] However, unlike the *Recognitions* and most earlier works that refer to the *regula*, he gives a very complete explanation of how it was derived, what it involves, and the results it produces when faithfully maintained.

He clearly connects the *regula* to the baptismal formula.[140] Baptism, and with it the rule of truth (and the reality that stands behind it), have come down to the Church from the apostles and their disciples,[141] and ultimately from the Lord Himself: 'But the Lord, having suffered, and bestowing the knowledge of the Father, conferred on us salvation…'[142] . As he expounds the *regula*, Irenaeus connects the redemption in Christ to God's creation and to His redemption of Israel:

> But as we follow the one and only true God, and possess his words as the rule of truth, we do all speak alike with regard to the same things; knowing but one God the Creator of this universe, who sent the prophets, who led forth the people from the land of Egypt, who in these last times manifested his own Son, that he might put the unbelievers to confusion, and search out the fruit of unrighteousness.[143]

Irenaeus does not see the *regula* as a merely external or legal concept, but rather a binding – and liberating – witness to how God has revealed Himself to humanity in His Son, thus ushering us into saving fellowship with Himself: 'In the first place (we must) believe not only in the Father, but also in His Son now revealed; for He it is who leads man into fellowship and unity with God.'[144]

Irenaeus frequently shows that the fellowship and unity with God is made a reality through the Trinitarian movement towards mankind: 'For God is powerful in all things, having been seen at that time indeed, prophetically through the Spirit, and seen, also adoptively through the Son; and he shall be seen paternally in the kingdom of heaven; the Spirit preparing man in the Son of God, and the Son leading him to the Father… and for this reason he (although) beyond comprehension and boundless, and invisible, rendered himself visible and comprehensible, and within the capacity of those who believe, that he might vivify those who receive and behold him through faith…'[145] 'Therefore God has been declared through the Son, who is in the Father, and has the Father in Himself – 'He who is' – the Father bearing witness to the Son, and the Son announcing the Father.'[146]

---

[139] Irenaeus, *Adv. Haer.*, II.27.
[140] Irenaeus, *Adv. Haer.*, I.9.4; *Demonstration of the Apostolic Preaching*, 3.
[141] Irenaeus, *Adv. Haer.*, I.10.1; III.12.7; IV.33.8.
[142] Ibid., II.20.3; also, IV.35.4.
[143] Ibid., IV.35.4.
[144] Ibid., IV.12.4.
[145] Ibid., IV.20.5.
[146] Ibid., III.6.2.

Similarly, in his *Demonstration*, Irenaeus connects our regeneration to the three points of the *regula*: 'For this reason, the baptism of our regeneration proceeds through the three points: God the Father bestowing on us regeneration through his Son by the Holy Spirit...'[147] Much of Irenaeus' exposition of the points contained in the *regula* was to answer the various Gnostic systems, and that was also the case with Clement of Alexandria.

Clement of Alexandria and Origen

Clement mentions the *regula veritatis* as testimony against the Gnostic heresy with its modernity, and hence its constant and shifting confusion. Writing around the year 180, Clement says: 'The [the Church] preserves the tradition of the blessed doctrine derived directly from the Apostles.'[148] The Church holds to the first article of the rule of truth, which is that God is the Creator of the world, over against the Gnostic denial of God's connection with creation.[149] Those who deny this rule of truth are likened by Clement to one drugged by Circe: 'So [is] he who has spurned the ecclesiastical tradition, and darted off to the opinions of heretical men.'[150]

The successor of Clement in the Catechetical School of Alexandria, Origen, gives a full exposition of the *regula veritatis* in his *De Principiis* (c. 225), which is reminiscent of Irenaeus in his *Adversus Haereses* (I.10.1, 2). Origen stresses the same three elements of apostolocity, unity, and three Persons of the Trinity in their creative, redemptive activity.[151] In his *Homilies on Jeremiah*, Origen mentions the rule of truth; though there his intention is not to expound its contents so much as to state the results it brings to those who hold it: 'Quando vero secundum ecclesiae regulas et sanae doctrinae propositum particeps communionis, non solum circumcisus es, verum etiam circumcisus es Deo.'[152]

Hippolytus of Rome

Hippolytus of Rome, who was already a renowned teacher of the faith while Origen was still a student, is in the same line as the other Fathers as concerns his understanding and use of the rule of truth. He seems particularly in the line of Irenaeus in this regard. In his *Philosophumena* (c. 222–235), Hippolytus – after enumerating in detail many of the confusing heresies of the day – then makes reference to the only remedy from confusion and falsehood: '... We have frequently propounded demonstrations for those willing to learn the rule of truth...'[153] In the same treatise, Hippolytus shows that the rule of truth is a witness to the nature of God: '... Executing our treatises

---

[147] Irenaeus, *Demonstration of the Apostolic Preaching*, 7.

[148] Clement of Alexandria, *Stromateis*, I.1.

[149] Ibid., IV.1.

[150] Ibid., VII.16.

[151] Origen, *De Principiis*, I.2,4 (Preface).

[152] Origen, *In Jer.*, V.14 – 'When you in truth participate in the fellowship according to the rules of the Church and the setting forth of its sound doctrines, not only are you circumcised, but truly are circumcised to God.'

[153] Hippolytus, *Philosophumena*, X.1.

in knowledge of truth and good sense, our object being the demonstration of his [nature].'[154]

In the sections of *Philosophumena* immediately following,[155] he goes on to discuss the nature of the Creator and the Logos. In his work, *Contra Noetum*, he turns to 'an exhibition of the truth itself.'[156] The content of this exhibition is none other than the Father, the Son and the Holy Ghost: 'The knowledge of whom we gain from Scripture.'[157] Hippolytus understood the historical connection between the *regula veritatis* and baptism:

> Go ye and teach all nations, baptising them in the name of the Father, and of the Son, and of the Holy Ghost (Matt. 28:19). And by this he showed that whosoever omitted any one of these, failed in glorifying God perfectly. For it is through the Trinity (*triados* [τρίαδος]) that the Father is glorified. For the Father willed, the Son did, the Spirit manifested. The whole Scriptures then, proclaim this truth.[158]

Tertullian

Tertullian, who was writing in North Africa while Hippolytus was writing in Rome, appears to make reference to the rule of truth in his treatises more often than any other of the Fathers. His many references to it can be subsumed under one or more of the four major points: its apostolicity (and dominicity), its content, its unity and its connection to salvation. Tertullian most often uses the *regula* to establish the apostolicity of the doctrine that is held in the true churches, over against the lateness – and thus, non-apostolicity – of heretical teaching. He shows in *Apologeticum* that the rule of truth is in fact dominical, in contrast with heresy.[159] In *De Praescriptionibus Haereticorum* he shows it to be both dominical and apostolic.[160]

In company with Irenaeus, Tertullian is impressed with the Roman Church, which has always held to the *regula*, and is 'doubly apostolic.'[161] In two other places, he mentions the recentness of heresy, and the necessity of being apostolic in order to know the truth.[162]

As to the content of the *regula*, Tertullian is no different from the other early witnesses of the Church. The content is the three Persons of the Trinity in their creative, redemptive activity. A representative sample of his exposition of the contents of the *regula* is found in *De Praescriptionibus Haereticorum*:

> Now with regard to this rule of faith ... it is, you must know, that which prescribes the belief that there is one only God, and that he is none other than the Creator of the world, who produced all things out of nothing through his Word, first of all sent forth; that this Word is called his Son ... at last brought down by the Spirit and Power of the faith into the Virgin

[154] Ibid., X.27.
[155] Ibid., X.28, 29.
[156] Hippolytus, *Contra Noetum*, 8.
[157] Ibid., 9.
[158] Ibid., 14.
[159] Tertullian, *Apologeticum*, 47.
[160] Tertullian, *De Praes. Haer.*, xx, xxi.
[161] Ibid., xxxvi.
[162] Tertullian, *Contra Hermogenem*, 1; *De Carne Christi*, xii,xiii.

> Mary; was made flesh in her womb ... having been crucified, he rose again the third day; having ascended into the heavens, he sat at the right hand of the Father; sent instead of himself, the power of the Holy Ghost to lead such as believe; will come with glory to take the saints ... to condemn the wicked... This rule, as it will be proved, was taught by Christ, and raises amongst ourselves no other questions than those which heretics introduce, and which make men heretics.'[163]

Tertullian is agreed with the other catholic Fathers in linking this one tradition to the salvation of humanity. He states: 'Now faith has been deposited in the rule; it has a law and salvation... To know nothing in opposition to the rule is to know all things.'[164]

Cyprian and Dionysius of Alexandria

Two other fathers of the early third century give a similar witness to the *regula veritatis*. Cyprian of Carthage, in an epistle to Jubianus, brings out the connection between baptism, the great commission of Christ and the three points of the rule of truth.[165] In another epistle, he congratulates Januarius for holding 'the truth and certainty of the catholic rule.'[166] Dionysius of Alexandria in a polemical letter against Novatian of Rome to Dionysius of Rome, also establishes the relationship between baptism and the rule of truth.[167]

The Church Fathers, therefore, put great emphasis upon this rule of truth, which was later to be enshrined in the 'Apostles' Creed' and the Nicene Creed. It is the basis of the Trinitarian confession of the Church. Novatian of Rome, a schismatic, though always formally orthodox, followed the earlier Fathers in holding to the rule of truth. He mentions it in chapter 1 of his *De Trinitate*, as well as in several other places, including the next-to-the-last chapter. In chapter 1, it is mentioned in connection with God the Father.[168] In four other places the *regula* is connected with the Godhead of the Son.[169] Then in chapter XXIX, it is related to God the Holy Spirit, who 'explains the rule of truth.'[170] Thus we see that in Novatian, in common with the other Fathers of the Church, the *regula veritatis* has a triune structure, and thus Trinitarian thought passed into the life and piety of the early Christian Church, by means of baptismal and confessional practice of countless congregations, both East and West.

Reformational version of the 'regula veritatis'

No doubt the reality of the *regula veritatis* lies behind what the sixteenth-century Protestant Reformers of the Church called 'the marks of the Church'

---

[163] Tertullian, *De Praes. Haer.*, xii, xiii.
[164] Ibid., xiv.
[165] Cyprian, *Epistle to Jubianus* (LXXI).
[166] Cyprian, *Epistle to Januarius* (LXIX).
[167] Dionysius of Alexandria, cited in Eusebius, *Church History*, VI.45.
[168] Novatian, *De Trinitate*, I.1.
[169] Ibid., IX.46; XI.61; XVII.95; XXI.121.
[170] Ibid., XXIX.163.

in their disputations with the Roman Catholics of their time as to how one could identify the true Church. Both Martin Luther and John Calvin, in response to the Roman Catholic hierarchy's denial of the term 'Church' to the Protestant Reform movement, argued that one could find two 'marks' by which one could identify 'the true Church'. These were: the true preaching of the Word of God and the pure administration of the sacraments.

While John Calvin in his *Institutes* (IV.1.9) followed the 1530 Lutheran Confession of Augsburg in mentioning only pure preaching and pure administration of the sacraments as the two marks of the Church, Robert M. Kingdon has shown that actually Calvin also held to discipline as a 'third mark of the church'.[171] Calvin speaks of discipline as the third mark of the Church in his famous 1539 'Reply to Sadoleto'.[172]

Both Calvin and his colleague, Pierre Viret, were cast out of their ministries for a time (Calvin from Geneva and Viret from Lausanne), on this very issue: that of the Church (rather than the city council) determining who was fit to come to the Lord's Supper. Thus it is clear that the Reformed practice considered discipline of life by the Church to be inseparable from 'the pure administration' of the sacraments. That was certainly the case with the Reformed churches in France and Switzerland in Calvin's time. And John Knox and the Scottish Reformation followed their lead in Scotland.

The 1560 Scots Confession said:

> The notes, signs, and assured tokens whereby the spotless bride of Christ is known from the horrible harlot, the false Kirk, we state, are neither antiquity, usurped title, lineal succession, appointed place, nor the numbers of men approving an error... The notes of the true Kirk, therefore, we believe, confess, and avow to be: first, the true preaching of the Word of God, in which God has revealed himself to us, as the writings of the prophets and apostles declare; secondly, the right administration of the sacraments of Christ Jesus, with which must be associated the Word and promise of God, to seal and confirm them in our hearts; and lastly, ecclesiastical discipline uprightly ministered, as God's Word prescribes, whereby vice is repressed and virtue nourished.'[173]

But in spite of the fierce controversy between Roman Catholic and Protestants, all were agreed that the truth of God is found and understood properly only within the Church, which – as St. Paul taught – is 'the pillar and ground of the truth' (1 Tim 3:15). And this church always bases its doctrine upon the apostolic truth of the Holy Scriptures, as Paul wrote to Timothy: 'And that from a child thou hast known the holy scriptures, which are able to make thee wise unto salvation through faith in Christ Jesus. All scripture is given by inspiration of God, and is profitable for doctrine, for reproof, for correction, for instruction in righteousness; that

---

[171] Robert M. Kingdon, 'Préface' to *Registres du Consistoire de Genève au Temps de Calvin*, publiés par Thomas A. Lambert et Isabella M. Watt, sous la direction de R. M. Kingdon avec l'assistance de Jeffrey R. Watt, Tome I (1542-1544), vii. See also Robert M. Kingdon, "The Church: Ideology or Institution?", *Church History* 50, p. 84-88.

[172] See 'Reply to Sadoleto' in *Calvin Theological Treatises* (*Library of Christian Classics*, vol. xxii) (London: SCM Press, 1954), 219-256.

[173] *The Scots Confession* ch. xviii.

the man of God may be perfect, throughly furnished unto all good works' (2 Tim. 3:15-17).

We find in both Church Fathers and Reformers that God and His truth are known (1) in a particular community; (2) historically; and (3) through reconciliation with 'the Truth'.

(1) God and His truth are known in a particular community

In company with Fathers and Reformers, the twentieth-century French Reformed scholar, Auguste Le Cerf, wrote that 'we know in the church':

> ... in the ordinary course of events, he [i.e. the Calvinist believer] derives his knowledge of God from the Church, which communicates to him the revelation that she has received. The first representatives of the Church, for him, are ordinarily his parents or teachers. The Church is the mother of the faithful, says Calvin,[174] it is she who brings them forth as believers. The isolated individual – except for a miracle of the sovereign liberty of God – is nothing, no more in the sphere of the spiritual life than in that of terrestrial and merely human existence. 'Faith cometh through hearing', says the Apostle, 'and hearing through the Word of God' (Rom. 10:17). The Church claims indeed to draw from the Word of God written that which she teaches to her children. It is the province of exegesis and dogmatics proper to justify this affirmation of the Reformed Church. But it is always the Word of God, the contents of which are sealed in the heart of the child by the testimony of the Holy Spirit, that she teaches in her official catechisms and confessions...[175]

The Christian Church, in continuity with Israel, is *a particular community*. The philosophy of the Enlightenment has had an aversion to 'particularity', preferring instead supposedly universal ideas drawn by rootless, individual thinkers from concepts that the human spirit extracts from self, from nature and from history (in varying combinations). An illustration is found in the 'thought societies' of pre-revolutionary France, whose concepts were in many respects vague and antithetical parodies of the doctrine of the Catholic Church, which they sought to replace.[176] That God should be known by a particular revelation in a particular community of faith was abhorrent to them, and in many respects their hostility to the particularity of the revelation of God's truth has constituted the deep, underlying fault-line dividing Western culture from the eighteenth to the twenty-first century.

The particularity of revelation is because it comes from a personal God to a community called into personal fellowship with Him. One assumes that at least part of the Enlightenment (and especially Idealist) hostility to Israel and the Church comes from their perception that accepting this revelation would necessarily call them into personal contact with a holy God. Thus they take refuge in gods of their own making; gods who do not threaten their sinful self-sufficiency. Certainly that was part of the appeal of ancient Gnosticism, as it is of 'the New Age.'

---

[174] Calvin *Institutes* IV. 1. 4.

[175] Le Cerf, op. cit., 236.

[176] See *L'Esprit du Jacobinism*, already discussed in Appendix to Chapter Two.

What Happens in the Community of Faith

However, if one wants to meet with the real God, it has to be on His terms. He will be met with in the community of faith which He established, and which He maintains personally by His Word and Spirit; a community which, in turn, bases its life and teaching upon that divinely revealed, particular word in a community that lives by the Spirit. So to meet Him is not primarily theoretical; it is most personal and practical, and profoundly searching: 'For the word of God is quick, and powerful, and sharper than any two-edged sword, piercing even to the dividing asunder of soul and spirit, and of the joints and marrow, and is a discerner of the thoughts and intents of the heart. Neither is there any creature that is not manifest in his sight: but all things are naked and opened unto the eyes of him with whom we have to do' (Heb. 4:12,13).

Even to come into a service where believers are worshipping the Triune God strips away pretence, causing one to be frighteningly unveiled before the Holy One. That is the argument Paul uses to require that speaking be carried on in Church in a known tongue and in orderly fashion: 'But if all prophesy, and there come in one that believeth not, or is unlearned, he is convinced of all, he is judged of all: And thus are the secrets of his heart made manifest; and so falling down on his face he will worship God, and report that God is in you of a truth' (1 Cor. 14:24, 25). For such reasons, multitudes tragically prefer false gods who have been fabricated by other sinners, so as to keep themselves from being embarrassed by an honest exposure of who they really are, and potentially humbled and changed before the true God. But the kind of embarrassment that all of us sons and daughters of Adam find before the Holy One of Israel is soon succeeded by the joy of all sins forgiven, and the sweetness of lasting fellowship with the God of all grace; the one who said through Isaiah: 'Though your sins be as scarlet, they shall be as white as snow; though they be red like crimson, they shall be as wool' (Isa. 1:18).

In other words, the very purpose of divine revelation of truth is for personal fellowship in a believing community with the tri-personal, one God. To demand truth somewhere else: whether from our own minds or from the world's culture with its humanly fabricated religion and philosophy, would defeat the purposes for which God has spoken His Word and called together His people. He will not allow long-term success to this kind of proud unbelief, though it may prosper in the short-run as a kind of judgment to an apostate society; a judgment that is intended to call the people to repentance. To persist in it is 'to hew oneself out broken cisterns that can hold no water' (Jer. 2:13). It is 'to offer strange fire' that instead of affirming one's religious actions, actually destroys those who finally reject God's proffered way of grace (as was the case with Dathan and Abiram, sons of Aaron, who were burned up by the self-kindled fire they offered, having refused the divinely appointed fire of the sanctuary, as they sought to overthrow the spiritual leadership of Israel in the wilderness – Num. 16 and Deut. 11:6).

But the particularity of the faith communities of Israel and the Church to whom and through whom the divine revelation was originally and definitively given, continues to be a necessary part of how the faith expands within the world. That is, the grasping of the gospel with that knowledge of God in Christ which is 'life eternal' (John 17:3), is still personal and particular within the community of faith. This finding of the life of God and satisfying of the soul is not a possibility given to human philosophy and religion, as long as these are separated from the continuing particularity of the community of faith. Otherwise, God could be found impersonally and generally, rather than personally and particularly. Such would be inconsistent with who He is, and thus does not – so far as we limited humans generally know – happen,[177] much as the Enlightenment would have it otherwise.

Stăniloae summarizes the position well:

> In supernatural revelation, God makes himself known clearly as person, inasmuch as he calls and sends out a particular person to a particular human community. This person arrives with a responsibility awakened powerfully by God. On the one hand, God confirms the natural evidence that our being possesses about the future fulfilment of its meaning in union with God and, on the other hand, he shows man that this union will not come about nor is it being prepared in isolation, but rather in the solidarity of each man with his neighbour. Hence, this preparation does not come about only through situations interpreted by man in isolation, but through the mission of a person who draws the attention of all to the content of his mission. It is not isolated individuals whom God wishes to save through supernatural revelation, but the great multitudes of believers in a mutual and common responsibility towards himself, for all must help one another on the way of progress towards the goal of perfection and eternal life, and help strengthen their own communion based on communion with God. In fact, the communion among them is a constitutive part of their own perfection and of their progress towards that perfection.[178]

As Karl Barth has written that God is known only in the chosen community of faith, because He is always consistent with who He is, and has determined the grounds where He gives Himself to be known:

> God has limited Himself to be this God and no other, to be the love which is active and dwells with men at this point and in this way, in Jesus Christ. God has bound Himself in His own Son to be eternally true to His creation. But He has done this Himself, and the fact that He has acted in this and not in any other way has its basis in and from Himself.

Barth then notes two facts:

> The first is that what did and does happen to and for creation in Jesus Christ must be understood as God's free decision. As He has in fact effected this, we cannot and should not form any conception of God in abstraction from what He has effected, His reality in Jesus Christ...

---

[177] Other than, as A. Le Cerf has said: '...except for a miracle of the sovereign liberty of God...', op. cit., 236.

[178] Stăniloae, op. cit., 24.

> The second insight is complementary, that what has taken place and takes place in Jesus Christ must be understood as a necessary decree of God… By the very nature of the case we cannot try to seek or find Him except where and how He has given Himself to be sought and found.[179]

(2) God and His truth are known historically

Ancient Gnosticism held that God is to be known in terms of general principles of 'secret knowledge', rather than through His mighty deeds in creation, revelation, incarnation in and through the Spirit-constituted Church. Modern Idealism also eschewed a historical revelation and a corporately revealed truth. 'The accidents of history' were rejected in the interests of the supposed 'eternal truths of reason.' But such truths are insubstantial and unreal; they do not and cannot reveal God and His salvation to mankind.

Indeed, even rationality itself never exists on its own. Stăniloae explains:

> It is impossible to think of a rational order as existing objectively on its own. It is always a rationality communicated or received by a person. It is impossible to think of a rationality without a hypostatic reason which thinks and communicates its thought or which receives a communicated thought. And it is impossible to imagine a person without the will to communicate himself or to receive a communication in a fully meaningful way, in a way that is rational or intelligible. This is how, in fact, the person breathes spiritually. It is impossible to think of a rationality without a person or a person not under the necessity of communicating himself in some rational or intelligible way. The separation of the person and the rational results in the fantastic notion of a self-engendered rationality which is devoid of meaning, and a person as a sentient life-force, blind and devoid of meaning… The things of the world are communications exemplifying the rational thoughts of the supreme Person, at a level of discernment which is in keeping with human understanding. Cognitive human reason itself is the creation of this supreme cognitive Reason, created to understand the thoughts communicated by means of things.[180]

Thus, as T. F. Torrance has written, we cannot know the truth unhistorically:

> We cannot forget here that the divine and human natures of Christ are united in *One Person*, and that this Person is the *One Word* of God. He is the Truth of God in the form of Personal Being, Word of God is identical with His Person… Therefore we do not just learn of Christ, we learn Christ…We think a Person, the Person, and in doing that we are adapted to personal thinking and gain true subjectivity. He certainly communicates truths to us, but they are truths that inhere in His Personal being and are not detachable from Him…We cannot know this Truth unhistorically or statically, therefore, by seeking to pass behind or beyond His action and life *in* time to what we may imagine to be the Truth in Himself, for there

[179] Karl Barth, *Church Dogmatics* II/1 (ET), 518.

[180] D. Stăniloae, 'Jesus Christ, Incarnate Logos of God, Source of Freedom and Unity' in *The Ecumenical Review*, XXVI, Jan. – Oct. 1974, 405-406.

> is no other Truth of God for us than this Truth in life and action who decisively intervenes in our human existence and pours Himself out in love to redeem us from our plight. He is not to be found or known except as He gives Himself to be known in space and time, that is, as He becomes flesh, as He lives His life in time and action on earth for our sake, as He *dies* upon the Cross for our salvation, and as He *rises again* from the dead for our justification. The Truth of God cannot be separated from the whole historical Jesus Christ, for time, decision, action, history belong to the essential nature of this truth.[181]

Two sides of this matter of truth and history should always be held together: (1) God's truth is not finally abstract and impersonal, but historically founded, and at the same time, (2) the historical nature of the revelation of truth should be strongly contrasted to Western historicism. Western historicism subsumes dogmatic/historical truth to the impersonal historical process (as one sees in 'process theology').[182]

(3) God's truth is known only through reconciliation with 'the Truth'

Since the Triune God is personal and we are persons, we cannot know Him properly while we are still at enmity with Him, for we instinctively turn our faces away from His holy light. That is part of what the Apostle Paul teaches about the dynamic of the reconciliation of sinners with the Holy God of love and grace in 2 Corinthians 4 and 5. The 'hidden things of dishonesty' that make us 'walk in craftiness and handle the word of God deceitfully' have to be renounced (2 Cor. 4:2). The 'god of this world' who blinds the minds 'of them which believe not' is to be forsaken in order to perceive 'the light of the glorious gospel of Christ, who is the image of God…' (2 Cor. 4:4). This means focusing on Christ, and the needs of others, and not on self (2 Cor. 4:5). This renouncing and forsaking of dishonesty and false deities can occur only through our identification by faith with God in Christ. 'And all things are of God, who hath reconciled us to himself by Jesus Christ, and hath given to us the ministry of reconciliation: to wit, that God was in Christ, reconciling the world unto himself, not imputing their trespasses unto them: and hath committed unto us the word of reconciliation' (2 Cor. 5:18,19).

Reconciliation is both vertical and horizontal

We must note here that the reconciliation brought us in Christ works both vertically and horizontally. 2 Corinthians 5 gives us the vertical aspect: we are reconciled with God. 2 Corinthians 4 gives us the necessarily accompanying horizontal aspect: we are reconciled with our human neighbours. 1 John 4:7-12 teaches the same two-sided aspect of true reconciliation:

---

[181] T. F. Torrance, *Theological Science*, 207,208.

[182] See the important work of Cardinal Siri on Western historicism and Vico: *Gethsemane* (Chicago, IL: Franciscan Press, 1981).

> Beloved, let us love one another: for love is of God; and every one that loveth is born of God, and knoweth God. He that loveth not knoweth not God: for God is love. In this was manifested the love of God toward us, because that God sent his only begotten Son into the world, that we might live through him. Herein is love, not that we loved God, but that he loved us, and sent his Son to be the propitiation for our sins. Beloved, if God so loved us, we ought also to love one another. No man hath seen God at any time. If we love one another, God dwelleth in us, and his love is perfected in us.[183]

How could one relationally know the God of truth while still His enemy? God does not parcel out His saving truth apart from His own reconciling presence. That is why the Church is commissioned to beseech the lost world to be reconciled to God (2 Cor. 5:20). That marvelous reconciliation, though free to us sinners, was accomplished at highest cost to God, through what He did in His well-loved Son: 'For he hath made him to be sin for us, who knew no sin: that we might be made the righteousness of God in him.' That divinely wrought reconciliation of sinners with God's holy truth operated by means of what John Calvin called *mirifica commutatio* ('wondrous exchange').[184]To refuse to be reconciled with the truth is to shut the only door against knowing the ultimate and saving truth. For Jesus said, 'I am the truth' (John 14:6); finally to refuse the gracious offers of His freely given gospel is to refuse access to the truth, though that door is still open to those who will pray (cf. Rev. 3:20: 'Behold, I stand at the door, and knock: if any man hear my voice, and open the door, I will come in to him, and will sup with him, and he with me').

T. F. Torrance has noted how our coming face to face with God's truth in Christ causes a collision with 'our natural forms of knowing and speaking.'[185] But,

> If the conflict they involve is intended and unavoidable, the ultimate intention they embody is reconciliation. The reason for this is that they are statements in the mode of the Word and Truth of God as it is in Jesus and in accordance with His activity of justification and reconciliation. In Jesus Christ the Truth of God has broken into our human life and history in such a way as to involve our crucifixion on His part as He endures the contradiction of sinners against Himself, and 'crucifixion' on our part as we take up the Cross and follow Him in an act of obedience in which we repent of our untruth and are changed in adaptation to the Truth of God.'[186]

---

[183] James says much the same in terms of faith in God always being accompanied by good works towards humans (James 2:14-26).

[184] Calvin, *Institutes*, IV.xvii.2: 'This is the wondrous exchange which, out of his measureless benevolence, he has made with us; that, becoming Son of man with us, he has made us sons of God with him; that, by his descent to earth, he has prepared an ascent to heaven for us; that, by taking on our mortality, he has conferred his immortality upon us; that, accepting our weakness, he has strengthened us by his power; that, receiving our poverty unto himself, he has transferred his wealth to us; that, taking the weight of our iniquity upon himself (which oppressed us), he has clothed us with his righteousness.'

[185] T. F. Torrance, *Theological Science*, 180.

[186] Ibid., 180, 181.

We know 'in Christ'

Ultimately this means that God is truly known in and through Christ, who is the supreme revelation of His truth in the flesh, by whose Person and work we are reconciled to that truth. The Church Fathers constantly showed that 'we know in Christ.' In the second century, Irenaeus made it clear that in the incarnation of Christ, God adapted Himself *to our human language* so that we could know Him there clearly:

> There is therefore one God, who by the Word and Wisdom created and arranged all things; but this is the Creator (Demiurge) who has granted this world to the human race, and who, as regards His greatness, is indeed unknown to all who have been made by Him (for no man has searched out His height, either among the ancients who have gone to their rest, or any of those who are now alive); but as regards His love, He is always known through Him by whose means He ordained all things. Now this is His Word, our Lord Jesus Christ, who in the last times was made a man among men, that He might join the end to the beginning, that is, man to God. Wherefore the prophets, receiving the prophetic gift from the same Word, announced His advent according to the flesh, by which the blending and communion of God and man took place according to the good pleasure of the Father, the Word of God foretelling from the beginning that God should be seen by men … and should be present with His own creation, saving it, and becoming capable of being perceived by it, and freeing us from the hands of all that hate us, that is, from every spirit of wickedness; and causing us to serve Him in holiness and righteousness all our days (Luke 1:71, 75) in order that man, having embraced the Spirit of God, might pass into the glory of the Father.[187]

In the fourth century, St. Hilary made essentially the same point, showing that the incarnation was God's gracious miracle 'to bring Himself within the range of our understanding':

> Thus He is the only-begotten, perfect, eternal Son of the unbegotten, perfect, eternal Father. But those properties which He has in consequence of the Body which He took, are the fruit of His goodwill toward our salvation. For He, being invisible and bodiless and incomprehensible, as the Son of God, took upon Him such a measure of matter and of lowliness as was needed to bring Him within the range of our understanding, and perception, and contemplation. It was a condescension to our feebleness rather than a surrender of His own proper attributes.'[188]

Earlier, St. Athanasius had commented on Matthew 11:27 ('All things are delivered unto me of my Father: and no man knoweth the Son, but the Father; neither knoweth any man the Father, save the Son, and he to whomsoever the Son will reveal him'; cf. Luke 10:22) as follows:

> For to Him [i.e. Christ], as to a physician, man 'was delivered' to heal the bite of the serpent; as to life, to raise what was dead; as to light, to illumine the darkness; and because He was Word, to renew the rational nature (*to logikon*). Since then all things 'were delivered' to Him (Luke 10:22), and He is made

[187] Irenaeus, *Adversus Haereses* IV.20.4.
[188] Hilary, *De Trinitate* III.3.

> man, straightway all things were set right and perfected ... the Word has been made flesh (John 1:14), and put it on, in order that 'in Him' all should be set right. Suffering Himself, He gave us rest, hungering Himself, He nourished us, and going down into Hades He brought us back thence... For man, being in Him, was quickened: for this was why the Word was united to man, namely, that against man the curse might no longer prevail.[189]

Knowledge by grace of union with Christ

John Calvin explains it in terms of Christ's having come down to make real 'a mutual connection' in being and knowledge between God and His people. Calvin speaks of our otherwise 'hopeless situation' – owing to God's holiness, and our sin and our lack of a Mediator:

> The situation would surely have been hopeless had the very majesty of God not descended to us, since it was not in our power to ascend to him. Hence it was necessary for the Son of God to become of us 'Immanuel, that is, God with us' (Isa. 7:14; Matt. 1:23), and in such a way that his divinity and our human nature might by mutual connection grow together. Otherwise the nearness would not have been near enough, nor the affinity sufficiently firm, for us to hope that God might dwell with us. So great was the disagreement between our uncleanness and God's perfect purity! Even if man had remained free from all stain, his condition would have been too lowly for him to reach God without a Mediator... Who could have done this had not the self-same Son of God become the Son of man, and had not so taken what was ours as to impart what was his to us, and to make what was his by nature ours by grace?'[190]

Karl Barth explained the same reality in terms of the *gratia unionis* ['union by grace']:

> When God gives Himself to us to be known in the truth of His self-knowledge as the triune God, He permits some one of His creatures or a happening in the sphere and time of the world created by Him to speak for Him. The basic reality and substance of the creatureliness which He has commissioned and empowered to speak of Him, the basic reality and substance of the sacramental reality of His revelation, is the existence of the human nature of Jesus Christ. *Gratia unionis*, i.e. on the ground of and through its union with the eternal Word of God, this creature is the supreme and outstanding work and sign of God. Because the eternal Word Himself became flesh, because the revelation of God took place once and for all in Jesus Christ, we know the same revelation of God, wherever it is attested in expectation and recollection... That the eternal Word as such became flesh is a unique occurrence. It happened only once. It is not therefore the starting-point for a general concept of incarnation. But its attestation through the existence of the man Jesus is a beginning of which there are continuations; a sacramental continuity stretches backwards into the existence of the people of Israel, whose Messiah He is, and forwards into the existence of the apostolate and the Church founded on the apostolate...Here we have the function which can be repeated in the confirmation and proclamation of that unique happening of the unity of Creator and creature; and in the

---

[189] Athanasius, *In Illud Omnia* 2.

[190] John Calvin, *Institutes* II.xii.1, 2.

> Church of Jesus Christ, the Church of the old and the new covenants, it actually is repeated...'[191]

T. F. Torrance summarizes the entire work of the Nicene Fathers as explicating the reality implied in Luke 10:22 and Matt. 11:27:

> As they sifted through the New Testament Scriptures, those who met at Nicaea were convinced that the relation of the Father to the Son and of the Son to the Father constitutes the basic ontological relationship or reciprocity in the Godhead in which all the language of the gospel is finally rooted and shaped. 'All things have been delivered unto me of my Father: and no man knows who the Son is, save the Father; and who the Father is, save the Son, and he to whom the Son wills to reveal him' (Luke 10:22; Matt. 11:27). That is to say, a mutual relation of knowing and being obtains between the Father and the Son in the Godhead, and it is as that relation is actualized through the incarnation between Jesus Christ and God the Father that it becomes possible for us to know God in and through Jesus Christ in such a way that our knowledge terminates on the ultimate Reality of God himself.[192]
>
> We could not know the Truth of God had he not condescended in Jesus Christ to be one with us in our human nature, and thus to present himself to us within the lowliness of our creaturely capacity and at the same time to lift us up in Jesus Christ to know him in some measure as he is in himself. However, even when we do apprehend the Truth of God in this way, we are quite unable to comprehend him, for he infinitely transcends all our human conceptions of him.[193]

To know God's truth is to know God, and we know God truly only to the extent that we *participate* in His life by grace. Stăniloae has stated this point well: 'We only know the attributes of God in their dynamism and to the extent to which we participate in them.'[194] In other words, this true knowledge of the personal God is by definition personal:

> If God offered his love beforehand to conscious creatures through the things of creation and through his uncreated energies, in Christ he gives himself to them as hypostasis [i.e. as a person]. In Christ the divine hypostasis [i.e. Person] is accessible to us on our own human level for the sake of full communion. Christ overcomes in himself the interval between divinity and humanity, and between himself as God and ourselves. This state is made real for us at present, however, only potentially and, as it were, through a process of maturation.[195]
>
> Through the incarnate Son we enter into filial communion with the Father, while through the Spirit we pray to the Father or speak with him as sons. For the Spirit unites himself with us in prayer. 'It is the Spirit in whom we worship, and in whom we pray... Therefore, to adore or to pray in the Spirit seems to me to be simply himself offering prayer or adoration to himself.'[196] But this prayer which the Spirit offers, within us, he offers to himself in our name, and into this prayer we too are drawn. Through grace the Spirit

[191] Barth, *Church Dogmatics* II/1 (E.T.), 53, 54.

[192] T. F. Torrance, *Reality and Evangelical Theology*, 111, 112.

[193] Ibid., 119.

[194] Stăniloae, *The Experience of God*, 126.

[195] Ibid., 169.

[196] Stăniloae quotes Gregory Nazianzus, *Oration* 31.12.

> identifies himself with us so that, through grace, we may identify ourselves with him. Through grace the Spirit eliminates the distance between our 'I' and his 'I', creating between us and the Father, through grace, the same relating he has by nature with the Father and the Son. If in the incarnate Son we have become sons by grace, in the Spirit we gain the consciousness and boldness that come from being sons.[197]

The transforming knowledge of the Triune God through Christ, given us in the Holy Spirit as we participate in the saving community of faith, is vouchsafed to us in the Holy Scriptures. As we follow them, we will always be in line with what the Church has known as 'the rule of truth'. All of this is the gift of God to the undeserving within the bounds of the Covenant of Grace. And they are commissioned to invite all others into it.

---

[197] Stăniloae, *The Experience of God*, Vol. I, 248.

Chapter Six
Appendix One

Where Was the Covenant Before the Sixteenth Century?

Within a generation of theological work after the sixteenth-century Protestant Reformation, emphasis on the covenants of Holy Scripture became very pronounced. This raises a fair question: if covenant theology is as significant as the Post-Reformation taught, then why was it neglected before that time? That is, is covenant theology a valid part of the ancient Christian tradition, or is it a Protestant innovation?

In 1534, Heinrich Bullinger, ministerial and theological successor of Zwingli in Zurich, wrote a major work on the covenant: *De Testamento seu Foedere Dei unico & aeterno Heinrychi Bullingeri brevis expositio.*[1] In Bullinger's *Epitome* of 1565, he saw the covenant as the key to summarizing history from creation to the destruction of Jerusalem in A.D. 70. By the 1570s and 1580s, Ursinus and Olevianus, German Reformed theologians, who had written the Heidelberg Catechism (published in 1563), were developing the concept of covenant much more fully (little had been said about it in the Heidelberg Catechism). From there it passed into widespread usage among Continental and British Calvinists for the next four centuries.

But where was covenant theology before 1534? So far as I know, the best answer to this question is found in a still unpublished PhD dissertation from Edinburgh University by the Rev. Dr. J. Ligon Duncan, The Covenant Idea in the Ante-Nicene Fathers (1995).[2] With his kind permission, I reproduce directly and in full the abstract to his dissertation, in hopes that it may help those who wish to research the ancient background of covenant theology within the undivided Christian tradition.

'This thesis argues that the covenant idea was more significant in the writings of particular ante-Nicene theologians than has generally

[1]For an English translation, see J. Wayne Baker and Charles McCoy, *Fountainhead of Federalism: Heinrich Bullinger and the Covenantal Tradition. With a Translation of De Testamento seu foedere Dei unico et aeterno (1534) by Heinrich Bullinger* (Westminster/John Knox Press: Louisville, 1991). For Bullinger's theology of the covenant, see also J. Wayne Baker, *Heinrich Bullinger and the Covenant: The Other Reformed Tradition* (Athens: Ohio University Press, 1980).

[2]Dr. Duncan is senior minister of the First Presbyterian Church of Jackson, Mississippi, and was formerly a professor of systematic theology at Reformed Theological Seminary in Jackson, Mississippi.

been admitted in patristic research or general surveys of the history of the covenant idea in the Christian tradition. Indeed, this survey of the covenant idea in the ante-Nicene period demonstrates a significant usage, development, and modification of the covenant concept as it is found in the OT and NT writings, and early Judaism. This investigation reveals that the covenant idea functions in several arenas of early Christian thought. It is employed 1) to stress moral obligations incumbent upon Christians; 2) to show God's grace in including the Gentiles in the Abrahamic blessings; 3) to deny the reception of these promises to the Israel of the flesh, that is, Israel considered merely as an ethnic entity; 4) to demonstrate continuity in the divine economy; and 5) to explain discontinuity in the divine economy.

'In reviewing the role of early Christian covenant thought in these areas, this thesis argues that 1) the pre-Nicene theologians usually take OT covenant passages (not NT passages) as the starting point in their applications of the covenant concept to Christian living. 2) The early Christian use of the covenant idea evidences that they understood the covenant to be both unilateral and bilateral, promissory and obligatory, to bring divine blessings and entail human obedience. 3) These writings also show that, from the very earliest times, Christian authors (following OT and NT examples) have employed the covenant concept as a key structural idea in their presentations of redemptive history. 4) Contrary to the suggestions of previous studies, there is no evidence of a gap in the usage of the covenant idea after the era of the NT writings. 5) The covenant idea was closely linked to the early Christian self-understanding as the people of God. 6) The covenant idea is not monolithic in the thought of the authors surveyed. It is employed with differing emphases and takes on varying shades of meaning in their respective writings. 7) Genetic connections in specific usages of the covenant idea can be found in different pre-Nicene authors (e.g., Justin, Irenaeus, Tertullian).

'The argument of this thesis proceeds by first reviewing the role of the covenant idea in the writings of the NT, Apostolic Fathers, and Justin. This provides background for comparison and contrast with subsequent theological reflection on the covenants in Christian theology. Then we consider, in turn, the covenant idea in Melito, Irenaeus, Tertullian, Cyprian, Origen, Clement of Alexandria, Hippolytus, and Novatian. In each, specific employments of the covenant idea are inventoried. In the epilogue, our findings are summarized and conclusions are drawn.

'This study is significant for at least these following reasons. 1) It confirms current research on the Jewish matrix of early Christianity, from a vantage-point not yet exploited. 2) It reviews in greater detail the early Christian covenant thought which is now being acknowledged to have been influential on the sixteenth-century Reformers (such as Bullinger and Calvin). 3) As the first extensive patristic survey of the covenant idea, it fills a significant lacuna in the history of ideas. 4) It lays the groundwork for more detailed considerations of the covenant concept in the pre-Nicene and post-Nicene eras.'

Chapter Seven

The One Lord Exists as Three Persons

The identity of the three distinct Persons within the one beatific Being of God indicates that God's very Being subsists through relations. That is to say, the ontological is understood through the relational. The Christian Church had to think through the Trinity because Jesus is God, the Father is God and the Holy Spirit is God, and yet there is only One God. We examine central New Testament passages which exhibit the Triune nature and mission of God, as do many other triadic formulae. While not yet clearly revealed in the Old Testament, God's inner diversity of related persons is definitely prefigured there in wide-ranging fashion. 'Elohim', 'God and God', hypostatizations of Word, Wisdom, Spirit, Name, Face and Glory point to an inner fellowship of divine Persons within the Being (or substance) of the one God. The same diversity of persons within divine oneness is adumbrated by the Angel of the Lord, by theophanies, by the Messiah and by many Old Testament triads.

Relational terms signify who God is

The one eternal LORD exists as a communion of holy love within Himself, and this means personal existence; that is, the inter-communion of three equally divine and holy Persons. For God to be is to be in relationship within Himself. As John Zizioulas has written concerning the essential oneness of Father and Son: 'To say that the Son belongs to God's substance implies that substance possesses almost by definition a relational character.'[1] Or as St. Augustine says: 'For God it is not one thing to be, another to be a person, but it is absolutely the same thing.'[2]

In his 'Second Dialogue On the Trinity', Cyril of Alexandria explains that mentioning such true attributes of God the Father as unbegotten, incorruptible, immortal and invisible, while necessary and correct, do not signify who He really is.[3] To know who God most essentially is, one must look at the relational terms concerning Himself that are given us,

---

[1]John Zizioulas, *Being as Communion*, 95.

[2]Augustine, *De Trinitate* VII.6.11.

[3]Cyril of Alexandria, *Dialogues Sur La Trinité* (French translation by G. M. de Durand, Paris: Sources Chrétiennes, 1976), II. 422b (p.237).

particularly in the baptismal formula of Matthew 28. Thereby, we may discern most deeply who God is in His own inner-Trinitarian relationships as Father, Son and Holy Spirit. His being is expressed most clearly for us in these eternal relationships.[4]

St. Augustine seems to have the same thing in mind when he writes that God can be spoken of relationship-wise or substance-wise. If Father could be thought of apart from Son, and Son apart from Father (that is, only in relationship to themselves alone), they would, in effect, be different substances.

> But since the Father is only called so because he has a Son, and the Son is only called so because he has a Father, these things are not said substance-wise, as neither is said with reference to itself but only with reference to the other… Therefore, although being Father is different from being Son, there is no difference of substance, because they are not called these substance-wise but relationship-wise…[5]

In other words, the Trinity of Persons in organic relationship one to another within the one Being (or substance) of God is constitutive of who God is from all eternity, without 'amounting to' more than one substance (or more than one essence of God, or more than one God). Augustine summarizes his position several paragraphs later, when he writes: 'Each meaning [i.e. "begotten" and "unbegotten"] belongs to the predication that is called relationship. And what is stated relationship-wise does not designate substance, because just as son refers to father, and not son to not father, so begotten must refer to begetter, and not begotten to not begetter.'[6] And he adds in a note to Book VII.9, that God the Father 'subsists by way of relationship, just as he begets by way of relationship…'[7] Or, as Zizioulas has said above, the substance of God is inherently relational, so that within the Triune God we find one Being (or substance), who always exists ontologically, and thus, as three related Persons.

Who is Jesus?

St. Athanasius showed that the Christian doctrine of the Holy Trinity originally comes from the Church's scriptural reflection upon the Father/Son relationship. In Book 3 of his *Orations Against the Arians*, he brings out the central basis of the gospel as reposing in the fact that through the Son we know who the Father is in His own being. 'We are allowed to know the Son in the Father, because the whole Being of the Son is proper to the Father's being… For whereas the Form of the Godhead of the Father is in the being of the Son, it follows that the Son is in the Father and the Father is in the Son.'[8] And, 'The Godhead of the Son is in the Father's, whence also it is indivisible; and thus there is one God and none other but he. And so since

---

[4]Ibid., 422b (p. 239).

[5]Augustine, *De Trinitate*, Edmund Hill, translator, V.6 (p. 192).

[6]Ibid., V.8.

[7]Ibid.,VII.9 (p.227).

[8]Athanasius, *Contra Arianos* 3.3.

they are one, and the Godhead himself is one, the same things are said of the Son as are said of the Father, except his being said to be Father.'[9]

It is significant that the Apostles' Creed and the Nicene Creed place God's Fatherhood before His being Creator. That is, God was always Father, but not always Creator. Hence Athanasius writes in *Contra Arianos*: 'It would be more godly and true to signify God from the Son and call him Father, than to name God from his works alone and call him Unoriginate.'[10] Thus, creation is to be understood in light of the eternal Triune relations within the One God, as John 1:1-3 suggests ('In the beginning was the Word, and the Word was with God, and the Word was God. The same was in the beginning with God. All things were made by him; and without him was not any thing made that was made').

The Church was constituted by the events of Christ's incarnation, and by the outpouring of the Holy Spirit at Pentecost. Thus, they had to seek to understand who this Christ and Holy Spirit were, who brought them into the saving community of Israel. Jaroslav Pelikan of Yale takes us back to the central question raised for the Christian Church by who Jesus was:

> ... for the early Church, 'God' was an appropriate name for Jesus. The oldest surviving sermon of the Christian Church after the New Testament opened with the words: 'Brethren, we ought so to think of Jesus Christ as of God, as of the judge of the living and the dead. And we ought not to belittle our salvation; for when we belittle him, we expect also to receive little.' The oldest surviving account of the death of a Christian martyr contained the declaration: 'It will be impossible for us to forsake Christ ... or to worship any other. For him, being the Son of God, we adore, but the martyrs ... we cherish.' The oldest surviving pagan report about the church described Christians as gathering before sunrise and 'singing a hymn to Christ as though to [a] God.' The oldest surviving liturgical prayer of the church was a prayer addressed to Christ: 'Our Lord, come!'... amid all the varieties of the response to the Gnostic systems, Christians were sure that the Redeemer did not belong to some lower order of divine reality, but was God himself.[11]

The Church then had to think through who the one God really is as to His innermost being. The basic issue in the life and theology of the early Church was the reality and significance of who Jesus is. Being convinced that He was the very Son of God, the Church had to seek to understand His relationship to God the Father, as a matter of first priority. As we shall soon see, this was happening in the years surrounding the Councils of Nicea (A.D. 323) and Constantinople (A.D. 381). Heretics wanted to make the Son in various ways inferior to the Father, but the Church understood that His full deity was essential to the accomplishment of the salvation of fallen humanity.

In his *Lord Jesus Christ*, Larry Hurtado states:

> Moreover, an exalted significance of Jesus appears astonishingly early in Christian circles. Well within the first couple decades of the Christian

[9]Ibid., 3.5.

[10]Ibid., 1.34.

[11]Jaroslav Pelikan, *The Christian Tradition: The Emergence of the Catholic Tradition* (vol. I), (Chicago and London: The University of Chicago Press, 1974), 173.

> movement (i.e., ca. 30-50 C.E., to make this point in the discussion a deliberately modest chronological claim) Jesus was treated as a recipient of religious devotion and was associated with God in striking ways. In fact, as we will see later in this study, we probably have to posit a virtual explosion of devotion to Jesus toward the earlier end of this short period. I have proposed that in this development we have what amounts to a new and distinctive 'mutation' or variant form of the monotheistic practice that is otherwise characteristic of the Jewish religious matrix out of which the Christian movement sprang.[12]

Probably more than any other, Athanasius worked through most clearly what this meant to the inner being of God. T. F. Torrrance summarizes: 'Through the *homousion* [i.e. the Son is of the "same being" as the Father – the central affirmation of the Nicene Creed] the incarnational and saving self-revelation of God as Father, Son and Holy Spirit was traced back to what God is enhypostically and coinherently in himself, in his own eternal being as Father, Son and Holy Spirit.'[13]

In other words, if the Son – as the Nicene Creed confesses – is *homoousios* [i.e. of the same substance] with the Father, then both the Father and the Son are God. And the Church later goes on to confess that the Spirit is *homousios* with the Son, so that Father, Son and Spirit are all God. But then, as Dr. John Zizioulas points out, the question arises: 'What does it mean to say that God is Father, Son and Spirit without ceasing to be one God?'[14] Thus, as Leonard Hodgson states, a way of thinking had to be found which would preserve biblical monotheism, yet maintain the distinctness of the Persons of Father, Son and Spirit.[15]

Before we address this question, we must note that the New Testament writers were just as monotheistic as those of the Old Testament. B. B. Warfield of old Princeton made this plain, in noting that the New Testament writers did not think that their doctrine of God was alien in any way to the Old Testament:

> ... its writers [the New Testament] felt no incongruity whatever between their doctrine of the Trinity and the Old Testament conception of God. The New Testament writers certainly were not conscious of being 'setters forth of strange gods.' To their own apprehension they worshipped and proclaimed just the God of Israel and they laid no less stress than the Old Testament upon His unity (John 17:3; 1 Cor. 8:4; 1 Tim. 2:5). They do not then place two new gods by the side of Jehovah as alike with Him to be served and worshipped; they conceive of Jehovah as Himself at once Father, Son, and Holy Spirit ... Without apparent misgiving they take over Old Testament passages and apply them to Father, Son, and Spirit indifferently. Obviously they understand themselves, and wish to be understood, as setting forth in the Father, Son and Spirit just the one God that the God of the Old Testament revelation is...[16]

---

[12]Larry W. Hurtado, *Lord Jesus Christ: Devotion to Jesus in Earliest Christianity* (Grand Rapids, MI: Wm. B. Eerdmans, 2003), 2.

[13]T. F. Torrance, *The Trinitarian Faith*, 199.

[14]Zizioulas, op. cit., 36.

[15]Leonard Hodgson, *The Doctrine of the Trinity*, New York: Charles Scribner's Sons, 1944), 99-100.

[16]B.B. Warfield, *Biblical Foundations*, London: The Tyndale Press, 1958), 88.

In the same essay, Warfield rightly says that 'the fundamental proof of the Trinity' lies in the incarnation of God the Son and the outpouring of God the Spirit:

> ... all the evidence of whatever kind, and from whatever source derived, that Jesus Christ is God manifested in the flesh, and that the Holy Spirit is a divine Person, is just so much evidence for the doctrine of the Trinity ... and when we go to the New Testament for evidence of the Trinity we are to seek it, not merely in the scattered allusions to the Trinity as such, numerous and instructive as they are, but primarily in the whole mass of evidence which the New Testament provides of the Deity of Christ and the Divine personality of the Holy Spirit.[17]

Warfield notes the basic methodology presupposed by all orthodox Christian theology: (1) one finds that the New Testament insists on the unity of the Godhead; (2) one finds that the New Testament recognizes the Father as God, the Son as God and the Spirit as God. And (3) these three are presented to us as Persons.

New Testament Evidence regarding the Trinity

The Trinitarian witness of crucial passages

The great commission given by the risen Lord to the Church admonishes us 'to baptize all nations in the name of the Father and of the Son and of the Holy Ghost' (Matt. 28:19). This indicates three divine Persons who are equally God and yet only one God. This prime baptismal formula has served as the heart of the basic Trinitarian theology of the Christian Church from the beginning of its life and mission to the world. The Pauline benediction, given in 2 Corinthians 13:14, is clearly Trinitarian: 'The grace of the Lord Jesus Christ, and the love of God, and the communion of the Holy Spirit, be with you all.' Embedded in St. Paul's famous passage on spiritual gifts is found this Trinitarian formula: 'Now there are diversities of gifts, but the same Spirit. And there are differences of administrations, but the same Lord. And there are diversities of operations, but it is the same God which worketh all in all.' (1 Cor. 12:4-6)

In Galatians 4, Paul presents the climax of the long history of redemption in Trinitarian terms: 'But when the fullness of the time was come, God sent forth his Son, made of a woman, made under the law, to redeem them that were under the law, that we might receive the adoption of sons. And because ye are sons, God hath sent forth the Spirit of his Son into your hearts, crying, Abba, Father' (verses 4-6).

In Ephesians 4, the Apostle to the Gentiles speaks of the life and unity of the Church in terms of its connection with the Trinity: 'There is one body, and one Spirit, even as ye are called in one hope of your calling; One Lord, one faith, one baptism. One God and Father of all, who is above all, and through all, and in you all' (verses 4-6). Similarly, Ephesians 2:13, 14, 16, 18, which shows how Jew and Gentile are brought together as one

[17] Ibid., 92.

people by Christ's Person and work, is also Trinitarian: 'But now in Christ Jesus ye who sometimes were far off are made nigh by the blood of Christ. For he is our peace, who hath made both [i.e. Jew and Gentile] one, and hath broken down the middle wall of partition between us... And that he might reconcile both unto God in one body by the cross, having slain the enmity thereby... For through him we both have access by one Spirit unto the Father.'

T. F. Torrance writes, concerning such passages: 'It is significant that in these formulations reference to the Father, to the Son, and to the Holy Spirit is not always made in the same order, which suggests that already in the apostolic mind there was lodged an implicit belief in the equality of the three divine Persons.'[18]

Other triadic formulae

We find other 'triadic formulae' elsewhere in the New Testament as well.

Acts 2:32, 33: 'This Jesus hath God raised up, whereof we all are witnesses. Therefore being by the right hand of God exalted, and having received of the Father the promise of the Holy Ghost, he hath shed forth this, which ye now see and hear.'

1 Peter 1:2: 'Elect according to the foreknowledge of God the Father, through sanctification of the Spirit, unto obedience and sprinkling of the blood of Jesus Christ: Grace unto you, and peace, be multiplied.'

2 Thessalonians 2:13, 14: 'But we are bound to give thanks always to God for you, brethren beloved of the Lord, because God hath chosen you to salvation through sanctification of the Spirit and belief of the truth: whereunto he called you by our gospel, to the obtaining of the glory of our Lord Jesus Christ.'

Such passages indicate an underlying Trinitarian theology. As B. B. Warfield stated:

> Paul clearly so writes, not because 'gifts,' 'workings,' 'operations,' stand out in his thought as greatly diverse things, but because God, the Lord, and the Spirit lie in the back of his mind constantly suggesting a threefold causality behind every manifestation of grace. The Trinity is alluded to rather than asserted; but it is so alluded to as to show that it constitutes the determining basis of all Paul's thought of the God of redemption.[19]

The New Testament includes a number of 'triadic formulae' where the three Persons of the Trinity are in evidence, without however mention of the kind of co-ordinated relationship amongst them that we found in the passages above. Such texts are: Matthew 11:25-27; Luke 10:21, 22; Acts 2:38, 39; 11:17; Romans 1:3, 4; 5:5, 8; 8:3, 4, 8, 9, 11, 16, 17; 15:16, 30; 1 Corinthians 6:11; 12:4ff.; 2 Corinthians 1:2f.; 3:3f.; Galatians 3:13f.; Ephesians 3:14-16; Philippians 3:3; Colossians 1:6-8; Titus 3:4-6; Hebrews 6:4f.; 10:29; 1 Peter 4:14; 1 John 5:6-12; Jude 20f.

Various passages in the Gospel of John are the outflow of Trinitarian relationships, which are perhaps more assumed than explained.

---

[18] T. F. Torrance, *The Christian Doctrine of God*, 71.

[19] B. B. Warfield, 'The Biblical Doctrine of the Trinity,' (Chapter 3) in *Biblical Foundations*, 159.

> Then answered Jesus and said unto them, 'Verily, verily, I say unto you, The Son can do nothing of himself, but what he seeth the Father do: for what things soever he doeth, these also doeth the Son likewise. For the Father loveth the Son, and sheweth him all things that himself doeth: and he will shew him greater works than these, that ye may marvel' (John 5:19,20).

> 'And I will pray the Father, and he shall give you another Comforter, that he may abide with you for ever; Even the Spirit of truth; whom the world cannot receive, because it seeth him not, neither knoweth him: but ye know him; for he dwelleth with you, and shall be in you. He that hath my commandments, and keepeth them, he it is that loveth me: and he that loveth me shall be loved of my Father, and I will love him, and will manifest myself to him… If a man love me, he will keep my words: and my Father will love him, and we will come unto him, and make our abode with him. He that loveth me not keepeth not my sayings: and the word which ye hear is not mine, but the Father's which sent me. These things have I spoken unto you, being yet present with you. But the Comforter, which is the Holy Ghost, whom the Father will send in my name, he shall teach you all things, and bring all things to your remembrance, whatsoever I have said unto you' (John 14:16-21, 23-26).

> 'Howbeit when he, the Spirit of truth, is come, he will guide you into all truth: for he shall not speak of himself; but whatsoever he shall hear, that shall he speak; and he will shew you things to come. He shall glorify me: for he shall receive of mine, and shall shew it unto you. A little while, and ye shall not see me: and again, a little while, and ye shall see me, because I go to the Father'(John 16:13-16).

> Then said Jesus to them again, 'Peace be unto you: as my Father hath sent me, even so send I you. And when he had said this, he breathed on them, and saith unto them, Receive ye the Holy Ghost…' (John 20:21).

Joint working of the Persons of the Trinity

In addition to specifically Trinitarian formulae, we also notice the presence and working of all three Persons of the Godhead on a number of occasions; particularly connected with the incarnation and ministry of Christ. In Matthew 1, at the annunciation of the conception of Jesus to the Virgin Mary's betrothed husband, Joseph, the Angel mentions the Holy Ghost (v. 20), Jesus (v. 21) and God the Father – i.e. 'the Lord' (vv. 22, 23). It is the same in Luke with the salutation of the Angel Gabriel to the Virgin. God the Father is mentioned (vv. 30, 32, 35); God the Son (vv. 31, 32, 33), and the Holy Ghost (v. 35).

In each of the four Gospels, all three Persons of the Trinity are referred to at the Baptism of Christ by John in the River Jordan (Matt. 3:16,17; Mark 1:8-11; Luke 3:21-22; John 1:29-34). In various places both Father and Holy Spirit are directly connected to the final passion and atoning death of the Son: e.g. Christ speaks to the Father in Gethsemane (Matt. 26:39, 42, 53; Luke 22:42), and there he speaks of the Father (John 18:11). Christ speaks of the Father at his trial (Luke 22:69, 70). He speaks to the Father from the cross (Matt. 27:46; Mark 15:34; Luke 23:34, 46). In Hebrews 9:14, we are told that Christ's atoning work on Calvary was accomplished through the Holy Spirit: 'How much more shall the blood of Christ, who through the eternal Spirit offered himself without spot to God, purge your conscience from dead works to serve the living God?'

The New Testament attributes the bodily resurrection of Christ to the Father, to the Son himself, and to the Holy Spirit. As Louis Berkhof writes:

> In distinction from others who were raised from the dead, Christ arose through His own power. He spoke of Himself as the resurrection and the life, John 11:25, declared that He had the power to lay down His life, and to take it up again, John 10:18, and even predicted that He would rebuild the temple of His body, John 2:19-21. But the resurrection was not a work of Christ alone; it is frequently ascribed to the power of God in general, Acts 2:24,32; 3:26; 5:30, 1 Cor. 6:14; Eph. 1:20, or, more particularly to the Father, Rom. 6:4; Gal. 1:1; 1 Pet. 1:3. And if the resurrection of Christ can be called a work of God, then it follows that the Holy Spirit was also operative in it, for all the opera ad extra are works of the triune God. Moreover, Rom. 8:11 also implies this.[20]

Revelation 1:4, 5 greets the churches in Trinitarian fashion:

> John to the seven churches which are in Asia: Grace be unto you, and peace, from him which is, and which was, and which is to come; and from the seven Spirits which are before his throne; and from Jesus Chirst, who is the faithful witness, and the first begotten of the dead, and the prince of the kings of the earth. Unto him that loved us, and washed us from our sins in his own blood…

The Father is referred to as 'him which is, and was and is to come'; the Spirit as 'the seven Spirits before his throne'; and then Jesus Christ is described.

B. B. Warfield summarizes faithfully the New Testament teaching of the One God as always existing in three Persons as fully consistent with the Old Testament, of which it is the fulfillment:

> It is clear, in other words, that, as we read the New Testament, we are not witnessing the birth of a new conception of God. What we meet within its pages is a firmly established conception of God underlying and giving tone to the entire fabric. It is not in a text here and there that the New Testament bears its testimony to the doctrine of the Trinity. The whole book is Trinitarian to the core; all its teaching is built on the assumption of the Trinity; and its allusions to the Trinity are frequent, cursory, easy and confident. It is with a view to the cursoriness of the allusions to it in the New Testament that it has been remarked that 'the doctrine of the Trinity is not so much heard as overheard in the statements of Scripture.' It would be more exact to say that it is not so much inculcated as presupposed. The

---

[20]Louis Berkhof, *Systematic Theology* (New Combined Edition), with a New Preface by Richard A. Muller (Grand Rapids, Mich.: Wm. B. Eerdmans Publ. Co., 1996), 346, 347. See Karl Barth's discussion of this question of 'Jesus Christ as the Son of God … associated with the Father as the Subject of His own resurrection …' in *Church Dogmatics* IV/1, 303-09. Barth places the emphasis here on the work of the Father in this matter, rather than the co-operation of the Son as an Acting Subject.

> doctrine of the Trinity does not appear in the New Testament in the making, but as already made.[21]

In like fashion, St. Augustine based his faith in the Trinity on the Holy Scriptures of Old and New Testaments, as understood in the Catholic Church:

> The purpose of all the Catholic commentators I have been able to read on the divine books of both testaments, who have written before me on the trinity which God is, has been to teach that according to the Scriptures Father and Son and Holy Spirit in the inseparable equality of one substance present a divine unity; and therefore there are not three gods, but one God; although indeed the Father has begotten the Son, and therefore he who is the Father is not the Son; and the Son is begotten by the Father, and therefore he who is the Son is not the Father; and the Holy Spirit is neither the Father nor the Son, but only the Spirit of the Father and of the Son, himself co-equal to the Father and the Son, and belonging to the threefold unity.
>
> It was not however this same three (their teaching continues) that was born of the Virgin Mary, crucified and buried under Pontius Pilate, rose again on the third day and ascended into heaven, but the Son alone. Nor was it the same three that came down upon Jesus in the form of a dove at his baptism, or came down on the day of Pentecost after the Lord's ascension, with a roaring sound from heaven as though a violent gust were rushing down, and in divided tongues of fire, but the Holy Spirit alone. Nor was it this same three that spoke from heaven *You are my Son*, either at his baptism by John or on the mountain when the three disciples were with him, nor when the resounding voice was heard, *I have both glorified it* (my name) *and will glorify it again*, but it was the Father's voice alone addressing the Son; although just as Father and Son and Holy Spirit are inseparable, so do they work inseparably. This is also my faith inasmuch as it is the Catholic faith.[22]

Why did not the Old Testament clearly reveal the Trinity?

Gregory Nazianzus and other theologians in the East suggested that the Trinity was not clearly revealed in the Old Testament in order to prevent the Jewish people from being tempted to polytheism, with the idea that to have spoken plainly of a plurality within God might have encouraged a belief in more than one God. There may be something to that, but I believe that B. B. Warfield is much more to the point when (in line with Galatians 4:4) he states the following:

> The real reason for the delay in the revelation of the Trinity, however, is grounded in the secular development of the redemptive purpose of God; the times were not ripe for the revelation of the Trinity in the unity of the Godhead until the fullness of the time had come for God to send His Son unto redemption, and His Spirit unto sanctification. This revelation in word must needs wait upon the revelation in deed, to which it brings its

---

[21]B. B. Warfield, 'The Biblical Doctrine of the Trinity' (in *Biblical Foundations*) 143.

[22]Augustine, *De Trinitate*, translated by Edmund Hill, O.P., as *The Trinity* (Brooklyn, NY: New City Press, 1991), I.7 (pp. 69,70).

> necessary explanation, no doubt, but from which also it derives its own entire significance and value.[23]

Yet Gregory Nazianzus himself was not far from this insight, when he wrote concerning the gradual revelation of the Trinity in Old and New Testaments:

> The Old Testament proclaimed the Father openly, and the Son more obscurely. The New manifested the Son, and suggested the Deity of the Spirit. Now the Spirit Himself dwells among us, and supplies us with a clearer demonstration of Himself. For it was not safe, when the Godhead of the Father was not yet acknowledged, plainly to proclaim the Son; nor when that of the Son was not yet received to burden us further (if I may use so bold an expression) with the Holy Spirit; lest perhaps people might, like men loaded with food beyond their strength, and presenting eyes as yet too weak to bear it to the sun's light, risk the loss even of that which was within the reach of their powers; but that by gradual additions, and as David says, goings up, and advances and progress from glory to glory, the Light of the trinity might shine upon the more illuminated.[24]

How much was intimated concerning the Trinity in the Old Testament?

Since the Christian Church is in direct continuity with Israel in the one Covenant of Grace, the Scriptures of the New Testament are to be seen as fulfilling those of the Old Testament, not contradicting them, nor inconsistent with them, for the One God is not divided in His Being nor in His revelation. Therefore, from the vantage point of the coming of Christ in the flesh and the outpouring of the Holy Spirit at Pentecost, we can look back and see that the Old Testament teachings on the being and activity of God are consistent with who God shows Himself to be in the New Testament, although in the ongoing development of revelation, more light is shone than previously 'in the fullness of the times…' And from that perspective, the Fathers and later teachers of the Church have found intimations of the Trinity in the Old Testament, even where it was not yet clearly revealed.

God and creation

The very first verse of the Old Testament speaks of God as *Elohim* (Gen. 1:1), which – as we saw earlier – is a plural form for God. We noted that there is a numerically singular word for God – Eloah – and yet the plural is used here and throughout the Old Testament. By itself, this usage would not be sufficient 'to prove' that God is Triune, but it does seem to indicate a diversity within the being of the One God who created all things. The related verb in Genesis 1:26, 'Let us make man in our image, after our likeness …' again does not constitute a clear proof of the Trinity, but it is consistent with the plural nature of the subject, and – from the New Testament perspective – places the creation of man in the context of the inter-personal relationships

---

[23]Warfield, op. cit., 91.
[24]Gregory Nazianzus, *Oration* 31.26.

of the Holy Trinity. St. Thomas Aquinas brings this out in his comments on the Old Latin version of Genesis 1:26, 'Let us create man unto our image...'[25] And, of course, Thomas was following Saint Augustine in this matter, although he considerably developed the understanding of image in the Trinitarian context.[26]

Thomas writes, for instance in De Trinitate: 'Both let us make and our are said in the plural, and ought not to be received except in terms of relative names. For it was not that gods might make, or make after the image and likeness of gods, but that the Father, and Son and Holy Spirit might make after the image of the Father, and Son, and Holy Spirit, that man might subsist as the image of God. And God is the Trinity.'[27]

Elohim usually takes the singular verb (as in Gen. 1:1), but can also take the plural, as in Genesis 20:13; 35:7; Nehemiah 9:18, and Isaiah 16:6. This usage seems to imply that God is not a solitary 'individual', but that within His life is a rich diversity of relationship, although on its own, it is not enough to prove it clearly.

The creation account definitely implies a certain diversity within the being of the Creator. In Genesis 1:1 we find Elohim who creates the heavens and the earth; in verse 2, we find the Spirit of God who broods over the waters, and in verse 3, the word of God which commands 'Let there be light.' Herman Bavinck suggested that the 'ontological Trinity' was necessary for the 'economical' work of creation to have occurred 'outside the being of God': '... without generation [i.e. of the Son, eternally, by the Father] creation would not be possible. If in an absolute sense God could not communicate himself to the Son, he would be even less able, in a relative sense, to communicate himself to his creature. If God were not triune, creation would not be possible.'[28]

Athanasius had also, long before, interpreted the divine actions of the creation within a Trinitarian framework in *De Incarnatione*: 'It is, then, proper for us to begin the treatment of this subject [*sc*. the incarnation] by speaking of the creation of the universe, and of God its Artificer, that so it may be duly perceived that the renewal of creation has been the work of the self same Word that made it at the beginning. For it will appear not inconsonant for the Father to have wrought its salvation in Him by Whose means He made it.'[29]

God and God

The Hebrew word used for the oneness of God in the 'Shema' of Deuteronomy 6:4 ('Hear, O Israel, the LORD our God is one LORD') is the oneness of unity (*echad*). There is another word for numerical individuality

---

[25] See D. Juvenal Merriell, *To the Image of the Trinity: A Study in the Development of Aquinas' Teaching* (Toronto: Pontifical Institute of Mediaeval Studies, 1990).

[26] See Merriell, op. cit., 13-35.

[27] St. Thomas, *De Trinitate*, 7.6.12.

[28] Herman Bavinck, *In the Beginning: Foundations of Creation Theology*, ed. John Vriend and John Bolt (Grand Rapids: Baker, 1999), 39.

[29] Athanasius, *De Incarnatione*, 1. See also ibid., 3,12,14.

(*yachid*), but it is not used here. This usage is entirely consistent with a plurality of persons within the One God.

Thus, it is not surprising that in a few Old Testament texts, we find 'God and God' together, indicating a mysterious diversity within the one being of God, that will only be made clear in the New Testament. Such is the case with Psalm 110:1, where the Lord Himself addresses the Lord Himself: 'The LORD said unto my Lord, Sit thou at my right hand, until I make thine enemies thy footstool.' This 'Lord' of David is addressed by none less than the LORD, the 'I AM'. This text is addressed elsewhere in this volume.[30]

Or Psalm 45:6, 7: 'Thy throne, O God, is for ever and ever: the sceptre of thy kingdom is a right sceptre. Thou lovest righteousness and hatest wickedness: therefore God, thy God, hath anointed thee with the oil of gladness above thy fellows.' The Psalm envisions a royal wedding in which the persons involved are more than human royalty; deity is in evidence. One of them is spoken of as God in verse 6, and then in verse 7, God is anointed by God. Psalm 45 does not tell us who this is, but the New Testament shows us. For there we find who it is at the Jordan River and on the Mount of Transfiguration.

In the call of God to the prophet, Isaiah, the holy seraphim are praising the Lord with a threefold praise: 'Holy, Holy, Holy, is the LORD of hosts…' (Isa. 6:3). The fact that the same threefold praise is offered to God by the angelic beings in Revelation 4:8, and that God is presented as triune in person in this context of Revelation, does make it most likely that the one is an adumbration of the other.

Hypostatization of Word and Wisdom

B. B. Warfield speaks of beings in the Old Testament that are in some sense identified with God, and yet are distinguished from Him. At times it may be a 'hypostatization' (or 'personification') of his attributes. This is the case with the Word of God, 'by whom the heavens were made' (Ps. 33:6). God often 'sent out' His Word (cf. Ps. 147:18). His word goes forth from His mouth to accomplish that for which he sent it (Isa. 55:11).

> It is widely thought that the use of the term 'Logos' in [John] 1:1-18 was influenced by, and was intended to allude to, biblical and Jewish traditions about God's Word and Wisdom, sometimes pictured as the uniquely intimate and efficacious agent of divine purposes. It is important to note that God's 'Word' and 'Wisdom' are sometimes linked in Jewish tradition of the time. Of various references, perhaps the parallel-structure statement in Wisdom of Solomon 9:1-2 is a particularly good example of this: 'O God … who has made all things by your word [*en logo sou*], and by your wisdom [*te Sophia sou*] has formed humankind.'[31]

Psalm 33:6 states that the world was made 'by the word of the LORD and by the breath of his mouth…' Proverbs 8, much used (and at times abused) by the Church Fathers, hypostatizes the Wisdom of God as a being in related persons (identified in vv. 1-3 as female), who was somehow associated with

---

[30]See chapter 3 for discussion of this messianic text.

[31]Hurtado, op. cit., 366.

God in the work of creation. Many Church Fathers saw this personified wisdom as the pre-existent Christ, but to take it literally raised problems, for the Arians employed it to argue that, therefore, Christ was a creature, although the first-born of creation (vv. 22, 23).

They were answered well by Athanasius in *Contra Arianos*. Most of 'Discourse II' in that treatise answers the Arian charge that Proverbs 8:22, 23 teaches that Christ is merely a creature (though the first one). In 'Discourse I', Athanasius spoke of how the Arians refused to expound the true sense of Scripture, and instead '... laying down their own irreligion as a sort of canon of interpretation, they wrest the whole of the divine oracles into accordance with it.'[32] In 'Discourse II', he notes how the heretics put terms above the realities they are meant to express, thus leading to severe misunderstanding: 'For terms are not prior to essences, but essences are first, and terms second.'[33] From Chapter XVI of Discourse II to Chapter XXII, Athanasius expounds the true sense of Proverbs 8, so that the reality of the Person of God the Son gives us the clue as to how the terms are used, rather than a merely human understanding of the terms precluding us from grasping the divine Reality: 'For it is written, "The Lord created me a beginning of His ways, for His works" [Prov. 8:22]; since however, these are proverbs, we must not expound them nakedly in their first sense, but we must inquire into the person, and thus religiously put the sense on it. For what is said in proverbs is not said plainly, but is put forth latently, as the Lord Himself has taught us in the Gospel according to John, saying, "These things have I spoken unto you in proverbs, but the time cometh when I shall no more speak unto you in proverbs, but openly" [John 16:25]. Therefore it is necessary to unfold the sense of what is said ... plainly...'[34]

Athanasius shows that this passage of Proverbs 8 refers to the creational/redemptive economy of Christ, not to His eternal ontological Being: 'For in this passage, not as signifying the Essence of His Godhead, nor His own everlasting and genuine generation from the Father, has the Word spoken by Solomon, but on the other hand His manhood and Economy towards us. And as I said before, He has not said "I am a creature," or "I became a creature" but only "He created".'[35]

Athanasius explains that the form of words in Proverbs 8, dealing with creaturely realities in familiar terms – like the rest of Scripture – are to enable us creatures to understand higher realities:

> ... and thus the words 'He created' are for our sake. For because of our need, the Word, though being Creator, endured words which are used of creatures; which are not proper to Him, as being the Word, but are ours who are created in Him... For though no works had been created, still 'the Word' of God 'was,' and 'the Word was God' [*sc.* John 1:1]. And His becoming would not have taken place, had not the need of men become a cause. The Son then is not a creature.[36]

---

[32]Athanasius, *Contra Arianos*, Discourse I. xii.52.

[33]Ibid., II.xiv.2.

[34]Ibid., II, xix.44.

[35]Ibid., II.xix.45.

[36]Ibid., II.xix.56.

Such terminology is 'because of the Word's condescension to the creatures, according to which He has become the "Brother" of "many" [*sc.* Heb. 2:9-13].'[37] In other words, Athanasius seeks to make sense of a poetic passage of Proverbs in light of clearer, didactic passages in John and Hebrews. In that way he is assessing the words in light of the scope of the realities.

From a somewhat different perspective, Augustine argued – in a rather complex meditation on 1 Corinthians 1:24 ('Christ the power of God and the wisdom of God') – that 'wisdom is a being word' and 'Word is a relationship word'; that is, both Father and Son can rightly be called 'wisdom', but only the Son can be called Word.[38]

On the other hand, Proverbs 3:18 clearly taught that wisdom was an attribute of God by which He made the world, and Paul in 1 Corinthians 1:30 identified wisdom with Christ. And indeed, Augustine did go on (in his meditation on 1 Corinthians 1:24) to state that in Scripture, wisdom is nearly always appropriated to the Son inasmuch as the Son reveals to us most fully the Father, whom we should imitate.[39]

Hypostatization of Spirit

The Spirit of God in the Old Testament is very widely referred to, and in general seems to be an attribute of God, or an intermediary by which He works in the created order. It usually carries the sense of 'the breath' of God, and bears God's presence into the world. In most cases, it would not appear to refer clearly to a distinct Person within the Godhead, although Psalm 139:7 could be taken as making the Spirit the same high being as the LORD.

The Spirit, somehow being 'breath', gives life (Gen. 1:2; Ps. 33:9), as is most notably seen in Ezekiel 37 when He breathes upon the dry bones in the valley to bring them to life (vv. 8-10). He equips the people of God for service (Num. 27:18; Judg. 3:10; Exod. 31:3); He anoints and enables the Messiah (Isa. 11:2, 3; 42:1; 61:1). He helped the prophets see the future (as Joseph in Genesis 41:38 and Daniel in Daniel 5:14). He was with penitent David (Ps. 51:11). He would be poured out on God's people in the future to give them faith and repentance in their LORD (Zech. 12:10).

---

[37]Ibid., II.xix.62.

[38]Augustine, *De Trinitate* VII.3: 'So the Father and the Son are together one being and one greatness and one truth and one wisdom. But the Father and the Son are not both together one Word, because they are not both together one Son. Just as the Son is referred to Father and is not said with reference to self, so too Word is referred to him whose Word it is...He is Son in the same way as he is Word...it follows that the Father and the Son are not both together one Word. And therefore the Son is not Word in the same way as he is wisdom, because he is not called Word with reference to himself, but only in relationship to him whose Word he is, just as he is Son in relationship to the Father; but he is wisdom in the same way as he is being. And therefore one wisdom because one being. But because wisdom is also Word, though not Word in the same way as wisdom (for Word is to be understood relationship-wise, wisdom being-wise... When we use these two words "born wisdom," the first of them, "born," can be understood as signifying Word and image and Son, and none of these names indicates being, because they state a relationship; but the second word, "wisdom", having only a self-reference (it is wise with itself), indicates being, and its being is the same as its being-wise.'

[39] Ibid., VII. 4,5.

T. F. Torrance shows that it takes the incarnation of the Son of God for many distinctive features of the Old Testament to become understandable to the Jews themselves:

> For Jews it is finally only in the light of what has taken place in God's incarnate self-revelation in Christ in fulfilment of his covenant promises to Israel that distinctive features in the knowledge of God given in the Old Testament itself unfold their full significance. This applies above all to the Word and the Spirit of the living God which are not created intermediaries between God and mankind but are immediate emanations and agencies of his personal presence and power, and as such point to real distinctions within the invisible oneness and fullness of God in his regular designation in the Hebrew Scriptures as Elohim. But if Christians are properly to grasp the Trinitarian understanding of God within the unitary structure of his self-revelation they must also take seriously what the Old Testament Scriptures have to say about the Word and the Spirit of God which figure alongside of the one Lord God as hypostatic extensions of his presence and agency and yet clearly belong to what God is in himself, and sometimes like 'the Name' or 'the Face' of God take on the role of a 'double' for God. This is true also of what is said of the personalized role of Wisdom in creation which is another designation for the mighty Word of God.[40]

The name of God

At times the Old Testament seems to personify the name of God as though it were actually God in person. It is not my concern here to survey the various names given to God in Holy Scripture, but we may simply note that the third commandment ('Thou shalt not take the name of the Lord thy God in vain…' – Exod. 20:7) so identifies the name with the holy presence of God that to defame the one is to defame at the same time the other. 'To call upon the name of the LORD' (Ps. 116:17) is to seek personal contact with God Himself. Proverbs 18:10 ('The name of the LORD is a strong tower: the righteous runneth into it and is safe') shows the identity of God's name with Himself, for otherwise, how could one run into a mere 'name' unless it meant the person himself? Thus, God's name saves us (Ps. 54:1) and gives us joy as we trust in it (Ps. 33:21). The Lord our Shepherd leads us in paths of righteousness 'for his name's sake' (Ps. 23:3).

Isaiah shows 'the name of the Lord' 'sifting the nations' and giving songs to his people as 'the mighty One of Israel' (Isa. 30:27-29). One of the tasks that Moses said would be given to the pilgrim people of Israel as they came out of the wilderness into the Promised Land would be to seek God 'in the place which the LORD your God shall choose out of all your tribes to put his name there, even…his habitation' (Deut. 12:5). Solomon's prayer at the dedication of the Temple identifies God's saving presence in the Holy House with His name being there: 'That thine eyes may be open toward this house night and day, even toward the place of which thou has said, My name shall be there: that thou mayest hearken unto the prayer which thy servant shall make toward this place' (1 Kings 8:29).

---

[40]T. F. Torrance, *The Christian Doctrine of God*, 69.

When Moses requested to see directly the glory of the Lord, God made 'all his goodness pass before him and proclaimed the name of the LORD before him' (Exod. 33:18,19). The Psalmist connects the heathen 'fearing the name of the LORD' with 'all the kings of the earth fearing his glory' (Ps. 102:15).

The name of God is, as George A. F. Knight says, 'an alter ego of God.'[41] Hence, according to these texts and many others, the name of God is God Himself, and yet in some sense is distinguished from Him. This usage can be thought of as 'a forerunner' of the later-to-be-revealed truth of the diversity of personhood within the One God.

The New Testament unhesitatingly sees Christ, as well as 'He who is' (Yahveh or Jehovah), participating fully in 'the Name'. B. B. Warfield summarizes the evidence:

> A side-light is thrown upon the high estimate which was placed among these early Christians on Jesus' person by the usurpation by it of the Old Testament pregnant use of the term 'Name.' As in the Old Testament we read continually of 'the Name of Jehovah' as the designation of His manifested majesty, and even of simply 'the Name' used absolutely with the same high connotation, so in Acts we read of the Name of Jesus Christ, to the exclusion of the old phrase, and again of simply 'the Name' (Acts 5:41, cf. 3 John 7) used absolutely of Jesus. Those who were persecuted for His sake we are told rejoiced 'that they were counted worthy to suffer dishonour for the Name' (Acts 5:41, cf. 3 John 7). In the Old Testament this would have meant the Name of Jehovah; here it means the Name of Jesus. 'The Name,' as it has been truly remarked, 'had become a watchword of the faith, and is consequently used alone to express the name of Jesus, as it stood in former days for the Name of Jehovah (Lev. 24:11).' Nothing could more convincingly bear in upon us the position to which Jesus had been exalted in men's thoughts than this constant tendency to substitute Him in their religious outlook for Jehovah.[42]

To have knowledge of 'the Name' involves participation in the Covenant of Grace, as Karl Barth has shown:

> To have knowledge of the name of Yahweh, and to that degree knowledge of Yahweh Himself, and to participate in His revelation, is to be a partner in the covenant made by Him… It is so much the more direct [*sc* as opposed to shadowy Old Testament hypostases] that especially the notable position and significance of the name of Yahweh may be regarded quite simply and yet at the same time quite meaningfully, as the Church has always maintained against Judaism even if only from this standpoint, as a prophecy of the fulfilment present here. Into the place, not of Yahweh on Sinai or in heaven, but of the name of the Lord, which finally dwells very really in a house of stone in Jerusalem, there now comes the existence of the man Jesus of Nazareth. At one of the high points of the New Testament message He is called 'my Lord and my God' (John 20:28).[43]

---

[41]George A. F. Knight, *A Biblical Approach to the Doctrine of the Trinity*, 13.

[42]B. B. Warfield, *The Lord of Glory* (Grand Rapids, Mich.: Zondervan Publ. House, no date), 218, 219.

[43]Barth, *Church Dogmatics* I/1, 318.

The face of God

> The word for Face in Hebrew is *panim* [פָּנִים]. It is regularly conjoined with the preposition l [לְ] to mean 'before'. However, it is striking how often the composite word can only be translated by 'in the presence of' both man and God. In such cases the LXX normally translates it by the word *prosôpon* [προσώπον], the ordinary Greek word for 'face'. For example in the Psalms alone the LXX understands it in this sense some 63 times out of a total occurrence of 91 times... Almost every book in the OT, moreover, uses it in this sense.[44]

For instance, Jonah fled before the face of the Lord (Jonah 1:3,10). According to Nahum, the earth was upturned at the face of the Lord (1:5). In 2 Chronicles 7:20 God said that He would cast away His house from before His face. Judah was removed from before God's face (1 Kings 24:3). The Aaronic benediction signifies God's blessing as 'the LORD make his face shine upon thee...' (Num. 6:25). The Psalmist prays to God: 'Hide not thy face from me' (Ps. 102:3), and asks 'Whither shall I flee from thy face?' (Ps. 139:7). In Exodus 33:14,15, God promises: 'And he [God] said, My face shall go with thee, and I will give thee rest. And he [Moses] said unto him, If thy face go not with me, carry us not up hence.' Often this usage of 'face' is not evident in the English Authorized Version, for there it is frequently translated 'presence' – which in a sense makes the point that God's face is also an alter ego of God.[45] Isaiah 64:7 essentially identifies God's name and face: 'And there is none that calleth upon thy name, that stirreth up himself to take hold of thee: for thou hast hid thy face from us, and hast consumed us because of our iniquities.'

As George Knight notes:

> The face of God then means the Presence of God. But God was present in His Name in the Tabernacle and the Temple. Evidence that the Name was conceived also as the Face of God arises from the fact that in the OT what we call the Shewbread is in reality, in Hebrew, Bread of the Face. It would seem that it was so called because it was bread set before the Face of God in the Temple, the place where His Name dwelt. The term Face of God is thus just as significant theologically as is its sister term, the Word of God... Let us be content with the saying that since this OT pictorial representation of the Nature of God is true to our knowledge as we have it revealed to us in Christ, it means that the mystery of the Holy Trinity was not entirely hidden from the minds of God's people even before His coming to earth.[46]

Walter Kaiser connects the Old Testament usage of 'the Face' to other aspects of the divine presence:

> Yahweh's divine presence was so central and significant in the Mosaic era that four other forms are used to speak of it: the 'face,' 'appearance,' or 'presence' of the Lord (*panim*); His 'glory' (*kabod*); the 'angel of the Lord' (*mal'ak* YHWH); and His 'name' (*sem*). The passage that connects most of these divine presence themes is Exodus 33. There Moses had asked God to

---

[44] G. Knight, op. cit., 29.

[45] Ibid.

[46] Ibid., 31,33.

show him His "glory" (v. 18) so that he might be assured that God's "face," i.e., "presence" (vv. 14-15) was indeed going before him. To this request God acceded by causing all His 'goodness' to pass before Moses, and there God proclaimed in front of Moses the 'name' Yahweh (v. 19). Protected by the 'hand' of God while he waited 'in the cleft of the rock,' the reality of God's presence was verified by Moses as he saw the 'aftereffects' ('my back,' *'ahoray*) of the radiance (glory) of God's presence after it had passed in front of him (vv. 21-23).[47]

The glory of God

The Old Testament usage of the glory of God is another indication of a certain diversity within the Being of the One God, which is suggestive of personal distinction within the Deity. George A. F. Knight writes:

> It will be remembered that the one Hebrew word *kabod* [כבד] serves for the two English ideas of 'honour' and 'glory'. Originally, the root of this word signified the idea of being heavy. The noun then was used to describe one who was heavy with possessions. Consequently it could mean 'riches'. But if a man were rich, then he received honour. Thus the noun came to mean 'honour' as well. If a man receives honour, he receives glory. Again, the same growth in meaning was made when the word was applied to God. The 'garment of the living God' (Ps. 104:2) is none other than God's glory. 'The heavens declare the glory of God' (Ps. 19:1). They are 'the likeness as the appearance of' the fullness of glory not yet revealed.[48]

Hurtado shows that the New Testament usage of the Old Testament concept of glory, especially in the Gospel of John, borrows heavily from Isaiah 40-66.[49]

> ... throughout Isaiah 40-66 in particular, 'glory' is frequently used in statements about a future manifestation of God that will involve redemption for Israel and even the illumination of Gentile nations. For example, note the statement in Isaiah 40:5 that 'the glory of the Lord shall be revealed, and all people shall see it.' We know from the Johannine application of Isaiah 40:3 to John the Baptizer in John 1:23 that the author considered this chapter of Isaiah predictive of the events that he narrates... As Brockington puts it, in Isaiah *doxa* serves as an appropriate special terms 'to use in relation to the appearance of God in theophany.'[50]

The Jewish exegetes of the early Christian centuries, who were doing their theologising at the period of the great Christological controversies in the Church, developed a noun, *shechinah*,[51] from this Hebrew verb, 'to dwell', and used it to describe this indwelling of the Face of God in the midst of Israel. The corresponding word in the Aramaic for shechinah is *mashkan*, and that word was actually used as a name for the Tabernacle in the Targum of Onkelos, the second-century Aramaic translation of the Pentateuch. And so, although this is not a directly biblical word, but one used in the Jewish translations of the OT into Aramaic, here we have still another way

---

[47]Walter Kaiser, *Toward an Old Testament Theology*, 120.

[48]Knight, op. cit., 38.

[49]Hurtado, op. cit., 378.

[50]Hurtado, op. cit., 379 refers to L. H. Brockington, "The Greek Translator of Isaiah and His Interest in DOXA." Vetus Testamentum 1 (1951): 23-32.

[51]*Shechinah* often refers to the 'glory cloud' over the Tabernacle in the wilderness wanderings, and the glory of God that came down in the Temple. John 1:14 identifies the incarnate Christ with

of representing what Canon Phythian-Adams has been the first to call 'the Tabernacling Presence' of God.[52]

The angel of the Lord

Angels in both Old and New Testaments are usually 'messengers of God', often 'ministering to those who are heirs of salvation' (Heb. 1:14). They are created spirits who can at times appear in human form. But they can also be identified with God Himself. Such is the case with the angel who speaks to Hagar, promising "I will multiply thy seed exceedingly' (Gen. 16:7). Then, after the angel leaves, Hagar 'called the name of the LORD that spake unto her, Thou God seest me…' (v. 13). At the sacrifice of Isaac (which was divinely prevented), the angel of the LORD said to obedient Abraham: 'I know that thou fearest God, seeing thou hast not withheld thy son, thine only son from me' (Gen. 22:12). Not to withhold Isaac from the angel was not to withhold him from God Himself. Thus, the angel is identified with the Lord. Jacob in his strange night of wrestling with 'a man' in Genesis 32:30 (who is termed 'angel' in Hosea 12:4) says: 'I have seen God face to face, and my life is preserved.' The 'angel of the Lord' speaks to Jacob in Genesis 33:10-31, and makes it clear that He is the same as 'the God of Bethel.' Moses met the angel of the Lord in the burning bush, which was the same as meeting the Lord (Exod. 3:2-6). After the people of God had entered into the Promised Land, the angel of the Lord says: '… I made you to go up out of Egypt, and have brought you into the land which I sware unto your fathers; and I said, I will never break my covenant with you' (Judg. 2:1). Malachi 3:1 identifies the messenger (or angel) of the covenant with God Himself: 'Behold, I will send my messenger, and he shall prepare the way before me: and the Lord, whom ye seek, shall suddenly come to his temple, even the messenger of the covenant, whom ye delight in: behold, he shall come, saith the LORD of hosts.'

As Herman Bavinck writes:

> … the subject which speaks through the angel of Jehovah far surpasses a created angel. The church-fathers before Augustine were unanimous in explaining this Angel of Jehovah as a theophany of the Logos…So much is clear: that in the *Mal'akh Yhwh* who is pre-eminently worthy of that name, God (esp. his Word) is present in a very special sense. This is very evident from the fact that though distinct from Jehovah this Angel of Jehovah bears the same name, has the same power, effects the same deliverance, dispenses the same blessings, and is the object of the same adoration.[53]

Thus, the mysterious appearance of the angel of the Lord indicates a certain diversity within the one Being of God, for He is at the same time

---

this tabernacling glory, when 'the Word became flesh and dwelt [in Greek, 'tabernacled'] among us, and we beheld his glory, the glory as of the only begotten of the Father, full of grace and truth.'

[52]Ibid., 44.

[53]Herman Bavinck, *The Doctrine of God*, translated by William Hendriksen (Edinburgh: The Banner of Truth Trust, 1979 reprint), 257.

both distinct from God and also one with God. Such passages indicate that God's Being is not an impoverished monad. Instead, His Being has a rich inner diversity.

Theophanies

Some of the appearances of holy angels are traditionally called 'theophanies' (i.e., manifestations of God). 'In these theophanies we should note that on occasions the A.V. or the LXX speak of an angel, and sometimes the angel. This is no discrepancy, of course, but merely two ways of translating the Hebrew construct state.'[54] Knight goes on to list fifteen theophanies. We have already discussed several of them (i.e., Gen. 16:7-14; 21:17-19; 22:11-18; 31:11-13; 32:4-10; Exod. 3:2-6; Judg. 2:1-5).

Following Knight, we look briefly at the others:

> (1) Gen. 18:1-22. 'In v. 10 the LXX renders *jhvh* [κυρίος] by *Theos* [θεός]. v 2 records a visit of three men; in v. 3 they are addressed in the singular as if they were one person; the LXX continues to use this singular in v. 9, though the MT continues with the plural.'[55]
>
> (2) Gen. 19:1 'speaks of two angels, who, in v. 13, are sent by Jahweh. But in v. 17 the LXX calls the two angels "two men", and turns "he" into "they"; while in vv. 18, 19, 21 the LXX disagrees about the number of divine visitants, though in the MT Lot addresses the two angels in the singular.'[56]
>
> (3) Gen. 21:17-19, identifies the Angel of the Lord with God.
>
> (4) Gen. 48:15-16. 'The Angel is identified with God in the action of, or as the instrument of, redemption. He is the *Goel* [גֹּאֵל] although according to Isa. 44:6 there is no *Goel* [גֹּאֵל] but God.'[57]
>
> (5) Exod. 14:19-22. 'The Angel is differentiated from Jahweh, "going before the camp of Israel." But in Exod. 13:21 we are told that it was Jahweh who went before the camp in a pillar of cloud. Yet in Num. 20:16 we are again told that it was an angel that did so. In Exod. 14:24 it is Jahweh once again who is in the pillar of cloud.'[58]
>
> (6) Josh. 5:13-16. 'A man' becomes 'Captain of the host of Jahweh.'
>
> (7) Judg. 6:11-24. 'In v. 12 the Angel is distinct from God, but in v. 14 he becomes Jahweh Himself. In v. 22 we have both aspects at once, but in v. 23 we have Jahweh alone. (N.B. The LXX vv. 14 and 16, reads *ho angelos kuriou* [ὁ ἄγγελος κυρίου] for *jhvh* [יהוה].'[59]
>
> (8) Judg. 13:2-23. While it is an Angel that appears to Manoah (v. 3), he is called 'a man of God' twice (vv. 6 and 8), and once 'the man' (v. 10). However, v. 22 identifies the Angel with *Elohim* [אֱלֹהִים].'[60]
>
> (9) Zech. Chaps 1-6. 'The angel spoke with me' is not identified with Jahweh in 1:12, but in 3:6-10 he becomes 'the Angel with Jahweh speaking.'[61]

As Knight summarizes:

---

[54]Knight, op. cit., 25.
[55]Ibid.
[56]Ibid.
[57]Ibid., 26.
[58]Ibid.
[59]Ibid.
[60]Ibid.
[61]Ibid.

> What we do see in these theophanies, however, is a groping effort to describe in pictorial terms an experience of God who could not be fully known till He revealed Himself in Christ. But when He did so, the NT revelation was found to be astonishingly akin to that dimly discovered in and through the OT.[62]

Before the rise of biblical higher criticism, the Christian theological tradition, both East and West, Catholic and Protestant, generally understood the Old Testament theophanies to be pre-incarnate appearances of the Second Person of the Trinity, Christ Himself. The nineteenth-century Swiss Reformed scholar, Louis Gaussen, helpfully summarized much of traditional biblical interpretation on this point, as we see in Appendix II to this chapter.

The Messiah

This important figure constitutes the substance for much of the hope offered by the Old Testament prophets to the people of Israel, and through them to the needy world, as we see in Isaiah 9:

> ... beyond Jordan, in Galilee of the nations. The people that walked in darkness have seen a great light: they that dwell in the land of the shadow of death, upon them hath the light shined...For unto us a child is born, unto us a son is given: and the government shall be upon his shoulder: and his name shall be called Wonderful Counsellor, the mighty God, the everlasting Father, The Prince of Peace. Of the increase of his government and peace there shall be no end, upon the throne of David, and upon his kingdom, to order it, and to establish it with judgment and with justice from henceforth even for ever. The zeal of the LORD of hosts will perform this (vv. 1c, 2,6-7).

Isaiah describes the Messiah as the Suffering Servant of the Lord, bearing the sins of the people, making intercessions for them, and obtaining the victory of 'seeing the travail of his soul and being satisfied' (Isa. 52:13; 53:4-6, 12, 11). The New Testament frequently applies texts from Isaiah 52 and 53 to the Lord Jesus Christ, thus showing who the Messiah really was – but only 'in the fullness of the time'.

As N. T. Wright notes,

> ... there was no one picture of 'the Messiah' within the Judaism of Jesus' day. The royal and/or messianic movements of the time show considerable freedom and flexibility within a broad concept; the idea of Israel's coming king was one that different movements and different claimants could quite easily reshape...[63]

However, on any reading, Messiah and King were closely related ideas:

> The political titles melek and messiah are avoided by the prophets when they speak of the coming of the prince of peace. But even so, the political conception of kingship is the main form their expectation takes so far as it comes to be personalized. In the extension of this political idea lies the picture of the human helper, comforter and lord sent by God, who some

---

[62]Ibid., 27.

[63]N. T. Wright, *Jesus and the Victory of God* (SPCK: London, 2004), 482.

> day, at the approaching end of time, will realize the promise of the covenant for this people.[64]

Larry Hurtado rightly connects the crucifixion of Christ with His (or His followers') royal Messianic claims: '... perhaps involving a threat to public order, which would certainly correspond to a perceived royal-messianic claim, whether made by him or his followers.'[65] But as Karl Barth saw, the necessarily political connotations of Messiah as king, found in both Old and New Testaments, were far surpassed, even in the Old Testament, by the Messianic hope of the one who would bring salvation:

> What is involved in Messianic expectation is not an intensifying but a sheer transcending of present political experience. It comes to this, that the conception of the king in particular can be described as the central form of Messianic expectation, but as such it is clearly too narrow to express all that is to be said of the expected bringer of salvation. The 'servant' in [Deutero-] Isaiah is much less a king than a prophet, and the son of David in Ps. 110 and the *tsemach* in Zech. 6 is priest and king at once. The 'son of man' appearing in the clouds of heaven in Dan. 7 shows all the characteristics of a ruler, but, naturally, the ruler who makes an end of the world powers and of world power as such...[66]

Old Testament triads

There are a number of triads in the Old Testament. Certainly by themselves they are not clear revelations of the Trinity, and yet perhaps they exist as a sort of reflection of Triune reality; with a sort of mysterious, ontological pressure giving rise to them. This is probably the case with the Aaronic benediction, which is probably the background of the apostolic benediction (already discussed): 'The LORD bless thee and keep thee; The LORD make his face shine upon thee, and be gracious unto thee: The LORD lift up his countenance upon thee, and give thee peace. And they shall put my name upon the children of Israel; and I will bless them' (Num. 6:24-27). Thus, LORD is repeated three times, as though there are three and yet only one.

Isaiah 48:16 mentions three, but with more defining distinctions than in Numbers 6:24-26: 'Come ye near unto me, hear ye this; I have not spoken in secret from the beginning; from the time that it was, there am I: and now the Lord GOD and his Spirit, hath sent me.' The previous verse (15) shows that the LORD ('I AM') is speaking. But He has been sent by 'the Lord GOD', along with 'his Spirit'. The revelation of the fullness of God's tri-personal Being in the New Testament makes it clear precisely who Isaiah 48:16 is referring to and was foreshadowing. It is similar in Isaiah 63:9-10, where we read of the Lord, of the angel of His presence, and of His Holy Spirit.

All of these passages taken together will demonstrate, as T. F. Torrance has stated, that the God of the Old Testament, even within the Old Testament, is not 'an absolutely undifferentiated oneness.'[67] Torrance suggests that the

---

[64]Karl Barth, *Church Dogmatics* I/2, 98.
[65]Hurtado, op. cit., 57.
[66]Barth, I/2, 99.
[67]T. F. Torrance, *The Christian Doctrine of God*, 70.

post-New Testament Rabbinical Judaism is at this extremely important point different from Old Testament Judaism:

> It is quite otherwise with traditional Rabbinic Judaism. In spite of the strange plurality with which God (Elohim) speaks of himself in the Old Testament, he is regarded as a God of absolutely unfigured undifferentiated oneness who cannot be apprehended in himself at all, or even named by human beings. What may be known of God, it was explained, does not have to do with what he is in himself but only with his moral and metaphysical attributes as they are manifested in his historical interaction with Israel, his covenant people, and in his external relations to the world he has created.[68]

Karl Barth writes along the same lines, referring to 'the enigma of the self-distinction in God Himself which makes this self-unveiling possible' [i.e. the Father's unveiling Himself in the Incarnation of the Son].[69] He adds:

> Has not the rejection of Jesus by the Jews made it shatteringly clear that it was possible to accept the God of the Old Testament in what seemed to be the most profound reverence and the most zealous faith, and yet in fact to deny Him to the extent that His form, now become quite concrete, became an offence to the righteous? Or what other objection could Israel bring against Jesus apart from the divine self-unveiling which now, not for the first time, but for the first time unequivocally, encountered it, making, as it were, bodily contact with it? In thinking that it has to defend against Jesus as against a blasphemer the name of God dwelling in the house of stone in Jerusalem, it denies this very name, and thus separates itself from it and from its own Holy Scripture, which is one long witness to this name as God's real presence and action in the human sphere.[70]

Extra-biblical triads

Herman Bavinck, among many others, has discussed extra-biblical 'triads'.

> But even outside of Scripture the number three is prominent. Not only the mediating entities of Jewish theology and the Sephiroth of the cabalistic system: the Crown, Wisdom and Understanding (Kether, Chokmah and Binah) furnished analogies for the Christian doctrine of the trinity but indications and vestiges of the trinity were also found in the realm of heathendom: the Triumurti of the Indians: Brahma, Vishnu, and the Siva; the three forms of the Chinese Tao; the three chief gods of the Germans: Odin, Thor, and Loki; and in various Chaldean, Egyptian, and Grecian ideas concerning the gods. A passage in the Hermetic Books was quoted with predilection and reference was made to the three principles accepted by Plato in his explanation of the universe: the highest 'mind' (that which exists, the good), the universe of ideas, and 'matter.' But inasmuch as all these analogies are polytheistic it is difficult to connect them with the Christian doctrine of the trinity.[71]

Bavinck then makes reference to analogies taken from nature, so popular with the early Apologists and Fathers:

---

[68]Ibid.

[69]Karl Barth, *Church Dogmatics* I/1, 318.

[70]Ibid., 318,319.

[71]Herman Bavinck, *The Doctrine of God*, 322.

> The physical analogies taken from the realm of nature are of greater value. Philo, and afterward Justin Martyr, used the illustration of the flame that kindles another but remains the same. Tertullian said that God brings forth the Logos 'just as the root produces the fruit, just as the fountain produces the river and just as the sun produces the sunbeam,' and he spoke of the fountain, the rivulet, and the stream; root, trunk, and branches, etc.[72]

Bavinck goes on to discuss the later ideas of some Church Fathers on triads built into all physical existence:

> As similitudes of the Christian trinity, the following were called into service: the three dimensions of space; the three measurements of time; the three kingdoms of nature: matter, spirit, and the union of the two in man; the solid, fluid, and gaseous state; the power of attraction, repulsion, and equilibrium; the three functions of the human soul: mind, will and moral nature; the three factors that constitute a family; the three classes in society: teachers, soldiers, and peasantry...; the three ideals: the good, the true, and the beautiful; the three tones in music: key-tone, tierce-tone, and quint-tone; the rainbow and its many colors; the sun with its quickening, illumining, and warming energy; the three basic colors: yellow, red, and blue, etc.[73]

Barth makes reference to Bavinck, and adds other 'triads':

> We single out the fact that the ancient Babylonians had two triads of gods, a cosmic: Anu, Enlil and Ea (the gods of heaven, earth and water) and then a superior and sidereal triad: Shamash, Sin and Ishtar (sun, moon and the planet Venus). The ancient Egyptians also had the divine family of Osiris with his spouse Isis and their son Horus, and in a similar relationship the ancient Cananites, Syrians and Carthaginians knew a supreme God, then the magna mater later worshipped under the name Cybele, and the Son of God known, e.g., as Attis or Adonis, while again, presumably in a similar relationship, ancient Etruscan Rome had the so-called Capitoline triad, Jupiter optimus maximus, Juno regina and Minerva. Later Brahmanism has the so-called Trimurti: the mystical unity of Brahma, who brings forth the world, Vishnu, who upholds it, and Siva (or Rudra), who destroys it. To this day the confession of a convert to Buddhism runs: 'I take my refuge in Buddha, I take my refuge in Dhamma, I take my refuge in Sangha' (the 'three jewels'), Buddha denoting personality, Dhamma teaching and Sangha the community of the founder of the religion.[74]

Barth correctly writes about these extra-biblical triads that this material

> is not to be overrated, not to be used as a proof in the strict sense, because we need to know and believe the Trinity already if we are really to perceive its *vestigia* as such in the microcosm and the macrocosm, but still to be valued as supplementary and non-obligatory illustrations of the Christian Credo which are to be received with gratitude... What happened, then, was not that they tried to explain the Trinity by the world but on the contrary that they tried to explain the world by the Trinity in order to be able to speak about the Trinity in this world...But they did have confidence that the Trinity can reflect itself in things, and all the more or less felicitous discoveries of *vestigia* were an

---

[72]Ibid., 322, 323.
[73]Ibid., 323.
[74]Barth, *C.D.* I/1, 337.

> expression of this confidence, not of confidence in the capacity of reason for revelation but of confidence in the power of revelation over reason.[75]

Hence, the scriptural testimony in both Testaments indicates a richness, a diversity within the Being of the one God. He always lives in relationship within Himself, so that for Him to be is to exist eternally as three Persons in one Godhead. His diversity in oneness has even impressed something of its reality in non-biblical thought and religion. But most of all, His people of all ages in knowing the one God, have also constantly been savingly and transformingly confronted with the gracious and holy presence of the Father, the Son and the Holy Spirit.

[75]Ibid., 338, 341.

Chapter Seven Appendix One

St. Augustine's Psychological Analogies of the Trinity

Since St. Augustine holds that the human personality is created in the image of the Trinity, not just in the image of the Father, he seeks to find reflections of the Trinity in human personality.[1] In Chapter 9 of Book X (of his *De Trinitate*), he suggests that mind, knowledge and love are in humans a Trinitarian reflection, and in Chapter 12 of XIV, he writes that the mind 'can also remember, understand, and love Him by whom it was made'.[2]

Various triads suggested by St. Augustine

With this in view, he offers other psychological analogies between the divine Trinity and various triads in men. For instance, in the realm of the human mind experiencing material reality, he mentions the triad of object, sense-perceptions and attention.[3] Or in the realm of man's imagination, he suggests the triad of memory, inward vision and the will which unites both.[4]

But probably his most famous psychological analogy is found in Chapter 11 of Book X, where he speaks of memory, understanding and will as a reflection of the three Persons in the one Godhead.

> Since then, these three, memory, understanding, will, are not three lives, but one life; not three minds, but one mind; it follows certainly that neither are they three substances, but one substance. Since memory, which is called life, and mind, and substance, is so called in respect to itself; but it is called memory, relatively to something. And I should say the same also of understanding and of will, since they are called understanding and will relatively to something; but each in respect to itself is life, and mind, and

---

[1]*De Civitate Dei*, XI.26.

[2]Augustine, *De Trinitate* XIV.12.15.

[3]Ibid. XI.1.2 (dealing with the object we see, the act of seeing, and the attention of the mind 'that keeps the sense of the eye in the object seen').

[4]Ibid., XI.3.6. After discussing the process of vision, Augustine then draws an analogy to the threeness and oneness of the Trinity: '... the vision of a concipient is to the image of the body established in the memory, from which the eye of the mind is informed; and what the intention of the will is towards a body seen and the vision to be combined with it, in order that a certain unity of three things may therein take place, although their nature is diverse ... in order that here too a certain unity may take place of three things, not now distinguished by diversity of nature, but of one and the same substance; because this whole is within, and the whole is one mind' (XI.4.7).

> essence. And hence these three are one, in that they are one life, one mind, one essence; and whatever else they are severally called in respect to themselves, they are called also together, not plurally, but in the singular number. But they are three, in that wherein they were not equal, and this not only each to each, but also each to all, they certainly could not mutually contain each other; for not only is each contained by each, but also all by each…
>
> And therefore, while all are mutually comprehended by each, and as wholes, each as a whole is equal to each as a whole, and each as a whole at the same time to all as wholes; and these three are one, one life, one mind, one essence.[5]

Analogies related to the realities of love have been of far more interest to the Church since the time of Augustine (to mention only Richard of St. Victor and Bonaventura, among many). St. Augustine does mention the triad of lover, loved and love in Book VIII. 10. 14, but does not take it very far (possibly, because of its generally sexual connotations).[6]

An Eastern Orthodox Response to Augustine's triads

From the Eastern theological perspective (in the context of debate against the Augustinian/Western Filioque), Richard Haugh finds a common dialectic in all of Augustine's varied triadic, human analogies. Haugh sees four basic elements:

1. *essentia* – about which the dialectic is.
2. *essentia* – manifesting itself (the Father).
3. *essentia* – as manifested (the Son).
4. *essentia* – uniting that which manifests itself with that which is manifested (the Holy Spirit), or the expression of the unity of that which manifests itself with that which is manifested.[7]

He then argues that the Filioque necessarily follows from this same dialectic.[8] If Haugh is right, the Filioque is rendered necessary in the thought of Augustine because of this dialectic, not because it is clearly taught in Scripture.

While I would wish to affirm that there may be some truth and usefulness in Augustine's varied analogies of triadic reflections of God within human experience, I do find these texts the least convincing of all his argumentation in the great *De Trinitate*. Probably his suggestion of lover, beloved and love would have been more convincing, but St. Augustine does not seriously explore this one.

It seems to me that in all of these analogies (except for lover, beloved and love), it is much harder to demonstrate the distinctness of the triads, rather than their united operations and being. As Herman Bavinck insightfully suggests (paraphrasing St. Thomas Aquinas): '… the universe is the work

---

[5]Augustine, *De Trinitate* X.11.18.

[6]Augustine hurriedly says about the triad of lover, loved and love: 'What, then, is love, except a certain life which couples or seeks to couple together some two things, namely him that loves, and that which is loved? And this is so even in outward and carnal loves. But that we may drink in something more pure and clear, let us tread down the flesh and ascend to the mind' (Bk. VIII.10.14).

[7]R. Haugh, op. cit., 202.

not of one single person but of all three: hence it reveals the unity of God's essence but not the distinction of the persons.'[9]

Varied responses of Reformation and Post-Reformation to these triads

As far as Western Christianity is concerned, some of the Protestant Reformers made use of Augustine's speculative analogies, while others generally avoided them. So far as I know, no one denied that there was at least some truth in them, although they were to be used more for illustration and confirmation than for outright proof. Lutheran and Reformed scholars over the generations varied considerably in their assessment of these analogies.

Philip Melanchthon

Philip Melanchthon, the scholarly colleague and successor of the German Reformer, Martin Luther, referred to some of St. Augustine's Trinitarian analogies and made use of them, and, in fact, added some more of his own. In his *Explicatio Symboli Niceni* (1550–1561), Melanchthon paraphrases Augustine in comparing the various mental faculties of man to persons of the Trinity: mind represents the Father, the image or concept which is formed in the human spirit in the act of intellection represents the Son, and the will represents the Holy Spirit.[10]

Melanchthon suggested other analogies, such as one illustrating the distinction between the Son and the Holy Spirit. By this analogy, he proposes the Logos, being the image of the Father, who knows Himself, and the Holy Spirit as source of life, since He is presented as 'the mover'; the one who brings about movement. He then suggests that the distinction within humans between the cognitive and affective, and the duality of the two physical organs where they are seated: brain and heart, suggest distinct persons within the Trinitarian life.[11] He comes up with even more analogies than Augustine: organic activities of the soul; various classifications of the physical organs, etc.[12] So, far from being hesitant about following Augustine's speculative Trinitarian analogies, it seems that Melanchthon actually tries to outdo him!

John Calvin and some of his successors

But we see a different spirit in Melanchton's younger friend of France (and then Geneva), John Calvin. While largely following Augustine in his central Trinitarian doctrine, Calvin expresses his hesitancy about speculations beyond reflecting on the revealed truths of Scripture: 'The whole fifth book of Augustine On the Trinity is concerned with explaining this matter [*sc.* Father and Son; person and essence]. Indeed, it is far safer to stop with that

---

[8]Ibid., 202-05.

[9]Herman Bavinck, *The Doctrine of God*, 328.

[10]Philip Melanchthon, *Explicatio Symboli Niceni* (1550-1561), *CR* 23, 399s, quoted in Dino Bellucci, *Science de la Nature et Réformation*, 210.

[11]See Melanchthon, *Liber et Anima CR* 13, 10-11, quoted in Bellucci, op. cit., 405.

[12]Ibid., 401-408.

relation which Augustine sets forth than by too subtly penetrating into the sublime mystery to wander through many evanescent speculations.'[13]

Yet Calvin's Reformed colleague and close friend, Pierre Viret of Lausanne, thought highly of some of Augustine's psychological analogies of the Trinity. He did not invent new analogies beyond the classical ones of Augustine, but he definitely followed several points of Augustinian analogy. In particular, Viret makes use of Augustine's analogy of memory, intelligence and will, but he changes the order, putting intelligence before memory: 'There is only one God and a sole divinity as we see in our soul in which we find intelligence, memory and will.'[14]

Calvin's theological successor in seventeenth century Geneva, Francis Turretin (whose *Institutes of Elenctic Theology* served as standard academic textbooks in Presbyterian and Reformed seminaries and universities in Scotland and in the United States until the beginning of the twentieth century), was more like Calvin than Viret, in refraining from using these 'natural' analogies (though without denying their possible validity):[15]

> IV. But as this mystery far transcends the reach of the human reason, so it can be solidly demonstrated from the revealed word alone. Whatever proofs of it some are wont to adduce from nature and reason, or from the perfection and power of God, or from his understanding, or from the communication of good (although on the supposition of a revelation, they may with respect to believers serve in some measure to illustrate it), yet they cannot convince and obtain the force of solid proof. The same is the case with the various similitudes usually employed here; from the human soul, the rainbow, a tree, a fountain, the sun and light. These seem to afford some resemblance to the Trinity, though very obscure as they always labour under a great dissimilitude. Thus they ought to be proposed soberly and cautiously, not for the purpose of convincing adversaries, but for confirming believers and showing them the credibility at least of this great mystery.[16]

Wilhelmus à Brakel (1635–1711), the Dutch Calvinist scholar and pastor, is even less appreciative of these psychological analogies than Turretin, for he writes:

> Thirdly, it should be understood that the Holy Trinity cannot be known from nature, but has only been revealed in Scripture. Therefore one should refer only to Scripture and in all simplicity believe its testimony. One must not exalt his wisdom above that which has been written; he must set all human reasoning aside and avoid all imaginary comparisons to tangible objects. Such comparisons, rather than shedding light upon the issue, result

[13]John Calvin, *Institutes* I.xiii.19.

[14]Pierre Viret, 'Exposition familière de l'oraison de nostre Seigneur Jesus-Christ' (Genève, 1548, p. 165) quoted in Georges Bavaud, *Le Réformateur Pierre Viret: Sa Théologie* (Genève: Labor et Fides, 1986), 62.

[15]As Calvin had written: 'And let us not take it into our heads either to seek out God anywhere else than in his Sacred Word, or to think anything about him that is not prompted by his Word, or to speak anything that is not taken from that Word. But if some distinction does exist in the one divinity of Father, Son and Spirit – something hard to grasp – and occasions to certain minds more difficulty and trouble than is expedient, let it be remembered that men's minds, when they indulge their curiosity, enter into a labyrinth. And so let them yield themselves to be ruled by the heavenly oracles, even though they may fail to capture the height of the mystery' (*Institutes* I.xiii.21).

[16]Francis Turretin, *Institutes of Elenctic Theology, Vol. 1: First Through Tenth Topics* (Phillipsburg, NJ: P & R Publishing, 1992), translated by G. M. Giger; edited by J. T. Dennison, 266.

> in more obscurity and tend to divert from, rather than promote, a proper understanding of this mystery. May the Lord sanctify and guide me in writing, and you in reading or hearing.[17]

And yet, the famous American colonial Calvinist scholar, pastor, and later President of the College of New Jersey, Jonathan Edwards (1703–1758), gladly made use of St. Augustine's psychological analogies of the Trinity. In his Miscellany 390, Edwards sees (somewhat like Tertullian) analogies of the Trinity in the sun and the rainbow. But especially in the soul of man, he traces a reflection of the Trinity in the mind, its understanding (or idea), and its will (or affection).

St. Augustine's modesty

To his credit, Augustine does not claim that any of these analogies prove the Trinity; they are only possible illustrations from the visible, created world of the supreme reality which is invisible and uncreated, and they must always be evaluated in the light of the revealed faith.

As he states in the early part of *De Trinitate*:

> Wherefore, our Lord God helping, we will undertake to render, as far as we are able, that very account which they so importunately demand: viz., that the Trinity is the one and only and true God, and also how the Father, the Son, and the Holy Spirit are rightly said, believed, understood, to be of one and the same essence; in such wise that they may not fancy themselves mocked by excuses on our part, but may find by actual trial, both that the highest good is that which is discerned by the most purified minds, and that for this reason it cannot be discerned or understood by themselves, because the eye of the human mind, being weak, is dazzled in that so transcendent light, unless it be invigorated by the nourishment of faith…[18]

> And I would make this pious and safe agreement, in the presence of our Lord God, with all who read my writings, as well as in all other cases as, above all, in the case of those which inquire into the unity of the Trinity … because in no other subject is error more dangerous, or inquiry more laborious, or the discovery of the truth more profitable…[19]

> Let him, therefore, who finds this fault with my discourse, see whether he can understand other men who have handled the similar subjects and questions, when he does not understand me: and if he can, let him put down my book, or even, if he pleases, throw it away; and let him spend labour and time rather on those whom he understands.[20]

I believe that St. Augustine offered such analogies with tentativeness and in considerable humility, as is indicated in the brief prayer with which he concludes his *De Trinitate*:

> O Lord the one God, God the Trinity, whatever I have said in these books that is of Thine, may they acknowledge who are Thine; if anything of my own, may *it be pardoned both by Thee and by those who are Thine. Amen.*[21]

---

[17]Wilhelmus à Brakel, op. cit., 140.
[18]Augustine, *De Trinitate* I.1.4.
[19]Ibid. I.3.5.
[20]Ibid.
[21]Ibid., XV.28.51.

Chapter Seven Appendix Two

The Traditional Christian Interpretation of Old Testament Theophanies as Pre-incarnate Appearances of Christ (as summarized by Louis Gaussen)

In the main part of Chapter 7 we considered some Old Testament passages that speak of the mysterious angel of the Lord, and understood them to be intimations of the pre-incarnate Son of God. But more remains to be said about this foreshadowing of the Holy Trinity. Dr. Louis Gaussen has carefully explicated the appearances of the angel of the Lord in relatively brief compass.

In a sermon on Judges 6:17-24, 'Gédéon devant l'Ange de l'Eternel' ('Gideon before the Angel of the LORD'), Louis Gaussen, a noted Calvinist scholar of nineteenth-century Geneva, clearly summarized the traditional Christian interpretation of Old Testament theophanies as appearances of Christ before His incarnation.[1] Concerning the holy angel who appeared to Gideon, Gaussen writes:

> Who then was this person? Was it a man? Was it a created angel? ... Was it God Himself?
>
> The Scripture, in verses 11 and 12 [of Judges chapter 6] calls Him the Angel or the Messenger of the Eternal God; then, in the verses which follow, it does not hesitate to give Him the further name of THE LORD, JEHOVAH! It is THE LORD[2] who looks upon Gideon; it is THE LORD, who says to him: Have I not sent thee?
>
> Perhaps if this event were an isolated one in our Scriptures, it should cause us some surprise; but we constantly find in both Testaments so many similar scenes and witnesses of the same sort, that it will become simple for us, in recalling briefly here several very simple principles, by which we may grasp in a very precise and certain manner the right opinion on this important subject.
>
> The **first** of these principles is nothing else than one fact; here it is: every time in the Holy Bible that we are faced with appearances of this mysterious Angel, whom the Holy Spirit calls 'the Angel of the Face' (Isa. 63:9); 'the Angel of the Covenant' (Mal. 3:1), or 'the Angel of the LORD God' or 'Angel of Jehovah',[3]

---

[1]Louis Gaussen, *Sermons par Gaussen*, Nouvelle Edition (Paris: Chez Delay, Librarie, Rue Tronchet 2, 1847), 'Gédéon devant l'Ange de l'Eternel', pp. 45-79 [my translation].

[2]Dr. Gaussen follows the French versions in rendering the Hebrew name for God (in most of these references, jhvh – Yahveh or Jehovah) as 'L'Eternel'. But following the English versions, I render God's name as 'the LORD.'

[3]Several versions translated 'Angel of the LORD' as 'Angel of Jehovah': see, Genesis 22:15; 31:11, 13; 32:24-30; ch. 18; ch. 19; 16:7-13; Exodus 3:2-5; 4:5; 13:21; 19:19, 24; (12:12); 19:9; 23:2-23; 33:9-11; Joshua 5:13-15; 6:1-3; Leviticus 16:2; Judges 6:11, 14-33; 11:1; 13:18; Isaiah 63:9, 10, 11, 14; Malachi 3:1; Daniel 3:25; 10:5,6; Ezekiel 1:1-6, 26, 28, (Revelation 1:12-13).

one understands Him to be attributing constantly all the most incommunicable names of the omnipotent God; and not only the names, but also His attributes and works; and not only His attributes, names and works, but also the worship which everywhere God claims for Himself alone.

It is thus, to cite only a rather small number of examples among many others, that you will see that the Angel of the LORD who appeared to the Patriarch Abraham under the oaks of Mamre (Gen. 18), and who came to tell him that Sarah would have a son, is constantly called by the name of THE LORD, and that he does not cease speaking of Himself as almighty God.

You will understand the Angel of the LORD, who appeared to Jacob in Mesopotamia, saying to this patriarch: 'I am the mighty God of Bethel. I am the LORD, the God of Abraham thy father, and the God of Isaac.'[4]

You will understand the Angel of the LORD who appeared to Moses on Mount Horeb (Exod. 3), crying out to him: 'I am the God of thy fathers, I am He who is called I AM. Go to thy brethren that they may know that THE LORD has appeared to thee.' And Moses hid his face, because he feared to look upon God.

You will see that the Angel of the LORD, who led the people of Israel through their journey in the wilderness, is called by the great name of JEHOVAH; and you will hear the Angel or the Messenger of God who, upon Sinai, spoke to Moses (Acts 7:30), pronouncing these words: 'Hear, O Israel, I am the Lord thy God, who has brought thee out of the house of bondage, thou shalt have no others god before me' (Exod. 19; 20:1-3)!

And if you wish to gather together even more witnesses, you will understand a completely similar terminology, when this same Angel of the Face appears to Hagar in the wilderness,[5] to Joshua on the banks of the River Jordan (Josh. 5:13-15), to the parents of Samson in the fields of Tsorah,[6] and to all the people of Israel in the valley of Bohim.[7]

Here now is our **second** principle.

If there is one truth which the Old Testament is jealous to proclaim above all others, it is the principle of the divine unity. It is by this dogma that Israel for two thousand years differed from all other people in the world. Elsewhere, people worshipped everything but God, whereas Israel worshipped nothing but God. And if it were ever permitted to speak of Moses as the true lawgiver of all humanity, he would say that here lies the dominant thought and the cornerstone of his whole religious system. To it he constantly returns; of it he is jealous with a holy jealousy.

It is I, says the LORD, it is I alone; there is no other God beside me! There is no other righteous GOD and SAVIOUR but I. Thus speaks the LORD, the GOD of Israel and its REDEEMER: I am the first, and I am the last: there is

---

[4]Compare Genesis 31:11-13; 28:11-22; 35:7-15; 48:15, 16, and also 32:24, 28, 30; Hosea 12:4, 5.

[5]Genesis 16:13; she also calls Him 'Thou God seest me.'

[6]Judges 8. Here THE ANGEL OF THE LORD who appeared to Manoah, and whom the Scripture calls JEHOVAH, takes upon Himself the name that the Holy Spirit (in Isaiah) assigns to the ONLY-BEGOTTEN SON OF GOD, when he announces that 'a virgin will conceive, and will bear IMMANUEL, and that she shall call his name WONDERFUL, the mighty and powerful God, the eternal Father, the Prince of Peace (Isa. 7:14; 9:5). Why do you ask for my name? says the Angel of the LORD to Manoah. It is WONDERFUL. And when the Angel ascended into the heavens in the flame of the altar, Manoah knew that it was the Angel of the LORD; he bowed down his face to the ground, and cried: We shall surely die, because we have seen God.'

[7]Judges 11:1-5. 'In all the afflictions of His people, the LORD was afflicted,' says Isaiah, 'and THE ANGEL OF HIS FACE delivered them; He Himself delivered them because of His love and His mercy' (Isa. 63:9).

> no other God. Certainly, there is no other rock: I know no other! All the ends of the earth look unto me, and you will be saved, for I am the mighty God, and THERE IS NONE OTHER![8]

Now, our **third** principle will be only one assertion, which flows directly from the first two, and which is nearly the same as they. Here it is:

> The Being who, in the Bible, attributes to Himself the names, the works, the characteristics, and even the worship of almighty God, cannot be a creature.
>
> 'There is none like unto the LORD' is often repeated. 'The eternal! That is my name, and I shall not give my glory to another' (Isa. 42:8)! He is 'the great and jealous God' (Exod. 20:5); The angels hide their faces before Him and tremble in His presence; thus, could anyone be found in heaven above or earth beneath, who would dare to usurp such language in order to apply it to the one who was speaking to Gideon! Every time that anyone wished to offer the slightest worship to [a mere angel], they were immediately rebuffed. 'Beware, lest thou do it! He cried to them. I am only thy fellow servant! Worship God!'[9]

After these three assertions, here now is a **fourth**, which is no less unquestionable: THE ANGEL OF HIS FACE, who appears so often to the elect of God in the Old Testament, could not be God the Father.

> The person of the Father, in the whole course of the divine revelation, has always conserved the character of 'the invisible God', as Saint Paul calls Him several times.[10] He never revealed Himself to mankind except in His Son. The apostle says, 'He dwells in light inapproachable that no man has seen, neither can see' (1 Tim. 6:16); 'No one can look upon my face and live,' says the LORD Himself (Exod. 33:20). Our Lord says: 'You have neither heard his voice, nor seen his face' (John 5:37; 1 John 4:12,20).
>
> Thus, it was never the person of the Father who manifested Himself in the Old Testament. And who, therefore, was this mysterious Angel?

Here my brethren, is our **fifth** principle and last assertion:

> It was the Angel of the LORD, O Christians, it was the same Saviour, the same Master, the same Comforter, whom we are commissioned to proclaim in the flesh; and also it was therefore already He who was appearing before His incarnation, in preparation for His mission of incomprehensible abasement in which He would come down at a later time in order to save us.
>
> It was He who is called 'THE IMAGE OF THE INVISIBLE GOD! The out-raying of His glory, the express image of His person' (Col. 1:15; Heb. 1:3). It was He of whom Saint Paul says to us: 'Let all the angels of God worship Him' (Heb. 1:6). It was He whom Paul calls 'our great God and Saviour, Jesus Christ.'[11]
>
> And note well, my brethren, that this is not at all a mere presumption on my part, nor a human interpretation. It is a scriptural principle, of which the Holy Spirit has not wished to leave us the slightest doubt.

---

[8]Isaiah 44:8; 45:5, 19, 21, 22; 46:9; Deuteronomy 32:39; 4:35, 39.

[9]Revelation 22:9; 19;10, and similarly Acts 10:26; 14:14, 15; Colossians 2:18; Matthew 6:10; Hebrews 1:5, 7, 13, 14.

[10]1 Timothy 1:17; Hebrews 11:27; Colossians 1:15.

[11]Titus 2:13…

Listen, indeed, to how Saint Paul declares to us that Jesus Christ was the Angel of the LORD who led the Israelites in their wilderness journey: 'Do not tempt Christ,' he says to us, 'as the children of Israel in the wilderness, when they were destroyed by fiery serpents. For the rock which followed them in the wilderness was Christ,' and Moses, in becoming their leader, 'esteemed the reproaches of Christ greater treasure than the riches of Egypt.'

Hear Saint Peter, who testifies to us that it was Christ who inspired all of the ancient prophets (1 Pet. 1:11).

Hear Saint John tell us that when Isaiah, after the death of King Uzziah, saw the LORD seated on His throne, before whom the angels hide their faces in their wings, then the Eternal cried out to his prophet: 'Go, and speak to this people: You shall hear and shall not understand; you shall see and not perceive.' Listen to Saint John declare to us in his twelfth chapter, 'that Isaiah said these things, when he saw the glory of Jesus Christ and spoke of Him' (Isa. 6; John 12:39-41).

And if you are astonished to hear the LORD speak, both as He who sends, and as He who is sent, then hear these words of the LORD in the second chapter of Zechariah: 'Rejoice with a song of triumph, O daughter of Sion; for behold, I come, and I shall dwell in the midst of thee, SAYS THE LORD; then shall many nations become my people, and thou shalt know that the Lord of hosts HATH SENT ME to thee.'

But finally, hear above all, Jesus Christ Himself. Listen to Him speak to the Jews: 'Before Abraham was, I AM! Abraham desired to see my day, and he saw it, and was glad' (John 8:56-58).

Listen to Him replying to Philip, when he said to Him: 'Lord, show us the Father. What, Philip, have I been with you for so long, and you have not known me? Philip, he that hath seen me hath seen the Father; how can you therefore say, show us the Father' (John 14:8, 9). 'I and the Father are one' (John 10:30).

In effect, 'no one has ever seen God,' says Saint John;[12] but the Only begotten Son who is in the bosom of the Father has manifested Him to us. The Father works continually, and the Son does also (John 5:17). 'And the Word was in the beginning with God and was God. All things were made through him; and this Word became flesh and dwelt among us' (John 1:1, 2, 14).

Thus, my brethren, you see that we can abundantly conclude who the one was who appeared to Gideon under the oak of Hophra, and who said to him: 'Be not afraid, for I am with thee; thou shalt conquer the Midianites,' for that was the one who, thirteen hundred years after Gideon… appeared again to Paul in the city of Corinth, and said to him: 'Fear not, Paul, for I am with thee; but speak and be not silent' (Acts 18:9, 10). It is He who…appeared to John in the Isle of Patmos, and said to him: 'Be not afraid! I am the first and the last. I am He that liveth forever; but I was dead; and all the churches shall know that I am He who searches the heart and the reins' (Rev. 1:17, 18; 11:23). It is He who declares to us still today that 'where two or three gather together in my name, there am I in the midst of them' (Matt. 18:20).[13] In a word, it is God the Saviour, manifested in both Testaments. 'He was in the world, and the world was made by him,' says Saint John, 'but the world knew him not. He came unto his own, and his own received him not. It is He who is the true God and the eternal life' (John 1:10,11, and 1 John 5:20).

---

[12]John 1:18; compare with Numbers 12:18.

[13]Notice well that He already made this promise while He was still in the flesh, and that He went from place to place with nowhere to lay His head.

> This thought, my brethren, this grand thought is like the sun of the Old Testament; it enlightens it totally; it spreads upon it a blessed light; it manifests there for believers the grandeur and imposing harmony of every divine revelation. It makes them all a living letter, and reveals in them a Saviour who is ever living and ever the same. With the awareness of this truth, the entire Old Testament is explained, the entire book is opened; without awareness of this truth, it is inexplicable; it astonishes; it seems to contradict itself; it is closed and – to speak with Isaiah – 'It is thus a hidden book, that one would give to a man while saying to him: we beg you, read this! And he will reply: It is hidden; how could I read it?'
>
> But, how powerful it is, on the contrary, how mighty is this thought of the divinity of his Saviour, for the faithful, who, holding in his hands the book of the Old and New Testaments, lifts his eyes up to heaven and says to himself: He is thus ever the same! He is thus with me in this chamber where I seek Him; He who 'gave himself for my sins' (Gal. 1:4); He who says to me in his Word: 'Come unto me, all ye who labour and are heavy-laden, and I will give you rest' (Matt. 11:28)! How powerful this is on the heart of the believer, this simple thought contained in the response of Jesus to Nathaniel: 'Nathaniel, before Philip called thee, when thou wast under the fig tree, I saw thee' (John 1:47-49)... And Nathaniel cried out with transport: 'Thou art the Son of God; thou art the King of Israel!'[14]

Most Old Testament scholars for the last century (even conservative ones) have been considerably more restrained in definitely identifying all appearances of the angel of the Lord as the pre-incarnate Christ. Even if Gaussen is at times overconfident in focusing the scope of all the passages he quotes exclusively to the Second Person of the Trinity, still, I cannot see that he is essentially wrong either exegetically or theologically, in assuming that in most cases of theophanic appearances of the angel of the Lord, the pre-incarnate Christ is most likely referred to. Many Church Fathers, medieval scholastics, and sixteenth-century Reformers held to much the same understanding of the angel of the Lord, and I can find no compelling reason to part company with them on this point.

[14]Gaussen, op. cit., 55-64.

Chapter Eight

The Christian Church Thinks Through how God is One Being and Three Persons

Thus, the Christian Church, as heir of both Testaments, had to seek clearer understanding of the Trinity as 'One Being, Three Persons.' This involved the creation of new theological vocabulary, such as 'homoousios' and 'perichoresis', which enabled a clearer expression of the concept of Person, as the nature of Being was enriched in light of the eternal inter-trinitarian relationships. The meaning of Trinitarian Personhood is the basis for our own created personhood, and alone gives us significance both for this earthly life and the eternal realm to come. An Appendix considers the differing approaches of East and West to God's Being and His Triune Personhood.

'One Being, Three Persons'

By the time of the Christian writer of North Africa, Tertullian (in his treatise of A.D. 213, *Adversus Praxean*) Church theologians were stating the basic Trinitarian relationship in this formula, which was generally deemed to represent faithfully the New Testament testimony to who God is: God exists as 'three Persons in one substance' [or 'being', or 'essence', or 'reality'].[1] For several years, there was misunderstanding between theologians of the East (Greek) and West (Latin) on the meaning and usage of these terms.[2] But after discussion in A.D. 362, there was generally a mutual agreement on this terminology as being faithful to the intent of scriptural teaching on the issue. The great theologian of the East, Athanasius, used this Trinitarian formula (*mia ousia, treis hupostaseis* – μία οὐσία, τρεῖς ὑποστάσεις), as did the great theologian of the West, Augustine (*una substantia, tres personae*) and they were followed throughout the Church.[3]

---

[1]In Latin, *tres personae, una substantia*; in Greek, *treis hypostaseis, mia ousia* [τρεῖς ὑποστάσεις, μία οὐσία]

[2]See G. L. Prestige, God in Patristic Thought, (London: SPCK, 1952), chapter IX.

[3]Athanasius, *Ad Ant.*, 5-6; Augustine, *De Trin.*, V. 2.

'Homoousios'

As we have seen, the central issue at the Council of Nicea (A.D. 325) was this: who is Jesus Christ? Is He (as the heretical Arians would have it) merely 'like the Father' (i.e. *homoiousios* [ὁμοιούσιος] – of 'like substance', but not of 'the same substance' or reality – hence, *homoousios*), or is he (with the Orthodox Church, East and West) of 'the same substance' as the Father; that is, is the incarnate Christ as much God as the Father is God? Does His essential being belong to the side of uncreated, infinite Being, or to the side of created, finite being? No issue in the Church was ever of such great importance as this one. The Church Fathers understood the continuing validity of the saving gospel to ride upon the answer given to this question.

The Arians (not unlike the eighteenth-century Enlightenment in its rejection of clear scriptural and Church authority in favor of merely human speculation) denied that Christ is of the same high reality as God the Father Almighty. Like the Enlightenment Deists, they presupposed an unbridgeable split between the being of God and the natural world, which even God Himself could not bridge; thus, Jesus Christ could not be God incarnate. For that philosophical, presuppositional reason, they had to reject the *homoousios*. Like many 'Modernists' today, they held that Jesus is 'the best of men,' but ultimately for them, he stood on the creaturely side of the gap they posited; not on the Godward side. They even claimed that there was a time when Christ, the Son, did not exist; that the Father had created Him, so that ultimately He was an inferior sort of deity.

The Nicene Council answered this anti-biblical heresy with the term *homoousios*: that Christ is of the same high reality or being as God the Father Almighty, Creator of heaven and earth. Athanasius developed an understanding of the Son as *homoousios* with the Father in *Contra Arianos*, as the only way to explain the full scope of the rich biblical evidence concerning the Person and work of Christ, and His relationship in Person and work to the Father. Later, Athanasius worked through the *homoousial* relationship of the Spirit to the Being of the Father and the Son in his *Letters on the Holy Spirit to Serapionem*. Athanasius demonstrates that Holy Scripture forces us to the conclusion that the Holy Spirit is *homoousios* with the Son, as the Son is 'of the same substance' with the Father, and so that the entire Trinity is *homoousios* with one another within itself.

Athanasius and his co-workers, the two Cappadocian Gregories, as well as Basil, Epiphanius and others in the fourth century, constantly made clear the saving importance of this most central doctrine of Christianity: *homoousios*. They showed that if Christ is not fully God, then God has not come all the way to where we are in our fallen, space/time history and condition. If Christ is not as much God as the Father is God, then His death on the cross would not have infinite value and thus our sins are not forgiven; we face death and judgment without hope, so that the gospel itself is a cruel illusion. They knew that the essential oneness of the Son's being with that of the Father is absolutely essential to human salvation, and thus they fought for it at all costs.

John 1:1 speaks of 'Another' who was with God the Father from all eternity: the Word or *Logos*. John's Prologue goes on to make clear that this *Logos* is God's Son: an eternal, co-equal Person with the Father. The fact that the eternal Son of the Father is called Word or *Logos*, seems to mean, among other things, that there is – and has been from all eternity – talk, sharing and communication in the innermost life of God. The true God is not silent; He talks. At the back of the universe is not an empty black hole, or a chance configuration of spiraling atoms outside any personal control of their motion. It is not – to employ the imagery from ancient Greek drama – the sharp cutting scissors of impersonal, meaningless fate. No! Behind the universe is a Person with a face. God the Father Almighty on His Throne has shown us His very heart in the face and words and actions in our space/time realm in the Lord Jesus Christ.

That is what the evangelist John asserts in 1:18, '... the only begotten Son which is in the bosom of the Father, he hath declared him.' The Greek word for 'declared' is here literally 'exegeted'; which means to bring out the true meaning of a text. Jesus has brought out the Father from the glories of heaven on the rainbow-circled throne, down to the manger of Bethlehem, the ministry of teaching and healing, the cross of Calvary and the empty tomb. Jesus has truly 'made the Father known.' The Son has revealed the very heart of the Father.

The heart of the Father is seen in the face of the Son

Seeing the heart of the Father in the face of the Lord Jesus Christ is the fullest glory of the New Testament revelation. In the Son, the love of the Father has taken on flesh and blood in our nature, that in some measure we can get hold of. That is precisely why the early Church was so insistent upon the full deity of the Lord Jesus Christ. If He were not fully God, then the Father had not come all the way to where we are, and we still do not know who God really is.[4] But if, as the New Testament declares, He has become fully human without ceasing to be God, then eternity has broken through into time, and God is with us in pardoning mercy, so that in Jesus, we do know God the Father as He truly is in Himself.

Many Church Fathers (as we saw earlier in Athanasius) laid heavy emphasis on the passages in Matthew 11:27 and Luke 10:22, that 'no man knoweth the Son, but the Father; neither knoweth any man the Father, save the Son, and he to whomsoever the Son will reveal him.' This means that since they are fully God, the Son and the Father as infinite Persons truly and fully know each other. But the Son has come to earth and taken on true human flesh precisely in order to raise up human nature, so that in saving union with Him, His people might

---

[4]See T. F. Torrance, 'The Hypostatic Union', unpublished class notes, Edinburgh University, 1960s.

also share in the mutual knowledge of Father and Son to the limits of their finite capacity.

That is why Jesus said: 'I am the way, the truth and the life; no man cometh unto the Father except by me' (John 14:6). That is why also He said: 'I am the door of the sheep' (John 10:7). Or as Peter stated it, speaking of the results not just of the incarnation, but of Christ's death and resurrection: 'For Christ also hath once suffered for sins, the just for the unjust, that he might bring us to God, being put to death in the flesh, but quickened by the Spirit' (1 Pet. 3:18).

Jesus came and lived and died and rose and intercedes so that we can know who God is; indeed, so that we can know God in His inmost self as our reconciled heavenly Father. H. R. Mackintosh of Edinburgh University expressed it this way:

> When I look into the face of Jesus Christ and see the face of God, I know that I have not seen that face elsewhere and could not see it elsewhere, for he and the Father are one … All creation in heaven and earth, all the divine ways of history, all time and eternity – they meet and converge in this one transcendent figure.[5]

Mackintosh was not far from St. Irenaeus, who said: 'By the Word made visible and palpable, the Father was being shown, even though all did not equally believe him. But all saw the Father in the Son; for the Father is the invisibility of the Son, and the Son is the visibility of the Father.'[6]

'Homoousios' involves two different, but complementary truths at the same time

'Homoousios' meant not just one thing, but two things at the same time. It meant most obviously that the Father and the Son were of the same high reality or substance (*ousia* – οὐσία), but also that there was a genuine distinction between them. T. F. Torrance quotes St. Basil's Epistle 52.3: 'For nothing can be homoousios with itself, but one thing is *homoousios* with another.'[7] He adds that while ὁμοούσιος τῷ Πατρί clearly proclaims the full deity of the Son, at the same time, it also implies that the Father and the Son 'are eternally distinct for the Father is unchangeably the Father and not the Son, and the Son is unchangeably the Son and not the Father.'[8]

He states more fully: 'If the Son is eternally begotten of the Father within the being of the Godhead, then as well as expressing the oneness between the Son and the Father, homoousios expresses the distinction between them that obtains within that oneness.'[9] Elsewhere he notes that this term (*homoousios* - ὁμοούσιος) when used with the Trinity has a transformed meaning, which not only 'carried with it a revised concept of *ousia* [οὐσία] as being considered in its internal relations, and of hypostasis [ὑπόστασις]

---

[5]H. R. Mackintosh, quoted by T. F. Torrance, 'Hugh Ross Mackintosh, Theologian of the Cross,' in *Scottish Bulletin of Evangelical Theology* 5 (1987), 163.

[6]Irenaeus, *Adversus Haereses* IV.6.6.

[7]T. F. Torrance, *The Trinitarian Faith*, 125.

[8]Ibid.

[9]Ibid.

as being considered in its objective relations…'[10], but also 'carried within it the conception of coinherent relations within the one being of God…'[11] This significant concept of 'coinherence' or *perichoresis* [περιχώρησις], as we shall see immediately, was a way of addressing how the substance could be one, while at the same time involving three Persons within it.

That is, to affirm that God exists in one Being (or substance, essence, *ousia* or reality) and at the same time, as three Persons, raised the most mind-stretching questions as to how this could be, or at least, what could such an affirmation mean for us, who have no precise natural illustration or analogy of it? Ultimately, the Church came to see that when we speak of 'substance', 'ousia' [οὐσία], or 'being' in God, the meaning of the word has to be stretched almost infinitely beyond our human experience of it. This is just what happened in the development of the massively important Trinitarian concept of perichoresis [περιχώρησις], ('circumincessio' in Latin; 'coinherence' or 'mutual indwelling' in English).

'Perichoresis' or 'Mutual Indwelling' or 'coinherence'

What the Church had to think through has been summarized simply, as we saw earlier, by John Zizioulas: 'What does it mean to say that God is Father, Son and Spirit without ceasing to be one God?'[12] The Patristic doctrine of perichoresis made this possible, by enriching the word ousia or 'substance' when referring to God. 'Perichoresis derives from *chora* (χώρα), the Greek word for "space" or "room", or from *chorein* (χώρειν), meaning "to contain", "to make room", or "to go forward". It indicates a sort of mutual containing or enveloping of realities, which we also speak of as coinherence or coindwelling.'[13]

According to Torrance, this word seems first to have been used by Gregory of Nazianzus to speak of the way in which the divine and human natures of Christ dwell in one another.[14] From there it was taken by St. Hilary to apply to the relationship in which the three divine Persons mutually dwell in one another while retaining their distinctness: 'They [i.e. the three Persons] reciprocally contain one another, so that one should permanently envelope, and also be permanently enveloped by the Other, whom yet he envelopes.'[15]

A few centuries later, John of Damascus wrote:

> The subsistences [i.e. 'persons'] dwell and are established firmly in one another. For they are inseparable and cannot part from another, but keep to their separate courses within one another, without coalescing or mingling, but clinging to each other. For the Son is in the Father and the Spirit: and the Spirit in the Father and the Son: and the Father in the Son and Spirit, but there is not coalescence or commingling or confusion.[16]

---

[10]Ibid., 10.
[11]Ibid., 305.
[12]Zizioulas, op. cit., 36.
[13]T. F. Torrance, *The Christian Doctrine of God*, 102.
[14]T. F. Torrance, *The Trinitarian Faith*, 234.
[15]Hilary, *De Trinitate* III.1.
[16]John of Damascus, *De Fide Orthodoxa* I.14.

Perichoresis ('circumincession' or 'mutual indwelling') was a way of saying that the Father, the Son and the Holy Spirit inhere in one another; co-exist eternally, entirely and perfectly, so that where one is, the others are, and what one is involved in doing, the others are also involved in doing. What Jesus says in John's Gospel, chapter 5, illustrates perichoresis. After Jesus had healed a lame man on the Sabbath day,[17] and had forgiven his sins, the Jews wished to kill Him, for breaking the Sabbath and making God His Father (John 5:16-18). Jesus responded: 'My Father worketh hitherto, and I work' (v. 17). Then he adds a further explanation of the Father/Son relationship, both in activity (19-25) and being (26):

> ... the Son can do nothing of himself, but what he seeth the Father do: for what things soever he doeth the Son doeth likewise. For the Father loveth the Son and sheweth him all things that himself doeth: and he will shew him greater works than these, that ye may marvel. For as the Father raised up the dead, and quickeneth them; even so the Son quickeneth whom he will. For the Father judgeth no man, but hath committed all judgment unto the Son: That all men should honour the Son, even as they honour the Father. He that honoureth not the Son honoureth not the Father which hath sent him...For as the Father hath life in himself; so hath he given to the Son to have life in himself; and hath given him authority to execute judgment also, because he is the Son of man ... because I seek not mine own will, but the will of the Father which hath sent me (John 5:19-23, 26-27, 30).

In answer to Philip's request for Jesus to show him the Father, the Lord replies: 'Have I been so long time with you, and yet hast thou not known me, Philip? He that hath seen me hath seen the Father... Believest thou not that I am in the Father and the Father in me? The words that I speak unto you I speak not of myself; but the Father dwelleth in me, he doeth the works. Believe me that I am in the Father, and the Father in me: or else believe me for the very works' sake... At that day ye shall know that I am in my Father, and ye in me, and I in you' (John 14:9-11,20). In John 10:30 Jesus teaches that 'I and the Father are one', and in 10:38 that 'the Father is in me, and I in him.'

In His high priestly prayer, Jesus prays concerning His oneness with the Father, and then the oneness of His people with Him and the Father: 'That they all may be one; as thou, Father, art in me, and I in thee, that they also may be one in us: that the world may believe that thou hast sent me' (John 17:21).

It is similar with the Holy Spirit; the Spirit brings the very knowledge of God Himself into the believer. For the Spirit to be there is for God the Father to be there:

> But God hath revealed them [i.e. the things which God has prepared for his people – v. 9] unto us by his Spirit: for the Spirit searcheth all things, yea, the deep things of God. For what man knoweth the things of a man, save the spirit of man which is in him? Even so the things of God knoweth no man, but the Spirit of God. Now we have received ... the spirit which

[17]There are textual problems within this pericope, but none of them changes the joint working of Father and Son.

> is of God; that we might know the things that are freely given to us of God (1 Cor. 2:10-12).

After His ascension, Jesus comes back to be with His people in the Holy Spirit; for the Holy Spirit to be with them is for Christ to be with them: 'And I will pray the Father, and he shall give you another Comforter, that he may abide with you for ever ... but ye know him, for he dwelleth with you, and shall be in you. I will not leave you comfortless: I will come to you' (John 14:16-18). In verse 16, Jesus promises the coming of he Comforter (the Spirit of God); in verse 17, he says 'I will come to you.' Romans 8:9 speaks in the same verse of the indwelling of the Spirit of God and also of the Spirit of Christ. Romans 8:10 speaks both of Christ being in you, and the Spirit being your life within the same verse. The Apostle Paul at one time can speak of 'Christ in you, the hope of glory' (Col. 1:27), and another time of our being 'an habitation of God through the Spirit' (Eph. 2:22).[18] This is *perichoresis*.

T. F. Torrance unfolds this transformed sense of *ousia* within the Trinitarian thought of the Church – when used of God – from the Greek impersonal concept of being to the Christian personal sense.[19]

> Its application to the doctrine of the Trinity ... enables us to recognize that the coinherent relations of the Father, the Son and the Spirit ... are not temporary manifestations of God's nature, but are eternally grounded in the intrinsic and completely reciprocal relations of the Holy Trinity. In this way the concept of *perichoresis* serves to hold powerfully together in the doctrine of the Trinity the identity of the divine Being and the intrinsic unity of the three divine Persons.[20]

This perichoretic relationship of the three divine Persons with one another was not a mere 'linking or intercommunication of the distinctive properties of the three divine Persons but a completely mutual indwelling in which each Person, while remaining what he is by himself as Father, Son, or Holy Spirit, is wholly in the others as the others are wholly in him.'[21]

This can be stated in another way: we can say that the whole undivided essence (*ousia*) of God belongs equally to each of the three Persons. That is, the divine essence (or substance) is not 'divided' among the three Persons, but is wholly with all its perfection in each one of the Persons so that they have a numerical unity of essence or being. And yet, they are still three conscious Persons, not just one Person.

St. Thomas Aquinas taught that the one being of God is, in fact, the relationship of the three Persons:

> In God essence is not really distinct from person; and yet ... the persons are really distinguished from each other. For person signifies relation as subsisting in the divine nature. But relation as referred to the essence does not differ therefrom really; but only in our way of thinking; while as referred

---

[18]See James S. Stewart's now classical lectures on this subject: *A Man in Christ* (London: Hodder & Stoughton, 1935)

[19]T. F. Torrance, *The Christian Doctrine of God*, 103.

[20]Ibid., 102.

[21]T. F. Torrance, *The Trinitarian Faith*, 305.

> to an opposite relation, it has a real distinction by virtue of that opposition. Thus there are one essence and three persons.[22]

Stăniloae states it this way:

> No kind of attenuation of the divine nature is conceivable among the persons. All three are perfectly one in the other, together possessing in common the whole of the divine nature with no weakening of the continuity between them. In order to have even any understanding of this we must keep in mind that the divine nature is entirely spiritual, and that its spirituality is of a kind that transcends all spirituality known or imagined by us. As such the divine hypostases are free of any of that impermeability or persistent tendency to annex the other from which human hypostases – whom we have according imagined as knots on a string – are never wholly exempt.[23]

Or with Torrance:

> Not only is the divine consciousness proper to the nature of the one God common to Father, Son and Holy Spirit alike, but each divine person in virtue of his distinctiveness shares in it differently and appropriately, so that we would have to say that while Father, Son and Holy Spirit constitute one indivisible God, they do so as three conscious subjects in mutual love and life and activity. That is to say, coinherence applies fully to the three divine Persons as conscious of One another in their distinctive otherness and oneness. Such a view could only be taken along with the idea that we must think of God himself as Person, but of this one Person as existing and meeting us in the triunity of Persons in one God.[24]

In other words, God's substance inherently involves personal relationship with co-equals in that same substance. The three divine Persons are not superficially linked like three separate persons on earth in a sort of chain. Rather, perichoresis affirms 'a completely mutual indwelling in which each Person, while remaining what he is by himself as Father, Son or Holy Spirit, is wholly in the others as the others are wholly in him.'[25]

Dumitru Stăniloae speaks of perichoresis as 'transparency within the interiority of perfect love':

> The divine hypostases are totally transparent one to another even within the interiority of perfect love. Their consubstantiality is neither preserved nor developed by those fine threads which, on the human analogy, might unite them as bearers of the same being. Rather, each one bears the entire nature in common with the others. They are thereby wholly interior to one another and have no need to leap over even the thinnest of bridges between them so as to achieve a greater unity among themselves by means of such communication. The infinity of each leaves no possibility for any such attenuation of the divine nature among them. They might be likened, after the fashion of the Fathers, to three surpassingly bright and transparent suns which are reciprocally comprised in and appear in one another, bearing

---

[22]Thomas Aquinas, *Summa Theologiae*, I.39.1.

[23]Stăniloae, *The Experience of God*, 255.

[24]T. F. Torrance, 'Towards an Ecumenical Consensus on the Trinity' in *Trinitarian Perspectives: Towards Doctrinal Agreement* (Edinburgh: T & T Clark, 1994), 97.

[25]T. F. Torrance, ed., *Theological Dialogue Between Orthodox and Reformed Churches* (Edinburgh: Scottish Academic Press, 1985), 85

undividedly the whole of a single and infinite light. 'He who has seen me has seen the Father… Believe me that I am in the Father and the Father in me,' said our Saviour (John 14:9,11), and Saint Basil declares:[26] 'He who has, as it were, mental apprehension of the form of the Son, prints the express image of the Father's hypostasis … gazing at the unbegotten beauty in the Begotten.[27]

Trinity and person

The concept of person only arose in the declining classical world after the incarnation of Christ and the outpouring of the Holy Spirit; that is, after the clear revelation as God as triune. As Eric Von Kuehnelt-Leddihn noted: 'it is well to recall that the concept of person as we know it did not exist in antiquity. It appeared in the Western world – with the advent of Christianity.'[28]

St. Augustine's fourth-century *Confessions* manifest an intense sense of inward, personal life; marking perhaps the first 'autobiography' of a 'person' in the West. Of course, 'persons' existed in the world from the time of the creation of Adam and Eve, and it seems that the Old Testament idea of *panim* [פָּנִים] or 'countenance' (as in the Aaronic benediction), that is, 'face to face' with another, was the pre-conceptual bearer of personal reality.[29] However, the full concept of personhood came into the consciousness of the West as a result of the impact of the gospel through the mission of the Church, where one came 'face to face' with God the Father, through the Son, and in the Holy Spirit, and also into intimate, caring relationship with brothers and sisters in the faith.[30] This reality led to reflection within the Christian theological tradition on the meaning of personal being. It took a number of centuries before formal definitions were attempted, and as is generally the case, the reality was instinctively grasped and practiced long before the definition was forthcoming.

Boethius on person

Boethius, the Christian philosopher of sixth-century Northern Italy, offered a definition of 'person' in terms of the specific instance of a general reality (in line with Aristotelian philosophy). He wrote: 'persona est rationalis naturae individua substantia' ('a person is the individual substance of

---

[26]Basil, 'Letter' 38.8.

[27]Stăniloae, *The Experience of God*, 255.

[28]Eric Von Kuehnelt-Leddihn, op. cit., 34.

[29]Discussing the Hebrew usage of 'the face of the Lord', Harry F. Van Rooy notes that: 'Most of the uses of the (noun) also appear at Qumran. Especially important is the expression he'ir panim, used for the divine enlightenment of the righteous (I QH 3,3; 4,5). In the LXX prosopon is the usual translation of the (noun), encompassing the normal usages of the Heb. (noun): face, side, front, surface. When the LXX speaks of the face of the Lord it usually points to a relationship between God and man, e.g., his gracious turning to man. It appears also frequently in cultic language related to the temple' in Van Gemeren, *Dictionary of OT Theology & Exegesis*, vol.III, 639.

[30]H. F. van Rooy notes: 'The G word prosopon follows the OT usages in the NT. It is used for the face of a person (Matt. 6:16) and also metaphorically (Matt. 17:6). In 2 Cor. 1:11 it denotes a person. In Luke 21:35 it is used for the surface of the earth. It is also used for the face of God or Christ. For the believer the glory of God appeared in the face of Christ (2 Cor. 4:6)' in Ibid., 639.

rational nature').[31] That is, the general concept is that humans are rational animals, and the specific instance is this or that human being, or person.

This definition however cannot take sufficiently into account the three Persons of the Holy Trinity, for they are not 'three individual substances'. And since the triune God is the source of human personhood, Boethius' definition left much to be desired, as Richard of Saint Victor pointed out.[32]

Richard of St. Victor on Person

About six hundred years later, another Trinitarian theologian, Richard of Saint Victor in France (of Scottish origin), derived a more accurate definition of person from meditating on the communion of love in the one Being of God, among Father, Son and Holy Spirit. Personhood within God was the analogy by which Richard understood personhood within humankind. Thus, Richard's definition of a human person was: 'persona est...intellectualis naturae incommunicabilis exsistentia' ('a person is the incommunicable existence of intellectual nature').[33]

His definition of divine Person is: 'divina persona est naturae divinae incommunicabilis exsistentia.'[34] He derived his understanding of personality theologically, rather than in terms of Aristotelian philosophy (with its genera and species, or individual members of that species). Theologically, in terms of 1 John 4:8 ('God is love', which love takes more than one person so that it may be shared), Richard traces the three Persons of the Godhead to the communion of love in the Being of God (which Being is the relationship of the Persons), so that the Father, the Son and the Holy Spirit wholly interpenetrate and coinhere in one another in such a way that their personal distinctness as Father, Son and Holy Spirit remains inviolate.[35]

This means that although relationship with other persons is inherent in being a person, still there is something 'irreducible' or 'incommunicable' about oneself that is not dissolved, lost or merged in relationship with others. Hence, although Father, Son and Holy Spirit coinhere in one another, their distinct conscious subjectivity is not lost in one another or merged into an impersonal unity.

It is similar with human persons, created in the divine image. They are constituted as persons in relationship to God and to one another, but there is an 'incommunicable existence' about them that is never lost or merged into a general 'lump' or 'monad' of humanity. Richard understood that behind human personhood stood the Triune God, who is not only a fullness of personal being in Himself, but is also a person-constituting Being.

That is to say, only God is personalizing person (persona personans), while humans are personalized persons (i.e. persona personata). Torrance explains:

---

[31]Boethius, *De Personis et duabus Naturae* III.

[32]Richard of Saint Victor, *De Trinitate* IV.21.

[33]Richard of Saint Victor, *De Trinitate* IV.16, 22, 24.

[34]Ibid., IV.22.

[35]T. F. Torrance, *Reality and Evangelical Theology*, 43.

> ... in Epiphanian and Cyrillian language, the human nature of Jesus was personalised or given enhypostatic (ἐνυπόστατος) reality in the Person of the Son of God become man. That took place in Jesus in an utterly unique way. Yet we are all persons in our creaturely beings, for through the personalising activity of the Word and Spirit of God we have authentic personal existence in relation to God and in relation to one another. We are persons, however, not in an independent, but in a dependent or contingent way, as personalised persons. Each human being is a *persona personata*, to use the Latin; but God alone is properly and intrinsically Person... He alone is personalising Person, *persona personans*.[36]

T. F. Torrance has summarized Richard's insight on the relationship of Trinity and personality:

> It was from a theological understanding of God's personal and personalizing self-communication, creating personal reciprocity between us and himself, that the Christian concept of the person arose, which is applicable in a creaturely way to persons in relation to one another, but which reflects the transcendent way in which the three divine Persons are interrelated in the Holy Trinity.[37]

Torrance suggests that this 'onto-relational' way of thinking has in a certain sense reappeared fruitfully in some areas of modern physics:

> It is highly significant that it was an onto-relational way of thinking of this kind to which James Clerk Maxwell appealed in the decisive change he initiated in the scientific conception of the structure of the physical universe. Under the regulative force of his Christian beliefs in the nature of God's creative activity as discerned from the perspective of the Incarnation and in the concept of person, he made use of being-constituting relations in his development of a dynamical theory of the electromagnetic field, thereby rejecting a mechanical explanation of it and breaking away from the Newtonian tradition in a mechanistic and deterministic conception of nature. It was from Clerk Maxwell's unification of our understanding of electricity, magnetism and light on this basis and his establishment of the independent reality of the field through his famous equations, that Einstein first crystallized his theory of relativity and went on to bring about the great revolution in modern physics. I refer to this development from Clerk Maxwell to Einstein because when we find a relational way of thinking coming back at us from modern science, it must not be regarded as irrelevant or strange, for it has long roots in the history of Christian theology to which, under God, it calls us back.[38]

Duns Scotus on Person

T. F. Torrance has noted that Duns Scotus (c. 1266–1308) followed Richard of St. Victor's understanding of person:

> In the thought of Duns Scotus it is the nature and the mode of the Being of God as personal that is all-important here. It will be sufficient to recall his criticism of the Boethian notion of persona in which Duns followed

---

[36] T. F. Torrance, *The Trinitarian Faith*, 230.

[37] T.F. Torrance, *Reality and Evangelical Theology*, 143.

[38] T. F. Torrance, *The Mediation of Christ*, 58,59.

> up the teaching of Richard of St. Victor.[39] The difficulty with the Boethian notion of persona was that it was logically derived through abstraction of essence from existence; it presented to Duns the same problem as that in the logicalisation of the concept of being. Thus for Duns the proper notion of the person, derived from reflection upon the Holy Trinity,[40] is at once a relational and an ontological notion, for the relationship is not just a determination of our understanding (*aliqua relatio rationis*)[41] but an inherent and ontological determination of personal existence.[42]

Duns is like Richard of St. Victor[43] in distinguishing between the Trinity as *communis exsistentia* and the *incommunicabilis exsistentia* of the Three Persons of the Trinity.[44] That is, the three Persons exist in common relationship, while having an incommunicable reality about each one in particular. As Richard Cross says,

> Scotus builds on foundations laid by Richard, and he does so in a very metaphysically sophisticated way… In doing so, it seems to me, he develops one of the most compelling and powerfully coherent accounts of the Trinity ever constructed. For Scotus, as for Richard, incommunicability is the key concept.[45]

Cross then refers to Scotus's exposition of incommunicability:

'[5]
1. Something is said to be communicable either by identity, such that that to which it is
2. communicated is it, or by information, such that that to which it is communicated is
3. not it, but is by it (*ipso*).
4. In the first way, the universal is communicated to the singular, and in the
5. second way form [is communicated] to matter. For any nature, considered in itself
6. and under the description of nature, is communicable in either way – that is, to many
7. supposita of which each is it, and also as that 'by which' (*quo*), as a form, by which
8. the singular or suppositum is being quidditatively (*ens quiditative*), or something
9. that has a nature. And a suppositum is incommunicable with the opposed twofold
10. incommunicability.'[46]

Richard Cross helps us make some sense of this difficult and complex text, and I follow him here. He shows that:

---

[39]Torrance notes Duns Scotus *Ordinatio* I d. 23 n. 15: *Reportata Parisiense* I d. 23 q. un. N. 7; Quaestiones Quodlibetal q. 3 n. 17.

[40]Duns Scotus, Rep. I d. 25 q. 2 n. 5. 6. 7. 14; *Quodl*. Q. 3 n. 17.

[41]Duns Scotus, Ord. I d. 4 n. 11-13; Rep. I d. 25 q. 2n. 5. 14; d. 26 q. 5n. 5; Quodl. q. 3n. 4. 6. 9; q. 4n. 20; q. 19n. 20.

[42]T. F. Torrance, *The Hermeneutics of John Calvin* (Edinburgh: Scottish Academic Press, 1988), 9.

[43]Richard of Saint Victor, *De Trinitate* IV.22.24.

[44]Duns Scotus, *Ordinatio* I.23.1.

[45]Richard Cross, *Duns Scotus on God* (Aldershot: Ashgate, 2005), 159.

[46]Duns Scotus, *Ord*. I.2.2.1-4, nn. 380-1, quoted in Cross, op. cit., 159, 160.

> Scotus is distinguishing two sorts of communicability: by identity and by informing [5.1-3] and two corresponding sorts of incommunicability, the negations of these two types of communicability [5.9]. 'Something is communicable by identity if it is really the same in various different supposita [5.4], and this (as we discover elsewhere) can happen in one of two ways: either by being an extramental universal (immanent in each suppositum), or by existing as a concept that equally well represents various different supposita...Scotus believes that only the divine essence can satisfy the first of these descriptions...
>
> Clearly, part of the point of calling something 'individual' is to highlight its not being a common or shared nature; it is not the sort of thing that can be divided into further instances. For Scotus – as for all medieval thinkers – the divine nature is like this: it cannot be divided into further Gods. But the divine nature...is shareable in the sense of being fully exemplified in each person that possesses it. By preferring 'incommunicable' to 'individual' as a description of a divine person, Scotus is basically highlighting the metaphysical fact that no person is exemplifiable in the way that the shared (universal) divine essence is.'[47]
>
> This account of incommunicability helps us to see just what Scotus thinks Richard of St Victor's definition of 'person' adds to Boethius's. Scotus ... distinguishes two ways in which natures are shared by their supposita; by division (communicability ut quo), and by what we might call mere repetition – numerically one and the same nature in each exemplification (communicability ut quod). Scotus wants to draw attention primarily to the latter of these two sorts of relation, and deny it of a divine person. Scotus, as it happens, does not believe that the divine persons are individuals at all – presumably because he believes that anything individual is eo ipso communicable...[48]
>
> ... the (broadly logical) impossibility of communication ut quo must be the result of some additional real property; as Scotus puts it, 'some positive entity' added to the nature or essence. The reason is that a block on communication [i.e. incommunicabilis] requires some real explanation over and above the nature or essence of the relevant thing.[49] In the case of a divine person, this positive entity is the personal property of the divine person. The personal properties are thus the explanations for the persons' incommunicability.'[50]

According to T. F. Torrance, the work of Richard and Duns (both Scots) passed into the Reformed theology of Scotland:

> Here we have a distinctive element in Scottish and Reformed theology which dates back to Duns Scotus' development of the concept of the person as it emerged from the Trinitarian teaching of Richard of St. Victor, and was passed on through Duns Scotus' Commentaries on the Sentences of Peter Lombard to John Major in Paris and then to John Calvin and back, not least through the *Syntagma Theologiae Christianae* of Amandus Polanus to Scotland.[51]

---

[47]Cross, op. cit., 160.
[48]Duns Scotus, *Quod.* 3, n. 17, quoted in Cross, 162.
[49]Duns Scotus, *Ord.* 3.1.1, n. 10; *Quod.* 19, n. 20, quoted in Cross, 163.
[50]Cross, op. cit., 163.
[51]T. F. Torrance, *Transformation & Convergence in the Frame of Knowledge*, 230.

Torrance notes that 'The *Syntagma* of Polanus was prescribed reading for Scottish theologians for some two centuries. Evidence of its knowledge is found even in David Hume's *Dialogues on Natural Religion*, in ideas he put into the mouth of the interlocutor *Philo*.'[52]

The definition of divine Person by Polanus is thus in line with Richard and Duns, and Gregory Nazianzus and Epiphanius behind them. He writes: '*Persona Deitatis* is a subsistence in the divine essence, having in itself by nature the whole of that divine essence, but distinguished by its incommunicable attribute from the other *personae* to which it is related.'[53]

St. Thomas on Person

St. Thomas Aquinas defined person (in *Summa Theologiae*) as '*subsistens distinctum in natura rationali*' ('that which subsists as distinct in a rational nature').[54] In *Summa Contra Gentiles*, he showed that relationship is essential to the definition of divine Person: 'one must not speak of one person by reason of the unity of the subsisting essence, but of many persons by reason of the relations.'[55]

Paul Vanier shows in his *Théologie Trinitaire chez Saint Thomas D'Aquin* a development of thought on the concept of what 'person' is by Saint Thomas from his early *De Potentia* to his late *Summa Theologiae*. Vanier calls it 'un approfondissement marqué entre la théologie trinitaire du *De Potentia* et celle de la *Somme*.'[56] Particularly on the subject of how relationship manifests the divine Persons, Vanier considers the later thought of Thomas to be 'le développement du point crucial de la théologie trinitaire augustinienne.'[57] He specifies how this was worked out:

> En montrant comment la relation constitue exclusivement la personne divine tant comme subsistante que comme opposée aux autres personnes et distincte d'elles… [In showing how the relation constitutes exclusively the divine person insofar as it subsists over against the other persons and distinct from them…] (Thomas thus achieves this development of Augustine's thought). … Il est à la fois en possession de ce qui distingue les personnes entres elles et de ce qui distingue pour notre esprit chaque personne de l'essence commune aux trois… [It at the same time possesses that which distinguishes the persons between themselves and that which distinguishes for our spirit each person out of the essence common to the three…]
>
> … Encore: pour montrer la simplicité de la personne divine, il rappelle que, en elle, c'est la relation qui subsiste et distingue [… Again: in order to demonstrate the simplicity of the divine person, he recalls that in itself, it is the relation which subsists and distinguishes]:

---

[52]Ibid., p. 240, n. 61.

[53]Polanus, *Syntagma* III.2, cited in H. Heppe, Reformed Dogmatics, revised by Ernst Bizer and translated by G. T. Thomson (Grand Rapids: Baker, 1978 reprint), 111.

[54]St. Thomas, *Summa Theologiae* I, q. 30, a. 3; a. 4.

[55]St. Thomas, *Summa Contra Gentiles* Book IV, ch. 14, par. 6 (C. J. O'Neil translation: Notre Dame, p. 99).

[56]Paul Vanier, S.J., *Théologie Trinitaire chez Saint Thomas D'Aquin: Évolution du Concept D'Action Notionnelle* (Montréal: Institut D'Etudes Médievales, 1953), 9.

[57]Ibid., 76.

> Personae sunt *ipsae relationes subsistentes*. Unde non repugnant simplicitati divinarum personarum, quod relationibus distinguantur – Relatio si ut subsistens [...] *secum fert distinctionem* [suppositorum] – Proprietates personales [...] secum ferunt sua supposita, in quantum *sunt ipsae personae* subsistentes.' (*Summa Theologiae* Ia, Q. XI, a. 2, c and a. 3. c).[58] [Persons are *the subsisting relationships themselves*. Whence they are not repugnant to the simplicity of the divine persons, which is distinguished by relationships – Relationship if it be subsisting [...] *with itself brings distinction* [of underlying reality] – Personal properties [...] (which) the underlying realities bring with themselves, insofar as *they are subsisting persons themselves*.]

All of this should be understood to mean, I think, that the Persons of the Trinity do not exist without the relationships.

Karl Barth, however, is less appreciative of St. Thomas's achievement at this point than was Vanier. Barth shows that Thomas certainly understood the difficulty of accepting Boethius' definition of person as 'the individual substance of rational nature' (referring to Thomas's *Summa Theologiae* I. qu. 29, art. 1-2):

> Thomas is also familiar, of course, with the even more important objection, raised already by Augustine and Anselm, that a plurality of persons necessarily involves a plurality of essences as well, and therefore, when applied to God, a plurality of divine essences, or at least a division of the one divine essence. He has thus to state, in a way which is materially correct but which is also a threat to his concept of person, that the *personae* of the Trinity are *res subsistentes* (i.e. in the one) *divina natura*. Thomas cannot help conceding that the *hupostasis* of the Greeks is in this respect nearer the facts than the Latin *persona* and that he avoids it only on account of the fatal translation *substantia*. But the *res subsistentes in divina natura* are also, according to him, nothing but *relations*, intradivine relations (Ibid. qu. 29, art. 4; qu. 30, art. 1)...If Thomas has provided a true explanation, within the bounds of the possible, for what the three involve in triunity, he has done this, not in the form of an interpretation of the concept of person, but by means of the concept of relations.[59]

Note on Thomas's development of Augustine's doctrine of Person

According to Paul Vanier, St. Thomas carried forward far more thoroughly and clearly Saint Augustine's preliminary understanding of divine Persons as involving relationship. He writes:

> Rélatifs, ces noms propres aux personnes, peuvent distinguer réellement les personnes divines entres elles, sans rien ajouter à l'essence divine: telle est presque la solution d'Augustin. Il ne l'explicite cependant jamais. Il parait soupçonner seulement l'apport capital pour la théologie trinitaire de ce concept de relation. Mais la vision implicite de cet apport ne semble le diriger qu'inconsciemment, pour lui faire éviter sans cesse les affirmations qui favoriseraient tantôt le modalisme, tantôt l'arianisme. [*Relatives*, these proper names can really distinguish the divine persons among themselves, without adding anything to the divine essence: that is almost the solution of

---

[58]Ibid., 76,77.

[59]Karl Barth, *Church Dogmatics* (E.T. by Bromiley, 1973), I/1, 356, 357.

> Augustine. However, he never makes it explicit. He appears only to suspect the crucial help for Trinitarian theology of this concept of relation. But the implicit vision of this help seems to lead him only unconsciously, in causing him constantly to avoid those affirmations which would lead him to favour modalism on the one hand, as much as arianism on the other].[60]

As we saw earlier, Augustine distinguished between speaking of the Being of God 'substance-wise' and 'relationship-wise.' Speaking of the Father and the Son, Augustine said:

> But because son does not have reference to son but to father, it cannot be what he is called with reference to the Father that makes the Son equal to the Father. It remains that what makes him equal must be what he is called with reference to himself. But whatever he is called with reference to himself he is called substance-wise. So it follows that he is equal substance-wise. Therefore the substance of each of them is the same. And when the Father is called unbegotten, it is not being stated what he is, but what he is not. And when a relationship is denied it is not denied substance-wise, because the relationship itself is not affirmed substance-wise.[61]

But Augustine never worked this out with any clarity. That, according to Vanier, was the contribution of St. Thomas, as we saw above. And the Thomist account of Augustine's doctrine of Trinitarian Person, was – as Vanier states – 'universally accepted in the Medieval world', at least in the sense that 'from relationship comes every personal aspect within the Trinity'[62] (although Duns Scotus and others defined it rather differently).

With his development of St. Augustine's doctrine of the relational nature of the persons of the Trinity, it may well be that Thomas, in a certain sense, was actually closer to the concept of person as relationship found in Gregory Nazianzus in the fourth century,[63] and in Dumitru Stăniloae and John Zizioulas of the twentieth, than could have been realized by Barth at the time he was writing this first volume of *Church Dogmatics*. At least, Thomas's final concept of person seems to fit more easily into the Christian theological tradition than Barth's functional replacement of 'person' by 'Seinsweisen' or 'modes of being', which we must now consider.

Karl Barth on Person

Alan J. Torrance has done remarkable work on Barth's concept of Person within the Trinity, and much of this section gladly follows his research.[64] Barth expounds the Trinity in terms of 'a more personal conception of the revelation event.'[65]

Barth writes:

---

[60]Vanier, op. cit., 17.

[61]Augustine, *De Trin.* V.7.

[62]Vanier, op. cit., 35.

[63]See Gregory of Nazianzus, *Oration* 29.16, where he speaks of relation or *sxesis* as the element that constitutes the persons of the Trinity.

[64]Alan J. Torrance, *Persons in Communion: Trinitarian Description and Human Participation*, with special reference to Volume One of Karl Barth's Church Dogmatics (Edinburgh: T & T Clark, 1996).

[65]Ibid., 59.

> God reveals Himself. He reveals Himself through Himself. He reveals Himself.' If we really want to understand revelation in terms of its subject, i.e., God, then the first thing we have to realize is that this subject, God, Revealer, is identical with His act in revelation and also identical with its effect. It is from this fact ... that we learn we must begin the doctrine of revelation with the doctrine of the triune God.[66]

In that context, Barth speaks of the Triune Persons as Revealer, Revelation, and Revealedness (or 'being revealed'):

> The work of God is the essence of God as the essence of Him who (N.B. in a free decision grounded in His essence but not constrained by His essence) is revealer, revelation and being revealed, or Creator, Reconciler and Redeemer... The revelation of God attested in Scripture...shows us God in His work as revealer, revelation and being revealed, or as Creator, Reconciler and Redeemer, or as holiness, mercy and goodness. In these distinctions we can and should perceive the distinctions in the divine modes of being in the truth allotted and appropriate to us.[67]

Barth expounds this event of revelation as 'the reiteration of God'. That is, in revealing Himself as Lord, God says the same thing three times.[68] He writes:

> The name of the Father, Son and Spirit means that God is the one God in threefold repetition, and this in such a way that the repetition itself is grounded in His Godhead, so that it implies no alteration in His Godhead, and yet in such a way also that He is the one God only in this repetition, so that His one Godhead stands or falls with the fact that He is God in this repetition, but for that very reason He is the one God in each repetition.[69]

But Alan Torrance points out that "...'saying the same thing in a threefold way' may be construed as undermining further the notion of an intra-Trinitarian communion which would appear to be necessary if we are to identify what God is in himself with what God is toward us."[70]

Torrance goes on to suggest that Barth's replacement of 'person' by '*Seinsweise*' or 'Mode of Existence' weakens the important concept of communion between the three Persons. Let us see how this works out.

Barth speaks of 'the same God who in unimpaired unity is the Revealer, the revelation and the revealedness' as being ascribed 'in unimpaired differentiation within Himself this threefold mode of being.'[71] He states that he does not absolutely reject 'person': '... by preference we do not use the term 'person' but rather 'mode (or way) of being,' our intention being to express by this term, not absolutely, but relatively better and more simply and clearly the same thing as is meant by 'person.'[72]

He wrote a few pages earlier:

---

[66]Barth, *C.D.* I/1, 296.
[67]Ibid., 371, 372.
[68]Ibid., 332.
[69]Ibid., 350.
[70]Alan J. Torrance, op. cit., 107.
[71]Barth, *C.D.* I/1, 299.
[72]Ibid., 359.

> What we hear when with our human ears and concepts we listen to God's revelation, what we perceive (and can perceive as men) in Scripture, what proclamation of the Word of God actually is in our lives – is the thrice single voice of the Father, the Son, and the Spirit. That is how God is present for us in His revelation. This is how he obviously creates a *vestigium* of Himself and His triunity.[73]

Alan Torrance rightly notes that

> If the metaphor of repetition is to be used to establish the singularity of the divine identity in the threeness, this requires to be qualified by a much more profound doctrine of perichoresis than Barth seems willing to offer in this context… Barth's concept of the Trinitarian *Seinsweisen* obscures the concept of communion in God. Whereas the heart of the New Testament suggests that there is communion between the Father, the Son and the Holy Spirit, we find ourselves asking whether there is or can be communion between *Seinsweisen* – as Cornelius Plantinga expresses it, 'modes do not love at all. Hence they cannot love each other.[74] …[75]
>
> … If Barth is to adopt the term *Seinsweise* because of its apparent neutrality he risks the charge of naivete here through his failing to appreciate the extent to which *Seinsweise* is less than neutral – to the extent that it undermines the notion of mutuality and of relatedness within the divine identity as these are conveyed by the term person when it is given proper theological currency.[76]

In a further discussion of Barth's concepts of the Being of God and analogy, Alan Torrance notes that:

> The weakness in Barth's argument here, which, as we shall suggest, is similar to that reflected in his opting for *Seinsweise* as opposed to Person, is his refusal to lay claim to the fact that 'being' may be given theological reinterpretation in dynamic, relational and personal terms. There is no need, therefore, to be as suspicious as Barth was of the terms 'being' or, indeed, 'person'… The kind of theological apperception for which Barth strove required an insistence on a relational reinterpretation of 'being' as also of 'personhood' when used to interpret the intra-trinitarian life. This end was not served by departing from these terms in these two central areas…[77]
>
> … Barth underestimates the extent to which the language of *Seinsweise* risks sterilising rather than communicating an appreciation of the dynamic, perichoretic and participative presence of the Triunity.[78]

Alan Torrance properly notes that, nonetheless, Barth was neither a true modalist nor a Subordinationist.[79] Barth clearly speaks against both heretical views of the Trinity in *Church Dogmatics* I/1, 4. 'The Meaning of the Doctrine of the Trinity.'[80] As Alan Torrance goes on to say, Barth is against the basic

---

[73]Ibid., 347.

[74]Cornelius Plantinga, 'The Threeness/Oneness Problem of the Trinity,' *Calvin Theological Journal* 23, no. 1 (April 1988), 49.

[75]Alan Torrance, op. cit., 115, 116.

[76]Ibid., 116.

[77]Ibid., 186. 187.

[78]Ibid., 232.

[79]Ibid., 187.

[80]Barth, *C.D.* I/1. 375-83.

premise of classical modalism, that there is an unknown something behind God that gives rise to a medium, between God and man, three modes that are not fully and personally God:

> God does not exist behind that which reveals God. God is not mediated by that which is not God, God is nothing less than identical with God's revelation.[81]

> ... the fact that God takes form does not give rise to a medium, a third thing between God and man, a reality distinct from God that is as such the subject of revelation. This would imply that God would be unveilable for men, that God Himself would no longer need His revelation, or rather that God would be given up into the hands of men, who, God's form being given Him, could more or less control God as he does other realities.[82]

Thus, although Barth is opposed to modalism, yet the concepts involved in his reworking of the doctrine of the Trinity in terms of *Seinsweisen* or Modes of Being, in place of interpersonal communion, do tend to lead him at times in a certain modalist direction.

Barth to some degree is influenced by the expression of St. Basil, *tropos huparxeos* ('mode of personal subsistence of Father, Son and Spirit in the one being of the Godhead').[83] Certainly, Basil did not use this expression to advance modalism! And yet, this expression could not convey the full reality of the three co-equal persons in the one being of God. T. F. Torrance notes how this full personal reality of the three persons was conveyed far more accurately by Epiphanius:

> The teaching of Epiphanius, however, was not without its own characteristic nuances. (1) Unlike the Cappadocians, he did not speak of the different Persons of Father, Son and Holy Spirit as 'modes of existence' in the one being of God, but preferred to speak of them as 'enhypostatic' (ἐνυπόστατος) in God, that is, as having real, objective personal being in God and as coinhering hypostatically in him...(2) His understanding of the *homoousion* as applying not only to each Person but to the inner relations of the Trinity as a whole, deepened his notion of the coinherence of Father, Son and Holy Spirit in their enhypostatic relations...[84]

As T. F. Torrance has shown, it was not only Epiphanius who went in a different direction from the *tropos huparxeos* [τρόπος ὑπάρξεως] of Basil, but also – even earlier – Basil's Cappadocian colleague, Gregory Nazianzus had done so:

> It is significant that Gregory avoided the Basilian notion of *tropos huparxeos* [τρόπος ὑπάρξεως] altogether, for as he understood them the relations between the divine Persons are not just modes of existence but substantial relations which belong intrinsically to what Father, Son and Holy Spirit are in themselves as distinctive hypostatic realities as well as in their objective reciprocal relations with one another. The relations between them are just as substantial as what they unchangeably are in themselves and by themselves.[85]

---

[81]Alan Torrance, op. cit., 102.

[82]Barth, *C.D.* I/1, 321, cited in A. Torrance, op. cit., 103.

[83]Basil, *De Spiritu Sancto*, 46.

[84]T. F. Torrance, *The Trinitarian Faith*, 221,222.

[85]Ibid., 321.

But for all his rich discussion of the doctrine of the Trinity, in choosing 'modes of existence', Barth does not seem to have been able to benefit very much at this point from the work of Gregory Nazianzus, Epiphanius and Cyril of Alexandria on the objective inter-Trinitarian relations of the three Persons in the one Being of God (though he did benefit from them at many other points).

Specifically, Barth expounds the unity of the Trinity as one Lord, which he identifies as the essence of God. He sees the Father, Son and Spirit as a single Thou.[86] He explains the threeness as a threefold repetition of the single divine Person.[87]

But as Alan Torrance asks, following Peter Brunner: '… why is there no consideration of the possibility that reference may be made to what Peter Brunner refers to as a "divine 'we'"?'[88] Torrance adds:

> What Barth's conception of unity fails to take due cognisance of is the extent to which the New Testament accounts make it difficult to avoid affirming that God is a Thou to himself and an I in relation to himself, and that this eternal mutuality is opened to the world so that we are brought into communion within the union not of a 'we' but of the one, eternal and primordial We – 'The Father and I (i.e. 'we') are one.' … The notion of God as an indissoluble, single subject is not required by Christian monotheism…and fails of itself to allow sufficiently for the kind of distinctions which require to be made here.[89]

Karl Rahner on Person

Particularly since the publication in 1970 of Karl Rahner's very influential *The Trinity*, where he follows Barth's departure from the usage of 'Person', the continued viability of the terminology of 'Person' within the Trinity has been widely discussed.[90] As far as I know, the fullest response to Rahner's abandonment of 'Person' has come from T. F. Torrance's 'Toward an Ecumenical Consensus on the Trinity', in *Trinitarian Perspectives*.[91] Alan Torrance has also addressed Rahner's view of the person in Trinitarian theology in his (now frequently quoted by me) *Persons in Communion*.[92]

Rahner rightly seeks to overcome the traditional scholastic division between 'the two treatises' of 'the One God' (*De Deo Uno*) and 'the Triune God' (*De Deo Trino*), so critiqued by Barth and also by many modern Roman Catholic theologians. He noted that this traditional division led to serious abstraction, and could not properly deal with 'God as experienced in salvation history in his free relations to his creatures.'[93]

Rahner overcomes this abstractive division between the One God and the Triune God by this identity statement: 'The 'economic' Trinity is the

---

[86]Barth, *C.D.* I/1, 348.

[87]Ibid., 350.

[88]Alan Torrance, op. cit., 219.

[89]Ibid., 220.

[90]Karl Rahner, *The Trinity* translated by Joseph Donceel (London: Burns & Oates, 1970).

[91]T. F. Torrance, *Trinitarian Perspectives: Toward Doctrinal Agreement* (Edinburgh: T & T Clark, 1994), 77-102.

[92]Especially, pp. 262-306.

[93]K. Rahner, op. cit., 17-18.

'immanent' Trinity, and the 'immanent' Trinity is the 'economic' Trinity.'[94] As T. F. Torrance comments concerning this crucial statement of Rahner:

> The Economic Trinity is already the Immanent Trinity, because the basic event of the whole economy of salvation is the self-communication of God to the world through the Incarnation of the Son and the sending of the Spirit, and because all that God the Father is to us in Jesus Christ the Son and in the Holy Spirit would not really be the self-communication of God if the two-fold mission were not intrinsic to him, as 'processions' or 'outgoings' of his Being bringing with them the distinction of the three Persons in God himself.[95]

Alan Torrance notes:

> Two features of Rahner's argumentation are immediately significant. He insists that: 1) a proper interpretation of grace sees it as the 'self-communication of God (not primarily as 'created grace') in Christ and in his Spirit; and 2) 'there is at least *one* 'mission', *one* presence in the world, one reality of salvation history which is not merely appropriated to some divine person, but which is proper to him… There has occurred in salvation history something which can be predicated only of one divine person.[96]

Rahner's programme at this point has much to commend it, but as T. F. Torrance points out,

> Most of Rahner's discussion appears to relate to the second part of that axiom, the Trinity ad intra is the Trinity ad extra; but much more attention must be given to the first half of the axiom, the Trinity ad extra is the Trinity ad intra. … That is indeed the powerful implication of Rahner's point, already made so strongly by Barth, that the Incarnation of the Son of God in our world falls within and not without the inner Life of God,[97] for that forces us to operate with the essential openness of the contingent world, created and upheld by the Son in the Spirit, to God the Father.[98]

It appears to be this very point, of the *ad intra* relational nature of the three Persons within the one Godhead, that is to some degree weakened by Rahner's exposition, particularly as he rejects the traditional Christian term 'Person' as proper for God's inter-Trinitarian life. Although Rahner does not wish to deny this reality as such, he moves in that direction by his statements that (1) 'there is properly no mutual love between Father and Son, for this would presuppose two acts,'[99] and (2) Hence within the Trinity there is no reciprocal 'Thou'.[100]

These denials of objective inter-Trinitarian personhood are reflected in his replacement of 'Person' by 'distinct modes of subsisting' ('Subsistenzweisen'):

> The one self-communication of the one God occurs in three different manners of given-ness, in which the one God is given concretely for us in himself,

---

[94]Ibid., 21.
[95]T. F. Torrance, *Trinitarian Perspectives*, 100, 101.
[96]Alan Torrance, op. cit., 264,265, cites Rahner, op. cit., 22-3.
[97]See Rahner, op. cit., 23.
[98]T. F. Torrance, op. cit., 101.
[99]Rahner, op. cit., 106.
[100]Ibid., 76.

> and not vicariously by other realities through their transcendental relation to God. God is the concrete God in each one of these manners of given-ness – which, of course, refer to each other relatively, without modalistically coinciding. If we translate this in terms of 'immanent' Trinity, we may say: the one God subsists in three distinct manners of subsisting.[101]

Later, Rahner adds:

> The one God subsists in three distinct manners of subsisting; the manners of subsisting of Father, Son and Holy Spirit are distinct as relations of opposition; hence these 'three' are not the same one; the Father, Son and Spirit are the One God each in a different manner of subsisting and in this sense we may count 'three' in God ...[102]

But as T. F. Torrance comments:

> ... the abstract character of Rahner's new concepts and formulations does nothing to deepen the communion of the faithful with the Father through the Son and in the Holy Spirit, or therefore to promote the understanding of the Blessed Trinity within the heart of Christian experience, worship and mission as Rahner himself desires.[103]

In particular, Rahner's reinterpretation of Trinity in terms of 'Subsistenzweisen' instead of objective Persons, weakens the Church's grasp of being in direct communion with the Father, the Son and the Holy Spirit as *real persons* whom we can know personally in the experience of salvation. This is certainly a large part of the problem when Rahner denies a distinct center of consciousness and will of each of the divine Persons. T. F. Torrance replies, explaining why – on the contrary – we must assume distinct consciousness of all three divine Persons:

> However, the concrete personalisation of God's self-communication to us in Jesus Christ and in the distinct identity of the Holy Spirit does require us to give *consciousness* some real place in the notion of person as applied to the three Persons in God. Not only is the divine consciousness proper to the Nature of the one God common to Father, Son and Holy Spirit alike, but each divine Person in virtue of his distinctiveness shares in it differently and appropriately, so that we would have to say that while Father, Son and Holy Spirit constitute one indivisible God they do so as three conscious Subjects in mutual love and life and activity. That is to say, *coinherence* applies fully to the three divine Persons as conscious of one another in their distinctive otherness and oneness. Such a view could be held only along with the idea that we must think of God himself as Person, but of this one Person as existing and meeting us in a triunity of Persons in one God.[104]

Both of the Torrances, T. F. and his nephew, Alan, correctly state that Rahner has neglected thinking through the implications of *perichoresis* for a truer account of the three Persons of the Holy Trinity (i.e. the Trinity *ad intra*). T. F. writes:

---

[101]Ibid., 109.
[102]Ibid., 113, 114.
[103]T. F. Torrance, op. cit., 96.
[104]Ibid., 97.

> This requires much fuller use of the patristic concept of *perichoresis* than Rahner seems to entertain, if a richer concept of personal being involving consciousness is to be appropriate and helpful, and not to lead in the tritheistic direction which he fears. It would bring into the concept of the person a deeper ontology according to which a person precisely as person is understood to be free to go outside of himself while remaining in himself in relation to others what he distinctively is.[105]

Alan Torrance states:

> It is precisely here and here alone that we discover the irreducibly Trinitarian meaning of the statement 'God is love.' And it is as we discover this that we may begin to understand the extent to which this involves an appreciation of the integration at the deepest level of the divine self-relatedness and selflessness as these characterise the communion of the intra-divine life.[106]

Some Reformers and Puritans on Person

Martin Luther on Person

The major sixteenth-century Protestant Reformers continued firmly in the Patristic and Catholic tradition in their basic exposition of Trinity and divine personhood. What was stated in the Smalcald Articles (1537) about the Trinity is typical of the lifelong attitude of Luther (who helped draw up these Articles). In Part I – The Trinity, it is stated: 'That Father, Son and Holy Spirit, three distinct persons in one divine essence, are one God, who created heaven and earth.'

At the end of this brief, opening section, these important words are added: 'These articles are not matters of dispute or contention, for both parties [i.e. Roman and Lutheran] confess them. Therefore, it is not necessary to treat them at greater length.'

Luther's doctrine of Trinitarian personhood was traditionally Catholic, because – he believed – profoundly biblical. In light of the whole tradition, Luther saw Person in terms of personal relations within God:

> The Father is my and thy God and Creator, who hath made thee and me, the selfsame work that thou and I are, the Son hath also made, and is as much thy and my God and Creator as the Father. Thus the Holy Ghost hath also made the same work that I and thou art, and is my and thy God and Creator as much as the Father and the Son. Yet there are not three Gods or Creators but one single God and Creator of the twain of us. Here by this faith I guard myself against the heresy of Arius and his like, that I divide not the single divine essence into three Gods or Creators, but in true Christian faith retain no more than the one God and Creator of all creatures. Again, if I now pass beyond and outside creation or the creature into the inward, incomprehensible essence of the divine nature, I find, as Scripture teacheth me (for reason is naught here), that the Father is a different person from the Son in the one undivided eternal Godhead. His distinction is that He is the Father and hath not divinity from the Son nor from any one. The Son is a distinct person from the Father in one and the same Fatherly Godhead.

---

[105] Ibid., 98.

[106] Alan Torrance, op. cit., 281.

> His distinction is that He is the Son and hath divinity not from Himself nor from any one but only from the Father as eternally born of the Father. The Holy Ghost is a distinct person from the Father and the Son in one and the same Godhead. His distinction is that He is the Holy Ghost that proceedeth eternally from the Father and the Son together, and He hath Godhead neither from Himself nor from any one, but from both the Father and the Son together, and all this from eternity to eternity. With this faith I here guard myself against the heresy of Sabellius and his like, against Jews, Mahomet, and all that are wiser than God Himself, and mix not the persons into one person, but in true Christian faith retain three distinct persons in the one divine, eternal essence, all three of which, to us and creatures, are one God, Creator and Worker of all things.[107]

Luther is clear that when we meet Jesus Christ, we meet the Triune God; that in Him the entire Godhead is present, for one Person is not divided from the others: 'Since Christ, who is one undivided person, God and man, speaks to us, we are sure that God the Father and the Holy Spirit – that is, the whole divine majesty – is also present and speaking. So God is entirely comprehended in this one person, and you need not nor dare not search elsewhere.'[108]

And he employs the traditional Patristic terminology: one God in three Persons: 'We have no alternative but to use this little word 'person' here as the Fathers also used it: it means the same thing as a hypostasis (an essence or substance complete in itself) that is God. There are three distinct persons, but only one single Godhead; there is but one single God.'[109]

Philip Melanchthon on Person

Martin Luther's younger colleague, Philip Melanchthon, also followed in the traditional Patristic and Catholic understandings of Trinity and Person, although Karl Barth felt that 'he did not at least incorporate the concept of relation in his definition [of person] but usually introduced it, if at all, only by way of later explanations.'[110] Thus he thought that at times Melanchton unintentionally phrased these issues in a way that tended towards tritheism.

However, we can be certain that Melanchthon's intention was fully that of traditional orthodoxy, as a reading of Article II of his *Loci Communes* (first published in 1521, and finally revised in 1555) – 'Of the Three Persons, Eternal Father, Eternal Son, and Eternal Holy Spirit, who are One unified Divine Being' – will show.

> The ancient Church used hypostasis for the term 'person', and this is to be understood in the way in which I have just explained.[111] Thus, one says that the Son of God is a person; that is, he is not simply an imagined thought

[107]'Von den letzten Worten Davids', W.A., 54, 58, 4, cited in Karl Barth, *Church Dogmatics* I/1, 365.

[108]Martin Luther, *W.A.*, 45, 550, 22.

[109]Luther, *W.A.*, 46, 550, 16.

[110]Barth, *C.D.* I/1, 365.

[111]i.e. 'Person is not a part or a detachable thing, but is instead an essence, a living thing, which is not sustained and supported by any other being as if it were but an addition to it' – *Loci Communes*, Article II.

> but is truly a unified, distinct, rational entity [Ding], and is begotten by the Father…For this reason we must know that in the divine Being there are three persons, no more, no less…[112]

John Calvin on Person

John Calvin's significant work on the Holy Trinity, including his understanding of person, is very much in harmony with the Patristic tradition, especially with Gregory Nazianzus and St. Augustine, as we shall see. B. B. Warfield notes that the Reformers had no wish to distance themselves from the traditional teaching of the Catholic Church on the basic doctrine of God and the Trinity.[113] Calvin defines 'person' in his Institutes:

> 'Person' therefore I call a 'subsistence' in God's essence, which, while related to the others, is distinguished by an incommunicable quality. By the term 'subsistence' we would understand something different from 'essence.' For if the Word were simply God, and yet possessed no other characteristic mark, John would wrongly have said that the Word was always God [John 1:1]. When immediately after he adds that the Word was also God himself, he recalls us to the essence as a unity. But because he could not be with God without residing in the Father, hence emerges the idea of a subsistence, which, even though it has been joined with the essence by a common bond and cannot be separated from it, yet has a special mark whereby it is distinguished from it. Now, of the three subsistences I say that each one, while related to the others, is distinguished by a special quality. This 'relation' is here distinctly expressed: because where simple and indefinite mention is made of God, this name pertains no less to the Son and the Spirit than to the Father. But as soon as the Father is compared with the Son, the character of each distinguishes the one from the other. Thirdly, whatever is proper to each individually, I maintain to be incommunicable because whatever is attributed to the Father as a distinguishing mark cannot agree with, or be transferred to, the Son. Nor am I displeased with Tertullian's definition,[114] provided it be taken in the right sense, that there is a kind of distribution or economy in God which has no effect on the unity of essence.[115]

Thus, Calvin, like Gregory Nazianzus, sees Father, Son and Holy Spirit as eternal subsistent, personal relations in God. Gregory writes: '… the Father is not a name either of an essence or an action…But it is the name of the Relation in which the Father stands to the Son, and the Son to the Father. For as with us these names make known a genuine and intimate relation, so, in the case before us too, they denote an identity of nature between Him that is begotten and Him that begets…'[116]

---

[112]Philip Melanchthon, *Loci Communes* (1555 edition) translated and edited by Clyde L. Manschreck as *Melanchthon on Christian Doctrine: Loci Communes 1555* (New York: Oxford University Press, 1965), 12.

[113]With particular reference to Melanchthon (but also including his younger friend, Calvin), Warfield writes: 'The Reformation movement was, of course, at bottom a great revival of religion. But this does not mean that its revolt from Scholasticism was from the doctrines of God, of His unity and His trinity, of the mystery of creation, of the mode of the incarnation' [referring to Melanchthon's *Loci*, Augusti's edition of 1821]. Cited in B. B. Warfield, 'Calvin's Doctrine of the Trinity,' *Calvin and Augustine* (Philadelphia: Presbyterian and Reformed, 1956 reprint), 195.

[114]Tertullian, *Against Praxeas* ii. 9.

[115]Calvin, *Institutes* I. xiii. 6.

[116]Gregory Nazianzus, *Orations* 29.16; see also 23.8, 11; 30.11, 19; 31.9, 14; 42.15.

In addition to Gregory Nazianzus, Calvin follows Augustine as well, who carefully investigated the terms 'person' and 'substance', without denying the difficulty of doing so in our limited human language:

> And so, for the sake of talking about inexpressible matters, that we may somehow express what we are completely unable to express, our Greek colleagues talk about one being, three substances, while we Latins talk of one being or substance, three persons, because as I have mentioned before, in our language, that is Latin, 'being' and 'substance' do not usually mean anything different. And provided one can understand what is said at least in a puzzle, it has been agreed to say it like that, simply in order to be able to say something when asked 'Three what?' That there are three is declared by the true faith, when it says that the Father is not the Son, and the Holy Spirit which is the gift of God is neither the Father nor the Son. So when the question is asked 'Three what?' we apply ourselves to finding some name of species or genus which will comprise these three, and no such name occurs to our minds, because the actual transcendence of the godhead quite surpasses the capacity of ordinary speech. God can be thought about more truly than he can be talked about, and he is more truly than he can be thought about…
>
> Perhaps then it is more correct to say three persons than three substances. But we must inquire further into this, in case it looks like special pleading for our own usage against that of the Greeks. Now exactly the same arguments hold in the case of persons; it is not one thing for God to be and another for him to be person, but altogether the same. If he is said to be with reference to himself, and called person by way of relationship, then we could call Father and Son and Holy Spirit three persons in the same way as we talk about three friends…
>
> So the only reason, it seems, why we do not call these three together one person, as we call them one being and one God, but say three persons while we never say three Gods or three beings, is that we want to keep at least one word for signifying what we mean by trinity, so that we are not simply reduced to silence when we are asked three what, after we have confessed that there are three…
>
> But in the case of the being of the trinity, it is quite impossible for any other person at all to emerge out of the same being. Finally, with these ordinary things, one man is not as much as three men together, and two men are something more than one man… But that is not how it is in God; Father and Son together are not more being than Father alone or Son alone, but those three substances or persons together, if that is what they must be called, are equal to each one singly; which the sensual man does not perceive (1 Cor. 2:14).[117]

Calvin was also influenced by the definition of Richard of St. Victor, holding that within the Trinity, Persons means 'incommunicable subsistence or existence,' rather than the definition of Boethius, that Person is 'individual substance of rational nature.' As T. F. Torrance points out: 'It is highly significant that like Gregory Nazianzen Calvin would have nothing to do with the Basilian and Amphilochian notion of 'mode of being' (*tropos hyparxeos*), or with Augustine's speculative deployment of natural analogies or human similitudes.'[118]

---

[117]Augustine, *De Trinitate* VII. 7, 11.

[118]T. F. Torrance, *Trinitarian Perspectives*, 50.

We may note here, that while Calvin was very hesitant to follow Augustine's psychological analogies of the Trinity within human nature, his Lausanne colleague and friend, Pierre Viret, made considerable use of these analogies.[119] But Calvin did borrow heavily from Augustine's exposition of substance, Persons and relationship, as we have just seen.

Later, Calvin adds (with the same kind of humility as Augustine as to the limited capacities of human language):

> Again, Scripture sets forth a distinction of the Father from the Word, and of the Word from the Spirit. Yet the greatness of the mystery warns us how much reverence and sobriety we ought to use in investigating this. And that passage in Gregory of Nazianzus vastly delights me: 'I cannot think on the one without quickly being encircled by the splendour of the three; nor can I discern the three without being straightway carried back to the one.'[120] Let us not then, be led to imagine a trinity of persons that keeps our thoughts distracted and does not at once lead them back to that unity. Indeed, the words 'Father,' 'Son,' and 'Spirit' imply a real distinction – let no one think that these three titles, whereby God is variously designated from his works, are empty – but a distinction, not a division.[121]

In summary, and in company with the Church Fathers, Calvin writes:

> Therefore, let those who dearly love soberness, and who will be content with the measure of faith, receive in brief form what is useful to know: namely, that, when we profess to believe in one God, under the name of God is understood a single, simple essence, in which we comprehend three persons, or hypostases. Therefore, whenever the name of God is mentioned without particularization, there are designated no less the Son and the Spirit than the Father; but where the Son is joined to the Father, then the relation of the two enters in; and so we distinguish among the persons. But because the peculiar qualities in the persons carry an order within them, e.g. in the Father is the beginning and the source, so often as mention is made of the Father and the Son together, or the Spirit, the name of God is peculiarly applied to the Father. In this way, unity of essence is retained, and a reasoned order is kept, which yet takes nothing away from the deity of the Son and the Spirit.[122]

Or, as B. B. Warfield summarizes: '…there is but one God; the Father, the Son, the Spirit is each this one God, the entire divine essence being in each; these three are three Persons, distinguished one from another by an incommunicable property.'[123] This justly famous article by Warfield shows that although, as a result of harsh controversies on the Trinity – especially that with Pierre Caroli (who falsely accused Calvin of deviating from the Church doctrine of the Trinity) – Calvin refused to be ordered by Caroli to sign the ancient creeds:

---

[119]See P. Viret, *Exposition familière de l'oraison de nostre Seigneur Jésus-Christ…* (Genève, 1548), 62, 63, 165, etc. See the chapter (V) 'Le Mystere de la Sainte Trinite' in Georges Bavaud, *Le Réformateur Pierre Viret (1511-1571) Sa Théologie* (Genève: Labor et Fides, 1986), 59-66.

[120]Gregory of Nazianzus, *On Holy Baptism, Oration* 40. 41.

[121]Calvin, *Institutes* I.xiii.17.

[122]Calvin, op. cit., I.xiii.20.

[123]Warfield, op. cit., 232.

> Calvin refused to subscribe the ancient creeds at Caroli's dictation, not in the least because he did not find himself in accord with their teaching, but solely because he was determined to preserve for himself and his colleagues the liberties belonging to Christian men, subject in matters of faith to no other authority than of God speaking in the Scriptures. He tells us himself that it was never his purpose to reject these creeds or to detract from their credit;[124] and he points out that he was not misunderstood even by Caroli to be repudiating their teaching...
>
> Calvin's refusal to be confined to the very words of the old formulas in his expression of the doctrine of the Trinity did not carry with it, therefore, any unwillingness to employ in his definition of the doctrine the terms which had been beaten out in the Trinitarian controversies of the past. These terms he considered rather the best expressions for stating and defending the doctrine...He had only to point to the first edition of the 'Institutes' (1536), in which he had not only freely used the terms in question, but had defended at large the right and asserted the duty of employing them, as the technical language by which alone the doctrine of the Trinity can be so expressed as to confound heretical misconceptions.[125]

We must examine later Warfield's discussion of Calvin's clarity and theological contribution in his exposition of the doctrine of the aseity of the Son of God.[126] And this matter must be considered rather more fully than even Warfield did, in light of the work done over a thousand years before Calvin by Gregory Nazianzus, Epiphanius, Cyril of Alexandria and others.[127]

John Owen on Person

The great English Puritan theologian of the seventeenth century, John Owen, at one time Vice-chancellor of Oxford University and Chaplain to Oliver Cromwell, did not devote very large sections of his voluminous writings to the doctrine of the Holy Trinity, but everywhere he assumes an orthodox Catholic position on it, and does deal with it in some relatively brief treatises. In these concise writings on the Trinity, we will find Owen in line with the teaching of John Calvin, Augustine, and the Eastern Fathers such as Gregory Nazianzus.

In his 'Greater Catechism' (1645), he devotes all of Chapter III to the Holy Trinity. It includes seven questions. He defines person as follows:

> Q. 2. *What mean you by person?*
>
> A. A distinct manner of subsistence or being, distinguished from the other persons by its own properties – John 5:17; Heb. 1:3. [Owen adds a footnote, worthy of Gregory Nazianzus, Hilary, Augustine or Calvin, to 'subsistence': 'This is that mysterious ark that must not be pried into, nor the least tittle spoken about it, wherein plain Scripture goeth not before'.]

---

[124]Calvin 'Adversus F. Caroli calumnias,' *Opera Calvini* vii. 315 and letter to Farel, Oct. 8, 1539 in Herminjard, vi. (1883), 53.

[125]Warfield, op. cit., 207, 211.

[126]Ibid., 233ff.

[127]See the following section of this chapter on the question of subordinationism.

> Q. 6. *Are these three one?*
>
> A. One every way, in nature, will and essential properties, distinguished only in their personal manner of subsistence – John 10:30; Romans 3:30; John 15:26; 1 John 5:7. [Owen adds another footnote to the question on person, something that goes beyond what Calvin or Luther would have said: 'This only doctrine remained undefiled in the Papacy.'][128]

In 1669, Owen published 'The Doctrine of the Holy Trinity Explained and Vindicated' as an antidote to the radical fringe of seventeenth-century Protestantism, among Socinians and Quakers, as well as for the edification of the ordinary people of God. He expounds:

> ... *how God is one*, in respect of his *nature, substance, essence*, Godhead, or divine being; how, being Father, Son, and Holy Ghost, he subsisteth in these three distinct persons or hypostases; and what are their mutual relations to each other, by which as their peculiar properties, giving them the manner of their subsistence, they are distinguished one from another...[129]

Owen, in line with every good theologian, noted that one has to use non-scriptural terms in order to bring out and safeguard scriptural truth:

> Wherefore, in the declaration of the doctrine of the Trinity, we may *lawfully*, nay, we must *necessarily*, make use of other words, phrases, and expressions, than what are literally and syllabically contained in the Scripture, but teach no other things.[130]

And of course, for that reason, Owen with the best of the Church Fathers and Reformers has to give attention to the non-scriptural term, 'Person.'

In line with Gregory Nazianzus, Augustine, Calvin and others on 'Person' in the Godhead having distinction by relationship with the one Being, Owen writes:

> ...it is revealed, also, that these three are *distinct* among themselves, by certain peculiar *relative properties*, if I may yet use these terms. So that they are distinct, living, divine, intelligent, voluntary principles of operation or working, and that in and by internal acts one towards another, and in acts that outwardly respect the creation and the several parts of it. Now, this distinction *originally* lieth in this, – that the Father begetteth the Son, and the Son is begotten of the Father, and the Holy Spirit proceedeth from both of them.[131]
>
> The *distinction* which the Scripture reveals between Father, Son, and Spirit, is that whereby they are three hypostases or persons, distinctly subsisting in the same divine essence or being. Now, a divine person is nothing but *the divine essence, upon the account of an especial property, subsisting in an especial manner*...[132]

I think it is well worth quoting at length Owen's answers to several objections raised in his time (apparently by Socinian thinkers) against

[128]*The Works of John Owen* (London: Banner of Truth Trust, 1966 reprint), vol. I, 472.
[129]*The Works of John Owen*, vol. II, 378.
[130]Ibid., 379.
[131]Ibid., 405.
[132]Ibid., 407.

taking seriously the traditional doctrine of the Trinity. Although Owen was in controversy with seventeenth-century Unitarians (or Socinians), Augustine had dealt with some of these same objections in his fifth-century *De Trinitate*. Owen responds to five objections:

1. *'How can these things be? How can three be one, and one be three? Every person hath its own substance; and therefore, if there be three persons, there must be three substances, and so three Gods.'*

   Answer. Every person hath distinctly *its own substance*, for the one substance of the Deity is the substance of each person, so it is still but one; but each person hath not its own distinct substance, because the substance of them all is the same, as hath been proved.

2. They say, *'That if each person be God, then each person is infinite, and there being three persons, there must be three infinities.'*

   Answer. This follows not in the least; for each person is infinite as he is God. *All divine properties*, such as to be infinite is, belong not to the persons on the account of their personality, but on the account of their nature, which is one, for they are all natural properties.

3. But they say, *'If each person be God, and that God subsists in three persons, then in each person there are three persons or Gods.'*

   Answer. The collusion of this sophism consists in that expression, *'be God,'* and *'that God.'* In the first place the nature of God is intended; in the latter, a singular person. Place the words intelligibly, and they are thus: If each person be God, and the nature of God subsists in three persons, then in each person there are three persons; and then the folly of it will be evident.

4. But they farther infer, *'That if we deny the persons to be infinite, then an infinite being hath a finite mode of subsisting*, and so I know not what supposition they make hence; that seeing *there are not three infinities, then the Father, Son and Spirit are three finites, that make up an infinite.'*

   Answer. The pitiful weakness of this cavil is open to all; for finite and infinite are properties and adjuncts of beings, and not of the manner of the subsistence of any thing. The nature of each person is infinite, and so is each person because of that nature. Of the manner of their subsistence, finite and infinite cannot be predicated or spoken, no farther than to say, an infinite being doth so subsist.

5. 'But you grant,' say they, *'that the only true God is the Father, and then if Christ be the only true God, he is the Father.'*

   Answer. We say, the only true God is Father, Son, and Holy Ghost. We never say, the Scripture never says, that *the Father only is the true God*; whence it would follow, that he that is the true God is the Father. But we grant the Father to be the only true God; and so we say is the Son also. And it doth not at all thence follow that the Son is the Father; because, in saying the Father is the true God, we respect not his paternity, or his paternal relation to his Son, but his nature, essence, and being. And to say, that because each person is one God, one person must be another,

> is to crave leave to disbelieve what God hath revealed, without giving any reason at all for their so doing.'[133]

John Owen's practical application of the Trinitarian personhood to the spiritual life

Of course, Owen's great contribution to Church and theology was *not* any sort of restatement of the traditional doctrine of the Trinity (as Calvin had done), and thus no rethinking of 'Person', but rather his pastoral and practical *application* of Trinitarian spirituality to the daily life and disciplines of the Christian Church. For the sake of encouraging Christian spiritual discipline in our own time, it will be worth extracting a few points he raises; all of which are placed within a context of the Trinitarian Persons.

He sees the foundation and expansion of the Church as Trinitarian:

> Concerning the church, while the eternal purpose and love of the Father is presupposed as is the mediatory work of the Son ... there yet remains the *actual application* of all to the souls of men, that they may be partakers of the grace designed in the counsel of the Father, and prepared in the mediation of the Son. From the sequential order of this work, after the Son has been in the flesh ... the carrying and finishing of the whole work of the grace of God in our salvation concerns the sending of the Spirit to do and perform what he also had undertaken.[134]

Along with the Cappadocian Fathers, Owen knows that new spiritual life in believers comes 'from the Father, through the Son and in the Spirit':

> The Spirit gives *life* and *quickening* – Romans 8:11; Ephesians 1:19; 'According to the exceeding greatness of the power of God, which he wrought when he raised Christ from the dead.' There are two things in this quickening: (1) The *actus primus* or life itself bestowed. By nature 'We are dead in sins and trespasses' – in our quickening we have a new spiritual life communicated to us – Colossians 3:4: 'When Christ, who is our life, shall appear'; Galatians 2:20. (2) Secondly the *operations* of that life in them on whom it is bestowed: 'It is God that worketh in you...'[135]

Owen addresses the Christian's lifelong duty of mortification of sin in Trinitarian terms:

> The Spirit alone in mortification clearly and fully convinces the heart of the evil, guilt, and danger of the lust to be mortified. (1) The *first thing* that the Spirit doth in order to the mortification of any lust whatever – it convinces the soul of its evil. (2) The Spirit alone reveals unto us the *fulness of Christ* for our relief; which is the consideration that stays the heart from false ways. (3) The Spirit alone establishes the heart in expectation of relief from Christ, which is the great sovereign means of mortification. (4) The Spirit alone brings the *cross* of Christ into our hearts with its sin-killing power. (5) The Spirit alone is the author and finisher of our sanctification. (6) In all the soul's addresses to God in this condition, it hath supportment from the Spirit.[136]

---

[133]Ibid., 409-411.

[134]*Works of John Owen*, vol. III, 190.

[135]*Works*, vol. XI,341.

[136]Vol. VI, 85,86.

Owen also places the operation of vivification of the believer in a Trinitarian context, with special reference to the Spirit and the Son:

> He (the Spirit) doth it by communicating the grace of Christ to us – *all the fruits* of his purchase, all the desirableness of his person, as we are interested in him. The grace of Christ hath two heads: his person and work. By both these doth the Holy Ghost administer consolation to us – John 16:14. He glorifies Christ by revealing his excellencies as 'Altogether lovely' – and shows the things of Christ – his love, grace, fruits of his death, resurrection, intercession – and with these supports their hearts and souls.[137]

This means, in terms of *perichoresis*, that the Holy Spirit 'supplies the bodily absence of Christ': 'Thus the Holy Spirit *supplies* the bodily absence of Jesus Christ, and *effects* what he hath to do and accomplish towards his people in the world: so that whatever is done by him – it is the same as if it were wrought *immediately* by the Lord Christ in his own person, whereby all his holy promises are fully accomplished towards them that believe.'[138]

And John Owen correctly brings out the truth – again in terms of *perichoresis* (which he terms here *concurrence*) that in the Church's act of worship, to render worship to any one person of the Trinity is to worship the whole Godhead:

> In that *heavenly directory* which we have, Ephesians 2:18, this whole business is declared. Our access in worship is said to be 'to the Father;' and this 'through Christ,' or his mediation; 'by the Spirit,' or his assistance. Here is a distinction of persons as to their operations, but not at all as to their being the object of our worship. For the Son and the Holy Ghost are no less worshipped in our access to God than the Father himself; only the grace of the Father, which we obtain by the mediation of the Son, and the assistance of the Spirit, is that we draw nigh to God for. So that when, by the distinct dispensation of the Trinity, and every person, we are led to worship (that is, to act faith on or to invocate) any person, we do herein worship the whole Trinity; and every person, by what name soever, of Father, Son, or Holy Ghost, we invocate him. So that this is to be observed in this whole matter, – that when any work of the Holy Ghost (or any other person), which is appropriated to him (we never exclude the concurrence of other persons), draws us to the worship of him, yet he is not worshipped exclusively, but the whole Godhead is worshipped.[139]

Francis Turretin on Person

Francis Turretin (1623–1687), pastor in the Church and Professor of Theology in Geneva, lived in the same approximate time frame, and taught the same orthodox Protestant, Scholastic Calvinism as John Owen and the other British Puritans. His influence on both British and American Calvinism was immense for well over two centuries (e.g. his *Institutio Theologiae Elencticae* were the main theological text books in such American Presbyterian Seminaries as Princeton in New Jersey, and Union in Virginia

[137]Vol. II, 263.
[138]Vol. III, 199.
[139]Vol. II, 269.

throughout the nineteenth century), as well as in many other educational institutions.

His 'Third Topic' is 'the One and the Triune God,' and he devotes 'Questions' XXIII to XXXI to The Holy Trinity. He too is thoroughly Patristic in his understanding and definitions of Trinitarian concepts. He certainly understands the Persons of the Trinity in relational terms: 'The absolute consideration of God (as to his nature and attributes) begets the relative (as to the persons)...'[140] Turretin makes reference to Basil's *tropos huparxeos* (without naming Basil) as a 'mode of subsisting.'[141] He is well aware of the difficulties of the early Church in deciding on what the various terms for Person meant in Greek and Latin.

> To designate this subsistence the Greeks employed the word *hypostaseos*, which formerly gave occasion to great disturbances in the church on account of the equivocal sense of the word. For among the Fathers, it is taken either generically and wisely for the very substance of a thing... He (*Athanasius*) prudently and happily put a stop to the sharp controversy arising from this cause between Eastern and Western parties, the Greeks and Latins (which Gregory Nazianzus notices in his *Oration* 21, 'On the Great Athanasius')... According to the testimony of Augustine, they were accustomed to say *mian ousian, treis hypostaseis*, viz. 'one essence, three subsistences' (*The Trinity* 5.8). But afterwards, lest the ambiguity of the word might give occasion to error (as Aquinas remarks, *ST* I, Q. 29, Art. 2, p. 157), the opinion of the Greeks (who use *hypostasin* for subsistence) obtained, and this is now the common opinion received by all. Further, Scripture appears to precede us here, for in comparing the person of the Son with the person of the Father (whose image he bears), it calls him 'the express image' of the subsistence of the Father (Hebrews 1:3).[142]

Turretin notes a difference in emphasis on 'Person' between Calvin on the one side, and Melanchthon and Ursinus on the other, and comes down on the side of Calvin:

> Hence arose a twofold distinction of a divine person: one abstractive, employed by our Calvin (*ICR* 1.13.6, p. 128) defining a person to be a 'subsistence in the essence of God by which (related to others) he is distinguished by an incommunicable property' – having followed here Justin and John of Damascus who called it *tropon hyparxeos* ('a mode of subsisting') (cf. [Pseudo-] Justin Martyr, *Quaestiones et Responsiones ad orthodoxos*, Q. 139 [488 C] in *Corpus apologetarum Christianorm* [ed. J. Otto], 5.224,225; John of Damascus, *Exposition of the Orthodox Faith* 1.8 ... cf. also his *contra Jacobitas* 52 [PG 94.1461]); the other concretive, given by Melanchthon and Ursinus, who define a person as 'the individual that subsists, is living, intelligent, is not sustained by another, nor is a part of another.' The former expresses more fully the perfection of the divine persons; the latter more clearly sets forth the truth of their subsistence.[143]

---

[140]Francis Turretin, *Institutes of Elenctic Theology*, translated by George M. Giger, edited by James T. Dennison, Jr. (Phillipsburg, NJ: P & R Publishing, 1992), Vol. I, First Through Tenth Topics, 253.

[141]Ibid.

[142]Ibid., 254.

[143]Ibid., 255.

It is not the case, however, that Calvin ever followed the definition of *tropos hyparxeos*. But probably the point Turretin wishes to make is that Calvin understood that divine Person is inherently relational, and that about each of the three divine Persons there is something 'incommunicable.'

Turretin also affirms the Patristic and Calvinian belief in the *perichoresis* (or as Turretin terms it, *emperichoreseos*):

> Here belongs the word *emperichoreseos* which the fathers frequently used... But that it was not used without reason to describe the intimate mutual union of the persons can be inferred not obscurely from Scripture itself when 'the Son is said to be in the Father, and the Father in the Son' (John 10:38; 14:11). They thought this mystery could not be better expressed than by the phrase *enallelon emperichoresin* (i.e., a mutual intertwining or inexistence and immanence), so as to designate thus that union by which the divine persons embrace *each* other and permeate (if it is right to say so) each other. So that although always remaining distinct, yet they are never separated from each other, but always coexist; wherever one is, there the other also really is. And if believers are said to dwell in God and he in them (1 John 3:24; John 14:23) on account of the intimate presence of the Spirit (who is the strictest bond of their communion with God), does it not follow that such an *emperichoresis* can be attributed to them? There is the widest difference between the mystical union of believers with God and the divine union of the persons of the Trinity in nature, or of the human and divine natures in the person of Christ.[144]

The infinitely great reality of the eternal existence of God as three Persons, one Being, engaged the highest devotion and energetic scholarship of the universal Christian Church for nearly four centuries, as it sought to develop a theological terminology that would – to some degree – express faithfully the biblical truth of who God is; or at least, not misrepresent it. The Holy Trinity – three uncreated Persons, one Substance – is the basis for our own created personhood, and it alone gives us significance for this earthly life and eternal hope beyond it.

---

[144]Ibid., 257.

Chapter Eight Appendix One

The Differing Approaches of the Cappadocians and Augustine to the Trinity

So far in this volume, we have relied upon theologians of the East (particularly the Cappadocians) and of the West (particularly Augustine) to seek a fuller understanding of the one God who always exists as three Persons. It is my opinion that they are not very far apart as to the basic realities of who God is, yet there are strong differences in their approaches to that final reality.

The Cappadocians tend to work from the threefold personhood of God to the oneness, whereas Augustine (and most of the West) tends to work from the oneness of God's essence to the threefold personhood. Neither approach is necessarily contradictory to, nor exclusive of, the other. It is valid to start with the oneness of essence or to start with the threeness of personhood as long as both oneness and threeness are considered of equal ultimacy within the Godhead. For all their differences in methodology, I believe that this was the true intention of both East and West.

Aristides Papadakis is correct when stating the starting-point of the East (in the context of the refutation of the pro-Filioque Council of Lyon of 1274 by the Patriarch of Constantinople, Gregory II of Cyprus):

> In general, Gregory's thought is based on the biblical-personalist approach of Photius and the Cappadocians who, as has been said, first see God as a trinity of persons subsisting in the divine essence, and then confess Him to be essentially one God. Moreover, it is the person of the Father (as opposed to some abstract essence) who provides the concrete principle of unity without in any way undermining the ultimate equality of the three... The Father, then, is the source of their common possession of the same essence, and, indeed, the pledge of their unity. Trinitarian unity is grounded in the person of the Father, not in some philosophically conceived abstract essence of God.[1]

Augustine begins with the simplicity of God's essence

And as Richard Haugh points out, Saint Augustine starts with the one God and then moves to the diversity of Persons within the Godhead:

[1]A. Papadakis, *Crisis in Byzantium: The Filioque Controversy in the Patriarchate of Gregory II of Cyprus* (1283-1289), 119, 120.

> Augustine's doctrine of *Filioque* follows logically from his entire perspective of God. Greek patristic thought began with the principle that there is God and He is God the Father. Augustine begins with the principle that there is God and in Him there is fatherhood.[2]

Irénée Chevalier similarly summarized the different starting-points between Saint Basil and Saint Augustine (and Saint Thomas Aquinas who followed Augustine), with the former beginning with the persons, and then moving to the one essence, and the latter beginning with the one essence, and then moving to the three Persons:

> This difference comes from a divergence of viewpoint which is most important. The two traits (σχέσις οἰκέωσις[3]) by which Saint Basil characterizes the divine generation does not represent in his thinking exactly the same hierarchy of ideas found in Saint Augustine and the Scholastics. For the Greek doctor the issue is that community of nature which exists between a father and a son, by virtue of generation. It is this issue of origin, the only cause of the difference between the Father and the Son, which far from destroying their identity, confirms it and explicates it. But Basil does not intend to say that when one presupposes the unity and the identity of the divine essence, the immanent generation can only entail a distinction of relations. He begins with the matter of generation in order to reach by that means a community of relations, whereas Thomas Aquinas, for instance, begins with the divine simplicity in order to conclude with purely relative [or relational] terms of procession. This last point of view is that of Saint Augustine … Basil accepts these relations, but once given, so to speak, their divine subjects and above all their source, the generation 'ex natura' and the procession, he moves to the unity of essence. Augustine accepts the divine identity, but given that the processions are revealed, he moves to the relations. These are identical truths, but contemplated from different points of view. There is nothing surprising in that![4]

That is to say, Augustine begins with the absolute simplicity of God's essence, and then considers just how there may be three distinct hypostases without compromising that essence. He does this in terms of relations within the essence, especially in Book V of his *De Trinitate*. His basic solution is found in his distinction between absolute terms (*ad se*), which refer to God's essence, and relative terms (*ad alium*), which refer to the properties of each divine Person.

> Paternity in God is truly other than filiation, but it is not a different substance. The personal properties by which the divine persons are distinguished are relations of origin, not of substances. The unity [one] and the number [three] do not point to identical references; in spite of these distinctions, the [triune] consubstantiality is safeguarded; even more so, by reason of the nature of these distinctions, the unity of essence is required.[5]

Augustine is not unlike the Eastern Fathers in teaching that within God the distinction of Persons comes from the processions. Thus, the properties of

---

[2]Richard Haugh, *Photius and the Carolingians: The Trinitarian Controversy*, 204.

[3]'Relations' or 'mode of relations resulting from an origin' and 'common or family origin'.

[4]Irénée Chevalier, *S. Augustin et la Pensée Grecque: Les Relations Trinitaires* (Librairie de l'Université: Fribourg en Suisse, 1940), 168,169.

[5]Ibid., 67.

the three divine persons issue from their processions or internal relations: the Father is unbegotten; the Son is begotten and the Spirit proceeds or is breathed out from God. 'Person' with Augustine implies relationship within God. He writes: '... relative quaeque persona ad alteram dicitur...'[6] Similarly, in Book XV of *De Trinitate*, he summarizes what he meant by relations in his earlier Book V:

> In the fifth [*sc.* Book], – with a view to those who think that the substance of the Father and of the Son is therefore not the same, because they suppose everything that is predicated of God to be predicated according to substance, and therefore contend that to beget and to be begotten, or to be begotten and unbegotten, as being diverse, are diverse substance, – it is demonstrated that not everything that is predicated of God is predicated according to substance...but that some things also are predicated relatively, i.e., not in respect to Himself, but in respect to something which is not Himself; as He is called the Father in respect to the Son...[7]

In other words, the personal distinctions within God are constituted by eternal relations, indicated by Father, Son and Spirit; or, by begetting and proceeding (or being breathed out). There is a distinct relation belonging to the generation of the Son and to the procession of the Spirit, but it is in no sense opposed to Their absolute identity of nature or essence. Each of the three divine Persons can, according to Augustine (especially, as we have noted, in Book V of *De Trinitate*), be considered from two different perspectives: one, *absolutely*, in terms of the transcendent divine essence, and the other, *relatively* (or relationally), in terms of Their distinct personal properties (which are constituted by the inner-Trinitarian processions). Chevalier speaks of these two perspectives in Augustine's Trinitarian theory as 'two orders of attribution'.[8]

Hence, Augustine holds that the distinction of the three consists only and wholly in these inner-Trinitarian relationships, so that the names of Father, Son and Holy Spirit are terms of real and distinct relations, while the divine essence is 'simple' and identical. This is fairly close to what Didymus the Blind states in his *De Spiritu Sancto* (probably finished before 380, which Chevalier shows to have definitely influenced Augustine.[9] St. Jerome had made a Latin translation of it by 389, and by 419, Augustine quoted this work by Didymus[10]). Whether or not Augustine was acquainted with Didymus' *De Trinitate* (written between 386 and 392) is not known, but some things he writes in his own *De Trinitate* are close to it, and probably come from a common pool of ideas.

Didymus the Blind and two orders of attribution

In particular, Didymus, somewhat like Augustine did later, deals with two orders of attribution (κατά σχέσιν κατ̀ οὐσίαν), and shows that the persons of the Trinity refer to the order of relations (κατά σχέσιν), rather than to the

---

[6]Augustine, *The City of God*, XI.10, cited in Chevalier, op. cit., 61.

[7]Augustine, *De Trinitate* XV.3.5 (from The Nicene and Post-Nicene Fathers, First Series, vol. III, 200).

[8]Chevalier, op. cit., 132.

[9]Ibid., Ch. VI – 'Didyme L'Aveugle (313-398), 153-163.

[10]Ibid., 154.

essence (κατ̓ οὐσίαν). In Didymus' *De Trinitate*, he does so in terms of relations between a father and his son regarding the education of the son:

> The meaning of the word 'to make' is not always determined by comparison with 'to create'; one can understand it in terms of a relation (κατά σχέσιν). Take someone who is already a master within himself (κατ̓ οὐσίωσιν). A father makes him master of his sons, while the master begins to instruct the sons (there is then in this master a mode of being in terms of relationship with his sons, in addition to his mastery κατ̓ οὐσίωσιν); someone makes his son a soldier or an orator (there is then in this son a mode of being in terms of relationship to a trade where he works).[11]

Certainly, Augustine goes much further than Didymus in working out the details of defining the three Persons by means of mutual relations within the simple essence. But his insight here is not inconsistent with the idea of Didymus that the persons of the Trinity refer to the order of relations. Augustine then goes on to state that within the oneness of God the persons are only distinguished by their mutual 'relations of opposition'. Everything is absolutely identical within the divine being except for these relations: 'Simplex dicitur, quoniam quod habet hoc est, excepto quod relative quaeque persona ad alteram dicitur.'[12]

The Cappadocians begin with the three hypostases

A. Papadakis summarizes their starting-point clearly:

> Historically, the trinitarian theology of the Byzantine Church was first enunciated in the fourth century at the Council of Nicaea. Athanasius was its original champion, while the Cappadocian Fathers, Basil the Great, Gregory of Nyssa, and Gregory of Nazianzus, brought the process to its conclusion. As is well known, it was their technical theological definition – that God is one essence in three hypostases, or persons – that led to the final defeat of Arianism at the close of the fourth century...God is a Trinity of persons who is first met in Scripture as three agents of salvation and only then acknowledged as one God...it was ultimately true to man's experience of the mystery of the deity as revealed in Scripture and the incarnation of Christ. For it is in the coming and revelation by Christ of His own person, or hypostasis, that the other two hypostases in turn are revealed and manifested to us. As such, the *personal* revelation of God in Scripture is the point of departure for all trinitarian theology, both for the Cappadocians and for all Byzantine theology.[13]

But not only are starting-points of East and West somewhat different (though not contradictory or mutually exclusive), the way they seek to account for the reality of three Persons in one essence is also somewhat different (though again, neither contradictory, nor mutually exclusive). As Papadakis has pointed out, Saint Augustine accounts for the three Persons by means of mutual relations, while the Cappadocians account for them by means of cause.[14]

---

[11]Didymus, *De Trinitate* c. 844c, 845a; quoted in I. Chevalier, op. cit., 156.
[12]Augustine, *De Civitate Dei*, XI, ch. 10.
[13]A. Papadakis, op. cit., 85,86.
[14]Ibid., 113.

In the eighth century, John of Damascus summarizes the Cappadocian view of the Trinitarian persons in the context of cause:

> [We believe] in one Father, the principle and cause [ἡ ἀρχή] of everything ... Father of only one by nature, his Only-Begotten Son ... and Projector [προβολή] of the most Holy Spirit ... The Holy Spirit proceeds from the Father ... For this is the teaching of Holy Scripture ... We also believe in the Holy Spirit ... who proceeds from the Father and rests in the Son ... proceeding from the Father and communicated through the Son ... the begetting of the Son and the procession of the Holy Spirit are simultaneous ... Therefore, all that the Son and Spirit have is from the Father, including their very existence. Unless the Father exists, neither the Son nor Spirit exists. And unless the Father possesses a specific quality, neither the Son nor Spirit can possess it ... *We do not speak of the Son as Cause* ... We speak of the Holy Spirit as from the Father and call him the Spirit of the Father. And we do not speak of the Spirit as from the Son, although we call him the Spirit of the Son.[15]

Mutual criticism of East and West on Trinitarian theology

Many of the Eastern theologians criticised Augustine (and his successors) on various grounds, but I shall mention only two of the main ones here.

Augustine is said to give an 'impersonal' essence priority over the three hypostases

First, some of them held that Augustine's account of the Triune personhood as internal relations within God's essence seemed to give simplicity or essence an unnecessary primacy over the three hypostases. Patriarch Photius, for instance, in his arguments against the procession of the Spirit from the Father *and the Son* (the *Filioque*), maintains that Augustine's view undercut the Father's monarchy in the interests of an abstract view of God's essence. As Papadakis explains:

> He [Photius] was particularly disturbed by the fact that this [*Filioque*] entailed an understanding of the Trinity as simple essence, in which essential unity had primacy over personal diversity; the three persons were reduced to internal relations within the single deity. Such a priority of the essence over the three hypostases was positively improper and inadmissible. For, like the Cappadocians, he attributed the cause and origin in the deity, not to the essence, but to the hypostasis of the Father. It is the Father who is the principle of unity alone – *a Patre solo*. Although this formula was verbally novel, it was, for the most part, nothing more than an affirmation of the Cappadocian teaching of the Father's 'monarchy'.[16]

Of particular significance is the different understanding of the ultimate source of the Persons, as seen in the East and in the West. In general, the Cappadocians are correctly represented by Photius, in stating that the source of the Son and the Spirit is the *Person* of the Father, whereas Augustine and the West state that the source of the Son and the Spirit is the *Being*

[15]John of Damascus, *De Fide Orthodoxa* I, 8 (*Patrologia Graeca* 94, 805ff.), quoted in R. Haugh, op. cit., 18, 19.

[16]A. Papadakis, op. cit., 113.

of the Father. As we note in another chapter, there is some evidence that Athanasius, Gregory of Nazianzus and Epiphanius looked to the *Being* of the Father as source of the Trinity, and if so, it can be said that Augustine was to a degree in line with their conception (although he goes beyond them in positing the *Filioque*).[17]

But on the other hand, most of the East followed Gregory of Nyssa, who clearly teaches that the source of the Persons of the Trinity is not the common essence of the Father, but the Person of the Father: 'The difference between them is by way of "cause" and "caused," and by this alone can we conceive of one Being distinguished from the other, namely, by the belief that one is "cause" and another from the "cause." In the case of those who are from the cause, we recognize a further difference; one is derived immediately from the first, and the other through that which comes immediately from the first.'[18]

This was certainly the case with a leading medieval theologian of the Greek Church, Gregory II of Cyprus (Patriarch of Constantinople, 1283–1289). He wrote: 'The hypostasis of the Father is the source of divinity, and the natural principle, and the root of Son and Spirit.'[19] Papadakis comments:

> The doctrine in question insists that the *origin* of the persons within the deity is not the common essence, but the hypostasis of the Father – the unique cause and principle of the unity of both the Son and the Spirit. For the Father is not only unbegotten, He is without cause (*anarkos*)... Specifically, the one real point of distinction within the deity is causality, which is to be identified with the Father, the first cause; from this one cause – the guarantee of the unity of the three – the other two are derived.[20]

Papadakis suggests that Augustine's doctrine of the three Persons coming from the common essence of God assumes that the divine essence is ultimately *impersonal*:

> In this perspective, not only has the essence assumed a logical priority to the person of the Father, but the trinitarian concept of God (in which the Father is the principle of unity and the unique cause – according to His hypostasis – of Son and Spirit) becomes 'irrelevant and unintelligible'.[21] The personal God of revelation has become a philosophically impersonal essence.[22]

In response, it appears to me that this is **not** the way Augustine saw it. Like Athanasius before him, he considered the common essence to be precisely the essence *of the Father*. Athanasius had spoken of the confession of 'a whole Trinity, but one Godhead, and one *Arche*, and that the Son is of one Being with the Father, while the Holy Spirit is proper to and inseparable from the Being of the Father and the Son.'[23]

---

[17]See Chapter 9, pp. 540-545.

[18]Gregory of Nyssa, *To Ablabius*, ed. W. Jaeger, *Gregorii Nysseni opera dogmatica minora, III*, pt. 1 (Leiden: E.J. Brill, 1958), 56; quoted in Papadakis, op. cit., 87.

[19]Gregory II of Cyprus, *On the Procession of the Holy Spirit*, PG Tomus 142.271A.

[20]A. Papadakis, op. cit., 86, 87.

[21]Quoting Martland, 'A Study of Trinitarian Methodology,' 257.

[22]Papadakis, op. cit., 87.

[23]Athanasius, *Ad Antiochenos* 5.

It is in this spirit, I believe, that Augustine seeks to explicate the three divine Persons as relations within the one essence (i.e. the essence of the Father). He teaches that the essence is the personal relations. So far as I can understand his *De Trinitate*, he does not appear to posit first an impersonal essence, and then later, one that is constituted by relations. On the contrary, in Augustine's doctrine, the essence of God is the essence of Father, Son and Holy Spirit; thus, a personal essence in and through the relations of the three divine Persons. As he writes in *De Trinitate* VII.6.11, comparing the Greek usage of 'three hypostases' to the Latin terminology:

> Although they [the Greeks] also, if they pleased, as they call three substances three hypostases, so might call three persons three 'prosopa,' yet they preferred that word which, perhaps, was more in accordance with their language. For the case is the same with the word persons also; for to God it is not one thing to be, another to be a person, but it is absolutely the same thing…

Some in the Eastern tradition, however, have responded that Augustine's identification of the Persons with the Being is still finally positing an impersonal essence in God, since he speaks of the persons only 'relatively' and not 'absolutely.' Thus, according to this interpretation, if the Persons are only relative, and God is by definition absolute, then the essence must be absolute: that is, not relative and hence, not personal.

Richard Haugh, for example, draws this conclusion: 'For Augustine, existence is not in itself personal, for whatever is personal in the Divinity is not absolute but relative. Person is ad se identical to essence. Person becomes merely another aspect of existence; for God to exist is the same as to be Person, just as it is the same to be good, just, and wise.'[24]

This criticism is not unreasonable in terms of how 'absolute' and 'relative' are generally used in theology. Yet I think that if one looks closely at the peculiar way in which Saint Augustine employs these terms in *De Trinitate*, one will conclude that he really does not teach that the essence of God is ever impersonal. But at first glance, it would certainly appear that when Augustine speaks of the Persons as only 'relative', then the absoluteness of God is strictly reserved for the essence, which, is of course, not 'relative', and by that same token, not 'personal.'

But Augustine is employing these terms – relative and absolute – in a rather idiomatic way in order to overcome, on the one hand, Arianism (which radically subordinated the Son and Spirit to the Father), and on the other, Sabellianism (which finally identified the being of the three so absolutely, that no personal distinctions were left). In both popular heresies, one is left with a unitarian God; not the Triune God of Holy Scripture and Christian tradition. The Greek Fathers fought these same heresies in one way, and Augustine and his followers in the West fought them in a somewhat different way (at least as far as their terminology is concerned).

Augustine seeks to hold to the true distinctiveness of the three divine Persons by considering them to be three real relations with their own

[24]R. Haugh, op. cit., 199.

personal properties, while affirming their substantial oneness by speaking of the essence of God as absolute and source of the Trinity. That is to say, for these purposes, Augustine generally restricts the term 'relative' to the Persons, and 'absolute' to the essence, as his way of confessing the ultimate harmony of the three and the one.

Perhaps Edmund Hill's translation of these terms as used by Augustine as *relationship-wise* and *substance-wise* is more helpful in conveying accurately what Augustine meant than saying simply *relative* and *absolute*.[25] If one takes into account the peculiar terminology of Augustine's Trinitarian thought, one will see – as Irénée Chevalier points out – that in fact, Augustine thinks of the 'relative' persons as at the same time also 'absolute'.

Chevalier explains:

> Relation as a thoroughly abstract word, is thus isolated from every other conceptual element: this is a disadvantage [of his terminology], but from the speculative point of view, one gains in both clarity and precision. Thus, one will not say that the relation is relative; but they are subjects which, by this relation, become relative one to another. 'Relation' is the formal abstraction, while 'relative' is the concrete subject affected by the 'accidental' [i.e. not 'substantial'] relationship, and so in God, this means the subsistent person, at once both absolute and relative…[26]
>
> It will appear as one goes further, that to these relative terms, such as Father and Son, one may attribute absolute terms, which pertain to the divine substance: thus, these relations are identified with the unique divine substance, that they are identical to the simple reality of the substance, and are not extrinsic [to it].[27]

If that is the case, then Augustine does not really consider the essence (or substance) of God to be impersonal, but rather as constituting three Persons, who are not extrinsic to it, but intrinsic. The Being of God in his thought is nothing but personal, although his peculiar usage of 'relative' and 'absolute' may sound otherwise. Nevertheless, although Augustine holds the very being of God to be personal, still his general emphasis tends to be upon God in general, rather than upon the three Persons of the Trinity. Thus, Olivier Du Roy has suggested, with some justification, that as Western piety followed Augustine in this regard, '… it became less and less centered upon the Father or upon the Trinity, so that prayer tended to be addressed to God, without distinction of persons, or to Christ, but not generally to the Father by the Son and in the Spirit, even though the liturgy continued to invite the faithful to do so.'[28]

Eastern criticism of Augustine's doctrine of Filioque

In another appendix, the important and long-lasting controversy between East and West on the *Filioque* is discussed in some detail, so I need not

[25] In Hill's translation of Augustine's *De Trinitate*, as in V.6.

[26] Chevalier, op. cit., 72.

[27] Ibid., 75.

[28] Olivier Du Roy, *L'Intelligence de la Foi en la Trinité selon Saint Augustin: Genèse de sa Théologie Trinitaire jusqu'en 391* (Paris: Etudes Augustiniennes, 1966), 462.

repeat it here.[29] That is, no doubt, the primary reason why many in the East have been suspicious of Augustine. I assume that this is one reason why Augustine is known in the East as 'Beatus' rather than 'Saint.'[30] It has to be noted, however, that Patriarch Photius, who argues strongly against the *Filioque* of his contemporary Western, Carolingian theologians, is very respectful of the good reputation of Augustine and the Western Fathers.[31]

But, let us now, on the other hand, look at the Western criticism of the Cappadocians. We deal here on with the major issue from the Western/ Augustinian point of view.

Western Criticism of the Cappadocian concept of 'cause' within the Trinity

Much of the Western theologians' criticism of the Eastern Trinitarian theology is in the context of debates over the *Filioque*. All I shall mention here is the serious Western hesitation concerning the Cappadocian usage of the concept of **cause**. Indeed, this hesitation is not merely a Western one, for we also find it in Gregory Nazianzus, Cyril of Jerusalem and Epiphanius.[32] Gregory of Nazianzus said, for instance, that to subordinate any Person of the Trinity to another was to overthrow the doctrine of the Trinity.[33] And Cyril of Alexandria taught that to assume a causal status of the Father would subordinate the other two Triune Persons.[34]

Even with 'Western' eyes, however, I do not think that Basil the Great, Gregory of Nyssa and the later Photius and Gregory II of Cyprus ever intended to subordinate the Son and the Spirit to the Person of the Father in terms of eternal or absolute cause. What A. Papadakis says is very relevant to this issue: 'The argument that this doctrine of causality, or "monarchy" of the Father, masks a potentially dangerous subordinationism, is countered by the fact that the concept of time is inapplicable to the eternal life of God.'[35]

Richard Haugh states similarly:

> If one takes seriously the Biblical and patristic vision of the Spirit proceeding from the Father through the Son, or proceeding from the Father together with the Son and remaining on or in the Son, then an eternal relationship between the Son and Spirit is mandatory. But this eternal relationship does not have to be existential. There can be eternal relations in the life of the Holy Trinity which are not existentially *causal* relations.[36]

Probably the tension between the Eastern insistence on cause within the Trinity (or the Monarchy of the Person of the Father) and 'eternal relations'

---

[29]See Chapter 9, Appendix I of this work.

[30]See Chapter VIII of Fr. Seraphim Rose's *The Place of Blessed Augustine in the Orthodox Church* (Saint Herman of Alaska Brotherhood, 1996), 'Opinion of Blessed Augustine in Modern Times', 75-81.

[31]See Richard Haugh, op. cit., 136-137, 151-154.

[32]Their approach is discussed in Chapter 9, (b) Gregory of Nazianzus, Cyril of Alexandria and Epiphanius (pp. 542-545).

[33]Gregory of Nazianzus, *Oration* 43.29.

[34]Cyril of Alexandria, *Thesaurus de Trinitate* in Migne, P.G., 75. 144,177.

[35]Papadakis, op. cit., 87.

[36]Richard Haugh, op. cit., 176.

of full equality is to some degree resolved by their distinction between the essence and the energies of God. That is discussed elsewhere in this volume.[37] I believe that Paul Evdokimov is assuming this distinction, when he states in his work on the Holy Spirit that 'in the Trinity there is neither "before" nor "after," for the three in God transcend all mathematical unity.'[38]

---

[37]See Chapter 4, Appendix I.

[38]Paul Evdokimov, *L'Esprit Saint*, Paris: Flammarion, 1969), 44.

Chapter Nine

The Full Co-equality of the Trinitarian Persons: No Subordinationism

What was implicit in Holy Scripture was made theologically explicit as the Holy Spirit guided the Church for the first four foundational centuries into a clear understanding of the full co-equality of the Trinitarian Persons. That is, the Church, after passing through stormy controversies over several generations, came to express theologically what it already really knew: that all Persons of the Trinity are co-equal; none is ontologically subordinate to the other. In that light, classical Christian theology has made distinctions between the ontological and economical Trinity; as well as distinctions in modes of personal existence within the Trinity, and in historic-redemptive work by the the Trinitarian Persons. Negatively, the true Church ruled out both Unitarianism and Polytheism, and positively, has invited humanity to share in the Trinitarian Life, and thereby to find with the Trinitarian reality eternal life and communion, and a fruitful balance between 'the one and the many' in this world and in the world to come. The pastoral and cultural significance of this sort of Trinitarian theology continues as much as ever to be a river of vitality for the Church directly, and for society indirectly. Above all other issues, direct, personal knowledge of this Triune God, from the Father, through the Son, and in the Spirit is available by sheer grace to all who will ask for it. In an appendix, we examine carefully and hopefully the Filioque Controversy between East and West (the Western addition to the Nicene Creed – that the Spirit 'proceeds from the Father and the Son').

The Westminster Shorter Catechism (1640s) is in line with the best of the Trinitarian theology of the ancient Church when it states in the answer to Question 6: 'There are three Persons in the Godhead; the Father, the Son, and the Holy Ghost; and these three are one God, the same in substance, equal in power and glory.' Church Fathers, medieval Scholastics and Protestant Reformers understood that the Son and the Spirit are equally ultimate and original as is the Father in the Godhead.

But it took considerable discussion in various languages[1] over some centuries clearly to establish this pivotal doctrine. (1) This discussion

[1] See Hilary, *De Synodis*, 9, where he discusses the difficulty of Latin translations of the bishops of the East, who wrote in Greek: 'Much obscurity is caused by translation from Greek to Latin, and to be quite literal is sometimes to be partly unintelligible.'

involved 'false starts' raised by some early Church writers which tended to subordination of the Son and the Spirit to the Father, and (2) these 'false starts' were answered and overcome by the mainstream of the Orthodox Fathers of the Church, both East and West. We must consider these two stages.

(1) Subordinationist concepts of some Church writers

The 'Logos theologians' (including such writers as Justin Martyr and Tertullian) tended to place the Son (or Logos) on a somewhat lower plane of being than the Father, and the Spirit on the same plane as the Son, or slightly lower. Of course, it is necessary to remember that the Trinitarian theology of the Church at that time had not yet received the clarity of thought and terminology that it did by the fourth century, so the intentions of several of these writers were no doubt more orthodox than their statements would have been at a later time. And also it must be noted that other Church writers at the same time as (or earlier than) Justin, Tertullian and Origen held to the equality of the Persons of the Trinity.

Non-subordinationist Apologists

Ignatius of Antioch

Ignatius of Antioch,[2] for instance, while holding a certain 'Logos' Christology, was not subordinationist. He wrote: 'There is one God, who has manifested himself by Jesus Christ his Son, who is his Word proceeding from silence, who obeyed the one who sent him.'[3] He calls Christ 'the mouth of God', 'the knowledge of God', and 'the intention of God'.[4] He identifies Christ as God.[5] Ignatius ascribes the very attributes of God to Christ: 'Look for him who is above time – the Timeless, the Invisible, who for our sake became visible, the Impassible, who became subject to suffering on our account and for our sake endured everything.'[6]

Polycarp and Athenagoras

And Polycarp (martyred c. 156) wrote this Trinitarian prayer: 'For this reason I praise thee for all things, I bless thee, I glorify thee through the everlasting and heavenly High Priest, Jesus Christ, thy beloved Child, through whom be glory to thee with him and the Holy Spirit both now and for the ages to come. Amen.'[7]

Athenagoras spoke (c. 177) of 'The Son being in the Father and the Father in the Son by the unity and power of the Spirit.'[8] He, unlike Justin Martyr, clearly avoids subordinationism:

> But if, in your surpassing intelligence, it occurs to you to inquire what is meant by the Son, I will state briefly that he is the product of the Father, not as having been brought into existence – for from the beginning, God, who

[2] Ignatius was sentenced to death under the Emperor Trajan (between A.D. 98-117).

[3] *Letter to the Magnesians* 8.2.

[4] *Letter to the Ephesians* 3.2; 17.2; *Letter to the Romans* 8.2.

[5] *Letter to the Ephesians* 7.2.

[6] Ignatius, *Letter to Polycarp* 3.2.

[7] J. Quasten and J.C. Plumpe, eds., *Ancient Christian Writers* (Westminster:MD: Newman Press, 1950), 14.3.

[8] Athenagoras, *Leg.* 10 and 24.

> is the eternal mind, had the Logos in Himself, being from eternity instinct with Logos (λογικὸς) – but inasmuch as he came forth to be the idea and energizing power of all material things, which lay like a nature without attributes, and an inactive earth, the grosser particles being mixed up with the lighter. The prophetic Spirit also agrees with our statements: 'The Lord,' it says, 'made me the beginning of his ways to his works.[9]

Melito of Sardis

Between Ignatius and Athenagoras, Melito of Sardis clearly taught the full deity of the Son. In his famous *Pascal Homily* (perhaps the earliest preserved Passion sermon outside Holy Scripture – A.D. 169), he does not hesitate to identify Christ as God:

> For born as a son, and led forth as a lamb, sacrificed as a sheep, buried as a man, he rose from the dead as God, being by nature God and man. Who is all things: in that he judges, Law, in that he teaches, Word, in that he saves, Grace, in that he begets, Father, in that he is begotten, Son, in that he suffers, the sacrificial sheep, in that he is buried, Man, in that he arises, God. This is Jesus Christ, to whom belongs the glory to the ages of ages.[10]

Irenaeus of Lyon

St. Irenaeus of Lyon was also in the line of early Christian apologists who firmly maintained the eternal deity of the Son and Spirit. Unlike Justin, whom to some degree he followed, Irenaeus – the great champion of the faith against the Gnostics (a sect which taught a series of levels of being or 'aeons', coming down from the transcendent God, who by means of these aeons was personally separate from the creation) – denied intermediary beings between God and the creation.

Irenaeus shows – contrary to the subordinationist theologians – that one cannot read back human language and creaturely analogies into the Being of God, thereby limiting God in terms of merely human concepts. The Logos, for instance, cannot be limited and reduced to what happens in the expressions of a human mind: 'And this [examination of judgement] *remaining in the mind* is most properly termed Logos, from which the spoken Logos proceeds.'[11]

> He [the Logos] is however *above* these properties, and therefore *indescribable*. For he may well and properly be called an Understanding which comprehends all things, but he is not like the understanding of men; and he may most properly be termed Light, but he is nothing like that light with which we are acquainted. And so, in all other particulars, the Father of all is in no degree similar to human weakness. He is spoken of in these terms according to the love, but in point of greatness, our thoughts regarding him *transcend* these expressions.[12]

> For they [the Gnostics] maintain that Logos and Zoe [life] were sent forth by him (i.e. Nous – mind) as fashioners of this pleroma; while they conceive of an emission of Logos, that is, the Word *after the analogy of human feelings*, and rashly form conjectures respecting God, as if they had discovered something wonderful

[9] Athenagoras, *Apol.* 10.
[10] Melito of Sardis, *Pascal Homily* 8-10.
[11] Irenaeus, *Adversus Haereses* II.13.2.
[12] Ibid., II. 13.4.

> in their assertion that Logos was produced by Nous. All indeed have a clear perception that this may be logically affirmed with respect to man. But in him who is God over all, since he is all Nous, and all Logos, as I have said before, and has in himself nothing more ancient or late than another, and nothing at variance with another, but continues altogether equal, and similar and homogenous, there is no longer ground for conceiving of such production in the order which has been mentioned... [He then condemns] those who transfer the generation of the Word to which men gave utterance to the eternal Word of God, assigning a beginning and course of production [to him] even as they do to their own word.[13]

Thus, Irenaeus clearly sees that wrong views of the Triune God, in which one Person is subordinated to or caused by another, comes from people's reading onto God the creaturely limitations of their own beings and understandings: 'For they ascribe the things which happen to men, and whatsoever they recognize themselves as experiencing, to the divine reason; they seem to those who are ignorant of God to make statements suitable enough.'[14] 'Those things which are everywhere acted in the theatres by comedians with the clearest voices they *transfer to their own system*, teaching them undoubtedly through means of the same arguments, and merely changing the names.'[15]

Thus in contradistinction to human ways of reading the uttering of a word from a creaturely mind into independent and inferior existence, Irenaeus makes clear that Christ is of the full Being of God; not an intermediary or inferior being: 'The gospel, therefore knows no other Son of Man but him who was of Mary, who also suffered; and no Christ who flew away from Jesus before the passion; but him who was born it knew as Jesus Christ the Son of God, and that this same suffered and rose again... Foreseeing these blasphemous systems which divide the Lord, as far as lies in their power, saying that he was formed of *two different substances*.'[16]

Far from limiting transcendence only to the Father, Irenaeus ascribes it to the whole Being of God, including of course the Son, even in his incarnation: 'There is therefore, as I have pointed out, one God the Father, and one Christ Jesus, who came by means of the whole dispensational arrangements and gathered together all things in himself. But in every respect too, He is man, the formation of God; and thus He took up man into Himself, the invisible becoming visible, the incomprehensible becoming comprehensible, the impassible becoming capable of suffering, and the Word being made man, thus summing up all things in Himself.'[17]

This Trinitarian understanding of both God and the history of redemption was no peripheral matter to Irenaeus. He knew that only the Creator could redeem the creation in the person of his Son through the power of the Spirit:

> There is therefore one God, who by the Word and Wisdom created and arranged all things, but this is the Creator, who has granted this world to the human race ... but as regards His love, He is always known through Him by

[13] Ibid., II.13.8.
[14] Ibid., II.13.10.
[15] Ibid., II.14.1.
[16] Ibid., III.16.5.
[17] Ibid., III.16.6.

> whose means He ordained all things. Now this is His Word, our Lord Jesus Christ, who in the last times was made a man among men, that He might join the end to the beginning, that is man to God … announced His advent according to the flesh, by which the blending and communion of God and man took place according to the good pleasure of the Father … that God … should be present with His own creation, saving it and becoming capable of being perceived by it … in order that man having embraced the Spirit of God, we might pass into the glory of the Father.[18]

Irenaeus taught that the incarnate Christ adapted our human nature to receive the Holy Spirit, whose presence enables believers to share in the relation of mutual knowing between the Father and the Son. In adapting our human nature to true communion with God in the Holy Spirit, Christ 'the Last Adam' recapitulated the experience of the 'First Adam', and in so doing, restored our nature to the holiness of obedient fellowship with the Father. Only one who was equal with the Father could accomplish this:

> For I have shown that the Son of God did not then begin to exist, being with the Father from the beginning; but when He became incarnate, and was made man, He commenced afresh the long line of human beings, and furnished us, in a brief, comprehensive manner, with salvation; so that what we had lost in Adam – namely, to be according to the image and likeness of God – that we might recover in Christ Jesus.[19]

> For, in what way could we be partakers of the adoption of sons, unless we had received from Him through the Son, that fellowship… unless His Word, having been made flesh, had entered into communion with us? Wherefore also He passed through every stage of life, restoring to all communion with God…[20]

And the gift of the Spirit in the fellowship of the Church brings us into communion with Christ, and thus we share in His knowledge of the Father. Only a Spirit who is fully of the being of God could do this: 'For this gift of God [the Spirit] has been entrusted to the church, as breath was to the first created man, for this purpose, that all the members receiving it may be vivified; and the [means of] communion with Christ has been distributed throughout it, that is the Holy Spirit, the earnest of incorruption, the means of confirming our faith, and the ladder of ascent to God.'[21]

Subordinationist Apologists

Theophilus of Antioch

Theophilus of Antioch, however, teaches a subordination of the Logos to the Father in his distinction between 'the internal Word' (*Logos endiathetos* [Λόγος ἐνδίαθετος]) and 'the uttered Word' (*logos prophorikos* [λόγος προφορικος]), as he discusses the origin of the Logos (in his *Ad Autolycum* c. 180): 'God, then, having his own Word internal (*logon endiatheton* [λόγον ἐνδίαθετον]),

[18] Ibid., IV.20.4.
[19] Ibid., III.18.1.
[20] Ibid., III.18.7.
[21] Ibid., III.24.1.

within his own bowels begot him, emitting him along with wisdom before all things. He had this Word as a helper in the things that were created by him, and by him he made all things.'[22] He holds that the Logos is the 'first originated being', or the 'first creature', whereas the Father has no beginning.[23]

Both Theophilus[24] and Justin Martyr[25] hold that the Old Testament 'theophanies' were appearances of Christ, not of the Father, on the grounds that the Son is of a certain lower order of Being, who thus can enter the world. Theophilus seems to believe that there were stages in the development of the Logos: at one time He was internal to the thought of God (His Counsellor), and later – before the creation – is outside of the Father so as to execute His works: 'For before anything came into being he had him as a counsellor, being his own mind and thought. But when God wished to make all that he determined on, he begot his Word, uttered (*prophorikos* [προφόρικος]) the firstborn of all creation, not himself being emptied of the Word, but having begotten Reason, and always conversing with Reason.'[26]

It is clear that Theophilus, Justin Martyr and the other Apologists were Trinitarians (for they worked within the Church's 'regula veritatis', based on the Trinitarian baptismal formula that is reflected in the early Creeds, such as the Roman Creed, standing behind the 'Apostles' Creed'). On occasion, what Justin writes concerning the Trinity could be fully in accord with the Church's full-fledged affirmation of the New Testament implications of the equality between the three Persons, as long as what he says is understood to refer to *economic* or *ad extra* aspects of the Triune Being and revelation: 'And that we reasonably worship him, having learned that He is the Son of the true God himself, and holding Him in the second place, and the prophetic Spirit in the third, we will prove…'[27]

Justin Martyr

But a closer reading of Justin will show a definite subordinationism of Logos and Spirit to the Father. In the following passage, he claims that the Son was begotten 'by an act of will' of the Person of the Father:

> God begat before all creatures a beginning, a certain *rational power* from himself who is called by the Holy Spirit, now the Glory of the Lord, now the Son, again Wisdom, again an Angel, then God, then Lord and *Logos*; and on another occasion calls Himself Captain, when He appeared in human form to Joshua, son of Nave…He was begotten of the Father by an act of will … just as we see happening among ourselves. For when we give out some word, we beget the word; yet not by abscission, so as to lessen the word in us … just as a fire which has not lessened when it has kindled another.[28]

---

[22] Theophilus, *Ad Autolycum* 2.10.
[23] Ibid., 22.
[24] Ibid., 2.22.
[25] Justin, *Dialogue with Trypho* 127.
[26] Theophilus, op. cit., 2.22.
[27] Justin, *First Apology* 13.
[28] Justin, *Dialogue with Trypho* 61.

A large part of Justin's (and other Apologists') problem with formulating a clear doctrine of the Trinity was that while they ascribed transcendence to the Father, they seem to have not been aware of his omnipresence within the creation.[29] This was almost a very early form of the kind of disjunction between God and the world that would become known as *Deism*. Hence, there had to be some kind of intermediary being between God the Father and his created order, and they took this to be Christ and the Holy Spirit. The assumption was that if these two could interact with the creation, then they could not have been on the same high order of the eternal God, although they did come from Him and were very close to Him.

Origen

In the great Origen of Alexandria, this 'deistic' assumption of Justin and Theophilus was magnified. As T. F. Torrance explains:

> [From his Commentary on St John's Gospel, he carries on two errors]... First, he clearly taught there that the Spirit came into being through the Word, although he is revered more than any other creature that has come into being through the Word of the Father. Secondly, Origen carried over, as an axiomatic assumption into his teaching, the Hellenistic disjunction between the real world of the intelligible and the phenomenal or shadowy world of the sensible, i.e. the *chorismos* between the *kosmos noetos* and the *kosmos aisthetos* (*In Ioann*. 1. 25f.). While Origen himself appeared to apply to his doctrine of the Spirit the notion of eternal derivation from the Logos which he had applied to his doctrine of the Son in his eternal generation from the Father, nevertheless the axiomatic assumption of the *chorismos* between the intelligible and sensible worlds, together with his stress upon the immutability of God which that assumption was meant to guard, was bound to provoke the question: on which side of this dichotomy are we to think of the being of Christ, and therefore of the Son or Word of God?[30]

On the one hand, Origen (c. 185–253) sought to be Trinitarian. In his *Discussion with Heraclides*, found at Toura near Cairo in 1941, Origen interrogates Bishop Heraclides, who was displeased with Origen's formula 'two Gods' as a description of the relation between the Father and the Son. In terms of John 10:30 ('I and the Father are one'), he raises these questions:

> Origen said: Is not the Father God?
> Heraclides answered: Yes.
> Origen said: Is not the Son another (*heteros* [ἕτερος]) than the Father?
> Heraclides answered: How could he be simultaneously Son and Father?
> Origen said: Is not the Son who is another than the Father, also God Himself?
> Heraclides answered: He is also God Himself.
> Origen said: Do not therefore the two Gods become one?
> Heraclides said: Yes.
> Origen said: We confess therefore two Gods?
> Heraclides answered: Yes, but the power is one.[31]

---

[29] Justin, op. cit., 127.

[30] T. F. Torrance, *Theology in Reconstruction*, 211.

[31] J. Scherer, 'Entretien d'Origen avec Héraclide et les êveques ses collegues sur le père, le fils, et l'âme' (Cairo: Publications de la Société Fouad I de Papyrologie, Textes et documents IX, 1949). Cited in Johannes Quastern, *Patrology*, vol. II (Antwerp: Spectrum Publishers: Utrecht-, 1965), 63, 64.

Yet on the other hand, Origen denies the equality of Father and Son. In his *De Oratione*, he says that one can pray only to the Father, not to any creature, and thus not to the Son: 'Those simple-minded who thoughtlessly and inconsiderately pray to the Son with the Father or without the Father, commit a sin of ignorance.'[32] In line with this, he holds that the Father alone is incomprehensible, but that He can be made comprehensible through the Son, for He can be perceived through his creatures.[33] He teaches that the Son proceeds from the Father not by division, but as the will proceeds from reason:

> For if the Son do all those things which the Father does, then, in virtue of the Son doing all things like the Father, is the image of the Father formed in the Son, who is born of Him, like an act of His will proceeding from the mind. And I am therefore of opinion that the will of the Father ought to be sufficient for the existence of that which He wishes to exist…[34]

Yet unlike the later Arians, who in many respects followed him and exaggerated his teaching, Origen maintains that since everything is eternal in God, this generation of the Son is thus eternal.[35] Contrary to the Arians (who taught that 'there was a time when he was not'), Origen holds that the Son had no beginning.[36] Still, Origen's teaching on the relationship of Father and Son seems confused. He maintains the inferiority of the Son: 'We who say that the visible world is under the government of Him who created all things, do thereby declare that the Son is not mightier than the Father, but inferior to Him.'[37]

This means that Origen (like Justin) assumes that only the Father is fully transcendent; the Son and Holy Spirit are intermediate beings between God and mankind:

> As for us, who believe the Saviour when He said: 'The Father, who sent me, is greater than I,' and who for that reason did not allow that the word 'good' should be applied to Himself in its full, true and perfect sense, but attributed it to the Father and gave Him thanks, condemning him who would glorify the Son to excess – we say that the Saviour and the Holy Spirit are without comparison and are very much superior to all things that are made, but also that the Father is even more above them than they are themselves above creatures even the highest.[38]

It was not a very far step for the Arians to take, when they did what Origen would not have done: identify Son and Spirit as creatures.[39] This seems to have happened through Lucian of Antioch, teacher of Arius. T. F. Torrance says:

> In answer to this basic question [i.e. on which side of the deistic gap between God and the world are Son and Spirit] the Arians insisted on the creatureliness

---

[32] Origen, *De Oratore* 16.1.
[33] Origen, *De Principiis* 1.1.6.
[34] Ibid., 1.2.6.
[35] Origen, *De Prin.* 1.2.4.
[36] Ibid., 1.2.4.
[37] Origen, *Contra Celsum* 8.15.
[38] Origen, *In Johan.* 13.25.
[39] Athanasius discusses how the Arians placed the Son of God on the creaturely side of being in *De Synodis* 46.

> of the Son even if he were in some way the image and power of God; and the semi-Arians went on to teach the creatureliness of the Spirit. However, when the Council of Nicea formulated the doctrine of the *homoousion*, it rejected the assumption of a radical dichotomy between the two worlds (i.e. of the *real* and the *phenomenal*), and set in its place the very different biblical distinction between the Creator and the creature, and the freedom of the Creator to be present and active in his creation, which gave *reality*, but not eternity, to the creature, and at the same time it taught that in Jesus Christ God the Son in his own divine Being and Person has come into our creaturely existence, revealing himself to us and reconciling us to the Father.[40]

Tertullian

Tertullian is a sort of border-line figure; while he is subordinationist, he points the way forward to a clearer Trinitarian understanding which would be followed by the whole Church, especially in his anti-modalist treatise, *Adversus Praxean*. The modalist theologians tried to explain the three members of the Godhead by saying that God was only one 'Person' at the same time, who 'evolved' as first, Father, then Son, and then Holy Spirit. Praxeas was a modalist, against whom Tertullian formulated the pivotal definition of the Trinity: God is one substance in three Persons.[41] That is, the three Persons of the Trinity co-exist *at the same time*. He shows that the distinction of persons is required by the New Testament. Father, Son and Spirit speak to one another and refer to one another, as for example at Jesus' baptism.[42] For instance, he speaks of Jesus as a person: 'For whatsoever the being of the Word was, I call it a person, and I claim the name 'Son' for him…'[43] The three have personal names, and thus are not three transmuted manifestations of only one Person.[44] He interprets Genesis 1:26 ('Let us make man in our image') as involving all three divine Persons.[45]

It is always Tertullian's concern in *Adversus Praxean* to hold together 'the Monarchy' (i.e. the one being of God) with 'the Economy' (i.e. the dealings of God with humanity in the history of redemption). He wrote: 'It is the economy … which disposes the unity into trinity.'[46] As he thinks through these two realities together, in spite of his subordinationism, at times he comes close to grasping the *perichoretic*, inner-Trinitarian life:

> 'And the Word was with God' [John 1:1] and never separated from the Father or different from the Father, because 'I and the Father are one' [John 10:30]. This will be the projection of truth, the guardian of unity, by which we say that the Son was brought forth from the Father, but *not* separated. For God sends forth the Word…as the root does the shrub, the source the river, and the sun the ray… The Spirit is the *third* with respect to God and the Son, even as the fruit from the shrub is third from the root… Thus the Trinity running down from the Father, through stages linked and united together, offers no obstacle to monarchy, and conserves the established position of the economy.[47]

---

40 T. F. Torrance, *Theology in Reconstruction*, 211, 212.
41 Tertullian, *Adversus Praxean* 9.3.
42 Ibid., 11.9-10.
43 Ibid., 7.
44 Ibid., 7.9.
45 Ibid., 12.3.
46 Ibid., 2.4.
47 Ibid., 8.

Yet he is definitely still subordinationist: 'For the Father is all being, but the Son is a tributary of the whole... "For the Father is greater than I."'[48] Yet he rises above Justin's and Origen's conception of the Logos having been distinctly emitted only at the beginning of the work of creation. As D'Alès brings out in his *Théologie de Tertullien*, 'Tertullian is the only one to distinguish clearly this phase [that is, the birth of the Word in the act of the creation] from the preceding [that is, the generation of the Word before all creation]; but by this distinction, the theory of the temporal generation of the Word attains its full development, and it includes in it the key to a terminology otherwise obscure.'[49]

Novatian: hesitant steps towards a doctrine of co-equality within the Trinity

Within a generation, Novatian of Rome (in *De Trinitate*, c. 250) would 'abandon the theory of the temporal generation of the Word and profess very clearly the eternal generation.'[50] Although he led a schism, it was more for personal reasons of power within the Church; his teaching was clearly in the bounds of strong orthodoxy. He was the first from the Roman Church to write in Latin, and his writing was very influential in the West (though in the Middle Ages, printed within the works of Tertullian, owing to the Novatianist schism).

Novatian sought to establish the co-equality of the Father and the Logos: 'The Son, then, since He is begotten of the Father, is always in the Father. When I say "always", I do not maintain that He is unborn, but that He is born. Yet He who is born before all time must be said to have always existed in the Father, for a date in time cannot be fixed for Him who is before all time. He is eternally in the Father; otherwise the Father were not always Father.'[51]

He goes on to affirm the full Godness of Christ: 'He proceeded from the Father at whose will all things were made, God, assuredly, proceeding from God, constituting the Second Person after the Father, as Son, yet not robbing the Father of the unity of the Godhead.'[52] He identifies Christ as 'the Lord our God': 'The same rule of truth teaches us to believe, after the Father, also on the Son of God, Christ Jesus, the Lord our God, but the Son of God – of that God who is both one and alone, to wit the Founder of all things...'[53]

Novatian confesses Christ to be both God and man: 'For Scripture as much announces Christ as also God, as it announces God Himself as man. It has as much described Jesus Christ to be man, as moreover it has also described Christ the Lord to be God... So that being of both, He is both, lest if He should be one only, He could not be the other.'[54]

---

[48] Ibid., 9.
[49] D'Alès, *Théologie de Tertullien*, (Paris: Beauchesne, 1905), 91.
[50] Ibid., 96.
[51] Novatian, *De Trinitate* 31.
[52] Ibid.
[53] Ibid., 9.
[54] Ibid., 11.

He states that there is no 'inequality of divinity' between the Father and Son: 'And His [i.e. Christ's] divinity is thus declared, that it may not appear by an dissonance or inequality of divinity to have caused two Gods.'[55]

Yet in Novatian's concern to affirm the unity of the substance of God against any sort of ditheism, and his concern to avoid modalistic monarchianism (according to which Christ is only a temporary manifestation of the Father), he still employs as his solution the Logos subordinationism of Tertullian (whom he follows, and indeed, surpasses in certain ways). That is, he maintains the unity of the substance of the One God at the price of the subordination of the Son:

> At the same time, the Father is antecedent to Him, for the Father must be of necessity before the Son, as Father, inasmuch as He who knows not an origin must of necessity exist before Him who has an origin. Of necessity, too, the Son must be less than the Father, for He knows Himself to be in the Father; He has an origin, in that He is born, and through the Father, in some mysterious manner, although He has an origin, as born, He is germane to him, in the matter of His birth, seeing that He is born of the Father, who alone has no origin... The Father is shown to be the One God, true and eternal; from Him alone this power of divinity issues, and though it is transmitted to the Son and centred upon Him it runs its course back to the Father through their community of substance. The Son is shown to be God, since divinity is manifestly delivered and granted to Him; yet none the less, the Father is proved to be the One God, while step by step the same majesty and divinity, like a billow returning upon itself, sent forth again from the Son Himself, returns and finds its way back to the Father.[56]

But as we see in the quotation above (from chapter 31 of *De Trinitate*) this is no 'Arian' subordination of the Son to the Father. He sees Christ as inferior to the Father in terms of origin and of being sent, but still he is personally God, and remains so even when he becomes man. Along these lines, Novatian refers Christ to the 'community of substance' with the Father, and to a birth 'beyond all time'.[57] With much insight, he teaches that in Christ we find the very bosom of the Father: 'And He [Christ] is the angel, in that He declares the bosom of the Father, as John sets forth. For if John himself says, that He Himself who sets forth the bosom of the Father, as the Word, became flesh in order to declare the bosom of the Father, assuredly Christ is not only man, but angel also; and not only angel, but He is shown by the Scriptures to be God also.'[58]

Novatian's work on the Holy Spirit has little new to offer, beyond what is found in Tertullian. As we have seen, in the interests of safeguarding the unity of the Godhead, he makes the Spirit inferior to Christ, who in turn

---

[55] Ibid., 31.
[56] Ibid.
[57] Ibid.
[58] Ibid., 18.

is inferior to the Father: 'But if he [the Paraclete] has received from Christ what He may declare to us, Christ is greater than the Paraclete, because the Paraclete would not receive from Christ unless He were less than Christ. But the Paraclete being less than Christ, moreover, by this very fact proves Christ to be God, from whom He has received what He declares...'[59]

(2) Historic Orthodoxy affirms the co-equality of the three Persons of the Trinity

We have seen that the Council of Nicea (325) affirmed the full deity of the Son of God (in the *homoousios*), and following that, the Council of Constantinople (381) made clear the full deity of the Holy Spirit, especially on the basis of the earlier work of Athanasius in his *Letters on the Holy Spirit to Serapion*. But this question remained to be worked out: granted the co-equality of the three divine Persons, where is the oneness of the Being of God to be anchored?

We find two different lines of approach amongst the Orthodox Fathers of the fourth century: (a) Basil, Gregory of Nyssa and Amphilocius on the one hand, and (b) Gregory Nazianzus, Cyril of Alexandria and Epiphanius on the other. We shall see, that (c) over one thousand years later, Gregory of Nazianzus, Cyril and Epiphanius were followed by the sixteenth-century Reformer, John Calvin.

(a) Basil, Gregory of Nyssa and John of Damascus

These theologians anchored the deity of the Son and Spirit in the Person of the Father, thereby continuing a certain subordinationism in that they set up a 'causal series' or 'structure of dependence' among the Triune Persons, in which the second and third Persons were unequally dependent, or even 'caused' by the first Person (although 'cause' is being used in a way that precludes any coming into existence out of nothing, for these theologians say that the Son and the Spirit are equally eternal with the Father[60]).

Nevertheless, these theologians do speak of cause within the Trinity. Gregory of Nyssa writes in *Against Eunomius*: 'For as the Son is bound to the Father, and while deriving existence from Him, is not substantially after Him, so again the Holy Spirit is in touch with the Only-begotten, who is

---

[59] Ibid., 16.

[60] Basil denies the sense of 'time' in God that we experience in natural causation: '...In what sense do they say that the Son is "after the Father"; later in time, or in order, or in dignity?... And indeed so far as our conception of human relations goes, it is impossible to think of the Son as being later than the Father, not only from the fact that the Father and the Son are mutually conceived of in accordance with the relationship subsisting between them, but because posteriority is predicated of subjects separated by a less interval from the present, and priority of subjects farther off ... is it not really the extremist folly to measure the existence of the life which transcends all time and all the ages by its distance from the present? Is it not as though God the Father could be compared with, and be made superior to, God the Son, who exists before the ages...' (*De Spiritu Sancto* 14).

Gregory of Nyssa writes in a like vein: 'On the one hand, because the existence of the Son is not marked by any intervals of time, and the infinitude of his life flows back before the ages and onward beyond them in any all-pervading tide, he is properly addressed with the title of Eternal... Extensions in time find no admittance in the Eternal Life; so that, when we have removed the thought of cause, the Holy Trinity in no single way exhibits discord with itself; and so to it is glory due' (*Against Eunomius* I.42).

conceived of as before the Spirit's subsistence only in the theoretical light of a cause.'[61] He says in *That There Are Not Three Gods* '…while we confess the invariable character of the nature, we do not deny the difference in respect of cause, and that which is caused, by which alone we apprehend that one Person is distinguished from another; – by our belief, that is, that one is the Cause, and another is of the Cause; and again in that which is of the Cause we recognize another distinction. For one is directly from the first Cause…'[62] And Basil said much the same in his treatise *Against Eunomius*.[63]

In one of his Letters, Basil spoke of the Father as 'the cause of the cause of all things': 'On the other hand there is a certain power subsisting without generation and without origination, which is the cause of the cause of all things… But God, who is over all, alone has, as one special mark of his own hypostasis, his being Father, and his deriving his hypostasis from no cause…'[64]

John of Damascus is in their line of thought when he writes:

> But if we say that the Father is the origin of the Son and greater than the Son, we do not suggest any precedence in time or superiority in nature of the Father over the Son (for through his agency he made the ages) or superiority in any other respect save causation. And we mean by this that the Son is begotten of the Father and not the Father of the Son, and that the Father naturally is the cause of the Son: just as we say in the same way not that fire proceedeth from light, but rather light from fire. So then, whenever we hear it said that the Father is the origin of the Son, and greater than the Son, let us understand it to mean in respect of causation.[65]

And yet, as we have noted with Basil and Gregory of Nyssa, John of Damascus, who follows them, is using 'cause' in a particularly limited way. For he specifies that it never implies bringing into existence out of non-existence:

> … and when we say He was before all the ages we show that his birth is without time or beginning: for the Son of God was not brought into being out of nothing…But always He was with the Father and in Him, everlastingly and without beginning begotten of Him. For there was never a time when the Father was and the Son was not, but always the Father and always the Son, who was begotten of Him, existed together. For He could not have received the name Father apart from the Son: for if He were without the Son, He could not be the Father…[66]

T. F. Torrance summarizes the problem raised by this teaching:

> Thus the Cappadocian rebuttal of the charge that their differentiation between three hypostaseis [ὑποστάσεις], with their distinct modes of existence, implied three ultimate divine Principles (*archai*) [ἀρχαί], and their attempt to secure the oneness (*henosis*) [ἕνωσις] of the Godhead by referring the three

---

[61] Gregory of Nyssa, *Against Eunomius* I.42.

[62] Gregory of Nyssa, *That There Are Not Three Gods* (Nicene and Post-Nicene Fathers, vol. V, 336).

[63] Basil, *Against Eunomius* 1.19,25.

[64] Basil, *Letter* 38.4.

[65] John of Damascus, *De Fide Orthodoxa* I.8.

[66] Ibid.

> Persons to a single Principle (*archē*) [ἀρχή] or Cause (*aitia*) [αἰτία] in the Father, were made at the expense of a damaging distinction between the Deity of the Father as wholly underived or 'uncaused', and the Deity of the Son and of the Spirit as eternally derived or 'caused'. Moreover, in differentiating the Persons of the Holy Trinity they cast the internal relations between the Father, the Son and the Holy Spirit into the consecutive structure of a causal series or a 'chain' of dependence 'through the Son', instead of conceiving them more, like Athanasius, in terms of their coinherent and undivided wholeness, in which each Person is 'whole of the whole'.[67]

This coinherent 'whole of the whole' is, of course, not to deny that there is order within the Trinity. That is, the Father is unbegotten, the Son is begotten, and the Holy Spirit proceeds. Yet the being of the Son of the Father and of the Spirit is the same being.

(b) Gregory of Nazianzus, Cyril of Alexandria and Epiphanius

These theologians on the contrary understood the unity of the substance of God to be anchored in the *Being* of the Father, the Son, and the Holy Spirit, rather than in the *Person* of the Father. Hence, Gregory of Nazianzus came to deny:

> ... the application of the concept of 'principle' or *arche* to the Father *alone* in distinguishing him from the Son and the Spirit, for that appeared to import the impossible idea of precedence in honour and even of unequal degrees of Deity within the Holy Trinity. Gregory Nazianzus felt strongly that to subordinate any of the three divine Persons to another was to overthrow the doctrine of the Trinity. He was thus returning to the more unified conception of the divine *arche* advocated by Athanasius, who had also rejected any idea of degrees of Deity in the Trinity.[68]

So, Gregory of Nazanzus wrote in *Oration* 40, that each of the three Persons of the Trinity is fully God Himself:

> ...neither increased nor diminished by superiorities or inferiorities; in every respect equal, in every respect the same; just as the beauty and the greatness of the heavens is one; the infinite conjunction of three infinite Ones. Each God when considered in Himself; as the Father so the Son, as the Son so the Holy Ghost; the Three One God when contemplated together; each God because consubstantial; one God because of the Monarchia.[69]

He draws back from using the word 'origin' within the Trinity: 'I should like to call the Father greater, because from him flows both the equality and the being of the equals (this will be granted on all hands), but I am afraid to use the word origin, lest I should make him the origin of inferiors, and thus insult him by precedencies of honour. For the lowering of those who are from him is no glory to the source.'[70]

Gregory teaches that to subordinate any Person of the Three is 'to overthrow the Trinity': 'For he [Arius] did not honour the Father, by

[67] T. F. Torrance, *The Trinitarian Faith*, 238.
[68] T. F. Torrance, *Trinitarian Perspectives*, 30.
[69] Gregory Nazianzus, *Oration* 40.41.
[70] Gregory Nazianzus, *Oration* 40.43.

dishonouring His offspring with his unequal degrees of Godhead. But we recognize one glory of the Father, the equality of the Only-begotten; and one glory of the Son, that of the Spirit. And we hold that to subordinate any of the three is to destroy the whole.'[71]

Gregory taught that the unity of the Godhead is complete not just in the Person of the Father, but in each Person as well.

> But when I say God, I mean Father, Son and Holy Ghost. For Godhead is neither diffused beyond these, so as to bring in a mob of gods; nor yet is it bounded by a smaller compass than these, so as to condemn us for a poverty-stricken conception of Deity; either Judaizing to save the Monarchia, or falling into heathenism by the multitude of our gods.[72]

> ... acknowledging the unity in the essence and in the undivided worship, and the Trinity in the Hypostases or Persons (which term some prefer)... That they are three, who are distinguished not by natures, but by properties [i.e. they have the same essence as God, but are distinguished by personal properties].[73]

Thus, he states that the Monarchy is not limited to one Person.[74]

In this, he was following Athanasius, who taught that the unity of the Godhead, or the Monarchy, was not limited to the Person of the Father alone, but to the whole being of the Trinity, so that in this sense he identifies the *Monas* with the *Trias*.[75] Athanasius also held that the Father cannot be considered the *Arche* apart from the Son.[76] He ascribed the *arche* to the whole Godhead, in confessing 'a Holy Trinity, but one Godhead, and one Arche, and that the Son is of one Being with the Father, while the Holy Spirit is proper to and inseparable from the Being of the Father and the Son.'[77]

In preference to the concept of causation of one Person by another, Gregory spoke of the three Persons as relations (σχέσεις) who subsist in God, 'beyond all time' (ἀχρόνως), 'beyond all origin' (ἀνάρχως), and 'beyond all cause' (ἀναιτίως).[78] Evdokimov, in our own time, carries through this understanding in stating in his work on the Holy Spirit that in the Trinity there is neither 'before' nor 'after', for 'the Three in God transcend all mathematical unity'.[79]

Like Athanasius and Gregory of Nazianzus, Cyril of Alexandria (d. 444) denies subordination of one Person to another within the Trinity, but holds to a full co-equality. He says in his second Dialogue On The Trinity, discussing the significance of the three names given us in the baptismal formula of Matthew 28:

> ... He [Christ] chose and preferred those names above others which would be able to present us with the sharpest clarity the proper existence of each one

---

[71] Ibid., 43.29.
[72] Ibid., 38.10.
[73] Ibid., 42.16.
[74] Ibid., 29.2.
[75] Athanasius, *Contra Arianos* 4.1,3.
[76] Athanasius, Ibid. 4.1.
[77] Athanasius, *Ad Antiochenos* 5.
[78] Gregory of Nazianzus, *Oration* 29.3.
[79] Evdokimov, *L'Esprit Saint*, 44, cited in Stăniloae, op. cit., 277.

> of those who are designated by these names. This would be to express the common traits of the whole divinity, if I may so speak, rather than to discuss what belongs by nature to the supreme substance; and to name the divine nature is immediately to designate for us in a word the integrity of the Holy Trinity, such as it is conceived in a unique divinity, but not yet the personal distinction of each one in particular. When one says 'Father, Son and Holy Spirit', one is no longer, [as indicated in the formula], starting from that which is indivisibly the entire nature of the divinity, but rather one is starting off in a way that allows one to discern the identity of substance of the Holy Trinity in the three proper hypostases. The language refers then to each of the beings indicated by the name which belongs to him and it establishes in their proper hypostases those who are united by substance… [He who is begotten of the Father's nature is] a Son who is not in an inferior situation to the Father as concerns the shining forth in beauty of his own nature, who co-exists with him eternally, who is on the same level with him in every point, except for being begotten… Finally, you would qualify the Holy Spirit as he who by nature flows out from the Father through the Son, who under the image of breath coming out of one's mouth, manifests his proper existence. With these things in mind, you may preserve in a clear manner and without confusion, the properties of the three hypostases in their own proper existences, all the while adoring the unique and consubstantial nature, king of all other beings.[80]

Elsewhere, in his *Thesaurus de Trinitate*, Cyril rejects the teaching of Basil and Gregory of Nyssa that, in order to avoid tritheism, one must affirm a causal status of the Father that subordinates the other two Triune Persons.[81] Instead, he holds that the entire Godhead is a completely personal Being in Himself; that is, God is a communion of personal Being, so that the whole undivided Being of God is in each Person, without any sort of causal priority or subordination.[82] Cyril taught that the Father can be held to be greater than the Son only *economically*, and thus excluded any *ontological* subordination.[83]

In his *Contra Nestorium*, Cyril teaches the *perichoresis*, in terms of which the three divine Persons coinhere in one another, so that they are consubstantially of the same Being.[84] T. F. Torrance summarizes:

> … the thought of Cyril of Alexandria in his view of the living and dynamic coinherence or mutual containing of the Father, the Son and the Holy Spirit essentially and enhypostatically within the Holy Trinity. He brought together the emphasis of Athanasius upon the one Being of the *homoousial* Trinity with Gregory Nazianzen's conception of an indivisible but internally differentiated Trinity of real hypostatic relations continuously and actively subsisting in the Godhead.[85]

Epiphanius

Epiphanius, whose teaching preceded that of Cyril of Alexandria and apparently influenced his, held that each Person of the Trinity is whole and

---

[80] Cyril of Alexandria, *Dialogues sur la Trinité*, tome I ('Dialogue II'), pp. 239-41. (My translation).

[81] Cyril of Alexandria, *Thesaurus de Trinitate* in Migne, Patrologia Graeca, 75.128.

[82] Cyril, *In Joannis Evangelium*, 15.1.

[83] Cyril, *Thesaurus de Trinitate* in Migne, Patrologia Graeca, 75.144, 177.

[84] Cyril, *Contra Nestorium*, 4.3 in Migne, P.G., 76, 190-192.

[85] T. F. Torrance, *The Christian Doctrine of God*, 171,172, where in note 16, he refers to Cyril's comments on John 1:1, 3 & 18; 10:30 & 38; 10:10.

perfect God.[86] He wrote: 'We call the Father God, the Son God, and the Holy Spirit God... When you pronounce the homoousion, you declare that the Son is God of God and the Holy Spirit is God of the same Godhead.'[87] He did not use the terminology of Basil and Gregory of Nyssa that the three Persons were 'modes of existence', but spoke of them as enhypostatic in the Godhead, where they coinhered in one another.[88]

Against subordinationism, he affirmed that the Being of the Persons of the Trinity is 'beyond beginning and beyond time (ἀνάρχως καὶ ἀχρόνως), with no 'before' or 'after' in God.[89] He refers the Monarchia to the entire Trinity, not just to the Father: 'In proclaiming the Monarchia [Μοναρχία] we do not err, but confess the Trinity, Unity in Trinity and Trinity in Unity, one Godhead of the Father, Son and Holy Spirit.'[90] He ascribes self-existence to Christ Himself as Yahweh (יהוה).[91] Thus, the Son, as well as the Father, is *autotheos*.

(c) John Calvin on the full equality of the Triune Persons

Cyril of Alexandria's and Epiphanius' teaching that Jesus Christ has self-existence was followed, and developed, by John Calvin over a thousand years later. In a colloquy at Neuchatel with other Reformed ministers, Calvin speaks of Cyril's teaching that 'the Father has nothing of himself which the Son does not have of himself.'[92] And in the line of Epiphanius,[93] Calvin attributes self-existence (*autousia*) to Christ.[94] He says: 'I assert each to be true, both that Christ is from the Father, so that he is the second Person, and that he is from himself, if we have regard to his divine Being *simpliciter*.'[95] He states that 'for the reason that Christ is rightly said to be the one eternal God, he is said to be self-existent.'[96]

In his *Institutes*, he argues against Valentine Gentile, who held that the Father 'gave essence' to the Son and the Spirit, so that they had merely a derived deity. Calvin answers:

> For if we consider no one but the Father to be God, we definitely cast the Son down from this rank. Therefore whenever mention is made of deity, we ought by no means to admit any antithesis between Son and Father, as if the name of the true God applied to the latter alone. For of course the God who manifested himself to Isaiah (Isa. 6:1) was the true and only God, the God whom nevertheless John affirms to have been Christ (John 12:41)...[97]

Having strongly affirmed the full deity and *autotheos* of Christ, Calvin then must discuss in what sense the Father and the Son are distinct from

---

[86] Epiphanius, *Haer.*, 62.3ff.
[87] Epiphanius, *Anc.*, 2.
[88] Ibid., 5-10.
[89] Ibid., 46.
[90] Epiphanius, *Haer.*, 62.3.
[91] Ibid., 69.
[92] Cyril of Alexandria, *De Trinitate*, 3, referred to by Calvin in Opera Calvini XI. 560.
[93] As above, Epiphanius, *Haer.*, 69.
[94] Calvin, *Opera Calvini*, VII.322 and 323,4.
[95] Ibid., XII.18.
[96] Ibid., VII.322.
[97] Calvin, *Institutes* I.13.20.

one another, since he denies all forms of Modalism. In the same passage, he adds:

> Conversely, there must be some mark of differentiation in order that the Father may not be the Son. Those who locate that mark in the essence clearly annihilate Christ's true deity, which without essence, and indeed the whole essence, cannot exist. Certainly the Father would not differ from the Son unless he had in himself something unique, which was not shared with the Son. Now what can they find to distinguish him? If the distinction is in the essence, let them answer whether or not he has shared it with the Son. Indeed, this could not be done in part because it would be wicked to fashion a half-God. Besides, in this way they would basely tear apart the essence of God. It remains that the essence is wholly and perfectly common to Father and Son. If this is true, then there is indeed with respect to the essence no distinction of one from the other...[98]

Calvin, with all of the orthodox Fathers, shows that the distinctions within the Trinity lie *not* in the essence (which is one), but in Person (which are three).[99]

Calvin adds that since the essence of God is one, the essence itself of all three Persons is unbegotten, so that all three are equally eternal God without reference to cause or time. Yet one must speak of the Father as unbegotten and the Son as begotten with reference to the Persons, so that the priority of the Father is not in terms of their common essence, but in terms of their 'order of relations' as Persons:

> But because the peculiar qualities in the persons carry an order within them, e.g., in the Father is the beginning and the source, so often as mention is made of the Father and the Son together, or the Spirit, the name of *God* is peculiarly applied to the Father. In this way, unity of essence is retained, and a reasoned order is kept, which yet takes nothing away from the deity of the Son and the Spirit.[100]

> Yet we teach from the Scriptures that God is one in essence, and hence that the essence both of the Son and of the Spirit is unbegotten; but inasmuch as the Father is first in order, and from himself begot his wisdom, as has just been said, he is rightly deemed the beginning and fountainhead of the whole of divinity. Thus God without particularization is unbegotten; and the Father also in respect to his person is unbegotten.[101]

Dumitru Stăniloae explains it in terms of *perichoresis*:

> In God each 'I' is and contains all, but his perfect happiness consists in the fact that each 'I' who is the all contains the other 'I's' who are themselves also

---

[98] Ibid.

[99] 'Person, therefore, I call a "subsistence" in God's essence, which, while related to the others, is distinguished by an incommunicable quality. By the term "subsistence" we would understand something different from "essence." ... Now, of the three subsistences I say that each one, while related to the others, is distinguished by a special quality...whatever is proper to each individually, I maintain to be incommunicable because whatever is attributed to the Father as a distinguishing mark cannot agree with, or be transferred to, the Son. Nor am I displeased with Tertullian's definition, provided it be taken in the right sense, that there is a kind of distribution or economy in God which has no effect on the unity of essence.' He refers to Tertullian, *Adversus Praxean* 2.9 in his *Institutes* I.13.6.

[100] Calvin, *Institutes* I.13.20.

[101] Ibid. I.13.25.

> the all, each being the all in this reciprocal act of containing. These 'I's' do not encounter one another from the outside, as is the case with human 'I's', even though the latter are satisfying an inner necessity. From eternity they are completely interior to one another but not identical, just as human 'I's' aspire to become. The divine all (or the infinite divine being) is not multiplied externally, as is true with men, since if this were the case the Godhead would no longer be absolute. It remains perfectly one and nevertheless subsists in three personal modes, each mode containing perfectly in itself the other modes as well. The divine all exists within an ontological dialogue among the three. No partner in the dialogue furnishes any content from outside the dialogue. Each possesses the infinite divine all in dialogical communion with the other two 'I's.[102]

Some traditional Trinitarian distinctions

Classical theology has drawn certain distinctions regarding the Holy Trinity. The three main ones are: (1) distinction between the ontological and economical Trinity; (2) distinction in modes of existence; and (3) distinction in historico-redemptive work.

(1) Distinction between Ontological and economical Trinity

The Church of course has always confessed only one Trinity, but it has looked at the same reality in two different ways: ontological and economical. The ontological aspect refers to the eternal character of the Holy Trinity, antecedent to all creational and redemptive history, and in their ontology or Being, there is absolute and eternal equality. Athanasius, for instance, especially in *Contra Arianos*, frequently employs this sort of distinction to explain passages of the Gospels that seem to attribute inferiority to Christ, as does Hilary in *De Trinitate*. And both of them are following earlier Apologists, not least Irenaeus.

The economical aspect has reference to the creational, providential and historico-redemptive work of the Trinity, in which there is a certain historical order and temporary subordination among the Persons in terms of their work in bringing salvation. In this respect, the Father is first, the Son second, and the Holy Spirit third. Yet in the ultimate sense, this historical order does not mean that there is any antecedent inequality among the Persons of the Triune Being.

(2) Distinction in modes of existence as co-equal Persons

Reflecting upon various statements in Holy Scripture, traditional theology has distinguished the three Persons by their 'order of relations' (to paraphrase Calvin, above). That is, generation is an act of the Father (or, put another way, He is ingenerate), filiation is an act of the Son, and spiration belongs to the Spirit. Some such terminology seems required by Scripture, but still it does not tell us very much; only that there are 'incommunicable' personal distinctions that are best summarized this way.

---

[102] Stăniloae, op. cit., 263,264.

Here above all, we will do well to remember what John Calvin says, quoting Hilary:

> Here, indeed, if anywhere in the secret mysteries of Scripture, we ought to play the philosopher soberly and with great moderation; let us use great caution that neither our thoughts nor our speech go beyond the limits to which the Word of God itself extends. For how can the human mind measure off the measureless essence of God according to its own little measure, a mind as yet unable to establish for certain the nature of the sun's body, though men's eyes daily gaze upon it? Indeed, how can the mind by its own leading come to search out God's essence when it cannot even get to its own? Let us then willingly leave to God the knowledge of himself. For, as Hilary says, he is the one fit witness to himself, and is not known except through himself. But we shall be 'leaving it to him' if we conceive him to be as he reveals himself to us, without inquiring about him elsewhere than from his Word.[103]

In speaking of these internal Trinitarian relations of ingenerate, begotten and proceeding or sent, we also must remember this instruction from E. L. Mascall:

> I accept, of course, the dyadic [twofold] relations which are classical in Christian theism, for example that by which the Father eternally begets the Son. If, however, we remember that, in virtue of their common deity and equality, the filiality of the Son is as basic as the paternity of the Father, and if we remember, as East and West agree, that the Holy Spirit is the mutual love and the bond of love between the Father and the Son, we may be able to see these dyadic relations as included within the basic and comprehensive triadic Trinitarian relations whose co-subjects are the Father, the Son and the Holy Spirit.[104]

It is important to add here that the Holy Spirit, while certainly being 'the bond of charity between Father and Son,' is also a distinct person within the Trinity.

John Owen, some 1,300 years after Hilary, breathed the same spirit of reverent reserve, when he wrote concerning the inner-Trinitarian relations:

> We have, I say, words and notions about these things; but as to the things themselves what do we know? What do we comprehend of them? Can the mind of man do any more but swallow itself up in an infinite abyss, which is as nothing; give itself up to what it cannot conceive, much less express? Is not our understanding 'brutish' in the contemplation of such things, and is as if it were not? Yea, the perfection of our understanding is, not to understand, and to rest there. They are but the back parts of eternity and infiniteness that we have a glimpse of. What shall I say of the Trinity, or the subsistence of distinct persons in the same individual essence – a mystery by many denied, because by none understood – a mystery whose every letter is mysterious? Who can declare the generation of the Son, the procession of the Spirit, or the difference of the one from the other?[105]

---

[103] Ibid., I.13.21, quoting Hilary, *De Trinitate* I.18.
[104] E. L. Mascall, *The Triune God*, 83.
[105] John Owen, *Works*, vol. VI, 67.

Long before Owen, and even before Hilary, Athanasius had written similarly in his account of the Council of Nicea. Without ever seeking to explain the inner-Trinitarian relations, it was his concern to establish the foundational biblical principle that the Being of God is never impersonal, and thus that the Being and hypostases are one.[106]

Stăniloae makes the same point:

> The fact that we speak of the divine hypostases as subjects does not mean that we are reducing the divine nature to a nonsubjective reality. The person does not bring the character of subject (as though this character were something new) to divine nature. For the person is nothing other than the mode of real subsistence that belongs to a nature. But neither does this mean that there exists an impersonal being which gives itself the character of subject. Being does not exist really except in a hypostasis, or – in the case of spiritual being – in the conscious subject.[107]

With this in mind, Stăniloae goes on to explain the *joint Trinitarian nature* of filiation and procession:

> The Son is not passive in his generation from the Father, although he is not the subject who begets but the subject who takes his birth. Neither does the term 'procession' in reference to the Holy Spirit mark any passivity on the part of the Holy Spirit such as would make him an object of the Father. The Savior said that the Spirit 'proceeds from the Father' (John 15:26). The Spirit is eternally in the movement of proceeding from the Father, just as the Son exists eternally in the movement of taking birth from the Father. But neither does this mean that the Father is placed in a state of passivity. The Spirit proceeds, but the Father also causes him to proceed. The procession of the Spirit from the Father is itself an act of pure intersubjectivity of Father and Spirit, without there being any confusion between them. Moreover, as the Father in incomprehensible fashion is the source of both the Son and the Spirit, each of them together with the Father not only lives the act of his own coming forth from the Father, but also joyfully participates along with the other – though from his own position – in living that act whereby the other comes forth from the Father. All three in intersubjectivity experience the act of the Son's generation and of the Spirit's procession, but each from his own position. Once again, this forms a community between the three hypostases.[108]

(3) Distinction in historico-redemptive work

At times, particularly in the West, the Persons of the Trinity have been distinguished in terms of their particular share in the unfolding work of redemption: election and creation are ascribed to the Father, incarnation and redemption to the Son, and regeneration and sanctification to the Holy Spirit. Martin Luther's *Small Catechism* (1529) brought this tradition of appropriations into the magisterial stream of the Protestant Reformation.[109] There is certainly

---

[106] Athanasius, *De Synodis* 51.

[107] Stăniloae, op. cit., 256.

[108] Stăniloae, op. cit., 261,262.

[109] Martin Luther Small Catechism (1529) , from *A Short Explanation of Dr. Martin Luther's Small Catechism: A Handbook of Christian Doctrine* (Saint Louis, MO: Concordia Publishing House, 1965). Question 27: 'How are the three divine Persons distinguished from each other? The Father *has begotten* the Son from eternity; the Son *is begotten* of the Father from eternity; the Holy Ghost from eternity *proceeds* from the Father and the Son. – To the Father especially is ascribed the work of *Creation*; to the Son, the work of *Redemption*; to the Holy Ghost, the work of *Sanctification*.'

something to be said for this from various scriptural passages. But the way it was developed in part of the Church does raise problems.

In the medieval period in the West, there was a development of the 'law of appropriations', which T. F. Torrance suggests arose as a way of addressing 'an unbalanced essentialist approach to the doctrine of the Trinity from the One Being of God, which obscured the evangelical approach from the economic Trinity.'[110] That is, as Karl Rahner, among many others, has pointed out, 'The Augustinian-Western conception of the Trinity, as contrasted with the Greek conception…begins with the one God, the one divine essence as a whole, and only *afterwards* does it see God as three persons.'[111]

In other words, if one ascribes a particular attribute or activity to one of the three Persons rather than another in order to distinguish his hypostatic character, there may be a tendency to lose the wholeness of the Being and acts of the Trinity in unity. In the line of Augustine (who started with the One and went to the Three), St. Thomas appropriated power to the Father, wisdom to the Son, and goodness and love to the Holy Spirit.[112] But as Torrance objects: 'This law of appropriations depends on the concept of the Father as the *principium deitatis* which is similar to the Basilian understanding of the role of *APXH* [ἀρχή] in the unity of God and his threefold activities.'[113]

Karl Barth sought to overcome this problem by appropriating creation to the Father, reconciliation to the Son and redemption to the Holy Spirit in a way that makes it clear that God's 'economic' activities are grounded in the 'ontological' Trinity.[114] As Torrance points out from Calvin's doctrine of the Trinity (see above):

> In other words, all three divine Persons, who do not share with one another their distinguishing properties, nevertheless share together completely and equally, not partially, in the one indivisible Being of God: the whole Being of God belongs to each of them as it belongs to all of them, and belongs to all of them as it belongs to each of them…Thus while he [i.e. Athanasius] thought of the whole Being of God as dwelling in each Person, he thought of each Person and of all the Persons, with their differentiating properties and in their mutual interrelations, as dwelling hypostatically and consubstantially in the one indivisible Being of God.[115]

Stăniloae shows that the only way we can grasp this wholeness of Being and distinguishing (though never separate) particularity of missions from within the Trinity is to think of their actions towards us in light of *perichoresis*. For example, he – when speaking of Trinitarian inner-relations – would not simply ascribe 'goodness' to the divine being in terms of the Western 'law of appropriations': 'But in Scholastic dogmatics goodness is held to be an attribute of the divine being. The thought of the Fathers, however, is

[110] T. F. Torrance, *The Christian Doctrine of God*, 200.
[111] Karl, Rahner, *The Trinity*, 17.
[112] St. Thomas, *Summa Theologiae* I.39.7.
[113] Torrance, op. cit., 200, n. 130.
[114] Barth, *Church Dogmatics* I/1, 353ff.
[115] Torrance, op. cit., 202.

more complex. They do not conceive of the divine being separately from person; for them the goodness of the being shows itself in the relationship between persons.'[116]

As far as the acts 'appropriated' to the various Persons are concerned, Stăniloae states: 'The acts through which the divine persons, in their distinction and through perfect love, affirm one another reciprocally in existence are eternal acts and have a totally personal character, although they are acts in which the divine persons are active together.'[117] This perichoretic reciprocity in existence is also carried through in their operations in the created order. Stăniloae writes that 'The affirmation of the filial "I" through the paternal "I" and vice versa can be seen as it relates to creation not only in the identity of the will but also in the fact that all the works of the Father are accomplished by the Son and vice versa.'[118]

Or, in the words of E. Jüngel:

> Attribution is that procedure in which God in the concrete harmony of his modes of being assigns to himself his being *as Father, as Son* and *as Spirit*. Appropriation is attribution in so far as God assigns to himself his being as the triune God. In this way God corresponds to himself...God is concrete in the harmony of his modes of being as he who brings to speech, as he who he chooses to be. Shorter: God is concrete in that he himself assigns to himself his being *as* Father, *as* Son and *as* Spirit and so corresponds to himself.[119]

Trinitarian errors

Historically speaking, major Trinitarian errors tend to fall into one of two main categories: (a) those based on some kind of Unitarian presupposition, and (b) those based on some kind of polytheistic thinking. The early Church had to do battle with both types of erroneous thinking in a wide variety of forms as it wrought out a biblically faithful statement of Trinitarian relations. The Church understood that a misrepresentation of who God is would destroy the gospel it was commissioned to proclaim to the ends of the earth and the end of the age, and this understanding would explain the vehemence of the Trinitarian controversies.

(a) Unitarian assumptions

This basic assumption holds that God can exist only as one Person (if indeed personhood be ascribed to him) at one time. Part of the problem here is the belief that for one God to be more than one Person at the same time seems to violate human understanding of mathematical reality. Thus, the human mind is made the limit of what God can be in Himself. That probably puts the issue most starkly between heresy and orthodoxy.

Of course other assumptions entered in to the equation, and shaped the expression of Unitarian thinking in different directions. The Docetists (who claimed that Christ only seemed [i.e. Greek, *dokeo* 'to seem'] to be a man, by definition rejected the possibility of the incarnation of God in the

---

[116] Stăniloae, op. cit., 257.
[117] Ibid.
[118] Ibid., 265.
[119] Eberhard Jüngel, *The Doctrine of the Trinity*, 38,39.

flesh, because of the dualism which posited 'spirit' as good and flesh as inherently evil and unclean: no place for God to enter! But allied to this dualism was their 'Unitarian' unwillingness to consider that God the Father could at the same time co-exist with a Son (and Spirit) who was a distinct personal reality in communion with Him. This sort of approach seems already referred to in the First Epistle of John, and was firmly countered by the earliest Church writers.

The Ebionites, who came more from the Jewish realm than the Docetists (who were Hellenists), were prepared to accept some kind of incarnation of Christ, but denied His equality with the Father; again, on the presupposition that the true God can have no personal distinctions within Himself; that He can be only one 'person' (although they did not really have the concept of Person) at the same time. They too were fully answered by the writers of the Church in the early centuries.

The heresy of monarchianism is generally (at least since the nineteenth century) considered to have had two forms: 'dynamic monarchianism' and 'modalistic monarchianism.' 'Dynamic monarchianism' evidently maintained that at first Christ was a 'mere man', who was later 'adopted' by the Father at his baptism, or perhaps at his resurrection. This error was called 'Adoptionism' in the form held by Paul of Samosata (c. 260). Once again, it taught that only the Father can be fully and eternally God; the Son is of a lower order of being, on the side of creation, for only one can exist as true God at one time, although somehow he could 'promote' a man to a position closer to his status.

According to Jean Daniélou and Henri Marrou: 'The Monarchian doctrine appeared as the continuation of Jewish monotheism, treating the Son and the Spirit merely as powers of the one God, in the Judaic sense of the word. So it was the unique divine person who was manifest in Jesus Christ... Another Monarchian group is described by Hippolytus in his *Elenchos*, that of Noetus. Noetus was born in Smyrna. According to Hippolytus he was excluded from the Church there by the presbyters.'[120]

'Modalistic monarchianism' was far more influential in the third century than 'dynamic monarchianism', probably because at first sight it seemed to accept the deity of the Son and the Holy Spirit, which the 'dynamics' denied in obvious contradistinction to scripture. This position said that God changes His forms (or modes) of Being at different times. It was taught by such people as Noetus of Smyrna (c. 200), who was answered by Hippolytus in his *Contra Noetum* and *Philosophumena*, and Praxeas, who was answered by Tertullian (c. 213) in *Adversus Praxean*. Praxeas, for instance, had alleged that the Father had literally turned into the Son, so that it was actually the Father who was suffering and dying on the cross (hence his error was called 'Patripassianism').

Moltmann's explanation of this error is accurate:

> ... if Christ is our God, then the Father and the Son must be, not merely *one* but in fact *one and the same*. The One God is then called 'Father', inasmuch

[120] Jean Daniélou and Henri Marrou, *The First Six Hundred Years*, translated by Vincent Cronin (London: Darton, Longman & Todd, 1979), 107.

> as he makes himself the subject of his revelation. He is then called 'Son' and 'Holy Spirit', inasmuch as he becomes the object and power of his own revelation. An early form of maintaining God's simple unity in this way can be found in Syrian patripassianism: 'The Father himself appeared in the flesh by making himself the Son; he himself suffered; he himself died; he himself raised himself.' According to this thesis, the history of Christ can have only *one* subject. It is the one God who appears to us *as* Father, *as* Son and *as* Spirit. The *trias* only comes into being in the revelation of the *monas*.[121]

Tertullian in countering this erroneous thinking provided the Church, as we have seen, with the biblically faithful formula: 'one substance and three Persons,' as well as with the word 'Trinity.' He raised the right question: if God could be only one Person at the same time, then to whom was the Son praying when He was on earth? It is plain from the scriptural witness to the involvement of the three divine Persons in revelation and reconciliation, that God's Being is not Unitarian, but tri-personal.

(b) Polytheism

The other, not unrelated, assumption that excludes the Trinity is a sort of polytheism. The Arians were motivated by this unbiblical way of thought. As G. L. Prestige has written:

> Alexander [Bishop of Alexandria, and teacher of Athanasius] and the orthodox said that the Arians were putting forward a theory which, in effect, combined the views of Jewish Unitarians and pagan polytheists...Arius, though he recognized the divine Son as an inferior deity, reduced the Logos to an impersonality and by worshipping Christ, whom he regarded as a demigod of different substance from that of the Father, put himself in the same position as the polytheists.[122]

In opposing the Arians (followers of Arius, the heretical bishop and opponent of Athanasius in Alexandria in the fourth century), Athanasius pointed out certain false assumptions of the Arians which kept them from interpreting the Scriptures properly. Especially in his *Contra Arianos*, he noted that the Arians assumed (what we would call since the European Enlightenment) a 'deistic gap' between God and the world, so that God could not really interact with it. By definition, this meant that He could not become incarnate within it. If He should come into the world, then He would cease to be God. Therefore, the Son could not have been fully God, but was a 'secondary deity' (hence, a subtle form of polytheism).

Secondly, Athanasius noted that the Arian heretics worked with an assumption about the utter unknowability of the Being of God, by which God was precluded from revealing in words or in flesh and blood who He really was in Himself. Hence, statements of Christ such as 'I and the Father are one' (John 10:30) or 'He that has seen me has seen the Father' (John 14:9) have to be explained away as not meaning what they say.

---

[121] Jurgen Moltmann, *The Trinity and the Kingdom of God*, translated by Margaret Kohl (London: SCM Press, 1981), 135.

[122] G. L. Prestige, *God in Patristic Thought*, 146-47.

But on the other hand, the Arians would take literally such a statement of the Lord as 'The Father is greater than I' (John 14:28), and read it back into the essence of God, thus making Christ an inferior deity. But the orthodox Fathers showed that such texts are to be understood not ontologically, but economically (that is, in terms of Christ's voluntary condescension for our salvation), and that this is indicated by the very context of the passages of Scripture themselves.[123]

T. F. Torrance discusses how different the methodology of Athanasius was from the Arians with their unbiblical philosophical assumptions:

> Athanasius entirely rejected the cosmological and epistemological dualism of Hellenism, Gnosticism and Origenism – nowhere in his writings, for example, do we come across him deploying the (χωρισμός) [i.e. gap or disjunction] between the (κόσμος αἰθητός) [i.e. the world of experience or perception – the 'phenomenal world'] and (κόσμος νοητός) [i.e. the world of thought or ultimate reality – the 'noumenal world']...Above all, perhaps, he rejected the Platonic doctrine of God as 'beyond knowledge and being' which had been combined in Alexandria with a transcendental Judaism in its notion of the 'namelessness' of God and with an intellectual mysticism such as we find in Neoplatonism.[124]

The Christian Church answered the polytheistic Arians in the work of the two great fourth century Councils – Nicea (325) and Constantinople (381) – with the lasting and luminous formula that the Son is of the same substance with the Father (*homoousios*). This means that God has 'bridged the gap' between the heavenly and earthly worlds, and thereby has revealed His own inner Being in the Persons of His Son and Holy Spirit in our space/time conditions, thus lifting us up into truest knowledge of Himself.

Basic difference in attitude between orthodoxy and heresy

A great deal of the controversy between Christian believers and heretics through all the generations of severe conflict over the Trinity and over Christology could be summarized in their profoundly different attitudes to the mysterious teaching of Holy Scripture. Athanasius and Hilary both discussed this difference. Torrance has summed up well what they both said when they pinpointed the heart of the controversy. They saw that 'the epistemological principle of the Arians (was) ... that what men cannot understand cannot be true.'[125]

Basil rightly accused Eunomius of the same arrogant principle. He demonstrated that Eunomius assumed that what he could not comprehend by the limits of the human mind must be totally non-existent.[126]

Heretical thinking in all ages allows 'contemporary' patterns of thought to determine what can or cannot be true about the nature of God and of His salvation. Therefore, Scripture must be reinterpreted in order to fit into this mold. This attitude did not die with the Arians. It would reassert

---

[123] See Gregory Nazianzus, Oration 40.31; Cyril of Alexandria, *Thesaurus de Trinitate* in Migne P.G. 75.144-45.

[124] T. F. Torrance, *Theology in Reconciliation*, 217.

[125] Ibid., 61.

[126] Basil, *Contra Eunomium* 2.24.

itself with power during the Enlightenment and especially in the new form of Unitarianism (Socinianism) which arose after the Renaissance, during the early Reformation, and thus shortly before the flowering of the Enlightenment. It possibly gave some impetus to the Enlightenment.

John Calvin would spend much energy dealing with the Unitarian Socinians. And their kind of thinking (that man's mind determines what, if any, parts of Holy Scripture can be true) rose to great power in late eighteenth and early nineteenth-century New England, and from there eventually tended to dominate American intellectual life to the present. It lay behind early twentieth-century 'Modernism.'

It seems to me that the most effective response to this arrogant attitude was provided by Hilary of Poitiers (c. 350) in his *De Trinitate*. There he noted two important points for a proper attitude to grasping who God is. First, the true believer 'must take his stand upon the sure ground (*substantia*) of God, as holy Jeremiah says, that since he is to hear about that nature (*substantia*), he may expand his thoughts till they are worthy of the theme, not fixing some arbitrary standard for himself, but judging as of infinity.' Then Hilary adds that the human mind 'must not measure the divine nature by the limitations of his own, but must gauge God's assertions concerning himself by the scale of his own glorious self-revelation…Since we are to discourse of the things of God, let us assume that God has full knowledge of himself, and bow with humble reverence to his words.'[127]

Hilary and Athanasius before him had the humble attitude of letting one's understanding of who God is be shaped by the scriptural testimony, even when it stretched beyond anything the human mind could ordinarily conceive, rather than limiting God by human preconceptions of what is possible for Him. Athanasius summarized the whole position with power, and gave the Church of all ages a sure standing place when he wrote: 'When our minds are wearied with such problems as these, we must at last come to Holy Scripture. Here we must rest, and believe things exactly according to the obvious sense revealed there.'[128]

Practical application of Trinitarian doctrine

We shall consider, among many possible applications, how the reality of the Holy Trinity makes possible: (a) our sharing in the Trinitarian life, and (b) a fruitful approach to the ancient (and modern) problem of 'the one and the many.'

(a) Our sharing in the Trinitarian life

We have noted from the start of this work that God is known in community. This is not least because God is community within Himself; for Him to be is to be in relationship within His own Being from eternity to eternity. And God has created us from the beginning to be in a community of relationship to Himself and to one another. Another way to state this would be the words

---

[127] Hilary, *De Trinitate* I.17.

[128] Athanasius, *Contra Arianos* II.36.

of Jesus: 'And this is eternal life, that they might know thee, the only true God, and Jesus Christ whom thou hast sent' (John 17:3).

In Matthew 11:27, we are told that 'only the Son knows the Father' and that 'the Son reveals the Father to whom he will'. In John 14:9, Jesus says to Philip, 'He who hath seen me hath seen the Father.' That is, the Son has come down to earth to do all that was necessary to lift us up to a true knowledge of the Father, so that we share in the Son's knowledge of the Father.

Saint Irenaeus in the late second century taught that we know God through sharing in the knowledge He has of Himself.[129] Hilary said the same: 'To the Son only is he known, for no one knows the Father except the Son and he to whom the Son wills to reveal him, nor yet the Son except the Father. Each has perfect and complete knowledge of the Other. Therefore, since no one knows the Father except the Son, let our thoughts of the Father be at one with the only faithful witness who reveals him.'[130]

Athanasius saw that our true knowledge of God must conform to Jesus Christ since He is the perfect image of God, the one Form or *Eidos* of Godhead.[131] He stated that 'The Form of the Godhead of the Father is the *Being* of the Son.'[132] T. F. Torrance comments on Athanasius' and Hilary's expression of this truth:

> Careful examination [i.e. of passages such as Luke 10:22 and Matthew 11:27] disclosed that the mutual relation of knowing between the Father and the Son…involved a mutual relation of *being* between them as well, and not only between the eternal Son and the Father but between the incarnate Son and the Father. This implies that we are given access to the closed circle of divine knowing between the Father and the Son only through cognitive union with Christ, that is only through an interrelation of knowing and being between us and the incarnate Son, although in our case this union is one of participation through grace and not one of nature.[133]

To make this sharing (in a way appropriate to creatures) in the divine Being and knowing, the Son of God took on our flesh, lived the holy life of obedience to the Father that we should have lived, atoned for our sins on the cross, raised us with Him in His bodily resurrection, 'seated us in heavenly places' (Eph. 2:6) with Him, and thus prepared the way for us to share in His true knowledge and love of the heavenly Father. From His glorious seat on high with the Father, He and the Father sent down to us the Holy Spirit to baptize us into this union with incarnate deity in being and knowledge. Torrance describes this movement clearly: 'It is the Holy Spirit who actualises the self-giving of God in Jesus Christ and so enables us to receive and apprehend what is beyond ourselves altogether, the self-knowledge of God himself incarnate among us in Christ. This is what is actualised in the faith and worship and obedient devotion of the Church to God's self-communication through the Son and in the Spirit.'[134]

---

[129] Irenaeus, *Adversus Haereses* IV.11.1-5.
[130] Hilary, *De Trin*. 2.6.
[131] Athanasius, *In Illud Omnia* 5.
[132] Athanasius, *Contra Arianos* 3.3.
[133] T. F. Torrance, *The Trinitarian Faith*, 58,59.
[134] Ibid., 56.

Cyril of Alexandria wrote in his *Dialogues on the Trinity*, 'Sanctified by its union with the Spirit, the flesh is raised to the divine Word, and through Him to the Father…It is the Spirit who unites us and so to speak, makes us sympathize with God; His reception makes us partakers of the divine nature, and we receive this from the Son, and, through the Son from the Father.'[135] In other words, the stupendous grace of the generous God is such that He gives us knowledge – thus, saving relationship – with Himself, as He comes to us in Christ and in the Holy Spirit. Stăniloae explains:

> In Christ the divine hypostasis is accessible to us on our own human level for the sake of full communion. Christ overcame in himself the interval between divinity and humanity, and between himself as God and ourselves… The Son of God became man in order that, through our own movement, he might help us overcome the temporal interval that separates us from full communion with God. In some fashion he performs this movement together with us and because of this he finds himself within this interval still, although on the other hand he is above it.[136]

This saving knowledge in which we are given to share by divine and immeasurable grace is *brought down* from God and *takes us up* to God. To refer again to Stăniloae:

> Within the reciprocal knowledge of the Trinitarian persons as infinite subjects there is given in God, simultaneously with eternity, the basis for the possibility of the knowledge of other subjects, and hence also of the creation of subjects who are limited in themselves. Through this love which gives him knowledge, God comes down to the interiority found in created limited subjects, yet by means of his love God raises them up at the same time to their interiority in him, thus opening up for them the road towards his knowledge.[137]

John Calvin on our true knowledge of God in Christ

The Reformer John Calvin was in line with the best of the Church Fathers, and with Holy Scripture, in teaching that we truly know God through Christ and in the Holy Spirit. He states that although we are separated from God by space and time, the Holy Spirit overcomes those barriers to grant us true union with Christ, whom to know is to know God in His innermost Being.

Ronald S. Wallace in his *Calvin's Doctrine of the Christian Life* has summarized correctly Calvin's teaching on this important application of Trinitarian doctrine. I shall summarize what he brings out, with copious references to the statements of Calvin. He shows that the Holy Spirit as the omnipresence of God unites us believing humans to the humanity of the Lord, so that to know him is to know the Father:

Calvin teaches that our knowledge of the Father is possible only through union with Christ:

> Therefore, to share with us what he has received from the Father, he had to become ours and to dwell within us. For this reason, he is called 'our Head' (Eph. 4:15), and 'the first-born among many brethren' (Rom. 8:29). We also,

[135] Cyril of Alexandria, *De SS. Trinitate Dialogus* III in Migne, P.G. 75.837.
[136] Stăniloae, op. cit., 169.
[137] Ibid., 202.

> in turn, are said to be 'engrafted into him'(Rom. 11:17) and to 'put on Christ' (Gal. 3:27): for, as I have said, all that he possesses is nothing to us until we grow into one body with him.[138]

> It is true that we obtain this by faith. We know, moreover, that he benefits only those whose 'Head' he is, for…we 'have put him on' (Gal. 3:27). This union alone ensures that, as far as we are concerned, he has not unprofitably come with the name of Savior. The same purpose is served by that sacred wedlock through which we are made flesh of his flesh and bone of his bone, and thus one with him. But he unites us to himself by the Spirit alone.[139]

Calvin is clear that our union with Christ occurs through the supernatural operation in us of the Holy Spirit, who thus united us to Christ, and through him brings us to the Father. Again, he is close to Cyril of Alexandria in this teaching: 'The fullness given in us by the Father and the Son is realized (as one fullness) … by the Holy Spirit who fills us with divine charisms through Himself, and makes us partakers of the ineffable nature.'[140]

In Calvin's words: 'It is therefore the Holy Spirit alone who can effect this union [i.e. between God and mankind], for it is the Holy Spirit alone who can so join things in Heaven and things on earth that heavenly things can be grasped by human minds and that the life and virtue of what is in Heaven can be shared by those who are yet on earth. It is the Holy Spirit alone who can bring into real being that wonderful relation of mystery between Christ's heavenly body and His Church on earth which is so clearly depicted in the act of participation in the Lord's Supper and in Baptism ….'[141]

Here, Calvin is very close to Cyril of Alexandria who influenced him considerably. Cyril wrote: 'If, perchance, we were to be deprived of the Spirit, we would not even recognize that God might be in us; and had we not been enriched by the Spirit who places us among the children of God, we would in no way be children of God. For it is the Spirit who joins us together and so to speak, unites us to God; once He is received, we become partakers of the divine nature. And thus, through the Son and in the Son, we receive the Father Himself.'[142]

Calvin then shows that this participation through union with Christ is never apart from personal faith:

> Faith enables us to partake of the life made available through the death of Christ. But all this is possible only because faith actually unites us to Christ and inserts us into His body, creating the bond that enables us to receive, possess and enjoy Christ Himself – for the blessings which are His gifts cannot be received and enjoyed by us apart from communion with Himself by faith.[143]

> Faith is thus an entirely supernatural gift – a new capacity created within man whereby what is in Heaven is really possessed and enjoyed by him. It effects such a secret and wonderful communion with Christ that even

---

[138] Calvin, *Institutes* III.1.3.
[139] Calvin, *Institutes* III.1.1.
[140] Cyril of Alexandria, *Dialogue on the Trinity* III, in Migne, P.G. 75.800.
[141] Ronald S. Wallace, *Calvin's Doctrine of the Christian Life*, 20, 21.
[142] Cyril of Alexandria, *In Joannis evangelium* 11, 10 in Migne, P.G. 74.544.
[143] R. Wallace, op. cit., 21.

> though Jesus Christ remains entire in Heaven, He is nevertheless grasped so firmly and possessed so completely that He may be said actually to dwell in our hearts.[144]
>
> Faith has the power to reach through the humanity of Jesus even God Himself. Faith is able to rise from the flesh of Christ to His divinity, and to penetrate above all the heavens, even to those mysteries which the angels behold and adore. Faith unites man to God and makes God to dwell in man.[145]

We can summarize this teaching of Calvin on our experience of the whole Trinity in Christian salvation by referring once more to Cyril of Alexandria, whom Calvin so often followed. Cyril expresses the Christian experience of communion with God in terms of *beauty*: 'To this beauty, we too have been conformed, by receiving a filial imprint through the Son in the Spirit.'[146]

(b) A fruitful approach to the one and many problem

One of the most ancient questions in philosophy and in the ordering of human society is the question of the one and the many; which is more basic: the one (the overarching structure) or the many (the individual)? Far from remaining a merely philosophical problem, it has always been – and still is – a major problem for the political, governmental ordering of human society.

More than one Trinitarian theologian has seen that there is a fruitful approach to this question in the eternal existence of the Creator, who is at the same time both One (one Monarchy) and Many (three Persons). Colin Gunton in his 1992 Bampton Lectures to the University of Oxford has seen the right answer to this question as lying in the reality of God as one and many *at the same time*.[147]

He argues that in Western society since the Nominalist movement of the fourteenth century, God has been displaced by other universals.[148] This movement is destructive for human society,[149] for it leaves society without a balance between individual freedom and governmental structure. When the many are reduced to one, totalitarianism inevitably ensues.[150] As early as the fourteenth century, William of Occam was denying creational balance between the one and the many for the ordering of human life in society.[151] By excluding relationship to God within His creational orders, mankind was left with a sort of individualism that required collectivism.[152] Thus, modernism tended to suppress the particular (or the many).[153] This has led to our present malaise of soul-less homogeneity in Western

---

[144] Ibid., 22.
[145] Ibid., 22-23.
[146] Cyril of Alexandria, *Dialogue on the Trinity* III in Migne, P.G. 75.837.
[147] Colin Gunton, *The One, the Three and the Many* (Oxford: Clarendon Press, 1993).
[148] Ibid., 31.
[149] Ibid., 35,38.
[150] Ibid., 49.
[151] Ibid., 56,57.
[152] Ibid., 64.
[153] Ibid., 70, 71, 74.

consumer society.[154] Out of this 'knee-jerk' homogeneity has come the late twentieth-century 'Political Correctness' movement, which – not unlike the medieval Spanish Inquisition – sternly forbids, and frequently punishes, the expression of an alternative point of view to the reigning secularist, pluralistic orthodoxy of jaded Western society.

In displacing the true one and the many – the Triune God – modern society has 'liberated' society from Christianity into a depressing bondage of the shifting consensus of the secularist elite, who control to some degree the Western media. This is a bondage to the one, which brooks no rivals. In displacing the reality of God and eternity, it has focused all attention and all hopes on our brief life in this world. It has led to the widespread belief in the omnicompetence of politics,[155] which has produced massive intolerance by those who preach tolerance, or – in effect – a selective tolerance.[156]

Gunton shows that there is no way out of this horrid morass except a return to faith and obedience in the Holy Trinity: the One and the Many, whose presence and Word gives a fruitful and wholesome balance between liberty (of the many) and ordered structure (of the one moral reality).

From a rather different cultural and political point of view, though with some important theological commonalities, R. J. Rushdoony several years earlier had also seen the Trinity as the answer to the inescapable answer to the one and many problem that always confronts all humans. In his study, *The One and the Many*, he writes:

> Since both the one and the many are equally ultimate in God, it immediately becomes apparent that these two seemingly contradictory aspects of being do not cancel one another but are equally basic to the ontological trinity, one God, three persons. Again, since temporal unity and plurality are the products and creation of this triune God, neither the unity nor the plurality can demand the sacrifice of the other to itself. Thus, man and government are equally aspects of created reality. The locus of Christianity is both the believer and the church; they are not independent of or prior to one another. The wishes of husband and wife do not take priority over marriage, nor does the institution of marriage have primacy over the partners to it; marriage indeed is a type of eternal reality (Eph. 5:22), but man is himself created in the image of God (Gen. 1:26, 27). Education must be geared both to the individual and to society, but, above all, to God.[157]

Rushdoony explains the details of what this balance means in practical terms:

> In orthodox Trinitarian Christianity, the problem of the one and the many is resolved. Unity and plurality are equally ultimate in the Godhead. The temporal unity and plurality is on a basis of equal validity. There is thus no basic conflict between individual and community. The individual lives in community, and the community flourishes as the individual finds himself and grows in terms of consistently Christian faith. Instead of a basic philosophical hostility between government, believer and church, person

[154] Ibid., 101.
[155] Ibid., 73.
[156] Ibid., 105.
[157] R. J. Rushdoony, *The One and the Many* (Craig Press, n. p., 1971), 10.

> and family, there is a necessary coexistence. Neither the one nor the many is reducible to the other. They cannot seek the obliteration of the other, for it involves self-obliteration. The Augustinian and Calvinistic faith, with its hostility to subordinationism, holds, if developed, the possibilities for true social order, and to the extent that Augustinianism and Calvinism have been followed, Western culture has developed both freedom and order.[158]

Elsewhere, Rushdoony suggests some of the products of this kind of Trinitarian balance between the one and the many as: parliaments, universities and constitutions.[159] In his *The Nature of the American System*, he traces the constitutional balance between structure (the one) and local and personal liberties (the many) that took deep root in the American colonies back to the faith of most of the founding fathers in the Holy Trinity. He argues with considerable persuasiveness that insofar as faith in the Trinity is eclipsed in society, an imbalance towards the one (eventually resulting in various forms of political totalitarianism) is bound to follow.

Although not of the same theological persuasion in various respects, Colin Gunton's assessment of our contemporary dilemma is not essentially different – at least as to the origin of our current problem: formerly, perhaps, totalitarian Marxism in the East, but now a sort of soulless consumerist materialism (as equally hostile to the reality of the Holy Trinity as were the communists) – which is equally destructive of God-given human values – in the West, as Del Noce has shown us.[160]

A return to living faith in and cordial obedience to the Holy Trinity is the only hope for our sick society of both East and West. The high mission of God's Church is to point the way to restoration for every nation and culture; not as its main goal (which is always the glorification of God in the eternal salvation and sanctification of sinners into the body of Christ), but as a fruitful by-product or perhaps a certain temporal foretaste of a future cosmic renewal (which is not unrelated to final manifestation of 'the glorious liberty of the children of God' – Rom. 8:21). But until that great breaking of eternity into time, many different periods of history in many different cultures have shown that God-centered lives tend towards mercy and justice, beauty and truth. Thus, when large minorities (even when far less than a majority) in a land are 'walking in the Spirit', reformed and healthy societies (imperfect as they always are before the final 'manifestation of the sons of God') follow, as the day follows the night.

Of course, restoration within human cultures over the centuries of Christian influence has its ebbs and flows. But even when the tide of vital faith and godly practice seems to be at a low point in some nations, it may be rapidly rising in others (as seems to be the case today with the declining Western world, which has largely jettisoned its Christian belief – and is losing population – and the rising Christian spirituality in the African, Asian and Southern American spheres – which are growing in population). Yet through all these varied conditions which are constantly changing from

[158] Ibid., 16.

[159] Rushdoony, *Notes on World History*, (Vallecito, CA: Ross House Books, 1974), 170.

[160] See Chapter Three.

time to time and land to land, one majestic reality overarches them all, and makes life worth living in any of them at any time. It is a glorious reality open to all who wish it: the communion of holy love that constitutes the very life of the Triune God is available to those who recognize that they are unworthy and cannot save themselves from sin and death, and are willing to cry out to God for mercy. In a word, eternal life, lasting pardon and true liberation from the Father, through the Son and in the Spirit are gifts of the gospel that may still be received by simple faith.

Isaiah says that living waters can be purchased 'without money and without price' (Isa. 55:1). The Puritan biblical commentator, Matthew Henry, beautifully expounds this free invitation to those who can offer nothing in return:

> ... Though we be never so miserable and empty – empty of knowledge, empty of grace (*tohu and wohu*, Gen. 1:2 [i.e. transliterations of two Hebrew words – 'without form and void']) yet we have received from Christ, without money and without price (Isa. 55:1). The poor and the maimed are fetched in to the feast. Former barrenness and badness is no bar to this grace if we be truly penitent and come for grace. Poor and blind and naked are invited to Christ (Rev. 3:17, 18). Paul that had been a blasphemer yet received this grace. There's gifts received even for the rebellious (Ps. 68:18).[161]

Jesus says in the Gospel of John: 'And ye now therefore have sorrow; but I will see you again, and your heart shall rejoice, and your joy no man taketh from you. And in that day ye shall ask me nothing. Verily, verily, I say unto you, Whatsoever ye shall ask the Father in my name, he will give it you. Hitherto have ye asked nothing in my name ask, and ye shall receive, that your joy may be full' (John 16:22-24).

And above a changing world, the unchanging promise of our Lord still stands: 'For God so loved the world, that he gave his only begotten Son, that whosoever believeth in him should not perish, but have everlasting life. For God sent not his Son into the world to condemn the world; but that the world through him might be saved' (John 3:16,17).

---

[161] Matthew Henry's *Unpublished Sermons on The Covenant of Grace*, edited by Allan Harman (Tain, Great Britain: Christian Focus, 2002), 142,143.

Chapter Nine
Appendix One

On the Filioque

The Filioque ('and from the Son') controversy between the Eastern and Western branches of the Catholic Church has lasted from at least the fifth century down to the present. It concerns an addition to the Nicene-Constantinopolitan Creed (381) of the term 'filioque', by the West, specifying that the Holy Spirit proceeds 'from the Father *and the Son*' (*Filioque*). The Western branch of the Church added this phrase without having called an ecumenical council, and then sought to impose it upon the East. The difficulties and resentment caused by this non-ecumenical imposition have never ceased.

This addition came out of the context of the Arian and (later) Nestorian controversies. Orthodox Fathers of East and West reacted to the Arian and Nestorian heresies differently. Both wished equally to safeguard a sound doctrine of the Holy Trinity, but in a sense they reacted to somewhat different problems, and thus their solutions to the difficulties raised by these heresies 'went past' one another. T. F. Torrance has summarized accurately, I believe, the different concerns articulated by equally sound theologians in East and West. First, he explains the concern of the East:

> There were understandable reasons for the original divergence of the East and West on this issue. It was supremely important for the Eastern Church to insist upon the procession of the Spirit from the Father, the one Source (*arche*) and Fount (*pege*) of the Godhead and to avoid a procession from the Son, in view of the assertions of the Arians, Macedonians and Tropici, that the Spirit was a creature of the Son since he came into being through his mediation.[1]

Then he explains the concern of the West:

> For the Western Church, however, it was of the utmost importance to insist that the Spirit was truly the Spirit of the Son as of the Father, for unless the Father and the Son were held to be fully equal the doctrine of the *homoousion* could hardly be maintained... The *filioque* clause in the West had been intended to make clear the Lordship of the Spirit and the propriety of the Spirit to the Son, that is, the transcendent presence of God over the whole of his creation whereby he governs and disposes all things...[2]

[1]T. F. Torrance, *Theology in Reconstruction*, 229.
[2]Ibid.

We must first survey (a) the basic history of this issue; then (b) consider its theological aspects, and finally (c) see how it is being dealt with today.

(a) History of the Filioque Controversy

Bobrinskoy lists the early steps:

> It is in Spain that the *Filioque* appears for the first time in the fifth century, first in the liturgy at Toledo (446-447), and then, in 589, at the Third Council of Toledo, marked by the conversion of King Recared from Arianism to Orthodoxy. This event led to the unification of Visigothic Spain. In his profession of faith, Recared says that 'The Spirit proceeds from the Father and the Son.' The intention is anti-Arian, through this very strong affirmation of the divine Unity. This same council ordered the Symbol of Nicea (the Nicene Creed) to be changed during the liturgy – a new custom in the West. Undoubtedly, this newly chanted Creed included the addition of the *Filioque*. Thus, everyone believed that the Creed in its interpolated form was the original text, because the custom of chanting it before the *Filioque* had been added to it was unknown. But for a long time still, the Roman liturgy did not observe the addition of the Nicene-Constantinopolitan Symbol of Faith.[3]

This addition was used against the authority of the Eastern Church during the Carolingian Reign in order to bolster the authority of Charlemagne in the Western portion of the Roman Empire over against the government of the Empress Irene, so that he could claim sole leadership of the whole empire. The *Libri Carolini* (787) accused the Patriarch of Constantinople (Tarasius) 'of not being orthodox, because he does not say, according to the teaching of the Council of Nicaea: the Spirit who proceeds from the Father and the Son, but: through the Son.'[4] In 809, under the authority of Charlemagne (and his theologian, Alcuin of York), a Council was held at Aachen, which inserted the *Filioque* into the Creed. Pope Leo III declared that the *Filioque* was orthodox, but refused to add it to the Creed.

During this Carolingian period, an internal struggle was being waged within what we now call Western or Latin Christianity. This long struggle for control of empire and Church was between the Germanic Franks and the traditional 'Romans.' The Franks wished to distance themselves from the authority of the Eastern Roman emperor in Constantinople in order to establish their own feudal power, and to do so, sought to move the Church and papacy away from close fellowship with the East. John Romanides speaks of this split as 'a schism between Franks and Romans' (rather than between a Greek East and a Latin West).[5] He adds: 'The schism between Eastern and Western Christianity was not between East and West Romans. In actuality, it was a split between East Romans and the conquerors of the West Romans [*sc*. the Franks].'[6]

---

[3]Boris Bobrinskoy, *The Mystery of the Trinity: Trinitarian Experience and Vision in the Biblical and Patristic Traddition*, translated by Anthony P. Gythiel (Crestwood, New York: St. Vladimir's Seminary Press, 1999), 279.

[4]Ibid., 279,280.

[5]John S. Romanides, 'Franks, Romans, Feudalism, and Doctrine: An Interplay between Theology and Society' (first published in *Kleronomia*, 7 (1975), 285-334), p. 2.

[6]Ibid.

The Franks wished to distance the Church in their territory from the four patriarchies in the East in order to increase their control of 'old Rome.' The Franks began to speak of the Eastern part of the Empire as *Graecia*, and represented it as theologically different and unsound (for political reasons).[7] It was in the general context of this policy (of distancing the West from the East) that Charlemagne 'caused the Filioque to be added to the Frankish Creed, without consulting the pope.'[8] He then 'tried to pressure Pope Leo III into accepting it.'[9]

Richard Haugh devotes a chapter of his book to 'The Frankish Envoys and Pope Leo III.'[10] At this time, the papacy was not yet under the control of the Franks and their theologians (such as Alcuin, Ratramnus and Theodulphe of Orleans), and continued faithful to the ancient Creed, which did not include *Filioque*. Hence, Pope Leo 'considered the problem so serious that he had two silver shields engraved with the original Nicene-Constantinopolitan Creed in both Greek and Latin and then placed on each side of the Confession of St. Peter.'[11]

Some fifty years later, the Eastern Patriarch, Photius (810–895) and the Pope of Rome, Nicholas I, for various reasons (in large part political – concerning influence in Bulgaria; a disputed jurisdiction between East and West) entered into controversy over the *Filioque*.[12] Missionaries of Nicholas I imposed it upon Bulgaria, and in reaction, Photius denounced Nicholas to be promoting a heresy. Finally, the Council of Constantinople of 879 excluded the addition to the Creed of *Filioque*.

But as for 'the West,' the Franks eventually prevailed over what Romanides calls 'the West Romans' for control of Church and papacy. After this change, Pope Benedict VIII (1012–1024) inserted the *Filioque* into the Creed, 'but it was only at the Council of Lyons (1274) that this doctrine assumed dogmatic status among the Latins and was accompanied by anathematisms against its detractors. But upon the return to Constantinople of the Eastern delegates to the Council of Lyons, their approval of the *Filioque* was revoked.'[13]

The Council of Lyons had been stacked against the theologians of the East, before it even began, as Papadakis shows in careful detail.[14] It allowed no fair discussion of the issue of *Filioque*, but rather imposed it by force on the few Eastern delegates. 'It had been agreed upon long *before* the Byzantines had even set foot on French soil. The Greeks' "error" had been condemned without their approval or presence.'[15]

Patriarch of Constantinople, Gregory II of Cyprus (1283–1289), almost single-handedly led the Eastern Church back to its traditional position,

---

[7]Ibid., 6,7.
[8]Ibid., 6.
[9]Ibid.
[10]Richard Haugh, op. cit., chapter vi, 79-90.
[11]Ibid., 89.
[12]See Bobrinskoy, op. cit., 280, 281.
[13]Ibid., 281.
[14]A. Papadakis, op. cit., Chapter 1 (15-35).
[15]Ibid., 19.

especially by means of the Council of Blachernae and its explanatory *Tomus* (1285).[16] According to Papadakis: '… Blachernae may well be the most important contribution of the Byzantine Church to the *Filioque* controversy… It was then that the Byzantine Church, by endorsing Gregory's formula of the eternal manifestation of the Spirit by the Son, supplied the doctrine of the procession with that "conceptual clarity" which it had hitherto lacked.'[17]

That is to say, Gregory led the way in distinguishing procession and manifestation, essence and energy.[18] Instead of resting 'solely [in] Photius' exclusive formulation "from the Father alone",' Gregory's 'solution was to resolve the impasse in terms of an eternal manifestation (ἐκφανσις ἀίδιος) of the Spirit through the Son.'[19] Procession refers to God's incomprehensible essence, whereas manifestation refers to His energies by which He makes Himself known to the world. In the procession, Gregory (following Photius) holds that the Spirit proceeds from the Father, but in the manifestation, He is eternally manifested by the Son. Gregory then, deals with the relationship of the Son to the Spirit, and thereby fills in 'the blank' that had been left by Photius concerning this relationship.

> In trinitarian theology, therefore, two distinct realities are involved. If one level of reality denotes the *internal* life and nature of the Trinity itself – its self-existence – the other denotes the *external* life or self-revelation of God Himself, as it reveals perpetually the glory and 'splendour' that is common to the trinity of persons in the Godhead. (For every externalization in the order of the manifestation of the divine life includes the three – the Father, the Son, and the Holy Spirit.) God, in short, exists not only in His essence but outside His essence. But, since this antinomy is, in truth, a distinction within God's very being (both the manifestation and the timeless procession are *eternal*), the divine manifestation, as such, is neither alien nor 'without' God.[20]

As we have noted elsewhere (Chapter 4, Appendix I), the *Tomus* of Gregory of Cyprus summarizing the Council of Blachernae (1285) prepared the way for Gregory Palamas by clarifying the crucial distinction between essence and energy in God. On that basis, he would resist the Western doctrine of *Filioque* that was forced upon the East for a time, once again at the Council of Florence (1438-39).

> In the fourteenth century, negotiations for Union were conducted, and St Gregory Palamas wrote his two *Apodictic Treatises on the Procession of the Holy Spirit from the Father Alone*. At the council of Union of Florence (Ferrara-Florence, 1438-1439), Byzantium, with Ottoman pressure at its back, accepted the Western concept, at least verbally. After the rejection of the Union by the East, all dialogue ceased for centuries, until this time of contemporary negotiations and research.[21]

---

[16]See Papadakis, op. cit., Chapter 4 (83-105).
[17]Ibid., 10.
[18]Ibid., 49.
[19]Ibid.
[20]Ibid., 124.
[21]Bobrinskoy, op. cit., 281, 282.

(b) Theological Aspects of the Filioque

Apart from the powerful ninth and tenth-century Carolingian political interests, the underlying *theological* concern of the West seems to have been to maintain the full equality amongst the three Persons of the Holy Trinity, and to eliminate any possibility of subordinating the Persons of the Son and the Holy Spirit to the Person of the Father. That ultimately lies behind their willingness to add in the *Filioque*. In this they followed St. Augustine. They appear to have been reacting against the teachings of Gregory of Nyssa and Basil, which sought to anchor the unity of the Godhead in the *Person* of the Father, rather than in the *Being* of the Father. This implied to them a serious distinction between the deity of the Father and the deity of the Son and the Spirit, as though that of the latter two were definitely subordinate.

Cappadocian concept of 'cause' within the Trinity

In his *Theological Dialogue Between Orthodox & Reformed Churches*, Thomas F. Torrance has pinpointed this issue raised by two of the Cappadocians that may lie behind the *Filioque* reaction of the West:

> [The Cappadocians' use of *aitia* or 'cause'] was '... at the expense of a distinction between the Deity of the Father as wholly underived 'uncaused' Deity and the Deity of the Son and of the Spirit as eternally "caused" or derived. At the same time, this led to the tendency to identify "Father" = the Godhead with "Father" = the Person of the Father. It was, in my view, this Cappadocian distinction that provided the ground for the problem of the understanding of the procession of the Spirit when East and West split over the notorious '*filioque*' clause added by the West ... without the authority of an Ecumenical Council, and the Greeks responded by insisting on the procession of the Spirit from "the Father *only*" which implied "from the *Person* of the Father."... But if the Spirit does not proceed from the Son as well as the Father, then for the West, that would import a damage to belief in the unqualified Deity of the Son.'[22]

Eastern fear of 'two principles' within the Trinity

The major theological criticism of the *Filioque* by the East has been the claim that it introduces two principles or causes of the Spirit into the Trinity. Or to say it another way, the East holds that this Western clause makes not only the Father, but also the Son a source or cause of the Holy Spirit. Photius (810–885), Patriarch of Constantinople, wrote extensively against the *Filioque*, especially *The Mystagogy of the Holy Spirit*,[23] *Encyclical Letters* 2 and 15, and *Letter to the Patriarch of Aquilae*.

Photius argues that if there existed two causes or principles within the Divinity, it would destroy the unity of God's Being. Father Justin Popovitch summarizes the position of Photius against the *Filioque*:

> The Roman Catholic *Filioque* introduces into the Divinity a double principle, a dy-archy, and thus ruins the unity of the Divinity, the mon-archy. The

---

[22]T. F. Torrance, *Theological Dialogue Between Orthodox & Reformed Churches* (Edinburgh and London: Scottish Academic Press, 1985), 16.

[23]See Migne, *Patrologia Graeca* 102. 279-392.

> dyarchy makes the mon-archy impossible. By this teaching on the Filioque the hypostatic properties of the divine Persons are ruined; a dangerous and heretical subordination is thereby introduced among the totally holy Persons…[24]

However, some four centuries before Photius, Augustine had sought to make clear that he understood there to be only one *principle of origin* within the Godhead for the Holy Spirit, even while he confessed that the Spirit proceeds from the Father and the Son. In *De Trinitate*, he wrote:

> … in this trinity we call none Word of God but the Son, none Gift of God but the Holy Spirit, one of whom the Word is begotten and from whom the Holy Spirit originally proceeds, but God the Father. I add the word 'originally', because we learn that the Holy Spirit proceeds also from the Son. But this is part of what is given by the Father to the Son, not as already existing without it, but given to him as all that the Father gives to his only-begotten Word, in the act of begetting. He is begotten in such a manner that the common gift proceeds from him also, and the Holy Spirit is the Spirit of both.[25]

Western Councils deny 'two principles'

Centuries later, Western Councils specifically denied that the procession of the Spirit from the Father and the Son meant that He was from 'two principles'. The Council of Lyons (1274)[26] and the Council of Florence (1438–39)[27] both affirmed that the Spirit was from only one principle (although both Councils treated the East unfairly).

But as we have seen above in Popovitch's summation of Photius, this would not have been satisfactory to most of the East, for they considered any sort of *Filioque* to be a derogation from the monarchy of the Father. Photius wrote:

> If the Spirit who proceeds from the Father proceeds also from the Son, what reasoning will stand in the way of striking a blow at the immutability of the hypostatic properties? Indeed, the name of 'Father' … would be deprived of meaning, an empty word: the property which characterizes Him would no longer be His exclusively, and two divine Hypostases would be contracted, coalesced in one Person. And thus, Sabellius emerges again for us, or rather, some Semi-Sabellian monster.[28]

T. F. Torrance seeks to get behind the problem

In our own generation, T. F. Torrance has sought to cut behind the impasse between East and West on this issue of the monarchy of the Father, which – more than any other matter – divides Greek and Latin (and Protestant) Christians. In the train of Gregory of Nazianzus, Torrance suggests that the whole Trinity, and not just the Person of the Father, is the source of the Holy Spirit. That is, the monarchy resides not just in the Father, but in the whole Trinity. He quotes Gregory Nazianzus to this effect:

---

[24]Popovitch, op. cit., vol. I, 238.

[25]Augustine, *De Trinitate* 15. 26. 47.

[26]See Denzinger, *Enchiridion Symbolorum* (Barcinone: Herder, 1965), 850.

[27]Ibid., 1300.

[28]Photius, *De S. Spiritus Mystagogia* (P.G. m102. 289B), quoted in Bobrinskoy, op. cit., 287.

> To us there is One God, and One Godhead, and all that issues from him is referred back to him so as to be One with him, although we believe that there are Three. And One is not more and another less God, nor is One before and after another ... But differentiated as the Persons are, the entire and undivided Godhead is One in each Person, and there is one mingling of light, as it were of three suns joined to each other.[29]

Torrance then comments:

> Thus the fullness of the one Godhead applies to each of the three divine Persons as well as to all of them together... The incommunicable properties distinguishing them do not divide them from one another, but on the contrary integrate them in their subsequent reciprocal relations. The whole Being of God belongs to each Person as it belongs to all three Persons, and so the Unity of God, utterly simple though it is, is to be understood, not in an abstract generic way, not as an undifferentiated oneness, but as the indivisible consubstantial Communion of the Father, the Son and the Holy Spirit.[30]

The need to rethink the concept of cause within the Trinity

In the dialogue that he led between Greek and Reformed theologians (1979, 1981, 1983), Torrance stated:

> I had in mind fundamental theological dialogue beginning with the doctrine of the Holy Trinity in which discussion would centre upon the teaching of Athanasius and Cyril rather than upon the Cappadocians, who seemed to have occupied the main attention of Orthodox theologians in recent years, for in that way I believed we could cut behind certain disagreements between Eastern and Western theology, not least relating to the *filioque* clause of the Western Creed.[31]

Some Eastern Fathers do not use 'cause' within the Trinity

Torrance is correct, I believe, in stating that the concept of *cause* should not be brought into the relations within the Holy Trinity:

> It seemed clear that more attention would have to be given to the problems that gave rise to the *filioque* clause in the Western Creed, but that these should be appropriated through closer attention to the teaching of Athanasius and Cyril of Alexandria with their insistence that everything we say of the Father we must say of the Son except 'Father', and that notions of causality should not be introduced into our understanding of inner-Trinitarian relations ...[32]

Torrance goes specifically to the heart of the problem:

> The basic question I would set down for this discussion would be whether there is not a far-reaching difference between the teaching of Athanasius and Cyril on the one hand and that of the Cappadocians on the other hand. The problem is sharpest at the point where the Cappadocians speak of God the Father unreservedly in terms of *aitia* [cause], *pege* [source] and *arche* [source

---

[29]Gergory of Nazianzus, *Oration* 31.14.
[30]T. F. Torrance, *Trinitarian Perspectives*, 73,74.
[31]T. F. Torrance, ed., *Theological Dialogue Between Orthodox & Reformed Churches*, xi.
[32]Ibid., xxvi.

> or principle], but not of the Son or of the Spirit, whereas Athanasius' great principle ran that we say of the Son everything we say of the Father, except 'Father'.... The danger of the Cappadocian position was pointed out by Cyril of Alexandria in protesting against the use of aitia in intra-Trinitarian relations... It was, in my view, this Cappadocian distinction that provided the grounds for the problem of the understanding of the procession of the Spirit when East and West split over the notorious '*filioque*' clause...[33]

Professor Torrance believes that the way forward to resolving the *filioque* controversy lies in a return to the theology of the *Eastern* theologians, Athanasius and Gregory Nazianzus. In this regard, he refers to the five Theological Orations of Gregory Nazianzus in A.D. 380, which rely heavily upon Athanasius.

> The general Cappadocian view, however, seemed to import a modification of Athanasius' position in a way that clearly made Gregory Nazianzen uneasy. This seemed to imply a partial return to the Origenist notion that the Godhead is complete primarily in the Father alone, but mediately in the Son and the Spirit through their origination from the Father, against which Athanasius had insisted on the perfect equality of the Father, Son and Holy Spirit, in each of whom the Godhead is complete...What worried Gregory Nazianzen was the combination of the terms *arche* and *aitia* in speaking of the 'origin' of the Son, for it appeared to import 'superiority' and 'inferiority' in the Trinity (*Oratio* 40.41, 43) which conflicted with his own basic convictions (*Oratio* 21.10; 31 (5), 14; 40.41,43; 42.15f.; 43.30)... It is highly significant that when Cyril of Alexandria turned back to the teaching of Athanasius, rejecting like him all idea of a hierarchy in God, while accepting the Cappadocian formula, *mia ousia, treis hypostaseis*, he eliminated the ambiguity that had arisen, by rejecting the notion of causal relations within the Trinity as quite unbiblical (*Thesaurus*, MPG 75, 125, 128, 144f; *Dialogus* II, MPG 75, 744f; cf. 721 and 769; *Comm. On John* 14, 28). It is 'only economically' (*oikonomikos*) that we may speak of the Father as 'greater' than the Son (*Thesaurus*, MPG 75, 144). Here we have the full orthodox doctrine of the *Holy Trinity in one Godhead. One God in three Persons*, in which the Persons are understood as wholly coinhering in one another, as completely coequal and coeternal as well as consubstantial, with one authority, glory, power, will, activity and goodness, and who as such are *one arche*, as Athanasius had claimed (*Ad Antiochenos*, 5). This was wholly consistent with the statement of Gregory Nazianzen, 'When I say *God*, I mean Father, Son and Holy Spirit' (*Oratio* 38.8; 45.4)...[34]

The whole Trinity, rather than the Person of the Father, is the source of Trinity

This means that the whole Trinity, not just the Person of the Father, is the source of the Trinity:

> There cannot, of course, be two or three Sources or Origins any more than there can be two or three Fathers or Supreme Beings. The Father, the Son and the Holy Spirit are indivisibly One, eternally coinhering in one another as the Blessed and Holy Trinity, but with 'one Godhead and one Principle

[33] Ibid., 16.

[34] Ibid., 88,89.

> (μία θεότης καὶ Μία ἀρχή) (Athanasius, *Ad Ant.*, 5.6-11; *Con. Ar.*, 2.33; 3.1f, 15; *Ad Afr.*, 11, *In ill. om.* 5; *Exp. Fidei*, 11f; *In ill. Om.*, 6). That is to say, it is the *triune God*, the undivided Trinity, who is the one only ultimate Principle or (ἀρχή) of all things. Expressed otherwise, the one being of God is whole and complete not in the Father alone but in the Son and in the Holy Spirit as much as in the Godhead. Each is the whole God (ὅλος θεός) and wholly all that God eternally is as God (Athanasius, *De decr.*, 16ff., 22f; *Ad epis.*, 17f; *Con. Ar.*, 1.16-28; 2.33; 3.1ff; *Ad Afr.*, 4f; cf. also *Exp. Fidei*, 1f.; *In ill. Om.*, 6).[35]
>
> Or, to say it (with Epiphanius) another way: There is no suggestion of any subordinationism in God, for whatever the Father is, this the Son is and this the Spirit is in the Godhead. Their being of the Father and with the Father is beyond beginning and beyond time ἀνάρχως καὶ ἀχρόνως – there is no 'before' or 'after' in God (Epiphanius, *Anc.*, 46; *Haer.*, 57.4; 62.3; 69.36; 70.8; 73.36; 74.1; 76.6, 21. Cf., his reference to the Son and the Spirit as the one ultimate source, πηγὴ ἐκ πηγῆς, with the Father, *Haer.* 69.54).[36]

Any binding Christian theology reposes directly upon biblical evidence. The difficulty here in the age-old controversy between East and West is that the biblical evidence is neither voluminous nor luminously clear. Perhaps this relative lack of clear biblical evidence explains why Sergius Bulgakov followed Bolotov in considering the *Filioque* not to have the strength of dogma, but rather belonging 'in the realm of theology, of opinion, of *theologoumena*.'[37] And long before, Maximus the Confessor (580–662) had sought to explain to his Eastern colleagues the *Filioque* in an acceptable sense:

> The Westerners cited the constant testimonies of the Latin Fathers, as well as of Cyril of Alexandria in his commentary on the Gospel of St John. They showed thereby that they did not view the Son as cause of the Spirit, for they knew that the Father alone is the cause of the Son and of the Holy Spirit, but they showed that the Spirit proceeds through the Son, and thereby showed the conjunction of their nature, which is in no way different."[38]

Yet there is some biblical evidence, controverted though it is. John 15:26 says: 'But when the Comforter is come, whom I shall send unto you from the Father, even the Spirit of truth, which proceedeth from the Father, he shall testify of me…' Generally, the East rightly points out that this verse is in the context of the historico-redemptive missions of the Trinity. Thus, they state that it does not directly refer to the intra-Trinitarian relationships, but to those in 'the economy' of redemption.

Photius, for example, in response to the Carolingian theologians of his time, who used such verses to prove that the Spirit proceeded from the Son as well as the Father, countered that to state that the Spirit is the 'Spirit of the Son' does not mean that He proceeds from the Son:

---

[35] T. F. Torrance, *The Trinitarian Faith*, 80.

[36] Ibid., 222.

[37] Sergius Bulgakov, *Le Paraclet* (Paris: Aubier, 1946), 87, cited in Bobrinskoy, op. cit., 292.

[38] Maximus the Confessor, *Epistola ad Marinum*, PG 91.136AB, cited in Bobrinskoy, op. cit., 285.

> Paul … said the Spirit was sent by the Father. Say the same thing Paul said! For he is the Spirit of the Son … He did not say he proceeds from the Son… But if they think that because he is called the Spirit of the Son, he therefore proceeds [from the Son], then they will also teach that the Father proceeds from the Son, for the Father is everywhere called [the Father] of the Son.[39]

In a literal sense this is true, but if Karl Rahner is right that 'the economical Trinity is the ontological Trinity', then the historical missions must necessarily refer to the intra-Trinitarian relationships.[40] Such verses do not constitute final proof (since so much is determined by the presuppositions or framework with which one interprets them), but they can be seen as a strong indication that Father and Son are together in the procession of the Holy Spirit from within the inner being of God.

Interpretation of John 15:26 in this sense would be consistent with the 'Commentary: Agreed Statement on the Holy Trinity', which is the outcome of T. F. Torrance's *Theological Dialogue between Orthodox and Reformed Churches* (1993). This statement was the result of several years of dialogue between Reformed and Pan-Orthodox Christians. The 'Agreed Statement' was edited after a session in Geneva in 1991. The 'Commentary on the Agreed Statement' concludes by making the significant point that what God is in His missions to us, He is ontologically and eternally in Himself:

> Thus in the doctrine of the Holy Trinity we confess with the One, Holy, Catholic and Apostolic Church, that what God is toward us as Father, Son and Holy Spirit in his revealing and saving activity among us in salvation-history he is eternally in his One Being, and that what God is eternally in his One Being as Father, Son and Holy Spirit he is toward us in his revealing and saving activity.[41]

Other New Testament passages speak of 'the Spirit of Christ'(Rom. 8:9; Phil. 1:19; 1 Pet. 1:11, etc.) or 'the Spirit of his Son' (Gal. 4:6), as well as 'the Spirit of God' (e.g. Matt. 3:16; Luke 4:18; Acts 5:9; etc.) and 'the Spirit of your Father' (Matt. 10:20). But these do not definitively prove the point one way or the other.

Athanasius is eminently fair to the biblical evidence when he writes that 'The Holy Spirit proceeds from the Father and belonging to the Son is from him given to the disciples and all who believe on him;'[42] and 'The Spirit receives from the Son.'[43] He also says: 'If the Son is of the Father and is proper to his being, the Spirit who is said to be of God must also be proper to the Son in respect of his being.'[44] 'Because the Spirit is one and, what is more, is proper to the Word who is one, he is proper to God who is one and ὁμοούσιος with him… In nature and being he is proper to and not foreign to the Godhead and being of the Son and is thus of the Holy Trinity.'[45]

---

[39]Richard Haugh, op. cit., 135..

[40]Karl Rahner shows how a disconnection between the 'missions' and the intra-divine Life would be destructive of who God is, The Trinity, 39.

[41]T. F. Torrance, *Trinitarian Perspectives*, 142, 143.

[42]Athanasius, *Ad Serapionem*, 1.2.

[43]Ibid., 1.20.

[44]Ibid., 1.25.

[45]Ibid., 1.27.

Epiphanius called the Holy Spirit as being 'in the middle of the Father and the Son' and 'the bond of the Trinity'.[46] He writes: 'The Holy Spirit is ever with the Father and the Son, proceeding from the Father and receiving from the Son.'[47] He understood the Holy Spirit to proceed as Light and Truth from both the Father and the Son.[48] Like Didymus the Blind, he spoke of the procession of the Spirit from both Son and Father, but without any thought of two principles. On the contrary, Didymus makes clear that procession through the Son is in the context of perichoresis: that is, the inherence of the Spirit in the Son and their community of nature with the Father.[49]

Cyril of Jerusalem taught similarly:

> The Holy Spirit is ever one and the same, living and personally subsisting and always present together with the Father and the Son – not as if uttered like breath from the mouth and lips of the Father and the Son, only to be dispersed into the air – but as enhypostatic being, speaking and operating, dispensing and fulfilling the saving economy which comes to us from the Father, the Son and the Holy Spirit, and is indivisible, harmonious and one.[50]

Cyril of Alexandria in much the same way, stated that 'The Holy Spirit proceeds from the Father and the Son, for he belongs to the divine Being and inheres in it and issues from it substantially.'[51] Cyril believed that it is appropriate to think in this manner, for 'the Father has nothing of himself that the Son does not have of himself.'[52]

(c) How the Filioque is being dealt with today

Bobrinskoy

Boris Bobrinskoy writes that 'Modern Orthodox theology is divided between three main tendencies.'[53] These are (a) 'the rigid and absolute traditionalism of the schools' (as in nineteenth and twentieth-century manuals of dogmatic theology), largely based on Photius, who saw *filioque* as heretical;[54] (b) 'Those who give the *Filioque* a limited and relative value', such as the Russian church historian, B. Bolotov,[55] and (c) Those such as Vladimir Lossky, John Meyerdorff, Paul Evdokimov, Dumitru Stăniloae and other distinguished Eastern Orthodox theologians, who seek a more careful working out of issues raised by *Filioque* into the concepts of Gregory Palamas of eternal Trinitarian 'manifestations'.[56] The interested reader is referred to Bobrinskoy for the significant details of these three positions.

---

[46]Epiphanius, *Anc.* 4.7f; *Haer.* 62.4.

[47]Epiphanius, *Anc.* 6.

[48]Epiphanius, *Haer.* 62.4; 73.12, 16; 74.7f; 76.11.

[49]Didymus, *De Trin.*, 2.1; 2.2, 5; 2.26f; *De Sp. St.*, 26. See T. F. Torrance, *The Trinitarian Faith,* 243,244.

[50]Cyril of Jerusalem, *Catechetical Orations*, 17.5.

[51]Cyril of Alexandria, *Thesaurus de Trinitate*, PG 75, 577, 580, 585.

[52]Cyril of Alexandria, *De Trinitate*, 5.3.

[53]Bobrinskoy, op. cit., 291.

[54]Ibid.

[55]Ibid.

[56]Ibid., 292-95.

T. F. Torrance

We have already made considerable reference to the Eastern Orthodox and Reformed dialogues that have been on-going since the 1970s, under the guidance of Professor T. F. Torrance. In my view, these dialogues (and their resulting publications) are the most important steps forward in the *Filioque* controversy since the split between East and West in 1054. One may find the main points in two publications, edited or written by Torrance.[57] In another publication (though not a dialogue), Torrance had sought to address the *Filioque* problem at its roots in chapters 6 and 8 of his *Trinitarian Faith* (1988), where he deals with biblical and Patristic evidence to enable us to get behind the problem and potentially to surpass it.

It is not necessary here to give even an outline of these very important volumes, which may help Eastern and Western Churches eventually find their way through the difficult controversies surrounding *Filioque*, without either one giving away any of its most basic dogmatic beliefs. However, we may summarize in brief the approach of Torrance in the dialogical volumes.

The whole Trinity is the source of the Trinity

First, he believes that the whole Trinity must be considered the *arche* of the Son and the Spirit, rather than exclusively the Person of the Father. Thus he writes:

> The Father, the Son and the Holy Spirit are indivisibly One, eternally coinhering in one another as the Blessed and Holy Trinity, but with 'one Godhead and one Principle' (μία θεότης καὶ μία ἀρχή).[58] That is to say, it is the *triune* God, the undivided Trinity, who is the one only ultimate Principle or ἀρχή, of all things. Expressed otherwise, the one being of God is whole and complete not in the Father alone but in the Son and in the Holy Spirit as much as in the Godhead. Each is the whole God (ὅλος θεός) and wholly all that God eternally is as God.[59]

This means that the Son and the Spirit are from *the Being* of the Father, rather than from *the Person* of the Father. Torrance explains the significance of the difference in terms of the history of the Nicene Council:

> At first, when the Arians agreed to the formula that the Son is 'of God', as in 'Light from Light', the Nicene fathers insisted on defining the 'of God' or 'from God' as 'from the being of the Father' (ἐκ τῆς οὐσίας τοῦ Πατρός), thereby qualifying the analogies in the light of each other and of the objective relations within God to which they pointed beyond themselves. This meant that the Son is proper (ἴδιος) to the very being or substance of God, and is of God the Father, as creatures are not: he is *God of God*. But when the Arians and Eusebians, to their astonishment, seemed to agree to the phrase 'from the being of God' or 'from the being of the Father', they

[57] T. F. Torrance, *Theological Dialgoue Between Orthodox & Reformed Churches* (1985) and Torrance, *Trinitarian Perspectives: Toward Doctrinal Agreement* (1994).

[58] He refers to Athanasius, *Ad Ant.*, 5.6-11; *Con. Ar.* 2.33; 3.1f, 15; *Ad Afr.*, 11; *In Ill. Om.*, 5; *Exp. Fidei*, 1-4, in *Trinitarian Faith*, 80.

[59] He refers to Athanasius, *De decr.*, 16ff., 22f; *Ad epis.*, 17f; *Con. Ar.*, 1.16.28; 2.33; 3.1ff; Ad afr., 4f; cf. also *Exp. Fidei* 1f; *In ill.* om., 6, in *Trinitarian Faith*, 80.

> realized that they were going to interpret it in a sense in which it might be applied to human beings who are created not only as 'children of God' but 'in the image and glory of God'. The Council then decided to cut away all ambiguity and remove any possibility for misunderstanding by inserting the crucial expression 'of one being with the Father' (ὁμοούσιος τῷ Πατρί), which meant that the Son and the Father are equally God within the one being of God.[60]

Or in other terms, the Monarchy is referred not only to the Person of the Father, but to the entire Being of the Holy Trinity. That is how Torrance reads Athanasius:

> It is surely in this light also that we are to understand the *Tomus ad Antiochenos* in which Athanasius joined with others in acknowledging 'a Holy Trinity, but one Godhead, and one ἀρχη, and that the Son is of one being with the Father, while the Holy Spirit is proper to and inseparable from the being of the Father and the Son.'[61] While accepting the formulation of μία ὀυσία, τρέ ις ὑποστάσεις he had such a strong view of the complete identity, equality and unity of the three Persons within the Godhead, that he declined to advance a view of the Monarchy in which the oneness of God was defined by reference to the **Person** of the Father. While the Father was on occasion denoted as the αἴτιος and the ἀρχή of the Son that was meant to express the truth that the Father is Father of the Son and that the Son is Son of the Father, but not to withdraw anything from the complete equality of the Son with the Father, for the Sonship of the Son is as ultimate as the Fatherhood of the Father. 'The same things are said of the Son as are said of the Father, except his being said to be "Father".'[62]

In order to re-establish this profoundly biblical and orthodox understanding, Torrance suggests that the East move back in the direction of the theology of Athanasius, Gregory of Nazianzus, Cyril of Alexandria and Epiphanius, and away – at this point – from Basil and Gregory of Nyssa:

> We have to remember, as Hilary said, that revelation is not of the Father manifested as God, but of God manifested as Father.[63] This may well provide us with a further point of ecumenical convergence, as it might serve to cut out the false problematic which gave rise in different ways in East and West to the difficulties in respect of the procession of the Spirit: if we could agree that while the Son is from his Father, i.e. from God who is his Father, and say that the Holy Spirit proceeds not from God his Father but from God who is Father, then we might come closer together. For the Orthodox, however, that would mean accepting Cyril of Alexandria's rejection of the Cappadocian modification of the Athanasian doctrine of the Trinity, when in their determination to reject any tritheism that might be apparent in the formulation, 'one οὐσία, three ὑποστάσεις,' they spoke of a *causal* priority or superiority of the Father over the Son and the Spirit.[64]

---

[60]He refers to Athanasius, *De syn.*, 41 in *Trinitarian Faith*, 121, 122.
[61]He cites Athanasius, *Ad Ant.*, 5 in *Trinitarian Faith*, 312.
[62]He cites Athanasius, *Con. Ar.* 3.3f. in *Trinitarian Faith*, 312, 313.
[63]He cites Hilary, *De Trin.*, 3.22 in *Trinitarian Perspectives*, 82.
[64]T. F. Torrance, *Trinitarian Perspectives*, 82, 83.

The problematic Cappadocian distinction between the Being and energies of God

> ... the basic difficulty which ought not to have arisen comes from the Cappadocian distinction in the Trinity – which is, incidentally, allied at a second-order level to their distinction between the 'Being' of God and his 'Energies'. I would maintain that had the Greek Church remained steadfast to the Athanasian-Cyrilline basis, the whole problem, and the division that followed it, would probably not have risen: nor would the Greeks have lapsed into their characteristic Byzantine dualism. In other words, by returning to the impeccably Orthodox and non-dualist basis of Athanasius and Cyril we ought to be able to cut behind the schism between East and West over the *'filioque'*, and at the same time provide a deeper basis for the healing of the rift between Evangelical and Catholic wings of the Church, not to mention the rift between the Orthodox and the so-called 'Monophysite' Churches.[65]

More emphasis on Athanasius and Cyril than on Gregory of Nyssa and Basil

Professor Torrance's work in suggesting the rethinking of the Patristic tradition in a direction away from that of the Cappadocians (Gregory of Nyssa and Basil) and towards Athanasius and Cyril of Alexandria on the part of contemporary Eastern theologians is no simple task. For instance, even in the volume *Theological Dialogue Between Orthodox & Reformed Churches*, one of the dialogical partners, Metropolitan Emilianos Timiadis of Selybria, expresses problems with believing that '...if the Church had stayed with the Athanasian-Cyrillian Christological formula, no division would have been produced by the so-called pre-Chalcedonians, and the Byzantines would not have lapsed into their "dualism".'[66] Metropolitan Timiadis, however, expresses much respect for Professor Torrance's formulation concerning God's work in creation out of nothing, and his conferring upon the universe its contingent rationality.[67] It would appear that Archbishop Methodios (then of Thyateira and Great Britain) may have been in closer accord with Torrance's suggestion of a renewed emphasis on Athanasius and Cyril. But, at the best, much work remains to be done on this issue among leaders of the churches, although progress has certainly been made, not least by T. F. Torrance and his Eastern Orthodox colleagues.

J. Moltmann

In *The Trinity and the Kingdom of God*, Professor Jürgen Moltmann of Tübingen discusses the *Filioque*, and tenders the suggestion that it be replaced by: 'The Holy Spirit, who proceeds from the Father of the Son, and who receives his form from the Father and the Son.'[68] In explication, he notes that 'The Father "breathed out" the Holy Spirit in eternity as *the Father of the Son*, not as the monarch of the Godhead.' He goes on to show that this 'monopatrism' is as problematic as 'the dangerous Filioqueism'.[69]

---

[65]T. F. Torrance, *Theological Dialogue Between Orthodox & Reformed Churches*, 16, 17.
[66]E. Timiadis, 'God's Immutability and Communicability' in Torrance, *Theological Dialogue*, 21.
[67]Ibid., 47.
[68]J. Moltmann, *The Trinity and the Kingdom of God*, 187.

The particular problem of 'monopatrism' is related to the same issue raised by T. F. Torrance above: that of the concept of cause within the Trinity. Moltmann states:

> Even the concept of the Father as sole origin threatens to blur the concrete inner-trinitarian relationships. The concept of origin can therefore only be used in a transferred sense. It is not a general heading covering both generation [of the Son] and breathing out [of the Spirit].[70]
>
> By introducing the Aristotelian concept of cause (ἀρχή, αἴτια) into the doctrine of the Trinity, as the Cappadocians did (and this was not undisputed in the early church either), the uniqueness of the Father over against the Son and the Holy Spirit can certainly be emphasized. But if the Father is only named as the 'origin' of the divinity of the Son and the divinity of the Holy Spirit, then the specific difference between the generation of the Son and the procession of the Holy Spirit is blurred.[71]

'The Father of the Son' sends the Spirit

Thus, as we have seen, Moltmann proposes the following formula:

> The Father 'breathed out' the Holy Spirit in eternity as *the Father of the Son*, not as the monarch of the Godhead.[72]
>
> It would therefore be helpful to remove the concept of the First Cause from Trinitarian doctrine altogether, and to confine oneself to an account of the interpersonal relationships. For out of these the logical priority of the Father emerges all by itself.[73]

Hence, we may conclude this study of the *Filioque* by noting that even if *Filioque* be dropped from the Creed by the West, nothing significant would be lost so long as the whole Church follows the line of Athanasius and Cyril of Alexandria in avoiding the concept of cause with its potentially subordinationist overtones, and instead, emphasizes (1) that the two other divine Persons flow eternally from the Being of the Father, rather than the Person of the Father, and (2) that the Monarchy resides in the entire Godhead, rather than solely in the Person of the Father. As such, the Father always has priority by his very name as 'Father of the Son', but not a kind of causal priority. To move back in this direction is to rediscover the deepest roots of Eastern Orthodox theology in Athanasius, Cyril of Alexandria, Gregory of Nazianzus and Epiphanius. To do so would constitute healing for the entire Church.

---

[69]Ibid., 188,189.
[70]Ibid., 189.
[71]Ibid., 188.
[72]Ibid.
[73]Ibid., 189.

Bibliography

A
Primary Sources

1. Bible

Unless other wise stated, English Bible quotes are from the Authorized Version.

Biblia Sacra Utriusque Testamenti Editio Hebraica et Graeca. Stuttgart: Germany, 1994.

2. Other Jewish, Patristic, and Related Texts

Athanasius. *Ad Antiochenos. Nicene and Post-Nicene Fathers*, vol. iv. T & T Clark: Edinburgh, 1891.

Athanasius. *Contra Arianos. Ibid.*

Athanasius. *De Incarnatione. Ibid.*

Athanasius. *De Synodis. Ibid.*

Athanasius. *In Illud Omnia. Ibid.*

Athanasius. *Letters to Serapion Concerning the Holy Spirit.* Translated by C. . B. Shapland. London: The Epworth Press, 1951.

Athenagoras. *Apology. Ante-Nicene Fathers*, vol. ii. T & T Clark: Edinburgh, 1870.

Augustine. *City of God.* Translation by Henry Bettenson. Harmondsworth: Penguin Books, 1972.

Augustine. *Confessions.* Translated by R. S. Pine-Coffin. Harmondsworth: Penguin Books: London, 1961.

Augustine. *De Civitate Dei.* English translation by Henry Bettenson. Harmondsworth: Penguin Books: London, 1984.

Augustine. *De Correptione et Gratia*. Migne, *Patrologia Latina*, xliv.

Augustine. *De Doctrina Christiana.* Translated by R. P. H. Green. London: Oxford University Press, 1997.

Augustine. *De Natura Boni. Corpus Scriptorum Ecclesiasticorum Latinorum*, xxv. Vienna: Committee of Austrian Academy of Sciences, 1866.

Augustine. *De Trinitate*. Translated by Edmund Hill. Brooklyn: New City Press, 1991.

Augustine. *On Christian Teaching.* Translated by R. P. H. Green. Oxford: Oxford University Press, 1997.

Augustine. *The Literal Meaning of Genesis*. Vol. i. *Ancient Christian Writers* 41. Translated by John H. Taylor. New York: Newman Press, 1982.

Basil. *Aux Jeunes Gens Sur La Manière De Tirer Profit Des Lettres Hélléniques.* Paris: Société d'Edition 'Les Belles Lettres', 1965.

Basil. *Against Eunomius. Nicene and Post-Nicene Fathers*, vol. viii. T & T Clark: Edinburgh, 1894.

Basil. *De Spiritu Sancto. Ibid.*

Basil. *Epistle 233 to Amphilochius. Ibid.*
Clement of Alexandria. *Paedagogas. Ante-Nicene Fathers*, vol. iv. T & T Clark: Edinburgh, 1867.
Clement of Alexandria. *Stromata. Ibid.*
Cyprian. *Ad Donatum. Ante-Nicene Fathers*, vol. v. T & T Clark: Edinburgh, 1975.
Cyprian. *Epistle to Jubianus. Ibid.*
Cyril of Alexandria. *Contra Julianum* III; Migne, *Patrologia Graece*, 76.
Cyril of Alexandria. *Contra Nestorium*, 4.3 in Migne, *Patrologia Graece*, 75.
Cyril of Alexandria. *De SS. Trinitate Dialogus* III in Migne, *Patrologia Graece*,
Cyril of Alexandria. *Explanatio in Epist. Ad Rom.* I; Migne, *Patrologia Graece*, 74.
Cyril of Alexandria. *In Joannis Evangelium*, 15.1. Migne, *Patrologia Graece*, 74.
Cyril of Alexandria. *Thesaurus de Trinitate* in Migne, *Patrologia Graeca*, 75.
See also (in French translation) Cyril of Alexandria. *Dialogues Sur La Trinité.* Translation by G. M. de Durand. Paris: Sources Chrétiennes, 1976.
Cyril of Jerusalem. *Catechetical Lectures. Nicene and Post-Nicene Fathers*, vol. vii. T & T Clark: Edinburgh, 1893.
Didymus. *De Trinitate.* Migne, *Patrologia Graece*, xxix.
Epiphanius. *Ancoratus.* Migne, *Patrologia Graece*, xliii.
Epiphanius. *Haereses (Medecine Chest).* Migne, *Patrologia Graece*, xli, xlii.
Epiphanius. *The Panarion.* Translated by Frank Williams in *Nag Hammadi and Manichaean Studies*, Edited by J. M. Robinson & H. J. Klimkeit. Leiden: Brill, 1997.
Epistle to Diognetus. Ante-Nicene Fathers, vol. i. T & T Clark: Edinburgh, 1884.
Eusebius of Caesarea. *De Evangelica Praeparatione.* Translated and Edited by E. H. Gifford. Oxonii: E Typographeo academico Novi Eboraci: H. Frowde, 1903.
Gregory of Nazianzus. *The Fourth Theological Oration. Nicene and Post-Nicene Fathers*, vol. vii. T & T Clark: Edinburgh, 1893.
Gregory of Nyssa. *Against Eunomius. Nicene and Post-Nicene Fathers*, vol. v. T & T Clark: Edinburgh, 1892.
Gregory of Nyssa. *The Great Catechism. Ibid.*
Gregory of Nyssa. *To Ablabius.* Edited by W. Jaeger, *Gregorii Nysseni opera dogmatica minora, III*, pt. 1 (Leiden, 1958).
Hilary. *De Synodis. Nicene and Post-Nicene Fathers*, vol. ix. T & T Clark: Edinburgh, 1898.
Hilary. *De Trinitate. Ibid.*
Hippolytus of Rome, *Philosophumena* or *Refutation of All Heresies. Ante-Nicene Fathers*, vol. v, T & T Clark: Edinburgh, 1867.
Hippolytus. *Contra Noetum.* London: Heythrop College, 1977.
Ignatius. *Letter to Polycarp. Ante-Nicene Fathers*, vol. i. T & T Clark: Edinburgh, 1884.
Irenaeus. *Démonstration de la Prédication Apostolique*, Paris: Éditions du Cerf, 1959.
Irenaeus. *Adversus Haereses. Ante-Nicene Fathers*, vol. i. T & T Clark: Edinburgh, 1884.
John of Damascus. *De Fide Orthodoxa. Nicene and Post-Nicene Fathers*, vol. ix. T & T Clark: Edinburgh, 1898.
Justin Martyr. *First Apology. Ante-Nicene Fathers*, vol. i. T & T Clark: Edinburgh, 1884l
Justin Martyr. *Hortatory Address to the Greeks. Ibid.*
Justin. *Dialogue with Trypho. Ibid.*
Melito of Sardis, *Pascal Homily.* Translated and Edited by Campbell Bonner. *Studies and Documents*, 12. Eds. T. K. Lake and S. Lake: London, 1940.
Minucius Felix. *Octavius.* Translated by J. H. Freese. SPCK: London, 1919.

Novatian. *De Trinitate. Ante-Nicene Fathers*, vol. v. T & T Clark: Edinburgh, 1867.
Origen. *Contra Celsum.* Translated by Henry Chadwick. Cambridge: Cambridge University Press, 1980.
Origen. *De Oratore.* Translated by J. J. O'Meara. *Ancient Christian Writers*: New York: Newman Press, 1988.
Origen. *De Principiis. Ante-Nicene Fathers*, vol. iv. T & T Clark: Edinburgh, 1867.
Origen. *In Johanem.* 2 vols. Ed. A. E. Brooke. Cambridge University Press: Cambridge, 1896.
Philo. *De Congressu Quaerendae Eruditionis Studies* in *The Works of Philo*, New Updated Edition. Translated by C. D. Yonge. Hendrickson Publishers: Peabody, MA, 1993.
Photius. *La Mystagogie Du Saint Espirt. Ouevres Trinitaires.* Tome II. Paris: Fraternite Orthodoxe St. Gregoire Palamas, 1991.
St. John Chrysostom. *Homily on Colossians 5:3.* Migne, *Patrologia Graece*, 62.
Tatian. *Address to the Greeks. Ante-Nicene Fathers*, vol. iii. T & T Clark: Edinburgh, 1867.
Terrtullian. *Adversus Marcionem. Ante-Nicene Fathers, Ibid.*
Tertullian. *Ad Scapulam. Ante-Nicene Fathers*, vol. iv. T & T Clark: Edinburgh, 1885.
Tertullian. *Adversus Praxean. Ante-Nicene Fathers*, vol. iii. T & T Clark: Edinburgh, 1867.
Tertullian. *Contra Hermogenem. Ibid.*
Tertullian. *De Carne Christi. Ibid.*
Tertullian. *De Prescriptionibus Haereticorum. Ibid.*
Theophilus of Antioch. *Ad Autolycum.*
Migne, J. P. *Patrologia Graece*. Paris: Imprimerie Catholique, 1857-1866. 161 vols.
Migne, J. P. *Patrologia Latina*. Paris: Imprimerie Catholique, 1844-1855. 217 vols.
Corpus Scriptorum Ecclesiasticorum Latinorum. Vienna: Committee of Austrian Academy of Sciences, 1866 to the present.
The Ante-Nicene Fathers. Edited by Alexander Roberts and James Donaldson. 1885-1887. 10 vols. Repr. Peabody, Mass.: Hendrickson, 1994.
The Nicene and Post-Nicene Fathers. Edited by Alexander Roberts and James Donaldson. 1885-1887. 14 vols. Repr. Peabody, Mass.: Hendrickson, 1994.

3. Pagan Texts

Aristotle. *Metaphysics*. Translated by Stephen Makin. New York: Oxford University Press, 2006.
Aristotle. *Physics.* Translated by Robin Waterfield. New York: Oxford: at the University Press, 1946.
Arnim, Hans Friedrich August von. *Stoicorum Veterum Fragmenta.* Lipsiae, in aedibus B.G. Teubneri, 1903.
Cicero. *Academicus* in *Philosophical Treatises*, vol. xix. Translated by H. Wrackham. (Loeb Series) Harvard University Press: Cambridge, MA, 1956.
Cicero. *Finis* in *Philosophical Treatises*, vol. xvii. Translated by H. Wrackham. (Loeb Series) Harvard University Press: Cambridge, MA, 1931.
Diogenes Laertius. *Works. vol. II.* Translated by R. D. Hick. (Loeb Series) Harvard University Press: Cambridge, MA, 1925.
Pausanias. *Description of Greece.* 5 vols. Translated by W. H. S. Jones and H. A. Omerod. (Loeb Series) Harvard University Press: Cambridge, MA, 1931-1955.
Philostratus. *Life of Apollonius of Tyana*. 2 vols. Translated by F. C. Conybeare. (Loeb Series) Harvard University Press: Cambridge, MA, 1912.

Sextus Empiricus. *Against the Logicians*. Translated by R. G. Bury. (Loeb Series) Harvard University Press: Cambridge, MA, 1935.

Sextus Empiricus.*Outlines of Pyrrhonism*. Translated by R. G. Bury. (Loeb Series) Harvard University Press: Cambridge, MA, 1933.

B

Medieval to Modern Literature

Abbott, Walter M., ed. *The Documents of Vatican II*. New York: Guild Press, 1966.

Allison, C. F. *The Rise of Moralism: The Proclamation of the Gospel from Hooker to Baxter*. London: S.P.C.K., 1966.

Althaus, Paul. *The Theology of Martin Luther*. Translated by Robert C. Schultz. Philadelphia: Fortress Press, 1966.

Andrewes, Lancelot. *Sermon 15 "On the Nativity." Ninety-Six Sermons*, Vol. I. Edited by John P. Parkinson. Oxford: John Henry Parker, 1841.

Angold, Michael., ed. *Eastern Christianity*. Vol. 5 of *The Cambridge History of Christianity*. Edited by Michael Angold. Cambridge: Cambridge University Press, 2006.

Anselm. *Epistola De Incarnatione Verbi*. Bonnae : P. Hanstein, 1931.

Anselm. *Cur deus homo* in *Anselm of Canterbury: Trinity, Incarnation, and Redemption: Theological Treatises*. Edited & Translated by Jasper Hopkins & Herbert W. Richardson. New York: Harper Torchbooks, 1970.

Anselm. Introduction to *Liber Apologeticus*, Migne, *Patrologia Latina*, 158.

Anselm. *Proslogion*. Edited and Translated by M. J. Charlesworth. Notre Dame: University of Notre Dame Press, 1979.

Anselm: *Fides Quaerens Intellectum*. Paris: J. Vrin, 1978.

Aquinas, Thomas. *Quaestiones disputatae de veritae*. Ed. R. Spiazza. Turin: Marietti, 1949.

Aquinas, Thomas. *Summa Contra Gentiles: Book Four*. Translated by C. J. O'Neil. Notre Dame: University of Notre Dame Press, 1975.

Aquinas, Thomas. *Summa Contra Gentiles: Book One – God*. Translated by Anton C. Pegis. Notre Dame: University of Notre Dame Press, 1975.

Aquinas, Thomas. *Summa Theologica*. Edited by Brian Davies and Brian Leftow. New York: Cambridge University Press, 2006.

Arnold, E. V. *Roman Stoicism: Being Lectures on the History of the Stoic Philosophy with Special Reference to its Development within the Roman Empire*. Cambridge: The University Press, 1911.

Ayres, Robert H. *Language, Logic and Reason in the Church Fathers: A Study of Tertullian, Augustine & Aquinas*. Hildesheim: Olms, 1979.

Bainton, Roland H. *Erasmus of Christendom*. New York: Charles Scribner's Sons, 1969.

Baker, J. Wayne. *Heinrich Bullinger and the Covenant: The Other Reformed Tradition*. Athens: Ohio University Press, 1980.

Balthasar, Hans Urs Von. *The Glory of the Lord: A Theological Aesthetics*. 7 vols. Translated by Erasmo Leiva-Merikakis. San Francisco: Ignatius Press, 1982.

Balthasar, Hans Urs von. *The Theology of Karl Barth*. San Francisco: Communio Books, Ignatius Press, 1991.

Balthasar, Hans Urs Von. *Theodrama: The Dramatic Theory, vol. II: The Dramatis Personae: Man in God*. San Francisco: Ignatius Press, 1988.

Balz, H. and G. Schneider, eds., *Exegetical Dictionary of the New Testament*. 3 Vols. Grand Rapids, MI: Eerdmans, 1991.

Barbellion, Stephané-Marie. *Les 'Preuves' de L'Existence de Dieu*. Paris: Les éditions du cerf, 1999.

Barnes, Jonathan. *The Ontological Argument*. London and Basingstoke: MacMillan, 1972.

Barr, James. *The Old and New in Interpretation: A Study of Two Testaments*. London: S.C.M. Press, 1966.

Barrett, C. K. *The Epistle to the Romans*. New York: Harper & Row Publishers, 1957.

Barth Karl. *Anselm: Fides Quaerens Intellectum: Anselm's Proof of the Existence of God in the Context of his Theological Scheme*. London: SCM, 1960.

Barth, Karl and Emil Brunner. *Natural Theology*. Translated by Peter Fraenkel. London: G. Bles, 1946.

Barth, Karl. *Church Dogmatics I.1 The Doctrine of the Word of God*. Edited and Translated by G. W. Bromiley. Edinburgh: T & T Clark, 1975.

Barth, Karl. *Church Dogmatics I.2 The Doctrine of the Word of God*. Edited by G. W. Bromiley and T. F. Torrance. Translated by G. T. Thomson and Herold Knight. Edinburgh: T & T Clark, 1998.

Barth, Karl. *Church Dogmatics II.1 The Doctrine of God*. Edited by G. W. Bromiley and T. F. Torrance. Translated by T. H. L. Parker, et al. Edinburgh: T & T Clark, 1964.

Barth, Karl. *Church Dogmatics II.2 The Doctrine of God*. Edited by G. W. Bromiley and T. F. Torrance. Translated by G. W. Bromiley, et al. Edinburgh: T & T Clark, 1978.

Barth, Karl. *Church Dogmatics III.1 The Doctrine of Creation*. Edited by G. W. Bromiley and T. F. Torrance. Translated by J. W. Edwards, et al. Edinburgh: T & T Clark, 1998.

Barth, Karl. *Church Dogmatics IV.1 The Doctrine of Reconciliation*. Edited by G. W. Bromiley and T. F. Torrance. Translated by G. W. Bromiley. Edinburgh: T & T Clark, 1997.

Barth, Karl. *The Knowledge of God and the Service of God According to the Teaching of the Reformation*. Translated by J.L.M. Haire and Ian Henderson. London: Hodder and Stoughton, 1938.

Bauckham, Richard. 'Biblical Theology and the Problems of Monotheism.' In Craig Bartholomew ed. *Out of Egypt: Biblical Theology and Biblical Interpretation*. Grand Rapids: Zondervan. 2006.

Bavaud, Georges. *Le Réformateur Pierre Viret: Sa Théologie*. Genève: Labor et Fides, 1986.

Bavinck, Herman. *In the Beginning: Foundations of Creation Theology*. Edited by John Vriend and John Bolt. Grand Rapids: Baker, 1999.

Bavinck, Herman. *Our Reasonable Faith: A Survey of Christian Doctrine*. Translated by Henry Zylstra. Grand Rapids: Baker, 1977.

Bavinck, Herman. *The Doctrine of God*. Translated and Edited by William Hendriksen. Edinburgh: Banner of Truth Trust, 1977.

Beardslee, John W. III (editor and translator). *Reformed Dogmatics: J. Wollebius, G. Voetius, F. Turretin*. New York: Oxford University Press, 1965.

Bede. *Opera Historica*. Vol. 2. Translated by J. E. King. London: William Heinemann, 1976.

Behe, Michael J. *Darwin's Black Box: The Biochemical Challenge to Evolution*. New York: The Free Press, 1996.

Bellucci, Dino. *Science de la Nature et Réformation: La Physique au service de la Réforme dans l'enseignement de Philippe Melanchthon.* Roma: Edizioni Vivere In, 1998.

Benedict XVI (Joseph Cardinal Ratzinger). *Many Religions – One Covenant: Israel, the Church and the World.* San Francisco: Ignatius Press, 1999.

Berkhof, Louis. *Systematic Theology.* Grand Rapids: Eerdmans, 1996.

Bernard of Clairvaux. *On the Love of God* and *Sermons on the Song of Songs.* In *Late Medieval Mysticism*, Vo. XIII of 'The Library of Christian Classics.' Edited by Ray C. Petry. London: SCM Press, 1957.

Bernard of Clairvaux. *Saint Bernard on the Love of God.* Translated by Terence L. Connolly. Techny: Mission Press, S.V.D., 1943.

Berthoud, Jean-Marc. "La Révolution Francaise et les Révolutions" *Révolution et Christianisme.* L'Age d'Homme: Lausanne, 1992.

Berthoud, Jean-Marc. "Le traité d'alliance et son histoire dans la Bible." second lecture in the series *Cours de Formation Biblique.* Unpublished: Lausanne, 2007.

Berthoud, Jean-Marc. "Les Différentes Formes de Causalité et la Pensée de la Bible." *Positions Créationnistes* 25 (Septembre 1996). Lausanne: Association Vaudoise de Parents Chretiens, 1996.

Beza, Theodore. *Master Bezaes Household Prayers for the Consolation and Perfection of a Christian Life.* London: Printed for John Barnes, 1621.

Bielawski, Maciej. The Philokalical Vision of the World in the theology of Dumitru Stãniloae. Dissertatio ad Lauream in Facultate S. Theologiae apud Pontificiam Universitatem S. Thomae. Urbe: Romae, 1997.

Billington, James H. *Fire in the Minds of Men: Origins of the Revolutionary Faith.* New York: Basic Books, Inc., 1980.

Bobrinskoy, Boris. *The Mystery of the Trinity: Trinitarian Experience and Vision in the Biblical and Patristic Tradition.* Translated by Anthony P. Gythiel. Crestwood, NY: St. Vladimir's Seminary Press, 1999.

Boethius. *De Personis et Duabus Naturae* in *Theological Tractates.* Translated by H. F. Stewart and E. K. Rand. London: Heinemann, 1918.

Boethius. *On the Consolation of Philosophy.* Translated by Victor Watts. Penguin Books: London, 1979.

Bolzano, Bernard. *Wissenschaftslehre.* Edited by Wolfgang Schultz. Leipzig: F. Meiner, 1929.

Bonansea, Bernardino M. *Man and His Approach to God in John Duns Scotus.* Lanham, MD: University Press of America, 1983.

Borg, Marcus and Ross MacKenzie eds. *God at 2000.* Harrisburg: Morehouse Publishing, 2000.

Borg, Marcus. *Meeting Jesus Again for the First Time: The Historical Jesus & the Heart of Contemporary Faith.* San Francisco: Harper, 1994.

Boston, Thomas. *A View of the Covenant of Grace.* Choteau: Old Paths Gospel Press, 1990.

Boston, Thomas. *Human Nature in its Fourfold State.* Edinburgh: The Banner of Truth, 1989.

Bouillard, Henri. *Knowledge of God.* Translated by Samuel D. Femiano. New York: Herder and Herder, 1968.

Brakel, Wilhelmus à. *The Christian's Reasonable Service,* vol 1. Translated by Bartel Elshout. Grand Rapids: Reformation Heritage Books, 1999.

Brehier, Emile. *Histoire de la Philosophie.* Paris: Presses Universitaries de France, 1994.

Broadie, Alexander. *The Shadow of Scotus.* Edinburgh: T & T Clark, 1995.

Brockington, L. H. "The Greek Translator of Isaiah and His Interest in DOXA." Vetus Testamentum 1 (1951).

Bromiley, Geoffrey W. *Historical Theology, An Introduction.* Grand Rapids: Eerdmans, 1978.

Brookes, Derek R., ed. *Thomas Reid: Essays on the Intellectual Powers of Man.* University Park: The Pennsylvania State University Press, 2002.

Brown, Colin. Ed. *New International Dictionary of New Testament Theology.* 4 vols. Grand Rapids: Zondervan, 1986.

Bruce, F. F. *The Book of the Acts Revised Edition.* Grand Rapids: Eerdmans, 1989.

Bruce, Robert. *The Mystery of the Lord's Supper: Sermons on the Sacrament preached in the Kirk of Edinburgh in A. D. 1589.* Translated and Edited by Thomas F. Torrance. Edinburgh and Fearn: Rutherford House & Christian Focus, 2005.

Brun, Jean. *Révolution et Christianisme: Une Appréciation Chrétienne de la Révolution Francaise.* Lausanne: L'Age d'Homme, 1992.

Brun, Jean. *L'Europe Philosophe: 25 Siècles de Pensée Occidentale.* Paris: Clefs de l'Histoire, Stock, 1997.

Buber, Martin. *The Kingship of God.* London: Allen and Unwin, 1967.

Bulgakov, Sergius. *Le Paraclet.* Paris: Aubier, 1946.

Bullinger, Heinrich. *Fountainhead of Federalism: Heinrich Bullinger and the Covenantal Tradition.* Translation by J. Wayne Baker and Charles McCoy. Westminster/ John Knox Press: Louisville, 1991.

Bullinger, Heinrich. *The Decades: The Fourth Decade.* Cambridge: The University Press, 1851.

Burgess, Stuart. *He Made the Stars Also: What the Bible Says About the Stars.* Epsom: Day One Publications, 2002.

Calvin Theological Treatises. Library of Christian Classics. vol. xxii. London: SCM Press, 1954.

Calvin, John. 'Adversus P. Caroli calumnias,' *Opera Calvini* vii. and letter to Farel, Oct. 8, 1539 in Herminjard, vi. (1883).

Calvin, John. *Commentary on Acts.* Translated by William Pringle. Grand Rapids: Baker Books, 2005.

Calvin, John. *Commentary on Genesis.* Calvin's Commentaries. Translated by William Pringle. Grand Rapids: Baker Books, 2005.

Calvin, John. *Commentary on Isaiah.* Calvin's Commentaries. Translated by William Pringle. Grand Rapids: Baker Books, 2005.

Calvin, John. *Commentary on Romans.* Calvin's Commentaries. Translated by William Pringle. Grand Rapids: Baker Books, 2005.

Calvin, John. *Commentary on the Epistle to the Hebrews.* Translated by William Pringle. Grand Rapids: Baker Books, 2005.

Calvin, John. *Commentary on the Second Epistle to the Corinthians.* Translated by William Pringle. Grand Rapids: Baker Books, 2005.

Calvin, John. *Commentary on the Second Epistle to Timothy.* Calvin's Commentaries. Translated by William Pringle. Grand Rapids: Baker Books, 2005.

Calvin, John. *Institutes of the Christian Religion*, 2 vols. Edited by John T. McNeill. Translated by Ford Lewis Battles. Westminster John Knox Press: Louisville, 2006.

Calvin, John. *The Acts of the Apostles: 14-28.* Translated by J. W. Fraser. Edited by D. & T. Torrance. Edinburgh: Oliver & Boyd, 1966.

Calvin, John. *The Harmony of the Pentateuch.* Calvin's Commentaries. Translated by William Pringle. Grand Rapids: Baker Books, 2005.

Cameron, N. ed. *Dictionary of Scottish Church History & Theology*. Downers Grove: InterVarsity Press, 1993.
Cameron, Nigel. *Evolution and the Authority of the Bible.* Exeter: The Paternoster Press, 1983.
Carson, D. A. *The Inclusive Language Debate: A Plea for Realism.* Leicester: Intervarsity Press, 1998.
Casadei, Bernardino. *'Del Noce Interprète du XXe siecle: Une Introduction.* Paris: Catholica, 2002.
Cassirer, Ernst. *The Myth of the State.* New Haven: Yale University Press, 1946.
Catechism of the Catholic Church. San Francisco: Ignatius Press, 1994.
Chevalier, Irénée. *S. Augustin et la Pensée Grecque: Les Relations Trinitaires.* Librairie de l'Université: Fribourg en Suisse, 1940.
Chopp, Rebecca S. *The Power to Speak: Feminism, Language, God.* New York: Crossroad, 1989.
Christian Hymns. Bryntirion, Mid Glamorgan: Evangelical Movement of Wales, 1977.
Cochin, Augustin. *L'Esprit du Jacobinisme.* Paris: Presses Universitaires de France, 1979.
Cochin, Augustin. *La Révolution et la Libre-pensée*. Paris: Plon-Nourrit, 1924.
Cochin, Augustin. *Les Sociétés de Pensée et la Démocratie*. Paris: Plon-Nourrit et cie., 1921.
Cochin, Augustin. *Les Sociétés de Pensée et la Révolution en Bretagne.* Paris: H. Champion, 1925.
Cochrane, Charles Norris. *Christianity and Classical Culture: A Study of Thought and Action From Augustus to Augustine.* London: Oxford University Press, 1940.
Copleston, F. C. *A History of Philosophy.* 9 Vols. New York: Image Books, 1962.
Copleston, F. C. *Aquinas.* Harmondsworth: Penguin Books, 1961.
Courthial, Pierre. *Le Jour des Petits Recommencements: Essai sur l'Actualite de la Parole (Evangile- Loi) de Dieu.* Lausanne: Messages: L'Age d'Homme, 1996.
Cranfield, C. E. B. *A Critical and Exegetical Commentary on the Epistle to the Romans.* Vol. I. Edinburgh: T. & T. Clark, 1975.
Crossan, John, Dominic. *The Historical Jesus: The Life of a Mediterranean Jewish Peasant.* San Francisco: HarperCollins, 1991.
D'Alès. *Théologie de Tertullien.* Paris: Beauchesne, 1905.
Daly, Mary. *The Church and the Second Sex: With the Feminist Postchristian Introduction and New Archaic Afterwords by the Author.* Boston: Beacon Press, 1985.
Daniélou, Jean and Henri Marrou. *The First Six Hundred Years.* Translated by Vincent Cronin. London: Darton, Longman, & Todd 1979.
Daniélou, Jean. *Théologie du Judéo-Christianisme.* Paris: Desclée, 1958.
Davies, Brian and G. R. Evans, eds. *Anselm of Canterbury: The Major Works.* Oxford: Oxford University Press, 1998.
Davies, Horton. *Worship and Theology in England from Andrewes to Baxter and Fox, 1603–1690.* Princeton: Princeton University Press, 1975.
Davies, W. D. *Paul and Rabbinic Judaism*. Mifflintown, PA: Sigler Press, 1998.
Davies, W. D. *The Background of the New Testament and its Eschatology*. Cambridge: The University Press, 1956.
Deiss, Lucien. *Springtime of the Liturgy.* Collegeville, MN: The Liturgical Press, 1979.
Denzinger. *Enchiridion Symbolorum.* Barcinone: Herder, 1965.
Descartes, René. *Discours de la Méthode.* A Leyde, De L'Imprimerie de I. Maire, 1637. English translation: Everyman: London, 1949.

Descartes, René. *Works*. Translated by E. S. Haldane and G. R. T. Ross. Cambridge: Cambridge University Press, 1911.

Dewar, Douglas and H. S. Shelton. *Is Evolution Proved?* London: Hollis and Carter, 1947.

Dickson, David. *Therapeutica Sacra*. Translated by David Dickson. Edinburgh: Evan Tyler, 1664.

Dickson, David. *Truth's Victory Over Error*. Edited by John R. De Witt. Edinburgh: Banner of Truth, 2007.

Diderot et d'Alembert. *L'Encyclopédie ou Dictionnaire Raisonné des Sciences, des Arts et des Métiers*. Fairview: Pergamon Press, reprint of 1775 edition.

Diderot. *Réfutation suivie de l'ouvrage d'Helvétius intitulé l'Homme, Oeuvres Philosophiques*. Edited by A. Billy. Paris, 1952-.

Dods, Marcus. *Expositor's Bible, Genesis*. Edinburgh: T. & T. Clark, 1888.

Donne, John. *Sermons*. Edited by George R. Potter and Evelyn M. Simpson. 10 vols. Berkeley: University of California Press, 1953–1962.

Dooyeweerd, Herman. *A New Critique of Theoretical Thought*. Philadelphia: Presbyterian and Reformed, 1953.

Dooyeweerd, Herman. *In the Twilight of Western Thought*. Philadelphia: Presbyterian and Reformed, 1960.

Dostoevsky, Fyodor. *Demons*. Translated by Richard Pevear & Larissa Volokhonsky. New York: Vintage Books, 1995.

Dostoyevsky, Fyodor. *The Brothers Karamazov*. Translated by Andrew R. MacAndrew. New York: Bantam, 1981.

Dragas, George Dion. (Protopresbyter). *Saint Athanasius of Alexandria: Original Research and New Perspectives*. Rollinsford, NH: Orthodox Research Institute, 2005.

Du Roy, Olivier. *L'Intelligence de la Foi en la Trinité selon Saint Augustin: Genèse de sa Théologie Trinitaire jusqu'en 391*. Paris: Etudes Augustiniennes, 1966.

Dumbrell, William J. *Covenant and Creation: A Theology of the Old Testtament Covenants*. Carlisle: Paternoster, 1984.

Dunn, James D. G. *Jesus, Paul and the Law: Studies in Mark and Galatians*. Louisville: Westminster/John Knox, 1990.

Duns Scotus. *Ordinatio*. See "De Ordinatio I. Duns Scoti Disquisitio historica-critica" in *Joannis Duns Scotus Opera omnia*, vol. 1. Civitas Vaticana, 1950.

Edwards, Jonathan. *The Works of Jonathan Edwards*. Edinburgh: The Banner of Truth Trust, 1974.

Edwards, Jonathan. *The Works of Jonathan* Edwards. New Haven: Yale University Press, 1957-.

Edwards, Jonathan. *Miscellanies* in *The Jonathan Edwards Collection*, NavPress Software: www.WORDsearch.com.

Eichrodt, Walter. *Theology of the Old Testament*. English Translation. Philadelphia: The Westminster Press, 1961.

Evdokimov, Paul. *L'Esprit Saint*. Paris: Flammarion, 1969.

Evdokimov, Paul. *Les Ages de la Vie Spirituelle*. Paris: Desclée, De Brouwer, 1980.

Florovsky, Georges V. "Idea of Creation in Christian Philosophy." *Eastern Churches Quarterly* 8 (1949; Supplementary Issue: Nature and Grace): 46.

Frank, Joseph. *Dostoevsky: The Mantle of the Prophet*. Princeton and Oxford: Princeton University Press, 2002.

Funk, Robert W. and Gerhard Ebeling, eds. *Journal for Theology and Church*. New York: Harper & Row, 1965.

Funk, Robert W. and Roy W. Hoover. *The Five Gospels: The Search for the Authentic Words of Jesus*. New York: Macmillan, 1993.

Funk, Robert W., Bernard B. Scott, and James R. Butts, eds. *The Parables of Jesus: Red Letter Edition. A Report of the Jesus Seminar.* Sonoma, CA: Polebridge Press, 1988.

Garrigou-Lagrange, Réginald. *God, His Existence and Nature*. Translated by Bede Rose. St Louis: Herder, 1934.

Gaussen, Louis. *Sermons par Gaussen.* Nouvelle Edition. Paris: Chez Delay, Librarie, Rue Tronchet 2, 1847.

Gay, Peter. *The Enlightenment, An Interpretation: The Rise of Modern Paganism.* New York: Alfred A. Knopf, 1967.

Geisler, Norman. *Thomas Aquinas: An Evangelical Appraisal.* Grand Rapids: Baker Book House, 1991.

Gibbon, Edward. *Autobiography*. Edited by John Sheffield. New York: Buckland & Sumner, 1846.

Gibbons, William J. ed. *Seven Great Encyclicals.* Glen Rock: Paulist Press, 1963.

Gillet, Lev. *The Jesus Prayer by A Monk of the Eastern Church.* Crestwood, NY: St. Vladimir's Seminary Press, 2006.

Gilson, Etienne. *History of Christian Philosophy in the Middle Ages.* New York: Random House, 1955.

Gilson, Etienne. *Jean Duns Scot. Introduction à ses Positions Fondamentales.* Paris: Vrin, 1952.

Gilson, Etienne. *The Spirit of Medieval Philosophy*. Translated by A. H. C. Downes. London: Sheed and Ward, 1936.

Gilson, Etienne. *Thomism: The Philosophy of Thomas Aquinas.* Translated by Laurence K. Shook and Armand Maurer. Toronto: Pontifical Institute of Medieval Studies, 2002.

Goldberg, Steven. *The Inevitability of Patriarchy.* New York: Marrow, 1973.

Gore, Charles, ed. *Thoughts on Religion.* London: Longmans Green and Co., 1895.

Gotthelf, Jeremias. *L'Argent et l'Esprit.* Lausanne: L'Age d'Homme, 2000.

Grant, Jamie A. and Alistair I. Wilson, eds. *The God of Covenant: Biblical, Theological and Contemporary Perspectives.* Leicester: Apollos: Intervarsity Press, 2005.

Grant, Robert. *Gnosticism and Early Christianity.* New York: Columbia University Press, 1959.

Green, F. C. *'Deux Frères: Diderot et Jean-Jacques.* In vol III of *Diderot Studies.* Paris, 1962.

Green, F. C. *Jean-Jacques Rousseau: A Critical Study of His Life and Writings.* Cambridge: University Press, 1955.

Grudem, Wayne. *Evangelical Feminism & Biblical Truth: An Analysis of 118 Disputed Questions.* Leicester: Apollos, Intervarsity Press, 2005.

Grudem, Wayne. *Evangelical Feminism: A New Path to Liberalism?* Wheaton: Crossway Books, 2006.

Gunton, Colin. *Enlightenment & Alienation: An Essay towards a Trinitarian Theology.* Grand Rapids: Eerdmans, 1985.

Gunton, Colin. *The One, the Three and the Many.* Oxford: Clarendon Press, 1993.

Halyburton, Thomas. *Natural Religion Insufficient and Revealed Necessary to Man's Happiness in his Present State.* Edinburgh: Heirs of Andrew Anderson, 1714.

Hampson, Daphne. *Theology and Feminism.* Oxford: Blackwell, 1990.

Harnack, A. *History of Dogma.* Translated by Neil Buchanan. Boston : Roberts, 1897

Hartshorne, C. *The Logic of Perfection.* La Salle: Open Court, 1962.

Haugh, Richard. *Photius and the Carolingians: The Trinitarian Controversy.* Belmont, MA: Nordland Publ. Co., 1975.

Havens, George R. *Voltaire's Marginalia on the Pages of Rousseau: A Comprehensive Study of Ideas.* Columbus: The Ohio State University, 1933.

Hazard, Paul. *La Crise de la Conscience Européenne.* Paris: Librairie Antheme Fayard, 1981.

Henderson, G. D. *The Scots Confession*. Edinburgh: Saint Andrew Press, 1960.

Hendrickson, William. *More than Conquerors: An Interpretation of the Book of Revelation.* London: The Tyndale Press, 1973.

Henry, Desmond P. *Medieval Logic and Metaphysics.* London: Hutchinson & Co. Ltd., 1972.

Henry, Matthew. *Unpublished Sermons on The Covenant of Grace.* Edited by Allan Harman. Tain: Christian Focus, 2002.

Heppe, Heinrich. *Die Dogmatik der evangelisch-reformierten Kirche.* Edited by Ernst Bizer, 2d ed. Neukirchen: Neukirchener Verlag, K. Moers, 1958.

Heppe, Heinrich. *Reformed Dogmatics.* Revised by Ernst Bizer. Translated by G. T. Thomson. Grand Rapids: Baker, 1978.

Hodgson, Leonard. *The Doctrine of the Trinity*. New York: C. Scribner's Sons, 1944.

Holbach, Paul Henri Thiry. *Système de la Nature.* A Londres, 1770.

Hooker, Richard. *Ecclesiastical Polity.* Manchester: Carcanet, 1990.

Horton, Michael S. *Covenant and Salvation: Union with Christ.* Louisville: Westminster John Knox, 2007.

Horton, Michael. *Lord and Servant: A Covenant Christology.* Louisville: Westminster John Knox, 2005.

Hughes, Philip Edgecombe. *Lèfevre: Pioneer of Ecclesiastical Renewal in France.* Grand Rapids: Eerdmans, 1984.

Hume, David. *Dialogues on Natural Religion.* Edited by Norman Kemp Smith. Oxford: Clarendon Press, 1935.

Hume, David. *Enquiry Concerning Human Understanding.* Oxford: Clarendon Press, 1894.

Hume, David. *The Natural History of Religion*. Oxford: Clarendon Press, 1976.

Hume, David. *Treatise of Human Nature.* Edited by L. A. Selby-Bigge. Oxford: Oxford University Press, 1961.

Hurtado, Larry W. *Lord Jesus Christ: Devotion to Jesus in Earliest Christianity.* Grand Rapids: Eerdmans, 2003.

Jaki, Stanley. *The Road of Science and the Ways to God*. Chicago: University of Chicago Press, 1978.

James, I. *Basilikon Doron*. Cardiff: University of Wales Press Board, 1931.

Jenkins, Philip. *Hidden Gospels: How the Search for Jesus Lost its Way.* Oxford: Oxford University Press, 2003.

Jenkins, Phillip. *The Next Christendom: The Coming of Global Christianity.* Oxford: Oxford University Press, 2002.

Jensen, Robert W. 'The Church as Communio,' in *The Catholicity of the Reformation.* Edited by Carl E. Braaten and Robert W. Jenson. Grand Rapids: Eerdmans, 1996.

Johnson, Elizabeth A. *She Who Is: The Mystery of God in Feminist Discourse.* New York: Herder & Herder, The Crossroad Publishing Company, 2003.

Johnson, Phillip E. *Darwin on Trial.* 2d ed. Downers Grove: Inter Varsity Press, 1993.

Johnson, Phillip E. *Evolution as Dogma: the Establishment of Naturalism.* Dallas: Houghton Publishing Co., 1990.

Jonas, Hans. *Gnosis und spätantiker Geist: Teil I: Die Mythologische Gnosis, 3 Aufl age.* FRLANT, Neue Folge, 33 Heft, Göttingen: Van den Hoect & Ruprecht, 1965. English translation by the author. *The Gnostic Religion: The Message of the Alien God and the Beginnings of* Christianity. Boston: Beacon Press, 2001.

Jones, O. R., ed. *The Private Language Argument*. London: Macmillan, 1971.

Jouvenel, Bertrand de. *Du Pouvoir: Histoire Naturelle de sa Croissance*. Paris: Librairie Hachette, 1972.

Jüngel, Eberhard. *The Doctrine of the Trinity: God's Being is in Becoming*. Grand Rapids: Eerdmans Publishing, 1976.

Kaiser, Walter C. *Toward an Old Testament Theology*. Grand Rapids: Zondervan, 1991.

Kant, E. *Critique of Pure Reason*. Translated by Norman Kemp Smith. New York: Palgrave Macmillan, 2007.

Kassian, Mary. *The Feminist Mistake*. Rev. ed. Wheaton: Crossway, 2005.

Kearsley, Roy. *Tertullian's Theology of Divine Power*. Carlisle: Paternoster Press, 1998.

Kelly, Douglas F. *The Emergence of Liberty in the Modern World*. Phillipsburg: P & R Publishing, 1992.

Kelly, Douglas Floyd. *Novatian of Rome*. 2 Vols. PhD diss., University of Edinburgh, 1972.

Kenny, Anthony. *The Five Ways: Thomas Aquinas' Proof of God's Existence*. London: Routledge & Kegan Paul Ltd., 1969.

Kenny, Anthony. *Wittgenstein*. London: Penguin Books, 1975.

Kidner, Derek. *The Proverbs: An Introduction and Commentary*. The Tyndale Old Testament Commentaries. Edited by D. J. Wiseman. Downers Grove: InterVarsity Press, 1964.

Kittel, Gerhard, and Gerhard Friedrich, eds. *Theological Dictionary of the New Testament*. Translated by Geoffrey W. Bromiley. 10 Vols. Grand Rapids: Eerdmans, 1964-1976.

Kline, Meredith. *By Oath Consigned: A Reinterpretation of the Covenant Signs of Circumcision and Baptism*. Grand Rapids: Eerdmans, 1968.

Knight, George A. F. "A Biblical Approach to the Doctrine of the Trinity." *Scottish Journal of Theology: Occasional Papers* No. 1. (1953).

Koons, Robert C. *Realism Regained: An Exact Theory of Causation, Teleology, and the Mind*. Oxford: Oxford University Press, 2000.

Koyré, Alexandre. *Du Monde Clos à l'Univers Infini*. Paris: Presses Universitaries de France, 1973.

Kuehnelt-Leddihn, Eric Von. *Leftism Revisited: From de Sade and Marx to Hitler and Pol Pot*. Washington: Regnery Gateway, 1990.

Kütsch, E. *Verheissung und Gesetz*, BZAW 131 (Berlin: De Gruyter, 1973).

Kuiper, Herman. *Calvin on Common Grace*. Goes: Oosterbaan & Le Cointre, 1928.

Kusakawa, Sachiko. *The Transformation of Natural Philosophy. The Case of Philip Melanchthon*. Cambridge: Cambridge University Press, 1995.

Kuyper, Abraham. *De Gemeene Gratie*. Amsterdam: Hoveker and Wormser, 1902.

Kuyper, Abraham. *Lectures on Calvinism*. Grand Rapids: Eerdmans, 1978.

Kuyper, Abraham. *The Problem of Poverty*. Translated and Edited by James W. Skillen. Grand Rapids: Baker Book House, 1991.

LaCugna, Catherine Mowry, ed. *Freeing Theology: The Essentials of Theology in Feminist Perspective*. San Francisco: Harper, 1993.

Lake, K. and H. J. Cadbury. *The Beginnings of Christianity Part IV: The Acts of the Apostles*. London: MacMillan and Col, Ltd., 1933.

Leith, John H., editor. *Creeds of the Churches: A Reader in Christian Doctrine from the Bible to the Present*. Garden City, NY: Anchor Books: Doubleday & Company, 1963.

Law, William. *A Serious Call to a Devout and Holy Life*. London: Tenth edition, 1772.

Lebreton, Jules. *L'Histoire du Dogma de la Trinité: Des Origines au Concile de Nicee.* 2 vols. Paris: G. Beauchesne, 1927-28.

Lecerf. *An Introduction to Reformed Dogmatics.* London: Lutterworth Press, 1949.

Leibniz, *Monadology and Other Philosophical Writings.* Translated by Robert Latta. Oxford: Clarendon Press, 1898.

Levin, T. W. *Six Lectures Introductory to the Philosophical Writings of Cicero.* Cambridge: Deighton, Bell, 1871.

Lloyd, William Freeman. *The Church Hymnary: Revised Edition.* Oxford: Oxford University Press, 1930.

Locke, John. *A Paraphrase and Notes on the Epistles of St Paul.* Edited by Arthur W. Wainwright. vol. 2. Oxford: Clarendon Press, 1987.

Locke, John. *An Essay Concerning Human Understanding*. Edinburgh, 1798.

Locke, John. *The Reasonableness of Christianity with A Discourse of Miracles*. Edited by I. T. Ramsey. London: Adam & Charles Black, 1958.

Lonergan, Bernard. *The Way to Nicea.* Translated by C. O'Donovan. Philadelphia: The Westminster Press, 1964.

Lossky, Vladimir N. *In the Image and Likeness of God.* Crestwood: St. Vladimir's Seminary Press, 1974.

Lossky, Vladimir N. *The Mystical Theology of the Eastern Church.* New York: St. Vladimir's Seminary Press, 1978.

Luther, Martin. "Psalm 90" Edited by Jaroslav Pelikan. Translated by Paul M. Bretscher. Luther's Works 13. Philadelphia: Fortress Press, 1960.

Luther, Martin. "Small Catechism (1529)." In *A Short Explanation of Dr. Martin Luther's Small Catechism: A Handbook of Christian Doctrine.* St. Louis, MO: Concordia Publishing House, 1965.

Luther, Martin. *A Brief Instruction on What to Look for and Expect in the Gospels,* 1521. Luther's Works 35. Edited by Theodore Bachmann. Translated by E. Theodore Bachmann. Philadelphia: Fortress Press, 1960.

Luther, Martin. *Commentary on Romans.* Translated by J. Theodore Mueller. Grand Rapids: Kregel Publications, 1976.

Luther, Martin. *Three Treatises.* Philadelphia: Fortress Press, 1960.

Machiavelli. *The Prince.* Translated by Luigi Ricci. London: Oxford University Press, 1935.

Mack, Burton. *A Myth of Innocence: Mark and Christian Origins.* Philadelphia: Fortress, 1988.

Malcolm. "Anselm's Ontological Arguments." *Philosophical Review* lxix (1960): 41-62.

Maritain, Jacques. *Approches de Dieu*. Paris: Alsatia, 1953.

Maritain, Jacques. *Sept Leçons sur l'être et les Premiers Principes de la Raison Spéculative.* Paris, Tequi, 1932-33.

Marshall, I. Howard. *Acts of the Apostles.* Leicester: Inter-Varsity Press, 1996.

Martin, Xavier. *Nature Humaine et Révolution Francaise: Du Siècle des Lumières au Code Napoléon.* France: Dominique Martin Morin, 1994.

Marx, Karl. *Critique of Hegel's 'Philosophy of right.'* Cambridge : University Press, 1970.

Mascall, Eric L. *Existence and Analogy.* London: Darton, Longman & Todd Ltd., 1966.

Mascall, Eric L. *He Who Is.* London: Libia Books, 1966.

Mascall, Eric L. *The Triune God: An Ecumenical Study.* Princeton Theological Monograph Series. Edited by Dikran Y. Hadidiand. Allison Park, PA: Pickwick Publications, 1986.

McFague, Sallie. *Metaphorical Theology, Models of God in Religious Language.* London: SCM Press, 1982.

McInerny, Ralph. *St. Thomas Aquinas.* Notre Dame and London: University of Notre Dame Press, 1982.

McKenzie, Steven L. *Covenant.* St. Louis: Chalice Press, 2000.

Melanchthon. *Melanchthon on Christian Doctrine: Loci Communes 1555.* Translated and Edited by Clyde L. Manschreck. New York: Oxford University Press, 1965.

Mendenhall, George E. *Law and Covenant in Israel and the Ancient Near East.* Pittsburg: The Biblical Colloquium, 1955.

Merriell, D. Juvenal. *To the Image of the Trinity: A Study in the Development of Aquinas' Teaching.* Toronto: Pontifical Institute of Mediaeval Studies, 1990.

Merton, Thomas. *The Seven Storey Mountain.* New York: Garden City Books, 1948.

Meyendorff, John ed. *Défense des Saints Hesychastes.* Louvain: Spicilegium Sacrum Lovaniense, 1959.

Meyendorff, John. *Byzantine Theology: Historical Trends & Doctrinal Themes.* London & Oxford: Mowbrays, 1975.

Moltmann, Jurgen. *The Trinity and the Kingdom of God.* Translated by Margaret Kohl. London: SCM Press, 1981.

Morris, Thomas V. *Anselmian Explorations.* Notre Dame: University of Notre Dame Press, 1989.

Morris, Thomas V. *Our Idea of God: An Introduction to Philosophical Theology.* Downers Grove: Intervarsity Press, 1991.

Moulin, Pierre Du. *A Treatise of the Knowledge of God.* London: Printed by A. Mathewes, 1634.

Muller, Richard A. *Post-Reformation Reformed Dogmatics: Prolegomena to Theology.* Vol. 1. Grand Rapids: Baker Book House, 1987.

Muralt, André de. *L'Unité de la Philosophie Politique de Scot, Occam et Suarez au Libéralisme Contemporain.* Paris: Vrin, 2002.

Muralt, André De. *Néoplatonisme et Aristotélisme dans la Métaphysique Médiévale.* Paris: Vrin, 1995.

Murray, Andrew. *Waiting on God.* London: James Nisbet & Co, 1901.

Murray, John. *Collected Writings of John Murray: Professor of Systematic Theology, Westminster Theological Seminary, Philadelphia, Pennsylvania, 1937-1966.* 4 Vols. Carlisle: Banner of Truth Trust, 1976.

Murray, John. *Redemption Accomplished and Applied.* Grand Rapids: Eerdmans, 1955.

Murray, John. *The Covenant of Grace.* Phillipsburg: Presbyterian and Reformed, 1988.

Murray, John. *The Epistle to the Romans.* Grand Rapids: Eerdmans, 1968.

Neher, André and Renée. *Histoire Biblique du Peuple d'Israel.* 3e éd. Paris: Librairie d'Amérique et d'Orient, 1988.

Newton, Isaac. *Principia Mathematica.* Edited by F. Cajori. Berkeley & Los Angeles, 1966 reprint.

Newton, Isaac. *The Chronology of Ancient Kingdoms.* London: J. Tomson, MDCCXXVIII.

Noce, Augusto Del. *L'Epoque de la Sécularisation.* Translated by Philippe Baillet. Paris: Editions des Syrtes, 2001.

Noce, Augusto Del. *Reforma Cattolica e filosofia Moderna.* Bologne: Il Mulino, 1965.

Noce, Augusto Del. *L'Irréligion Occidentale.* Translated by Philippe Baillet. Paris: FAC-editions, 1995.

Nock, A. D. and A. J. Festugière. *Hermes Trismégiste: Corpus Hermeticum.* Tomes I–IV. Paris, 1954.

Nys, Hendrik. *Le Salut sans l' Evangile. Etude historique et Critique du Problème du 'Salut des Juifs fi Dèles' dans la Littérature Théologique Récente (1912-1964).* Paris: Cerf, 1966.

Oakes, Edward T. *Pattern of Redemption: The Theology of Hans Urs Von Balthasar.* New York: Continuum, 1994.

Oberman, Heiko. *The Harvest of Medieval Theology: Gabriel Biel and Late Medieval Nominalism.* Durham, NC: The Labyrinth Press, 1983.

Old, Hughes. *The Shaping of the Reformed Baptismal Rite in the Sixteenth Century.* Grand Rapids: Eerdmans, 1992.

Orr, James. *The Progress of Dogma.* London: James Clarke & Co. Ltd., 1901.

Ortiz, Jorge Ruiz. "L'Ancienne Alliance est-elle Révoquée? L'élection du People Juif Selon la 'Nouvelle Théologie' Catholique." PhD diss. Aix-en-Provence, 2005.

Osick, Carolyn. *Freeing Theology: The Essentials of Theology in Feminist Perspective.* Edited by Catherine Mowry LaCugna. San Francisco: Harper San Francisco, 1993.

Owen, John. *An Exposition of the Epistle to the Hebrews.* 7 vols. Edited by W. H. Gould. Edinburgh: Banner of Truth Trust, 1991.

Owen, John. *The Works of John Owen.* London: Banner of Truth Trust, 1966.

Owen, John. *Works of John Owen.* Edited by Andrew Thomson. Fearn: Christian Focus, 1996.

Owens, Joseph. *Thomas Aquinas on the Existence of God (Collected Papers of Joseph Owens).* Albany: State University of New York Press, 1980.

Packer, James I. *Among God's Giants: The Puritan Vision of the Christian Life.* Eastbourne: Kingsway, 1991.

Pagels, Elaine. *The Gnostic Gospels.* New York: Vintage Books of Random House, 1981.

Pannenburg, W. *Systematic Theology.* Vol. 1. Grand Rapids: Eerdmans, 1991.

Papadakis, Aristeides. *Crisis in Byzantium: The Filioque Controversy in the Patriarchate of Gregory II of Cyprus (1283-1289).* Crestwood, NY: St. Vladimir's Seminary Press, 1997.

Parker, T. H. L. *The Doctrine of the Knowledge of God: A Study in Calvin's Theology.* Grand Rapids: Eerdmans, 1959.

Pasternak, Boris. *Dr. Zhivago.* Translated by Max Harari. London: Collins Harvill, 1987.

Peel, Malcolm Lee. *The Epistle to Rheginos, A Valentinian Letter on the Resurrection.* Philadelphia: The Westminster Press, 1969.

Pelikan, Jaroslav. *Christianity and Classical Culture: The Metamorphosis of Natural Theology in the Christian Encounter with Hellenism.* New Haven: Yale University Press, 1993.

Pelikan, Jaroslav. *The Christian Tradition: The Emergence of the Catholic Tradition.* Chigaco: University of Chicago Press, 1971.

Persson, Per Erik. *Sacra Doctrina: Reason and Revelation in Aquinas.* Translated by Ross MacKenzie. Philadelphia: Fortress Press, 1970.

Phillips, Richard P. *Modern Thomistic Philosophy.* London: Burns, Oates, 1934-35.

Pinnock, Clark, Richard Rice, John Sanders, William Hasker and David Basinger. *The Openness of God: A Biblical Challenge to the Traditional Understanding of God.* Downers Grove: InterVarsity Press, 1994.

Plantinga, Alvin and N. Wolterstorff, eds. *Faith and Rationality: Reason and Belief in God.* Notre Dame and London: University of Notre Dame Press, 1983.

Plantinga, Alvin. "A Valid Ontological Argument?" *Philosophical Review* lxx (1961): 93-101.

Plantinga, Alvin. *The Nature of Necessity.* Oxford: Clarendon Press, 1982.
Plantinga, Alvin. *The Ontological Argument: Form St. Anselm to Contemporary Philosophers.* London: Macmillan, 1968.
Plantinga, Cornelius. "The Threeness/Oneness Problem of the Trinity." *Calvin Theological Journal* 23. No. 1 (April 1988): 49.
Pohlenz, Max. *Stoa und Stoiker, die Gründer, Panaitios, Poseidonios.* Zurich: Artemis-verlag, 1950.
Pohlenz, Max. *Die Stoa: Geschichte einer geistigen Bewegung.* Gottingen: Vandenhoeck & Ruprecht, 1955-59.
Polanyi, Michael. *Knowing and Being.* London: Routledge and Kegan Paul, 1960.
Polanyi, Michael. *Personal Knowledge. Towards a Post-Critical Philosophy.* London: Routledge and Kegan Paul, 1962
Polanyi, Michael. *Science, Faith, and Society.* London: Oxford University Press, 1946.
Popovitch, Père Justin. *Philosophie Orthodoxe de la Vérité: Dogmatique de l'Eglise Orthodoxe.* Vol. I: Collection La Lumière du Thabor. Paris: L'Age d'Homme, 1992.
Prestige, G. L. *God in Patristic Thought.* London: SPCK, 1952.
Purves, Jock. *Fair Sunshine: Character Studies of the Scottish Covenanters.* Edinburgh: The Banner of Truth Trust, 2003.
Rahner, Karl. *Mission and Grace: Essays In Pastoral Theology.* 3 vols. London: Sheed and Ward, 1966.
Rahner, Karl. *The Trinity.* Translated by Joseph Donceel. London: Burns & Oates, 1970.
Rahner, Karl. *Theological Investigations.* 23 vols. London: Darton, Longman & Todd, 1966.
Ramelet, Denis. "Pourquoi Dieu est-il Père et non mere?" *Contre-poisons: Cahiers de la Renaissance Vaudoise*, no. cxlv (2006).
Redpath, Peter A. *A Simplif ed Introduction to the Wisdom of St. Thomas.* Lanham, New York: University Press of America, 1980.
Reid, Duncan. *Energies of the Spirit: Trinitarian Models in Eastern Orthodox and Western Theology.* Atlanta: Scholars Press, 1997.
Reid, Thomas. *An Inquiry into the Human Mind.* Edited by Derek R. Brookes. Edinburgh: Edinburgh University Press, 1997.
Reid, Thomas. *Essays on the Intellectual Powers of Man.* Edited by Derek R. Brookes. University Park: The Pennsylvania State University Press, 2002.
Reid, Thomas. *The Works of Thomas Reid, D.D.* Vol. 2. Edited by Sir William Hamilton. Edinburgh: MacLachlan and Stewart, 1880.
Richard Cross. *Duns Scotus on God.* Aldershot: Ashgate, 2005.
Richard de Saint-Victor. *De Trinitate.* Paris: Éditions du Cerf, 1959.
Robert M. Kingdon, 'Préface' to *Registres du Consistoire de Genève au Temps de Calvin*, publiés par Thomas A. Lambert et Isabella M. Watt, sous la direction de R. M. Kingdon avec l'assistance de Jeffrey R. Watt, Tome I (1542-1544). Librarie Droz: Geneva, 1996.
Robertson, O. Palmer. *The Christ of the Covenants.* Phillipsburg, NJ: Presbyterian and Reformed, 1980.
Robinson, James M. ed. *The Nag Hammadi Library.* Harper & Row: San Francisco, 1977.
Romanides, John S. "Franks, Romans, Feudalism, and Doctrine: An Interplay between Theology and Society." *Kleronomia* 7 (1975): 285-334.
Rose, Seraphim. *The Place of Blessed Augustine in the Orthodox Church.* Platina, CA: Saint Herman of Alaska Brotherhood, 1996.

Rosenstock-Huessy, Eugene. *Out of Revolution*. Norwich: Argo, 1969.

Rousseau, J.-J. *Du Contrat Social* with an introduction and notes by G. Beaulavon. Paris, 1938 (5th edition).
English translation: *The Social Contract and Other Essays*, by G. D. H. Cole. Everyman's Library: London, 1913.

Ruether, Rosemary Radford. *Gaia and God: An Ecofeminist Theology of Earth-Healing.* San Francisco: Harper San Francisco, 1992.

Ruether, Rosemary Radford. *Women-Church: Theology and Practice of Feminist Liturgical Communities.* San Francisco: Harper & Row, 1985.

Ruokanen, Miikka. *The Catholic Doctrine of non-Christian Religions According to the Second Vatican Council.* Leiden: E. J. Brill, 1992.

Rushdoony, R. J. *Notes on World History.* Vallecito, CA: Ross House Books, 1974.

Rushdoony, R. J. *The Mythology of Science.* Nutley, NJ: The Craig Press, 1978.

Rushdoony, R. J. *The One and the Many.* Nutley, NJ: Craig Press, 1978.

Rushdoony, R. J. *The Politics of Guilt and Pity.* Nutley, NJ: Craig Press, 1970.

Rutherford, Samuel. *Lex, Rex.* 1644. Repr. Harrisonburg: Sprinkle Publications, 1980.

Rutherford, Samuel. *The Tryal & Triumph of Faith,* 1645. [reprint] Edinburgh: Banner of Truth, 2001.

Rutledge, Archibald. *Life's Extras.* New York and London: Fleming H. Revell Company, 1928.

Ryle, Gilbert. "Systematically Misleading Expressions." *Proceedings of the Aristotelian Society* xxxii (1931-2).

Ryn, Claes G. *America the Virtuous: The Crisis of Democracy and the Quest for Empire.* New Brunswick and London: Transaction Publications, 2003.

Salmon, Wesley. "Religion & Science: A New Look at Hume's Dialogues." *Philosophical Studies* 33 (1978): 176.

Sanday. "Recent Research on the Origin of the Creed." *Journal of Theological Studies* Vol. I (1899).

Sanders, E. P. *Paul, the Law, and the Jewish People.* Minneapolis: Fortress Press, 1983.

Sanders, E. P. *Paul: A Very Short Introduction.* Oxford: Oxford University Press, 2001.

Scherer, J. 'Entretien d'Origen avec Héraclide et les êveques ses collegues sur le père, le fils, et l'âme.' Cairo: Publications de la Société Fouad I de Papyrologie, Textes et documents IX, 1949.

Schmaus, M. *Die Psychologische Trinitätslehre des Heiligen Augustinus.* Munster: Aschendorff, 1967.

Scholem, Gershom. *Jewish Gnosticism, Merkabah Mysticism, and Talmudic Tradition.* 2d ed. New York: Jewish Theological Seminary of America, 1965.

Scott, Drusilla. *Everyman Revived: The Common Sense of Michael Polanyi.* Grand Rapids: Eerdmans, 1995.

Scotus, John Duns. *A Treatise on God as First Principle,* Translated and Edited by Allan B. Wolter. Chicago: Franciscan Herald Press, 1966.

Secher, Reynald. *Le Génocide Franco-Francais: La Vendée-Vengé.* Paris: Presses Universitaires de France, 1986.

Sherry, Patrick. *Spirit and Beauty: An Introduction to Theological Aesthetics.* Oxford: Clarendon Press, 1992.

Simon, M. Jules. ed. *Oeuvres philosophiques D'Antoine Arnauld*. Paris: Charpentier, 1843.

Skinner, Quentin. *The Foundations of Modern Political Thought: Volume One: The Renaissance.* Cambridge: Cambridge University Press, 1978.

Smith, Morton. *Clement of Alexandria and a Secret Gospel of Mark.* Cambridge: Harvard University Press, 1973.
Smith, T. V. *From Aristotle to Plotinus.* Chicago, University of Chicago Press, 1956.
Solzhenitsyn, Alexander. "A World Split Apart: Commencement Address given at Harvard University in May 1978." *National Review* (July 7, 1978).
Soskice, Janet Martin. *Metaphor and Religious Language.* Oxford: Clarendon, 1985.
Spanneut, Michel. *Le Stoicisme des Pères de l'Eglise: de Clement de Rome a Clement d'Alexandrie.* Paris: Editions du Seuil, 1957.
Spicq, Ceslas, ed. *Theological Lexicon of the New Testament.* 3 Vols. Translated by J. Ernest. Peabody: Hendrickson Publishing, 1994.
St. Gregory of Palamas. *The One Hundred and Fifty Chapters.* Edited and Translated by Robert E. Sinkewicz. Toronto: Pontifical Institute of Medieval Studies, 1988.
St. Photios. *La Mystagogie du Saint Esprit: Oeuvres Trinitaires II.* Paris: Fraternité Orthodoxe Saint Grégoire Palamas, 1991.
St. Symeon the New Theologian. *The First Created Man: Seven Homilies.* Edited and Translated by Fr. Seraphim Rose. Platina CA: St. Herman of Alaska Brotherhood, 2001.
Stahl, F. J. *Was is Die Revolution*? Berlin: W. Schultze, 1852.
Stãniloae, D. "Jesus Christ, Incarnate Logos of God, Source of Freedom and Unity." In *The Ecumenical Review*, XXVI, (Jan. – Oct. 1974).
Stãniloae, Dumitru. 'The Faces of our Fellow Human Beings.' *International Review of Missions* LXXI, 281 (Jan. 1982).
Stãniloae, Dumitru. "Jesus Christ, Incarnate Logos of God, Source of Freedom and Unity." *The Ecumenical Review* XXVI (Jan.–Oct., 1974).
Stãniloae, Dumitru. *Orthodox Dogmatic Theology: The Experience of God*. Translated and Edited by Ioan Ionita and Robert Barringer. Brookline, MA: Holy Cross Orthodox Press, 1994.
Steinmetz, David C. *Luther in Context.* Grand Rapids: Baker Books, 1995.
Swinburne, Richard. *The Coherence of Theism.* Oxford: Clarendon Press, 1986.
Swinburne, Richard. *The Existence of God.* Oxford: Oxford University Press, 1979.
Tamburello, Dennis E. *Union with Christ: John Calvin and the Mysticism of St. Bernard.* Louisville: Westminster John Knox Press, 1994.
Taylor, Alfred E. *Platonism and its Influence.* New York: Longmans, Green and Co., 1927.
Taylor, Alfred E. *Philosophical Studies.* London: MacMillan and Co., 1934.
Taylor, Alfred E. *The Faith of a Moralist: Gifford Lectures Delivered in the University of St Andrews*, Vol. 2. London: Macmillan, 1930.
Teigen, Bjarne W. *The Lord's Supper in the Theology of Martin Chemnitz (1522-1586).* Brewster: Trinity Lutheran Press, 1986.
Temple, William. *Christus Veritas.* London: Macmillan Co., 1934.
The Book of Common Prayer and Administration of the Sacraments and Other Rites and Ceremonies: Together with the Psalter or Psalms of David According to the use of the Episcopal Church. New York: The Church Hymnal Corporation, 1979.
The Second Helvetic Confession. In the PCUSA *Book of* Confessions. Louisville: Geneva Press, 1996.
Thiry, Philippe. *L'Existence de Dieu: Les Arguments de L'Agnosticisme, de L'Athéisme et du Theism.* Namur: Presses Universitaires de Namur, 1996.
Tindal, Matthew. *Christianity as Old as Creation.* London: [s.n.], 1730.
Toland, John. *Christianity Not Mysterious.* London: [s.n.], 1696.
Torrance, Alan J. *Persons in Communion: An Essay on Trinitarian Description and Human Participation.* Edinburgh: T&T Clark, 1996.

Torrance, James B. "The Covenant Concept in Scottish Theology and Politics and its Legacy." *Scottish Journal of Theology* 34. no. 3 (1981).

Torrance, James B. *The Principle of Analogy in Protestant and Catholic Theology.* The Hague: Martinus Nijhoff, 1963.

Torrance, T. F. "Hugh Ross Mackintosh, Theologian of the Cross." *Scottish Bulletin of Evangelical Theology* 5 (1987).

Torrance, T. F. "Towards an Ecumenical Consensus on the Trinity." In *Trinitarian Perspectives: Towards Doctrinal Agreement.* Edinburgh: T & T Clark, 1994.

Torrance, T. F. *Christian Theology and Scientific Culture.* New York: Oxford University Press, 1981.

Torrance, T. F. *Divine Meaning: Studies in Patristic Hermeneutics.* Edinburgh: T & T Clark, 1995.

Torrance, T. F. *Reality and Evangelical Theology: The Realism of Christian Revelation.* Downers Grove: InterVarsity Press, 1999.

Torrance, T. F. *Scottish Theology.* Edinburgh: T & T Clark, 1996.

Torrance, T. F. *Space, Time, and Incarnation.* Oxford: Oxford University Press, 1969.

Torrance, T. F. *The Christian Doctrine of God, One Being Three Persons.* Edinburgh: T & T Clark, 1996.

Torrance, T. F. *The Ground and Grammar of Theology: Consonance between Theology and Science.* Charlottesville: University Press of Virginia, 1980.

Torrance, T. F. *The Hermeneutics of John Calvin.* Edinburgh: Scottish Academic Press, 1988.

Torrance, T. F. *The Mediation of Christ.* Grand Rapids: Eerdmans, 1983.

Torrance, T. F. *The Trinitarian Faith.* London: T and T Clark, 1991.

Torrance, T. F. *Theological Dialogue Between Orthodox & Reformed Churches.* Edinburgh and London: Scottish Academic Press, 1985.

Torrance, T. F. *Theological Science.* London: Oxford University Press, 1969.

Torrance, T. F. *Theology In Reconstruction.* London: SCM Press, 1965.

Torrance, T. F. *Transformation & Convergence in the Frame of Knowledge: Explorations in the Interrelations of Scientific and Theological Enterprise.* Grand Rapids: Eerdmans, 1984.

Torrance, T. F. *Trinitarian Perspectives: Toward Doctrinal Agreement.* Edinburgh: T & T Clark, 1994.

Turretin, Francis. *Institutes of Elenctic Theology, Vol. 1: First Through Tenth Topics.* Edited by J. T. Dennison. Translated by G. M. Giger. Phillipsburg: P & R Publishing, 1992.

Upinsky, Arnaud-Aaron. *La Tête Coupée: Le Secret du Pouvoir.* 3. éd. Paris: Le Bec, 2000.

Ussher, James. *Annals of the World.* 1658. Reprinted and updated by Larry and Marion Pierce. Master Books: Green Forest, AR, 2003.

VanGemeren, William A, ed. *New International Dictionary of Old Testament Theology & Exegesis*, 5 vols. Grand Rapids: Zondervan, 1997.

Van Til, Cornelius. *Common Grace.* Philadelphia: The Presbyterian and Reformed Publishing Company, 1947.

Van Til, Henry. *The Calvinistic Concept of Culture.* Philadelphia: Presbyterian and Reformed, 1959.

Vanier, Paul, S.J. *Théologie Trinitaire chez Saint Thomas D'Aquin: Évolution du Concept D'Action Notionnelle.* Montréal: Institut D'Etudes Médievales, 1953.

Verbeke, Gérard. *L'Evolution de la Doctrine du Pneuma du Stoicisme à St. Augustin: Etude Philosophique.* Paris: D. de Brouwer, 1945.

Vico. *Gethsemane.* Chicago: Franciscan Press, 1981.

Vidler, Alec R. *Christ's Strange Work.* London: Longmans, Green and Co, 1944.

Viret, P. *Exposition familière de l'oraison de nostre Seigneur Jésus-Christ.* London: H. Middleton, 1582.
Viret, Pierre. *Instruction Chrestienne en la doctrine de la Loy et de l'Evangile.* Geneve: Jean Rivery, 1564.
Viret, Pierre. *Instruction Chrétienne, Tome Premier*, Édition Établie. Présentée et Annotée par Arthur-Louis Hofer. Lausanne: L'Age d'Homme, 2004.
Viret, Pierre. *Pierre Viret D'Après Lui-Même: Pages extraites des oeuvres du Réformateur à l'occasion du quatrième centenaire de sa naissance.* Par C. Schnetzler et al. Lausanne: Georges Bridel & Cie, 1911.
Virieux-Reymond, Antoinette. *L'Epistémologie.* Paris: Presses Universitaires de France, 1966.
Voetius, *Selectae Disputationes Theologicae Pars I - V.* Utrecht, 1648-1669.
Vogelin, Eric. *Science, Politics & Gnosticism.* Wilmington: ISI Books, 2004.
Voltaire. *Eléments de la Philosophie de Newton.* London: Printed for Stephen Austen, 1738.
Voltaire. *Du contrat social, Oeuvres* III. Edited by Moland (52 vols.). Paris, 1878-1885.
Von Rad, Gerhard. *Old Testament Theology.* New York: Harper, 1962.
Vos, Arvin. *Aquinas, Calvin, & Contemporary Protestant Thought: A Critique of Protestant Views on the Thought of Thomas Aquinas.* Grand Rapids: Eerdmans, 1985.
Vos, Geerhardus. *Biblical Theology: Old and New Testaments*. Grand Rapids: Eerdmans, 1948.
Wallace, Ronald S. *Calvin's Doctrine of the Christian Life*. Tyler: Geneva Divinity School Press, 1982.
Wallace, Ronald S. *Calvin's Doctrine of the Word and Sacrament*. Tyler: Geneva Divinity School Press, 1982.
Warfield, B. B. *The Lord of Glory.* Grand Rapids: Zondervan Publ. House, no date.
Warfield, B. B., 'Calvin's Doctrine of the Trinity,' *Calvin and Augustine.* Philadelphia: Presbyterian and Reformed, 1956 reprint.
Warfield, B.B. *Biblical Foundations.* London: The Tyndale Press, 1958
Waters, Guy Prentiss. *Justification and the New Perspectives on Paul: A Review and Response.* Phillipsburg: P & R Publishing, 2004.
Weaver, Mary Jo. *Springs of Water in a Dry Land.* Boston: Beacon Press, 1992.
Weinandy, Thomas G. *The Father's Spirit of Sonship: Recovering the Trinity.* Edinburgh: T & T Clark, 1995.
Weinfeld, Moses. "The Covenant of Grant in the Old Testament and the Ancient Near East." *Journal of the American Oriental Society* 90 (1970).
Wells, David F., ed. *Southern Reformed Theology: Reformed Theology in America.* Grand Rapids: Baker Book House, 1989.
Wells, Paul. *God and Gender*. 2005. (unpublished)
Wendebourg, Dorothea. *Geist oder Energie*. München: Kaiser, 1980.
Westfall, Richard. *Life of Isaac Newton.* Cambridge: Cambridge University Press, 1993.
Westminster Confession of Faith
Whyte, Alexander. *Lancelot Andrewes: And His Private Devotions.* Edinburgh and London: Oliphant Anderson and Ferrier, 1896.
Willborn, C.N. *Confessing Our Hope: Essays in Honor of Morton Howison Smith on His Eightieth Birthday.* Taylors, SC: Southern Presbyterian Press, 2004.
Witsius, Herman. *The Economy of the Covenants Between God and Man: Comprehending A Complete Body of Divinity.* 1677. Repr. London: R. Baynes, 1822.
Wittgenstein, Ludwig. *Philosophical Investigations.* Translated by G. E. M. Anscombe. Oxford: Blackwell Publishing, 2001.

Wolfson, H. A. *The Philosophy of the Church Fathers: Faith, Trinity, Incarnation.* Cambridge: Harvard University Press, 1976.

Wolter, Allan B., ed. *John Duns Scotus: A Treatise on God as First Principle*, Translated by Allan B. Wolter. Chicago: Franciscan Herald Press, 1983.

Wright, N. T. *Jesus and the Victory of God.* London: SPCK, 2004.

Wright, N. T. *The Climax of the Covenant.* Minneapolis: Fortress Press, 1992.

Wright, N. T. *The New Testament and the People of God.* Minneapolis: Fortress Press, 1992.

Wright, N. T. *What Saint Paul Really Said.* Grand Rapids: Eerdmans, 1997.

Yannaras, C. *De L'Absence et de L'Inconnassance de Dieu D'Après les écrits Aréopagitiques et MartinHeidegger.* Paris: Éditions du Cerf, 1971.

Zeller, Eduard. *Stoics, Epicureans and Sceptics.* London: Longmans, Green, and co., 1870.

Zizioulas, John. *Being as Communion.* Crestwood, NY: St. Vladimir's Seminary Press, 1985.

Scripture Index

Romans (cont.)

1 Corinthians

2 Corinthians

Galatians

Ephesians

Index of Names

Subject Index

The author gives cordial thanks to several faithful friends, who helped proof-read this large volume. Some of them are ministers and others are theological students. They are listed in alphabetical order.

Ministers: the Reverend Messrs.

Trevor Bowers
COLUMBIA, SOUTH CAROLINA

Wallace Bumpas
DYERSBURG, TENNESSEE

Murray Garrott
DURHAM, NORTH CAROLINA

Terry Johnson
SAVANNAH, GEORGIA

Bart Lester
MONTGOMERY, ALABAMA

Leo Markwat
CHARLOTTE, NORTH CAROLINA

Mark Miller
LANCASTER, SOUTH CAROLINA

Matt Miller
GREENVILLE, SOUTH CAROLINA

Carl Robbins
GREENVILLE, SOUTH CAROLINA

Dean Turbeville
CHARLOTTE, NORTH CAROLINA

Theological Students: Messrs.:

Taylor Ince
CHARLOTTE, NORTH CAROLINA

Mantle Nance
CHARLOTTE, NORTH CAROLINA

Blake Schwarz
CHARLOTTE, NORTH CAROLINA

Christian Focus Publications

Our mission statement –

STAYING FAITHFUL

In dependence upon God we seek to impact the world through literature faithful to His infallible Word, the Bible. Our aim is to ensure that the Lord Jesus Christ is presented as the only hope to obtain forgiveness of sin, live a useful life and look forward to heaven with Him.

Our books are published in four imprints:

CHRISTIAN FOCUS

Popular works including biographies, commentaries, basic doctrine and Christian living.

CHRISTIAN HERITAGE

Books representing some of the best material from the rich heritage of the church.

MENTOR

Books written at a level suitable for Bible College and seminary students, pastors, and other serious readers. The imprint includes commentaries, doctrinal studies, examination of current issues and church history.

CF4•K

Children's books for quality Bible teaching and for all age groups: Sunday school curriculum, puzzle and activity books; personal and family devotional titles, biographies and inspirational stories – because you are never too young to know Jesus!

Christian Focus Publications Ltd,
Geanies House, Fearn, Ross-shire,
IV20 1TW, Scotland, United Kingdom.
www.christianfocus.com